Women's Agency in Early Modern Britain and the American Colonies

THEMES IN BRITISH SOCIAL HISTORY
edited by John Stevenson

This series covers the most important aspects of British social history from the Renaissance to the present day. Topics include education, poverty, health, religion, leisure, crime and popular protest, some of which are treated in more than one volume. The books are written for undergraduates, postgraduates and the general reader, and each volume combines a general approach to the subject with the primary research of the author.

Currently available

THE ENGLISH FAMILY, 1450–1700
Ralph A. Houlbrooke

POVERTY AND POLICY IN TUDOR AND STUART ENGLAND
Paul Slack

CRIME IN EARLY MODERN ENGLAND, 1550–1750
J. A. Sharpe

GENDER IN ENGLISH SOCIETY, 1650–1850: The Emergence of Separate Spheres?
Robert Shoemaker

LITERATURE AND SOCIETY IN EIGHTEENTH-CENTURY ENGLAND
W. A. Speck

CRIME AND SOCIETY IN ENGLAND, 1750–1900 (Third Edition)
Clive Emsley

THE LABOURING CLASSES IN EARLY INDUSTRIAL ENGLAND, 1750–1850
John Rule

POPULAR DISTURBANCES IN ENGLAND, 1700–1832 (Second Edition)
John Stevenson

SEX, POLITICS AND SOCIETY: The Regulation of Sexuality since 1800 (Second Edition)
Jeffrey Weeks

HEALTH AND SOCIETY IN TWENTIETH-CENTURY BRITAIN
Helen Jones

NEWSPAPERS AND ENGLISH SOCIETY, 1695–1855
Hannah Barker

THE PROFESSIONS IN EARLY MODERN ENGLAND, 1450–1800
Rosemary O'Day

POPULAR CULTURES IN ENGLAND, 1550–1750
Barry Reay

THE ENGLISH TOWN, 1680–1840
Rosemary Sweet

Women's Agency in Early Modern Britain and the American Colonies

Patriarchy, partnership and patronage

Rosemary O'Day

Harlow, England • London • New York • Boston • San Francisco • Toronto
Sydney • Tokyo • Singapore • Hong Kong • Seoul • Taipei • New Delhi
Cape Town • Madrid • Mexico City • Amsterdam • Munich • Paris • Milan

PEARSON EDUCATION LIMITED

Edinburgh Gate
Harlow CM20 2JE
United Kingdom
Tel: +44 (0)1279 623623
Fax: +44 (0)1279 431059
Website: www.pearsoned.co.uk

First edition published in Great Britain in 2007

© Pearson Education Limited 2007

The right of Rosemary O'Day to be identified as author
of this work has been asserted by her in accordance
with the Copyright, Designs and Patents Act 1988.

ISBN: 978-0-582-29463-9

British Library Cataloguing in Publication Data
A CIP catalogue record for this book can be obtained from the British Library

All rights reserved; no part of this publication may be reproduced, stored
in a retrieval system, or transmitted in any form or by any means, electronic,
mechanical, photocopying, recording, or otherwise without either the prior
written permission of the publisher or a licence permitting restricted copying
in the United Kingdom issued by the Copyright Licensing Agency Ltd,
Saffron House, 6–10 Kirby Street, London EC1N 8TS. This book may not be lent,
resold, hired out or otherwise disposed of by way of trade in any form
of binding or cover other than that in which it is published, without the
prior consent of the Publishers.

10 9 8 7 6 5 4 3 2 1
11 10 09 08 07

Set by 35 in 10/13.5pt Sabon
Printed in Malaysia (CTP-VVP)

The publisher's policy is to use paper manufactured from sustainable forests.

Contents

	Preface	vii
	Abbreviations	x
1	General introduction	1

PART 1 Marrying: an active proposition

	Introduction	27
2	How and where were marriages solemnised?	28
3	What was marriage? What was its purpose?	41
4	Finding a partner among the landed aristocracy	67
5	Making marriages among women of the professional and the middling sorts	111

PART 2 Experience of marriage

	Introduction	141
6	Attitudes to marriage	146
7	Patriarchy	152
8	Partnership and separation	185
9	Mistress of the household: what wives did all day	205
10	Mothers	240
11	Wives and property	258
12	Widows and widowhood	280

PART 3 Culture and religion: women's preparation for and participation in contemporary culture

	Introduction	319
13	Women's formal and informal education	320
14	Women and religion	338

15 Contemporary culture: print and non-print, public
and private 372
16 Women's cultural lives: participation 397

Bibliography 429
Glossary 476
Subject index 481
Index of proper names 485

Preface

I was commissioned to write this book shortly before my husband (and soulmate) David Englander died. In their infinite wisdom administrators at the Open University suggested that I become acting and then actual head of department in order to overcome my grief. Partly as a result, this book has taken a decade to complete. I hope, however, that the long gestation period has produced a better book than I had at first envisaged. When he was dying, David advised me to find happiness where I could and especially in a return to early modern studies. He was right, and I did.

I owe so many debts of gratitude. First of all, I wish to thank the authors of the books, articles and theses that I have read. I have listed in the bibliography all works from which I quoted or drew significantly. Secondly, I thank the archivists and assistants, past and present, who have helped me at the various record offices: British Library, Bodleian Library, Lichfield Joint Record Office, William Salt Library and Staffordshire County Record Office, North London Collegiate School, Nottingham University Library, Shakespeare Birthplace Trust Record Office, Folger Shakespeare Library, Washington DC; Library of Congress, Huntington Library, San Marino, California. I must single out for special mention Dr Mary Robertson of the Huntington who has given generously of her time and expertise regarding the Egerton, Temple and Brydges families and their papers; Karen Morgan of the North London Collegiate School, for her immense cooperation; Mairi Macdonald of the Shakespeare Birthplace Trust for her generosity and Dorothy Johnston of the University of Nottingham Library for her interest and assistance. Thirdly, I thank especially Ian Harris, Barbara Donagan, Patrick Collinson, Dorothy Johnston, Anne Laurence, Gill Perry and the Gender in the Humanities Group at the Open University for their conversation, comments and support. I am particularly grateful to the Huntington Library for allowing me to work there for an extended period each year and to its fellowship committee for awarding me an Andrew Mellon fellowship in 2005/6. Financial support was also extended by The Open University, for which I am most grateful. I acknowledge the above libraries and record offices for quotation from documents in their possession. I gratefully acknowledge the Church Commissioners, North London Collegiate School and Stoneleigh Abbey Limited for other permissions.

I owe a great debt to Dr John Stevenson, editor of this series, for his enthusiastic support and helpful suggestions and to Dr Rachel Gibbons, my research assistant, for her bibliographical work and her generous comments. In addition I thank Christina Wipf Perry of Longman/Pearson for her help and patience.

Last but not least, I thank my family – Andrew O'Day and Dan and Matthew Englander – and my good friends Janet Dawson, Catherine Roe, Sheila Taylor, Meg Kesten, Yvonne Alton, Lee Stolzman and Sian Lewis for support when I was brought low by life's vicissitudes, and for listening patiently when I was eventually revived by this book.

Rosemary O'Day
The Open University, June 2006

I dedicate this book to my parents and siblings, with thanks
for their unfailing support and love:
My mother Beryl Robinson Brookes (1902–1989)
My father Thomas Henry Brookes (1895–1980)
My sister
Kathleen Mary Brookes Poole (1929–)
My brothers
Bryan John Brookes (1931–)
Neville Hugh Brookes (1936–)

Abbreviations

BL	British Library
CSPD	Calendar of State Papers Domestic
FSL	Folger Shakespeare Library, Washington, DC
HEH	Huntington Library, San Marino, California
HM	Huntington Manuscript
L.J.R.O.	Lichfield Joint Record Office
MHR	Maryland Hall of Records
MO	Montagu Papers
NLCS	North London Collegiate School
NLW	National Library of Wales
SBPTRO	Shakespeare Birthplace Trust Record Office, Stratford-upon-Avon
SCRO	Stafford County Record Office
ST	Stowe Collection
STT	Stowe Temple Papers
STB	Stowe Brydges Papers
UNL	University of Nottingham Library

Conventions

Spelling and punctuation in quotations have been modernised where necessary for clarity. Otherwise no changes have been made.

Citations are given in full for contemporarily published works. Citations for other items are abbreviated; full details of publication can be found in the Bibliography.

CHAPTER 1

General introduction

There is a good deal of interest in the history of women. This interest has produced excellent detailed work by historians, which has led to several exciting debates. It (and associated interest in the history of gender) has also led to a broadening of the perspective adopted by socio-economic, socio-religious and other historians, who now see women's history as an essential part of any historical writing, if only at the level of explaining why women's history plays a minor role in some political, diplomatic or military histories. At its best we see women as more than half the population of these countries, who were important agents in their social, economic, religious and cultural life and who exercised considerable influence, both direct and indirect, on their development.

What should such a book contain? At the very heart of this book is the idea that the history of women's experience is a central concern. It is certainly also important to learn about attitudes to women; there is necessarily a relationship between theory and practice both for the women themselves and the individuals and communities with whom they interacted. This was part of women's experience. While inevitably indebted to the work of many scholars in the field, such a book should be equally grounded in the author's own research into and understanding of the issues. In this case, research areas have included the history of the family and family relationships, the history of education and the social history of religion: and this book has, as a result, a rather different perspective on women's history than have many others.

When detailing the manner in which men and women conducted themselves in the past, there could be a temptation to assume that 'normal behaviour' within a society was 'natural' rather than socially and economically constructed. The inclusion of comparison across such a wide spectrum – not only across the kingdoms of the British Isles but also across the Atlantic and not only across 'old world' societies but also 'new world' – will possibly reveal not only that 'gender' is a social construct but also that different societies will create it differently, even when they have recently experienced another 'construction'. So we are not in the business of simply describing differences across these societies and these periods but also of pinpointing explanations for such differences.

There will always be the problem, of course, of distinguishing between, on the one hand, common patterns of behaviour and experience that could be described as 'characteristic' of a particular time and place and, on the other hand, the unusual behaviours and experiences. This is especially true for the medieval and early modern periods when documentation is relatively scarce. Similarly, there will be the problem of achieving some balance between how contemporaries considered that women should behave in society and how they actually behaved, between how contemporaries regarded women and between how women regarded themselves. Historians, however, will always at their best employ their own experiences, humanity and understanding to reflect upon and interpret the sources.

The truth has gradually been acknowledged by modern historians that, in order to understand women's history, we need to cast our net wider. Not only does this mean that we need to consider 'gender roles' of both men and women, it also means that we need to place both sexes in a more general social context. So some of the issues that we will consider in this book are not only, or even mainly, concerned with the lives of women but their resolution in all cases will also have a profound effect upon our interpretation of the experiences of women. For instance, there is an important debate concerning the prevalent laws of inheritance in all these societies. Historians differ in their views concerning whether and where primogeniture or partible inheritance ruled. They differ in their views about the economic dependence and independence of various categories of people – men, women, older sons, younger sons, daughters, widows, singletons. They differ in their views of who baked the bread and brought home the bacon. They differ in their views concerning the age at marriage. They differ in their views concerning the seasonality of marriage. They differ in their views on the relative importance of marriage and other forms of partnership in England, Scotland, Ireland, Wales and the British colonies. Upon their answers depend so many aspects of our picture of the place of women and experience of women in these societies.

One corollary of this is that a book about women cannot properly take the form of a narrative that simply describes the lives of women and conveys a sense of absolute certainty. Some things are certain, others are surmise based upon the latest scholarship.

Another central premise

A further basic premise is that people in the British Isles in the sixteenth, seventeenth and eighteenth centuries were interested in both men and women not as individuals but chiefly as role players in a household and a social hierarchy. The sixteenth and seventeenth centuries have been seen as a watershed between a peasant society and a capitalist one. For example, the German sociologist Max Weber remarked on the gradual movement from a 'clan' society to a 'household' society to a 'modern individualistic society'. He identified the seventeenth century as the period of transition between the final two stages.[1] Karl Marx and Frederich Engels saw the break-up of the 'household' society in place in the sixteenth century. In their view there emerged in the sixteenth century in Europe the preconditions of modern individualist society: separation between home and work; a large, landless labourer class; a change in ethic from dedication to the survival of the family/household to one of unlimited acquisitiveness, fostered by the religious reformer John Calvin's stress on the individual. Perhaps the most renowned British proponent of this idea was R. H. Tawney, author of *Religion and the Rise of Capitalism*. He saw a sharp distinction between the peasant and the capitalist family:

The household does not merely imply what we [today] mean by 'the family', a group of persons connected by blood but pursuing often quite separate occupations and possessing quite separate economic interests. It is, on the contrary, a miniature co-operative society, housed under one roof, dependent upon one industry, and including not only man and wife and children, but servants and labourers, ploughmen and threshers, cowherds and milkmaids, who live together, work together, just as one can see them doing in parts of Norway and Switzerland at the present day. When the economic foundations of their small organism are swept away by a change in the method of farming, the effect is not merely to ruin a family, it is to break up a business.[2]

More recently, Alan Macfarlane, a demographer and socio-economic historian, challenged the assumption underlying this position. He maintained that England's had not been a true peasant society since the thirteenth century and that the origins of capitalist society stretched back into the medieval period because England had had a large landless labourer class – a rural proletariat – for some two hundred years by 1500 and was fast urbanising. He demonstrated that the law already favoured individual rather than family rights. There was already a good deal of individual geographical, social and economic mobility. Although the family was important, marriage was late and was not universal. According to this view English and Welsh society was made up of free-moving individuals (presumably motivated by individual economic and social interest) rather than of household production units. If so, this was in sharp contradistinction with the situation in, for instance, Ireland or in Scotland where there was a strong land–family bond in the clan or lordship system.[3] England's according to Macfarlane was not an industrialised society but it was capitalist – exploitation of waged workers by the drones was already the order of the pre-industrial world before the Reformation.

Macfarlane's views have not gone unchallenged. R. W. Hoyle pointed out that although landowners could dispose of their land as they wished during their lifetimes and could disinherit presumptive heirs by will, they could also deny those rights to future generations by using instruments such as settlements and entails. 'Indeed' he wrote, 'it might plausibly be argued that disinheritance was most frequently used to maintain the integrity of lands when the next generation seemed careless of their preservation.'[4] He went on to demonstrate that although the right to sell was acknowledged, customs evolved to give the heir or kin first option to purchase. Both Hoyle and Govind Sreenivasen challenged Macfarlane and David Levine and Keith Wrightson's argument that land markets were active and that little property remained in the same family for more than two generations. Sreenivasen sought to prove that much land in fact remained within the family. Hoyle urged that it was more important to ascertain why farmers were selling their land. He concluded that this was because of economic and social distress.[5]

This apart, there is much to be said for the view that England and Wales underwent an early capitalist apprenticeship but very little for the view that this was an individualistic society. It was the household that mattered in that society. It was perhaps not a peasant household but it was a household. The individual within it who counted was the head of the household – commonly but not always the oldest male. Macfarlane unfortunately confused the concepts of capitalism and individualism. The two are by no means identical. Capitalism may take both individual and corporate forms. Even more importantly from our point of view, he equated the individual with the head of the household and totally forgot the people who were subsumed in and subordinate to him/her within the family. Even if families or households were acquisitive and competitive with one another, a different ethic applied *within* the household. The ethic of individualism did not apply to family relationships within the household, whether between the head of household and the rest or between the rest of its members. Neither did proto-industrialisation introduce this ethic.

At a time when historians of women rightly emphasise that women's history and history of the family are not the same, it could appear heretical to suggest that we cannot sensibly study the history of women without a profound understanding of the historical family and the role that women, of different status, were expected to play and did play within it. This family may be defined as those individuals dwelling together along with their servants in a household. Other individuals who are related to this 'family' are frequently called kin although I prefer to see them as a 'wider family'. The 'household society', frequently consisting of the nuclear family, relied for its success very heavily upon the roles of women, whether they were wives, mothers, daughters, or sisters. Even in a traditionalist clan society, women's roles were defined and important. While there may be some dispute about the nature of kinship and the extent of kin interaction in England, there can be little doubt that contemporary women in all these societies did also see that kinship whether close or distant brought with it certain obligations. Women acknowledged these obligations themselves and they also claimed them from others, whether distant cousins or step-relatives or even relatives and connections by marriage, whenever these women deemed it necessary.[6]

Laurel Thatcher Ulrich, in her brilliant short book *Good Wives* about women in seventeenth-century New England, expressed very well the fact that contemporaries did not emphasise the personalities but the roles of women and, moreover, that those roles changed according to circumstance.

Certain patterns of behaviour could be put on and taken off according to circumstances without altering the essential nature of the person; women could act as 'deputy husbands' or men as 'brides of Christ' without becoming any less 'submissive' or 'masterful' in other social relations.[7]

This approach to studying the lives of women draws not only upon Weberian understanding of the external ordering of family lives but also upon Foucauldian theories of the informal negotiation of power within the family.

History of women, not only the history of women in the family

This said, it is crucial to decide to what extent the individuality of women was important to themselves and to their kinfolk and friends. The history of women is *not* encompassed by the history of the family or the roles women played. It was, moreover, the case that society did gradually move towards the ethic of individualism that we know today. In this book I have attempted to show how far women's experience was determined by their family roles but also to show to what extent they existed as individuals and expanded their horizons. Contemporary correspondence and also accounts of friendship between women and women, and women and men, are explored from this point of view.

Nevertheless, contemporaries often set the development of a woman's individual personality, character, and accomplishments in the context of her family responsibilities. The book concentrates on the education of women and the cultural and religious roles of women. It was increasingly accepted that women required a degree of education if they were to be good wives and mothers and if they had to support themselves during periods as a singleton. Within the household women had special religious and cultural roles. Eventually this led to women exercising these roles and responsibilities outside the household, leading to a more individualistic approach. So we may regard the development of individualism as a by-product of the emphasis upon preparation for family responsibilities. When women exercised cultural and religious patronage they also exercised a social and economic power, which made them important as individuals.

So the contribution of individual women and women to the culture and belief of these societies in general is important to this book. How many women writers, painters, poets, sculptors or translators can you name? In all probability not many, and if you can name sixteenth- or seventeenth-century examples ten to one it's because they're also known for other things – for example Queen Elizabeth I because she was Queen, or Margaret Roper because she was Sir Thomas More's daughter. Why is this? Historians have uncovered the lives of many cultured women who made distinct contributions to the life of their contemporaries – from Bess of Hardwick to Cassandra Willoughby, from Mary Wroth to Mary Wollstonecraft – but many still had not been heard of until the later decades of the twentieth and the start of the twenty-first century – why? During the nineteenth and early twentieth centuries a number of women scholars made determined attempts to trace the cultural activity of particular women but, generally speaking, their efforts did not receive the imprimatur of a male academy and hence made little impression on general histories. As a result, their works did not enter the canon of literary or artistic study. But women should not be seen as important culturally solely because they produced critically notable works of music, art or literature. There were other ways in which they participated in and contributed to cultural life. Relatively recently the effort to uncover the ways in which women engaged with and helped shape their contemporary culture has been redoubled and has begun to have somewhat more recognition from both female and male social, religious and cultural historians and, especially, from literary historians.

But why was uncovering their contribution such a difficult process in the first place? Largely this was because historians of this period relied very heavily upon the written and especially the printed record. Where archives were used, they were generally those of central or local government or of male-dominated trades and professions. Professional historians were largely male and the notable female historians were active on the margins and were unacknowledged by them or their focus dismissed by them as 'not serious'. A few historians did push the boundaries further but found it difficult to gain ground in a profession dominated by political, institutional and diplomatic history. The opening of academia itself from the 1960s to large numbers of women with very different interests and an awareness of feminism spelt change. At the same time local and ecclesiastical archives were made more accessible, and by stimulating academic interest in socio-economic and religious history they created a more receptive environment within the profession.

Investigation of the cultural role of women also has a bearing upon the long-standing debate about public and private spheres. The idea that males completely dominated the public sphere and that women were relegated to the private, domestic sphere has most resonance when applied to the upper middle classes of mid-Victorian Britain and the United States of America and, even then, best describes a situation that some men desired rather than one that actually prevailed.[8] In the early modern period privacy was certainly hard to come by: domestic life was lived in a semi-public fashion. Nevertheless historians have accepted that elite males did dominate the political and economic arena to a great extent and that women lived in a society that presumed their dependence upon men in these areas and accorded them little 'voice' in society in their own right. Latterly historians have begun to modify this picture to show how women managed to manipulate their socio-economic and legal environment in order to survive and even prosper. Amy Louise Erickson's seminal study of women and property has shaped the way that historians now approach the subject. In the United States a number of historians have studied what they call the 'agency' of women in seventeenth-century colonial societies, contrasting them with the Anglicised societies of the later colonies. Yet women were also pivotal in the shaping of English society itself and the way in which both men and women conducted themselves in it. In *The Family and Family Relationships* I have shown how the women of the Ferrar family of Little Gidding fully participated in the family's decision-making, even to the extent of voting on important issues.[9] Susan Whyman's somewhat neglected *Sociability and Power in Late-Stuart England* demonstrates how during that period the 'control of manners increasingly fell to women' and that women played an important role not only in determining the formalities of social life in both public and private but also in giving political commentary and advice to menfolk in their social networks (drawn from their personal experience and observation). Study of the late sixteenth- and early seventeenth-century Temple family in this book indicates that this was not a new phenomenon (as Whyman implies) but rather something that had its roots in the earlier part of our period. And indeed the evidence of the Paston and Stonor correspondence in the fifteenth century may suggest that women acted in this way as soon as vernacular letter-writing became popular.

Structure and agency as explanations for the ways in which particular women and women in general lived and behaved

There has been much discussion of the 'dominant discourses of gender' that formed a background to and constructed women's lives.[10] There is more awareness than there once was, however, of the complex relationship that existed between theory and practice. There were multiple and competing ideas about the nature and role of women and of how women should behave. These ideas frequently differentiated between women of various types – single, married, mothers, widows, servants. Women themselves reacted in different ways to such discourses, sometimes internalising them but often modifying them, ignoring them or even, on occasion, explicitly rejecting them.[11] As this book indicates, their menfolk and their kin and friendship circles were frequently permissive.

Sara Mendelson and Patricia Crawford boldly state: 'Women had a limited range of scripts, or stories, by which they could understand their experiences. The stereotypical choices were sharply polarized.' They could be virtuous or they could be witches or whores.[12] These historians argue that stereotypically women were presented in an inferior light. Although individual women were often valued and lauded by their menfolk they were seen as exceptions to the rule. Women as well as men internalised this message and so accepted the generally negative view of womankind. There is much to be said for this interpretation but the same evidence can more convincingly be used to support alternative arguments. In their edited collection of essays treating women in Scotland after 1400, Yvonne Galloway Brown and Rona Ferguson argue that women did not internalise this stereotype but rather 'resisted repression' and that their deviancy expressed through political radicalism, unbalanced piety, brutality, and subversion added up to 'positive resistance and a force for change'.[13] Equally the evidence would support an interpretation that many women and men rejected such stereotypes in practice (or, at least, only fell back upon them when they were annoyed with one another), in much the same way as moderns regard jokes and comments about husbands, wives and mothers-in-law as containing part but only part of the truth about the sexes.

So, when women were relatively strong and assertive within a marriage (as for examples Honor, Lady Lisle, Hester, Lady Temple, or Margaret Cavendish, Duchess of Newcastle), was this just because their menfolk allowed them to be so? Well, yes, perhaps, but this would certainly suggest that these men (and perhaps their own birth families) also reacted in different ways to the 'dominant discourses' and that they presented alternative 'scripts' for their wives and female children to learn. The evidence that survives about the role of consecutive generations of women in particular families (for example, the Sidneys) suggests that different families had different cultures and attitudes to their womenfolk.

What this adds up to is that the lives and opinions of men and women frequently did not correspond closely with the model of social order presented by public commentators. Documenting the tension between the public and secret 'transcripts' of gender requires ingenious use of sources.[14]

Why a book that considers the history of women across the British Isles and Britain's colonies?

Women, like men, did exercise some individual choice or agency in their lives and relationships but this choice was considerably restricted by society, economy, religion and culture. Even within a society differences in social and economic status, for example, had considerable bearing upon the roles women were conditioned to play. The wife of a nobleman had to be a mistress of a large household and a patroness as well as a wife and mother; the wife of a landless labourer had no real household to run and did not have the necessary 'power' to be a patroness. Some historians argue that differences in ideology and in religious belief were also directly reflected in the roles women played. Comparison across these Old World and New World societies presents an additional challenge – unless the societies were identical there would have been differing constraints on female agency.

There has been something of a renaissance in Scottish, Welsh and Irish historical studies recently, which has produced some important work particularly touching on marriage, inheritance and witchcraft. It will be some time before the volume and depth of such work matches that for England.[15] Nevertheless Scottish (and, to some extent, Welsh and Irish) historians have now provided the all-important socio-economic, political and religious 'backcloth' for the lives of women which enables the historian to make some sensible and sensitive comparisons.

While the book does compare the lot of women in all these societies it does not pretend to give them attention equal to that accorded English women, who unashamedly form the heart of the book. In part the decision to give them this status was pragmatic: the book's length and its intended audience, the relative scarcity both of detailed sources and of scholarly study for, for example, Scotland and Ireland, and the dangers of repetition within the narrative all pointed towards this approach.[16]

A union of love? Similarities and differences between the three kingdoms and the principality

There is, however, a problem when treating the history of the British Isles which also stretches far beyond the bounds of women's history. Although this book is not the place to discuss the historiography of this problem in detail, readers should be aware of the nature of the debate, which has some impact upon our own comparisons of women in these societies. This problem is, in a nutshell, whether the Islands in any real sense shared cultural, religious, political and social norms, even after the union of the three kingdoms in the person of James VI and I. In other words, how similar were these societies? Taking Scotland as an example, some historians, notably Brian Levack, have emphasised that King James's aspirations to a union of love between the kingdoms of England, Ireland, and Scotland

and the principality of Wales had a certain credibility because of the successful 'union of the Welsh and English people after the constitutional union of 1536 and 1543'.[17] Jane Dawson detected that the relative success of protestant reformation in both England and Scotland created an Anglo-Scottish Protestant culture and 'a common language of print'. Both acknowledged, however, that religion contributed as much to division as to unity and diversity as conformity.[18] And these divisions were not only those marked by geo-political boundaries between states, they were very present within the states themselves. For instance, Jane Dawson found that evangelicals in the Highlands and Islands were not accepted as members of the same religious or cultural community by Lowland ministers, purely because they used Gaelic and not the language in which the Scriptures were printed. This was also true in different ways in the other kingdoms. Protestantism met with a patchy reception in England and parts of the kingdom clung to Catholicism; Protestantism made very slow progress in both Wales and Ireland. In Ireland there was a sharp division between Protestant settlers and non-Protestant native Irish. Steven Ellis attributes this situation to the central government's lack of interest in remote parts of the jurisdiction; the presence of relatively few educated clergymen in both Wales and Ireland until the later sixteenth century; limited contact between the Welsh and Irish and continental Protestants; and a failure on the part of missionaries to face up to linguistic challenges. In Ireland English reluctance to promote English-speaking residents of the Pale to positions of import in church and state probably strengthened loyalty to the Old Religion.[19] They (like Welsh Catholic gentry) sent their sons and daughters away to the Continent for education. In the case of Wales these educated young priests were most often sent to England to work whereas the Irish Catholic priests returned to Ireland to work. This relative weakness of the Catholic mission in Wales and its strength in Ireland has been adduced to explain the failure of resistance to evangelicalism in Wales and its success in Ireland.[20] In Ireland the Old English (as the Catholics came to be known) were excluded from government but created a strong economic and social presence in the country, reinforced by family networks.[21]

Nicholas Canny, a foremost authority, argues that while attempts to bring religious conformity throughout the kingdoms had patchy success, attempts to make English the common language among the ruling elites were much more successful, at least partly because of the enthusiastic support of local as well as 'national' elites, who supported the introduction of 'English' English as opposed to Scots (previously the language of literary composition) and Gaelic.[22] However, even here there was division and difference. Scots continued to be used as a spoken language and Gaelic persisted in the Highlands. In Ireland English had been on the decline from the fourteenth century onwards and so the advocates of the English language had a more difficult task than the Scots in converting those outside the elite to its use. Within the elite of the Pale, 'English' English was dominant in everyday life, reinforced by the presence of a multitude of English-born or educated settlers. There were parts of the kingdom, for example Ulster, where Scottish influence was so strong that Scots was the predominant language of discourse. There have been sharp differences of opinion between historians regarding the extent to which knowledge and use of English reached down to lower social levels. Nicholas Canny maintains that by the mid-seventeenth century knowledge and use of English was widespread, especially where British settlement was intense or where English had maintained a presence throughout the later Middle Ages.[23] Alone among the societies, Wales clung to its native tongue. It is estimated that around 90 per cent of Wales was Welsh-speaking throughout the sixteenth and seventeenth centuries. The Welsh elite continued to support Welsh culture and even the English authorities appear to have accepted that Welsh should be the language of print as well as speech when they authorised a Welsh-language Bible in 1588.[24]

The North American colonies

The historiography of the European settlement of North America has undergone considerable change since about 1970. Initially, (predominantly white) historians of European extraction concentrated upon the settlers as religious migrants, the innocent victims of persecution, or as commercial adventurers. Hardly anyone took seriously the existing settlements of the indigenous peoples of the Americas or the experiences of the non-white immigrants during the colonial period. Francis Jennings's *The Invasion of America: Indians, Colonialism, and the Cant of Conquest*, published in 1975, changed all that.[25]

This is in many respects a laudable development although it has tended towards an idealisation of life before the European invasion, a certain lack of objectivity in some quarters, a tendency to cast the Indians as victims who simply reacted to European settlers and their demands, and a turning away from studies of the European immigrants and their descendants. Black American history has until relatively recently also emphasised the way in which whites imposed their culture upon blacks and the ways in which a separate slave culture developed and survived notwithstanding.

Mechal Scobel has now introduced a new perspective, showing the extent to which there was interaction and symbiosis between the two cultures, so that historians cannot understand one without the other.[26] In itself this development seems to point to the wisdom of detailed study of white culture as well as of black and indigenous cultures.

'The European presence in America *was* an invasion, but it was also partly an invited settlement, partly a commercial interchange and partly a folk migration.'[27] The uneven migration to the thirteen British American colonies in terms of motivation, geographical and social origin, and timing and density makes comparing their development with that of the mother country problematic.[28] The fact that historians disagree considerably over the extent of white immigration in the seventeenth and eighteenth centuries does not help.[29] However, there does appear to be some general agreement now that between 278,000 and 486,000 immigrated in the period 1700–1780, although historians differ a good deal about the composition of that number in terms of origin, some claiming that half were from Ireland, for example.[30] It certainly makes for difficulties when attempting comparisons between the several colonies of the Atlantic seaboard and the component parts of the British Isles, already fraught enough! Notable already in the seventeenth-century colonies is the wide diversity in the colonial laws of inheritance, often as a result of the local origin of the immigrants, which had a direct impact upon the lives of women in the various colonies.[31] In her recent study of women in seventeenth-century Maryland Debra Meyers was able to 'situate her Marylanders as English women and men in a new locale'.[32] This situation was not to last. The predominantly English phase of colonial settlement ended in the later seventeenth century. Most scholars agree that large numbers of the eighteenth-century immigrants were Scots–Irish, Irish and German, although they differ as to the precise numbers involved. Smaller but still significant numbers arrived from France (Huguenot), the Netherlands and Wales.[33] These new immigrants also brought with them customs, traditions and attitudes that presumably had some impact upon their settlements, which tended to fall in particular colonies. For example, most immigrants from Germany entered the New World through the port of Philadelphia and spread out through Pennsylvania and adjacent colonies.

So, to avoid overmuch complexity, while trying to accommodate conclusions from the recent work on Indian and Black women in North America and accepting the moral force of the Jennings/Salisbury argument,[34] I have emphasised in this book the experience of white women of European (especially British) extraction. I have done this for several reasons, the most important of which are: the availability of high-quality research into the experience of women which, with honourable exceptions, favours work on immigrants rather than indigenous peoples; and the role of the North American example as a way of establishing whether 'British' patterns of female life were 'natural' and 'inevitable' and simply transplanted to the far side of the Atlantic or whether such patterns were changed in response to new circumstances.

A view of the difference between English and American women has crept into American popular history, in which patriarchy is seen as rigid in England and, at least at first, resisted in the Americas.

> [I]t appears that not one of the three groups had what we think of as 'traditional' sex roles. In Indian Virginia, for example, and in much of West Africa, women were the farmers. Among the English, meanwhile, ideas about the proper roles of women were often undermined by the fluid conditions of life and death in the New World. By 1700 the English had established dominion over Virginia, and English men were establishing increasingly effective dominion over women. But none of this was a foregone conclusion in 1607.[35]

During the second half of the twentieth century, American historians emphasised the comparatively favourable status of women in early modern America. As more and more work is done by British historians on the experience of English, Welsh and Scottish women, the stark contrast between 'oppressed' British women and 'liberated' American women in the seventeenth century is tending to disappear. Some American historians claim to have uncovered a tendency for colonial men to exercise *greater* dominion over their womenfolk in the period after 1650, at a time when others would argue that English women were still resisting patriarchy with effect.

The validity of such comparisons is also contestable on grounds of the sources available. Comparison of women in England with women in the American colonies is difficult because of the differing social structure. Until the 1730s, America, unlike England, Wales, Scotland and Ireland, was not dominated by elites. Early elite settlers soon returned to England and for a period in the seventeenth century society was fluid. The distribution of wealth was much more unbalanced in the south than in the north.[36] Local elites began to emerge from old English settlers by the late seventeenth century. Their composition varied considerably, however – Virginia, for instance, was dominated by planter families such as the Beverlies, the Carters, the Lees and the Byrds (which approximated in their lifestyle to that of rural upper-gentry families in England) while Massachusetts was ruled by merchant families such as the Sewalls and Hutchinsons who were rooted in urban communities and had more in common with England's urban oligarchs.[37] So there is a real problem of comparing like with like both within the colonies and between the colonies and the British Islands. Where there is source material for the seventeenth-century colonies, this most often refers to women who were comparable to working or middling-sort English women rather than the aristocratic English, Welsh, Scottish and Irish women with which this book is chiefly concerned. This means that it is only possible to make a confident and direct comparison between elites in the eighteenth century. It also means that much of the evidence cited by Americanists for the seventeenth century relates in fact to women of the middling sort who are more strictly comparable with middling-sort women of the Old World, among whom women also appear to have had considerable practical freedom of action.

English colonies in Ireland

As noted above, the nature of early modern Ireland has proved difficult for historians to determine, with its division into the 'English' lordship of the Pale and the Gaelic provinces that surrounded it. There are ongoing debates about the nature of Tudor rule and ambitions in Ireland, about the extent of the Gaelicisation of the Pale and the Anglicisation of the Gaelic lordships, and about the relationships between New English, Old English and Irish peoples which cannot but impinge upon any study of the women of this society. In Gaelic Ireland, for example, society was organised in clans which were agnatic groupings (that is, from a common male ancestor through male links) as opposed to the cognatic descent prevalent in England.[38] During our period the English colonised parts of Ireland (although Old English or Anglo-Norman families were to some extent already integrated into native Irish culture and society) and, certainly by the end of the sixteenth century, sought to impose English political rule over the whole island. The New English aristocrats who were now responsible for Ireland's rule more often than not did not bring their wives and families to live in Ireland. Much of the early Tudor colonisation involved large numbers of male soldiers, who had relationships with and married native Irish women. After this experience later colonisation encouraged male colonisers to bring with them English wives and create exclusively English enclaves. Varying degrees of segregation from the Irish population were envisaged. The final 1650s project was rather different because it involved soldiery once more and met up again with the problems caused by liaisons with the native women. Because of the dearth of documentation, historians have in the past often relied for information about indigenous women on the attitudes and opinions of the 'New English' colonial power.[39] More recently scholars have begun to use Gaelic sources to explore the position of native Irishwomen before, during and after the Tudor period. Simultaneously they have shown that in many respects the lordship system of Old Ireland (and with it the Gaelic law) had effectively collapsed by the early seventeenth century as a consequence of Anglicisation. This said, they have become more sensitive to regional differences, noting that Munster's ties with southern England were of growing importance at a time when Ulster was 'becoming an extension of south-west Scotland'.[40] Yet disagreements among historians of Ireland as to the chronology and character of colonisation certainly present a challenge to the historian of Irish women.[41]

Sources

Historians of women and womanhood have to be acutely aware of the provenance and purpose of the sources they use. Sara Mendelson and Patricia Crawford deliberately privilege women's writing and women's words. More survive than is commonly supposed, especially for the English experience.[42] These sources generated by women include letters, diaries, manuscript autobiographies, memoirs and works of fact and fiction and literary collaboration as well as published texts. There are, of course, also numerous documents written by men in which women figure. These offer a different view of women's lives, experience and importance which should not be overlooked. Historians may also use visual evidence to indicate ways in which the norms of expected female behaviour were conveyed to both men and women. In the fifteenth and sixteenth centuries, when manuscript illumination of books of hours and other works flourished and when cults of female saints were prevalent and were supported by images, we can see how women of all classes were constantly made aware of these norms against which to measure themselves.

Whichever society we are considering, historians have to take care that they do not mistake an increase in documentation for the eighteenth century for social change. Sometimes the evidence, even for England, is so thin for the fifteenth to seventeenth centuries that it is simply not acceptable to argue enormous change. This means that in some cases the question of change has to be left open.

There is certainly a more acute shortage of documentation for the study of women in Ireland and in the early American colonies. For Ireland few court records or personal and family papers survive before the 1660s. There survive for Gaelic Ireland a variety of sources, ranging from law tracts to poetry, and annals to genealogies but their study is still in its infancy as scholars strive to set them in historical context and some of this work is highly controversial.[43] The search for a clearly identifiable Anglo-Irish experience, separate from that of England, is also difficult and exemplified by the case of Elizabeth and Percy Freke. Peirce or Percy was born in Ireland near his family's castle at Rathbarry in 1643. His father Arthur had married Dorothy Smith of Youghal, daughter of Mary Boyle and niece of the powerful Earl of Cork. Percy, however, left for England twenty years later and became a student at the Middle Temple in 1663. Six years on he married 'Mrs Elizabeth Freake of Martin in the Fields' by licence but without her father's permission. They spent much of their married life in England but also spent considerable periods, both separately and together, in Ireland. Elizabeth's detailed remembrances, however, indicate that, while her husband's commitment to Ireland was genuine, she resisted his attempts to move permanently to Ireland. Between 1692 and 1694 the family lived together on the Rathbarry estate with their son but, despite their prominent position in the social life of County Cork and the shared English heritage of this society, Elizabeth felt so isolated that she took the dramatic step of leaving her husband and son in order to return to their Norfolk estates and make her own way. This instance reminds us that it is dangerous to assume that because a family had Irish possessions, residence and influence, the culture of its women was Irish.[44] For the New England and Chesapeake colonies there are legal court records and statutes but very little in the way of other documentation until the late seventeenth and eighteenth centuries. Mary Beth Norton and others have shown, for example, that several purported diaries of seventeenth- and eighteenth-century colonial women were, in fact, nineteenth-century fakes: Dorothy Dudley, Mary Titus Post and the 'Puritan Maid' Hester Shepard.[45] While some of Norton's reasoning about the fraudulence of Shepard's diary is itself suspect (for examples, the Oxford English Dictionary is not the last word on the first appearance of words either in the colonies or Britain; and, worse still, 'Young women – indeed *any* women – didn't keep diaries in 17thC America' is an argument against ever accepting evidence of the unusual!) she does prove that Hetty Shepard's diary is a fake by painstakingly checking the references and finding errors and anachronisms. Real colonial diaries date from the second and third quarters of the eighteenth century. Normally they fall into two categories: reflective religious journals and routine work or social diaries. During the revolutionary period women also wrote lengthy letters of a diurnal character to relatives and friends which are highly revealing of their lives. As a result historians of seventeenth- and early eighteenth-century America have been forced to approach the history of women more obliquely than they would have wished. Nevertheless, in the case of Ireland, Scotland and the colonies, some excellent work has been forthcoming, displaying considerable ingenuity in the exploitation of such sources as do exist.[46]

Women's writings have to be regarded as critically as those of men but some historians have urged that 'Women's words were . . . filtered through the barrier of men's expectations . . .'[47] and therefore require an even more critical approach. For instance, men perceived female criminality differently from that of male criminality. Also women themselves quite frequently curtsied to convention and apologised for nonconformist behaviour. Most images of women should be similarly viewed, they argue, especially as most were portrayed by men: the deliberate self-representation of a woman artist such as Mary Beale was very much the exception that proved the rule.[48]

Our eyes have been opened to the possibilities of many other types of evidence than the written and printed words of or about women. Historians are only now beginning to explore and exploit more fully the riches of women's contributions to the furnishings and decorations of their time – bed hangings, tapestries, clothing – and also to the buildings themselves and to their gardens.[49] Such sources may be used not only to demonstrate the important role women played in organising the lives of their families and structuring their environment and incidentally contributing to the overall landscape of Britain and her colonies but also to indicate how far women accepted or rejected the stereotypical views of the female gender. The needle as well as the pen could liberate a woman's creative powers.

Why a book that considers the history of women across more than two centuries?

In some ways the long chronological sweep of this book has proved a disadvantage, yet it alone gives an opportunity for tracing trends and changes in the experience of women, the roles of women, the attitudes towards, and of, women. Chronologically the book does focus upon the sixteenth and seventeenth centuries but makes forays into both earlier and later periods with respect to particular themes and debates. This approach has been adopted in the main to prevent overlength and to avoid repetition.

One of the disadvantages of the long time period is the temptation to substitute the broad, general picture and statistical summary for evidence of the lives of women themselves. There is here an attempt to counter this tendency by using relatively detailed case studies of particular women wherever appropriate. During the course of the book the reader will become acquainted with the lives of women of the period who left rich documentation such as Hester Temple of Stowe, and her daughters and daughters-in-law, Bess of Hardwick, Margaret Clifford, Cassandra Duchess of Chandos, Margaret Lucas Cavendish, Grisell Baillie, Lettice Bagot, Constance Fowler, Elizabeth Stout, Elizabeth Carey, Mary Sidney, Mary Wroth, Lady Katherine Boyle Jones, Viscountess Ranelagh, Elizabeth Freke, and Aphra Behn. In leaving such literary or other remains they were, of course, unusual and, untypically, they have as a result had some influence at least upon the canon but in other respects these women were not atypical. Their doings seem to point to and exemplify characteristics of the lives of many other contemporary women. It has not proved possible to balance these case studies of English and Anglo-Irish women with equivalents from the American colonies – although some attention is given to Ann Hutchinson, Phyllis Wheatley and Abigail Adams – as there are few surviving personal archives for American women before the American Revolution.

Women of all social classes?

For a variety of reasons this book concentrates upon the experience of elite and middling-sort women. This is, in a real sense, an advantage because it was at these higher reaches of society that one is led by traditional historians to believe that the hold of patriarchy upon women was tightest. In fact, the evidence for this seems far from compelling. Some men may have attempted to keep a stranglehold on their womenfolk but the evidence seems overwhelming that, if so, they failed miserably. What is clear, however, is that many, even most, women did subscribe willingly to the general commitment in society to the good of the family.

Where there are appropriate data, however, some attention is accorded to women of the lower sort but such data is patchy on the ground. In particular an attempt is made to provide a statistical demographic backdrop which includes all social groups in England and Wales where the sources permit. In the case of the colonies – Ireland and the North

American colonies – the book treats available data for the colonisers (and in the case of North America their imported black slaves and servants) rather than the indigenous peoples. This is in large part because the scholarly work to facilitate such a treatment of existing populations is at present insufficient. In small part it is because the scope of the book is already enormous and space simply does not allow for such a study.

Debates

Some areas of women's history have assumed greater importance because they have stimulated debates among historians. In a book intended for undergraduates and university teachers, it seems important not only to offer a synthesis of modern scholarship regarding women but also to preserve the distinctions between different positions. In this way the book acts as a companion to women's history of the period. Thus, although some of the chapters in this book focus on the 'ages' and 'stages' of women's lives, and others are organised around broad issues – such as, what religious role did women perform and what part did women play in the culture of their time and place? – the chapters themselves also try to give a flavour of debate where this is current and important. Overall there has been an attempt, nonetheless, to provide a readable, concise and accessible account.

Organisation

The present book is divided into substantial parts. Part One treats the business of marrying; Part Two the experience of marriage and widowhood; Part Three, containing chapters on the cultural and religious life of women, forms a bridge between the various phases of women's lives. This arrangement reflects a conviction that, while women's lives were dominated by the prospect of, or actuality of, marriage (even when they elected to, or were destined to, remain single) there was no sharp division in their lives when they passed from the single to the married state. Throughout their single years, girls and young women were prepared for their married lives and widowhood not only through formal education but also through training in the running of household, family and estates. (The type of such education and training varied according to social and economic circumstance.) During the same years young women developed cultural and religious lives that also affected their experience as wives and mothers. Each one of these parts is subdivided into shorter chapters. There follows a select bibliography.

One of the chief problems that any author of a history encounters is the fact that the material does not fall into neat categories. This, in the present instance, was because women's lives were not divided into compartments. In an age dominated by religion, almost every aspect of women's lives had a religious dimension and so to write a single chapter on 'women and religion' or belief must be artificial. Similarly 'power' relations were observable in many different aspects of women's lives. Women's role in contemporary culture was also not neatly compartmentalised. There has also, inevitably, had to be some repetition in order to explain the relevance of, for example, the laws and patterns of inheritance to women and their kin during different life stages. Nevertheless, in this book there are separate chapters on different dimensions of women's experience that add up to a particular interpretation. Students using the book will find this organisation convenient but should be aware that relevant material might be found elsewhere in the book and that careful use of the index is advisable.

Notes

1 Historians who sympathise with this view would nevertheless caution that western societies did not always develop at the same rate and that, for example, parts of Scotland were dominated by clan society until the eighteenth century.
2 R. H. Tawney (1912) p. 233.
3 J. Wormald (1985) *passim*; Liam Kennedy (1991) p. 478.
4 R. W. Hoyle (1995) p. 154.
5 Govind Sreenivasen (1991) pp. 3–37.
6 See Rosemary O'Day (1995) pp. 64–128; David Cressy (1986), 'Kinship and kin interaction in early modern England', pp. 38–69.
7 Laurel Thatcher Ulrich (1991) p. 185.
8 For standard accounts of the position of women in late eighteenth- and nineteenth-century Britain and America see Martha Vicinus (ed.), *Suffer and Be Still* (1972); Janet Wilson James (1954) pp. 34–64; Mary Beth Norton, (1984) pp. 593–619; Lauren Thatcher Ulrich (1991) pp. 103–5; Nancy Cott (1978–9) pp. 219–36; and Cott (1977).
9 Rosemary O'Day (1995) pp. 271–2.
10 I. Maclean (1980) was a pioneering work in this area; see also L. Woodbridge (1984); A. Fletcher (1995); S. Gosling (1999).

11 See R. O'Day (1995) *passim* and especially pp. 129–63.
12 Sara Mendelson and Patricia Crawford (1998) p. 17.
13 Yvonne Galloway Brown and Rona Ferguson (2002).
14 See James C. Scott (1990) p. 18.
15 For two interesting articles on early modern Scottish history see Allan I. Macinnes (1994) pp. 30–46; and Michael Lynch (1994) pp. 47–63.
16 Christine Peters (2004) succeeds brilliantly at the level of generalities in comparing women over four countries but it is more difficult to execute systematic comparison in detail.
17 B. Levack (1987) p. 179.
18 J. Dawson (1995) *passim*.
19 S. G. Ellis (1985) *passim*.
20 See S. G. Ellis (1985) pp. 108–27; and N. Canny (1995), 'Irish, Scottish and Welsh responses to centralisation, c.1530–c.1640' pp. 150–55, for an excellent summary.
21 See Canny (1995) pp. 153–5.
22 Ibid pp. 158–61.
23 Ibid p. 160; and A. Bliss (1979) for an opposing view.
24 Garthine Walker, 'Strange kind of stealing: abduction in early modern Wales', in M. Roberts and S. Clarke (eds), *Women and Gender in Early Modern Wales*, 2000, especially p. 69.
25 Francis Jennings (1975); see also Neal Salisbury (1982); James Axtell (1978), 'The ethno-history of early America' pp. 110–44; James Axtell (1981); Bruce G. Trigger (1982) pp. 139–55; Bruce G. Trigger (1979) pp. 205–23.
26 Mechal Scobel (1988) *passim*.
27 Quoted in James Axtell (1984) p. 645.
28 See Bernard Bailyn and Barbara DeWolfe (1986); and Bernard Bailyn (1986) for a general introduction to the varied development and demography of the thirteen colonies.
29 See Henry A. Gemery (1984) pp. 318–20.
30 John Higham (1984) p. 18.
31 George L. Haskins (1960); Marylynn Salmon (1986); Carole Shammas *et al.* (1987).
32 Maryland Debra Meyers (2003) p. ix.
33 For a good summary and suggested estimates see Aaron Fogleman (1992) pp. 691–1709.

34 I note especially the work of Mechal Scobel (1988).
35 Anon., *A Share of Honour. Virginia Women 1600–1945*, p. 11.
36 Paul Clemens (1980); Kenneth E. Lockridge (1970); Gary B. Nash (1979).
37 Richard Middleton (1992) pp. 224–5.
38 See Steven G. Ellis (1985) pp. 40–1.
39 Mary O'Dowd (1999) pp. 156–71.
40 Bernadette Cunningham (1986) pp. 152–64; Michael McCarthy Morrogh (1986) pp. 172–89.
41 See Introduction, Ciaran Brady and Raymond Gillespie (1986) pp. 11–17, for a brief but illuminating discussion of the historiography down to 1986. Steven G. Ellis (1985) provides a useful interpretation of the situation prior to the English rule of all Ireland imposed from 1603 onwards.
42 Patricia Crawford (1985); Sara Mendelson (1985); also James Daybell (ed.), *Early Modern Women's Letter-Writing 1450–1800*, 2001.
43 For a good discussion of the problems involved see Bernadette Cunningham (1986) pp. 148–70.
44 Raymond A. Anselment (2001) pp. 7–14.
45 Mary Beth Norton (1998) pp. 141–54; this problem is not unique to American sources, as some English diaries such as the published *Diary of Elizabeth Pepys* also appear to be fake, despite the editor's claim to have found the manuscript in an attic.
46 Mary O'Dowd (1999) pp. 156–71.
47 Sara Mendelson and Patricia Crawford (1998) p. 11.
48 Her self-portrait (painted in c. 1675) is reproduced in Sara Mendelson and Patricia Crawford (1998) p. 7.
49 Anne Laurence (1994, 2002 reissue) pp. 293–303.

PART 1

Marrying: an active proposition

Introduction

One of the key concerns for a young woman in each of these societies (and for her mother and father) was the question of her marriage. The specific vocations of the great majority of women were those of wife and mother, notwithstanding important recent work on other forms of partnership and on singletons. Those who did not marry felt obliged to explain their departure from the norm. For the historian of women, therefore, it is important to investigate how this question of marriage was settled, revealing in the process the variety of views and practices. It is also important to recognise that gender played a relatively small role in the way in which marriages were arranged: much of the evidence shows that the major distinction was that between 'parents' and 'family members' and 'friends' on the one hand and 'children' or 'young people' on the other.

Historians have focused upon issues which surround the purpose of marriage; the choice of marriage partner; the contractual arrangements surrounding promise, 'engagement' and marriage. These debates are closely linked and in this section each is not treated separately, which would be repetitive, but a series of short chapters attempt to show how treatment of these issues sheds light on the place of women in early modern society. These chapters are not equal in length: for some aspects there is much to be said, for others relatively little, largely owing to the paucity of documentation. The dearth of evidence makes it difficult to grapple with the question of change over time as well as the differences between these societies.

The question of whether marriage was equally important in each of these societies is broached and, in the process, definitions of marriage and indications of the ways in which it was arranged and solemnised are teased out.

CHAPTER 2

How and where were marriages solemnised?

Forasmuch as N and N have consented together in holy wedlock, and have witnessed the same before God and this company, and have therefore given and pledged their troth either to the other, and have declared the same by the giving and receiving of a ring, and by joining of hands, I pronounce that they be man and wife together.[1]

Introduction

In early modern societies marriages could be divided into 'regular' and 'irregular' unions. Regular unions obeyed rules set down by the state and/or the church. It is with these regular unions that this chapter is concerned. Irregular unions (often called clandestine or secret marriages) were valid but any ceremonial attached to them was by definition hidden from history. There were differences in the conduct of regular marriages between England and Scotland and between England and her American colonies. Some of these differences were due to religious differences between the societies. Others were shaped by the circumstances of settlement in the New World.

How and where were regular marriages conducted?

When Advent comes do thou refraine
Till Hillary set thee free again
Next Septuagesima saith thee nay
But when Low Sunday comes thou may
Yet at Rogation thou must tarrie
Till Trinitie shall bid thee Marry[2]

In Catholic countries where marriage, or holy matrimony, was a sacrament (that is, an outward and visible sign of an inward and spiritual grace), marriages took place in church at given seasons of the year and during daylight hours. Marriage was forbidden, for example, during Lent (the season of preparation for Easter), Rogationtide and Trinity (in the late spring), and Advent (the season when Christians prepared themselves for Christmas). Once England and Wales broke from Rome, the status of marriage as a sacrament was contested but the prohibitions on unseasonable marriages were retained. Only two sacraments were accepted by many Protestants – Baptism and the Eucharist or Lord's Supper – and even these were not seen as essential to salvation. In the more radical second Prayer Book of Edward VI's reign, the English marriage service nonetheless expresses the common Protestant view that marriage was a holy estate to be entered into before God and not lightly: 'And there the Priest shall thus say . . . we are gathered together here in the sight of God, and in the face of his congregation, to join together this man and this woman in holy matrimony, which is an honourable estate, instituted of God in Paradise . . .' By the later revisions of the Prayer Book marriage was reinstated as a sacrament and many of the Catholic practices reappeared.[3]

In Scotland, as we shall see in the next chapter, approaches to the question of a valid marriage varied. In Scotland handfasting arrangements appear to have been very common. Handfasting (betrothal) often consisted of public (and parentally approved) exchange of marriage vows, without the subsequent marriage ceremony before a minister. In 1562 the Aberdeen Kirk Session declared that such unions although legally valid were 'manifest fornication and whoredom'. In 1568 the Aberdeen Kirk Session forbade ministers to attend handfasting ceremonies, thus trying to rob them of ecclesiastical respectability. But in 1570 the Scottish General Assembly reversed this policy by insisting that handfasting took place in the Kirk and that sexual abstinence was practised thereafter until the marriage itself. In 1575 this policy was again reversed (with a ban on any other ceremonies than marriage itself) and the Kirk sessions eventually contented themselves with requiring couples applying for banns of marriage to take out bonds that would be declared forfeit if the bride was found to be pregnant prior to marriage. Marriage itself was to be performed by the minister in the Kirk.[4]

In the Middle Ages spousals and marriages were celebrated in the church porch: the Sarum Missal, which was widely used in southern England, specified that the service should begin 'before the door of the church, or in the face of the church', although people of high rank might be married in the nave of the church itself and all couples would come before the altar for a nuptial mass after they were wed standing beneath a pallium.[5] The spousals ring which had been given to the bride-to-be and worn on her right hand since the signing of the betrothal agreement some time earlier was now blessed with holy water and transferred to her left hand by the groom. Vows were exchanged and afterwards the couple were 'crowned' before they left the church. Weddings were followed by a breakfast in church of blessed wine, bread and cakes – literally a breaking of the fast insisted upon before the Eucharist.

Contemporary accounts of marriages themselves and the preparations for them show that throughout the period brides and grooms clad themselves in as much finery as they could muster. Leonard Wheatcroft went with his bride-to-be on a shopping spree as soon as the ink was dry on their marriage settlement. Some clearly spent to excess, at least in the opinion of those who were expected to foot the bills. So Margaret Harlakenden from Essex spent £120 in London on wedding attire and her father was 'exceeding angry . . . for her vanity'.[6] It may not always have been the parents who bore such expenses directly, however. Joyce Jefferies, a well-to-do Hereford spinster, for example, recorded in May 1641 'Anne Davies wedding gown which I gave her, she was married to Joshua Ailway on Whitsun Thursday' and in December 1643 she gave Eliza Acton, her god-daughter and maid £20 to 'pay for her wedding clothes'. In both cases Joyce Jefferies had been given charge of the girls' portions when they came to dwell with her as maids and a responsibility to pay for their weddings may have been part of the arrangement.[7] Grooms too attended to their dress as did attendants and guests. English brides customarily completed their outfits with garlands of flowers and carried floral bouquets. The flowers they bore had symbolic significance, indicating that marriage brought an end to strife and that the wife and husband would have particular virtues. Buckinghamshire rector Roger Hacket preached a marriage sermon that drew attention to the flowers in the bridal bouquet – primroses, violets, rosemary and maiden's blush – as recommendations of obedience, patience and faithfulness for the bride and wisdom, love and loyalty for the groom in their future life together.[8]

Following the break from Rome, marriages in England were supposedly all brought into the nave (main part) of the church building: 'the persons to be married shall come into the body of the church, with their friends and neighbours' instructed the Edwardian order of service. In fact there is some evidence that marriages continued to take place in the church porch. For example, licences issued in the midland diocese of Coventry and Lichfield in the 1660s stipulated that weddings must be solemnised 'in the face of the parish church'.[9] It was a public occasion, not just because the whole community should rejoice at this entry into a holy estate but also to prevent bigamous and other irregular marriages. Other measures were taken to guard against such irregularities: this was why marriages took place during daylight (between 8 a.m. and midday) during divine service;[10] why veils were lifted to expose the bride's face; why banns were ordered to be read during public service on three successive Sundays in the parishes where bride and groom resided and also during the marriage service itself, inviting anyone who had good reason why the marriage should not take place to come forward and explain themselves; why licences were contingent upon both parties swearing that they had entered into no prior contracts. This practice of reading the banns on three occasions was extended to the 'English' colonies of the Atlantic seaboard of America, albeit in colonies where there was civil marriage the banns had to be read or posted in writing in 'a public place' rather than necessarily in a church.[11] Scotland also maintained a similar system. All this reflected considerable anxiety concerning the problem of bigamous unions and/or outright desertion in these early modern societies,[12] and the need to avoid the resulting complications concerning establishing who were the legitimate heirs, and where the responsibility lay for the maintenance of both mothers and children. Although marriages were ordered to be recorded in the parish registers, it was not until 1653 that civil marriage was introduced into England for a brief period.[13]

Studies have shown that the English obeyed the prohibition against Lenten weddings throughout the period 1500–1760 but, although they more or less obeyed the other prohibitions against marriages during Rogationtide, Trinity and Advent throughout the sixteenth century, by the seventeenth century people were increasingly ignoring these rules regarding the season of marriage.[14] (Marriages during the prohibited seasons technically required a special licence but this rule often seems to have been disregarded.) In rural areas especially, though, harvest time in the autumn and also after lambing or calving in the spring proved highly popular times to celebrate a union, because food was plentiful and work had been done.[15]

The American colonies appear to have altered this Old World pattern of seasonality in many respects, at least partly as a reflection of the changed climatic conditions. Marriages in the late seventeenth-century/eighteenth-century New England colonies on the Atlantic seaboard were flat from

February through May, slumped in the summer and picked up again in October, peaking in the early months of winter. New Jersey also followed this pattern but marriages picked up and ended a month earlier than in New England (perhaps in an effort to beat the onslaught of bad weather further north). Examination of marriages among particular groups show more variation. For example, both New England and New Jersey Quakers displayed a surge in May marriages but New Jersey Quaker couples were much less likely to marry during the summer and showed a more dramatic and early preference for autumn–winter marriages. In Maryland there was a very marked preference for marrying in December, January and February (peaking two months after that in New England and a month after that in New Jersey) and avoidance of marriage during Lent and between May and October. French Canadians followed the French peasant disinclination to marry in Lent but whereas in France there was a marked mid-summer peak in marriages, Canadians preferred not to marry between May and September. A flurry of Canadian marriages in February perhaps represented an attempt to celebrate unions before the Lenten prohibition.[16]

Although the Church of England did not specify any particular day for marriages, English couples did prefer certain days of the week. Roger Schofield extrapolated from the reconstitution of twenty-six parishes across England (1538–1831) that whereas Sunday and Monday were the most popular wedding days in the period 1538 to 1575, there was a marked decline in their popularity between 1575 and 1660, with a commensurate rise in the popularity of Tuesday, Wednesday and especially Thursday. 32 per cent of marriages had taken place on a Thursday in the mid-seventeenth century, and this trend was especially dominant in agricultural parishes. From 1660 to 1780 Thursday became a much less favoured day (falling to 14 per cent of marriages) and Monday became the increasingly frequent choice. 'The rise of the Monday marriages, on so-called "St Monday", has been taken as the mark of the appearance of proto-industry, or of an urban working pattern, in which the working week ran from a Tuesday to a Saturday.' The modern preference for Saturday is a post-Second World War phenomenon.[17]

Marriage rituals and feastings

There had long been rituals connected with the ceremony, which the Catholic Church had tolerated and which the Church of England continued to wink at, allowing some to take place in the church porch. For example, in parts of the north of England the couple would be locked into the church and only allowed out once the groom had pushed a 'ransom' under the church door. In Yorkshire and Wales there was often a race from the church to the couple's new home. Here the winner could claim the bride's garter as his prize. In many places obstacles would often be placed in the couple's way and be removed only on the payment of fines. In Wales couples were even seized and roped together. Rough music (when the couple were mocked) was very common in all parts of England and Wales.

Typical was a procession of the youth of the parish, boys and girls, accompanied by fiddlers and/or pipers, to escort the bride and groom from church to wedding feast. This feast was followed by kissing and fondling. Fuelled by drink the young couple and their guests sang, danced and frolicked, and engaged in sexually explicit jesting and playing games that involved throwing around intimate items of clothing. There was no coyness here regarding the climax of the night!

O! Give them active heat
And moisture both complete:
Fit organs for increase
To keep and to release
That, which may the honour'd stem
Circle with a diadem.[18]

This climax was prepared for by the virgin bridesmaids who showered the couple with flowers and wheat as they left the church and at their new home scattered flowers on the marriage bed. Here the disrobing of the bride was performed in front of the young male and female attendants.

Late at night when the happy couple retired to bed they met with further obstacles and intrusion: the bed might contain branches and be short-sheeted; a band might strike up; rowdy visitors might burst into the chamber and pelt the couple with stockings filled with sand. In 1665 Samuel Pepys recorded invading a bridal chamber in order to kiss the bride in her bed, and more than a century later this custom was continuing. Puritans objected to these practices but there is small doubt that they continued until late in the nineteenth century in many parishes.

Once the happy pair were bedded the festivities continued for their friends and neighbours, sometimes for several days. When George Cely, a merchant, married Margery on Tuesday 18 May 1484, the groom provided feasting over about five days costing around £12 16s. (comparable to six months' normal housekeeping) that included liberal quantities of meat, poultry, fish and white wine, and delicacies such as rabbit, oranges and figs. In addition to the three dozen rabbits to be eaten at the wedding breakfast there were live rabbits to be let loose amongst the guests![19] Higher up the social ladder, the marriage festivities of Prince Arthur and Katharine of Aragon in 1501 were yet more lavish, including, as they did, disguisings and pageants.[20] Yet again 'many quick conies [rabbits] . . . ran about the hall and made very great disports'. On this occasion white doves and other birds were also released and this caused 'great laughter and disport'.[21] No matter what the social status of the couple, a great fuss was made of weddings and the humble wedding breakfast was augmented by feasts. In 1537 the entire parish turned out to celebrate the wedding of Margaret Timewell and William Taylor of Morebath, Devon, specially held on St George's Day which was a holiday when no one worked.[22] Such celebrations continued in some situations from the Reformation onwards. Henry Machyn described in his sixteenth-century diary the 'big weddings' of freemen of London, celebrated over several days, with processions, 'the trumpettes blohyng', formal feasts, dancing and merrymaking.[23] We know that the urban guilds made much of the weddings of their members: some of them, such as the chimney sweeps, continued well into the nineteenth century, with elaborate, noisy and colourful celebrations of members' weddings. The wedding of a London Alderman's son at Draper's Hall in 1675 lasted three days. In 1682 Ralph Thoresby attended a two-day wedding feast in Yorkshire and there is evidence that this practice was common in the north.

These festivities and the giving and receiving of invitations and of gifts and tokens such as gloves and trinkets served to consolidate the connection to which bride and groom belonged. The reading of the banns for three weeks before the wedding served to invite the whole parish to the public ceremony. By the late sixteenth century literate parents were also sending out personal written invitations to especial friends.[24] Many were individually invited by word of mouth. Colourful ribbons were distributed to all who attended the feast and were worn on hats or as garters. Customarily pairs of gloves were given by the happy couple to friends and kin. A pair of gloves, signifying the hand of friendship, would be sent to close family members who could not be present (in much the same way that modern couples send small portions of wedding cake to absent friends). The bride's garters were given away and treasured (as bridesmaids today treasure the bridal bouquet). The couple also entertained the guests to a feast (which in times of hardship would be highly valued).[25]

At the feast or during the wedding service the parents or guardians might give the bride's dowry or something symbolising the dowry. To the feast guests brought a variety of presents ranging from food, drink, money and plate to household goods. A major concern seems to have been to prolong the wedding celebrations themselves. So, in 1567, guests at the wedding of Surrey gentry Richard Polstead and Elizabeth More contributed birds such as capons, partridges, swans and woodcocks and game, fish, sweetmeats, puddings, cheeses and wine.[26] Even the clergyman who celebrated the wedding could be munificent, if the diary of the Sussex Restoration clergyman Giles Moore can be regarded as in any way typical, sometimes donating a sermon and forgiving the marriage fees, treating the fiddlers and pipers and so forth.[27] Doles were made by the bridal party to the poor. This was a practice followed from the beginning to the end of our period, and beyond.[28]

Protestant attitudes to marriage varied – was it a sacrament or wasn't it? Should it be a religious or a civil ceremony? Was the ring to be used or not? Should marriage be celebrated with feasting, drinking and dancing? One contemporary account suggests that these different views were echoed in the actual wedding practices of religious groups. Henri Misson, a Frenchman, commented of late seventeenth-century English weddings that they

[g]enerally vary according to the several customs of the countries, the rank or quality of the persons and their different religions. The Presbyterians profess so great a strictness, and such much a reservedness, that their weddings are very quiet [whereas those of the middling sort] invite a number of friends and relations; every one puts on new clothes, and dresses finer than ordinary; the men lead the women, they get into coaches, and so go in procession, and are married in full day at church. After feasting and dancing, and having made merry that day and the next, they take a trip into the country, and there divert themselves very pleasantly.[29]

The story of the Willoughby–Ridgway marriage in 1610 is one of the most detailed available for such an early date and it certainly suggests very elaborate festivities at this social level in Anglo-Irish Protestant circles. David Cressy has collected together many accounts of elaborate wedding festivities amongst the middling and upper sorts of people: from the court wedding of Sir Philip Herbert, the weddings of Cornish gentry, to the marriage of a shipwright's daughter to an apprentice in 1637 when the many guests were royally entertained under a 'marquis' (marquee) in the garden. Cressy, however, suggests that, although there are certainly examples of Puritan critique of contemporary excesses, Misson exaggerated the opposition of Presbyterians and other dissenters to wedding celebrations. Cressy argues that Christians could discern between acceptable festivity and unacceptable excess. He cites the examples of Oliver Heywood, a dissenting preacher, who married Elizabeth Anger in 1655 and 'feasted above an hundred persons of several ranks, ages and sexes'; of Ralph Josselin Puritan minister and diarist who wrote approvingly of a marriage feast that lasted three days; and of Leonard Wheatcroft of Ashover whose wedding deliberately echoed those of popular literature. Wheatcroft, married during the Protectorate (a time associated in the popular mind with austerity), held eleven feasts on eleven days. He entertained full two hundred people to breakfast, dinner and supper. There were merry bells in the morning, sweet music for dancers in the afternoon, choice tunes in the evening after supper.[30] Even jousting was laid on. All in all, the marriage feasting at Canaan provided a comforting New Testament model for all Christians to follow.

New World marriages

Some of the evidence from the New World suggests that Cressy is wise to be cautious in drawing too firm a divide along religious lines. The wedding of Governor Bradford of Plymouth Colony in 1623 suggests an adaptation of customary celebrations to accord with local circumstances for it was similarly marked with entertainment (on this occasion from native Americans) and a great feast of turkeys.[31] In this Puritan colony, however, weddings were civil ceremonies that mostly took place not in church but in the bride's home and were not marked by feasting. John Demos believes that such marriages were 'characterized by a kind of rough and ready spontaneity', being short and to the point. He argues that these Old Colony home weddings had little in common with developing traditions in neighbouring Massachusetts, of which New Plymouth Colony eventually became a part.[32] There marriage was also a civil institution but there are indications that they were accompanied by jollity and festivity.[33] By making marriage a civil institution, presumably Puritans felt justified in allowing celebration. It was in the marriage itself that the differences between 'Puritan' and other Christians (Catholic or Anglican) were really seen. Following the English example set in 1645 (whereby the reading of three sets of banns was a necessary prelude to a legal marriage) and the ruling of Oliver Cromwell in 1653 that marriage should be a civil ceremony performed by a magistrate before two witnesses, in the Puritan colonies of New England (Massachusetts, New Hampshire, Connecticut), civil marriage before a magistrate was the order of the day and it was a public affair. Calvinists in the southern colonies of Virginia, Maryland and the Carolinas seem to have continued the old English Puritan practices, refusing to use the ring in marriage and viewing marriage as a contract publicly entered into and preferably in a church. In Maryland for most of the propertied the old Catholic customs of celebrating a nuptial mass, of marrying under a pallium, of using a ring blessed with holy water and of crowning bride and groom persisted, however. Marriage for both Catholics and 'Anglicans' in Maryland remained a sacrament and the main distinction between Catholic and Anglican ceremonies lay in the fact that the Anglicans dispensed with the pallium and holy water. The various stages of marriage from betrothal through marriage settlement through reading of banns to marriage in church were followed. Large numbers of betrothal rings, duly inscribed with loving words, have been discovered in the former St Mary's City. Christians of both persuasions insisted on a religious ceremony even where no ordained priest was available to perform the marriage. In such circumstances couples copied the Prayer Book service and made their vows within a religious context. It was even relatively common for Catholic priests to marry Anglican couples when the couple could not find an Anglican priest. Quakers also sought religious marriages, approved of and witnessed by the Meeting and seem to have followed practices similar to those instituted in England by George Fox.[34] Although Maryland eventually (largely because of a shortage of ordained ministers of religion) instituted civil marriage and permitted Justices of the Peace to perform marriages, for many couples religious marriage persisted, and only the precise wording of the vows slightly modified the ceremony. The Maryland Assembly commanded that all marriages, whether civil or church, should use repetition of the traditional vows before two witnesses: 'I [A] do take thee [B] to my wedded [wife or husband] to have and to hold from this day forward for better or worse, for rich or for poor, in sickness and in health, till death us do part and thereto I plight thee my troth' and the magistrate or priest declared, 'I being hereunto by law authorised doe pronounce you lawful man and wife'.[35]

Conclusion

Whatever their religious affiliation early moderns regarded marriage as an occasion for rejoicing and celebration and for the confirmation of old and new alliances and connections. The differences in approach were to the rite of marriage itself. Within Catholic countries Holy Matrimony was a sacrament and was performed in church. Within Protestant countries there was controversy concerning its standing as a sacrament. The Scottish Presbyterians did not include it as a sacrament but did insist that it be performed in a church. The imposition of episcopacy and eventually of the English liturgy on Scotland in the reigns of James VI and I and Charles I meant that Anglican views and rites of marriage were introduced but were also robustly resisted. Within Anglicanism, matrimony remained one of the sacraments and there was an insistence that regular marriages be performed in church by a priest and according to canonical rules. Puritans disliked the ceremonies surrounding the rite (especially the use of the ring) and, while regarding marriage highly, did not see matrimony as a sacrament. In 1653 such views found their expression in the introduction of civil marriage by Oliver Cromwell. This experiment was short lived. Broadly speaking, the Puritan New England colonies followed Cromwell's lead whereas the Anglican and Catholic colonies of the Chesapeake region adhered to the traditional forms of marriage which returned to England at the Restoration. Local conditions – as in the case of the extreme shortage of ordained ministers – could and did lead to some modification of English practices.

Notes

1 Service of Holy Matrimony, Book of Common Prayer.

2 Mnemonic verse in the Everton, Nottinghamshire Parish Register, quoted by D. Cressy (1997) p. 299; and Meyers (2003) p. 50.

3 The two chief sacraments were those of Baptism and of the Holy Eucharist, which according to Article 25 of the 39 Articles of the Church of England of 1563 were differentiated as the 'two sacraments ordained of Christ . . . in the Gospel' from the 'five commonly called sacraments', including marriage, confirmation, penance, ordination and extreme unction. These Articles, themselves a slight revision of the 42 Articles of 1553, contained short summaries of the Anglican view of matters of contemporary controversy. David Cressy (1997) does not acknowledge this reversionary change.

4 A. E. Anton (1958) pp. 89–102, especially pp. 96–9; J. Stuart (1846); T. C. Smout (1981) especially pp. 211–12; see also C. Peters (2004) pp. 15–17 for a good summary.

5 This was a cloth or veil held over the bride and groom while they exchanged vows.

6 A. Macfarlane (1976) p. 410.
7 Account Book of Joyce Jefferies, BL Egerton MS 3054, fos 43v, 70v.
8 Roger Hacket, Rector of North Crawley, Buckinghamshire (1607) pp. 1–2.
9 See, for example, the licence for marriage of John Ryley and Mary Downy of Bradeley in the face of the parish church of St Mary's Stafford contained in L.J.R.O. B/C/6, Folder 4, no. 1, 1660.
10 See Canon 62 of 1603.
11 William Brigham (1836) p. 272; John Demos (1978) p. 159.
12 See, for example, L.J.R.O.
13 D. Cressy (1997) pp. 336–76, provides the best summary of what is known about the medieval and early modern marriage service and the rituals surrounding it. Another valuable, and more detailed, account is given by John R. Gillis (1985) which attends to northern as well as southern English practices.
14 E. A. Wrigley and R. S. Scofield (1981) pp. 298–305, 519–25.
15 Cressy (1985) pp. 1–21. See also A. Kussmaul (1990) especially pp. 3–4, 36–8, and A. Kussmaul (1981) pp. 755–79.
16 R. Schofield (1985) pp. 1–21; R. V. Wells (1987) pp. 299–307.
17 R. Schofield (2005) pp. 93–109, quotation from p. 104.
18 Robert Herrick, 'An Epithalamie to Sir Thomas Southwell and his Ladie' in F. W. Moorman (1921) p. 217. An Epithalamie was a nuptial verse. Herrick wrote a number of these, which can be read in the above edition of his works.
19 A. Hanham (1985) pp. 312–15.
20 Appearing in disguise and/or masks was very popular at court in the later Middle Ages and the early modern era.
21 John Leland (1770) p. 372. Cited in Hanham (1985) p. 314.
22 E. Duffy (2001) p. 7.
23 Henry Machyn (1847) pp. 243–4, 288.
24 William Vaughan (1609) book 2, ch. 6.
25 See D. Cressy (1997) pp. 365–7.
26 J. Evans (1855) pp. 36–44.
27 R. Bird (1971) pp. 300, 301, 316–18, 327, 333, 335.
28 T. F. Thisleton-Dyer, *Church-Lore Gleanings*, 1892, p. 123; and Anon. (N. H.) *Ladies' Dictionary, Being a general entertainment for the fair sex*, 1694, pp. 505, 740; both cited in Cressy (1997) p. 367.
29 Henri Misson (1719) pp. 349–51.

30 G. Parfitt and R. Houlbrooke (eds) (1986), pp. 83–8.
31 S. V. James (1963) p. 29.
32 J. Demos (1978) p. 163.
33 A. M. Earle (1894) pp. 73ff., R. S. Dunn (1998) pp. 37–8.
34 D. Meyers (2003) p. 53.
35 Browne, *Archives of Maryland*, 2, 523. The ampersand (&) was used indiscriminately in early modern manuscripts, frequently being mixed with the spelt-out version (and). Henceforth in this book, for convenience, the ampersand is spelt out.

CHAPTER 3

What was marriage? What was its purpose?

I did put her in mind of a young maiden that she had brought up in her house, the which I could like very well to be my wife and if I might have it so . . . To the which my words my gentlewoman said that she, for her part, was willing thereunto. 'But', quoth she, 'the maid is my husband's kinswoman, and therefore he will bestow her where he liketh. And if you would sue to him for his will to have her, I am sure it would be such a troublesome piece of work for you, as it would disquiet you very much . . . and therefore, if you will be counselled by me, do you never proceed any further in it.'[1]

Introduction

In the last chapter we considered how and where marriages were solemnised. During the discussion it became apparent that the issue of what constituted a valid marriage was important. This present chapter treats not the concept of patriarchy, which is dealt with later, but with the difference between legitimate and illegitimate unions summed up in the questions: What was marriage? What was its purpose?

Answers to these questions require examination from various perspectives, a good deal of delving in the archives, and are frequently elusive. From a twenty-first-century perspective the answers might seem obvious: marriage is a legally recognised, exclusive and registered life partnership between a man and a woman, arising from mutual desire, that is to be dissolved only by legal process. (Until recently the possibility of legalised partnerships between members of the same sex was not contemplated or countenanced.) If, however, we look back at the late medieval and early modern period with this definition in mind we will inevitably be totally confused by what we see. Until the eleventh century polygamy was the norm, concubinage was common, divorce simple. Illegitimate offspring – 'bastards' – and many half brothers and sisters stood in the wings to inherit property if the direct 'official' line failed. The eleventh-century church declared polygamy unlawful and insisted on betrothal (or spousals) and wedding. For secular society marriage was an entirely private affair, with no acknowledged role for church or central government. Landholding laymen saw marriage as a private property agreement or contract that also guaranteed some kind of protection to the widowed or divorced, and un-propertied laity saw it as a private contract between individuals, according to custom. Church ceremonies seemed unnecessary and expensive. Divorce was widespread and remarriage following divorce was common. Remnants of ancient customs persisted and were echoed in the secular laws. In the Middle Ages the Church continued to assert, with some success, the principles of monogamy and indissolubility, to bar bastards from inheritance, to forbid incest and to punish fornicators and adulterers. It did not, however, succeed in ensuring that all marriages took place in church, before a priest, and that all other 'marriages' were illegal.[2]

Early modern marriage: England

Marriage, the Church accepted, consisted of five stages: a legal contract setting out financial arrangements between parents; spousals (betrothal or engagement) before witnesses of the formal intention to marry; proclamation of banns in church (allowing those who knew of impediments to the proposed marriage to come forward); the wedding in church, allowing public verification of the marriage and its church blessing; and sexual consummation.

The Catholic Church regarded spousals and/or sexual consummation as just as legally binding as the church wedding. It was not until 1563 that the Catholic Church declared invalid all marriages that had not taken place before a priest. The Church in England (and after 1536 in Wales), however, retained the medieval canon (ecclesiastical) law of marriage, with all its confusions, until the mid-eighteenth century, except where it had specifically been changed by royal proclamation or parliamentary statute. This led to a situation in which Catholic marriage law was modernised whereas English (Protestant) marriage law was not. Regular marriages which followed the five stages were valid but so were irregular or clandestine marriages which did not. True marriages were made by consent, whether *verba de praesenti* (consent by both parties), or *verba de futuro* (statement of intention to marry in the future, followed by sexual intercourse) or by 'habit and repute', not just by church wedding ceremonies. The church courts were put in the position of actually declaring church weddings invalid where a prior contract or sexual union with another partner could be proved. (English civil courts, on the other hand, insisted that a church wedding must have taken place for a widow to have claim to a dower or her children to claim inheritance rights.)

Marriage in Scotland, Wales and Ireland

Some historians have argued that marriage was a weaker institution in Scotland and Wales than in England, chiefly because they see illegitimacy as having been more favourably treated in those societies. Yet the evidence for such a position seems less than convincing. Under Welsh law a young girl's virginity was jealously guarded until the day of her marriage and the goal of every father was to see his daughters formally contracted to marry and eventually married to another.[3] After 1536 this Welsh law no longer ran but historians are uncertain how Anglicised Welsh marriage customs became. It seems probable that Welsh girls still lived closely under parental supervision until they married, unlike Irish and English girls who were frequently fostered out.[4] Recent studies of Welsh wills indicate that in West Wales fathers had as strong a commitment as English fathers to providing dowries for their daughters to marry comfortably.

In Scotland the validity of a marriage was subject to the same tests as in England, and in the seventeenth and eighteenth centuries the rights of 'bastards' to inherit were hotly contested in the Edinburgh Commissary Court (the national court of Scotland dealing with such matters). Especially in the lowlands it seems unlikely that marriage was a weak institution. The Edinburgh court, like the English Church courts, also had on occasion to hear cases where the validity of an irregular marriage was asserted as against that of a regular union. For example, in 1639 or 1640 Dr Christopher Irving met and married Margaret Wisheart in Ireland. She had two children who were baptised as legitimate before the couple moved to Edinburgh and had further children. In 1670 Christopher left Margaret for Elisabeth Ker and had several children with her. He did not pay Margaret any maintenance and she eventually returned to her family in Ireland. In 1694 Christopher Irving junior claimed legitimacy under Scottish law in an action against Elizabeth Ker and her children, brought as much to protect his mother's reputation as his own estate. The commissaries declared that Christopher was legitimate because his father and mother had been lawfully married and that his father's subsequent union with Elisabeth Ker had been invalid and their children illegitimate.[5] Unions had to be permanent, bigamy was not allowed and the status of a church wedding over a handfast marriage or betrothal was a matter of legal debate.[6]

In Gaelic Ireland, as Katharine Simms has shown, bastard sons were eligible to inherit their fathers' property and this led to disregard of the Catholic Church's dictats, the development of divorce and even the practice of polygamy. By the seventeenth century, however, the introduction of the English common law into Ireland and the Catholic Reformation had combined to insist on the legitimacy of heirs to property and titles, monogamy and lifelong unions. In a sense married women were offered more protection, therefore, under English law than under Gaelic, although they lost the right to hold and administer their own property.[7]

Betrothal and handfasting

Contract would be followed by betrothal and then by marriage in church or the face of the church. Upon betrothal couples were held to have committed themselves to marriage – it was a solemn and legally binding 'engagement' to marry and individuals who refused to go on to marriage itself could be taken before the courts for breach of promise.

Some historians argue that handfasting was widespread throughout Britain. Couples who were handfasted consummated their union sexually. The union might be dissolved after a period of a year and one day. The Church acknowledged that handfasting in effect formed a valid marriage. In some cases, handfasting might take place even though the couple did not comply with the Church's rules regarding, for example, consanguinity and affinity (a person might not marry a relative by blood or affines). Before a church marriage might take place, a dispensation had to be obtained (for a fee) from the Church authorities, whether Catholic or, in the English case, Anglican. While these rules had been introduced for perfectly good reasons (to prevent incest or a man killing his wife in order to marry her sister or, on widowerhood, a man choosing to wed his step-daughter) dispensations became automatic (and a good source of revenue) once the principle had been conceded that only mutual consent was necessary for a valid marriage.

Clandestine 'marriage'

For a variety of reasons many couples failed to seal their marriage vows according to the Church's laws. Some couples handfasted. Some couples did marry in church, but covertly at night and, hence, against the Church's rules. Parties to such marriages might be seeking to employ a minister or priest of similar persuasion – a Catholic, for example, or a Puritan who wanted to be married without the ring. Or they might not be legally free to marry – the parties were under age, the parents' consent had not been obtained or a previous spouse was still alive. There appears to have been a sharp increase in the number of clandestine marriages in England in the late seventeenth century.[8] It has been suggested that this tendency was heightened in the 1690s by the introduction of a tax on London marriage licences.[9] Clandestine marriages at the Fleet became extremely popular: by 1740 there were about 6,000 Fleet marriages per annum compared to fewer than 7,000 regular marriages per annum in London. The Church, despite its canons, would acknowledge that these were valid marriages – as long as both parties had freely consented, a contract had been exchanged and the union had been consummated. No doubt, as today, some couples favoured simple cohabitation because of the freedom from mutual legal responsibilities and the ease of dissolution that it implied.

Handfasted marriages

During the sixteenth and much of the seventeenth century there was a divergence in marriage formation practices in Highland and Lowland Scotland. After the union of the Crowns of Scotland and England in 1603 there were concerted official attempts to end this divergence. Some historians have regarded these divergent practices as amounting to trial marriages in the Highlands.

Despite the protests of A. E. Anton that to portray Scottish males as wilfully and knowingly entering into trial marriages (by handfasting) with every intention of casting off their wives after a short period is an unwarranted slur,[10] it does seem that such trial marriages did exist in which menfolk had, as it were, the power of veto. In his *Description of the Western Isles of Scotland* Martin Martin described a practice of trial marriages:

It was an ancient custom in the islands that a man should take a maid to his wife, and keep her the space of a year without marrying her; and if she pleased him all the while, he married her at the end of the year, and legitimised these children; but if he did not love her, he returned her to her parents and her portion also; and if there happened to be any children they were kept by the father . . .[11]

Perhaps the practice was extended by some to take the form of short-term contracts of 'marriage'. This seems to be borne out by the wording of the Statutes of Iona. When the Crown and the chieftains agreed these in 1609 they determined that 'marriages contracted for a certain number of years' should be prohibited and the offenders punished as though they were fornicators.[12] The Statutes were reissued in 1616. Historians are uncertain whether this reform was effective. Its intention was to bring the more remote and traditionalist Highlands into line with lowland Scottish practice. Whether the reform was effective or not, its articulation suggests that temporary marriage was already unacceptable in the Lowlands by the early seventeenth century and perhaps before. Handfasting marriages (and subsequent divorces), where couples committed themselves to one another for a year before making a commitment to marry, occurred in Dumfries and Skye but were said to have fallen out of use by the seventeenth century. By 1695, when Martin wrote his description, the custom of trial marriage was said to have disappeared from the Western Isles.

There are indications that trial marriages and short-term contracts of marriage were once the custom in Wales also. Welsh law, which operated until 1536, saw marriage as consisting of two periods: the first seven years, during which the wife had no joint share in her husband's moveable goods, and the period thereafter when she had more rights. The marriage might be easily dissolved during the first seven years and, if it came to an end through no fault of the woman, she was entitled to a payment, the *agweddi*, on the basis of her father's status. After seven years the couple were fully married and on dissolution of the contract the wife was entitled to one-half of her husband's moveable goods. While Welsh law technically did not prevail after 1536 some historians believe that it shaped Welsh behaviour and expectations for many years to come.[13]

Toleration of (and even complicity with) such practices by the Church and the secular authorities seems hard to comprehend at first sight. It becomes easier when we realise that the Church was not in a strong position in these traditional Gaelic societies, just as it was not in many other parts of Britain. The situation in remote Scottish communities would have been echoed in many a remote English or Welsh village. In the seventeenth century in some parts knowledge of Christianity was minimal. There was an ongoing debate within the Church concerning the correct way to convert the people. Some believed in conflict but many churchmen felt that they had perforce to compromise in order to conquer. The more extreme customs of traditionalist societies were not blessed but they were regularised and modified. In 1610 the Revd Farquar Macrae claimed that when he preached in Lewis he had to baptise everyone under forty years old and marry 'a vast number who lived there together as man and wife, thereby to legitimate their children, and to abolish the barbarous custom that prevailed, of putting away their wives at the least discord'. Local ministers in seventeenth-century Kintyre divorced couples on grounds of adultery and permitted the parties to remarry and remain in communion. Such pragmatism was felt necessary if missions were to succeed in Christianising society and even the Franciscan Catholic missionary Cornelius Ward felt impelled to grant dispensations to marry to those whom the church would normally turn away – those who had formed illicit unions; those who had dissolved unions; and persons who were related to one another through blood or affinity.[14] Rome issued dispensations to many Scots who had handfasted despite the existence of impediments to their marriage – relieved that these couples had troubled to obtain the Church's blessing even if it was after the event.

Marriage on the Atlantic seaboard

What of the colonies on the Atlantic seaboard? Evidence for the seventeenth century is sparse but that which does exist suggests attempts by those determined to introduce order and government to regularise the institution of marriage in a manner adapted to the circumstances of colonial existence. In 1648 the Court of Massachusetts Colony pronounced a law for 'preventing all unlawful marriages' that repeated a law of 1639 ordering that 'no persons shall be joined in marriage' before the intention to marry 'hath been three times published at some time of public lecture or Towne meeting, in both the towns where the parties of either of them do ordinarily reside' or 'be set up in writing upon some post of their meeting house door in public view, there to stand so as it may easily be read by the space of fourteen days'.[15] Whereas in England banns were read in the church on three consecutive Sundays prior to the wedding, in Massachusetts they were published three times either at a public sermon or a town meeting or set on the meeting house door a fortnight before the ceremony. What in England was an ecclesiastical matter had in Massachusetts become a civil concern, a contract between two individuals. What is more, in a situation where young people were frequently far removed from parental supervision by migration, the civil magistrates acted legally *in loco parentis*. Care was taken, however, to ensure that parental authority was not thereby compromised. If any young man tried directly or indirectly to 'draw away the affections of any maid in this jurisdiction under pretence of marriage, before he hath obtained liberty and allowance from her parents or governors (or in absence of such) of the nearest magistrate' he would be fined for the first two such offences and for the third, if the parents or magistrate chose to make a complaint, imprisoned at the magistrates' pleasure.[16]

In seventeenth-century Maryland there are several examples of irregular marriages, which, as in England, were accepted as true marriages by the community, despite the rulings of the Catholic Church which, after 1563, insisted on religious marriages. In the American colonies it was sometimes difficult in any case for couples to celebrate their union in a church, with a properly ordained minister presiding. In Maryland, for example, a church and priest were frequently inaccessible. In such circumstances couples would invent their own ceremonies and simply marry themselves, using the old spousal customs. Elesabeth Lockett testified in a Maryland court in 1684 that she and Thos Bright had broken 'a peace of money . . . betwixt' them in front of witnesses. This would have been legally binding had not Thomas already been married to another.[17] Other couples based their ceremonies upon the prayer book.[18] Thus a layman named Thomas Seamor 'read the prayer and the matrimony' from the 1662 Book of Common Prayer over Mary Cole and Joseph Edlow before they 'did lie together'.

However, the overwhelming majority of Maryland colonists who owned land and other property apparently preferred legal marriages performed with a religious ceremony to ensure the safe transmission of that property to spouses and legitimate heirs without costly inheritance disputes.[19] Religiously sanctioned marriages also ensured that a household became accepted socially.[20] In this colony, established to provide a safe haven for Roman Catholics and members of the Church of England, many of the inhabitants also revered marriage as a sacrament.[21]

Unsurprisingly, the evidence suggests that in Tudor and Stuart England the propertied elite generally left nothing to chance and entered marriage using all five steps and taking care to see that the marriage was both valid and public. It is unclear how careful others were to abide by all the rules. The passing of laws against clandestine marriage in the colonies (and the wording of such laws) suggests that the authorities perceived an immediate and pressing problem as regards the normal population. For at least some in Scotland, the border counties, Wales and Devon and Cornwall, the betrothal ceremony or handfast was regarded in society as a whole as sufficient. In such avoidance of a church wedding, couples also avoided the need to publish the banns and invite scrutiny of their previous lives, and the expense and rigmarole of public marriage. The relative impermanence of pre-contracts probably also made them more attractive to contemporaries. Indeed Church marriages possibly became less common after the Restoration than before. In Tetbury in Gloucestershire, for instance, a full 20 per cent of marriages in the 1690s were conducted clandestinely, outside the Church altogether.[22] The big question remains: may we extrapolate from these figures for one county that a similar proportion of people in Britain never solemnised their marriages in church?

The purpose of marriage: England and Scotland

Any approach which examines the understanding of the purpose of marriage as a key to appreciating the place of women in the process of marrying must take into account different concepts of the institution of marriage itself, as indicated above.[23] Such concepts may be deduced from prescriptive literature – for example, conduct books – from social and religious commentaries; and from the descriptive evidence of marriage negotiations contained in family correspondence and marriage settlements.

The business of marrying for elite families certainly struck at the heart of property, particularly in England. Marriages were legal contracts and money and land and influence passed between the parties. William Stonor married three wives, the first two being wealthy widows and the third, Anne Neville, a niece of Warwick the Kingmaker and sole heiress to her father John Marquis of Montagu's estates. Anne Neville brought with her not only land but also an influential network and close association with the Marquis of Dorset.[24] For those who were obsessed with building, consolidating or maintaining an estate, the personal happiness of the parties to the marriage might play a very small part in determining whom a child should marry. At the very highest of social statuses the institution of the wardship presented a temptation. Wardships were chattels which could be bought, sold and bequeathed and even stolen, and they existed in Scotland as well as in England and Wales.[25] They gave the owner the rights of a father over the ward. If a ward refused to marry the spouse the guardian had selected, the ward had to pay a large fine. In 1576 the 8th Lord Glamis bought the wardship and marriage of his nephew John Kennedy, 5th Earl of Cassillis, who was the son and heir of his sister Margaret

Lyon and the recently killed 4th Earl of Cassillis. Glamis paid the Regent £10,000 for the privilege.[26] Humphrey Okeover was brought up as the ward of Elizabeth and Walter Bagot and married to their daughter when they were both 'imphants'.[27] When William Stonor married as his first wife Elizabeth Rich, the widow of a London mercer, one of the chief benefits their marriage brought to him was the lucrative wardship and marriages (of the four Fenn children) that she inherited.[28] In England and Wales when a minor child whose family property was held in knight-service was orphaned, as in the case of thirteen-year-old Mary Blacknall of Abingdon, he or she became a royal ward. Such wardships were sold. Wardship was not land but it was the promise of land. Wardship spelt control over the estate, education and marriage of the ward, who became potential prey to other families who saw him or her as an attractive marriage prospect. Sometimes, but not often, wardships were granted to close kin by the Court of Wards, although rarely to mothers on their own. In 1611 a ward's closest relatives were granted by reforms of the Court of Wards a period of one month in which to take up the option of the wardship before it was offered more widely. This was a matter which exercised parents considerably. In 1632 Sir John Temple, second son of Thomas and Hester, made a codicil to his will that if he should die before his heir came of age his second wife and her co-executor Thomas Tyrell of the Inner Temple should try to obtain the wardship and attend to his education.[29] In Mary Blacknall's case the claims of four of her own relatives were rebuffed and Sir Edmund Verney bought her wardship as the bride for his eldest son, Ralph.[30]

In 1549 the reformer Hugh Latimer had heard 'tell of stealing wards to marry their children to'.[31] As Latimer's comment implies, by no means a majority even of the elite accepted that this approach to marriage was correct. Some contemporaries criticised the whole system because it treated people – both men and women – like oxen. Sir Thomas Smith thought it to be 'very unreasonable and just, and contrary to nature, that a freeman and gentleman should be bought and sold like an horse or an ox'. This was, of course, not because male and female children were regarded as objects but because the man and the woman in a marrying situation *represented* actual property. As Hugh Latimer continued: 'This is strange kind of stealing, but it is not the wards, it is the lands they steal.' Garthine Walker has shown how Welsh mothers challenged others' rights of guardianship (and, therefore, marriage) 'in battles that could result in, or be construed as, abduction'.[32] If it could be proved that a marriage was the result of compulsion then it could legally be annulled.[33] Clearly quarrels over guardianship focused on property transmission (although, as this discussion shows, this obsession with property transmission was in the service of the family and its continuance and of the livelihood and protection of children and grandchildren).

It seems that in those parts of Scotland where a clan society existed marriage performed a rather different function, although historians disagree about its efficacy.[34] Marriages in the Highlands in the seventeenth century were used to increase clan solidarity in marked contrast to the Lowlands where the clan was much less important. Within the dominant Macdonald and Mackenzie clans marriages of the clan head and the heads of cadet branches were almost entirely within the clan. In the Lowlands less than 8 per cent of marriages occurred within the clan.[35] Where there were blood feuds, it was customary for the males of the dominant clan to marry females from the subservient in order to secure peace. It could also help to cement ties within the clan. See, for example, the way in which marriage in the 1590s between James Muir, son and heir to Auchindrain, and a daughter of Culzean was used to bring peace within the Kennedy clan so that they might resist external enemies.[36]

This seems to have had parallels in Ireland among the native population, where the society was also clan based. When Turlough Brasselagh O'Neill and Sir Brian Mac Phelim resumed their alliance in April 1571 'Turlough does take again Sir Brian's sister to his wife who before he had put away.'[37] In December 1572 the 'disorder' between the couple led to disaster for him: 'his wife . . . has carried away with her into Scotland the strongest part of the Scots'.[38] Then again, in January 1574 when Aqrt MacDonnell married Turlough Luineach O'Neill's daughter, the Earl of Essex revealed the significance of this move: he 'is ready to revolt to him' because of the marriage alliance.[39] The crucial importance of the wives of Irish chiefs was again acknowledged in a letter of Lord Deputy Fitzwilliam to the Earl of Leicester recommending the imprisonment for one year of the Earl of Desmond, his wife and his brother as a cure for unrest in Munster.[40]

But this evidence of the socio-economic effects of marriage, and of the ways in which it was used by families, has to be set against evidence of the perceived purpose of marriage. For the Christian Churches marriage was an institution designed for mutual satisfaction of both partners and for the procreation of humankind within a Christian family. Such a view was expressed in the marriage services of the Anglican, Presbyterian and Catholic Churches of the British Isles and England's colonies. A marriage was created when a man and a woman, who were 'free' to marry, entered into a marriage contract. This contract was in Catholic countries before the Reformation based upon mutual consent, irrespective of parental agreement. In 1469 the bishop of Norwich advised Margaret Paston against her marriage to the bailiff, Richard Calle, because by acting against her mother's opposition she had forfeited her assistance in future, but the actual contract of marriage was flawless and the union valid. William Hay, Professor of Theology and Principal of Aberdeen University from 1536 to 1542, made it absolutely clear in his lectures that it was consent that made a marriage. The Reformation did not bring change in this respect and later Scots writers elaborated that it was consent and not sexual union that 'facit matrimonium'.[41] Decrees of nullity were sometimes made on the grounds of incapacity to give consent.[42] Marriage which took place within a church service was regarded after 1439 by the Catholic Church and later by the Church of England as a sacrament – a sign and means of attaining grace. It was known as the state of 'holy matrimony'. The reformed churches did not see marriage as a sacrament although they too thought that it was an estate ordained by God.

The approach of the Church of England and of the Presbyterian Church of Scotland was ambiguous. Although the canons (laws) of the Church of England sought in 1604 to bolster the rights of parents in the making of Christian marriage – this forbade marriage within the Church without parental consent for those under the age of twenty-one and required consent for all except remarriages – the Church did not declare invalid marriages that flouted this law. This English approach was, for example, transported to Maryland, where priests did not inform parents of marriages performed without parental consent.[43] Similarly in Scotland's *First Book of Discipline* of 1560 parental consent was declared essential before a couple could marry but the Church of Scotland found it difficult to enforce this rule. Forte has shown that over three centuries in post-Reformation Scotland there were very determined efforts to make marriage a 'public institution, requiring the publication of banns and celebration by ordained ministers of its established church' but that, nonetheless, irregular marriages were recognised. The essential weakness of the Church's position is here apparent, a weakness that, in theory, did not prevail in Catholic countries after 1563.

In a detailed study of the Reformed Discipline in Scotland, Michael Graham explored the relationship between the emergence of the new reformed order and its concern over marriage and sexuality but has, in so doing, made observations of a more general relevance to the study of approaches to marriage throughout western Europe. Offences concerning sexuality were prevalent in the courts. Of 4,594 Kirk session charges, 2,523 (55 per cent) involved sexuality; for presbyteries, the figure was 572 out of 1,191 (48 per cent). Ministers and Elders were motivated in this by their desire to banish pauperism by discouraging illegitimacy but they saw a strong and clear connection between vagrancy and illegitimacy and irreligion. Christian marriage provided a nursery for a Christian life. James Melville complained of the growing swarms of vagrants 'godless and lawless, without marriage, baptism, or knowledge of duty to God or man'. Reasons for this concern were acknowledged as both economic and religious by the Canongate Kirk Session (1564) when it referred to fornication as both 'hurtful to the common wealth' and 'slander to the kirk of God'. Vagrancy in late sixteenth-century Scotland and indeed in western Europe was seen as a growing problem and illegitimacy among those already living on the margins of poverty was certainly a contributing factor. 'Sex outside marriage was nothing new, but in a context of diminishing resources and growing population it became less socially acceptable.' Elders and ministers tried to persuade cohabiting couples with children to marry; if they refused, usually because the male resisted, the session often ordered that a sum be set aside by the father for the child's upbringing.[44]

The Kirk was exercised over what made a legal marriage. There were concerted attempts to change marriage customs and to force those living together outside marriage to formalise their relationships by marriage according to the rules of the Church. The General Assembly (the largely ministerial national body ruling the Kirk) regularly reminded the Crown of the existence of a rarely used Act of Parliament of 1563 that ordered the death penalty for adulterers. It also considered questions of social discipline at its meetings, and passed resolutions concerning both sex and marriage. The first assembly in 1560 determined that sexual relations between the betrothed, but not yet married, couple constituted fornication and required public confession by the offenders. Graham observes that here the real target may have been irregular marriage, in which the clergy were not involved. This was continuing the stance of the Catholic Church in Scotland. Andrew Forman, Archbishop of St Andrews, had declared that handfast unions were 'an evil custom or corruption' increasingly prevalent in his diocese (1516–1521).[45] In a similar vein the crypto-Catholic Aberdeen Kirk Session ordered in December 1562 that all such 'handfast' couples, some of whom had been cohabiting for seven years or more, would have to marry formally by the following 'Festerans eve' (Shrove Tuesday). In such instances the self-interest of professionals was clearly to the fore. But Graham notes that the General Assembly's interest extended well beyond this concern. In March 1570 it took up seventeen questions, of which eight related to sexuality, including the quandary of whether two men who had slept with two sisters could marry each other's daughters, provided the latter were not the issue of either sister. By the 1580s and 1590s the General Assembly was turning its attention to other issues but at local level Kirk sessions were still obsessed with sexuality. Although action against poor couples was predominant, numerous examples of cases against the prominent and the wealthy show that the obsession with sexual propriety and regular marriage was not simply economic. In cases of fornication, adultery and incest both sexes were frequently required to do public penance, oftentimes in sackcloth and ashes. Ecclesiastical and economic sanctions were employed to bring offenders both to light and to justice. The Canongate session in November 1564 introduced fines for landlords who rented rooms to those guilty of fornication, for masters who turned a blind eye to the sexual liaisons of their servants, and for midwives who neglected to report all births. Midwife Molly Acheson in October 1565 when questioned about one woman, admitted that she 'was lighter of a bairn in harlatry'. On 5 November 1574 the Edinburgh session ordered immediate excommunication for masters who employed servants who had been convicted of fornication but had not yet done public penance: the merchant William Scot promptly delivered to the court Jonet Fyft, a servant who had thus 'defiled' his house. In an attempt to ensure that illegitimate children should not become a burden on the Church, it was ordered in August 1576 that no servants from outside the city could be hired without testimonials from the minister where they had previously dwelled.

How should Christians find marriage partners?

Christians, of course, were also citizens living within a state whose law accepted a different kind of marriage and among people who had married according to different dispensations. Recognising irregular marriages in England as in Scotland was a practical necessity. Neither society had the advantage of the post-Tridentine Catholic decree Tametsi of 1563 which nullified marriages that were not celebrated by an ordained priest in public, thus fulfilling the rules of the Church. Seventeenth-century English conduct books (frequently based upon the content of sermons) advocated an ideal situation in which children were matched with those whom they accepted as potentially compatible partners and in which parental consent was required if the marriage were to be regarded as Christian marriage. The writers of these conduct books, often Puritan preachers, saw parents as having divinely conferred powers of control over their children, who were literally dependent upon them for their livelihood. Parents were empowered to confer or withhold their consent for a child to become independent through a particular marriage. As William Whately wrote in his *Care-Cloth*, if a couple entered a marriage without first obtaining parental consent they could not 'be said to bee joined by God mediately', indicating an acceptance in his mind of something akin to a registry office or civil marriage today. But the implications were that parents should exercise that power of control and consent responsibly within the context of good Christian parenting. As parents they had a responsibility to guide their children in matters of education, vocation and marriage, all designed to provide for the child's eventual independence.

As we have already established, there was no legal requirement for prior parental consent for a marriage to be recognised as binding, except where one or both of the parties was under age. Even when an institution such as wardship granted the marriage of an heir to the guardian, an insistence by the heir on a contrary marriage resulted not in dissolution of the marriage but in payment of a hefty fine. The rule regarding parental consent for minors was certainly enforced. The licences contained in the Lichfield Court Book for the 1660s, for example, all stipulated that where parental consent was required because parties were under age, the licences were null and void if the marriage proceeded without this consent.[46] It was, however, custom and not law and threats of financial or emotional disinheritance which gave parents control over their children's marriages. The authors of conduct books described what was, in their view, the ideal balance of a marriage carefully chosen by the parties themselves and one engineered and facilitated by loving parents.

Such writers did not countenance irresponsible parental behaviour and the forcible marriage of children against their consent. The law of the land, however, gave parents and guardians ultimate control in some cases. It is worth noting that the English law of 1558, which imposed a punishment of two years' imprisonment upon those who abducted 'maidens that be inheritors' between the ages of twelve and sixteen, and five years upon those who raped or forcibly married the girl concerned, did not apply to the parents or guardians of such maidens who had control as of right, although it did apply to widowed mothers who were not granted wardship.[47]

The rights of mothers to influence whom their children married were, in practice, jeopardised when the father died. Maternal uncles were often awarded control. In Wales, especially, custom frequently discriminated against the rights of the mother. In England and Wales a widow's control was challenged when the husband had held land by knight-service. A very few mothers were granted wardship of their children, even after a law of 1611 gave close relatives a month's pre-emption on wardships. There was also a second-hand market in wardships, of which some of the richest mothers were able to take advantage. Garthine Walker has suggested that Welsh women were at a particular disadvantage when it came to retaining custody of minor children whether by wardship or otherwise because most gentle-male testators left guardianship of the children to close male relatives rather than to widows. She adds, though, that women could wield an informal influence over wardship negotiations. So Sir John Wynn complained of the influence of his stepmother and her former mother-in-law in the matter of the wardship of Thomas Salusbury because they 'so rule my father that he ratifieth what they think fit to be done'.[48] In many respects the best chance a widowed mother had of asserting her parental control lay with challenging the legality of the wardship itself. When in 1581 thirteen-year-old Jennett Thomas of Newport, Gwent was removed by her mother from her long-term guardian's keeping, this action was defended on the basis of the maternal claim that Jennett's inheritance was not through knight-service at all but through socage tenure from the lord of the manor. Sometimes, however, widowed mothers defended such action on the basis of the legal and natural rights of a widow to inherit the marriages of her children: custody 'properly belongs to me . . . [by] your majesties good and godly laws . . . and by the law of nature'.[49] While such cases demonstrate that the law did discriminate against mothers with respect to wardships they also indicate that mothers were prepared to go to considerable lengths, with or without male support, to win back control.

Late Tudor and Stuart preachers thought that arranging a marriage should not simply be based on concern for family aggrandisement and should certainly not involve forcing their children into intolerable matches. The preacher William Gouge was critical of parents who tried to push their offspring into early marriage for the sake of building an estate or a connection.[50] Samuel Hieron was particularly keen to condemn those who used the financial criterion as the sole test of a good match.[51] Such guidance would provide children with the benefit of experience and mature wisdom when they came to consider the matter of their lifetime partnership.[52] Simultaneously children were advised to demonstrate honour (respect) and obedience to their parents as ordered in the Ten

Commandments and to do this by accepting their advice in the matter of marriage.[53] This was not a gendered obligation: the duty of giving advice and guidance and consent belonged to both parents together and children of both sexes were regarded as equally subservient to their parents in this matter.

While such authors did not see family furtherance as an acceptable rationale for Christian marriage they did counsel that it was the parents' duty to see that the young couple were 'economically viable' as a potentially independent household. Even Samuel Hieron thought that balancing the partners in terms of age, social status and income to achieve 'an even yoke fellow' was incumbent upon parents.[54] What part then should young people play in choosing their marriage partners? There was a conflict here between the insistence that both partners must find the match to their liking and give their consent – that is, that they were the parties to the contract and that they must enter it freely – and the belief that the young were ill-equipped to make such a decision and that parents gave consent on their behalf. William Gouge believed that young people were guided chiefly by lust, 'heady and rash for want of experience', and not aware of the prerequisites for finding 'a good lasting help for themselves'. The secret lay perhaps in creating in children a willingness to take heed of their parents' advice and in parents a determination to ensure that the young people developed a real liking one to another so that affection and love between them was a long-term possibility.[55] Although historians have come to accept that both men and women gave their consent to marriages and participated in the making of them, there is a continued reluctance to accept that young women played more than a passive role. 'The woman's role was passive, but not entirely powerless.'[56] Later in this section examples are adduced to contradict this argument.

Counsel about the role of parents in the making of marriage came from prescriptive literature, which is difficult to use as a guide to actual behaviour. However, it is true that there is a relationship between prescriptive and descriptive literature: the authors of these conduct books considered that the situations and practices they criticised were sufficiently prevalent to require correction and for their arguments to strike a chord among their natural audience – the elite and middling sorts.[57] Having acknowledged this relationship, we should not be misled into thinking that it was a simple one in which the readers of such books of advice unquestioningly accepted and followed it or in which many did not already attempt to arrange marriages in a similar way.

The purpose of marriage in the context of colonisation

The population of England and Wales in the mid-1540s was about 3 million; by 1603 this had risen to 4,156 million, by 1676 to around 5 million and by 1750 to about 5.5 million. London, the largest city, grew from 60,000 in 1500 to approximately 120,000 in 1582 and 200,000 in 1603. By 1700 a full 10 per cent of the population lived in the metropolis. There were a number of other provincial capitals of some size even in the seventeenth century which had grown explosively in the eighteenth century. These included Norwich, Bristol, York, Exeter and Salisbury. There were also many county towns and centres fashionable with the local 'gentry' such as Bath, Tunbridge Wells, Bury St Edmunds and Buxton.

In comparison, colonial settlements were tiny. Examples here are drawn from the early seventeenth-century English settlements.[58] Plimouth Colony was founded by 101 Pilgrims in 1620. In 1624 the population of New Plimouth stood at 124; by 1630 it had swollen to 300 and by 1637 there were 550 inhabitants. At this point the Pilgrims began new towns, all of them small.[59] The Massachusetts Bay Company, dominated by John Winthrop, settled Salem from 1629 onwards. By the end of 1630 there were eleven townships with somewhat over a thousand inhabitants overall. Other settlements were established in Rhode Island (when Roger Williams was expelled from Massachusetts), Maine and Connecticut. In 1643 the United Colonies of New England were founded, combining all these colonies. About 20,000 people had emigrated to New England in the 1630s but such emigration virtually ceased after 1640. The population did increase considerably so that the twenty-one settlements in existence in 1641 grew to thirty-three by 1647.[60] In 1637, 250 people had emigrated from the Old World and eventually settled and built the town of New Haven – originally a colony separate from Connecticut. The entire New Haven Colony (which included some other townships) in the 1640s had, at most, about 2,000 white inhabitants. By 1701 when New Haven was made co-capital of the Connecticut colony (with Hartford) the county of New Haven population stood at 5,000. About 1,500 of these people lived in New Haven itself and as few as fifteen families in its smallest township of Durham. From then on the settlements each increased by about 28 per cent per decade: by 1770 New Haven's population had risen to 8,295, Wallingford's to 3,700 and Durham's (the smallest of the eight townships in the county) to 800.[61] Boston in the early eighteenth century had a population of a mere 16,000 or so and even Philadelphia, the largest

North American town, had a population of only 40,000 in 1770 and New York city only 25,000.[62]

During the first half of the seventeenth century the tiny numbers of English settlers in Virginia were swamped by more than 40,000 native peoples. In 1650, while the number of natives was declining, the entire colony of Virginia contained a non-indigenous population of a mere 14,000, 500 of whom were black slaves. During the period of the English Civil Wars it became a haven, as did neighbouring Maryland, for Royalist Cavaliers. By 1700 this population had swollen to 63,000, of whom black slaves numbered between 6,000 and 10,000. At the close of the seventeenth century York County, Virginia had a population of 1,900, which, sparse though it was, itself marked a great increase over the second half of the seventeenth century through immigration of indentured English servants and slaves from the Caribbean.[63] Virginia also by now boasted a 'city' – Williamsburg – although this was small and provincial in comparison with English cities.

Maryland, founded to further the ambitions of the Catholic Lord Baltimore, ironically became a tiny colony riven by tension between Catholics and Puritans. In the late 1630s the population stood at about 500 and by the mid 1640s this had fallen to 400. It was swollen again by the expulsion from Virginia of about 400 Puritans.

The population of Ireland stood at one to one-and-a-half million in 1600, just as it had during the reign of Henry VIII. Historians have identified deliberate attempts to exterminate the Catholic Irish by Lord Mountjoy during the years 1602–1607 and Oliver Cromwell and the generals between 1649 and 1653 which perhaps led to a slump in the population to 900,000 in the mid-seventeenth century. Thousands were also deported to the West Indies. In the 1690s the wars of William III devastated Ulster. In 1700, despite a high fertility rate and settlement by Protestants, the population had only recovered its 1,600 peak. The only towns of note in Ireland before the Plantation were Carrickfergus and Newry. Belfast and Londonderry were the result of the Plantation but their growth was sluggish: Belfast still had only 4,000 inhabitants at the end of the seventeenth century, although its population exploded in the eighteenth century.[64]

The colonising powers sought to populate the areas that they controlled, and marriage and the family became central to this effort. It was not simply that marriage and procreation went together (although that was important) but also that marriage and the family and the role of women within them were thought to guarantee the survival and perpetuation of what was considered to be a superior Christian civilisation. In 1623 it was recommended that the Irish match their sons with British daughters of old English families because 'the child follows more the mother than any in his language and manners'.[65] Henry Carey, Lord Falkland, Lord Deputy of Ireland in the 1620s, asked that only educated English women be permitted to settle in his plantation for they 'would make a good nation in time, for those will maintain the language to their children and then it is no great matter of what nation the men be, so the women be English'.[66] The characterisation of indigenous Irish women as 'harlots' and 'camp followers', licentious, lustful, deceitful and dirty rejected them absolutely as suitable wives for Englishmen and as uncivilised. They were also seen as potential spies who could not be trusted and who eventually undermined colonies.[67] The Munster plantation of the 1580s attempted to segregate the plantation entirely from the native population and the early seventeenth-century Ulster plantation planned to clear the natives from the land and settle them with British people, dedicated to procreation.[68]

On the Atlantic seaboard of North America the intention to populate the land with 'civilised Christian people' was dominant. Some 40,000 Puritans are said to have made their way to what came to be called New England, often in family groups. This emigration was at its peak in the 1630s when an alarmed Charles I strove without success to stem the flow, at the same time that he authorised the commercial venture of the Massachusetts Bay Company. The concern of the Puritan emigrants was to be able to follow their religion and, in order to do so, they had to master their environment. Tiny groups of immigrants were fighting against enormous odds, as the beleaguered early settlements of Roanoke (Carolina) and Plymouth (Cape Cod) showed. Maryland was founded by Lord Baltimore to provide a haven for Catholics and Arminian Anglicans, fleeing from England's oppressive protestant regimes. The southern colony of Virginia originated as a commercial adventure but it, no less than the 'religious' colonies, felt the need to expand in order to survive. People were needed to work the land and to produce artefacts and also to defend the settlement. People were imported but procreation was the order of the day. And to those committed to the ideals of an ordered society, marriage was the preferred institution in which such procreation should take place.

Marriage had importance for demography and economy, then, but it was also a vehicle for ordering society. This was not only to ensure the clear transmission of property from generation to generation but also the allocation of responsibility for the accommodation, care and maintenance of all individuals. In all these early modern societies the ideal was for the exclusive and regular cohabitation of married couples and for them to maintain equally exclusive sexual relationships. Within the household they should live harmoniously. Patriarchy itself was envisaged as a means to these ends.[69] It is easy to see how attractive such an ideal of harmonious, exclusive relationships was to contemporary governments, whether civil or ecclesiastical, at a time when the powers of centralised government in church and state were relatively weak. Court records show how hard the authorities fought to maintain the kind of marital order that made social harmony possible. The English and Welsh Church courts and the Scottish Kirk sessions were kept busy by this category of work throughout the period from the Reformation to the end of the seventeenth century. This was as, or even more, true of the American colonies, where central control and record-keeping were yet weaker. 'In addition to enforcing laws about illegal marriage, seventeenth-century New England colonies also punished fornication more consistently and severely than their English counterparts.'[70] In the context of civil marriage, the General Court of Plymouth Colony was as keen as any English or Scottish court to stamp on irregular marriages. There were several cases of men being punished for joining themselves in marriage 'disorderly'.[71] The conduct of the lives of married couples was also policed. For example, the court of Plymouth Colony in 1659 ordered Goodwife Spring to return from a lengthy sojourn in Scituate to live with her husband, a resident of the Bay Colony, or 'give a reason why she doth not'; the penalty would probably have been banishment from the colony.[72] Certainly, in the colonies which sanctioned divorce, lengthy desertion by one partner was regarded as one of the grounds for divorce, as was bigamy. In 1670 James Skiff was granted a divorce because his wife had deserted him and had married another husband in Roanoke, 'in or at Virginia'. The courts would also interfere when peace and harmony did not reign in a marriage: so George and Anna Barlow were 'severely reproved for their most ungodly living in contention one with the other, and admonished to live otherwise'.[73] Rarely, though, did incompatibility result in divorce.[74]

Conclusion

Marriage and the patriarchal family it created were important institutions because they provided a means of ordering society and transmitting its Christian values. As such both church and state wanted to control marriage. Despite arguments to the contrary, marriage was seemingly as strong an institution in Scotland and Wales as in England although the picture is somewhat clouded by the confusion caused by the existence of irregular as well as regular unions.

The Catholic Church stipulated a five-point marriage process, which began with a financial or property settlement and ended with the marriage ceremony itself. The Scottish Presbyterian Church and the American colonies adopted some of the same key features – especially the character of the ceremony as open to public scrutiny, and the essential component of willing consent. The English elite appears to have complied with the five-point process (to ensure the transmission of property without dispute). Celebration of contracting was advocated by English Puritan writers such as Richard Greenham and William Gouge. Their works were in part motivated by a perception that 'handfasting' or formal 'contracting' was in decline already in the general population by the late Elizabethan period. This decline may best be explained by the fact that handfasting was not legally necessary for a valid marriage and found no place in the Book of Common Prayer. In Scotland, however, many well-born couples appear not to have got past the contract and espousals stage (known as 'handfasting').

Even though in England only minors were required to obtain parental consent prior to marriage, in fact most young people sought the approval of their parents or guardians. While preachers and writers in the sixteenth and seventeenth centuries emphasised that marriage was a holy estate and that church marriage and parental consent were important, in fact clandestine or irregular marriages were accepted as valid as long as the parties had entered the marriage willingly. On a family level, marriage played an important part in the transmission of property and the creation of dynasties and affinities (connections). Most crucially, however, marriage helped secure the present and future (material and emotional) of children, especially daughters. This relieved parents of an economic burden but there is evidence that there were many caring parents for whom the future of the children was an equal concern.

In Ireland and the American colonies, marriage and the family provided an essential layer of society which linked central or community government and geographically remote individuals. Unions, both regular and irregular, served also to populate the colonies and to provide care for young and old. We have to remember that these were all societies in which there were no accurate records of the population, no electoral rolls, no nationally kept records of births, marriages or deaths. In England parishes kept records of baptisms, marriages and funerals from the third decade of the sixteenth century. But these records and the ceremonies that surrounded their creation were open to chiefly local scrutiny. Regular (and therefore publicly registered) marriages helped to guard against bigamy, which had always been a problem and appears to have been even more so as men and women moved between the Old and New Worlds and became part of a fragmented and fluid society.[75]

Notes

1. J. M. Osborn (ed.), *Autobiography of Thomas Whythorne*, p. 95.
2. L. Stone (1977) pp. 30–2.
3. C. McAll (1980) pp. 7–10.
4. Ibid pp. 8–10.
5. L. Leneman (2001) pp. 45–62.
6. See Chapter 2.
7. K. Simms (1991) pp. 32–42.
8. R. B. Outhwaite (1995) pp. 54–73.
9. J. Boulton (1991) pp. 15–29.
10. A. E. Anton (1958) pp. 89–102.
11. Martin Martin (1695).
12. G. Donaldson (1970) p. 173; cited in C. Peters (2004) p. 10.
13. R. R. Davies (1980); Peters (2004) p. 12.
14. C. Giblin (1964) p. 57.
15. R. S. Dunn (1998) p. 37, law of 1639.
16. Ibid p. 37, law of 1647.
17. Maryland Hall of Records (hereafter MHR) Prerogative Court Wills (Wills) Book 4: 153 (1684) cited in D. Meyers (2003) p. 43.
18. Meyers (2003) p. 44.
19. Ibid p. 45.
20. Ibid.
21. Ibid.
22. E. A. Wrigley (1973) p. 15.
23. There is a more detailed consideration of 'marriage' as an institution in Chapter 2.

24 It also brought him considerable danger and exile, although he was restored to favour under Henry VII.
25 Joel Hurstfield suggested that in Wales the system of wardship was perhaps grafted onto an earlier Welsh system. See Hurstfield (1973 edn) pp. 18–27, 96, 104, 145.
26 Keith M. Brown (1996) pp. 168–96 (e.g. from p. 170).
27 Folger Shakespeare Library, Bagot Collection.
28 C. Carpenter (1996) pp. 57–8 and nos 180, 185 and 208.
29 HEH, STT Personal Box 8, Folder 21, 18 Sept 1632 Will and probate (copy) of will of Sir John Temple of Biddlesden, Berks.
30 M. Slater (1984) p. 13.
31 The standard work on the institution of wardship remains Hurstfield (1973 edn). See also F. Heal and C. Holmes (1994) pp. 144–5; Garthine Walker (2000) pp. 55–62; B. Harris (1998) p. 11.
32 G. Walker (2000) pp. 59–60.
33 D. Cressy (1997) p. 256.
34 See Keith M. Brown (1996) p. 195. He questions the cohesiveness and solidarity of agnatic kindreds and lordships during the period, showing that unquestioning loyalty to a lord was never to be assumed.
35 I. Carter (1973) pp. 51–2; L. Stone (1977) p. 127.
36 Keith M. Brown (1996) p. 183.
37 M. O'Dowd, *CSP Ireland*, 2000, Document 13.1, pp. 14–15, Nicholas Bagenal to Lord Justice Fitzwilliam, 14 April 1571, SP 63/32, no. 13 (i).
38 O'Dowd, *CSP Ireland*, 2000, Document 396, p. 239, Lord Deputy Fitzwilliam to Elizabeth I, 7 December 1572, SP 63/38, no. 49.
39 O'Dowd, *CSP Ireland*, 2000, Document 805, p. 473, Walter Devereux, Earl of Essex, to the Privy Council, 16 January 1574, SP 63/44, no. 7.
40 O'Dowd, *CSP Ireland*, 2000, Document 214, p. 141, Lord Deputy Fitzwilliam to Robert Dudley, Earl of Leicester, 16 March 1572, SP 63/35, no. 33.
41 A. D. M. Forte (1984) p. 105.
42 See the case of Leith v. Elphinstoun, 1523 cited in Forte (1984) p. 105.
43 Meyers (2003) p. 45.
44 M. Graham (1996).
45 A. E. Anton (1958) p. 96.
46 L.J.R.O., B/C/6 and B/C/7.

47 Statutes of the Realm, 4 and 5 Philip and Mary, c. 8.
48 G. Walker (2000) p. 59.
49 G. Walker (2000).
50 William Gouge (1622) pp. 563–6.
51 Samuel Hieron (1613) pp. 8–11.
52 William Gouge (1622) p. 449.
53 Dudley Fenner (1592).
54 Samuel Hieron (1613) pp. 8–11.
55 William Gouge (1622) pp. 449.
56 See D. Cressy (1997) pp. 252–63 and especially p. 254.
57 M. O'Day (1995) pp. 29–63 and especially pp. 44–5; S. Gosling (1999) p. 262 for further discussion of the complexities of the relationship between prescription and practice.
58 The Carolinas, Georgia, Pennsylvania and New Hampshire were established in the late seventeenth century; Georgia was founded in 1730, Delaware was originally included in Pennsylvania and New Jersey did not become a fully fledged royal colony until the reign of Queen Anne.
59 R. Middleton (1992) p. 50, citing figures provided by William Bradford, Governor of the Colony.
60 Middleton (1992) p. 67.
61 C. H. Dayton (1995) pp. 52–8, using back projection from the 1756 census.
62 E. B. Greene (1932) p. 59; B. C. Daniels (1979) p. 160.
63 T. Snyder (2003) p. 9.
64 Kevin Phillips (1999) p. 572.
65 George O'Brien (1923) p. 50; cited in M. O'Dowd (1999) p. 159.
66 Instructions to settlers printed in G. T. Cell (1982) pp. 244–5, cited in O'Dowd (1999) p. 159.
67 V. P. Carey (1985) pp. 255–6.
68 N. Canny (1978) pp. 17–44; M. McCarthy-Morrogh (1986) p. 177; P. Robinson (1984).
69 See Chapter 5 for a detailed discussion of the insistence upon parental consent for a valid marriage in the colonies.
70 R. Bloch (2003) p. 85.
71 That is, against the laws of the colony. These were probably cases of handfasting, which ignored the insistence that a marriage to be valid required

the publication of banns and the services of a magistrate. J. Demos (1978 repr.) pp. 162–3.

72 *Plymouth Colony Records*, III, p. 174 and V. p. 33; quoted by J. Demos (1978 repr.) pp. 92–3.

73 *Plymouth Colony Records*, IV, p. 10.

74 Demos (1978 repr.) p. 94.

75 For examples of bigamy cases see L.J.R.O.

CHAPTER 4

Finding a partner among the landed aristocracy[1]

I hear he is vehemently [opposed] on the divers part (I mean Percival Willoughby) by one John Fox, whose wife is his ally, and by one both an attorney his nephew who is the agent for my brother Willoughby. He is the man upon whom dependeth all the matter, wherefore if he be firm I hope well of the rest. Wherefore I pray you good cousin be earnest with him and if the like happen to any of yours I will be ready to requite this kindness.[2]

Introduction

In the last quarter of the twentieth century historical accounts of the processes of courtship and marriage were dominated by the work of the historian Lawrence Stone, beginning with his monumental *Family, Sex and Marriage in England*. In this book Stone argued that the family 'evolved' during the early modern centuries towards the modern 'domesticated nuclear family' in which affective individualism flourished. Stone believed that the early Tudor period was characterised by the 'open lineage family' in which the individual was regarded as unimportant, there was little family 'affection' and the collective interests of family, kin and community were paramount. According to this model, marriages were made to further the interests of the 'house' (seen as a 'clan') and involved property and connection. This situation gradually changed so that after the Reformation the nuclear family, and within it 'patriarchy', dominated but, although the earlier impersonal aspects of marriage formation were overtaken by warmer, affective relationships between parents and children, the internalisation of teachings regarding filial and parental obligations and the need to achieve marriages which served the wider interests of the family ensured that 'personal choice' was relatively low down on the list of factors influencing marriage. Stone thought that during the late sixteenth and early seventeenth centuries the growing affective relations within propertied English families led to parents allowing their children at least a veto over the choice of marriage partner.[3] He suggested that by the late seventeenth century affective relationships within the nuclear family had the upper hand and led eventually to freedom of choice. Stone's thesis was based entirely upon a study of elite families, broadly defined. It suggested that young people's private feelings, whether they belonged to young men or young women, were under the Tudors and early Stuarts subjugated to the interests of those families.

Stone was aware that his model was based upon the behaviour of elite families and believed that, because the system of arranged marriages was based on the exchange of property, 'children lower down the social scale would enjoy greater freedom of choice'. It has frequently been asserted that young people in the elite had little influence upon their choice of marriage partner although 'freedom of choice increased as social status and means diminished.'[4] Mendelson and Crawford accepted this argument, quoting from contemporary ballads in support.

Would I had been a scullian-maid
Or a servant of low degree,
Then need not I have been afraid,
To ha' loved him that would love me.[5]

The relatively late age of marriage and the removal of the plebeian young woman from her parental home from adolescence onwards meant that she had greater initiative and control in the matter of her marriage than did her elite counterparts.[6]

This view has in part been contested. On the one hand it has been suggested that those with little if any property were just as keen to form marriages that produced financial stability as those who had a good deal. Parents and relatives remained involved. Few marriages at any social level, we are told, were based entirely upon 'romantic love'.[7] Sentiments such as those quoted above from the ballad *Love's Downfall*, represent the ignorance of one class about another. Fathers throughout society believed that they owned their daughters and could dispose of them as they wished. In a letter to Lady Hester Temple, William Harte (who was her social inferior) put it bluntly when discussing her attempts to find a match for his daughter: '<u>whilst she is mine</u> she shall be at your Ladyship's command.'[8]

On the other hand, it has been shown that elite youth (male and female) did exercise a real choice over their first marriage partners (rather than a mere veto) and that somewhat older elite individuals, who had often been married previously and who formed a significant proportion of newly-weds each year, were to the fore in finding their own spouses.[9] Elite daughters too, frequently spent at least part of their own adolescence away from their parents. Sometimes there is evidence of an eldest son being allowed (even encouraged) to marry for love rather than property. This was the case when Sir Percival and Lady Bridget Willoughby arranged the marriage of their son Francis to Cassandra Ridgeway, a younger daughter of the Earl of Londonderry, who brought with her small fortune but great charm:

Well, all's well yet, that ends well. [wrote her father in 1610] The best and truest news that I can tell you is that your Francis and my Cassandra are hail fellow well met already, that they like and love well as they both tell me or as we all may well enough tell them that they will be married for better for worse, for richer for poorer, in sickness and health, on what day it shall best please you and your lady, me and my comfort, for my part I'll appoint no day but whenever it is it shall be solemnly and substantially performed to the proof God send them and us all joy of it (whereof I doubt not) my wife dotes on him, every man likes him, and for my poor Cassandra she is one of the best jewels in our cabinet and though I say it who best knows it, fit for his wearing.[10]

It should be said, moreover, that there is little evidence to support Stone's schematic view of changing family 'models' during the sixteenth and seventeenth centuries, which produced a dramatic change in the amount of choice exercised by elite individuals: kin and connection[11] were as important in late sixteenth- and seventeenth-century upper-class families as they had been in the early sixteenth century.

It is necessary also to pose a more philosophical question: how much 'freedom of choice' *could* an individual exercise? Not only did young men and women internalise the views common in their families, communities and society but also they lived in controlled environments and met potential partners from within restricted social, geographical, religious groups. This was true at all social levels at least until the mid-seventeenth century. James Rosenheim has suggested, however, that geographical endogamy was uncommon among the nobility after 1650 (partly owing to a 'demographic dip' which reduced the chances of marrying well locally). He points to the lively extra-local marriage market.[12] However, more detailed studies are required to show that the connections between spouses and their families were not in fact being obscured by far-flung land and titles. For example, when James Brydges married Cassandra Willoughby in 1713 it appeared that an aristocrat from London and Hereford was marrying an heiress from Nottinghamshire – yet the two were first cousins, and mixed in some of the same social and geographical circles.

Although marriages within a locality were not invariably the rule they were prevalent for much of our period. In England marriage alliances were not influenced so much by the county of origin of both parties but by the social networks (which frequently crossed county boundaries) in which they were caught up. In the 1740s Catholic Jacobites from the south were seeking spouses of the same persuasion from the north, for example.[13] There were boundaries, political and geographical, which were difficult to cross. In Wales, the economic weakness and the remoteness of the country is said to have stood in the way of Anglo-Welsh marriages across much of the border (with the possible exception of that between Wales, Lancashire and Cheshire). When Sir John Wynn from Gwydir sought to marry his son John to an English girl in the early seventeenth century, both Sir Baptist Hicks and Sir Henry Bainton refused the match because Wales was so remote and, wrote Bainton, it was also irreligious.[14] Wynn himself was not certain that a wedding with an English girl was always desirable. English society, he wrote, accorded young women considerable liberty and they tended to be reluctant to give this up when they came into Wales.[15] Despite the Union of Scotland and England achieved by James VI and I's simultaneous rule, marriages between Scots and English were not overwhelmingly popular, except in the setting of the English court where James's Scottish favourites sought English brides. Nonetheless between 1603 and 1642 over a fifth of Scottish noble marriages were to English women.[16]

Late medieval and early modern English society was characterised by great fluidity, and status groups never became rigid castes. Nevertheless, there was intense class consciousness and some taboos operated.[17] Kim Phillips has suggested that young women in medieval times were required not only to preserve their virginity but also not to cross the boundaries of 'social status, religion, kinship and age' when finding a partner. Margery Paston was cast out of her family when she married their servant Richard Calle. While the bishop certainly upheld the validity of the marriage, he strove to make her aware of the taboo she had disobeyed and its implications for her future. He put her 'in remembrance how she was born, what kin and friends that she had, and should have more if she were ruled and guided after them, and if she did not, what rebuke and shame and loss it should be to her'.[18]

There was general concern, especially among the parents of marriageable daughters, that partners should be equally socially and economically matched. 'Matching in marriage must be with equality' and 'Like blood, like good, and like age make the happiest marriage'.[19] A union with social inferiors led to 'disparagement' of the superior partner by association. This was especially serious for a well-born wife who married a socially inferior husband for she automatically assumed the status of her spouse. In an abduction case heard in Wales the parents of a young girl suffered 'great grief and heart breaking' when in 1597 she was abducted and married to a man 'without credit',[20] and an alleged felon. To make matters even worse, there had already been a 'perfect and full agreement' that she should wed the eldest son of a gentleman.[21]

This said, early modern evidence suggests that more pragmatic considerations were uppermost in parents' minds. Relatives were sometimes exercised by the personal problems attendant upon making a match above their kin's station. Elizabeth Freke in the mid-1690s voiced this concern about the proposed match between her son Ralph and Lady Alice Moore, Lord Drogheda's daughter, who would have brought with her £3,000. Elizabeth thought Alice had 'nothing to be objected butt her quality, which I thought too much for a gentleman'.[22] Elizabeth was, interestingly, worrying about her own future relationship with such a daughter-in-law: 'A fine lady she was, but I cared nott to be a servant to anyone in my old age.'[23] This is by no means an isolated example and it affected both sexes. In 1591 when he was trying to negotiate a marriage for John Temple's niece, Miles Sandys wrote that the suitor's father 'thought it was too high a match for his son his fortune during his life shall be but l li [£50] and meat and drink'.[24] In the seventeenth century, the Greville manuscripts reveal a father's considerations concerning a match between his son and a younger daughter, aged fourteen, far above him in social standing. Parents were above all things practical and realistic. Mostly they were not gold-diggers but in search of parity of fortune and expectation. It is a mistake to view the careful financial and property investigations and negotiations that preceded any elite marriage as evidence purely of attempts at aggrandisement. 'But it's the greatest concern I have in the world to settle you happily and that immediately concerns you more than me. I pray God's providence may make you happy in a marriage. My part shall not be wanting.' The objections in this case largely concerned not the youthful bride's age but the payment of her portion and the capacity of the bride's settlement to provide sufficiently for the resulting expected expensive life style: 'She may reasonably expect a coach and six horses, page and lackeys and other servants which will not be kept for £400 per annum. One of lower birth with as good a fortune may be content with a coach and pair of horses ordinarily . . . and with much fewer servants.' If the match went ahead, would the bride snub her husband's family? – 'her quality being so great she may slight and disesteem you and all your relations (which would be very grievous to me and your Dear mother, And though she be at present very good and humble yet hereafter by suggestion of others is her every reflection she may think she hath undervalued herself and that may create unkindness and utter unhappiness to you and your posterity.' Would his relations have to live more expensively to accommodate her tastes when she and her family visited them? (At a time when lengthy family visits were so much part of life, this could be a major financial encumbrance.) Would her parents slight his family or even himself, 'which I doubt you can ill beare'? Would suitable 'high' places and matches be found for their children without inordinate expense? His father would consider such a match only if these financial problems were resolved and even then would be concerned because 'These objections have such might with me that I could hardly bring myself to consent to it (if the portion were ready) though I do believe in my conscience she is in person and disposition very deserving yet she is much above us and in time (though not at present) she may think so. For time and circumstances alter the very nature and reasons of things.'[25] Small wonder that arrangements made within a neighbourhood or network were greatly favoured.

Religion also could bring together or divide young couples and their wider families. Cassandra Willoughby declared that in her family archive were 'a great many [late sixteenth-century] love letters between Margaret, Sir Francis's third daughter and her Cousin Griffin Markham, at first Sir Francis seems rather for than against their marrying, he allows her to be much with him, and to stay for some time in the house with Mr Markham's father and mother, they I suppose were Roman Catholics, because Mrs Markham expressed a dislike to love her cousin Willoughby because he differed from her in religion, and therefore she was against the match. Lady Willoughby too writes earnestly to persuade her daughter against marrying her cousin Markham, and after some time Sir Francis is against her marrying him, and Mrs Margaret Willoughby herself foreseeing that she should be very unhappy with such a mother in law, resolves not to marry him But married Robert le Spenser.'[26]

There are many other examples of what could happen when an individual married 'out' and of the distress it caused parents and friends. For example, in 1666 Sir Heneage Finch wrote to his son Daniel of Dr Betts who

hath long been a concealed Catholic, and presently after he was married converted his wife, who breeds up all her children so, and is become a great bigod. This is an inexpressible grief to her mother and all her friends; it was but lately known to us, and now your mother, who was godmother to two of the children, hath a scruple of conscience how she shall discharge herself. I think if it had not been for my irregular name, I should have been involved in the same case. But I wonder how the Doctor absolves himself for suffering his child to be heretically baptized, and to take two such heretical gossips as my brother Dering and my wife. Surely it was more for dissimulations sake then for lucre, but absolutions in that church are very cheap and easy . . .[27]

Some historians emphasise the business of marriage as just that – a union designed to improve estates. To an extent this is very true but we should stress that its motivation was to provide appropriately for the male and female offspring in the future. This was not idle amassing of riches. The very survival of a family such as the Temples of Buckinghamshire, Northamptonshire, Warwickshire and Leicestershire depended upon wise marriage decisions.[28] As such negotiations involved careful investigation of the estates of both parties, the chances were that marriage settlements would in fact be honoured and portions and jointures supplied, and expectations met.[29] Into this business were drawn all manner of friends and relatives and not simply parents and grandparents.

A cluster of letters, copies of which are preserved at the Huntington Library, show how entire families were drawn into the marriage negotiations surrounding the match between Francis Willoughby and Emma Barnard in 1667/8.[30] These letters also indicate that in the opinion of some, both bride and groom should have their say. Cassandra Willoughby the elder (mother of the bridegroom) tried to increase Emma Barnard's £6,000 marriage portion.[31] In retaliation Henry Barnard, father of the bride, tried to retain for Emma an interest in the estate. This had repercussions for Barnard's elder daughter Elizabeth and her husband Sir James Brydges. Brydges opposed the alteration of the settlement post hoc and corresponded with Barnard about it. Eventually Francis Willoughby was so tired of the affair and the ructions that it had caused that he declared that he would prefer to drop the subject. However, he resented the fact that the terms had been fixed before either he or Emma had had a chance to influence them.

There being hardly any match that is fairly made but the young wooer has liberty to goe back and consult with his friends . . . [because the terms were fixed] without the consent of her whom it most concerned I should have thought my self bound in conscience to have disputed it a little more before our marriage but that my mistress absolutely forbad me the making of any disturbance, which seeing what has followed, she repents she did.[32]

The matter was to have almost immediate relevance for Emma Willoughby. In his will of 1671 her husband Francis granted Emma the final £2,000 payment of her marriage portion 'to make her some compensation for my too rashly accepting conditions to her disadvantage at marriage.'[33]

Respected relatives well esteemed in county and/or national affairs were especially useful members of the connection. For example, Anthony Shugborough of Staffordshire wrote several letters to his cousin John Temple in Buckinghamshire asking him and another cousin to produce an honest survey of the lands which were being offered to provide Shugborough's daughter with a jointure. 'I would wish that the value of the whole particulars had been set down.'[34] Siblings also expressed their views about particular matches: two of Peter Temple's married sisters expressed their satisfaction at his second marriage (to Christian Leveson).[35] Margaret Longueville deemed him a 'joyful man' because Christian is 'a handsome, good, sweet dispositioned lady, and far beyond my expectation she is to have four thousand pound: and her uncle Sir Richard Leveson's land is all tied to her if he have no children, which we conceive to be very unlikely . . .', thus demonstrating her own practical appreciation of the chief criteria for a happy match – good and compatible personal qualities and a considerable fortune and prospects.

Marriages were formed to unite 'houses' and 'property' and to do so through the production of heirs. The production of healthy children was one of a married woman's most important contributions to the economy. Sons *and* daughters helped create not only estates but also networks of influence and contemporaries; while they certainly wanted a son and heir, they also valued daughters.[36] This was true throughout the British Isles and North Atlantic colonies. Ensuring the future of the family by producing several children and ensuring that that family was properly provided for demanded a skilful balancing act of parents. An apparently wealthy and influential county family such as the Temples did not achieve this balance. Eleven children who survived into adulthood was difficult enough – even though most married reasonably well – but the family was always land-rich and cash-poor. Moreover lands brought into the Temple family by a succession of brides (from Susan Spencer to Hester Sandys to Anne Throckmorton to Christian Leveson) had to support long-lived dowagers such as Susan and Hester Temple and to underwrite the spendthrift activities of Thomas and Hester Temple's heir, Sir Peter.

This was a time when the lifespan of Europeans was short (and that in the American colonies still shorter) and old age came early. It was natural, therefore, that first marriages would take place at a relatively young age, while the women especially would fall within the childbearing age and the males have some chance of surviving sufficiently long to provide for their children. The well-documented existence of a certain age differential between males and females on marriage suggests a cultural norm and could even be indicative of an accepted tradition of seeking spouses within a given age range.[37]

There are indications that the pattern of education and training for men of all classes affected their age at marriage. Apprenticeship of seven years or more was incumbent upon men of the middling sort and apprentices might not marry. For an increasing number of young gentle and aristocratic men, formal education at grammar school and university, followed by a grand tour of England and/or Scotland and the continent, lengthened their dependence. For example, John Kennedy, fifth Earl of Cassillis, in 1596 signed a marriage contract but postponed his match with the eldest daughter of the Earl of Glencairn, while he toured Italy, France and England.[38] Also in the late sixteenth century, but this time in Kent, Percival Willoughby contracted to marry Bridget Willoughby but left her in his parents' house while he went on his grand tour.[39] When, in the second decade of the seventeenth century, Percival's young daughter Elizabeth contracted to marry John Gell of Derbyshire, she seems to have remained in her father's house while John studied at Oxford.[40] These patterns were at least in part the product of a conviction that, while it was appropriate to form a lifelong union when both partners were minors, it was not acceptable for the young couple to live together as man and wife for yet awhile. Elite families had the wherewithal to achieve this delay; non-elite families did not.

Historical demographers have revealed patterns of marriage formation in northern European and American societies that can help us understand the parameters within which marriages were formed. Men and women in Europe generally delayed marriage to the mid- and late twenties.[41] Earlier marriages occurred largely among the titled elite although, paradoxically, by the eighteenth century many English aristocrats were delaying marriage until the male was in his early thirties.[42] The European pattern appears to have been continued in seventeenth-century Dedham, Massachusetts, where men married at about twenty-five years and women at twenty-three years.[43] In seventeenth-century Virginia most of the female population consisted of indentured servants who were not allowed to marry until their contracts expired. Once this happened they hastened to the altar. In some of the colonies, age at first marriage was significantly earlier than in New England and Virginia although there were considerable local differences. In early eighteenth-century Perquimans, North Carolina, a majority of women married between the ages of seventeen and twenty-one whereas in New Hampton, New Hampshire, a similar majority married between the ages of nineteen and twenty-three. In the same communities a majority of men married at age twenty to twenty-four (Perquimans) and twenty-two (New Hampton).[44] Such differences may have had more to do with the 'class' of the population and the sex ratio and profile than with individual preferences or even cultural norms. The desire to form independent households and to increase the sparse population as fast as possible was dominant. In the British Isles men were more likely to marry women older than themselves than was the case in the colonies, but this was probably a result of the much older population profile in England, Scotland and Ireland. In New Hampshire, the middle colonies and North Carolina in the early eighteenth century there was clearly a normal age for marriage but the individual's age and maturity were considered more important for the decision to marry than was the age of the partner. Men would generally seek wives who were younger than themselves (across the Atlantic seaboard the mean differential was between 3.3 and 4.3 years) but, when such younger women were absent or unsuitable, they were prepared to marry women of the same age or older, just as in the Old World. As explained in the next section these demographic realities sometimes could have a marked effect upon the natural authority relations within resulting marriages.

Arranged marriages

Arranged marriages were the order of the day but the term covered many meanings stretching on a continuum – from the marriage arrangement with which the young woman gladly complied and indeed encouraged, or that where one or both parties was compelled to come to the altar surrounded by formalities such as contracts and settlements, to that which was less encumbered and more simply entered into.

Its meaning varied according to the social standing of the parties. The marriage of a royal princess had great diplomatic importance.[45] In a gentle or noble family, marriage impacted on both landed property and patronage in a quite amazing way. This was true in a different way of families of the middling sort and was less obviously true of the labouring or the pauper classes, although recently historians have shown that it did have a considerable impact upon the survival of the apparently 'unpropertied'.

What qualities would be looked for in a wife chosen by parents for a son? These varied not only according to social status but also according to generation. For example, middle-aged Puritans of the middling sort emphasised rather different qualities than did their younger counterparts. Martindale the elder tried to match his eldest son with a young woman with a portion of £140, of suitable age, who would 'make an excellent wife'. His son, however, preferred 'a young wild airy girl, between fifteen and sixteen years of age; an huge lover and frequenter of wakes, greens, and merry-nights, where music and dancing abounded. And as for her portion it was only forty pounds.' Parental consent was grudgingly given and, in the event, 'she proved above all just expectation not only civil, but religious, and an exceeding good wife'.[46] Another son, Hugh, married a papist, emigrated to Ireland and was never seen again.[47] Adam Martindale, his third son, married Elizabeth Hall the second daughter of a respectable 'Christian' yeoman and 'freeholder of good rank'.[48]

In gentle and noble families in England and Wales and Scotland and among the New English in Ireland the making of a first marriage, especially one that involved a young person, was carefully prepared for and researched by the parents and other relatives and friends or godparents of both parties.[49] Quite frequently a marriageable daughter would be sent into the great household of a prominent lady, probably a well-chosen godmother, who would train the girl up and, if appropriate, show her off to the parents and relatives of possible suitors. In 1533–34, Anne and Mary Basset, Honor Lisle's adolescent daughters from her first marriage, were sent to live with the aristocratic De Riou and De Bours families in northern France, where they might be educated and prepared for their future lives at court. John Temple's eighteen-year-old daughter Katherine was sent in 1591 to stay in London with Edward, Baron Wootton and his wife, with a view to finding her a match.

Sir, your daughter Katherine is (thanked be God) come hither very well, and to us very welcome indeed. She is (as you told me) very fair and well to be liked, and I doubt not but as good as fair. For the green sickness, which, indeed, she seemeth to be a little entered into, I doubt not but by

God his help the exercise which she shall take with my daughter her bedfellow and companion will soon rid her of it. At your next coming to London, we will travail further of the matter I brake unto you, till when and ever I recommend you and all yours to the Lord's holy protection. From London the 23 of March 1591.[50]

The matter of which Wootton 'brake' was a match between Katherine Temple and Sir Nicholas Parker of Willington, Sussex that was secretly agreed in 1593.[51] Lettice Willoughby, fourth daughter of Sir Percival and Lady Bridget Willoughby, spent much of her girlhood in the 1620s in the care of Lettice, dowager Countess of Leicester, who busied herself with marrying the girl off.[52] Much later another descendant of Sir Percival, his great granddaughter Cassandra, Duchess of Chandos, acted in the same capacity for her own and her husband's god-daughters, nieces and cousins.[53] The package they offered these young women included education, introductions to appropriate young men, and initial negotiations for marriage settlements. In addition, the small marriage portions of most of these women were invested in stocks in the hopes that their attractiveness would grow commensurately. The eldest daughter of Cassandra's parents-in-law (the 8th Lord and Lady Chandos), Mary, had been left with Lady Chandos's mother when her parents went to live in Turkey.[54] Mary and Anne Collet, Mary Ferrar's grandchildren, spent a good deal of time in the households of their older sister Susanna Mapletoft, of her children and of their aunt Mary. Historians have probably underestimated the impact of siblings, grandparents and godparents upon the upbringing and marrying of girls. Certainly such moving about served to widen a girl's circle of potential suitors and in some cases to advance her fortune. The age at which a daughter might be sent to live elsewhere seems to have varied considerably, probably governed by a number of circumstances.

Marrying was a family affair. Although the details differed the pattern was broadly the same. Members of the family and their agents sought the names of possible partners. The credentials of these 'candidates' were carefully investigated, listed and considered. When a decision was made that a given individual met, as it were, the 'job specification', there would be discussions with the family of the other party or its agents and with the young person concerned. Probably at this stage, if not before, there would be 'viewings' and 'interviewings' which involved the families and 'meetings' between the young people themselves. There are indications that in some cases such interviewings took the form of reasonably lengthy 'stays' with prospective in-laws to test compatibility.[55]

Even when the young person was independent (orphaned and of adult age) his or her existing close family considered a marriage to be a family concern and maintained their right to intervene. Francis Willoughby, a younger son who as a boy inherited his father's estates in Nottinghamshire, was on excellent terms with his sister Lady Arundel until he began in 1564 to negotiate a marriage with Elizabeth, daughter of Sir John Littleton of Frankley, Warwickshire. Lady Arundel wrote him several letters seeking to dissuade him from the match until 'at last Sir Francis suspects his sister covets his estate and for that reason expresses herself so much against his marrying, which Sir Francis takes very unkindly from her, on this account Lady Arundel writes a long letter to justify herself to her brother, and in it gives her reasons why she is against this match, because she thinks Sir John Littleton an ill man, a great dissembler etc.'[56] There are examples from Scotland too of freely given family advice. Much later, in 1700, we find Anna Graham remonstrating with her cousin Thomas Graham, Laird of Potento, against his proposed marriage to the widowed Lady Kinloch because Anna believes Lady Kinloch is now barren.[57] And the death of a father did not necessarily leave his unwed daughters free to marry whom they chose. Sir Arthur Throckmorton of Paulerspury, Northamptonshire, for example, in his will of 1623 left his daughter all of his stock of cattle as long as she was ruled by her mother and married with her mother's agreement. He assumed that Katherine would live with her mother till marriage and, in those circumstances, gave her maintenance of £50 a year. This amount would be raised to £100 a year if Katherine left her mother's home.[58]

This description of the process obscures more than it reveals, however. Frequently the young people belonged to families which already had a connection with their own and certainly which had similar social status and lifestyles.[59] Often the young people in a proposed match knew one another already and may have viewed one another as prospective partners from childhood.

Let us examine closely some examples of such marriage-making. The evidence lies largely in family correspondence and is often difficult to piece together. Rarely, if at all, do we see the efforts of both parties and their families and this may, in some circumstances, skew our understanding of the process and the role of both sexes within it.

First of all we see the initial stages of investigating a possible partner. When, in 1629, Lady Jane Bacon (formerly Cornwallis) was seeking a partner for her son Frederick Cornwallis, the initial groundwork was done by a close friend and relative, Dorothy Randolph, at her behest.[60] She met with one Mr Chilting to discuss the suitability of a niece of Sir Thomas Barrington (possibly Joan Meux) as a match for Frederick. Chilting suggested that a portion of £7,000 might come with the girl but Dorothy had to arrange a meeting with Lady Judith, wife of Sir Thomas Barrington, to establish the situation. As Dorothy Randolph reported, the portion was, in fact, one of £1,000 in money 'and a hundred pounds a year land in inheritance' on property valued at £5,000. Dorothy noted that she was sure that Lady Jane 'would not accept of so small a portion with any body' and that she would prefer money to land. She had, therefore, made Lady Judith aware that this was unlikely to prove attractive so that Lady Jane need not follow up if she preferred not to.[61] During the meeting with Lady Judith Barrington, however, Dorothy had met Sir William Curteen, a Dutch merchant, and two of his daughters. Talks with Lady Judith Barrington indicated that one of these daughters would be a potential match for Frederick providing that she brought with her £10,000 in cash. Dorothy was assured both of the family's wealth and of Lady Judith's assistance in promoting such a marriage.[62] Dorothy Randolph continued to search for other potential matches and to report back to Lady Jane on her progress. She suggested looking into the matter of the Lord President of Wales's daughter, for example, but Lady Jane was not keen to marry her son into the nobility.[63] Then Dorothy and her husband Ambrose investigated the possibility of a match with an orphaned young gentlewoman who had £600 a year. There were disadvantages, for the girl had to pay £1,800 to her grandmother for her wardship and freedom to marry, but Ambrose had inspected her personally and found her to be 'very handsome, and sixteen years old'.[64]

In this case it is startling that those active in searching for a partner for Frederick were almost all female. Perhaps this was particularly the case here because Frederick was a child of Jane's first marriage and because his father was dead. Similarly, Brilliana Conway Harley's aunt, Lady Vere, was instrumental in her marriage, first suggesting the possibility to Sir Edward Conway after fully investigating Harley's parentage, intelligence, religious affiliation, as well as his financial worth. When in the 1650s

TABLE 4.1 *17th-century daughters' portions by socio-economic class of fathers*[65]

Fathers' social class	Lower limit of portion	Upper limit of portion
Nobility	£5,000	£10,000
Upper gentry	£1,000	£5,000
Country gentry	£500	£1,000

Lady Christian Temple tried successfully to arrange a marriage between her daughter Frances and the Earl of Londonderry, she did not hesitate to instruct her husband as to the best action to take:

Sweet Hart . . . now I desire you to put forth all your interest with your mother to get her to assign over two thousand pound of her statute: for we have no other security which is possible for any council to accept for the present: and what you can get her to do let it be done as soon as possible may be: Procter can tell you what shire the land is in and how many tenants upon the great manor and thus being in hast is all I have to say for the present but that I am your wife that truly loves you.[66]

Some authors have used such evidence to argue that women in general played a prominent part and even assumed control in this area.[67] Certainly there are multitudinous examples of females playing a role. In the 1670s Sir Edward Dering negotiated with the mothers of three young women in the interests of his heir.[68] Sarah Churchill, Duchess of Marlborough, notably initiated marriages.[69] This was not exclusively a female area, however. Research pertaining to the Temple family of Stowe, Buckinghamshire, in an earlier period, shows the people involved in the initial inquiries were male and presumably related to the prospective bride by marriage.[70] Miles Sandys, connected to John Temple the elder by reason of Sandys' daughter Hester's marriage to Sir Thomas Temple, had been asked to investigate the suitability of a particular match for John's female relative.[71] He wrote to John reporting how he 'found a time when the party was at home and rode to him, and brake with him of their marriage'. It is intriguing that he saw his role as that of 'broker'. Perhaps Miles was conveniently placed geographically to make the approach. A broker (and of course Dorothy Randolph fulfilled the identical role) was useful not only from a practical point of view but also because he or she kept the parties at arm's length and minimised the opportunities for hostility if the match did not materialise. While the gentleman that Sandys visited here was encouraging in the matter of what jointure would be settled upon his daughter-in-law, Sandys 'could not of himself learn his favour, but a near neighbour of his told him that he knoweth very near 500 marks of by year of his land'.[72] It was only *after* the credentials of the potential suitor had been established and checked that the women of the family were drawn into the process. 'The father told me he thinks his son is free, I promised, to feel on your side whether she be free, and what shall be given with her and so to certify, and then an interview may be had if both parties friends like.' The offer of an interview was referred back by Sandys to the girl's friends. If they wanted an interview they should write back 'with speed' and he would arrange it, if they wished, in his house. This order of events made good sense – possibilities were explored and, only if they appeared exceptionally promising to both families, were allowed to reach interview stage.[73] John Temple responded by sending his son that 'you may understand my full mind in all points touching the matter you have written of' and by promising to come himself on the following Monday.[74] Sandys then contacted the other party with reassurances regarding the financial implications of the match.[75]

Sometimes members of the bride's or groom's families disagreed about the matches projected for the young people. It was difficult to find good matches for the two daughters of Henry Percy, 9th Earl of Northumberland, a great northern Catholic landowner, and his wife, a sister of Robert Devereux, Earl of Essex.[76] Percy was thrown into prison for treason in 1605 and a match with his family was therefore unattractive. Lady Northumberland began to seek a match for the elder daughter, Dorothy, when the girl was fourteen, using her connections with James I's queen, Anne of Denmark. Dorothy made her court debut in 1613 directly against the wishes of her father, at the wedding of Princess Elizabeth. Here she attracted the attentions of Count Henry of Nassau, but this came to nothing. In 1614 a match with Walter, 2nd Lord Scott of Buccleuch also proved unsuccessful. In 1615 the Earl tried to negotiate a marriage for Dorothy with Robert Sidney, son of Viscount de Lisle, but these negotiations were quickly broken off over the amount of Dorothy's dowry.[77] But Lady Northumberland, unknown to her husband, resumed the talks, using a neighbour, Sir Francis Darcy, as facilitator, and Dorothy and Robert, who had been friends since childhood, seemed to favour the match. The affair almost came to grief because Lady Northumberland, a married woman, could not transfer her property as a dowry without her husband's explicit consent. The Lisles even tried to negotiate another marriage for Robert but, in the end, Robert and Dorothy got their way and married in early 1616, completely without her father's knowledge. Meanwhile, Dorothy's younger sister Lucy, 'the most lovely damsel in all England', had also entered the marriage market. In 1615 the Countess of Northumberland, abetted by the Countess of Bedford, had allowed the flamboyant Scottish courtier Sir James Hay to present his suit to her daughter Lucy Percy. Hay was a widower with two children. The couple had reached an 'understanding'. Lucy's father, however, tried to influence Lucy's choice. Lucy hurriedly betrothed herself to Sir James. In February 1617, when Dorothy was already pregnant and Lucy betrothed, the two sisters took the news of the fait accompli of their matches to their father in the Tower. Percy accepted the Sidney marriage without great objection but tried to bribe Lucy (with the promise of a £20,000 dowry) not to marry Hay, who had no lineage or lands. When she refused, Percy refused to let her leave the Tower. When Northumberland discovered that Lucy and James were having secret rendezvous he disowned her. The two eventually wed. No doubt the peculiar circumstances of the family, with a father absent in prison and a strong-willed mother ruling the roost back home, and a Devereux family tradition of runaway marriages and affairs, explained to some extent the independent stance of these two young women and their mother and the ineffectual orders from their father. Nevertheless, taken with other evidence this example suggests that neither mothers nor daughters were necessarily passive in the face of male directives.[78]

Marriage negotiation was a delicate and secretive affair. Neither party wished to publicise the early stages of the process. This, as the following example indicates, could be for several reasons – not least being the temptation it offered to other, perhaps more attractive, suitors to emerge, or the implications for the future of the advertisement of failure.[79] So in spring 1593 Arthur Langworth confided to William, a younger son of John Temple the elder, that he had achieved an agreeable match between William's older sister Catherine and Sir Nicholas Parker, in which Edward, Baron Wotton had acted for Parker. This was an excellent match for Catherine, and Arthur wanted to keep it very quiet. Partly this was because 'I have brought it to pass contrary to some of my great good friends liking for that they meant to match him an other way. I have don it secretly no man yet knoweth but Sir Edward Wotton and I.' The conclusion waits upon John Temple: 'this resteth nothing but Mr Temple's coming up to finish all things' but 'I pray keep this letter safe. My Lady Compton your daughter and all that house is well. No body knoweth any thing of this matter but if they did it would fly and perhaps be crossed yet' and 'shall lose some great friends.'[80] Thus marriage was a family affair but it involved members of the networks of both families and had repercussions for their own livelihoods. On this occasion Arthur Langworth made it clear that he expected compensation for his good efforts on Temple's behalf and more than just a verbal acknowledgement: 'Mr Temple said nothing to me but that he was in my debt'; one word was not enough and William should forgive his plain speech in this regard for 'plain dealing of friends is a jewel'.

There are strong comparisons here with the situation in the southern colonies of North America. David Jordan, for example, has shown how the gentry of Maryland (1632–1715) built their own identity through a combination of participation in public life and the construction of kin networks following a pattern very similar to that of the Temples and other English families.[81] Here, as in England and Wales, the construction of the network was as important for lesser as for greater members.

Re-examination of the native Irish response to the challenge of the Tudor conquest has also shown that married and marrying women (such as the daughters and wives of the Fitzgeralds, Butlers, Burkes, O'Neills, O'Donnells, O'Connors and MacCarthys) played a crucial role in sustaining and extending alliances through the generations.[82] All sides used this strategy. Margaret Cusacke, daughter of the Pale reformer Sir Thomas Cusacke, married the 3rd Baron Inchiquin specifically to bind him to the Dublin government.[83] Eleanor Butler, daughter of Lord Dunboyne, was married in 1565 to Butler the last Earl of Desmond in order to ally the two great Munster families; her second marriage (to Donough O'Connor Sligo) in 1596 was probably arranged by Lord Burghley in order to mediate between O'Connor and the Dublin government.[84]

One other point emerges from the Temple/Sandys correspondence and that is that these negotiations (regarding the freedom of the young people to marry, the interest of their parents in such a match and the attractiveness of the conditions, financial and other, on the table) were preliminaries to the real business – the interview. As Sandys put it, when seeking to facilitate a marriage for Mary Temple to John Farmer in September 1591:

Wherefore me thinks there wanteth nothing but the principal point and that is that some interview may be had between the young parties upon whose good liking all the rest doth depend for if that be not perfect I say cease of and if it fall out to be good neither of you [or I] can do any thing . . .[85]

In this interview the role of the prospective mothers-in-law was crucial. 'Touching an interview if you will have it here I will procure my sister [Susan Temple, Sandys' sister-in-law] and her daughter [Mary] to come hither where you may with Mistress Farmer and all your children meet and be most heartily welcome. If you will have your son go thither my son shall accompany him but hear I hold the best place for you and Mistress Farmer may also see and judge and help your son's judgment and choice.' Sandys' choice of words suggests that he would have fully concurred with the advice given by Gouge and others that it was the parents' duty to assist their children to make the right choice of partner and not to impose such a choice upon them.[86]

Prospective in-laws who were keen on a particular match would do whatever they could to ensure that an interview reached a successful conclusion. Sir Thomas was not afraid to negotiate with the young woman in question, Lady Anne Throckmorton, who wished to marry his son Peter in 1613. In one letter Thomas expressed willingness to take the initiative even though he had expected the approach to come from her father. Then he advised discretion about their discussions and that the young people cease to see one another until her father's consent has been obtained and the final interview arranged. In so doing he acknowledged the crucial part that Sir Arthur played in achieving the match but also his own role and that of the young couple in 'managing' Sir Arthur.

It remained especially that wariness be had (wherein I doubt not of your discretion) that no hurt happen by interviews, whereby occasion may be given to Sir Arthur not to yield consent to that is mutually desired, from which meetings there may be the better abstinence for a time, till such consent be obtained, testimony being given of each party's constancy.[87]

A particular marriage could also be to the long-term advantage of the facilitators. So Miles Sandys thought when he brokered the match in 1591 between John Farmer and Mary Temple, John Temple the elder's daughter: 'I wish all happy success to this enterprise and motion of mine for love to you both and for love of mine own comforts which hereby may be greatly increased for if this match go forward then mine shall be linked in affinity with both yours and his as they be with his already.'

The key part played by the young people themselves in the concluding phases of a marriage arrangement is, however, evidenced over and over again. Sir William Ashcomb reported in his diary how, during his teen years, he rejected three suitors in as many years:

[1608] I was much importuned to marry my Lady Garrards daughter, of Dorney by Windsor. Mrs Martha Garrard; a fine gentlewoman truly. I saw her and no more.

[1609] I was importuned to see a brave spirited gentlewoman named Mrs Rachel Howard being one of the two daughters and heirs of the Viscount Bindon's brother. I saw her not far from Bath, was earnestly solicited to proceed being half afraid of the greatness of her spirit I did not; she was since more worthily bestowed and she was most worthy so to be.

[1610] I was wished unto a fine gentlewoman – I saw her – upon further acquaintance I disliked, and did not proceede.[88]

Aged twenty-two, and no longer needing parental consent for a church marriage, William, 'seeing so much wickedness in the world, and so much casualty among men, thought good to choose out a companion for me in an honest cause and take a wife'. His choice was Katherine Temple, fourteen-year-old daughter of Sir Thomas Temple, lawyer of Lincoln's Inn, and Lady Hester Temple.

As the Temple/Throckmorton case (of about the same time) suggests, there is absolutely no suggestion that this consent had to be given by the male party only. Other evidence supports such a view. In 1594 Anthony Shugborough expressed the view that the jointure arrangements for his daughter proposed by the relatives of Mr Stanton were far from generous 'yet considering the goodwill between the young couple, and the good liking I have of the gentleman I will not refuse it'.[89]

Some historians have argued that by the seventeenth century parents of the upper classes were merely giving their children a negative veto with regard to a marriage partner.[90] This could in some cases have been so. For example, Mary, Countess of Warwick arranged a match between her niece Essex Rich and Daniel Finch, son of the Lord Keeper, later the Earl of Nottingham; then she explained the advantages of the marriage to her niece and gave 'her free choice to choose or not, to do as she liked or disliked'. After the interview the Countess reported with satisfaction that Essex had 'consented to have him'.[91]

This presents the role of the young people as passive but in the background the young were often very active in urging on the conclusion of a match that they especially favoured. Francis Willoughby chose Cassandra Ridgeway, younger daughter of Thomas Ridgeway, Lord Treasurer of Ireland, as his bride; Francis wrote that his father 'never . . . have been seduced with an unquenchable or insatiable desire of lucre . . . but ever least valuing and esteeming that had chiefly my own liking, and contentment in which match of mine. I think it hath so fortunately chanced that for a father-in-law and mother, with a wife they are matchless again; whose love I perceive daily to be more and more testified.'[92] Their granddaughter concurred: 'Sir Percival showed his exceeding great care of his welfare in not pressing him to choose a wife that might bring a great fortune but such a one as he might live contentedly with.'[93] When Miles Temple, youngest son of Thomas and Hester Temple of Stowe, sought a wife of his own choosing, his parents were secretly relieved when the young lady in question matched elsewhere but they did not veto his choice.

[Y]ou shall perceive that our letters lately received from Hamburg: do bring news that Mr Witham's daughter is lately contracted to one Boothby and so my cousin Miles hath utterly lost his sweetheart, and so those fears concerning that matter are now past, which to hear I dare say you will be glad, as I was when I first heard it.

Indeed his cousin's assumption is that Miles is expected to take the initiative in the matter of his marriage. As a younger son, probably Miles was allowed more freedom than were his elder brothers.

I shall write his master by the first conveyance my mind concerning your son Miles at large, that now he is clear of this match, he may take heed to come upon any other/And so with my kind respects to your self and Sir Thomas remembered . . .[94]

Much later, in Scotland Sir John Clerk (1676–1755), advocate and second baron Penicuik, rejected two young women 'found' for him by his father and successfully negotiated a match (with his father's approval) with the 'very handsome' Lady Margaret Stuart, sister of the Earl of Galloway, 'one with whom I thought I could be very happy' and with whom he had 'contracted a friendship and familiarity . . . in the space of five or six months'.[95]

As approximately half of all young men and women had lost their fathers by the time they contemplated marriage (and many of them had also lost their mothers) we should assume that the young were often extremely active in pursuing matches for themselves.[96] Lawrence Stone argued that even more of the sons of the titled aristocracy – three-quarters – were fatherless when approaching marriage.[97]

The saying 'Marry thy daughters in time lest they marry themselves' suggests that as girls grew older they became less governable by their parents in this as in other matters.[98] Some did not wait that long to govern themselves.[99] Mary, Countess of Warwick (née Boyle) and Mary Wortley Montagu (née Pierrepoint) had as girls both defied their parents to marry their chosen suitors.[100] Mary Boyle was the daughter of the Earl of Cork. When she was just fourteen she resisted her father's attempt to marry her to Mr Hamilton, son of Lord Clandeboys. She refused to marry because her 'aversion to him was quite extraordinary'. For two years she continued to turn down every match her father suggested and then she fixed her eyes on Charles Rich, younger son of the Earl of Warwick. After horrendous scenes her father gave way and permitted the marriage.[101] Dorothy and Lucy Percy were in their mid-teens when they stood out for independent choice.[102] Mistress 'Sesell' [Cecil] spurned the determined wooing of Dorothy Bacon's melancholy son in the early 1620s. It was Anne Throckmorton who approached her future father-in-law on more than one occasion to step in and sort out the problems experienced by Peter Temple and herself at the hands of her own father. By February 1613/14 matters had progressed considerably with Peter Temple apparently living with the Throckmortons on a 'son-in-law' and 'husband' trial basis but the course of true love was not running smooth, as Anne explained to Sir Thomas: 'ever since your being here Sir Peter Temple and I hath endured much and my father will have his one mind . . . or there shall bee no match between your son and me in the which I shall think my self very unhappy because it was my own beginning at the first unknown to them.' Then she went on to deal with the practical issue that was causing Sir Arthur to think again: 'now, Sir, this my earnest request to you is that the difference being no greater but whether the females estate shall lie in per[son]al Lands or in Dasset.'[103] Although Sir Thomas sees Sir Arthur's agreement as pivotal, nowhere does he suggest that it is inappropriate or unacceptable that Anne should involve herself in the negotiations or active promotion of the match. He seems to be quite happy to correspond, and indeed collude, with her. The rather obscure wording of his letter of December 1613 suggests, however, that he thinks that Sir Arthur Throckmorton would not share his views and would see both the potential bride and the potential groom in a more passive light.

Why was this consent of the parties to a marriage so eagerly sought? In part this was because, ultimately, no marriage arrangement was safe if it did not have the willing consent of both parties.[104] In the mid-eighteenth century the second Duke of Argyll made his daughter Mary marry a promiscuous son of the Earl of Leicester against her will. Her behaviour prior to the wedding made her new husband refuse to bed her on the wedding night. In retaliation Mary refused to sleep with him at all, thus denying him a son and heir. Eventually, after her house imprisonment at Holkham Hall during which the servants referred to her as 'Our Virgin Mary', a separation resulted.[105] Confrontations such as this benefited no one and families normally sought to avoid them. When, in the seventeenth century, Hester Temple was arranging a match for her daughter with a young man who had been a ward she was assured that because the 'gentleman cometh and obtained the good will of your daughter and marryeth her not by your taking or enforcing', they are free from fears of litigation.[106] If nothing else, the existence of a marriage settlement or contract carefully negotiated by the parents of both bride and groom, guaranteed the future economic security of the couple and, looking to the future, the widowed wife. In part, though, and perhaps the largest part, parents were concerned for the happiness of their offspring and for the family harmony that such contentment promised. Sometimes, though, they did not play their cards aright. Sir Francis Willoughby of Middleton and Sir Thomas Willoughby of Boreplace, Kent, negotiated a marriage between Francis's eldest daughter Bridget and Sir Thomas's elder son Percival when the couple were very young. Percival was enthusiastic but Bridget opposed the match. Her great granddaughter, privy to letters surrounding the match and its aftermath, surmised that at least a part of the problem was that 'she was never consulted in it [the match] and therefore took a prejudice to Sir Percival'. She may also have suspected Percival of philandering. Percival after the ceremony went abroad on his grand tour, hoping that they would be reconciled. His passionate love letters and the welcoming reception accorded her by her new in-laws appear to have won her round.[107] Sir Thomas Temple expressed his love for his future daughter-in-law Anne Throckmorton for as long as she made his son Peter happy: 'This my estimation of you, your worthiness and the affection which I trust you will show to my son, hath obtained, and I will not deny but such unworthiness (as I do think, it is impossible you should be stained withal) will only lose the same'.[108] Even if love did not enter into their calculations, and it often did, parents were anxious that the union should last and that it should produce heirs so that the connection between the two estates and families achieved by the initial union would be continuing and strong. Attraction between the young couple made this outcome a possibility. The interview also provided an opportunity for the parties to assess the health and physical suitability of the prospective partners. Anne Throckmorton was quite open about her ability to bear healthy children as a major asset in her eligibility:

That you will be pleased to conclude quickly or else I shall see a present desolving of this matter which I hope I shall not live to see and I do not doubt but god will send me heirs males of my own body for all your lands so hoping of your favour here in I leave with hopes and rest no less yours than you expect Ann Throckmorton.[109]

Sir Thomas Temple's reply indicates, however, that a match might falter even at a late stage, when both future bride and groom's affections had been engaged and when the relatives have high opinions of the union: '[I have] already consented to more than others ordinarily for the like portion have required. And truly I would not for the like preferment condescend to any other so much as I have done in regard of the price I make of your worth and kindness and not without great hope of heirs males of you.'[110]

Romantic love and courtship among the elite

We would have fetched ambrosia down from heaven
That sweet celestial food, but see how Jove
Willing to grace this worthy company
Sends his cup bearer Lovely Ganimead
With cup of nectar to the brim
For to carouse a health to you fair bride
Whose nuptials to solemnize you have deigned
To make of this Good Himens Holiday
Then take it noble Chichester begin
And those that pledge in love the new made wife
Let it be so much blood unto their life.[111]

The examples so far have shown that parents and relatives considered that a match depended ultimately on the liking the young people had for one another but not that it depended on the presence of love. Throughout the period, however, romantic love certainly played a part in some elite liaisons which led to marriage. The young people involved thought that it provided the natural basis for a successful formal union and sometimes in otherwise inauspicious circumstances. 'He who marries where he doth not love, will soon love where he doth not marry.'[112] (Contemporary theatre such as Shakespeare's *Romeo and Juliet* echoed and supported their beliefs.) There are, of course, the famous examples of Henry VIII's passion for Anne Boleyn and Charles I's love for Henrietta Maria but there are many others. In February 1477 the prospects of success for Margery Brew's marriage to John Paston III seemed poor because her father refused to improve her portion. Margery wrote to John of her love for him and her wish that his love for her should outweigh her lack of adequate fortune: 'if that you love me, as I trust verily that you do, you will not leave me therefore; for if that you had not half the livelihood that you have . . . I would not forsake you.' Eventually, despite the appearance of another, richer woman in John's life, Margery married her 'Valentine'.[113] Arthur Lisle, an illegitimate son of Edward IV, clearly was in love with his second wife Honor (Grenville) Basset, when he wrote, 'I think so much on you I cannot sleep i' the night. When I think on you, in two hours after there was never child thought so long for his nurse as I do for you.' He called her 'mine own' and 'sweetheart' while she reciprocated with 'mine own sweet good lord' and 'good mine own' and signed herself 'By her that is more than all your own.'[114] In the 1670s none could deny the devotion of Daniel Finch to his wife Lady Essex (Rich) Finch.[115] The tempestuous relationship between Henry 2nd Duke of Chandos and his first wife Mary Bruce was founded in mutual passion and affection: 'My dearest C . . . Indeed in spite of all our disputes I love you sincerely and whether with you or from you shall ever wish you happiness tho mine I fear is lost for ever Oh that we might be happy or that Heaven would put an end to my sufferings . . .' and, somewhat later, 'Indeed I am quite tired of sleeping alone and long much for your return.'[116] Her letters are saucy and forthright. In one she declares herself ready 'to scold to rangle to bite to fight and to scratch to quirell in short to coak a Pug or any such but say my prayers go to the Devell'.[117] Henry's father, James Brydges, had clearly loved his first two wives very dearly. On Cassandra's death in 1735 he told a close friend through his secretary that he could not write himself because of 'an inexpressible load of affliction'.[118] Her death, he told another, had deprived him of 'all prospect of happiness or even comfort in life'.[119]

Parents tried to explain to their children the meaning of such love. Because traditionally historians have cited examples of advice to young women on their conduct within marriage it seems appropriate to emphasise here that fathers, like mothers, counselled their sons. Sir Thomas Temple bade his son Peter follow King Charles's and King James's example of faithful love by loving his own new wife, Christian (Leveson) Temple to the exclusion of all others and by acknowledging the practical obligations that such love implied on his part as well as his wife's:

I wish also you will rather imitate him also and King James his father, that loved their wives as they ought to do and for the Latin proverb Englished is, that the whole world followeth the example of the king, and not of lords as Sir Clement Throckmorton truly said, that it is not so great a benefit to have a good wife, as to love her. These things I will pray you [p. 1v] to endeavour for her, which is that she surfeit not: for the old saying is true (that more die with surfeitt than with the sword): that she take not cold, that she ride no more in the coach then she must needs do. To these I will add, that she foresee and avoid mischances.[120]

Historians have often observed that a double standard operated in medieval and early modern times, whereby women were expected to love their husbands exclusively and their menfolk were permitted much more latitude. Sir Thomas, a devout member of the Church of England, took the marriage vows seriously and expected his son to do likewise and to remember his father's counsel. He attached as much importance to the husband's chaste behaviour as to that of the wife:

I pray you keep and peruse this paper as an earnest of my endless love Let these three posies on our name put in mind to hearken to my said lines, that is one by a Batchelor of Arte and good scholar on my name: . . . Thou that bearest a Temple in name, and are a Temple in spirit, see that thou be of the holy ghost a Temple . . . my son Thomas his posy is, my name is god's house.

Katherine Thimelby and Herbert Aston were 'in love' in the 1630s. Katherine's letters revealed the depth of that love. They found a willing ally in Herbert's sister, Constance, who promoted their marriage:

I dare swear there was never two creatures so like, so perfectly alike as you two are in dispossessions and natures. Oh 'tis a thousand pities you should be parted: she is just you, and so you her, that may I be miserable if I do not think you will be the happiest lovers in the world, if you have the happy fortune to match with one another, the world might justly then envy you, but could not show your equals.[121]

In the sixteenth century headstrong Margaret Bagot fell in love with William Trew and married him in secret.[122] Her nephew Lewis wanted to marry his cousin Jane Throckmorton, with whom he had formed a relationship.[123] Once this relationship ended Jane went on to form another attachment, this time to Simon Rugeley, then a student at Cambridge.[124]

That said, in the cases of the Fowlers, the Astons, the Bagots and the Throckmortons, the importance of obtaining parental consent or approval was still acknowledged as a key to the success of the marriage. Constance Fowler urged Herbert to tell his family that he was interested in Katherine in order to stop her brother trying to make a match elsewhere and to ascertain from their father what settlement would be available.[125] Margaret Bagot came to her father and mother after the event and apparently secured acceptance by the family.[126] Lewis and Jane accepted the verdict of Walter Bagot that their marriage was not to be.[127]

Also all three examples should make us ponder the extent to which these relationships between the young were 'freely' formed. The Fowlers and the Astons were members of the Catholic Staffordshire gentry who moved in a close and controlled circle. Margaret Bagot, daughter of an ally of the Earl of Essex, married William Trew a member of Essex's entourage. Lewis and Jane were cousins, thrown into proximity by their wider family; and Simon Rugeley came from another local family that belonged to the Bagot connection. 'So that without we can bring him to undertake the payment of the portion, it can never be paid. The fund the father charges to pay it out off not being sufficient.'[128] In 1590, approached by a marriage broker with an eye to a match between Mr Pope of Oxfordshire and Wotton's daughter, Baron Wotton explained: 'Because the men were to me unknown, and I not acquainted with the gentleman, I knew not what to say unto them.' Only his friend John Temple's testimony will satisfy him that the proposal should be considered seriously: 'understanding you had been made privy to their purpose, I said I would expect the information you would give me of the gentleman, before I could make them any direct answer and therefore I pray you by your next to let me know what you think unfainedly both of the young man and his living'.[129] Family, religion and geography all played a major part in restricting the circle from which individuals could select a mate. If the families were not known to one another then the references of a network of friends and relatives were called into play.

There are many examples of both men and women gladly seeking parental consent to a match and indeed parental help in finding suitable partners. In those cases where young people went ahead against their parents wishes and married for love, they had almost always sought parental consent initially.

Elite parents faced with independent-minded young people had to bolster their authority by threats and cajolery. The Earl of Northumberland tried hard, but unsuccessfully, to dissuade (through bribery) his younger daughter Lucy from marrying a parvenu courtier.[130] He also tried in vain to end his heir Algernon Percy's plans to marry Anne Cecil, daughter of Northumberland's old enemy the Earl of Salisbury.[131] As late as the end of the seventeenth century, Bishop Richard Kidder of Bath and Wells tried to prevent the physician Claver Morris from courting his daughter. Finally Kidder approved the match but he told Morris that 'he would not oblige himself to do so much for a child that chose for herself, as one that in that affair should be governed by him'.[132]

There is evidence that young people were greatly exercised about this issue. In the seventeenth century Dr Richard Napier recorded that 40 per cent of his patients were troubled by courtship, many of them suffering physical and mental problems caused by parents witholding consent.[133] In the 1690s female correspondents in the *Athenian Mercury* were especially troubled by the wishes of their parents and kin with respect to their marriages.[134]

It should be noted that it was *parental* consent that was sought and this did not mean that it was only the *father's* agreement that mattered. Probably one of the most detailed accounts of a mother's determined and initially effective opposition to a marriage concerned the Willoughby family in the later sixteenth century. Winifred, a younger daughter of Sir Francis and his lady, formed an attachment to Ned, her brother-in-law (confusingly also named Willoughby). Sir Francis was won round to the match when Ned's father settled property upon him.

[T]he greatest difficulty still remained, and that was gaining Lady Willoughby's consent; Ned writes that when it was first proposed to her she flew into violent passions both with Sir Francis and her daughter Winifred and would by no means be prevailed with to hear of such a match and for fear least Winifred should steal away to marry privately, she kept her locked up by such hands as he could not convey a letter to her or get one from her and used her most sadly, in so much that in one of Ned's letters to Sir P W he writes that he fears by my Lady's severity poor Winifred will be lamed. (March 18th 89)[135]

Winifred could only escape this maternal refusal of consent by secretly marrying Edward. Her mother, hearing of it, fell into a rage and replied that imprisonment and death would be his portion with Winifred but her other children seem to have maintained contact. Winfred's mother was a very difficult and, possibly, seriously deranged woman and her reactions should not be considered typical but what is important here is that her husband Sir Francis considered her consent to be essential. Moreover there are other examples of mothers refusing consent throughout the period and at different social levels. In 1710 Peg Adams, a poor relative of the Verneys, had an offer of marriage from a man she loved but her *mother* forbade the match. She appealed to John Verney to intervene but, after one attempt to speak on her behalf, John told her to obey her mother.[136]

It is worth noting also that in the eighteenth century when the first Duke and Duchess of Chandos sought marriage partners for their many nieces and cousins they accepted that the final decision rested with the parents and the young woman, no matter what the Duke and Duchess perceived the advantages to be. Chandos was infuriated by the reluctance of his widowed brothers-in-law to accept nominated matches for their young (and relatively poor) daughters. (This indicates that historians need to be careful to establish whether both parents were alive before reaching conclusions about the shared responsibility of both parents for such important decisions.)[137] He was equally frustrated by the tears and tantrums displayed by the daughters themselves, often packing them off to their parents, but the Duke nevertheless surrendered to their wishes, because he and his wife thought detestation of one's spouse was not the perfect recipe for marriage.[138]

It is often impossible to discern whether the anxiety displayed by some young women at the prospect of marriage was an objection to marriage in general or to a specific match. Sarah Mendelson has collected together examples of young women who apparently viewed their change of state with apprehension if not revulsion. So Mary Boyle 'still continued to have an aversion to maridge . . . I was unwilling to change my condition'.[139] Elizabeth Delaval (b.1649) sank into profound depression during preparations for her happy day and Sarah (Henry) Savage (1664–1745) worried considerably about enforced absence from her family and friends.[140] Alice Thornton reflected that 'for my owne perticuler, I was not hastie to change my free estate without much consideration . . . wherein none could be more sattisfied'.[141] Yet when the cases are examined closely it often seems that the objection was to a forced match, as when Mrs Delany exclaimed of her marriage to a much older man in 1718: 'when I was led to the altar, I wished from my soul I had been led . . . to be sacrificed' but later wrote 'Why must women be driven to the necessity of marrying? A state that should always be a matter of choice!'[142]

Marriages between children

Instances of child marriage provide the ultimate example of arranged marriage. In the fifteenth century child marriage in royal houses (to form diplomatic alliances) had been common. We are in danger, however, of either underestimating or overestimating the significance of this practice even in the Middle Ages and Tudor period. It has been claimed that the system of wardship encouraged child marriage among the aristocracy, either because parents sought to marry their children to avoid a possible wardship situation, where family influence on the marriage would be prevented, or because feudal guardians married their young wards off to the highest bidder at the earliest opportunity. Child marriages in the sixteenth century were never in the majority and in fact the percentage of child marriages among the peerage (where they were most common) fell from 21 per cent between 1540 and 1599 to 12 per cent between 1600 and

1659.[143] 'Jan 22nd 1581/2 Arthur Dee and Mary Herbert, they being but 3 year old the eldest, did make as it were a shew of childish marriage, of calling each other husband and wife . . .'[144] Such marriages involved boys below the age of fourteen and girls below the age of twelve. Even when they did occur, child marriages were often only 'technical' marriages until the parties were well beyond the contemporary ages of consent: the young people were formally betrothed and contracted but marriage and/or consummation was delayed.[145]

Although we know that marriages at so young an age were not prevalent in England and Wales by the sixteenth century and that when they did occur they tended to involve the propertied classes, they were legal throughout the period and were not rare.[146] The records of the Chester ecclesiastical courts show that between 1561 and 1564 twenty-seven couples sought to have their child marriages annulled. It is, of course, impossible to say what proportion of marriages contracted below the age of consent would be adjudged unsuccessful enough to be brought before the consistory court in this way but presumably there were many more such marriages that survived.[147] There were still instances of youngsters being married before they came of age in the 1680s and the ecclesiastical lawyers kept at their finger tips the procedures necessary and the precedents available for dealing with them. Dr Richard Raines, Chancellor of the Diocese of Lichfield, noted in his letter book 'when a girl dissents to the marriage after she comes to age – how to proceed'.[148]

There were, then, remedies for the children involved. The Chester cases indicate that the young people involved believed that because the marriages had been made without their consent, they were not true marriages until this consent was freely given when they came of age. Many of the suits were filed when the boys reached the age of consent (fourteen). Often they were supported by claims that there had been no consummation of the union, no acknowledgement of the marriage by the parties and no love or affection between them. Although children might marry early, before the ages of consent, this did not mean that they consummated the union and lived as man and wife in an independent household. Parents perhaps persuaded the children to agree to the 'marriage' by pointing out to them that they would be able to make a final decision once they reached the age of consent. So Christian Hope was said to have told her son Peter (aged twelve) that 'if he and Alice Ellis . . . could not agree when they came to lawful age, that the said Peter should be at liberty, and the matrimony should be void'.[149] When Simonds D'Ewes negotiated a match with thirteen-and-a-half-year-old Anne Clopton (not by contemporary standards a child bride), her grandmother initially refused to countenance immediate marriage because of the dangers to her granddaughter's health and the possibility that her love for Simonds was only temporary. She only agreed to the match once Simonds promised not to consummate the marriage sexually for a given period.[150] In many if not all cases the young people involved would remain resident in their parents' houses. They might later refuse to cohabit and decline to accept the marriage as valid. The church's insistence on the principle of consent freely given by both parties certainly proved useful to individuals of both sexes who objected to the child marriages arranged by their relatives: the procedures in Chester in the mid-sixteenth century, that Raines was still using in a neighbouring diocese in the 1680s, favoured the children involved and this had been true throughout the period. The children involved had to prove that theirs was not a true marriage at all. What they were seeking was annulment and not divorce.[151] In about 1586 Sybil Bancroft and Thomas Waterhouse were both ten years old when they were married at the instigation of their parents. Despite her tender years Sybil refused to live with her husband, 'but by all means she could devise did deny and forsake him and so still does, and cannot be any means be persuaded to cohabit with him'. Her brother Robert revealed to the ecclesiastical court her rebellious attitude to her father, who 'did labour by all means to drive the said parties together and to have them live together as man and wife that the more he endeavoured to bring it to pass, the more forward she was in so much that diverse times she ran away from her father upon these occasions and kept her out of his sight so long, that at some times they were afraid she had drowned herself or done some other mischief to herself to be delivered from the said Thomas'. Even the neighbours were called in to help. She would always say that she would have none of Thomas, 'she could not fancy him And if she could not live in quiet there in the country she would leave that place and dwell some where else'. She left home and went into service rather than agree to cohabit with Thomas.[152] Higher up in the social scale Humphrey Okeover was able to renounce his Bagot bride when he reached the 'age of consent' and to marry his own choice, a member of the Cheyney family. In some cases marriage was forced upon a young woman utterly against her will. Some of the most startling examples of the abduction of and forcible marriage of young women have been uncovered by Garthine Walker for early modern Wales. She has, however, demonstrated that the young women concerned resisted such treatment and used Welsh law to do so.[153] Remedies existed for child brides and grooms which they were not slow to employ.

TABLE 4.2 *Age at marriage of the nine daughters of Sir Thomas and Lady Hester Temple, 1605–1630*

Name of daughter	Married	Date of birth	Year of marriage	Approx. age
Susan Temple	Edward Clark	September 1587	by 1606	19
Hester Temple	John Rous (Sir)	November 1589	November 1605	16
Bridget Temple	John Lenthall (Sir)	August 1591	by 1606	14
Martha Temple	Thomas Penistone (Sir)	January 1594	July 1611	17
Elizabeth Temple	Henry Gibbs (Sir)	1596	between 1606 and 1614	18
Katherine Temple	William Ashcombe (Sir)	November 1599	1613	14
Anne Temple	William Andrewes (Sir)	March 1601	April 1617	16
Margaret Temple	Edward Longueville	c.1607	c.1627	c.20*
Millicent Temple	Thomas Ogle	c.1609	c.1629	20

* HEH STT 1750 John Rous to Hester Temple 20 Jan 1629/30 refers to 'my brother and sister' Longfield (i.e. Edward and Margaret Longville) and 'my new married sister' Millicent. Another letter HEH STT, 21, Anne [Temple] Andrews to Hester Temple c.1630 refers to her sister Margaret's 'litel greate belly' and to her sister's 'litel Kate' indicating that Margaret had probably married in 1627 or 1628.

Not that such remedies were necessarily required. There can be few such enchanting examples of affection as that expressed by Thomas Betson's playful letter of suit to his future wife thirteen-year-old Katheryn Rich in 1476: 'and therefore I pray you, mine own sweet cousin, even as you love me, to be merry and to eat your meat like a woman . . . I sent you this ring for a token'. Much later in the seventeenth century Symonds D'Ewes was devoted to his young bride.

These were remedies for child marriages as defined by ecclesiastical law. However, no unusual remedies were available for the many young people in the propertied classes who consensually formed lifelong unions during their teen years. Of the nine daughters of Thomas and Hester Temple, for example, there are details of ages at marriage for eight and all were married before they were twenty years of age and four by sixteen or under. The remaining daughter Margaret was certainly married by the time she was twenty-three (by which time she had at least one child) and probably by the time she reached twenty.[154]

Second marriages

Second and third marriages were extremely common in all these societies. Those entering into second marriages unsurprisingly appear to have exercised much more initiative in the marriage process. In part this could have been the result of their greater independence within the wider family.

Many had already achieved their majority, inherited estates and raised families. The women had experience of managing their own households and governing their own children and had some financial security as a result of their first husband's provision. For instance, when they decided to marry, the widower Sir Thomas Barrington had three young children and the widow Lady Judith Smith had two young children. The two had formed a relationship entirely outside the circle of their families and Thomas Barrington declared his love for Judith in letters in which he had to describe his future bride and her circumstances to his parents.[155]

Despite this, both Thomas Barrington and Judith Smith felt it desirable and/or necessary to gain the approval of Sir Thomas's parents. 'She sayeth she humbly desires that if we proceed we may have your approbation and my mother's along with us.' To achieve this effect, he sent a person 'who hath known her, and her education, and her courses as a child' to argue her suitability and he explained that, although Lady Judith's late husband had been a dubious character, Judith herself was possessed of personal virtue, gossip notwithstanding.[156]

Why were the couple (who were both mature individuals) concerned to obtain parental approval? First, the existence of children from both first marriages proved a complicating factor and made this marriage still very important to the wider Barrington family. Both partners had to show that the interests of Sir Thomas's three young children would not be harmed.[157] Second, the reputation of the Barringtons had to be maintained and, therefore, Sir Thomas had to demonstrate his wife's honour.[158] Third, the families wanted to live in harmony with one another for material as well as affective reasons.[159]

Occasionally archives reveal the agonising choices before suitors. These seem to have varied enormously from person to person. For instance, Sir Nicholas Poyntz recounted to his sister Mistress Heneage in 1575 (who was acting as broker of the match) what was uppermost in his mind as he considered Mistress Denny's suitability as a wife. On the plus side were her fortune and the fact that she did not already have a child. On the minus side was the profligate character of her father. Her own character would be decisive. For Nicholas, love did not enter into the calculations but neither was money uppermost in his mind.[160]

As to my marrying, I shall never marry any women in regard to her favour and personage. What my state and ability of living is you know well, but how well and quietly I can pass my time with a little, what malice I bear to ambition and how I despise and detest vanity, now had in veneration and practiced in place of civility and godliness, God doth only know.

Now for Mistress Deny, her portion is to defray something more than her charge she will bring me, for except I be falsely informed she hath the park she dwelleth in and a 116l. rent besides her park, and some woods in the forest, the certainty whereof I would be glad I did know. She hath no child in her care. This shall satisfy me if she be a good woman and will be an obedient wife. But if Mr Deny with this little living hath given her his prodigal heart, then is she not for me, for so would it be the spoil of my children, and the beggery of such as I might have by her . . . If you proceed for me, let me not win her love like a fool, nor spend long time like a boy. As God shall help, I am much troubled to think I must speak to any woman one loving word.

Those entering the married state on a second or further occasion were required to obey the law in so doing in all these societies. Barrington's first marriage was ended by death and the way was clear for him to remarry. The same was not true of Scottish Lady Janet Wemyss who had been unsuccessful in having her first marriage annulled and was not, therefore, free to marry. She and John seemed shocked that the St Andrews Kirk Session in 1566 viewed their partnership as 'hurdom'[161] and they were outspoken in their description of the elders as 'mer[e] layik and ignorant persons for the most part'. The elders were undeterred by her protests and excommunicated them anyway for their refusal to separate and perform public repentance.[162]

Conclusion

In the later twentieth century work on the formation (and purpose) of aristocratic marriages was dominated by Lawrence Stone's work and reactions to it. This dominance has since disappeared. Close reading of the sources is necessary to establish precisely how and why marriages were arranged and who the main actors were. Detailed case studies of the formation of marriages give the lie to Stone's contention that bride (and groom) could merely exercise a veto and indicate that, while marriages within a network and with family approval were the norm, the young people of the marriage, including the prospective bride, were often actively involved. Even when family opposition to a particular match was vehement, determined young women usually succeeded in getting their way and in doing so demonstrated a good knowledge of property and law.

The incidence of child marriages annulled when the children came of age and withdrew their consent shows how important this principle of willing consent was to early modern marriage. The huge number of second marriages were entered into by mature and independent men and women who, at the top end of society, nonetheless sought family and particularly parental approval for their matches. This was not because the law or the Church required this of them but out of respect for and involvement in the affairs of the 'house' and a recognition of the important role that marriages played in its continuance and security.

Notes

1. This term includes the hereditary nobility and the upper gentry. It avoids the clumsiness of repeatedly including terms such as 'noble' and 'gentle'.
2. HEH, STT 1837 Robert Spencer from Althrop to John Temple 31 Aug 1597 – regarding enpanelling of his brother Peter Temple and Mr Makepeace of Dassett on the jury 'for the finding of Sir Francis Willughbyes office for the county of Warwicke' on 19 Sept 1597; quotation taken from STT 1838 Robert Spencer from Althrop to John Temple 3 Sept 1597 in which he explains that since writing above he has discovered that Peter Temple is not his brother but his 'neere kinsman'.
3. L. Stone (1977) pp. 69–299, pp. 127–36.
4. For example, R. Houlbrooke (1986) pp. 4–7.
5. *Love's Downfall*, in W. Chapell and J. Ebsworth (eds), *Roxburghe Ballads*, 9 Vols, London and Hertford, 1866–99, Vol. VI, p. 267.
6. S. Mendelson and P. Crawford (1998) pp. 110–12.
7. D. O'Hara (2000) p. 2.
8. HEH, HM 46390 William Harte to Hester Temple from Burton Dassett 14 Jan 1631/2. The underlining is mine.
9. S. Gosling (1999) pp. 124–6, pp. 138–41.
10. HEH, STB Box 2, Book 3, p. 22: London Derry to Sir P:W: on St James's eve, 1610.
11. Often referred to by contemporaries as 'affinity' or 'alliance'.
12. J. M. Rosenheim (1998) pp. 24–6.
13. P. Monod (1988) pp. 24–41.
14. J. Gwynfor Jones (1995) pp. 124–6.
15. K. W. Swett (1996) p. 226.

16 Keith M. Brown (1993) pp. 543–76.

17 Kim M. Phillips (2003) p. 156.

18 N. Davis, *Paston letters and papers*, 1999 edition, 1, letter 203.

19 Popular sayings quoted by David Cressy (1997) p. 255.

20 A term often used to mean 'good reputation'.

21 Garthine Walker (2000) p. 61. The term 'hypergamy' is used to describe women marrying above their station.

22 Raymond A. Anselment (2001) p. 62.

23 Ibid p. 230.

24 HEH, STT 1777 Miles Sandys to his 'brother' John Temple at Stowe from London 16 Sept 1591.

25 HEH, STG Personal Box 3 (folder 18).

26 HEH, STB II.

27 HMC Report, Finch MSS, (415) Sir Heneage Finch to his son, Daniel Finch, 13/23 April, Good Friday, 1666.

28 The situation was no different at the end of our period. See below for a discussion of the 1st Duke and Duchess of Chandos's marriage plans for their female cousins and nieces.

29 For example, one of the reservations that was expressed in HEH, STG Personal Box 3 (18) was that the now-deceased father of the prospective bride had left a fund insufficient to pay the portions of his five daughters and that her brother had paid only half those due to three of her married sisters.

30 HEH, STB Box 2, Folder 1, 1–3.

31 Ibid.

32 Ibid, 2 May 1670.

33 UNL, Mi 4/149/5; I am grateful to Dorothy Johnston for this point.

34 HEH, STT 1797 and 1798, Anthony Shuckburgh of Shugborough Staffs from Stowe to John Temple absent from Stowe his cousin Oct >1594.

35 HEH STT 1412 Margaret Longueville to Lady Hester Temple c.1631–1637. This seems to relate to Sir Peter's marriage to Lady Christian Leveson and should be dated c. June or July 1630; STT 21 Anne Andrewes to Hester Temple c.1630. Margaret Temple Longville had married in 1627 and already has one child, Kate, by this date.

36 For an example of festivities on the birth of daughters see HEH, STT 2350 20 Jan 1618/19 from Stowe, Bucks regarding 'this occasion of god's bounty to me' by 'the safe delivery of a daughter'. The catalogue misattributes this letter to Sir Thomas Temple, but it was almost certainly from Sir Peter Temple,

Thomas's son and heir, regarding the birth on 9 Jan 1618 of his first daughter and child, Anne, who was baptised at Stowe, according to the parish register, later that month. Thomas's last child, Millicent, had been born in c.1609.

37 J. M. Gallman (1984) p. 609.
38 Keith M. Brown (1996) pp. 177–9.
39 HEH, STB, Box 2, Book 2, p. 20 and Book 3 unpaginated – reverse of Willoughby/Ridgeway marriage papers recount Percival and Bridget Willoughby's troubled courtship.
40 A. C. Wood (1958) p. 43.
41 P. Laslett (1977) p. 13.
42 T. H. Hollingsworth (1957) pp. 4–26.
43 K. Lockridge (1970) p. 66.
44 J. M. Gallman (1984) pp. 615–16.
45 For an intriguing comment on the potential power of marriageable princesses, see F. Downie (1999) pp. 170–91.
46 Richard Parkinson (1845) p. 16.
47 Ibid p. 21.
48 Ibid p. 72.
49 See L. Stone (1977); P. J. Greven (1977); N. Canny (1982).
50 HEH, STT 2583 Edward Wotton, 1st Baron Wotton from London to John Temple 23 Mar 1591/2.
51 HEH, STT 1222 Arthur Langworth to Sir Wm Spencer at Yarrington 13 Apr 1593 re a marriage treaty between Catherine Temple (b.1574) and Sir Nicholas Parker.
52 A. C. Wood (1958) p. 59.
53 NLCS, Copy Letter Book of Cassandra, Duchess of Chandos. See Rosemary O'Day, *Cassandra Brydges*, 2007.
54 HEH, STB Box 10 (6) 10 October 1681. 'I left my eldest Daughter [Mary Brydges aged about 17] with my mother [her Grandmother and Godmother] the Lady Barnard.'
55 See, for example, the cases of Cassandra Ridgeway and Francis Willoughby and of Anne Throckmorton and Peter Temple.
56 HEH, STB Cassandra Willoughby's book on the Ridgeway–Willoughby marriage, pp. 16–17.
57 HMC Report 5, HMSO, 1909: Manuscripts of Sir John James Graham of Fintry, ed. Mrs S. C. Lomas, p. 258.

58 HEH, STT Personal Box 7 Folder 16, 3 June 1623. Copy will and probate of Sir Arthur Throckmorton of Paule[r]sperry, Northamptonshire; this was a very small portion according to the table on p. 80.

59 The Willoughbys, a rather extreme case, were forever marrying or trying to marry Willoughbys from different branches of the family in the sixteenth and seventeenth centuries. In the late sixteenth century, Bridget of the Nottinghamshire branch married Percival of the Kent branch while in the early seventeenth century Elizabeth Willoughby of the Grendon, Northamptonshire branch was seeking to arrange a match with Sir Percival's fourth daughter Lettice. HEH, STB Box 2, Book 3, p. 41.

60 R. Griffin, Lord Bray Brooke (1842) p. 208; Cassandra Willoughby, writing retrospectively in the early eighteenth century, assumed that Lettice Knollys, Countess of Leicester, was Lettice Willoughby's godmother not only because they shared the same name and because young Lettice spent so much time in the Countess's household but also because Lady Leicester expended so much energy in trying to find a match for her in 1614 (HEH, STB Box 2, Book 3, p. 42).

61 R. Griffin (1842) p. 208.

62 Ibid pp. 209, 221.

63 Ibid p. 213.

64 Ibid p. 227.

65 This table is based on data provided by A. L. Erickson (1993) pp. 88–9 and A. Macfarlane (1986) p. 264. Compare with p. 124 which gives figures for the lower (country or parish) gentry, merchants, professionals, craftsmen, tradesmen, farmers and labourers.

66 HEH, STT, Box 13, 1914 Lady Christian Temple from London to Sir Peter Temple at Stowe 4 Sep 1650.

67 S. Gosling (1999) p. 94; see also marriage in 1724 of Catherine, sister of Theophilus, 9th Earl of Huntingdon, which was arranged by Lady Betty Hastings, their half-sister, because her father was dead and her brother abroad, in F. Bickley (1934) p. 2.

68 M. F. Bond (1976) pp. 122–33, 114, 116. Also cited in J. M. Rosenheim (1998) p. 32.

69 Rosenheim (1998) p. 32.

70 HEH, STT 1777 Myles Sandys to John Temple from London, 16 Sept 1591.

71 This was probably the match with John Temple's relative Elizabeth Akers. She eventually married Thomas Thornton, who worked at Lincoln's Inn alongside Thomas Temple and was known as 'Cousin Thornton' in the seventeenth century – see HEH STT 2364 Elizabeth (Akers) Thornton to

Mr Andrew, 12 May 1591 [misattributed to 1581 by catalogue] from Stowe, Bucks regarding her entry 'into some [inclination[?] of mariage] with one Mr Thorneton whoe stayeth here about that matter'. Confusingly, at around the same time Sandys was broker for a marriage between John Temple's younger daughter Mary with John Farmer, for which see STT 1778 Myles Sandys to [Farmer]? from London 18 Sept 1591.

72 £100.

73 When Lady Leicester proposed several good matches for Sir Percival Willoughby's fourth daughter Lettice he turned them all down before his daughter was even alerted to them because he could not raise the money to pay 'her fortune'. She married two husbands of humbler degree. (HEH STB Box 2, Book 3, p. 42.)

74 HEH, STT 1939 John Temple to Myles Sandys on 17 Sept 1591.

75 HEH, STT 1778 Myles Sandys to ? from London 18 Sept 1591 to ?

76 Daughter of Lettice Knollys, wife first of Robert Dudley, Earl of Leicester, and then of Thomas [?] Devereux, Earl of Essex; and sister of Penelope (Devereux) Rich, and Robert Devereux, Earl of Essex.

77 Viscount de Lisle, brother of Sir Philip, was Lady Northumberland's nephew by marriage.

78 L.-R. Betcherman (2005) pp. 3–47.

79 The Temple Papers indicate some of the times when Sir Peter Temple made serious but ultimately unsuccessful proposals for first and second marriages. See HEH, STT Personal Box 6, Folder 9, 11 Feb 1609/10 Notes of agreement taken by Mr Thorneton at Lincoln's Inn re the proposed marriage of seventeen-year-old Peter Temple and Anne Neale, daughter of Sir Thomas Neale which never materialised. A letter of Hester's in 1614 perhaps refers to this lady: 'Poor Peter's lady was married the last Monday gretly to his greif, God help him take it.' The negotiations for his marriage to Anne Throckmorton also almost came to grief: for which see, STT Personal Box 6, Folders 23 and 24, 1614 which indicate the demands made by the bride's father and the Temple reaction to them, and letters quoted here on pp. 89, 91–2. The actual marriage settlement survives in the collection (STT Personal Oversize Box). Anne Throckmorton died in January 1619/20, leaving Peter with an infant daughter, and a search for a second wife was initiated. Sometimes negotiations would proceed as far as the legal contract of the settlement and still break down: see STT Personal Box 7 Folders 11 and 12, 1620–1622, Draft Marriage Agreement between Sir Peter Temple and Anne Sackville, Lady Beauchamp, widow. See also STT 2421, Sir Edward Tyrrell, 6 July 1624, to Sir Peter Temple regarding a proposed second match with one of Lady Manners's daughters. Finally Peter married Christian Leveson, co-heiress of her grandfather: HEH, STT Personal Box 8, Folder 14, 30 May

1630, Agreement re jointure of Lady Christian Leveson, second wife of Sir Peter Temple 2nd Bt.
80. HEH, STT 1222 Arthur Langworth to Sir Wm Spencer at Yarrington 13 Apr 1593 re a marriage treaty between Catherine Temple (b.1574) and Sir Nicholas Parker.
81. D. W. Jordan (1987) *passim*.
82. C. Brady (1991) pp. 76–7.
83. Ibid p. 78.
84. Ibid pp. 80–81.
85. HEH, STT 1778 Myles Sandys to ? from London 18 Sept 1591 to ?
86. W. Gouge (1622) p. 449.
87. HEH, STT 2303 Sir Thomas Temple 1st Bt to Lady Anne (Throckmorton) Temple, 1613.
88. HEH, HM 30665, Diary of William Ashcombe of Berkhampsted, Berks 1591–1625 – bears the title Memorable Accidents – also contains some accounts, fos 3r and 3v.
89. HEH, STT 1797 Anthony Shuckburgh 15 Oct 1594? To John Temple and STT 1798, 22 Oct 1594? Anthony Shuckburgh to John Temple re the jointure. See also The Letters and Will of Lady Dorothy Bacon, 1597–1622, Norfolk Record Society, Volume LVI, 1991, Letter 8 [?1619 to 1622] where Lady Dorothy indirectly counsels her son to be cautious in his choice of a bride and to consider carefully the alternatives of Mistress Barny and Mistress Gawdy.
90. L. Stone (1977) abridged version pp. 69–299, pp. 127–36.
91. T. Crofton Croker (1848) pp. 35–6.
92. HEH, STB, Box 2, Notes on Ridgeway–Willoughby Marriage in 1610.
93. HEH, STB, Box 2, Book 3, p. 35.
94. HEH HM 46485 Carew Saunders to Hester Temple Feb 26 1626/7 from London.
95. J. G. Fyfe and R. S. Rait (1928) pp. 370–71.
96. See J. Smith and J. Oippen (1993) pp. 306–8.
97. L. Stone and J. Fawtier Stone (1984) p. 76.
98. Sir John Oglander (1612) in C. Aspinall-Oglander, *Nunwell Symphony* (1945) p. 48.
99. See also *The Letters and Will of Lady Dorothy Bacon, 1597–1622*, Norfolk Record Society, Volume LVI, 1991, Letter 8 [?1619 to 1622] where Lady Dorothy says 'the father gave him a cortyars [courteous] conclusyon as from his daughter that she did never affecke him which hee was very sory for.'

100 S. Mendelson and P. Crawford (1998) p. 113.
101 T. C. Croker (1848) pp. 2–13.
102 L.-R. Betcherman (2005) pp. 1–54.
103 HEH, STT 1910 Lady Ann (Throckmorton) Temple to Sir Thomas Temple 1st Bt in February 1613/14.
104 See below.
105 J. A. Home (1889) I, pp. lix–lxvi, cxxiii, cited in L. Stone (1977) pp. 186–7.
106 HEH, STT 1516 Roger Nicholls to Hester (Sandys) Lady Temple c.1600.
107 HEH, STB, Box 2, Book 2 of Cassandra's Account of Ye Willughbys of Wollaton, pp. 20–23 and Book 3.
108 HEH, STT 2303 Sir Thomas Temple 1st Bt to Lady Anne (Throckmorton) Temple, 1613.
109 HEH, STT 1910 Lady Ann (Throckmorton) Temple to Sir Thomas Temple 1st Bt in February 1613/14.
110 HEH, STT 2304 Sir Thomas Temple 1st Bt to Lady Anne (Throckmorton) Temple on 4 March 1613/14 in reply to her last.
111 HEH, STB Box II, 'The speech made to ye Ld Deputy and Councell at ye marriage of Sir Francis Willoughby with ye Lady Cassandra Ridgeway at Ruthfarnam in Ireland By Mr George Withers ye poett Feb: 1610'.
112 Cited in B. Capp (1979) p. 125.
113 Norman Davis (1971) letters 415 and 416. For further comment see Kim M. Phillips (2003) pp. 182–5.
114 M. St Clare Byrne (1983) p. 18 and also letters between Arthur Lord Lisle and Honor Lady Lisle, September to November 1538.
115 HMCR (1922) Vol. 2, Item 24.
116 HEH, STB Box 3 Letters from Mary Bruce to Henry Brydges, Marquis of Carnarvon c.1729–1738, nos 34 and 39.
117 HEH, STB Box 3 no. 46.
118 HEH, ST 46, p. 153 To Sir Hungerford Hoskyns London 22 July 1735.
119 HEH, ST 46, p. 162 To William Leigh 25 July 1735.
120 HEH, STT 2326 Sir Thomas Temple from Dassett to Sir Peter Temple at Stowe 7 Aug 1631.
121 A. Clifford (1815) p. 124.

122 R. O'Day (1995) p. 148.

123 Folger Shakespeare Library, Bagot Collection, L.a. 852, Jane Skipworth to Lewis Bagot, 14 April 1610 and L.a. 854, Jane Skipworth to Walter Bagot, 19 September 1610.

124 Folger, Bagot Collection, L.a. 771, Richard Rugeley to Walter Bagot, 31 March 1621.

125 A. Clifford (1815) pp. 124–5.

126 R. O'Day (1995) p. 148.

127 FSL, Bagot Collection, L.a. 852, Jane Skipworth to Lewis Bagot, 14 April 1610 and L.a. 854, Jane Skipworth to Walter Bagot, 19 September 1610. Other examples of love matches, this time among the nobility, include those of Algernon Percy, 10th Earl of Northumberland (to Anne Cecil), and his sisters Dorothy Sidney, Countess of Leicester, and Lucy Hay, Countess of Carlisle. See L.-R. Betcherman (2005) pp. 4–50 and p. 117.

128 FSL Bagot Collection, L.a. 628, 25 November 1569.

129 HEH, STT 2582 Edward Wotton 1st Baron Wotton from Pickering House to John Temple 18 Nov 1590.

130 L.-R, Betcherman (2005) pp. 44–8.

131 Ibid p. 117.

132 A. E. Robinson (1924) pp. 134–44.

133 M. MacDonald (1981) pp. 88–9.

134 H. Berry (2003) p. 162.

135 HEH, STB Box 2, folder 1, Book 1, p. 36, 18 March 1589.

136 S. Whyman (2001) p. 187.

137 HEH, ST 57, e.g. Vol. 14, pp. 136–7 Letter to Brother Charles Walcot 2 Aug 1716.

138 NLCS, Copy Letter Book of Cassandra Brydges, no. 17. pp. 11–12 To my sister Walcot Aug the 25th 1716; no. 88, p. 46 To my sister Walcot [Undated c. September 1720]; For Cassandra's gentle approach see no. 35 p. 21 Copy of part of a letter to niece Bourchier 23 Sept 1718; the Duke described her dealings with tearful Betty Brydges (his brother's eldest daughter) in HEH, ST 57, Vol. 29, p. 170 To Dr Brydges from London 2 Feb 1726/7.

139 BL, Add. MS 27357, fo. 4v cited in S. Mendelson (1985) p. 192.

140 D. G. Greene (1975) pp. 177–9, 185–6; Sarah Savage's Diary fo. 5v; cited in Mendelson (1985) p. 191.

141 C. Jackson (1875) p. 76 cited in Mendelson (1985) p. 192.

142 Ruth Haydn (1980) p. 24, cited in Laurence (1994 reissue 2002) p. 57.

143 T. H. Hollingsworth, 'The Demography of the British Peerage', *Supplement to Population Studies*, 18, 1964, p. 20.

144 James Orchard Halliwell, *The Private Diary of John Dee*, Camden Society, 1845, p. 14.

145 F. Downie (1999) pp. 172–3. The age of consent was fixed at 12 for girls and 14 for boys. See below, pp. 170–76 for the way in which parents sought to delay the setting up of a separate household.

146 Peter Laslett suggests that they represented half a per cent only of marriages contracted in the early modern period, see P. Laslett (1965) p. 86. They were probably more common in the sixteenth than in the seventeenth century. To be legal such marriages had to be with parental consent.

147 Frederick J. Furnivall (1897); Gary G. Gibbs (1988) pp. 32–42.

148 L.J.R.O., B/A/19.

149 G. G. Gibbs (1988) pp. 35–6.

150 J. O. Halliwell (1845) I, pp. 352–4, 363.

151 This was a significant distinction. After divorce (*divortium a mensa et thoro* or legal separation) the parties were not allowed to remarry. After annulment (*divortium a vinculo matrimonii*) marriage was allowed because the original marriage was declared never to have been valid.

152 L.J.R.O., B/C/.

153 G. Walker (2000).

154 HEH STT Personal Box, folder 7, Hester Temple: the dates of birth of her children from 5 Sept 1587 to 11 Sept 1602; Extracts from the Stowe parish registers.

155 BL Egerton MS 2644, fos 218–20, Sir Thomas Barrington to Sir Francis Barrington, 11 October 1624; see S. Gosling (1999) pp. 137–40 for an excellent treatment of this case.

156 BL Egerton MS 2644, fo. 217, Sir Thomas Barrington to Sir Francis Barrington, undated.

157 BL Egerton MS 2644, fo. 218, Sir Thomas Barrington to Sir Francis Barrington, 11 October 1624; Essex Record Office, D/Dba F19, Draft regarding the marriage agreement between Sir Thomas and Lady Judith, undated.

158 BL Egerton MS 2644, fo. 217, Sir Thomas Barrington to Sir Francis Barrington, undated; he pleaded his new wife's case by citing references on her behalf, e.g. fo. 209.

159 See Chapter 7 for an account of the interdependence of households.
160 *Report on the Manuscripts of Allan George Finch Esq. of Burley-on-the-Hill, Rutland*, volume 1, ed. S. C. Lomas (London, HMSO, 1913), (21) Sir Nicholas Poyntz to his sister, Mistress Heneage from Chanon Row, 19 May 1575.
161 That is, whoredom.
162 M. Graham (1996).

CHAPTER 5

Making marriages among women of the professional and the middling sorts

Mr Harbach Senior: I think it is fitter for you to be married to a gentleman.
Mary Cudworth: I will not be married to a gentleman, for gentlemen usually live extravagant . . . and when they die leave their wives in poor condition.
Harbach: . . . what say you to a tradesman?
Mary: I will not have a tradesman, for if I should, my fortune will be put into his trade, and when he dies, his creditors may turn me out of all.
Harbach: . . . what think you of a clergyman, you being a clergyman's daughter yourself?
Mary: I will not have a clergyman, for they usually have nothing but their parsonages to live upon, and when they die leave their wives in mean conditions. My desire is to be married to an honest plain country-man, who has an estate of his own,
or in a probability of having an estate, and one whose house stands by itself.[1]

Introduction

Much less is known and has been written about making marriages among the lower (parish) gentry, professional families and the middling-sort of people, of England, Wales and Scotland, than those among the elite, although this situation is being rectified. The books of advice were directed in part to just such people and the laws of church and state applied equally to them. Although there is not the same amount of detail concerning the arrangement and brokerage of marriages for these classes of people either in the Old or the New World, there are indications that this business was taken just as seriously as it was by the elite. In England matchmakers and brokers played their part, especially for the well-to-do. A mid-eighteenth-century author counselled young men who did not trust their own judgement in finding a wife to consult the neighbourhood matchmaker, an experienced matron who 'knows to a tittle the exact rates of the market and the current prices of young women that are fit to marry'. In seventeenth- and eighteenth-century London, for example, scriveners seem to have acted for a fee as brokers of introductions with a view to marriage.[2] Haggling over the terms of a marriage settlement was a common feature in all these societies.[3] Families played their part in facilitating marriages.

Sources indicate that numbers of women from all social classes did not find marriage an attractive proposition and in some cases rejected it. Where marriage was contemplated, the evidence of actual marriage-making suggests that young women sought to exercise considerable independence in such matters, sometimes disregarding the advice and rebelling against the control of parents and family members and always consulting their own hearts and their own interests, financial and otherwise.[4] One such woman was Mary Cudworth, who initiated her own matches and whose business-like views on marriage and its effect on her portion (expressed to her prospective father-in-law) are quoted at the beginning of this chapter. Mary was well aware that her true power lay in her ability to make a choice of suitor and that she had better bestow herself wisely. Only thus could she secure her future. Her portion and not her face was her fortune. The church courts defended such independent choices, taking exception only to the incidence of young women entering multiple pre-contracts of marriage. Parents, anxious to control their daughters' marriages and lives, sometimes sought to exploit other instruments such as the will or simple threats to this end.

Knowledge of marriages among the very poor labouring classes and those who moved in and out of work is still sparse. Historians occasionally uncover examples of these unions but because of its patchy nature, such documentation does not provide a sound basis for comparison in this book. Parish authorities were anxious that their communities would not be overburdened by paupers and, as result, tried to prevent rash marriages which would not be financially stable.[5] Parents of the labouring classes as well as those from the ranks of husbandmen, yeomen and craftsmen probably shared a desire to 'provide' for the creation of another viable household, a desire that they rarely possessed the wherewithal to satisfy.

Comparisons between the Old World and the New suggest that the circumstances of colonisation (and in particular the demography of the individual colonies) had a marked impact upon the making of marriage. Marriage was encouraged by the governing bodies of the colonies. The absence of parents of many of the young immigrants made for the exercise of even greater freedom of choice than in England and Wales. When parents were present they rarely seem to have used other means, such as the will, to determine whom their children married. This perhaps indicates a greater acceptance of the child's freedom of choice or, where sons were concerned, reflects the paucity of choice available in male-heavy populations.

Proportions of married adult females in the English population, 1560–1720

It is hard to establish the number or proportion of single adult women in the population at any one time. According to Gregory King only a tiny proportion of women over the age of twenty-five remained unmarried (2.5 per cent). As Crawford and Mendelson point out, however, this amounted to 11,200 unmarried adult women. Wrigley and Scofield's work indicated that there were considerable fluctuations in the proportion of married women between 1560 and 1720, ranging from 5 per cent to 27 per cent of the adult single male and female population, rising to a peak in the third quarter of the seventeenth century. Only 9.2 per cent of those born in 1666 did not marry. In particular social groups there were also differences. Only 5 per cent of the daughters of peers were unmarried in 1600 but the number had increased to between 20 and 28 per cent by the late seventeenth and early eighteenth centuries. Many of these people who never married, however, probably entered into what are known as 'clandestine' or secret marriages – a practice that was probably much more common among the poorer sorts.

Whatever the true proportions, it is clear that a large minority of females did not marry in a society where marriage was regarded (by parents and preachers, writers of conduct books and teachers) as the desirable norm. Historians have variously explained this situation in terms of the changing sex ratios or the fall in real wages. Scotland lost a good many young men to emigration each year (perhaps as many as 20 per cent of its young men left), and this made it difficult for young women to find suitable matches.

The death rate among men was higher than among women. More young women flocked to the towns and cities, especially London, in response to demand for female servants, than did young men. During the seventeenth century there was less demand for male apprentices. Young men either remained in the countryside or looked to the colonies for a rosier future. As a result there was less chance of a young woman finding a suitable husband in these cities.

As Crawford and Mendelson have established, quite a few women expressed considerable reservations about the desirability of marriage, with most examples occurring in the seventeenth century. For example, Mary Evelyn was indifferent to marriage and Elizabeth Stout counselled her disabled daughter Elnor 'to remain single, knowing the care and exercises that always attended a married life, and the hazard of happiness in it'. Various Catholic women lauded celibacy and either entered convents abroad or remained in England to help with the home mission. Women within the Church of England sometimes wished to make vows of chastity but seem to have been advised by their chaplains and bishops to marry instead. For example in the 1630s two of the Ferrars of Little Gidding contemplated vows of chastity but Bishop Williams talked them out of it saying, 'Let the younger women marry was the best advice, that they might not be led into temptation'.[6] Outstanding examples of single women who led active and apparently happy single lives by choice include Joyce Jeffries in the period down to 1650 and Celia Fiennes who travelled through England for over thirty years and left a record of what she considered to be of interest.

Why might young women not wish to marry? For some, as indicated above, there could have been religious reasons. Some young women would not have been heterosexual. Others probably wished to retain their independence, particularly if they had means of support. A single woman could enter into contracts, sue and be sued in the courts and trade. Ironically, although aristocratic women probably had more chance of surviving independently of marriage than their sisters of the middling and lower sorts, they probably had more pressure put on them by parents and other relatives to enter into marriage. Families, at every social level, were frequently keen to keep at least one daughter at home as a guarantee against their own incapacity in old age or sickness. Elnor Stout might have been too disabled to handle married life but she was regarded as fully able to housekeep for her aged mother and her brother and to care for lively young nephews and nieces. When all the daughters married, other arrangements had to be made for the care of aged parents.

Sex and the single girl

Our emphasis in this chapter is upon marriage among the professional and middling sorts but it seems appropriate to consider what is known generally about the extent of sexual activity outside marriage in the English population as a whole. First of all, we do know that a high proportion of cases coming before the consistory (church) courts in the pre-civil war period were for pre-marital conception. Court cases, however, can be indicative of the concern of the authorities to stamp out a particular 'error' as well as of any rise in the occurrence of that error. Figures based on studies of the baptismal registers seem to hold out more hope of establishing how common illegitimate births were and also how common pregnancies were that began before marriage. Table 5.1 presents approximate percentages of both on a decade by decade basis.[7]

The indications are that young women were more sexually active during the sixteenth century than during the seventeenth, and that the seventeenth century saw a marked decline in both illegitimate births and pre-marital pregnancies. However, it is clear that some illegitimate children were not recorded as such by clergymen, that the children of vagrants were not baptised, that contraception was practised,[8] and also that many such pregnancies ended in abortion or still birth – so the above figures

TABLE 5.1 *Approximate percentages of illegitimate births and pregnancies that began before marriage*

Decade	Percentage of illegitimate births (Laslett)	Percentage of illegitimate births (Revised estimates based on more recent figures)	Pre-nuptial pregnancies
1590s	4.6% of baptisms	3.1%	c.32% of baptisms
1600s	3.6%	3.2%	c.21% of baptisms
1610s	3.1%	2.6%	c.21% of baptisms
1620s	2.5%	2.5%	c.21% of baptisms
1630s	1.9%	2.1%	c.21% of baptisms
1640s		1.7%	c.21% of baptisms
1650s	0.5%	0.9%	c.18% of baptisms
1660s			c.18% of baptisms
1670s			c.18% of baptisms
1680s			c.18% of baptisms
1690s			c.18% of baptisms
1700s			c.25% of baptisms
1710s			c.25% of baptisms
1720s			c.25% of baptisms
1730s			c.25% of baptisms
1740s	3%		c.25% of baptisms

provide just a rough guide to the extent of sexual activity outside marriage and in general are an underestimate.[9]

That some young unmarried women were, however, sexually active is clear. In being so they risked their reputation and futures but some saw this as a necessary prelude to finding a partner. We should not be misled by the statements of parents and preachers that young women always led submissive and secluded lives, exercising little or no initiative in their choice of partner or their behaviour. Early modern teens and twenty-somethings were as liable to rebel against the advice of their elders as those of our own day. Parents and courts could only enforce their authority to a limited extent as young women demonstrated their skilful manipulation of 'the system'. Personality, upbringing, the social milieu in which a particular young woman moved and the extent to which she was economically dependent on her parents and relatives all played their part but determined young women could and did have their own way.

Some women did engage in secret liaisons – sometimes with marriage in view. Frequently such young women were either women of property or promise of such. One such young woman was Mary Stenson of Breadsall, Derbyshire. Mary was a lively, independent girl, who enjoyed considerable sexual freedom and always had an eye to the main chance. Mary was the sole heir to, and lived with, her maternal grandfather who was a man of some property. She wanted to have affairs but she did not want them to jeopardise her inheritance. Mary, without telling her grandfather who, she thought, would disapprove of the match, entered a verbal contract of marriage with her 'mean' lover, Jonathan Troope, in autumn 1652. In June 1653 the couple quarrelled and when Mary refused to acknowledge the marriage Jonathan stormed off to join the parliamentary army. Some three years later Mary was stricken with guilt and invited Jonathan to a secret rendezvous in her grandfather's house. They renewed their marriage contract and for four years met clandestinely and engaged in bundling in her grandfather's home when the servants were not about. She declined to tell her grandfather and, she later claimed, always explained that the contract was conditional upon her coming into the legacy from her grandparent. In spring 1660 Mary again turned away from Jonathan and welcomed a new and, in her eyes, more socially and economically desirable suitor – William Henworth, a maltster from Derby. Once again Mary would not tell her grandfather and managed to persuade William to put up with what he considered the impropriety of bundling together once a week on the promise of future wealth. When Mary finally inherited in February 1662 she contrived to put William off for a further year while she settled her grandfather's estate; entered a verbal contract of marriage to be solemnised in church a year later; paid him, a mere tradesman, £300 to leave his trade and live as a gentleman; and proceeded to have a good time, apparently relishing her new-found freedom. Meanwhile Jonathan Troope tried to reassert his claims but to no avail. Mary sent him back his rings (a traditional way of breaking a verbal contract of marriage). Jonathan refused to accept them and brought a lawsuit to enforce their contract of marriage. In spring 1663 Mary married a third suitor, Gilbert Mundy, by whom she was now pregnant. William then also brought a court case for breach of contract. Jonathan's case was dismissed because he had no witnesses; William's case was dismissed because the court understood that to enforce a union that was actively resisted by one party (and that party bearing another man's child) was not sensible.

In assessing the extent to which young women participated in premarital sex we should not ignore the part played in such decisions by their prospective partners. Not all young men were prepared to engage in sex prior to marriage. The Elizabethan musician Thomas Whythorne made no secret of his sexual feelings for a particular widow but confided in his autobiography his conviction that indulging his passions before marriage would be a sin against God and a dishonouring of her, thus echoing the moral advice of Christian writers such as the Elizabethan Puritan Richard Greenham:

I promise you I was stiff. But yet, considering that the time was not like to be long to the wedding day; and also that the market was like to last all the year long and I loving her, meant not to attempt any dishonesty unto her, for a sinful act it had been, till we had been married, and we should have provoked God's heavy displeasure and wrath to have alighted upon us for our wickedness.[10]

Independent choices

The surviving documentation of marriage arrangements below the elite (largely drawn from ecclesiastical and other court records) indicates that there were strong echoes of elite patterns of marriage formation. The process was simpler because less property was involved but otherwise there were remarkable similarities. So Thomas Soley made initial approaches to Agnes Smith in 1571 after negotiating permission from her mother and her mother's kin.[11] The two 'talked together of matrimony to be had betwixt them two'.[12] Her mother agreed that Thomas might prove a suitable son-in-law and invited him to return, by which time she said she would have discussed the marriage with her friends and be able to give him her decision concerning consent.[13] On midsummer day the young couple remained in the house while the family attended the fair. The couple, left alone, agreed to marry, handfasted and, according to Thomas's testimony, 'he kissed her and put a ring on her finger'.[14]

Certainly by the early seventeenth century (and probably before this) young women were in the habit of personally entertaining (without supervision) a number of suitors and of entering contracts with whomsoever they chose. The agency of parents is less obvious, although the indications are that they still wished to exert control. So Elizabeth Hopper, a country woman of County Durham made a private contract of marriage with Robert Taler, despite the fact that her father wanted her to marry someone else. 'Setting her down upon her knees [she] said unto her father, good father give me I pray you leave to make my own choice of my husband, albeit I never get a groatsworth of your goods.' Her father replied 'I am willing thou satisfieth thine own mind.' It is noteworthy that Elizabeth was willing to run the risk of disinheritance in order to exercise free choice. In the event, the agreement between father and daughter over the marriage with Robert Taler proved academic as it was uncovered in court that Robert was already betrothed to another.[15] Much earlier, in the 1570s, it was alleged that Agnes Smith was not free to marry Thomas Soley because she had contracted to marry another. A witness stated that he had carried tokens to Agnes from William Headley at harvest time circa 1569 and another witness deposed that in the early evening of Easter Monday he had seen William and Agnes ritually exchange both coin and ring in a handfasting ceremony so that 'they two were man and wife before God and could have no other'. Agnes was presumably trying to extricate herself from this earlier match in favour of a more advantageous and parentally approved union with Soley.[16]

There is good evidence that young women of education and breeding themselves took a business-like approach to marriage and were sometimes able to protect themselves against familial intervention. They also strove to protect their portions against the designs of manipulative suitors. Mary Cudworth, daughter of the prosperous rector of Kinwarton, Warwickshire, had inherited a considerable sum of money from her deceased mother as a marriage portion. This was entirely under Mary's control and so she had a great degree of freedom over her choice of partner. In November 1680 Mary appears to have, on her own, negotiated a marriage contract with Robert Harbach, a yeoman from the next village. Her reasons for preferring a farmer to gentleman, tradesman or clergyman are intriguing.

But then Mary fell in love with John Brace, son of the rector of Doverdale, Worcestershire, and she entered a formal written contract of marriage in November 1681 and in this contract surrendered to John her marriage portion. Mary seems to have taken this unusual (and risky) step because of the pressure her father and brothers were putting on her, first to marry another suitor altogether and then to marry Harbach. Mary tried to forestall them by undertaking a clandestine marriage with Brace but she was in fact forced to go through with a church wedding to Harbach. However, she refused to consummate the marriage and when Brace brought a case in the ecclesiastical court he won Mary's hand in marriage.[17]

All the indications are then that young English women outside the elite played a very active role in arranging their own marriages, notwithstanding a general desire to remain in their parents' good books and retain their chances of keeping personalty and portions. By the late seventeenth century the conservative *Athenian Mercury* advised that a single woman involved in business 'could act independently of parental advice because she was "almost as much at her own dispose as a widow is".'[18] Women corresponding with the *Mercury* demonstrated, however, their need for advice about what was legal and/or desirable.[19] Women's knowledge and understanding of the ecclesiastical law regarding marriage contracts is debatable. It is also interesting to note that the Church court cases negated the above unions not because they were entered into without parental consent but rather because a pre-contract was proved to be in place which had been freely entered into by both parties, male and female.

There is little doubt, however, that some contemporaries found such developments reprehensible. The author of *The Whole Duty of Man* in 1684 expressed this view: 'Children are so much the goods, the possessions of their parents, that they cannot without a kind of theft, give away themselves.'[20]

While there is material for the seventeenth-century colonies this most often refers to women who were comparable to working or middling-sort English women rather than the aristocratic English, Welsh, Scottish and Irish women with which this book is chiefly concerned. This means that it is only possible to make a confident and direct comparison in the eighteenth century.

Engaged in the practicalities of marriage-making

These women were not alone in being concerned with the practicalities of marriage choice. Amy Louise Erickson has assumed that well-to-do fathers (lawyers, physicians, business men) normally negotiated marriages and that women came to the fore only during widowhood.[21] (As a third of young people before they reached the age of twenty-one were fatherless and half were fatherless by the time they married, this in itself means that female-arranged marriages were statistically extremely important.)[22] Erickson did discover some exceptions even to this rule – for instance, Green, a barrister, was still alive when his wife concluded a match for their daughter Peg in 1635. Given what we have discovered concerning the formation of landed and urban elite marriages, one might doubt the initial assumption and argue instead for the predominant role of womenfolk in marriage-making. We should also note that daughters aiming to marry at this level often did exercise considerable influence on their own marriages.[23] Although, in the absence of parents, a master and mistress would act *in loco parentis* in the matter of arranging a marriage, there is evidence that the young people involved were very much to the fore in collecting information about the intended partner. In or about 1581 Elizabeth Akers, who belonged to the household of the Temples of Stowe, Buckinghamshire, wrote to Mr Andrew, her uncle, further to inquire about the estate of one Mr Thornton, who was currently a guest at Stowe. She explained that she has 'by my master and mistress's consents entered into some [talk] of marriage with one Mr Thorneton who stayeth here'. She then indicated her anxieties about Mr Thornton's suitability, because of comments made by another aunt and uncle that 'Mr Thorneton's living is not xli by the year and that it is worst of all of little honesty'. She expressed her willingness to heed their advice, adding that 'I do assure my self my m[aste]r would not [?proceed] and I will take pause [?until from] either you or any other my friends I understand more of him'.[24] Apparently she was reassured because she married the lawyer Mr Thornton in due course. It may well be that the young woman concerned, because she was not a daughter of the house and was aiming to wed a lawyer, would be allowed or even expected to be more heavily involved in arranging a match and take upon her shoulders much of the work involved.

It is generally agreed that sons and daughters below this level in society – that is, children of yeoman and husbandman farmers, shopkeepers, craftspeople – commonly negotiated their own courtships and marriages.[25] Work on young women living outside the bounds of parental control in seventeenth-century London shows the degree of social freedom they enjoyed.[26] The conclusions of this detailed study are supported by evidence from diaries and correspondence. Nevertheless, this is not to say that the parents of such young women did not wish to influence their choice of spouse. Ralph Josselin, yeoman, of Cranham Hall, Essex (uncle of the well-known diarist Ralph Josselin) specified in his will in 1656 that his daughter Elizabeth should inherit his property 'provided that my said daughter shall not dispose of herself in marriage without the consent of Dorothy and Grace her sisters and of my cousin Ralph Josselin'.[27] When a daughter rejected such influence the penalty was often estrangement. Hannah Allan, for example, distanced herself from her father by refusing to marry the suitor he had chosen.[28]

As with the landed nobility and upper gentry, those of the urban elite and the urban and rural middling sort were concerned that prospective spouses were of equivalent wealth and status and that both parties brought sufficient 'property' to make the match viable in the long term. Studies of medieval women suggest that such concerns stretch back to the Middle Ages and involve the servant classes as well as the middling sort. In the 1360s Alice Redyng's marriage to John Boston was controversial because she was the daughter of a serf and because she had little money but her wages, supplemented by harvest labour. Attempts were made by the York consistory court to discover whether she had been freed and whether John was much wealthier than she, as she was suspected of hypergamy (marrying above herself). In 1394 Margaret Greystanes first of all refused to marry Thomas del Dale because she had no goods to bring to the marriage and was therefore unsuitable.[29] The groom's portion (brideprice) was as important as the bride's (dowry/portion) but did not always take the same form or make initially the same impact. For example, daughters would be given larger sums of cash as portions by their father's wills while younger sons would often receive an education and a profession in addition to a somewhat smaller cash portion. Eldest sons might be expected to rely entirely on property transferred during a marriage settlement or at some other time prior to the father's death.[30] By the eighteenth century it was often the bride's dowry that played the largest part in making the marriage economically viable from the start.

Equivalent work is not available for Scotland. The work of Leah Leneman, however, suggests that in seventeenth- and eighteenth-century Scotland the creation of marriages outside a 'network' was often problematic for the 'ordinary' women concerned. For young women (and indeed their parents or guardians) collecting information about a suitor if he was not part of their regular connection was often fraught with difficulties. Geographical mobility brought with it its own problems. In eighteenth-century Scotland (and there is no reason to believe that the situation in England was any different), for example, enlistment in the army figured large in the experience of many a young man, offering opportunities for moving about the country and indeed the world, for escape from poverty and unwelcome social situations, for easy dissolution of one union and entry into another. About 50,000 Scotsmen served in anti-Hapsburg armies during the Thirty Years War; there were 25,000 Scots in the armed service of the Swedes; and the army of the eighteenth century also drew away many young Scotsmen to foreign wars. Peter Wilson and Helen Kirk of Edinburgh had a daughter Margaret in 1743. Peter fled into the army when Helen became pregnant. When he returned from the army he married Isabella Kay and lived with her for about twelve years and began to raise a family. A friend of his from the army said that Peter's character was 'such that he would have taken a wife at every town where the regiment was', and another had prevented such a wedding when the parents of one young woman had sought information about his background.[31] At roughly the same time another soldier, John Napier, found a wife in Dumbartonshire when his regiment was stationed there, took her to, and discarded her in, Gibraltar, and gained two other wives (at different times) when living as a shopkeeper in Glasgow. Endless problems ensued for the women concerned and their descendants. (This was why personal knowledge through the family's social network was so very important.)

So it is possible to document the fact that young women, like young men, exercised choice when it came to finding a marriage partner. Recently, however, our attention has been once again drawn to the restrictions placed upon such choice. Drawing upon evidence from Canterbury diocese wills, Diana O'Hara has shown that in Kent many made financial arrangements for daughters on their marriage and that some of these arrangements were highly restrictive. For example, in 1498 Andrew Hawke of Wye, disapproving of his daughter Thomasine's plans to marry John Alcey, butler of Wye College, ordered his executors to pay her no more than 40s. if she married Alcey. If, on the other hand, she 'will be ruled and governed by my will and by the advice of my feoffees and executors and marry with some other man' she should be given an additional twenty marks and 'stuff of household'. A widow, Johana Alarde, in 1536 tried to promote her daughter's marriage to Mr Tucker by making a bequest of silver and household stuff contingent upon it.[32] Similar types of restriction were still to be found in clergy families in the midland diocese of Coventry and Lichfield in the first half of the seventeenth century. Alice Latimer, daughter of a clergyman, on her father's death in 1624 was to have twenty marks 'provided that she be ruled by her mother, her brother Henry Latimer and her Uncle Francis'.[33] Elizabeth Orgell, daughter of another clergyman, on her father's death in early 1647 received household stuff (a 'bottom drawer' of linen and implements) 'and if she will be dutiful and obedient to her mother in deportment and carriage, then I doubt not but that her mother will augment her portion accordingly'.[34] Ann Hallam's father stipulated in his will of 1626 that her portion of £120 was to be reduced to £20 if she married against her mother's wishes.[35] Mary Whitmore, daughter of the vicar of Chebsey, was expected to marry her father's successor (in a marriage which his executors would supervise) but provision was made for her in the event that this marriage did not materialise:

My will is that my daughter Mary should be married to the vicarage of Chebsey ... at the oversight of my executors ... and if it happens that my daughter Mary be not married unto it, that then my will be that she shall receive £60 per annum after my decease.[36]

Examples such as these certainly abound in England in the sixteenth and seventeenth centuries, and rather than confirming the power parents had to arrange marriages, on the contrary, they underline the weakness of parental control (and especially the control of widows) over the marriages and lives of their children. Men who made wills evolved strategies for shoring up the authority of their widows. The power of the purse had to be exerted when the power of patriarchy failed.

Marriage settlements

There is an extended discussion of wives and property in general in Part 2 of this book, in two chapters entitled, 'Wives and property' and 'Widows and widowhood'. Many of the observations made concerning the arrangement of marriages among the elite also seem to apply more generally. It seems appropriate here, however, to make some observations about the financial preparations made by the middling sort, including professionals and prominent business people, for their daughters at marriage.

Marriage settlements (made by legal contract) were common in seventeenth-century England and her colonies, at different social levels. Historians seem generally agreed that, for all except the very wealthy, marriage contracts were simple affairs, consisting mainly of a statement of the dowry (portion) and how and when it would be paid. Commonly a large sum was paid as a down payment, followed by the balance after six months or a year. But there were other arrangements too: for example, a London brickmaker contracted to pay carpenter Mintham Robinson a certain sum on his marriage in 1652 to his daughter Christian; he would then pay £13 a year for the first seven years of their marriage and £3 a year for the following nine years.[37] Some, like the marriage settlements of the landed elite, involved outright gifts of property and of jointures for the future provision of widows, but these were the exception rather than the rule. The ability to grant land as a marriage gift to a son depended to a great extent on the wealth and circumstances of a father. For example, in 1650 Governor Bradford of Plymouth made over entirely a large farm near Plymouth to his son, who was about to be married, and a little while later another colonist there promised 'to give sign and set over at present one third of all my lands to be my son Joseph's proper right for ever, to him and his wife's for ever also'.[38] Similarly the provision of a jointure for a widow required resource.

The dowries of English brides varied enormously according to their parents' wealth and status. Alan Macfarlane believes that the dowry of a daughter in the upper social level represented three years' annual income for her father while that of a husbandman's daughter represented just two years' annual income. Where families were large this could be a considerable financial burden for parents.[39] As already noted, daughters often accumulated their portions from a variety of sources (grandparents, godparents, uncles, aunts, brothers and sisters) and not only from their parents. Will-makers, who were often executors of the estate of others, on occasion acknowledged the fluidity of the situation as children died and altered the portions of surviving children, and fortunes ebbed and flowed – they frequently needed to update their wills to accommodate such changes: 'I may have often occasion to alter the portions of money given to my sister's children', wrote John Hill, rector of Elford.[40]

As Peter Earle has shown, in England the system of creating jointures through a formal marriage contract was not attractive to all by any means – not even to those who belonged to London's business elite. While it guaranteed that a wife would not starve in widowhood, a jointure tied up too much capital in land to be popular with parents. In about 15 per cent of Earle's sample, the husbands made provision to leave their widows

TABLE 5.2 *Seventeenth-century daughters' portions by socio-economic class of fathers*[41]

Fathers' social class	Lower limit of portion	Upper limit of portion
Country gentry/upper merchants and professionals	£500	£1,000
Clerks, merchants, wealthy yeomen and tradesmen	£100	£500
Prosperous yeomen, craftsmen and tradesmen	£50	£100
Majority of husbandmen, yeomen, tradesmen and labourers	£1	£50

a 'fixed capital sum, whether by jointure or bond'. Some prominent merchants and businessmen from London would, instead of immediately bestowing jointure land, thereby promise their wives or formally enter a bond to buy jointure land to a given value either on their retirement or as a first charge on the estate after death. When the Levant merchant Francis March married Mary Dunster in 1680 he covenanted to lay out £6,000 on lands for her jointure but these had still not been bought when he died in 1697 and, thinking land a poor investment, he bequeathed the money to trustees to 'place out for interest upon security'. An item in his inventory of 1699 reads 'to Mary March, relict . . . by her marriage articles for principle and interest from Christmas 1697 to Midsummer 1699 – £6540', a sum which represented 58 per cent of his net assets.[42] Others bound themselves to leave a particular amount of cash to the widow. Sir John Fryer gave a bond to his future father-in-law to leave his wife worth £1,500, just three times the portion she brought to him, to be a first charge on his estate. It would probably take at least twelve years (at a 10 per cent rate of growth) for a portion of £500 to grow to £1,500. Peter Earle believes that, assuming this ratio between portion and bond was typical, such arrangements could leave the remainder of a man's family 'in a desperate situation', especially if the groom died before the desired sum was achieved.[43] These types of bond did not always benefit the widow either. A London draper, for example, entered a bond to leave his wife £2,000 but, after his death, his net assets were worth only £694.

Marriage settlements were regarded as legally binding and final. Wills on both sides of the Atlantic were used to confirm previously made marriage settlements, although Erickson in her extensive study of English wills found only twenty-one, nearly all from the later seventeenth century, that mentioned marriage portions as such.[44] In Old and New Worlds they seem never to have undone prior arrangements, for 'a man can not by his last will and testament defeat and make void a gift of lands made unto his son and heir in frank marriage'.[45] The legally binding character of such formal settlements may account for their relative unpopularity.

In London, there were legal arguments aplenty when the widow's covenanted estate did not equal her right to customary thirds, which could happen if the husband was especially prosperous. James Tandin, a London pewterer, had bound himself to leave his wife £1,000 and the jewellery and clothing she had brought to the marriage, but when he died his net estate was worth between £6,000 and £10,000. The result was a long drawn-out suit in Chancery regarding whether the covenant prevented his widow claiming her thirds.[46]

The remaining 75 per cent of Earle's sample made no provision at marriage for the widow. In such cases the wife relied on her customary thirds to provide her with financial security once her husband died. This gave her a vested interest in helping her husband prosper his estate. It also made marriage to older, already rich, men seem extremely attractive.

In England, wills were frequently used to make marriage settlements. This was advantageous at a time when the will-maker knew his economic worth and the will could be updated. Erickson and O'Hara both concur that in these cases the portions bestowed upon daughters tended to be cash settlements rather than in kind.[47] Erickson was able to show that of 113 testators who left cash settlements, two-thirds favoured women.[48] Parents were concerned to provide for their daughters should they become widows. However, there are many examples of daughters, granddaughters, god-daughters and nieces being left mementoes, moveable goods and farm animals. In the colonies also, wills were used to pass on portions to children, male and female. In the case of a daughter this seems to have commonly consisted of a feather bed, bedding, table linen, household goods and clothing and variable amounts of cash.[49] The portions were usually, but by no means always, to be given them either when they reached the age of twenty-one years or on the eve of their marriage, whichever was the sooner. In English examples it seems to have been more common for daughters to receive their portions at a younger age than sons, probably in anticipation of their earlier marriages. There are certainly also some American examples of children receiving their portions at a younger age. In a will of 1647 Alexander Winchester of Plymouth Colony left half his property to his widow and the other half to be divided equally between his children when each reached the age of fifteen.[50]

There are occasional references to arrangements in the families of professionals in England similar to those made for elite couples. For example, Robert Freeman, clergyman of Ashley, had contracted to keep his daughter and son-in-law for three years following their marriage and by his will of 1606 he made provision to fulfil this bargain.[51] Such arrangements were specified very rarely in wills and we cannot argue from silence that they were common.

John Demos has described how, in Old Plymouth Colony, wills were often used to simply confirm or report outright gifts of land and portions that had been made some time before. 'I have already given my sons Simon and Samuel their full portions and deeds for their lands which I have settled on them', wrote Dolar Davis of Barnstaple.[52]

Networks

In describing middle-class marriages in late seventeenth- and early eighteenth-century London, Peter Earle observed that 'even when a business interest was not in the forefront of the relationship, sons and daughters were likely to marry the sons and daughters of business friends and acquaintances or at least of people of the same economic status. For these were the people whom they would meet or their parents would arrange that they would meet... it was easier for young people to play the field than it was in most countries [but]... like tended to marry like.'[53] This is an excellent reminder that networks were as important for middle-class marriage-making as for elite and, in all probability, for farmers and shopkeepers as for business people and professionals. Relatively little work has been done in this area but, what there is, is indicative. First of all, it is worth observing that the networks of the aristocracy and the gentry included many of lesser birth than themselves, from distant and not-so-distant relatives to friends and to servants and tenants. Sometimes networks were based on religious affinity. It has been possible to map a network of the nonconformist (Baptist) families of Steele, Cator, Froude, Gay, Attwater, Head, Drewitt and Whitaker in Somerset during the period 1680–1900 and to establish that members of these families married within this religious connection throughout.[54] Necessarily, marriage also formed and perpetuated networks and it is sometimes difficult to ascertain which came first, the marriage or the network.

What is known about the business of marrying in colonial America?

In colonial America, as in England, the selection of a spouse, at least in upper and middling families, was supposedly made within parameters determined by the parents and guardians. Young white women who were indentured servants contracted not to marry until their service period ended. Censure of those who broke their contract was under a law of master and servant, which may have been influenced by Scottish practice.[55] Whereas in England ecclesiastical courts policed marriages and sexual behaviours, the colonies did not institute such courts and left policing to the secular authorities. To a great extent they also sought to bolster the authority of parents.[56] All the New England colonies brought in legislation to this effect in the seventeenth century. Colonies of later settlement quickly enacted such laws so that by the late seventeenth century acts forbade fornication, adultery, sodomy and other types of illicit sex and insisted upon either the parents' or the master's consent, posting of banns and public wedding. Virginia legislated for parental consent as early as 1632 but only introduced effective penalties for breach of the rules gradually through revised versions of the law in 1646, 1661/2 and 1696. It had a sacred foundation: when William Byrd II's daughter threatened to refuse a match proposed by her father, he was quick to threaten to disown her for not performing 'the sacred duty you owe a parent'.[57] New York imported Dutch customs, which demanded paternal consent for first marriages of both sons and daughters whatever their age (or the mother's if the father were dead) and for the second marriages of daughters who were still under age. New Jersey in 1668 and 1682 passed laws insisting on the consent of parents and guardians, and Pennsylvania did the same from 1676 onwards.[58] Similar rules were belatedly introduced into England by Lord Hardwicke's Marriage Act of 1753, which, among other things, insisted that clergymen follow the secular rules (regarding the reading of banns, parental consent for those under twenty-one years old, public marriage and civil registration) for a marriage to be valid.

In some colonies, such as New Haven, the law stipulated that a suitor had to obtain the father's or master's consent even before making suit to a young woman. In Plymouth Colony a man had to obtain the father's or master's permission before he might pay court to a young woman, on pain of corporal punishment.[59] When Arthur Howland Jr tried to marry the Governor's daughter, Elizabeth Prence, 'making a motion of marriage to her . . . contrary to the parents' liking', the parents lodged a complaint in court in 1667 and tried to call a halt to the romance.[60] Ruth Bloch suggests that these laws owed a good deal to the English Abduction Law of 1558 but that the emphasis here was on preserving parental rights rather than, as in England and Virginia, on protecting inherited property from mercenary suitors.[61]

The same literature of advice to parents was available to the colonists as it was to their counterparts in the 'home country' and was presumably, because it was supported here by law, even more persuasive. Exceedingly close relations persisted between the colonists and the Old World during the pre-revolutionary years. (Although little work has been done by Americanists on links between emigrants from Germany, Ireland, Scotland, France and Holland with their homelands, there seems no reason to assume that these people had severed their links. Indeed the later history of the American Irish seems to support the idea that these links were very strong.) Individuals, families and communities maintained contact via correspondence. Individuals made visits to England surprisingly frequently, given the horrendous and hazardous conditions of the boat journey. Such contact tended to the perpetuation of old ideas and customs. Where children were living with or near their parents, such parents may well have 'arranged' their children's marriages in the early years of colonisation. When this was the case the views of women, in particular, seem to have been little solicited although, as in England and Wales, the evidence points to parents considering the potential compatibility of the couple emotionally and sexually as well as materially. Refusal of the spouse one's parents had chosen might then lead to disinheritance.

Marrying without parental consent was supposedly extremely difficult: most of the colonies as we have seen made the parents' consent statutorily obligatory. Unlike in England, rarely was an age limit for such consent stipulated.[62] Where parents were absent the civil authorities stood *in loco parentis*. And many young people who lived within families seem to have been content to obey their parents and actively seek their advice. Children and youth were conditioned to do so just as they were in sixteenth- and seventeenth-century England and Wales.

There is also a good deal of evidence that the seventeenth-century colonial courts, particularly those in New England, sought to implement the laws regarding consent. Fines of between £5 and £25 were frequently imposed on couples who disregarded the rules and went ahead with clandestine marriages. (There were also problems attendant upon young women, even children, being abducted and, legally, raped.) Most cases, however, that came before the courts involved the early stages of courtship and, when it was discovered that parental consent was denied, couples were prohibited to continue the relationship.[63]

However, such control as parents and civil authorities exerted was patchy at best. In that youthful society there were many young, single people who had uprooted from their home countries and their families and who chose their own partners and founded their own households. It was impossible to impose parental control over these immigrants and the wording of the laws intended to enforce control suggests a desperate attempt to forestall the inevitable. Determined young people in the New World as in the Old, whether geographically close to their parents or not, were able to get their own way in the end. Arthur Howland and Elizabeth Prence finally wore her parents down and were permitted to marry three years after Howland's initial proposal.[64]

The conditions of colonisation, rather than the law, engendered social change. By the late seventeenth century it was overtly accepted that youth generally exercised free choice in the matter of marriage. Indeed, the law followed where society led. The Pennsylvania marriage laws of 1693 stated that, to be valid, a marriage required parental consent but revisions bowed to social reality and asked for parental consent when this was 'possible' or convenient.[65] In general the eighteenth-century colonists were much less enthusiastic than those of the seventeenth century in their punishment of couples who offended against the marriage laws and/or engaged in 'fornication' outside regular marriage. Most of the colonies made no attempt to nullify irregular unions. A very few colonies had provided on their statute books for the nullification of irregular marriages and the illegitimacy of their offspring, but even there these laws were not taken seriously by the eighteenth century, and consensual unions were commonly accepted. For example, in 1665 Rhode Island granted an amnesty to couples living together as man and wife before the marriage act of 1647 and declared their children legitimate; in 1698 its legislature accepted that unregistered marriages were valid and their offspring legitimate.[66]

This meant that when greater numbers emigrated from Scotland, Ireland, and Germany in the eighteenth century, they did so into a society which already accepted that the young chose their own mates. In 1690 in New England, Fitz-John Winthrop wrote that 'it has been the custom of the country for young folks to choose'. This suggests that 'young folks' of both sexes made the choices but they could not do so for a number of years. In Virginia the majority of early settlers were indentured servants, male and female. The terms of indenture required that the servants remained single until the period of service was expired. Marriage was a breach of contract.[67] Indications are that the young women among them, once freed to marry, rapidly found partners. The period of service contracted for among emigrants from London to Maryland was generally four to five years.[68] Many emigrants to Maryland were not indentured

TABLE 5.3 *Laws stipulating that irregular marriages should be declared null and void*[69]

Colony	Nullification law	Modifications	Modification
Rhode Island	1647	1665	1698
New York	While still New Amsterdam	Never enforced	
Delaware	1676–1684	"	
Pennsylvania	"	"	
New Jersey	"	"	
Virginia	1661/2	1696	

but paid for their passage by agreeing to serve according to the colony's custom, which after 1661 for those who were aged twenty-two or above was for four to five years and for those who were younger much longer. It seems that more of these 'pay as you go' immigrants were more youthful than those who were indentured. These servants who came at a young age and without the protection of a contract were probably of a lower social status than those with indentures.[70] All these young people were remote from parental control and guidance, which effectively passed only temporarily to their masters. The dangers inherent in this situation seem to be borne out in the bastardy figures for Charles County, Maryland: here a full 20 per cent of the young women who immigrated between 1658 and 1705, only a handful of them free, were hauled before its court for bearing bastards.[71] These figures compare very unfavourably with those for England and were also two or three times the rate found in late seventeenth-century New England.

Before 1660 the sex ratio was extremely skewed because many fewer women immigrated than men. From 1660 onwards this situation began to right itself but the chances of a free woman finding a husband were very good and men were desperate to find wives. Virginia and Maryland were promoted as marriage markets for Old World spinsters. Maryland, in particular, was noted for its relaxed rules regarding marriage in the seventeenth century.[72] Female servants in the southern colonies could marry if their prospective husbands bought their freedom. Effective purchase of wives (that is, paying the masters of women servants for their freedom) was also commonplace throughout the seventeenth century.[73] There is no way of knowing whether these women were sold in marriage against their will, although some of the evidence suggests that young women could be tempted into illicit sex on promise of such marriage.[74]

Even when a second generation of southerners emerged, the choice of partners was apparently made without much reference to parents. In eighteenth-century North Carolina consensual unions seem to have been common and accepted, despite the fact that both civil magistrates and clergymen were enabled to perform marriages.[75] Debra Meyers, in her intriguing study of Maryland, argues that 'most landholding men and women in Maryland chose their life-long partners with care and did so largely free from overt parental coercion'.[76] So Governor Calvert was able to write to Lord Baltimore in 1672 'I am sorry my [cousin] Lukner thinks not of marrying yet, because that match would have brought a great deal of honour besides the advantages of a plentiful fortune'.[77] Meyers believes that Marylanders were confident that their children, well raised, would choose wisely, but it seems more probable that parents were realistic in accepting that the circumstances of colonisation in particular meant that parental authority could not be effectively enforced.[78] Less than 5 per cent of Maryland testators 1634–1713 sought to influence their children's choice of spouse by the provisions of their wills. In these cases the attempt seems to have been to bar particular suitors rather than to impose a more general control. A mother, Jane Long, for example, willed her daughter Tabitha twenty thousand pounds of tobacco, a bed, and some livestock, but only if she did *not* marry George Chany. John Phillips, ordered that his sons Thomas and Bennony 'shall not marry w[i]th any of [John] Robson's daughters' on pain of losing their inheritance.[79] This freedom also seems to echo the situation in England.

What else, though, could be the case when so many young people lived away from their parents? It was not only that in Virginia many of the first immigrants were young indentured servants, often drawn from among urchins, orphans and prisoners.[80] Bigamy was, perhaps predictably, a real problem in new societies constructed from such groups of supposedly single people. There are examples of Marylanders who had wives and families in England and mistresses and illegitimate offspring in the colony.[81] Dr John Wade, whose will was proved in Maryland in 1658, had a wife and two legitimate children in England but lived with Anne Smith and their illegitimate child in Maryland until she deserted him.[82] In Plymouth Colony too, however, in 1680 Elizabeth Stevens was granted a divorce when it was discovered that her husband had three other wives, one in Boston, one in Barbados and one in England.[83] In Massachusetts also there was awareness from the mid-seventeenth century onwards of the problem that 'both men and women' young and old were living away from those who knew them, including 'wives and husbands who are in England' who were giving way to the temptation to cohabit with others, and sometimes to marry bigamously; 'and some of them committing lewdness and filthiness here amongst us, others make love to women, and attempt marriage, and some have attained it'. In 1647 all persons who were in the colony without their parents or families were ordered to be sent back to their relations 'by the first opportunity of shipping upon the pain, or penalty of twenty pounds', unless they could show that they were 'come over to make way for their families, or are in a transient way only for traffic, or merchandise for some small time'.[84]

As the colonies were settled and generations reproduced themselves within their boundaries, perhaps this problem was proportionately less pressing although the possibilities of a bigamist simply 'disappearing' into another colony to avoid detection remained. In addition, whole extended families and even communities uprooted themselves from the Old to the New World, especially in New England. This had happened at the beginning of colonisation and it repeatedly occurred during successive waves of emigration. That some families sought out opportunities to emigrate together and – in so doing – acted upon information provided by colonists or visitors to the colonies, is apparent again in the second half of the seventeenth century with, for example, Quaker emigration to Pennsylvania, New Jersey and Delaware. Quaker merchant James Claypoole addressed his brother from London on 28 August 1681:

I desire thee to write at large what encouragement there is to remove from hence with a family to dwell in those parts, and what commodities is most proper and profitable to carry with one, and in what time a man may, if he arrives there in the seventh month, with the help of 3 or 4 servants, clear ground enough to afford corn and feed cattle for a family of 15 or 20, what safety or hazard may be expected from the Indians, in what time and with what charge with 10 or 12 rooms, and barns and stables etc. may be built . . . And whether New Jersey or Pennsylvania be most advisable to settle in.[85]

Claypoole went on to propose sending an attorney and some servants in advance, with his own son as overseer, 'to build and plant etc'. William Penn's method of granting land to immigrant Quakers actively encouraged the settling of whole families, to the extent that he 'that can settle some few families, I think about 6, may have his land altogether'.[86] In the event Claypoole removed his family to Pennsylvania in spring 1683. He planned to take many others with him in a ship that would accommodate up to 180 persons, including craftsmen of all kinds and whole families, from the Quaker community.[87] There are also examples of whole families uprooting themselves from one American community and moving to found another, as colonists sought to move back the frontier still further.[88]

When the native-born Americans became dominant in a population, the situation did change to some extent because the family unit became important once more. The consequences could be surprising. Philip Greven's research into family structure in seventeenth-century Andover, Massachusetts, has painted a picture of young married couples who were essentially still dependent upon their parents, waiting for their inheritance of the property that would render them independent until the father's death.[89] Evidence from a study of marriages in Higham, Massachusetts, seems to support this idea and, moreover, suggests that prior to 1780, sons were waiting to marry until their fathers had died, indicating that the generations were coexisting within the colony.[90] Possible explanations for this situation are: the fathers had refused the sons permission to marry and sons were unwilling to defy their parents; fathers had insufficient land to provide their sons with a viable farm; sons wanted to exercise complete control over whom they married. This all suggests that marriage before the Revolution was very much an economic decision and that, for whatever reasons, patriarchy in the sense of imposed paternal authority was already under threat in the colonies well before that time, contrary to accepted opinion.[91]

That this was a common pattern in the colonies seems doubtful, however. John Demos in his study of Plymouth Colony, argues that there was no general attempt by parents to use their ownership of property (and the implicit or explicit threat of disinheritance) to maintain effective control over their adult offspring. Parents very frequently during their lifetime distributed property and moveable goods to children.[92] The work of Debra Meyers indicates that the same was true of Maryland.

Conclusion

It is impossible to identify a single pattern of marriage-making in the classes immediately below the gentry. Urban elites probably came closest to gentry styles of marriage-making as they strove to achieve matches that were economically viable, offering long-term prospects for both sons and daughters. Formal marriage settlements were more common here than in middling-sort marriages but were still not the norm. The indications are that young women from slightly lower in the social scale (professionals, shop-keepers, farmers) were more able to initiate their own matches, although they still had to account to parents and guardians who believed that they *should* have control. This was true in the American colonies, where the law early insisted on parental consent for a valid marriage, as well as in England, where the consent of the parties made a marriage.

Certainly, in considering the issue of how non-aristocratic marriages were made, one needs to define what we might mean by 'freedom of choice'. Young people seem to have exercised much more freedom in their personal lives than historians would once have believed. Chaperonage was still considered important but seems often to have been both unenforced and unenforceable. Although advice specified that men should initiate courtship there is evidence that in practice this was rather different.[93] Young people formed liaisons, indulged in extra-marital sex and proposed their own matches. To assume that this freedom led only to love marriages or shot-gun weddings would be precipitate. Often it is unwise to speculate concerning motivation but the evidence reveals that the young could be as calculating as the old. Helen Berry has shown how young women in the London of the 1690s were using their family obligations to manipulate suitors and the timing of marriage.[94] 'The final choice of partner, while it frequently was motivated by personal liking or love, was still linked indissolubly to questions of family credit, economic worth and the successful handling of both courtship ritual and the sensitive negotiations that accompanied them'.[95] It was also governed by subtle factors, such as the demographic, geographical and economic range of a young person's social circle, and rather less subtle ones, such as the parent or guardian's or prospective partner's use of threats and/or cajolery to bend the young person's will to his or her own.

Notes

1 Hereford and Worcester County Record Office, Worcester CC Records, cited in L. Stone (1995) pp. 98–104.
2 P. Earle (1989) pp. 193–4.
3 See Edmund Morgan (1966) for a discussion of negotiations surrounding the marriage of Samuel Sewall.
4 The situation of widows is discussed in Chapter 12.
5 D. O'Hara (2000) p. 3.
6 J. Marshall (ed.), *The Autobiography of William Stout of Lancaster* (1967).
7 See Peter Laslett, *Family Life and Illicit Love in Earlier Generations*, 1977, pp. 117, 125, 137–42.
8 R. Thompson (1986) found examples of herbal abortifacients cited in court cases.
9 See E. Shorter *et al.* (1971) pp. 380–81.
10 J. M. Osborn (1962) pp. 150–53. See also R. Greenham (1599).
11 Family negotiation.
12 Interview.
13 Consent and settlement.
14 Betrothal. *Depositions* (1845) pp. 234–5; also cited in D. Cressy (1997) pp. 258–9.
15 Cressy (1997) p. 260.

16 *Depositions* (1845) pp. 236–40.
17 L. Stone (1995) pp. 98–104.
18 *Athenian Gazette or Casuistical Mercury*, 17, 24; 23 June 1695, cited in H. Berry (2003) p. 168.
19 Berry (2003) pp. 162ff.
20 Richard Allestree, *The Whole Duty of Man* (1684), p. 302.
21 A. L. Erickson (1993) pp. 93–4.
22 J. Smith and J. Oippen (1993) pp. 306–8; Erickson (1993) p. 93.
23 See above, Chapter 4.
24 HEH, Stowe Collection, Temple Correspondence, STT 2364 Elizabeth (Akers) Thornton to Mr Andrew, 12 May 1591 from Stowe, Bucks.
25 A. L. Erickson (1993) p. 94.
26 V. B. Elliott (1981) e.g. pp. 91–7.
27 Will of Ralph Josselin, Yeoman, dated 27 November 1656, PCC Wills, 1657, Ruthen 511.
28 H. Allen (1683) cited in Elspeth Graham (1989) pp. 217–19.
29 Kim M. Phillips (2003) pp. 157–8.
30 A. L. Erickson (1993) p. 92.
31 L. Leneman (2001) pp. 51–2.
32 D. O'Hara (2000) p. 195.
33 L.J.R.O., Will of Richard Latimere, vicar of Polesworth, W.P. 17 November 1624.
34 L.J.R.O., Will of Richard Orgell, vicar of Lullington, W.P. 1646/7.
35 L.J.R.O., Will of Nicholas Hallam of Shirland, Derbs, W.P. 3 August 1626.
36 L.J.R.O., Will of Humphrey Whitmore, vicar of Chebsey, W.P. 1617.
37 P. Earle (1989) p. 197.
38 J. Demos (1978) p. 168, citing *Mayflower Descendant*, XVI, 82; see also Demos, p. 160, *Mayflower Descendant*, II, 27–8, the deed of gift from Francis Cooke, the groom's father, entitled the 'conditions of marriage between Jacob Cooke and Damaris Hopkins' in 1646, which gave them land and livestock.
39 A. Macfarlane (1986) p. 264.
40 See p. 281. Also R. O'Day (1995) p. 118; L.J.R.O. Will of John Hill, rector of Elford, W.P. 16 January 1621/2.
41 This table is based on data provided by A. L. Erickson (1993) pp. 88–9 and A. Macfarlane (1986) p. 264. Compare with p. 80 which gives figures for the aristocracy (nobility and the upper gentry).

42 P. Earle (1989) pp. 194–7, for example, from p. 195.
43 Earle (1989) p. 195.
44 A. L. Erickson (1993) p. 87.
45 *Plymouth Colony Records*, V, p. 159.
46 Earle (1989) p. 196.
47 D. O'Hara (2000) p. 200; A. L. Erickson (1993) p. 81.
48 Erickson (1993) p. 81.
49 See, for example, the portion passed on by will to Damaris Hopkins (mentioned in Note 36) *Mayflower Descendant*, IV, 115, cited in J. Demos (1978) pp. 160–61.
50 *Mayflower Descendant*, IX, p. 30, quoted in Demos (1978) p. 149.
51 L.J.R.O., Will of Robert Freeman of Ashley, 31 October 1606.
52 *Mayflower Descendant*, XXIV, p. 71, quoted in Demos (1978) p. 166. Several other wills contained similar statements.
53 P. Earle (1989) p. 192.
54 M. Reeves (1997) pp. 1–9 and *passim*.
55 I am grateful to Douglas Hay for this point.
56 R. H. Bloch (2003) p. 79.
57 J. Demos (1978) p. 150.
58 Bloch (2003) p. 80.
59 William Brigham, *Compact with the Charter and Laws of the Colony of New Plymouth* (1863), p. 61.
60 *Plymouth Colony Records*, IV, 140, cited by Demos (1978) p. 155.
61 R. H. Bloch (2003) p. 81–2.
62 Virginia designated 21 as the age limit in 1632; New Jersey did so in 1719; in the second half of the eighteenth century Pennsylvania and Massachsetts also introduced an age limit of 21. Bloch, p. 81.
63 Bloch (2003) pp. 84–5, 94.
64 J. Demos (1978) p. 155.
65 R. H. Bloch (2003) p. 89.
66 Bloch (2003) p. 83.
67 Abbot Emerson Smith (1947) p. 273.
68 L. G. Carr and L. S. Walsh (1978) p. 264.
69 Table based on data in Bloch (2003) pp. 82–3.

70 Ibid p. 265.
71 Ibid p. 266.
72 R. H. Bloch (2003) p. 87.
73 George Alsop, *A Character of the Province of Mary-land*, in C. C. Hall (1910) p. 358.
74 See, for example, R. Thompson (1974); and T. W. Tate and D. L. Amerman (1979).
75 Bloch (2003) p. 88.
76 D. Meyers (2003) p. 45.
77 The Calvert Papers (1889–99) I: p. 263 as quoted in Meyers (2003) p. 45.
78 Meyers (2003) p. 45.
79 Meyers (2003) p. 45, citing Maryland Hall of Records (hereafter MHR) Prerogative Court Wills, Book 7: 141, Jane Long: 1696; Book 12: 212: John Phillips: 1707/8.
80 R. Hume, *Early Child Immigrants to Virginia*; I owe the point about prisoners to Jason Peacey.
81 Meyers (2003) p. 42.
82 MHR, Wills 1: 101 (1658) cited in Meyers (2003) p. 42.
83 Plymouth Colony Records, VI, pp. 44–5.
84 R. S. Dunn (1998) p. 37, law of 1647.
85 M. Balderston (1967) pp. 69–70; see also ibid, pp. 101, 109, 110, 127, 196, 223 and p. 111 for family migration to New Deal, Delaware.
86 Balderston (1967) p. 93.
87 Ibid p. 196.
88 J. Demos (1968) pp. 40–57; A. Taves (1989) pp. 3, 7.
89 Philip J. Greven (1966), 'Family structure in seventeenth-century Andover, Massachusetts', *William and Mary Quarterly*, 3rd Series, XXIII, 234–56.
90 D. S. Smith (1973) pp. 423–4.
91 C. Degler (1980) p. 10; but see Chapters 6 and 8 for other ways in which patriarchy was reasserting itself in the eighteenth-century colonies.
92 Demos (1978) pp. 169–70.
93 See, for example, *Athenian Mercury*, 18, 9; 13 August 1695 cited in Berry (2003) p. 172.
94 H. Berry (2003) p. 178.
95 D. O'Hara (2000) p. 3.

PART 2

Experience of marriage

Introduction

There is no pleasure in the world like that of the sweet society of lovers, in the way of marriage, and of a loving husband and wife. Hee is her head she commands his heart, he is her Love, her joy, she is his honey, his Dove, his delight . . .[1]

Once she was married, the place of a woman within marriage was proscribed by the societal attitude to marriage itself and to the role of women within it, and by the more variable factors such as the age of husband and wife, their relationship with one another and their personalities, their position in society and their economic situation, and the environment in which they lived. In this part we discuss the following areas: the problem of patriarchy and ideas about the institution of marriage and the place of women within it; the relationship between these ideas and lived experience; other conditions and circumstances that could be argued to have determined or constrained the lot of the married woman – for example, her property or lack of it; the roles which women actually played within marriage and society.

Sources and approaches

The sources available are many and various but all have to be handled with great care and criticism. There is prescriptive literature, both printed and manuscript, about the institution of marriage and how men and women should behave within it. A good deal of this was written from a religious viewpoint by clergymen. It was also often written to correct what was considered to be unacceptable behaviour and relationships. A serious imbalance can result from taking such sources at face value. The authors possibly exaggerated the prevalence of the problem they sought to correct. They perhaps also recommended behaviours that were deplored or ignored by the majority. When using such literature historians have to be careful to establish the relationship between prescription and actuality. Occasionally it will be possible to read direct challenges to prescriptive literature. Otherwise the historian has to look at the evidence of relationships. The way to establishing this relationship might seem to lie in testing the theory with examples from the experience of 'actual' women. This is a path historians at times must take but it is fraught with its own dangers. Most of the rich archival documentation, as usual, exists for the married lives of elite women in England and Wales, and for Scottish and Anglo-Irish women of like class, and comes from their family muniment rooms. Anglo-Irish aristocratic women frequently had much in common with English women as they spent part of their own lives in England. Women married to members of the Irish 'court' normally remained behind in England. For much of our period there was no elite in the British colonies established on the Atlantic seaboard of America and in any event there is very little detailed primary source material for the women of the American colonies, whatever their social position. Scholars are able to study in some detail the lives of a few well-born women from each society.

Historians have displayed enormous ingenuity in using other types of source – for example, court and trial records, wills and marriage registers – to flesh out the picture for women of all social strata, on the one hand, and, on the other hand, to set the evidence from case studies of elite women against a semi-statistical background so that some sense of the typicality or otherwise of individual examples might be gained. Scholars have been slower to use visual sources but are currently more prepared to learn about the expectations held about married women from stained-glass windows, paintings, portraits, manuscript illuminations, tombs and memorials. Neither the case study approach nor the statistical approach is sufficient on its own. In addition the very real problem of interpreting the evidence appropriately has to be tackled. The historian brings to this task all manner of intellectual and philosophical baggage, much of it useful and much of it an impediment to reading the evidence. Feminism has brought much that is good to the discipline of history – women's history for a start! It has not, however, brought as part of its philosophy any attempt at objectivity and this has led to an ahistorical interpretation. It has been left to historians – many of whom do share feminist ideals – to stand back from the record and seek to interpret it historically. Goodness knows, that is difficult enough in itself!

It is fairly self-evident that the historian needs to take care regarding the choice of sources. The Paston letters of the fifteenth century taken alone suggest an England racked by conflict; the Stonor correspondence from the Thames Valley balances this picture with one of an England that enjoyed periods of calm and got on with its everyday business.[2] The implications for women's as well as men's lives during the Wars of the Roses are many. The lesson for the historian is that as numerous and diverse a range of sources as possible should be consulted. Even then there are problems of interpretation.

Just one example must suffice to demonstrate that the sources are not transparent and that they frequently support more than one possible interpretation. Lady Cassandra Willoughby drew together original letters in the later Stuart period illustrating the domestic lives of her forbears in the sixteenth century. The letters from Sir Francis Willoughby and his wife (one of the Littleton family) and their daughters and their sons-in-law provided her with much information about the emotional lives of her ancestors. Sir Francis Willoughby married Mistress Littleton in about 1570. For a while they lived together and she bore him several daughters. In 1575–78, however, after acrimonious disputes concerning his sister, Lady Margaret Arundel, his servants, the children, Sir Francis's authority and the government of the household, in which her father Sir John Littleton sought to reconcile them, the couple separated, and Lady Willoughby was not given access to the children. There was a reconciliation in the 1580s which resulted in uneasy cohabitation. So far so good.

Interpreting the letters in such a way as to uncover the 'true' situation is not, however, easy. Did Sir Francis unreasonably side with his sister and his evil servants against his wife, as she and her father alleged? Or was she violent and paranoid and suffering from some psychic disturbance? She was accused of having gone to Buxton for a fortnight and of being liable to wander off thereafter. Was she denied access to her home and her children by an unreasonable and cruel husband or by a sensible father and master seeking to protect his children and servants against a mentally unfit mother and mistress? In Sir Francis's orders for his household at Coventry in 1578, during his own prolonged absence in London, he instructs: 'That those persons I have discharged from my house doe not repaire thereto nor have any conference with my wife or any of her friends till my return. That shee shall have nothing to doe with ye children but yt they be ordered by such as I shall appoint for yt purpose, that ye household be ordered by ye discretion of Dracot . . . that [my wife] shall not discharge or receive any servant nor strike or evil entreat any servant . . . that [she shall not use horses, buy anything without receipts, send any message and] that ye children doe go to bed strait after 8 a clock and are made ready before 8 in the morning, and yt after it is 9 a clock at night no body must be in ye great chamber, but yt ye fire be raked up and ye door locked'.[3]

A balanced approach, using just these letters, suggests that there was some fault on both sides. Sir Francis was probably unduly influenced by his servants and was overly protective of his position as 'master' of the household and of his wife. Lady Willoughby was of 'turbulent spirit', accused her husband of adultery with the children's nurse, and confronted her husband with what she described as 'disrespectfull speeches, which she is sorry for'. It seems to have taken her appeal to his need for a male heir 'to ye House of Willoughby' to make him agree to reconciliation by 1588.

The introduction of other evidence could lead us, however, to be more critical of Sir Francis's behaviour and more accepting of Lady Willoughby's position. Also contained in the Willoughby muniment room was a note suggesting that Sir Francis had indeed had an illicit union with Katherine Deverell:

William Deverell alias Willoughby son of Katharine Deverell and as she hath confessd him ye son of Sir Francis Willoughby knt of Nottinghamshire Baptized ye 4th day of March 1584.

This is a true copy taken out of ye register of Laughton in Le Morthing in ye county of York, and attested by

Robert Barnard Vicar.[4]

There were also several submissive and apparently rational letters from his wife 'sealed with my heart' and letters from family members that showed that others were complaining of Sir Francis's vitriolic temper and impetuous behaviour and over-reliance on ambitious servants. Some time after the death of his first wife and after a quarrel with his son-in-law Percival Willoughby, Sir Francis reputedly rushed out and remarried specifically to ensure that Percival and his wife Bridget did not inherit the estate. In the letters relating to this behaviour Percival, his wife and her sisters all commented on the malevolent influence that Sir Francis's servants wielded. Perhaps Lady Willoughby had been more sinned against than sinning.[5]

It is difficult enough to describe contemporary marriages and to correctly apportion blame in such cases but when four and more centuries intervene between the event and the imperfect evidence and ourselves the task is even more forbidding. The historian seeks to offer an honest interpretation of evidence that is itself biased and incomplete and to remain open to contrary sources and arguments.

Notes

1 Robert Croft, 'Eulogy' (1638), as cited in C. Belsey, 'The Serpent in the Garden', p. 6.
2 C. Carpenter (1996).
3 HEH, STB Box II, p. 24.
4 HEH, STB Box 2, Book 2.
5 HEH, STB Box 2, Ridgway–Willoughby marriage.

CHAPTER 6

Attitudes to marriage

Tho' Adam's wife destroyed his life,
In manner that was awful;
Yet marriage now we all allow
To be both just [right] and lawful . . .

Since it doth stand each man in hand,
To happify his life,
I would advise each to be wise,
And choose a prudent wife.[1]

Introduction

Marriage was encouraged in all the societies under study by secular and ecclesiastical governors. It was seen as an estate ordained by God for the procreation of mankind, the upbringing of children, and the proper ordering of society. In New England as in Old England a family was viewed as a 'little church, and a little commonwealth' and families were created by marriage. The recent in-depth study of marriage in Maryland has stressed that, where views on marriage were concerned as in much else, 'Marylanders [were] English women and men in a new locale'.[2] The extent to which adult life outside marriage was accepted or tolerated depended rather more upon demographic reality and ancient custom than upon doctrine.

Recent work on the situation in Scotland and Wales suggests that while marriage may have been encouraged in those societies it was a relatively weak institution when compared with informal unions and concubinage. In the Highlands of Scotland trial marriages of 'a year and one day' were possibly the norm rather than the exception and historians think that they could also have occurred elsewhere in Scotland.³ In Wales people seem to have moved in and out of partnerships with ease and monotonous regularity and the widespread acceptance of concubinage even extended to the clergy. Christine Peters suggests that within the ancient clan system of Scotland marriage was relatively unimportant until the 'commercialisation of clanship' when marriage became more important amongst the lairds as a means of accumulating and transmitting property.⁴

Marriage was a fact of life for most English women who survived to their twenties and thirties, even if they never entered the state of matrimony themselves. It was not the only fact of their lives but its anticipation dominated the lives of young and middle-aged single women and, as we have seen in an earlier chapter, the consciousness of their close relatives and friends. Lady Mary Wortley Montague expressed her horror (and that of many other women) of remaining an 'old maid'.

I have a moral aversion to be an old maid, and the decayed oak before my window, leafless, half-rotten, and shaking its withered top puts me in mind every morning of an antiquated virgin, bald, with rotten teeth, and shaking of the parrot.⁵

In the American colonies population was sparse and women few and far between. In theory women of marriageable age were in an advantageous position in such 'market conditions'. When people could pair off, they married young. There were attempts to bring in marriageable girls to supply the shortfall. Once they arrived it was important that they married quickly. Both women and men were encouraged to tie the knot, often with the use of financial incentives. In Connecticut, for example, bachelors were fined a pound for every week that they lived alone and in Maryland bachelors were subject to high taxation.⁶ The very existence of such strictures perhaps suggests that marriage was not always seen as desirable or essential by individuals.

In England in the late sixteenth and earlier seventeenth centuries the population was increasing and the age at marriage relatively late (on average age twenty-five for women, twenty-seven for men) for all except the elite, although there were local variations on this pattern. About 10 per cent of the population never married at all over the period as a whole and by the mid-seventeenth century it is thought that as many as 18 per cent of the population were single, never-married women over the age of twenty-five. Most married women had had a short period as single adults prior to marriage. Both these facts had an impact upon the experience and expectations of married women. The sex ratio was low, women's position on the marriage market was disadvantageous and surplus young women either lived alone and worked in other people's households or they sought husbands overseas by emigrating; on the other hand women had to accept some capacity for independence and even self-sufficiency if only for a short while.[7]

Paradise and the fall

For these women life was full of contradictions. When she entered and lived the married state a young woman learned to negotiate these paradoxes. The surviving works of her hands and her mind show how she did this – diaries, letters, embroidery, tapestry, accounts, writings. She was a meek helpmeet for her masterful husband. She was also his companion. She was a 'masterful' mistress of her household. She was to know about survival and sustenance and be able to rise to the challenge of difficult physical and emotional circumstances. She was a 'powerful' matriarch. She was an example of piety and submission for her daughters. The balance between these roles would vary from person to person and circumstance to circumstance. Laurel Thatcher Ulrich, in her brilliant short book *Good Wives*, expressed very well the fact that contemporaries did not emphasise the personalities but the roles of women and, moreover, that those roles changed according to circumstance.

Certain patterns of behaviour could be put on and taken off according to circumstances without altering the essential nature of the person; women could act as 'deputy husbands' or men as 'brides of Christ' without becoming any less 'submissive' or 'masterful' in other social relations.[8]

Contemporaries saw marriage as both ideal and idealised. Thomas Becon described it as 'an high, holy and blessed order of life, ordained not of man, but of God' when Adam was without sin.[9] Eve was given to Adam to perfect his life. Over the Tudor and Stuart centuries the medieval Catholic view of celibacy as the way of perfection steadily gave way to the ideal of companionate marriage. Marriage spelt a happy ending. Yet at the same time contemporaries saw the ideal married state as something that was not easy to attain. Men compared marriage to Eden but saw within the garden the serpent, woman the tempted temptress, and the eventual fall from grace. 'There's no mischief in the world done, but a woman is always one.' So the difficulties that beset marriage were not seen as they are today as related to the personal characteristics of the partners and their possible incompatibility, or even to the unlikelihood of two people living together in close proximity and perfect harmony for a lifetime. Rather, the difficulties lay in the nature of the partnership that God had willed upon man and the nature of 'Eve' herself. A woman was not easy to understand: in the words of Shakespeare, 'Who can read a woman?'[10]

As historians turn to contemporary artefacts for evidence of the approach of men and women to marriage, they note that even in the marital bedchamber there was evidence of this contradiction within marriage in many parts of the British Isles in the two hundred years or so before the Restoration of Charles II. An illuminated manuscript of the later Middle Ages shows Adam and Eve as companions in the garden and then as victim and temptress in another part of the page. A good later example is provided by the Isaak Walton and Rachel Floud marriage chest at Warwick Castle. Another is the bedstead at the Ancient High House at Stafford, where the headboard shows the temptation of Adam. George Washington's great, great-grandmother, Amphyllis Twigden, in about 1640 worked a tapestry around an oval painting of Eve tempting Adam in a glorious garden.[11] Similarly Dame Dorothy Davenport's marriage bed tapestry of 1610 at Capesthorpe Manor, Cheshire shows the fall. This tapestry, celebrating marriage and procreation, has death in its final scene. A set of valances from the late sixteenth century show a skeleton triumphing over the expulsion. North of the border there was a similar association of marriage with ideal partnership, paradise and generation on the one hand, and misery, the fall and death on the other. A mid-sixteenth-century Scottish valance belonging to Colin Campbell of Glenorchy and his second wife, Katherine Ruthven, who married in 1550, also depicts the fall. One recent historian describes the marriage beds, with their furnishings, as 'archetypal marriage furniture with their association with process of generation' and the decoration of them with scenes of Paradise and the fall as showing 'a wife, God-given and beautiful, but at the same time dangerously seductive, and thus equivocal, her meaning undecidable'. The theme was repeated on other artefacts associated with the act of marriage. For example, the Victorian and Albert Museum possesses a marriage dish dated 1635 that depicts the fall. The proliferation of such symbolism in home furnishings seems to support a view that men and women internalised this ambiguous message about marriage and the woman within it, as conveyed by contemporary religious teaching through the word and the image.[12] (Conversely, of course, it also speaks volumes about the ways in which husbands were regarded as both figures of authority and power and as figures of weakness.) 'Woman is the woe of man' and at best 'a necessary evil' but she is also, when virtuous, 'a goodly prize' and 'the ornament of her house'.[13] Women were portrayed in late medieval manuscripts not only as Eve the companion and temptress but also as the seven virtues, the arts of theology, logic, arithmetic, geometry and music, the figure of justice, and, above all, the mother of God.

The imagery of Adam and Eve and the garden was as common in eighteenth-century New England bedrooms as in their earlier Old World counterparts, as women themselves embroidered panels highlighting the contradictory message.[14] Laurel Thatcher Ulrich, however, has argued that the idealised figure of Eve was transformed in both Old and New England in the period between 1650 and 1750 from being Adam's Helpmeet to the 'lovely fair' creature of Milton's poem.[15] Mary Bulman of York, Maine, spent five years working bed hangings depicting a floral paradise, into which she wove a poem by Isaac Watts that spoke of the higher love between Christ and Christian, which transcended the earthly love of the marriage bed:

Sweet muse descend and bless the shade
And bless the evening grove
Business and noise and day are fled
And every care but love.[16]

But hence ye wanton young and fair
Mine is a purer flame
No Phillis shall infect the air
with her unhallowed name.

Jesus has all my powers possest
My hopes my fears my joys
He the Dear Sovereign of my breast
Shall still command my voice.

Ulrich uses portraiture to demonstrate the change: seventeenth-century portraits of husbands and wives show 'sturdy mates and fellow travellers on the road to salvation'; a few of Greenwood's and Copley's portraits of the eighteenth century continue to show these 'yoke fellows in the puritan tradition' but the majority of eighteenth-century portraits display the idealised sexuality, youth and innocence of the women. In 1729 John Smibert painted Elizabeth, the fifty-one-year-old wife of the honourable Daniel Oliver, with the flowing tresses of a maiden and the pinch-waisted, plunge-necked dress of a young bride.

Conclusion

Evidence from popular culture suggests that, while the role of Eve in the fall was fully appreciated and discussed, the God-ordained nature of marriage and the good woman's ability to make a man happy and complete was the dominant message. A distinction between good and evil women could be drawn. Later in this book a contrary argument is presented: that eighteenth-century women were more commonly prepared and educated to make a useful contribution to the household and family and that taking their portraits as evidence of their lives is tantamount to people today using school portraits as accurately representing the status of schoolgirls today.

Notes

1 Ballad, c.1786.
2 D. Meyers (2003).
3 See below for a discussion of the debate surrounding this idea.
4 C. Peters (2004) p. 8.
5 R. Halsband (1967), Vol. 1, p. 112.
6 S. Coontz (1988) p. 83; J. C. Spruill (1938) p. 137.
7 R. Thompson (1974); L. Stone (1973).
8 L. T. Ulrich (1991 edn) p. 185.
9 Thomas Becon, *Worckes*, 1560–1564, I, DCXVI.
10 See C. Belsey (1996) pp. 5–6, 13–16; J. Ray (1678) p. 60.
11 Now framed in the great bedroom at Sulgrave Manor, Northamptonshire.
12 This interpretation is based on Belsey (1996) pp. 7–18.
13 M. P. Tilley (1950) pp. 742, 744, 747 and J. Ray (1678) p. 58.
14 See, for example, panel from Newbury, c.1760 in the Wadsworth Athenaeum, Hartford, CT, illustrated in L. T. Ulrich (1991). For more detail see L. E. Hawes (1963) pp. 279–81; A. P. Rose (1973) pp. 101–68. The Adam and Eve motif was less prevalent in eighteenth-century English bedrooms, where men and women appeared in pastoral guise and where human figures were frequently absent from scenes of gardens. See the furnishings of Sulgrave Manor, Northamptonshire.
15 L. T. Ulrich (1991) pp. 113–17.
16 Bedhangings from the Old Gaol Museum, York, Maine; Isaac Watts, 'Meditation in a grove' from his *Horae Lyricae*, 1706, cited in Ulrich (1991) p. 117.

CHAPTER 7

Patriarchy

By the law of God, of nature, of reason and by the common law, the will of the wife is subject to the will of the husband.
                                            Lord Chief Baron Hale, 1663

Nothing is more gratifying to the mind of man than power or dominion: and this I think myself amply possessed of, as I am the father of a family. I am perpetually giving out orders, in prescribing duties, in hearing parties, in administering justice, and in distributing rewards and punishments ... In short, Sir, I look upon my family as a patriarchal sovereign, in which I am myself both king and priest.[1]

Introduction

Scholars have been interested in patriarchy in several contexts. In the case of England they have been fascinated by the parallels between a state governed by a monarch, normally male, and families governed by a head, also male. This has led to several studies which concentrate on the composition and conduct of families, mainly in the middle and upper echelons of society. Often the unspoken assumptions (in a society in which democracy and feminism are fashionable) have been that patriarchy permeated the whole of society and that it provided a wholly negative experience for all but males. In the case of the American colonies the debate has focused on the prevalence of patriarchy: was it on the increase or decrease before the American Revolution? The underlying assumptions here have been that the colonies were fundamentally anti-monarchical and favourable to egalitarian and democratic ideas.

Patriarchy has proved difficult for historians and other scholars, students and general readers to handle. According to the law in early modern

England, when a woman married she exchanged one household for another and one authority (her natural father) for that of another (her husband). A wife 'owned' no property, could not make a will without her husband's explicit consent or sue in a common law court without his permission.[2] Children and servants of both sexes stood in a like relation of subjection to the head of the household. Some historians – most notably Lawrence Stone – have emphasised the actual as well as the theoretical subjection of wives and female children to the male heads of household. As far as the state and community were concerned the husband was the monarch and the wife his subject. Taken out of context, a pledge such as that proposed by Griffith for married women to recite seems to prove the point.

Mine husband is my superior, my better; he hath authority and rule over me. Nature hath given it to him, having formed our bodies to tenderness, men's to hardness . . . His will is my tie and tether even of my desires and wishes. I will not strive against God and nature. Though my sin [the original sin of Eve in the Garden of Eden] hath made my place tedious, yet will I confess the truth. My husband is my superior, my better.[3]

The principle of legal coverture is emphasised to demonstrate that women have no rights to sue in the courts of law. Instances of strong, independent women are in such studies seen as anomalies, examples of unusual defiance, exceptions that prove the rule. These historians tend to stress the misogynistic aspects of the 'patriarchal system' – the ways in which early modern men lorded it over their womenfolk, deprived them of education, opportunity and responsibility and diminished their confidence and their abilities.

Feminist historians and literary scholars have often found that this concept of 'restrictive patriarchalism' fitted well with their view of the oppression of women. Patriarchalism, they argue, had wholly negative implications for the lives of contemporary women and their daughters. Suzanne Hull, for instance, pronounced that 'women were told over and over again that they were inferior, that they had lesser minds, that they were unable to handle their own affairs'.[4] K. Walker argued that women such as Lady Jane Cornwallis and Lady Brilliana Harley constructed their identities as women according to advice meted out by conduct books.[5] These interpretations have become an essential underpinning for studies of early modern literature and culture, and appear in bald form in popular history.[6] Even those historians of women who have attained most understanding of early modern society have frequently, in the face of contrary evidence, found it difficult to free themselves from such assumptions and from an obsession with the ideas of 'obedience', 'powerlessness', 'drudgery' and 'dependence', and sometimes even frivolity and fragility.

A few scholars from the mid-1980s have been wrestling more successfully with the evidence of both contemporary opinion and the way early modern people lived. Anthony Fletcher, advantaged by his deep knowledge of early modern English society as a whole, grappled with, for example, the relationship between prescription and practice; the ways in which 'the hierarchies of age and class [and marital status] continually cut across that of gender'; and the manner in which women themselves negotiated patriarchies.[7] Rosemary O'Day examined the active cooperation of men and women, husbands and wives, sons and daughters, brothers and sisters, in English families, again emphasising experience rather than prescription and parental rather than patriarchal authority.[8] Susan Dwyer Amussen, another social historian, has shown how capable, independent-minded women found their own way to a tolerable life by 'grooming' rather than defying their menfolk or the system.[9] Bernard Capp has also argued that most early modern women chose the path of 'accommodation', that is, softening and circumventing male authority without challenging it outright.[10] On the other hand, Amussen has also shown that some women openly resisted dominance: for example, in 1615 Alice Kemp told Faith Docking that 'if you beat cuckold your husband again about the home, we will have a better riding than we had before'. Such rough music or skimmingtons show how the community enforced its value system but the occasion for them also demonstrates how some women would not subordinate themselves to their husbands.[11] In her brilliant study of *The Patriarch's Wife* (which focuses on Anne Filmer, the wife of the most famous exponent of patriarchal theory, Robert Filmer) Margaret Ezell has shown, moreover, that patriarchy was no straitjacket for seventeenth-century women and that men as well as women were actively engaged in a 'lively dialogue' about its proper application:

The theory of patriarchal authority underwent intense scrutiny and debate during the seventeenth century by the very sex it supposedly benefited. Its principal tenet, the unquestionable authority of the male head of the house, was severely criticized from within the ranks of male writers as part of the larger issues of power and governance. At no time . . . does one find authoritarian, rigidly patriarchal, or misogynistic opinions in theological or satirical writings left unchallenged . . . male defenders of the female sex are actively engaged in sawing through the very supports of domestic patriarchal authority.[12]

Certainly there were misogynistic writings such as the anti-female satires, which include the much quoted *Arraignment of Lewd, Idle, Froward and Inconstant Women*.[13] There were also books which stressed the role of woman as the good, obedient wife:

To keep him good, his wife must be
Obedient, mild, her huswifery
Within doors she must tend; her charge
Is that at home; his that at large; . . .[14]

Yet Ezell showed that conduct books emphasised the partnership of husband and wife and, within this interdependent relationship, the *importance* of the wife's role in the household.[15] This importance extended to domestic government, where the wife has authority. She should 'rule over her children and servants. This the woman may do, as much as God hath made them subject to her'.[16] Although the good wife is aware of her duty to husband and family and the furtherance of their well-being she is not represented as 'feeble, incapable, or servile', in fact as just the opposite. In her discussion of the contributions of Filmer and Mary More to the debate, Ezell pointed to the important distinction between patriarchal and parental authority in the family, which some, perhaps most, males and females drew.[17] Judith Bennet's influential review of the historiography of patriarchy suggested that 'patriarchy . . . existed in many forms and varieties', inspired many different reactions from both men and women, and affected both sexes in many ways.[18] Sally Gosling concluded in her study of sex and gender roles in early modern England that while male supremacy shaped thinking on power relationships in printed works such as conduct books and formed a reference point in personal documents, the actual exercise of power within the household revolved around ensuring that family interests were effectively secured. 'Pragmatism overrode ideology'.[19]

A study of conduct books has, moreover, shown that most of the virtues recommended to women – virtue, self-effacement, education, diligence, neatness of apparel, generosity, grace, civility, and rationality – were certainly not the opposite of the recommended male virtues. The emphasis was not on differences occasioned by gender (although there were some) but upon what was necessary to 'preserve the social hierarchy and respect for the wisdom of age'.[20]

It should be noted also that not only women but also men were subject to the authority of a patriarch. Such males included not only male children and servants but also to some extent younger brothers (even when married) and others within the wider family network. And some of these males also acknowledged the authority of the patriarch's wife.

The truth about patriarchy?

This should leave historians asking many new questions. Was patriarchy, in essence, oppressive and restrictive? How did different women and men negotiate patriarchy? Were there different forms of patriarchy or was there simply one system, correctly or incorrectly applied? Is a typology of forms of patriarchy possible or are so-called case studies merely paradigmatic of themselves? What motivated such negotiation? How prevalent was such modification of the 'system'? If negotiation was frequent and successful, how effective then was patriarchy?

Patriarchy was not in essence oppressive – it provided women with protection which, if the husband failed in his duty of love and care, was to be given by fathers and brothers. The evidence from 'personal sources' (such as diaries, memoirs, funeral sermons, autobiographical writing, family histories, genealogies, marriage negotiations and settlements, some kinds of account books and correspondence) overwhelmingly supports the view that patriarchy, for a very large proportion of the population of England, was *protective* rather than overly restrictive and oppressive in its intent and its impact.[21] Individuals of both sexes saw themselves as engaged in a partnership for mutual benefit. Wives and male and female children were protected by the male head of the household. They had, however, 'useful' roles within both public and private life – roles which, in the case of children, prepared them for their future positions, and in the case of wives were a fulfilment of society's expectations. The absence of early Scottish, Welsh, Irish and American women's diaries seriously impedes comparison.

The Elizabethan Court of Requests and the ecclesiastical courts certainly saw themselves as restoring to hard-done-by wives the protection which normally was accorded them under marriage. A minority of married women were in this position. The Court of Requests, an equity court, generally upheld coverture when it was evoked by litigants *except* in cases of wives separated from their spouses whether *a mensa et thoro* or by imprisonment, banishment or mental incapacity of the husband.[22] Such wives were seen as legally competent and were even permitted, from the 1540s to the 1600s, to sue their husbands. Joan Morgan was one of a dozen or so middle to late Tudor wives who took advantage of this even though she had not yet won a divorce: she asked the Masters of Requests to come to her aid because her husband had fallen into a 'fransey' and threatened her life; she asked that they prevent her husband from selling the couple's farm until such time as she could discover whether she might be 'lawfully divorced from him'.[23] The Court of Chancery also chose in certain circumstances to treat married women as legally competent femes soles although hardly any examples have been found of married women suing under their own names in that court.[24] It was the ecclesiastical or church courts that effectively recognised women as legally competent during marriage. Prior to the Restoration they adjudicated disputes between husbands and wives and had the power to grant divorce *a mensa et thoro* and to impose a maintenance order on the husband for his separated wife and minor children. While these Courts Christian could only enforce maintenance orders by excommunication, by this time a weak tool indeed, they could and did insist on the husband entering into a bond for payment which could, in the event of non-payment, be sued for at common law. Because no married woman might sue in the common law courts, such a bond had to be made in the name of one or more of the woman's male relatives or friends who would, if required, sue on her behalf.[25] Women who had already obtained a separation order also might sue for payment in the Court of Requests, which probably played a large part in the development of a system of alimony.[26]

Was patriarchy as effective in the Americas? The law of marriage and divorce differed from colony to colony. American scholars have long contended that New England's law was more liberal than that of England and Wales and the other American colonies, largely because, we are told, the view of marriage was itself different. In New England, marriage was a contract in which each partner had certain rights and responsibilities. 'Thus, while the relationships were hierarchical, the duty of the subordinate partner to obey or submit was conditional on the superior partner's fulfilment of the covenant'.[27] But, while the English did not necessarily use contractual language to describe the relation between husband and wife, many certainly viewed each partner as having specific rights and responsibilities, which could be enforced by law, and sought to safeguard the future well-being of both partners through carefully drawn-up marriage settlements which were contractual in nature. Recently Debra Meyers's detailed study of Maryland marriages from the 1630s to the early eighteenth century has led her to suggest a sharp difference between Catholic and free-will Quakers and Anglican marriages on the one hand and predestinarian-Calvinist unions on the other.[28] She argues that this division 'made an important difference in the social freedom of women in the Maryland colony. While Calvinist Predestinarians tended to be hierarchical and patriarchal in their family structures and very controlling of and among their women, Free Will Christians supported more egalitarian structures and their results in terms of social, political (in the broad sense), and economic equality for women.' She shows that 'Free Will women, who were "yoke-fellows" with their men, owned land and property, managed it with aplomb, executed wills, and had their day in court.' If this division really did exist it would do much to explain disparities in the actualities of marriage within all of the British Islands and colonies. Such a hypothesis is, however, highly contentious. Taken to its extreme, it would argue that restrictive aspects of patriarchy were emphasised by Puritans and, perhaps, that the protective elements were stressed by believers in free will – perhaps, even, that the latter rejected patriarchy altogether. In the case of England this certainly seems improbable. It certainly stands oddly with a royalist and Arminian belief in parallels between king and father.

Quite a number of studies of colonial America have focused on the interest in bolstering patriarchy displayed by the emergent polities. The tendency is to see patriarchy as weak in the very early days of settlement. From the Restoration onwards Virginian males are seen as trying to reassert their rule. Terri Snyder's *Brabbling Women* shows the male rulers of the colony seeking with a series of laws to clamp down upon unruly women who were flouting patriarchy.[29] Her view echoes that of another major study of the Chesapeake region in the eighteenth century by Allan Kulikoff.[30] On the other hand, Daniel Blake Smith argues strongly that patriarchy was in retreat in Chesapeake planter households in the eighteenth century.[31] Several historians have linked this supposed decline of patriarchy with the questioning of all authority that led to the American Revolution.[32] The increasing tendency of younger sons to leave home and the rise in bridal pregnancies evident in eighteenth-century New England are also adduced to suggest a decline in patriarchy in the eighteenth century. Whereas during the seventeenth century pregnancies among New England brides never rose above 10 per cent, by the eighteenth century the percentage had risen to 30 per cent, indicating that fathers no longer had strict control over their daughters.[33]

It is necessary to examine how the protective patriarchal system operated in practice. Parents certainly counselled their children to behave responsibly in marriage. This applied equally to fathers counselling their sons as to mothers counselling their daughters. Sir Thomas Temple saw fit to intervene with fatherly advice in his eldest son's second marriage to Christian Leveson when he saw that Peter was neglecting her and, possibly, being unfaithful to her. Peter should follow closely the example of King James I and King Charles I, who loved their wives, rather than of his own cousin-german who had contracted the pox.

> [I]t is not so great a benefit to have a good wife, as to love her. These things I will pray you [fo. 1v] to endeavour for her, which is that she surfeit not: for the old saying is true (that more die with surfeit than with the sword): that she take not cold, that she ride no more in the coach then she must needs do. To these I will add, that she foresee and avoid mischances. So praying god to bless you, my daughter your wife . . .[34]

Sometimes, though, such counsel had no practical effect. Sir Thomas Tyringham, on 31 December 1625, received a visit at Tyringham Hall from his friend Sir Thomas Temple and Temple's cousin, another lawyer, Thomas Thornton.[35] Temple, convinced by his daughter's testimony that his son-in-law was abusing her, felt that it was naturally incumbent upon him as her father to protect her when her husband, in law her protector, had become her attacker. What these men told Tyringham inspired him to write immediately to William Andrewes because they 'doth inform me of much ill usage that your Lady hath lately received at your hands and because yet it is in my power to do you a neighbourly courtesy . . .' This neighbourly courtesy was to offer Anne and William mediation:

> [I]f you please to accept of it I make you this offer that if you will be pleased to take your self over presently hither with your Lady I will stay such counsels which otherwise I cannot, so not doubting hereof w[i]th my love to you I rest
> Y[ou]r loving frend and neig[hbour]
> Tho[mas]: Tyringham

The threat of further action should William not accept this offer was by no means veiled.[36] William was outraged and sent an answer by return of post, refusing to obey Tyringham's summons. These were 'false calumnations, no ways by [him] deserved' and Tyringham should 'spare . . . further censure until the truth shall appear whereby [he should] be disburdened of this scandal'. In fact, he says, Anne had deserved all she had got at his hands: 'And she be known to have worthily deserved far more than what she hath received, Nor upon such urging by me to be avoided nor by any man else.' What is more he anticipates that the law will condemn her and exonerate him: 'neither will he seek her out, nor accept of any other course then what the law shall set down wherein [he] will prove [him] self both just and honest'.[37]

Just a few days later, when he had been apprised of the situation by Tyringham, Thomas Temple wrote to his son-in-law, asking him to mend his behaviour and reconcile with his wife. Although Thomas certainly rebuked his son-in-law and defended his daughter's decision to retreat to Newport Pagnell for her safety and that of her two very young children, he left the way open for a reunion. He did not want to make the argument public because this would damage all concerned: 'for appeasing these matters I shall be so far from publishing the same, as that I desire the same for your credit [which] may as much as may be mitigated and reformed'. He expected that much was said and done in the heat of the moment that now might be regretted: 'And that you will upon mature consideration weigh the things which you in your choler and haste have said and done.' Finally he reminded his son-in-law of his obligations under God towards his wife:

Son Andrewes

. . . remember that you and your wife are one flesh and that by the law of God and your own affiance in your carriage you ought to love and cherish her and she you, which I wish and pray for, and do desire you to accept her and her children again and so to use them, as in law and conscience you ought which I still will hope you will do, And I pray you let me hear too lines of your purpose, which if it come from you with a loving heart, that shall give me great content and more and more to be your loving friend and father-in-law. And so hoping the best I commit you to God.

Whatever his commitment to eventual reconciliation and keeping matters private, Thomas had to find some way of offering his daughter and her family protection while William considered what he was going to do.

Son Andrewes

I am informed that your hard words and threatenings to your wife and children, together with your violent actions to her, . . . have put her in much fear for worse to come, and by these means you have enforced her for the safety of her self and children to go to Newport [Bucks] which cannot be for your credit nor my content And therefore for appeasing these matters I shall be so far from publishing the same, as that I desire the same . . . may as much as may be mitigated and reformed, And that you will upon mature consideration weigh the things which you in your choler and haste have said and done . . . your loving father in law.
Sir Thomas Temple to Sir William Andrewes, January 1625/6

Days before Thomas wrote to William, he had another son-in-law, John Lenthall, seek a warrant for William's arrest from the Lord Chief Justice. The Lord Chief Justice instead ordered that Sir Thomas Tyringham and Temple's brother-in-law, Sir Thomas Denton, both JPs and members of Temple's family and friends' circle, should 'carefully examine' William and 'if they found your allegations to be proved upon oath, then to bind him and his man with good sufficient surety to y[ou]r good behaviour . . .'[38] Writing about this examination to Tyringham Thomas Temple warned him of two things: first, 'that he is weaponed with swords in his parlour, that show it will be dangerous for a constable to serve your warrant on him and his said servant. The other care to be had, is that Sir Willim Andrewes wth 2 sureties be bound in great sums of money without which Sir William Andrewes will be careless.'[39]

Meanwhile Thomas, understanding that disputes between a husband and wife were the business of the Church courts, lost no time in having his second son John approach someone who had influence with the Archbishop of Canterbury. John reported that Newman would use 'divers ways employ your power with my Lord, to effect what good you could for my said daughter, and first you will in her behalf write your letter to my lord's grace'. Thomas would not leave matters there. He asked Newman 'to send to me your letter, with certain articles I have sent to you first to be seen by you' which Thomas himself or 'daughter or some other, will cause to be presented to his Grace'. He adds that he is enclosing the articles (allegations) and is expecting Richard to amend them appropriately: 'I have sent unto you at this time a draft of such articles as I had, purposing by oath and other wise to amend them very shortly, w[hi]ch so amended, you shall see also when it shall please you, yet the substance contained in these sent and so much as may give you much information of the matter, I thought it very necessary for this time to send them as they are to you.'[40] We do not know whether Anne appeared in person to plead her case before the Archbishop's court but later in the year, apparently after she had been granted a judicial separation and an alimony order for herself and her children, the elder of whom was under three years of age, Anne Andrewes personally petitioned the Archbishop:

The humble petition of Dame Anne Andrewes most humbly showeth: that about 9 years since your petitioner intermarried with Sir William Andrewes Kt and that he had in dowry with your petitioner the sum of £2,200 yet nevertheless hath notoriously in very ungratefully manner causelessly and cruelly used and abused your petitioner, but also forced the charge maintenance and education of two small children upon your petitioner and refuseth to give or allow any maintenance ether to your petitioner or the said children by means whereof your petitioner and the said children are much necessitated at this time.

Now for that the said Sir Wm Andrewes had such a portion with your petitioner as aforesaid, and for that he hath causelessly excepted against your petitioner as hath been manifested to your grace and others, and for that your petitioner and her children have been thought worthy of maintenance from him as appeareth under your Grace's hand that your Grace would be therefore pleased to give to your poor distressed petitioner and her children such good allowance of alimony as to her degree and your Grace's wisdom shall seem meet, and your petitioner and her children will ever pray for your Grace's health and happiness.[41]

Probably the precise details of this case were atypical: Keith Thomas has argued that the ecclesiastical courts rarely offered a remedy for unhappy wives.[42] Nevertheless case studies such as this demonstrate the way in which fathers and brothers fought the corners of their daughters and sisters.

The 'normal' way to ensure that patriarchy operated as intended was informal. If a wife were being abused by her husband she turned to her former patriarch (her birth family and friends) to come to her aid. Their instinct was to approach the husband, find out the truth of the matter and urge him to mend his ways. Only if he refused would they resort to some form of litigation. Anne's petition made it crystal clear that the dowry of £2,200 that William had received on marriage laid an obligation upon him to love, protect and support his wife and their children. Her dowry bought her rights commensurate with its size. If connubial harmony could not be achieved by the couple sharing a home together, then the husband was obligated to provide a separate home and sustenance. Sir Thomas Temple sought to protect his daughter because of his natural love for her but he could not accept responsibility for her maintenance. She had taken a handsome portion with her, a portion which Thomas, with his eleven surviving children and spendthrift son and heir, could ill afford. So it was now a matter for the courts to enforce. Unfortunately the Temple correspondence does not supply detail about the case from then on. William and Anne eventually achieved a reconciliation and were living together in 1634 when Sir William ended a letter to his brother-in-law Peter Temple, 'w[i]th my wife's love and service presented likewise to you and your worthy lady hoping to hear of y[ou]r health of you and all yours I rest, Your assured loving brother and servant to command.'[43] It is probably idle to speculate about the motives behind such a reconciliation but prominent in his mind would have been the economic disadvantages of maintaining two households and the socio-political disadvantages of losing the benefits of the Temple alliance of which his marriage was the cement. Anne herself was clearly aware of the debt she owed both of her parents, who had been there for her in her hour of need and had cared for her children: 'There is believe me no child you have would be more willing to manifest my true obedience and unforced love to you and my father than I would: I give you many thanks for my last being there, and all other kindnesses in which being so many to me, and my children I cannot express, But now I will ease you of that daily care which you have taken of my children, for now I [have] sent for them . . .'[44]

That this reliance upon fathers in cases of marriage breakdown was a consistent pattern is supported by several examples. For instance, in the 1580s Elizabeth (Littleton) Willoughby relied upon her father Sir John for 'comfort in my greife, assistance in my troubles, and succor in my necessities' during her quarrels with her husband. He intervened often on her behalf. Unfortunately, however, Elizabeth's own father was turned against her by gossip and accusations and she had to plead with him to 'take pitie of me as yor naturall childe, have compassion of me as a distressed woman'.[45] Another good example of a woman's appeal for protection against a violent and cruel husband is the case of the Earl and Countess of Pembroke in 1659. Philip appealed to Parliament in July 1659 against his wife's petition to the Commissioners of the Great Seal 'accusing him of unkindness, violence and cruelty, and praying for an order for maintenance out of petitioner's estate'.

In answer to this, he denied all acts of violence and cruelty, and desired (as he still desires) her again to cohabit with him, promising to receive her with all love and affection, and to provide for her as became her quality as his wife. The cause came to hearing on June 25th last, when Commissioner Fountaine behaved himself with so much passion that the petitioner could not in reason expect any justice from him; and without due consideration given judgement (together with Comr. Tirrill) according to the annexed paper. And although petitioner made it plainly appear that he had never given his wife any reason to complain against him and had received no portion with her, yet Commissioner Fountaine declared he would give her her whole jointure of 1,500l. a year, and if her jointure had been so much more, she should have had it . . . [Philip, Earl of Pembroke] . . . prays for consideration and relief.[46]

Here the state was assuming the role of patriarch.

Patriarchy, then, shielded wives and female children. On those occasions when the shield was ineffective a woman expected her birth family and the law to make it effective again. Moreover, when one patriarchal bond was weakened it was replaced as quickly as possible by another. A very large number of young women came from homes broken by death. In such circumstances patriarchal authority was frequently exercised by mothers, siblings of both sexes, and foster parents. It often passed from one person to another within a relatively short span of time. A young woman such as Lydia DuGard, for example, spent her early years in the crowded home of a London schoolmaster but when her mother, the daughter of a goldsmith, died in 1661, Lydia's father moved into the clergy community of Sion House and sent his daughter to live with her half-sister, Elizabeth, in Coventry where she tasted independence and a continuance of urban life during her early teenage years.[47] After a few years with her sister, Lydia removed to a safer environment to live with her uncle Thomas, rector of the tiny village of Barford, and his second wife, Mary. Lydia reluctantly accepted many of the restrictions placed upon her movements – which largely concerned her wishes to travel some distances alone along dangerously bad roads in an age before mobile phones and an AA service – but conducted a lengthy correspondence and romance with her first cousin from 1665 to their marriage in 1672.[48]

Was this protection oppressive and debilitating in itself? Other sections of this book provide a detailed consideration of the daily lives of women under patriarchy. No doubt many of these women, wives and daughters, struggled with aspects of the system, even when they lived in relative harmony with their menfolk. Others rebelled against the system outright. A couple of points need to be made. First, it is probably unwise to seize upon characteristic teenage rebellion and see this as incontrovertible evidence that women felt oppressed and unfulfilled. The jury is out. Second, nobody, least of all a father or a husband or a suitor, wanted a woman to be useless. There is abundant evidence that women were required to make an economic contribution to marriage that went far beyond that of the marriage settlement and producing and rearing one child after another. They were partners and they were often expected to be very active partners and full of initiative and skill.

Lawrence Stone's thesis of linear development from clan to patriarchal family to companionate marriage is far too simple. It seems improbable that there was any very considerable change in the protective nature of patriarchy over the period studied, although the increasing survival rate of evidence (especially diaries, autobiographies and letters) sometimes has the effect of suggesting such a change. What did alter was the theatre in which men and women were performing – an increasingly urban and mobile consumer society, with exciting opportunities for communication and expansion of horizons. This had the effect of making women make more demands of, and for, their lives. Historians have shown how, for instance, although girls did not attend the same schools as their brothers, they did receive some 'schooling' of various kinds, and interaction with their educated fathers and brothers and with social contacts indirectly led them to become readers, writers and communicators. Lydia DuGard was by no means alone in being able to conduct a highly literate correspondence. Literacy and education enabled many women to participate in the private and public spheres and in the patronage society.

The following example, taken from the English midlands in the 1640s, provides one striking example of the way in which patriarchy was interpreted differently by several parties: eminent contemporaries saw patriarchy as protective and sustaining by nature and standing out against the harsh actions of a father. A daughter was willing to defy a father and take him to the highest court in the land to obtain her 'rights' of inheritance. Peter Temple articulated the traditional view – that children belonged to their father and that defiance and disobedience were to be punished very harshly. Parliament took a different view: a daughter and a father had duties towards one another and it was against nature for a father to allow his disobedient daughter to starve. Anne Temple, only daughter of Sir Peter and Lady Anne (Throckmorton) Temple, had defied her father in order to contract a marriage with Thomas Roper, Lord Baltinglass. During the so-called 'Irish rebellion', her new husband's estates were devastated and Anne appealed to her father for money from her future estate. Sir Peter refused and Anne appealed to Parliament for assistance. The House of Commons, through the speaker, Sir William Lenthall, ordered Sir Peter to maintain his daughter. Peter's response is instructive.

Sir my daughter . . . suffered herself to be stolne from mee, and hath matched herself not only without, but much against my liking . . . [Despite cases brought by her in the equity Court of Chancery and a petition to the King in which Anne claimed he was an 'unnatural or at least an unkind father'] nothing appeared either in Law, equity, or common reason whereupon to ground relief. I could add to these some passages of unkindness (not to style them worse) as also how often I set them aside, when so ever my Daughter made her own addresses to my self, with the duties becoming a child to a father:

But these in the particulars would exceed the list of a letter and therefore I forbear them.[49]

In his view Anne Temple belonged to her father and was his to bestow on marriage to another. She owed him obedience. When she rebelled she cut herself off from him and had no rights to any relief. Appeals to her father brought no result, at least partly because what she was asking for would further deplete his heavily indebted estate. Anne's attitude to her father was certainly not servile. She did not acknowledge Peter's mastery over her. She asserted her right to choose whom she married; she sought to protect her interest in the Temple lands. Anne tried many legal avenues available to her to no avail. But she did have the right of appeal to Parliament, a route she took which bore favourable results.

Some marriages were clearly based upon this assumption that the exchange had taken place and that the wife was subject to the husband, although the ecclesiastical law did not fully support such a view. Evidence from Sir Peter Temple's second marriage, to Christian Leveson, suggests that Sir Peter, despite his harsh patriarchal attitude to his daughter's marriage and alleged poverty, had, after an inauspicious beginning, a happy and companionate marriage in which capable Christian effectively ran the estate at Stowe, Buckinghamshire and struggled to protect the family's future in London.[50]

The fact that men and women also did not necessarily accept an authoritarian patriarchy in any of the societies under study seems well supported by the evidence, moreover. Customs and laws that were intended to enforce patriarchal 'ownership' certainly existed – as evidenced here. Shaming rituals were used to persuade husbands, fathers and masters to discipline their households in the American colonies as in the 'mother country'. In England the magistrates were involved in exposing and punishing adulterers and fornicators and the ecclesiastical (Church) courts in correcting husbands and wives who were presented for the same offences by the church wardens. The courts of the American colonies frequently punished husbands for refusing to exercise authority over their wives, children and servants, although they distinguished between the position of the wife and that of the servant. New England tithing men were employed to report household heads who failed in their duty.[51] Laws were devised to curb contrary behaviour and resolve extraordinary situations. They suggest that a substantial number of husbands were not imposing their will on their wives or controlling their behaviour, whether by conviction or by lack of authority. Sarah Harrison and James Blair stood to be married before the officiating minister in Surrey County, Virginia, in 1687. Sarah, asked whether she would obey her husband, replied 'No obey'. The minister repeated the question twice but still the answer came back, 'No obey'. The minister continued and the answer stood.[52]

There are indications that by the late seventeenth century some women in London were expressing their reservations about patriarchy in public. In one letter a woman described her sister-in-law's view that 'the Lady should have during her life an independent jurisdiction over all her female children and servants, that her husband's authority should be confined to the males, and that he should never either directly or indirectly interpose in her administration'.[53] Her views may well have described practice in many households.

Patriarchy did not, of course, imply unhappy marriages. The big question is whether many or most early modern couples lived within patriarchy as a rigid and oppressive 'system'. I would argue that for many, if not most, a view of marriage as a contractual union blessed by God and/or personal emotional attachments between individuals softened patriarchy and *almost* made it redundant, except when there was recourse to the law. Abundant unions turned by affection and devotion into true companionate marriages. Both men and women bought into some aspects of patriarchy when they married. They became committed to each other and to the success and future of their family and household. Sara Mendelson found that of twenty-one English women's diary accounts of marriage, fifteen recorded loving, companionate partnerships and six unsatisfactory marriages.[54] Lady Joan Barrington stayed with her husband throughout his imprisonment in the Marshal sea 'and nothing but death shall part thee and me'. Adam Martindale's father was so distraught at the death of his wife, being much 'disordered in his head' thereby, that his married daughter Jane had him to live with her in London. Heigham Coke of Suckley, Worcestershire, begged 'Cosen Coke' in 1705, to use his influence to prevent Heigham being chosen High Sheriff, 'my wife being dead but some months ago, my house this year being the house of mo[u]rning, I hope I may be excused'. In the early 1700s James Brydges dreamt that 'my heart [was] ready to burst with grief'[55] when he realised that his wife was dead.

A good example of a marriage which certainly knew of its ups and downs and yet operated in many ways as a companionate partnership is that of Adam and Jane Eyre in the 1640s. At times Adam sought to control his wife on the basis of patriarchal authority but found to his cost that such 'mastery' was beyond him and that the only way to achieve part of what he wanted was by rational discussion, compromise and even contract. Adam had a circle of male friends and rarely a day went past when he did not drink at the alehouse with some of them, but he and Jane also had a joint social life with other couples and with a few single people. Sometimes they met just to 'be merry'. There were also trips to Denby and to Wakefield, walks in the countryside, dinners out and expeditions to hear noted preachers. In October 1647 'after I came home toward night, my wife went with mee, and we swam the scueball [skewbald horse] in a pitt'. This Yorkshire farmer was to be found in Barnsley, shopping at 'Greene shop things for my wife', making 'my wife a place for chickens' and 'blooding' his wife's sore foot which 'bled very well'. In her turn she acted as a willing go-between in negotiating a sizeable loan from her father in exchange for an increased jointure for her. The couple, however, also quarrelled, sometimes seriously, about her property, about her (in Adam's opinion) immodest attire, about his (in her opinion) excessive drinking and bowling.

This morn my wife began, after her old manner to brawl and revile me for wishing her only to wear such apparel as was decent and comely, and accused me of treading on her sore foot, with curses and oaths, which to my knowledge I touched not . . .

Finally, at dinner, he used sex (or rather the threat of withholding sex) to try to control her.[56] He told her he 'purposed never to come in bed with her till she took more notice of what I formerly had said to her, which I pray God to give me grace to observe'. Evidently he felt that abstinence would punish him as much as her! The situation became serious. She still refused to allow him to go out bowling; he contemplated separation; she locked him out 'and said she would be the master of the house for that night'. Eventually, on January 1, he formulated a new year's resolution (perhaps in the form of a contract) whereby she would 'forbear to tell me of what is past, and [he] promised her to become a good husband to her for the time to come, and she promised me likewise she would do what I wished her in anything, save in setting her hand to papers and I promised her never to wish her thereunto'. Apparently harmony was restored for a time once Adam promised not to touch her property.[57]

The Eyre paradigm is intriguing because it shows how one of the 'middling-sort' of women was simply unwilling to accept the more objectionable aspects of patriarchy (notably her husband's lifetime interest in her property) while gladly accepting its protective and companionate elements. It also demonstrates that Adam, keen at times to assert his patriarchal authority, was ultimately able to accept the limits of that authority in the face of his wife's own legal rights (the common law insisted that her husband could do nothing with her property without her express consent), his desire for a quiet life, and his love for his wife. His wife was not helpless: she exercised a very effective veto.

Kin groups

Women can be seen building lasting relationships with parents and siblings, uncles, aunts and cousins, which provided much needed support in time of trouble and of peace: Lettice Kinnersley turned to her brother Walter; Lucy Tyrell to her brother Sir John Barrington and his wife Dorothy;[58] Anne Dormer to her sister Elizabeth Trumbull; Mary Sidney to her brother Philip; Hester Temple's children to her, to their father and to one another; Aunt Gardiner to her brother Ralph Verney and her nephew John. The examples are drawn from the whole period. There is evidence that, when arranging matches for their daughters, parents attempted to ensure that geographical separation was not great. Certainly many upper-class wider families maintained relationships not only (or even mainly) via correspondence but also through regular and quite frequent visits.[59] Letter-writing certainly helped to fill the void when visits were impossible and provided at least one very good reason for young girls to be taught to write. As Sara Mendelson and Patricia Crawford observe, the physical isolation that Anne Dormer endured was regarded as unusual and unreasonable.[60]

Kinship in England and Wales and in the English settlements in America was defined by descent from both men and women. Thus all the descendants of one's ancestors are an individual's kin by consanguinity (blood). Kin produced by marriage were distinguished as affines. In these societies each individual formed a kin group, which might be selected for a variety of reasons.[61] Such kin groups were a matter of individual choice rather than of structure or law and it has been suggested that in some cases they might be 'artificial' and include non-kin as well as kin. John E. Crowley expressed the importance of this very well when he said 'A genealogical connection between two people does not necessarily indicate how they behave toward each other. The important questions concern whether relations with extended kin were really different from those with non-kin, and what kinds of kin and how many of them were significant to individuals.'[62] The evidence points to the importance of kin groups drawn from both consanguines and affines for women, in particular. In South

Carolina, for example, where kin groups were not particularly important for males, they were seen to be important for females. In England there is a good deal of evidence from the beginning to the end of the period that while married males drew into their circles many who were not actual kin,[63] wives' circles were more restricted to kin, whether by blood or by marriage. Lady Hester Temple, for example, appears to have corresponded largely, if not entirely, with near or extended kin. Kin groups were the oil of the patronage system but they often implied a reciprocal relationship. Evidence indicates that matriarchal figures might be as dependent upon the services of sons-in-law and nephews as vice versa.

Awareness of this networking and interdependence is important when we consider the position of women heads of household. It is true that such women, whether they be widows, divorced or separated women, or singletons, had 'authority' akin to that of a male head of household but they were not necessarily the main authority figure in a network. Sometimes they were truly independent but not always and the evidence is not always available to enable the historian to be certain.

Independent and interdependent households

If we are to understand the position of the wife we also need to appreciate the complicated relationships between the generations within the extended family. The claim of the demographic historians that most households in the west were small and nuclear in composition (that is, that they consisted in the great majority of cases of husband, wife and minor children plus servants) has obscured the fact that such households frequently belonged to extended networks of families and were, in many cases, far from being independent. Any historian examining the family correspondence of elite families among the nobility and gentry cannot help but be impressed by the fact that, throughout our period, even when the couple lived in a separate household, the contact with and influence of the birth and marriage families were extensive and pervasive. The layout of genealogies demonstrates the linking of two 'houses' and the hierarchical and interdependent arrangement of the generational 'households' within each house but it often fails to capture the lateral connections formed as a result of one marital union. Relations within wider families and connections were, of course, not always harmonious but they provided a 'strong reservoir of support'.[64] Such networking was probably even more prevalent in the American colonies. In Charlestown Massachusetts, for example, merchant planters formed 25 per cent of the population but controlled

70 per cent of the land and 'exerted power through an extensive network of intermarriage, socializing and child exchange, while the town's poor lived as boarders, often with their employers, or shared housing'.[65] Few were left as 'independent' as was Eliza Lucas.

In parts of colonial America women left in charge of huge estates *were* sometimes remote from family support. Eliza Lucas was only seventeen when in 1739 her father, Lt Colonel George Lucas of the British Army, was called to serve in Antigua and left her in sole charge of 5,000 acres in South Carolina for five years. Communication was poor and Eliza was left to her own devices. She developed into an enterprising businesswoman. Provided with seeds from the West Indies, she experimented with growing indigo and producing blue dye cakes for export, thus helping to transform the local economy. She also planted an orchard of fig trees in order to dry and export the fruit. When she planted oaks it was with an eye to the building of ships in the future. She also taught herself law and began to use her knowledge by drawing up wills for neighbours and acting as a trustee for a widow's estate. Eliza eventually married, had three children, and returned to England for a while. In 1658 she and her husband, Charles Pinckney, a wealthy lawyer and Carolina landholder, came back to South Carolina but, because her husband fell victim to a fatal attack of malaria, Eliza was once again left to run the estates. This she did so successfully that in 1779 she was able to lend the State of South Carolina a large sum of money.[66]

More typically, the case of Hester Temple, matriarch of Stowe in the first half of the seventeenth century, illustrates the way in which women fitted into the patronage system within the Temple family connection. Hester's clients were her children and their spouses, her grandchildren and her and their servants. But her own children, male and female, had their own clients and exercised their own patronage. These same children also had other patrons, for example, their fathers and fathers-in-law and mothers-in-law and powerful figures in church and state. Moreover, the children accessed the patronage of their parents, parents-in-law and siblings.

Clinging to birth family

It is important to note that, while there are discernible patterns in the way that marriage affected partners and especially the women, there are many such patterns.

For a section of the English elite, marriage did not bring with it immediate exchange of household and authority figure. It seems to have been far from uncommon for a youthful bride to remain for some time within her parents' home, apart from or with her spouse. This would be part of the marriage settlement and had obvious financial benefits for both sides. Sometimes the young couple lived with the parents of one or other spouse. Sally Gosling believes that it was normally with the groom's parents.[67] In the fifteenth century John Cotesmore, the under-age ward of Thomas Stonor II, and his young bride Thomas's daughter continued to live with the Stonor family in Oxfordshire for some time.[68] Often this arrangement was seen as attractive financially when it came to coming to an agreement of marriage. In May 1580 Robard Bacon was encouraged to accept a young woman in marriage on the lure of £80 per annum and a year's bed and board in her mother's house. In 1564 Francis Willoughby contracted to marry Mistress Elizabeth Littleton of Frankley, Warwickshire, partly because her father was providing three years' bed and board for the couple and their six servants.[69] Lady Elizabeth Masham was sceptical about the suitability of a match between her daughter Joan Altham and an unnamed suitor because his father was not prepared for the couple to live with him after marriage.[70] Anne Fitton, aged twelve-and-a-half, married John Newdigate, aged sixteen, in 1587. For seven years after their marriage the couple lived in her parents' home, while her husband spent much time at the university.[71] When Anne Finch married diplomat Edward Conway on 17 February 1651, correspondence indicates that Anne, aged twenty, continued to live at home in Kensington for the next few years, probably because of her ill health which made it impossible for her to travel abroad with her husband during his foreign postings.[72] The pattern of betrothal before the groom's education was complete seems to have been common in the early sixteenth century: William Blount, Lord Mountjoy was betrothed to an heiress, Elizabeth Say, before he went to Paris to extend his education; he was recalled in 1497 to marry Elizabeth but, as they were both still very young, she continued to live with her parents in Bedfordshire for a while.[73] Dorothy Percy was trained in housewifery in the household of her mother-in-law, the Viscountess Lisle – one of the purposes of the bride living with her parents-in-law was that she should learn the way their household was to be conducted. After her marriage to Robert Sidney, both while Robert was abroad completing his education and after he returned, the couple lived with his parents for some time.[74] Many another bride remained with her parents for a while, but this would be a temporary arrangement. Elizabeth Carey (Carew) (1585–1639), the only daughter of Sir Laurence and Lady Elizabeth Tanfield of Burford Hall Oxfordshire, married Sir Henry Carey in 1602 but was allowed to remain at her parents' home while Henry fought in the Netherlands. In 1603 her mother-in-law insisted that Elizabeth live with her new family.[75] Later, in 1636, Elizabeth Bassett, aged only fifteen, married nineteen-year-old John Egerton and remained at home alone with her family because she was 'too young to be bedded'. When the Civil War began she was with her mother and sisters, Jane and Frances, at Welbeck Abbey while William and his two sons, Charles and Henry, were fighting with the Royalist forces. When Elizabeth Willoughby married John Gell of Derbyshire in the early seventeenth century, he went to study at Oxford and she stayed with her father.[76] At around the same time, her brother Francis married Cassandra Ridgway; he departed for a Grand Tour shortly after the wedding and she stayed with her parents.[77]

Marrying a young bride seemed advantageous to the whole of the bridegroom's family. The young woman could be more easily accustomed by her mother-in-law and her husband to the ways of her new family. Elizabeth Clinton was one of three daughters and co-heiresses of Elizabeth Stumpe and Sir Henry Knevett (or Knyvett) of Charlton, Wiltshire. At the age of only ten, some time after 21 September 1584, Elizabeth was married to Thomas Clinton, who became 3rd Earl of Lincoln in 1616 and whose estate then included Tattershall Castle, Sempringham Manor (the principal home, it seems, of the family), and town houses in Boston and London. Their thirty-four-year marriage produced a phenomenal total of eighteen children, several of whom died young. In 1622 Elizabeth, now dowager Countess, encouraged Bridget (Fiennes) Clinton, her daughter-in-law and Countess of Lincoln, to breastfeed her children. In the context of the present chapter it is important to note that the teenage Elizabeth's own wish to suckle her own children had been overruled either by her husband or her mother-in-law and that she had lived to regret this for many reasons: 'partly I was overuled by another's authority, and partly deceived by some ill counsel, and partly I had not so well considered of my duty in this motherly office, as since I did, when it was too late for me to put it into execution'. Observing the example set by her daughter-in-law Bridget, she counselled breastfeeding. Typically she held back from arguing that women should have control over their own bodies per se and appealed instead to the teaching of the Bible that women should suckle their offspring. Following through her argument that maternal nursing is the will of God, husbands who assert their secondary authority over their wives by forbidding breastfeeding are contradicting the ultimate authority of God, to the peril of their souls and the health of their children.[78]

Parents frequently sought partners for their daughters relatively close at hand so that contact might be maintained. Elite couples, however, eventually had to face up to a greater geographical separation from their respective parents than did couples lower down the social scale, and arrangements such as those of the Ferrars and Collets of Little Gidding were unusual.

More common among the middling sort was delayed marriage until the young couple could afford a home of their own or until the male inherited property. (The emergence of a 'middling sort' and of new professions in Scottish burghs has been noted by historians and this might suggest a similar delayed marriage pattern.[79]) Young people experienced a period of semi-independence. They did not achieve true independence until they set up house together. Such independence might be more apparent than real, however. In tiny communities newly married couples frequently lived very close to their parents and maintained continuities and connections on a daily basis. In Myddle under the Tudors and Stuarts the daughters of tenant farmers perhaps did not marry parishioners but they generally married local Shropshire men and lived within a day's journey of their birth families.[80] Almost a half of the eighty-two families in Wigston Magna, Leicestershire, in 1670 had been resident there for over a hundred years.[81] On the other side of the Atlantic this pattern was preferred when circumstances permitted. When John Adams married Abigail Smith in 1760s Massachusetts they moved into a house John inherited from his father, only yards away from the house opposite where he had been living with his mother in Braintree. Abigail took with her one of her mother's black servants. Abigail was in many respects the archetypal independent, self-sufficient woman, yet she visited her parents (who lived but five miles distant) and her grandparents at least once a week and her sister even more frequently.[82]

This said, another pattern was also common enough to be observed by contemporaries. Young women moved well away from their parents' home, either because they spent time at boarding school or as servants in another house and for one reason or another never returned permanently to live at home, or because they moved away in search of fame and fortune. Circumstances on both sides of the Atlantic frequently militated against continued dependence on the wife's family. John Adams's political career meant that Abigail had to spend at least part of her married life in Boston. In the 1780s Abigail Bailey had to move with her husband Asa to the tiny nascent community of Bath, New Hampshire, away from the support of her birth family but in close proximity to her abusive husband's many relatives.[83] While migrants and emigrants often moved en masse as a family or group of families, this was not inevitable.

Poor labourers were probably those who clung least to their birth families (and labourers formed on average between one-third and one-half of the whole population) but the term 'labourer' covered a wide spectrum. Many 'labourers' were migrant workers who seized opportunities for housing and employment where they arose. Shropshire, with its woodlands and its waste, presented many from other places with an excellent opportunity for squatting and setting up independent cottages. These homes were often worse than those set up by colonists on the moving frontier of North America and were erected using local brushwood. For example, in the seventeenth century in Myddle the Chidlows lived in 'a poor pitiful hut, built up to an old oak' and two families lived in caves. Some labourers were previously husbandmen who had hit hard times. Some combined labouring with a craft. At the other end of the labourers' scale, however, were families such as the Hanmers who came from local farming families in the 1570s and built a solid one-room cottage in Myddlewood. Between that date and 1700 this was extended with another small ground-floor room and a one-acre garden. One can only speculate on the extent to which the Hanmers maintained the male connections with his birth family: they may well have earned their living labouring on the family holding. As time went by, however, relations with the labouring classes were cemented: Abraham Hamner married the only daughter and 'heiress' of another labourer.

Expectations of one another

Men and women frequently married for love and, even when romantic love was not present initially, they hoped and expected that love would be discovered during the marriage itself.[84] This seems to have been as true of the beginning of our period as of the end. The tomb of Edward Courtney, Earl of Devon, dated 1509 and situated in Tiverton church, is adorned with a verse that bears witness to his loving union with Katherine:

Lo, lo, who lies here?
'Tis I, the good Earle of Devonshire
With Kate my Wife, to me full dear,
We lived together fifty five year.
That we spent, we had;
That we left, we lost;
That wee gave, wee have.

This discovery and capture love and affection, of course, was not the same as marrying for love but Lawrence Stone's portrayal of medieval and Tudor marriages as loveless and cold bears little scrutiny. The prospect of mutual hostility was not relished.

Accounts of unhappy marriages are interesting because they often reveal that the expectations of both men and women were not being met. For example, Lettice (Bagot) Kinnersley drew her brother's attention to the problems in her own marriage because she knew that her husband's behaviour towards her (and the behaviour of her mother-in-law) would be regarded as unacceptable.

I borrowed of my neighbours as much as I could yet for all that the fault was laid all upon me: with many bitter curses and the charge of the house taken from me, and commanded to meddle with nothing: but keep my chamber: my servants discharged especially she that looks to my children: and is a bout my self.

We see that the blame for her husband's treatment of her was laid on her mother-in-law. 'He would never be half so ill, but for his mother, now her maid useth to stand at my door to hear what I say and then tells my mother in law and makes it more.' She knew that her husband's wrath would subside 'but she must have the over sight of all and then shall not I be able to stay'. This little tale of power relations within an elite family, on further examination, reveals something much more interesting. It was a tale constructed by Lettice herself. Taken on its own it tells of a violent marriage in which poor Lettice is the victim, Francis the ogre, his mother the wicked witch and brother Bagot Lettice's only refuge, but taken in the context of other Kinnersley–Bagot letters they tell a tale of a marriage which, if not happy, had been nonetheless at times a partnership. For in better times Lettice and her husband boarded with Margaret and William Trew in order to avoid the interference of Kinnersley's parents, and Lettice was wont to ask Walter for help to further Francis's interests. Moreover, Lettice describes a relationship with her husband and with her household which she sees, and expects her brother to see, as unnatural and intolerable. She and Francis do not have 'independence' because they live with the widowed matriarch. Lettice expected either Walter or Anthony to intercede with Francis on her behalf and negotiate a settlement whereby she would live elsewhere, in charge of her children, with a mere maintenance. In 1609 she displayed considerable initiative concerning financial matters when she reached desperate straits, asking her brother to arrange a lease to provide £100 for the maintenance of her younger sons (tactfully named for her brothers, Walter and Anthony). She did this, she explained, because 'my means is so small for house keeping, that my husband is weary of tarrying here, but it doeth not much trouble him, my wants and his poor children, which was never greater than now: and yet I fear, when my corn is gone, it will be worse: which will not be long to . . .' Not only is Lettice resourceful, she has a 'family' who will give her practical assistance in time of need. Married women with children could find themselves being treated like naughty children and need the support of their blood relatives.

Dorothy, the younger daughter of Sir Francis Willoughby, made a good match in the later sixteenth century to Henry Hastings, second son of George, Earl of Huntington, 'who used her barbarously, in so much that in some of her letters she says she is in fear of her life, and expects to be poisoned, she after writes that her husband denies her the use of his coach, and will allow her neither money nor clothes which forced her to write many begging letters to her sister Bridgitt Willoughby for such necessaries as she wanted. I find her husband would have forced her to sell her lands and her refusing it, I believe was the reason which made him use her so ill.'[85]

When Bridget Willoughby described *her* groom as her 'Master' he countered immediately that he was:

amazed to see her term him a Master to her, whom in heart he honours, in duty reverences, in love and loyalty faithfully serves and obeys, and of whom he always desired; and to his power deserved, to be entertained as a faithful friend and servant, remaining in her power and pleasure to be wholly commanded etc. He writes that we unadvisedly sowing ye seeds of our joys, are altogether ignorant when to make our harvest . . . doubt you not of this; that I love, and live, to be only yours.[86]

When all allowances are made for the effects of love in its first flush upon a young man, he was certainly expressing the complex relationship between a husband and wife. He was her master but she was also his mistress – each was the servant of the other.

When we examine the records of actual marriages, the patriarchal system accommodates the idea that in the conjugal partnership the partners were interdependent. This idea can be found from the top to the bottom of the social scale in England. More down-to-earth than the love-lorn Willoughby newly-weds, a bedridden London Porter, John Accors, in 1595 lamented how when the stairs were removed from his house 'his wife is debarred from his society, and comfort' thus depriving him of 'that attendance and looking unto which a man in his case ought to have but is in great misery'. He petitioned the vestry of St Saviour's to place him in a house 'wherein he may have the society of his wife to help to comfort him in this his extremity and also to keep him clean and sweet and to help relive him'. A wife would offer solace through her affectionate company as well as physical care.

It was not only the poor who valued such a relationship. Samuel Pepys relied on his wife as housekeeper but he also relied on her for conversation and missed her companionship when she was absent from him. John Evelyn depended on Mary, Thomas Temple on Hester and James Brydges on Cassandra. Ralph and Mary Josselin shared a comfortable and companionable married life.

This kind of expectation of compatibility and happiness also seems to have been common in the colonies. In the later eighteenth century, colonists in Massachusetts even assumed that loss of conjugal affection was a legitimate ground for divorce. Whereas between 1736 and 1765 petitioners never claimed the loss of a spouse's love as a grievance, between 1766 and 1786 one-tenth of petitioners did so. We read that 'he ceased to cherish her', 'she had almost broken his heart', 'all conjugal affection has fled'. If we look at the relationship between the future President, John Adams, and his wife, Abigail, we are struck by the reciprocity of their relationship.

Natural authority relations

In all these societies it was normal (although far from inevitable) that there should be an age gap between the husband and wife on first marriage – the bridegroom would be a few years older than the bride. In many cases this age differential was considerable and in those cases there was perhaps a natural authority relationship, because of age, between the husband and wife. It could be argued, moreover, that men's far greater access to education accentuated this natural authority relation. In many instances husbands tutored their wives and did so in ways congenial to themselves. The evidence is, however, susceptible to several interpretations. John Verney (1640–1717) married as his first wife in May 1680 sixteen-year-old Elizabeth Palmer. Initially they lived with her parents. When he leased a house for them in April 1681 he decorated the house and made all the decisions, relieving her of all responsibility.[87] Elizabeth was also his social inferior and this was probably one cause of this behaviour on his part; his house had to be appropriately fitted out for a polite society with which his young bride, the daughter of a 'mechanic' of the middling sort, was not familiar.

Young brides did not always regard their spouses with awe. The case of Mary Wroth springs to mind: she married Sir Robert Wroth when she was only seventeen and the pair had little in common.[88] She had abiding interests in literature while he was obsessed with hunting. Early in their marriage Robert reported to his father that 'there was some what that doth discontent him' intimating that this had something to do with 'her carriage towards him'.[89] It was unsurprising that Mary formed a secret and long-lasting liaison with her cousin William Herbert, with whom she had much more in common and by whom she bore two illegitimate children, although she and Robert were properly reconciled before his death in 1614.[90] Elizabeth Tanfield was only seventeen when she married Sir Henry Carey but she was always independent and determined to follow her own conscience, notwithstanding her husband's efforts. Not only did she openly embrace Catholicism against his wishes but also tried to use her influence with Queen Henrietta Maria to her husband's political advantage. He was not impressed:

For her abilities in agency of affairs, as I was never taken with opinion of them, so I was never desirous to employ them if she had them, for I conceive women to be no fit solicitors of state affairs . . . for my part I should take much more comfort to hear that she were quietly retired to her Mother's in the country.[91]

Barbara Harris has shown how relationships within a marriage also developed: Lady Anne Lestrange may have married as a child and played a marginal role in management of household and estates at first, but she grew into a force to be reckoned with, who cared for both household and estates when her husband found favour at court in the 1530s and when she herself had ceased childbearing.[92]

In such examples we could be facing variant family traditions – with some being reared in families that emphasised the companionate nature of marriage within patriarchy and the positive contribution to be made by capable women, and some being brought up in families that stressed the authoritarian relationship, with the contribution to be made by the wife strictly delineated by her husband. But we could also be looking at different stages in the typical 'marriage cycle'.

Conclusion

Patriarchy was a system not designed for oppression but for family-focused governance and protection, and the continuance of the line. There is no doubt that within patriarchy the individual's needs and wishes were sacrificed to those of the 'house' and that the ultimate authority lay with the household head, who was normally an adult married man. The circumstances of marriage have to be taken into account when considering the virtues and defects of the system – when many wives were inexperienced adolescents and when a family's survival chances were precarious. As with all human societies, there were extremes of behaviour – with men claiming absolute and God-given superiority and sometimes treating their wives, children and servants with extreme cruelty, and women resisting such oppression. It is small wonder that historians have given considerable attention to such instances, which are frequently couched in the colourful language of the controversial pamphlet or the court case. But these were examples of extreme behaviour and not an approved norm. The difference was between what we might term dysfunctional and functional families. On the whole, the system seems to have worked well and was acknowledged by contemporaries as doing so.

Notes

1 *Spectator*, 1712.
2 See 'Wives and property', Chapter 11 for a discussion of women's property 'rights' and related issues.
3 M. Griffith, *Bethel: or a forme for families in which all sorts of both sexes, are so squared, and framed by the word of God, as they may best serve in their severall places, for useful pieces in God's building*, 1633, p. 323.
4 S. Hull (1982) p. 140; see also H. Smith (1976) p. 177.
5 K. Walker (1996) pp. 31–3; I owe this point to S. Gosling (1999) pp. 31–2.
6 Examples include F. Nussbaum (1984); P. Malekin (1981); A. Fraser (1984).
7 A. Fletcher (1995); see especially pp. 401–13.
8 Rosemary O'Day (1995).
9 S. D. Amussen (1995) pp. 48–68.
10 Bernard Capp (1996) pp. 125–30.
11 Amussen (1995) p. 52.
12 M. J. M. Ezell (1987) p. 61.
13 Joseph Swetnam, *Arraignment of Lewd, Idle, Froward and Inconstant Women*, 1615. For an accessible edition of some of this literature see S. G. O'Malley (2004).

14 Patrick Hannay, *The Happy Husband*, 1622, cited in Ezell (1987) p. 37.
15 See R. O'Day (1995) pp. 64–128 and 137–45 for a discussion of partnership and parental authority in the household.
16 John Brinsley, *A Looking-glasse for good women*, 1645, pp. 38–9, cited in Ezell (1987) p. 39.
17 M. J. M. Ezell (1987) p. 143.
18 J. M. Bennett (1989) pp. 259–63.
19 S. Gosling (1999) p. 258.
20 Gosling (1999) p. 116; see Richard Braithwaite, *The English gentleman*, 1630; Richard Braithwaite, *The English gentlewoman*, 1631, dedicatory letter.
21 See N. Canny (1982) for a study of an elite family that was both patriarchal and affectionate.
22 Anon (T. E.) *The Lawes resolutions of womens rights*, p. 157 shows that the common law also provided for exceptions to coverture when a wife had been abandoned, whether through desertion, flight overseas or imprisonment.
23 T. Stretton (1998) esp. pp. 143–54; Johan Morgan v. John Andrewes, PRO Req 2/166/129, cited in Stretton p. 144.
24 J. Greenberg (1975) p. 178; A. L. Erickson (1993) p. 115.
25 M. Ingram (1987) pp. 219–91; Stretton (1998) pp. 144–5.
26 Stretton (1998) pp. 144–5; John Baker, *Introduction to English Legal History*, 1979, p. 562, n. 74.
27 J. T. Johnson (1971) pp. 107–18; A. Taves (1989) p. 11.
28 D. Meyers (2003) The quotations are taken from the foreword. Meyers studied well over 3,000 wills and many other types of documentation for her exciting study.
29 T. L. Snyder (2003).
30 A. Kulikoff (1986).
31 D. B. Smith (1980).
32 J. Fliegelman (1982); M. Yazawa (1985).
33 R. Middleton (1992) p. 220.
34 HEH, STT 2326 Correspondence Sir Thomas Temple from Dassett to Sir Peter Temple at Stowe 7 Aug 1631.
35 He is the lawyer who married Elizabeth Akers c.1591. See Chapter 4.
36 HEH, STT 2418 Sir Thomas Tyringham to Sir William Andrewes, 31 Dec 1625.

37 HEH, STT 40 William Andrewes to Sir Thos Tyringham at Tyringham 31 Dec 1625.

38 HEH, STT 1366 Sir John Lenthall to Sir Thos Temple at Biddlesden 4 Jan 1625/6.

39 HEH, STT 2342 Sir Thomas Temple to Sir Thomas Tyringham 11 Jan 1625/6.

40 HEH, STT 2273, 14 Jan 1625/6 Copy of letter from Sir Thomas Temple to Sir Richard Neuman 14 Jan 1625/6.

41 HEH, STT 17 Anne Andrewes to George Abbot Archbishop of Canterbury 1626.

42 Keith Thomas (1959) pp. 200–202.

43 HEH, STT 41 Sir William Andrewes to Sir Peter Temple, 13 Nov 1634.

44 HEH, STT 19 Anne Andrewes to her mother Lady Hester Temple c.1627–1637 (her father died in 1637).

45 BL Lansdowne MS 460, no. 30; also cited in A. T. Friedman (1986) pp. 549–50.

46 HMCR, Finch MSS, (77), Petition of Philip, earl of Pembroke, to Parliament (12 July 1659).

47 N. Taylor (2003) pp. 6–7.

48 Such marriages between cousins-german had been legal since 1563 but still provoked a good deal of controversy.

49 HEH, STT 2044 Sir Peter Temple to William Lenthall, Speaker 5 July 1643.

50 HEH, STT 2054 Sir Peter Temple from Barrow, [near Bristol] to Lady Christian Temple 9 May 1653.

51 S. Coontz (1988) pp. 111–12; E. Morgan (1966) p. 45.

52 *Virginia Magazine of History and Biography*, VII (January 1900) p. 278.

53 BL Add Ms 61, 687, fo. 175, Letter 36, c.1709, cited in H. Berry (2003) p. 42.

54 S. H. Mendelson (1985) p. 193.

55 HEH, STB 26. Vol. 2.

56 There are many examples of women using sexual blackmail to manipulate their husbands. See, for example, how Frances Berkeley treated Governor Thomas Berkeley when she returned to live with him in 1677: [I expect my 'feavour' but when Lady Frances] 'lay by me last night . . . God helpe us nothing but vocal kindnesse past betweene us'. (Sir William Berkeley to Francis Moryson, 21 Feb 1677, Coventry Papers, Vol. 77 fol. 426.)

57 H. J. Morehouse (1875) pp. 10, 12–13, 15, 19, 67–8, 116, 49, 39, 42, 49, 54, 84.

58 G. A. Loundes (1878) p. 40 transcription of letter from Lucy Tyrell to John and Dorothy Barrington, undated.
59 See below for the way in which frequent visiting established and cemented networks.
60 S. Mendelson and P. Crawford (1998) p. 146.
61 A. Macfarlane (1970) provides a highly accessible account of how such kin groups operated.
62 J. E. Crowley (1986) p. 561.
63 Although men also relied heavily on kin as the Temple correspondence testifies.
64 See Christine Carpenter (1996) p. 26. She shows that self-interest in most instances prevented family friction from getting out of control.
65 Ralph J. Crandall (1979), 'Family types, social structure and mobility in early America: Charlestown, Massachusetts, a case study', in V. Tufte and B. Myerhoff (eds), *Changing Images of the Family*, 1979.
66 Donna M. Lucey (2005) pp. 47–9.
67 S. Gosling (1999) p. 43.
68 Christine Carpenter (1996) p. 25, citing nos 109 and 110.
69 HL, STB, Box 2, Ridgeway–Willoughby descent, pp. 16–17.
70 BL Egerton MS 2645, f. 84, Letter from Lady Elizabeth Masham to Lady Joan Barrington, undated. Discussed in L. Stone (1977) p. 634.
71 Vivienne Larminie (2001) p. 95.
72 Marjorie Hope Nicholson (1992).
73 See Maria Perry (2002) p. 16.
74 L.-R. Betcherman (2005) pp. 34, 48.
75 S. P. Cerasano and Marion Wynne-Davis (1996) p. 43.
76 HEH, STB Box 2, Book 3, p. 15.
77 HEH, STB Box 2, Book 3, p. 42.
78 Elizabeth Clinton, *The Countess of Lincolnes Nurserie*, 1622, pp. 15–16.
79 See, for example, Helen Dingwall, *Physicians, surgeons and apothecaries: Medical training and practice in seventeenth-century Edinburgh*, 1995.
80 See, for example, Thomas II of the Formston family, who married the daughter of the local blacksmith in 1593 and whose two surviving daughters married local men. See David G. Hey (1974) p. 129.
81 W. G. Hoskins (1957) p. 96.
82 Lynne Withey (2000) p. 21.

83 Ann Taves (1989) pp. 6–7.
84 See the preceding chapter for further exploration of this idea.
85 FSL, Bagot Collection, L.a. 598, 14 September 1608, Lettice Kinnersley to Walter Bagot.
86 HEH, STB Box 2, Book 2, p. 21r.
87 Susan E. Whyman (2002 pbk) pp. 61–2.
88 S. R. Cerasano and M. Wynne-Davis (1996).
89 HMC, De L'Isle, III, 140 cited in J. A. Roberts (1983) p. 12.
90 J. A. Roberts (1983) p. 23.
91 M. O'Dowd (ed.), *Calendar of State Papers Ireland Tudor Period 1571–1575*, 2000, p. 63.
92 B. J. Harris (2002) p. 67.

CHAPTER 8

Partnership and separation

My father and mother were very industrious in their children's infancy, and in a few years had improved their estate . . . Our parents were very careful to get us learning to read . . . Our parents were of the communion of the Episcopal Protestant religion . . . and a good example to their children and servants and neighbours, and instructed us their children in the church catechism so called.[1]

Introduction

Contemporary English and Welsh Protestant preachers urged that marriage was a partnership. Their emphasis was not upon the marriage as property exchange or a relationship within the patriarchal system but upon marriage as shared responsibilities and joys. The male spouse was the houseband, the female was the housewife. Sometimes we can see this partnership in operation at all levels of society. Elizabeth Dickinson, aged twenty-eight, was the youngest of five daughters 'of substantial parents in good circumstances' in Hale, Westmoreland, when she married thirty-three-year-old Mr Stout, a yeoman of Lancashire in the late 1650s. Their second son William described their marriage as a partnership in the quotation that begins this present chapter. Of course, he does not comment directly on the equality of the partnership – there was no need to because the two persons joined in Christian matrimony were one person and equality was not an issue. As we saw in the preceding chapter on the process of marrying, everything was done to ensure that such unity was unimpeded and harmony guaranteed. Partners were preferably from the same social and economic strata and shared the same religion and culture.

Their families and friends thoroughly approved the match and the couple found one another suitable in every way. A similar kind of partnership operated in the slightly earlier marriage of Sir Thomas and Lady Hester Temple of Stowe, for instance. Examples can be found of such partnerships elsewhere throughout our period, in the case of the Americas perpetuating a tradition inherited from the Old World. One thinks of the marriage of the Reverend William Smith and Elizabeth Quincy in Weymouth, Massachusetts, in the 1730s and 1740s and their daughter Abigail's marriage with John Adams in pre-revolutionary Boston.

Sometimes marriages which had not been approved by relatives also resulted in lasting and effective partnerships and occasionally in a union where the wife seems to have been acknowledged as the more capable partner. Margaret Lucas, later Duchess of Newcastle, whose parents had married in awkward circumstances, was to reflect upon their cooperation and above all on her mother Elizabeth Leighton Lucas's role in managing the estate as well as rearing two sons and five daughters. Margaret described her mother as 'ver[y] skilful in leases, and setting of lands, and court keeping, ordering of stewards, and the like affairs'.[2]

Active partnerships

There are many examples of the ways in which married couples shared their lives. Already we have noted the example of the yeoman farmers, the Eyres, in Yorkshire in the mid-seventeenth century. The diary of a member of the elite, James Brydges, later Duke of Chandos, in the 1690s shows his closeness with his first wife, the extent to which they shared a social life and the degree to which they had semi-independent social lives. When his wife was ill in January 1697/8, James remained at home, anxiously watching over her. Male and female friends and relatives visited, and cheered the couple up with conversation about current affairs. Only when she was recovered sufficiently did he go to dinner with Lady Daws and Sir William Hooker at Greenwich. There was no post-prandial parting of the sexes and the women of the party contributed to the conversation: 'After dinner all our talk was of Mr Lumly, Lady Daws and Lady Hooker seemed to blame his conduct very much.' Then he returned home and caught up with news of his wife's visitors. About a week later 'my Mother, Sister Jacob, and sister Catharine came in to see us, and played at cards till half an hour after nine'. Other activities during that spring and summer included attending church and taking the sacrament with his wife, taking walks in the park, going shopping with her to purchase damask, viewing the portrait he was having painted of her, noting her blood-letting, numerous dinner and card parties and conversations and, when she was in good health, almost daily taking her out in the coach and dropping her off to see friends and then arranging to pick her up later to bring her home. There were activities that he did not share with her. For example, ladies had a separate box at the 'play' and, unlike their husbands, actually seem to have watched the performance rather than using the theatre as a convenient venue for catching up with current news. Similarly, Sir James toured the coffee houses on his own, presumably for the same reasons. Unlike some well-known diarists, he makes no mention of using the coffee houses and taverns to pick up whores.[3] Of course, the lives that the married Brydges led contrasted markedly with those of couples such as the Eyres, or even the Temples, who spent a good deal of their time managing their estates and other family business. The Brydges' days were days of being in society, often uncluttered by 'work' in the conventional sense but James was using his and Mary's 'social contacts' to obtain office and the point is that James and Mary did choose to spend a significant proportion of their leisure time together and in a society where this was considered the norm.

Thomas Tusser's manual made it clear for his readers that 'to thrive thou must wive'. In this book, primarily aimed at farmers, Tusser described the ideal traditional partnership. Wives worked in the house and also cared for the poultry and the dairy;[4] males worked outside the house in the fields and were also active in the community. Many farmers' families did not, however, abide by his prescription because they could not afford to. At sowing time, especially in the absence of day labour, wives and daughters were sometimes called upon to plough and sow; at harvest time they were prepared to lend their labour. This is not to say that they were expected to do the most strenuous work. For instance women were usually restricted to using the sickle rather than the scythe. Women went to market with their produce and shared in decision-making about the farm. Some married women acted as midwives, as nurses, as wet-nurses and as carers within the community. Tusser's manual, moreover, said nothing of the partnerships between day labourers (the large majority of the population), between craft and tradespeople, or partnerships between professional men and their wives or aristocrats and their wives. Cottagers' and day labourers' wives could not afford to remain at home when there was work to be had on the land. In Scotland, female day labourers were paid less than half the wages paid to men; in England women received about two-thirds of the average male wage. These disparities were probably in recognition of the heavier work done by men and of their increased dietary demands: it was accepted without question that males (and especially those involved in manual labour) needed twice as much food as women. Poor urban women, both single and married, might resort to prostitution and to occupations which shared its shady reputation. For instance, in 1580 the Edinburgh council tried to stop the activities of female water-carriers who were 'employed' by citizens. In the 1570s, pledge women or brogers went from door to door in Leicester reputedly selling second-hand clothing and household stuff and the authorities tried to clamp down upon this trade. Wives of craftsmen and tradesmen, along with their daughters, commonly shared in the manufacturing and retail side of the husband's enterprise. John Dunton, printer of the 1690s periodical *Athenian Mercury* described his wife Elizabeth as: 'Bookseller, cash-keeper, [she] managed all my affairs for me, and left me entirely to my own rambling and scribbling humours.'[5] In some cases this had led over the centuries to women carving out a distinct by-employment. Many women were involved in spinning and weaving cloth at home and made some cloth for sale. In seventeenth-century Wales they took their goods to a special cloth market.[6]

Not everyone approved of these kinds of partnership. Married women suffered as a result of both economic and moral pressure. In England, Scotland and Wales during the later Middle Ages, men produced the malt but women dominated the brewing and selling of ale, initially as a by-product of their domestic work. When these manufactures and trades were under economic pressure, there were attempts to exclude women.[7] Alewives became less common, however, not only as a result of guild regulations but also as a result of the introduction of beer made with hops, which was financially beyond most brewsters. In the sixteenth century what had been a virtual monopoly of brewing by married women (where women were acknowledged as brewsters by the guilds) became a largely male preserve; married women worked for their husbands and they sold ale bought from male brewers and sold in houses owned by men.[8] Henry Stocker of Salisbury said in 1585 that he 'mainly lives by selling and distributing ale wherein he employs his wife'.[9] Such developments probably occurred at different rates within the British Islands. Hop beer, for example, was very slow in arriving in Wales and Devon so that brewsters were common until the late seventeenth century but the pattern, albeit staggered, was a general one. In Scotland and elsewhere a moral panic was raised in the second half of the sixteenth century by the presence of so many female servants selling alcohol to males, and by suspected prostitution. This resulted in a considerable number of prosecutions of taverners for employing women to sell the ale.[10] As Christine Peters has observed, this led to increased efforts to exclude women from manufacture, retail and other jobs unless they were under the control of a husband or master.

Professionals such as clergymen relied upon their wives' labour within the home (and, in the case of rural clergy, on the glebeland) as well as within the parish. Small wonder that until the present day parishioners have looked askance at unmarried clergy – not only because they posed a threat to their daughters but also because a parson's wife engaged in a charitable ministry of her own among the elderly, the sick, the women and the children of the parish.

There is evidence that husbands throughout the period expected their wives to act as their deputies and also as channels of communication. When they were separated, women were expected to write to their husbands. When their husbands were away from home, the wives of men of property were left to take charge of both household and estates. When estates were spread out over several counties, a wife might be expected to take responsibility for particular estates and especially lands that formed part of her jointure. These women, like their husbands, had servants and stewards to assist them but they had overall control and responsibility and had to make plans and decisions, and communicate instructions. They learned how to read and write, at least in part, in order to pursue such duties. Wives also travelled to and from their country estates, often including the capital city in their routine both for business and pleasure.[11]

A wife could, as has been noted, also be an important business asset. For example, Elizabeth Stonor in the fifteenth century spent a good deal of her time in London away from her husband William and the family home in Oxfordshire. She had independent wealth and established business connections through her first husband, Master Thomas Rich, a London mercer. Indeed she may well have continued to act independently as a mercer after his death and her marriage to Stonor. In the 1470s she helped establish connections between Stonor and the merchant Thomas Betson, which led to a profitable business partnership in the wool-export area (which she helped coordinate) and the marriage of Thomas and their daughter Kathryn.[12] Her correspondence also shows her active involvement in household and estate affairs during her marriage to William Stonor.

There is every indication that this idea of active partnership informed marriages in the American colonies. Debra Meyers believes that this was especially true of marriages among Anglicans, Catholics and Quakers who shared a belief in free will and she argues that this was also true of England. 'Arminian Anglican women exerted authority in the household as partners in their marriages. Husbands consulted them about the important matter of the dispersal of wealth through the family . . . [and] also about substantive donations to the church.' When John Contee died in 1708, four witnesses declared that he had refused to sign his last will and testament until he was sure that his wife 'was satisfied' with it, and had asked her 'if there was anything she disliked saying it should be altered'. John Rousby, a Quaker of Calvert County, described in his will how he and his wife had varied his original bequests to children 'upon second thoughts and my wife's desire concerning my debts'. Other testators described their wives as 'yoke fellows' during life's journey and bore witness to their business acumen and flair for management. This language had parallels in English Anglican and Catholic wills of the period.[13] Meyers's statistical analysis of Maryland wills shows that Anglicans and Catholics frequently left their wives freehold property (often seemingly their jointure land) whereas Calvinists often did not and sometimes even left their wives with less than the thirds.[14] Meyers grants that very well-to-do Calvinists more closely conformed to the Catholic/Anglican pattern.[15] Significantly a majority of Anglicans and Catholics gave their wives power as executors whereas Calvinists did not. Calvinists more often assumed that their wives were incapable of caring for an estate.[16] Meyers has also discovered that more Quaker, Anglican and Catholic wives and widows made wills than did Calvinist.[17]

Reciprocal contract

Marriage in England and her colonies was a reciprocal contract. When he married, the man agreed to provide food, shelter and raiment for his wife. Women in all the areas studied expected that men would fulfil this obligation and complained vociferously (and often in court) if they did not. Lettice Kinnersley blamed her husband for the lack of provisions in the household. Seventeenth-century colonial records reveal that assertions that a man did not fulfil such obligations were regarded as slanderous and actionable. In Maryland in 1661, Isabella Barnes claimed that John Winchester had neglected his wife Margaret during her terminal illness. He responded by introducing a witness whom he had employed to keep watch over Margaret at nights, who testified that Margaret had been fed 'poultry stewed with butter and currents and she was shifted and tended and hur husband was as kind to her as any man Could be to his wife'. The saying 'to act like a man' was, in eighteenth-century New England, code for supporting your wife. Failure to provide such support was regarded as good grounds for cancelling the marriage contract.

Wives in New England pledged to their husbands good management and service in return. The contractual nature of the relationship is well evidenced in the American colonies and, according to Meyers, especially amongst those of the Calvinist persuasion. In 1760 Stephen Lufkin, a fisherman from Gloucester, Massachusetts, petitioned for divorce from his wife, Tabitha, alleging that she had wasted his property, committed adultery and conducted herself in ways unbecoming in a wife. Tabitha retorted that 'he had been an unkind husband, always checking up on her, finding fault, and getting angry, and only giving her to eat the food he liked, whether or not agreed it with her stomach; second he had refused to pay for a jug of cider she had bought in his absence, although she had drunk only water for seven or eight months; third he had argued with her about cloth she had bought for his coat, and had shut her out of the house until she, on her knees, begged him to be reconciled; fourth, he falsely accused her of wasting his goods, for they had little when they married . . .'[18]

English law had a more restrictive definition of legally actionable defamation and so the kinds of cases common in New England do not arise. As divorce was in practice only available to the well-to-do by private Act of Parliament, there is not the same rich seam of evidence concerning the failed marriages of the poor and middling sorts as there is in, for example, New England. In all these societies, however, marriages did collapse and it was normally the men who took the initiative in finally breaking the contract. Desertion was apparently quite common. In Norwich in 1570 there were a high number of deserted wives. Often the wife would be abandoned and have no idea where her husband had gone.[19] If, after investigation, the whereabouts of a spouse could not be discovered, there could be official presumption of death and the remaining spouse would be allowed to remarry. The old folk song in which the mariner husband has been lost for seven years and whose wife will yet not remarry indicates the predicament in which such women were placed by the uncertainty of desertion. But some were not so cautious: men and women sometimes married bigamously in their attempt to discover compatible partners when divorce was not a practicability and reacted angrily to those who disclosed their secrets.

When expectations were not met

It is often difficult for historians to discover the sources that would allow them to construct a picture of the intimate emotional lives of women. The series of late seventeenth-century autobiographical letters of the 1680s and 1690s from Anne Dormer, second wife of Robert Dormer of Rousham, to her sister Lady Elizabeth Trumbull is, therefore, all the more remarkable.[20] Anne Dormer, employing a common simile, thought her marriage was like a cage.[21] She attributed this both to her own natural 'softness of temper', as well as her husband's extremes of sexual jealousy and hatred of womankind, which she saw as a kind of insanity.[22] Over a period of years she was painfully aware that she was utterly dependent on her husband's will: 'I must not exasperate him, for I and my poor children are in his power'.[23] To avoid exciting his manic jealousy she determined never to go outside their garden and reported that sometimes she did 'not see another face for 2 months'.[24] On the surface she appeared to be the mistress of a large household with a staff of thirty, including some devoted maids, but underneath it all she had 'not a person to send', for the whole household was afraid of her husband. Like Lettice Kinnersley before her, she was forced to create a personal haven: 'my closet is a safe shelter but out of it is little quiet because he whose life is idleness is seldom from home'.[25] But there was little peace and security there either: 'my chamber when he is up he is always passing to and fro and in the nursery if I stay ½ hour he is in a fury; in winter he broke the door when he fancied I was there but I was not'.[26] The poet Katherine Philips in 1667 penned a work that extolled the spinster state and warned women of the onerous duties that accompanied marriage:

A virgin state is crowned with much contempt
It's always happy, and it's innocent
No blustering husbands to create your fears
No pangs of childbirth to extort your tears
No children's cries but to offend your ears
Few worldly crosses to distract your prayers
Thus are you freed from all the cares that do
Attend on matrimony – and a husband too.

Some women were not so defenceless when their own expectations of a partnership were not met, although the ability to 'do something about it' depended to a great extent on resources – finance, family and/or ferocity. Mary Farmer simply left her husband and child and set up home in her dower house.[27] Anne Andrewes went to her father and made allegations against her husband and was advised by him to petition the ecclesiastical courts for judicial separation. She moved out of the family home and went to live in Newport Pagnell with her children.[28] Sir Thomas Lorrain of Kirkharle was reputedly unable to go about his business as a JP in Scotland in the late 1680s because 'his lady . . . being in a passion, kicked him downstairs for selling four oxen and spending the price of them in drinking'.²⁹ Stifling marriages, terrifying marriages, unsatisfying marriages certainly existed in our period as in any other but to argue that Lettice Kinnersley's or Anne Dormer's marriages were typical would not be defensible. Indeed both women saw their circumstances as extraordinary and expected others to view them likewise.

It is more difficult to find detailed examples of the reactions of dissatisfied wives in the other societies under discussion because of the nature of the surviving evidence. Historians simply have to assume that developments in the early colonies echoed those of the mother country unless explicit evidence is found to the contrary. Court records have been used, however, to indicate that women were not averse to taking the law into their own hands to protect themselves against abusive husbands and masters. For example, in Maryland in the 1650s the wife of Clove Mace publicly threatened 'to cut his throat or poison him' or get John Harte to beat him because of his abusive behaviour, and eventually participated in beating her husband.³⁰ Terri Snyder's discussion of women's manipulation of the law in seventeenth- and eighteenth-century Virginia hinges on the resistance unhappy wives were prepared to offer their husbands, even to the extent of taking them before the courts.

*In courtrooms and neighbourhoods as well, the speeches of free and unfree women policed boundaries of sexuality and marriage, asserted their freedom and autonomy, and resisted legal and patriarchal authority. Legal officials faced women who refused to submit to their orders; neighbours of all ranks and both sexes complained that women's speeches threatened to 'undoe' them; and masters, both male and female, found themselves reproached by the words of their unfree women.*³¹

She argues that the tightening of laws against women in Virginia from 1662 onwards was a direct response to the perceived challenge women had made to the dominion of men before that date and beyond. Thus in 1662 the Virginia House of Burgesses ordered that 'women causing scandalous suites [are] to be ducked'.³²

Dissolution of marriage

Divorce and judicial separation

Legal divorce (in the modern sense of divorce, frequently granted on grounds of incompatibility, adultery or ill-treatment and permitting remarriage) was not available to most English, Welsh and Irish men and women in the period. In certain circumstances – which did offer women protection – a marriage might be annulled by the Church.[33] A very few highly privileged individuals had access to actual divorce through Act of Parliament. In Scotland the rules of the Catholic Church regarding annulment and separation prevailed until the Reformation. In Maryland, where the law remained much closer to English law (in contrast to the situation in Puritan New England) there was also no divorce (in this case until 1790).[34] This did not, however, mean that all men and women continued to live together when their relationships disintegrated. As we have noted above, judicial separation was acceptable in cases of incompatibility, adultery or ill-treatment.[35] The case for there having been a double standard in operation is not terribly persuasive. For instance, in Scotland, Grisell Baillie was granted official separation in March 1714 from her husband Alexander Murray of Stanhope on account of his 'dark moods, jealousy and ferocious temper'.[36] Robert Robins discovered the adultery of his wife and they agreed to separate. They both appeared before the county clerk in Maryland and made declarations:

I Robert Robins doe hereby disclayme my wife Elizabeth Robins for ever to acknowledge her as my wife and I do hear oblige myself and everie one from mee never to molest or trouble her any further.

In her declaration Elizabeth added that she would not ask 'for maintenance or any other necessaries'.[37]

In some cases women used the patriarchal 'system' to their own advantage, as in the case of Anne Andrewes in the English midlands in the 1620s when she, with her father's and brother-in-law's assistance, successfully petitioned for divorce *a mensa et thoro* and alimony.[38]

For others, and probably more, de facto separation for periods sufficed. In 1650s Maryland, when a husband and wife 'were minded to live asunder', the Provincial Court confirmed a division of assets that the couple had worked out and set down in a will.[39] Mary Farmer, Thomas Temple's sister, appears to have eventually reconciled with her husband after a period on her own in her dower house.[40] Elizabeth Freke had spent many periods apart from her husband Percy throughout their long marriage (some of them as a result of disputes) and determinedly separated herself from husband and son in 1696 but returned to care for Freke during his terminal illness. Their marriage ended not with divorce or judicial separation but with death.[41] Such marriages had their ups and downs and women demonstrated considerable resource in coping with adverse situations.

This means that historians have to be extremely careful when handling reports of a marriage at any one moment to make sure that that moment was representative of the marriage as a whole. In the 1560s and 1570s the early years of the marriage between Mistress Elizabeth Littleton and Sir Francis Willoughby appear to have been happy enough but the union turned sour because of his suspicious nature and the machinations of Willoughby's sister, Lady Arundel, and some of the servants. The two separated for some years, although they reunited for the last years of her life.[42] Elizabeth (Barnard) Brydges in one lengthy diatribe rebuked her husband for his wastrel nature, his drunkenness and gambling addiction, yet some years later she was to describe him as an ideal husband and a veritable saint.[43] Raymond Anselment has shown how, although Elizabeth Freke's marriage was certainly a troubled one, Elizabeth's own perception of both it and her husband changed according to circumstance and the marriage both began and ended with love. In this case, two accounts of the marriage, penned within a year of one another, presented it in very different terms. In the earlier account Freke portrays her husband as 'ill-tempered, grasping' and determined to have his own way; in the later she softens this emphasis on conflict by removing examples of his unkindness and refers to him as her 'deere husband'.[44]

The evidence for other strategies to which unhappy couples resorted is patchy but interesting.

Desertion

Historians have tended to look at the subject of desertion as it related to marriage. As is clear from the discussion in 'What was marriage?', in fact 'irregular marriages' and other forms of partnership were breaking down all the time and resulting de facto in desertion. The indications are that such partnerships were often preferred just because they were so easily dissolved. In some of those situations, as we have noted, attempts were made to protect the parties involved. How common, however, was desertion of one spouse by another and what, if any, sanctions were employed to enforce the rights of a wife or a husband to a continuance of the contract? Desertion, usually of wives by husbands, seems to have been relatively common in all these societies although 'hard' statistics are difficult to come by. In 1570 8 per cent of poor women in Norwich had been deserted by their husbands. The ecclesiastical courts tried to compel the errant husbands to return to live with their wives and they used economic penalties to enforce such decisions. (Of course, the economic implications were considerable if a wife and children were deserted, leaving the parish to support them.) Often such marriages were irreparable and it was, in any case, relatively easy for an individual to 'disappear' in a society with poorly kept records. Probably this was especially true of the poor and the unpropertied. Similarly there is much evidence of desertion of women by men in seventeenth-century Maryland, although from time to time a woman such as Elizabeth Johnson in 1669 might be so desperately unhappy that she would leave her husband and wander around, seeking shelter from neighbours. There seems to be some evidence that colonial men from time to time practised bigamy, maintaining one woman in the New and one in the Old country. Alexander Younger married Sarah, took all her goods, sold her land and escaped to England. Here he 'married' an English wife and told visitors from Maryland that Sarah was 'only his whore'.[45]

Wife sales

Some husbands, faced with wives with whom they were dissatisfied, were determined to make what economic benefit they could from the situation and formally transfer their property in their wives for payment. (Another view is that the money paid was economically insignificant and simply set a seal on the contract.) Moreover, by entering a formal contract a husband erroneously believed that he could avoid his obligations of supporting his wife and family, and any charge on him from the parish of her habitation for this support, and the purchaser mistakenly believed that he would avoid prosecution. Husbands of the 'lower sort' actually sold their wives at markets and in public houses. This form of poor man's divorce existed in England, Scotland, Wales and Ireland. Pope Gregory VII was complaining about this practice in either Ireland or Scotland as early as 1073 and there is evidence of the continuance and popularity of the practice in the British Isles throughout our period, although some historians have described it as 'a curiosity rather than a numerically significant phenomenon'.[46] Wife sales were frowned on by the church authorities who brought the offending males to book. For example, in February 1600 Ottiwell Andrew of Eyam, Derbyshire, confessed that at Easter he 'did buye the sayd Dorothie of her husband Michaell Ogden and gave unto him 44s for her'. He was ordered to do penance and to desist from cohabiting with Dorothy. Other examples survive from London in 1553; from Rickmansworth, Hertfordshire, in 1584 where both parties to a sale were made to do penance; from Great Warley, Essex, in 1585; from Fife in 1613; from Stirling in 1638 and again in 1646, from East Lothian in 1646 and from Warwick in 1642/3. It was even said in the mid-eighteenth century that the 2nd Duke of Chandos purchased his second wife (the daughter of an ostler).[47] Such examples probably represent the tip of an iceberg, for such private transactions were always difficult for the authorities to trace. By the late eighteenth century, while there is evidence that the practice was widespread, Smithfield Market in London seems to have been a centre for wife sales. Written contracts exist for the eighteenth century. These often state the terms of the transaction, which shed light on the expectations of a wife:

Oct 24 1766

Memorandum

It is this day agreed on between John Parsons, of the parish of Midsummer Norton, in the county of Somerset, cloth-worker, and John Tooke, of the same place, gentleman, that the said John Parsons, for and in consideration of the sum of six pounds and six shillings in hand paid to the said John Parsons, doth sell, assign, and set over unto the said John Tooke; with all right, property, claim, services, and demands whatsoever, that he, the said John Parsons, shall have in or to the said Ann Parsons, for and during the term of the natural life of her, the said Ann Parsons.

Marriages were thus ended because the spouses were incompatible. Very occasionally we can determine why the breakdown occurred from the wife-sale advertisements. In 1796 a man wrote of his wife in terms similar to those he might use if advertising a horse: 'she can sow and reap, hold a plow, and drive a team . . . she is damned hard mouthed and headstrong . . . She now and then, if not watched, will make a false step. Her husband parts with her because she is too much for him.'[48] Although such advertisements demonstrate the dissatisfaction felt by the husbands, it is not beyond the bounds of possibility that spurned wives preferred such a solution (when compared with the uncertainty of desertion or the pains of incompatability), which offered them male protection and the possibility of a happier partnership.

Jumping backwards over the broomstick

There were other forms of informal divorce to which both spouses were party. In Wales broomstick marriages were traditionally reversed by jumping backwards over the broomstick:

So let us be married, my Mary
If ever dislike be our lot,
We jump'd over the broom, then an airy
Jump back shall unfasten the knot!

Traditionally in Scotland and Ireland handfasted marriages were dissolved when the partners went to church and then left the building by separate doors after the service. As late as 1791 it was said that in the Kintyre region unhappy couples were invited annually to a ceremony at church where at midnight they were all blindfolded and made to wander about quickly; while they were still confused each man had to seize the nearest woman. She was his partner at least until the next opportunity to exercise choice came around.

By the late seventeenth century there is evidence that at least some women were being made aware of the grounds for legal separation.

Rights of separation and divorce were also allowed women in certain of the colonies in some circumstances. In Connecticut, for instance, a woman was entitled to a full divorce if her husband's adultery was proved or if he had deserted her for a minimum of three years. Not only did women bring successful divorce cases in Massachusetts between 1639 and 1692, they were also given generous settlements by the courts and allowed to keep their dower rights. In the South, where divorce was not legalised, separations were frequently formalised and maintenance payments to wives ordered. In England and in Maryland estranged wives were entitled to one-third of the estate.[49] Some husbands did try to avoid this obligation but the wives concerned had access to remedies at law. However, lest we become carried away, it is important to note that in Connecticut any woman who left the marital home in order to protest her husband's behaviour was not entitled to divorce. In the seventeenth century, magistrates tended to treat the woman in such a case gently, counselling mediation and arbitration, but by the eighteenth century judicial attitudes had hardened and a woman guilty of desertion was commonly pronounced 'rebellious' and guilty. Divorces on grounds of cruelty were denied by the eighteenth-century Connecticut courts.[50] Moreover, the principle of feme covert was not destroyed overnight. Until the eighteenth century the wife's parents were allowed to initiate divorce proceedings: her father possessed a legal identity she did not have and could fight her corner for her.[51]

In all these societies women (and men) were entitled to protection from abusive spouses – a protection which did not, however, amount to a right to judicial separation or, where it was available, divorce. As today, it was often difficult if not impossible for abused women to take advantage of the protection offered while they continued to cohabit. For example, Mrs Francis Brooke's husband beat her with wooden planks when she tried to eat food he had wanted for himself. Mrs Brooke was heavily pregnant at the time and, when her midwife Rose Smith observed that the newborn baby was badly bruised and questioned her as to the cause, she confessed that her husband had attacked her with metal fire tongs when she ate one of his stewed sheep's heads. Francis Brooke was questioned and said that his wife had sustained the injuries when she fell out of a peach tree. His wife, questioned in his presence, was intimidated and agreed that this was how she and the baby had been injured.[52]

Historians of England have, of course, argued vigorously that a double standard was applied in respect of the fidelity of spouses one to another. According to this view, men were allowed to sow their wild oats while the women were rebuked for allowing them to do so. However, the evidence does not really support such an argument. In England the ecclesiastical courts vigorously prosecuted males as well as females who committed adultery. In February 1600 a husband who had committed adultery and impregnated the woman involved was brought before the court because he had failed to perform several days of public penance wearing his white sheet and carrying a wand. He was ordered to perform the penance appropriately and to bring certification of this to the court in due course. It was also the males who were brought before the same court for making their wives pregnant before marriage. Husbands who had deserted their wives were ordered to return to cohabit with them and to support them. Evidence available for the American colonies gives some support for this reading. Sometimes indeed they suggest that it was as difficult for a man to obtain a judicial separation from an unfaithful wife as vice versa.[53] Robert Robins lived with a wife he claimed was frequently unfaithful – he called her a 'common whore'. Criticised by friends for tolerating this situation, he threw up his hands and asked, 'What would you have me do?' There was a 'good witness' to the public spectacle when 'William Herde rid her from stump to stump',[54] but Robert had few options – he could put up with it, desert her or sue for legal separation, 'a costly and time-consuming option'. He acted only when she bore another man's child, and sued for separation. This was granted only after two appeals and many favourable witness statements about him – he wanted separation and also to avoid financial responsibility for the child. The court deprived the wife of her right to a third of his estate and declared him free of any liability to her or the child.[55]

The differing attitudes to marriage, partnership and concubinage in Scotland, Wales and England are nowhere better signalled than in their attitudes to the question of illegitimacy. In Wales illegitimate children were treated as part of the family and given bequests. Sometimes at least concubines were given the 'thirds' of property and goods just as if they had been wedded wives. In Scotland the lairds accepted concubinage and nominated their own successors, not necessarily preferring legitimate over illegitimate offspring. In medieval times peasants, legitimate and illegitimate, were frequently rewarded with land from the chieftains. Some historians argue that as chieftains began to act as landlords, the rules of succession to tenancies became more fixed and this acted to the disadvantage of the illegitimate. Although many tenancies were held at will and there was no guarantee that a son would inherit, many were 'kindly' – that is, they were subject to hereditary succession – and this probably acted to favour legitimate offspring. In at least some parts of Scotland – for example, Glasgow – there was a lively peasant property market in kindnesses, however, and this meant that the issue of legitimacy was unimportant. After the Reformation, Scottish tenants were encouraged to nominate their successors (known as *feuing*) and this again did not discriminate against the illegitimate. In societies where the advantages of marriage were so few it was unsurprising that first the Catholic Church and then the English Church (in Wales) and the Kirk (in Scotland) had such limited success in encouraging people to celebrate their weddings in church and to turn their backs on the old ways. In Wales it was more expensive even for individuals to marry than to live in 'sin': a late sixteenth-century commentator noted that married persons had to give a tenth of their goods to the minister who joined them together in matrimony whereas, if they chose simply to cohabit, they just had to pay a 2s. fine. In England, where legitimacy was so important for inheritance of freehold property and for the security of widows and children, it was appropriate for landed society (including peasant landholders) to shun the paramour and for the authorities to obtain compliance with the practice of church marriage at this social level.[56]

Married women who found themselves in unpleasant or uncertain circumstances looked to their birth families for both financial and emotional assistance. Such help might be requested only at particularly difficult moments.

Conclusion

Whereas some contemporaries regarded marriage as a legal contract ensuring property transmission and the procreation of heirs, at least as common (and frequently coexisting) a view was that marriage was a loving and practical partnership between a man and a woman. Increasingly it became accepted that this contract was both consensual and conditional. Although the Church of England, like the Catholic Church, did not grant divorces after which both parties might remarry, it did grant judicial separations (divorce *a mensa et thoro*) in certain circumstances, and sometimes order generous maintenance of cast-off wives and children. Other unions were broken by desertion, wife sale or some other strategy. Some of the American colonies went one step further and built upon the short-lived Cromwellian policy legalising divorce. Favourable treatment of divorced and deserted wives in colonial courts seems indicative of the desire to support such women back into the marriage market.

Where there is full information concerning the lives of particular women, this suggests that contemporaries of all classes conceived of marriage as a partnership acted out (as were all family relationships) within the framework of protective patriarchy. Sometimes, as was inevitable in human society, a partnership was not harmonious but rather a forum for conflict. In some cases such conflict was temporary; in others it was continuous and sometimes led to total breakdown of the relationship. Equally, in some cases the partnership was not balanced – a husband or a wife was overly dominant and behaviour on one side or the other was unusually violent or submissive. Historians have to struggle to see such exceptions to the norm and to the ideal marital partnership as just that – exceptions. The relative scarcity of detailed examples from the sixteenth and early seventeenth centuries when compared with the later seventeenth and eighteenth centuries seems to indicate not an increasing trend towards partnership but rather the problems of discerning such trends when documentation is chronologically uneven.

Notes

1 J. Marshall (1967), *The Autobiography of William Stout of Lancashire*, p. 1.
2 Margaret Cavendish, *Natures pictures drawn by fancies pencil to the life*, 1656, pp. 369–70; S. H. Mendelson (1987).
3 HEH, ST 26, Vols 1 and 2 Diary of James Brydges.
4 See Chapter 9 for an indication of the content of this domestic work.
5 John Dunton, *Life and errors*, p. 79 cited in H. Berry (2003), *Gender, Society and Print Culture in Late Stuart England*, p. 55.
6 M. Roberts (2000), 'Gender, work and socialisation in Wales' p. 31.

7 For example, there were attempts in 1461, 1490 and 1511 to exclude women from weaving in Bristol, Hull and Norwich.

8 J. M. Bennett (1996); P. Clark (1983).

9 S. Wright (1985) p. 106.

10 C. Peters (2004) pp. 57–9.

11 R. Archer (1992) pp. 149–81; A. Truelove (2001) p. 48. See below for women of the Temple family in the period 1590–1650.

12 Truelove (2001) p. 44.

13 D. Meyers (2003) p. 150.

14 Ibid p. 139.

15 Ibid p. 145.

16 Ibid p. 152.

17 Ibid p. 148.

18 Cited in Nancy F. Cott, 'Eighteenth-century family and social life revealed in Massachusetts Divorce Records', *Journal of Social History*, 10, 1976, pp. 32–3. Also cited in Meyers (2003), pp. 149–50.

19 M. Pelling (1999) pp. 52–3.

20 S. Mendelson and P. Crawford (1998) pp. 138–9, citing BL Trumbull MSS, D/ED c. 13, Letter from Anne Dormer to Elizabeth Trumbull, 25 July 1689.

21 See also Margaret Cavendish, *Philosophical and Physical Opinions*, 1655, sig. B2v.

22 BL Trumbull MSS, Anne Dormer to Elizabeth Trumbull, 3 November 1688?, cited in Mendelson and Crawford (1998) p. 139.

23 Anne Dormer to Elizabeth Trumbull, 20 July 1688?

24 Anne Dormer to Elizabeth Trumbull, 28 January 1688/9?

25 Anne Dormer to Elizabeth Trumbull, 28 August 1686.

26 Anne Dormer to Elizabeth Trumbull, 3 November 1688?

27 HEH, STT Legal Cases.

28 HEH, STT Correspondence.

29 Extracts from Memoirs of William Veitch, J. G. Fyfe and R. S. Rait (1928) pp. 298–9.

30 William Hande Browne (ed.) *Archives of Maryland*, 72 vols, Baltimore, Maryland Historical Society, 1883–1972, Vol. 53 p. 628; also discussed in D. Meyers (2003) p. 39.

31 T. L. Snyder (2003) p. 3 *et passim*.

32 This was followed by more legislation in 1677 and 1699 limiting women's public role in the colony. See Snyder (2003) p. 21.

33 Marriages were, for example, annulled if the couple had been under-age and at maturity did not consent to the union, if the marriage was bigamous or incestuous (the latter being defined by the rules of consanguinity and affinity) or the result of force or deception. See R. O'Day (1995) pp. 58–60.

34 L. Walsh (1979) p. 129.

35 Confusingly called divorce *a mensa et thoro*.

36 R. Scott-Moncreiff (1911) pp. xxvii–xxviii.

37 Walsh (1979) p. 138.

38 See 'Patriarchy', Chapter 7 above, for a lengthier discussion of this case. HEH, STT 2418 Sir Thomas Tyringham to William Andrewes 31 Dec 1625; STT 40 William Andrewes to Sir Thos Tyringham at Tyringham 31 Dec 1625; STT 2255 Sir Thomas Temple to William Andrewes 3 Jan 1625/6; STT 1366 Sir John Lenthall to Sir Thos Temple at Biddlesden 4 Jan 1625/6; STT 2342 Sir Thos Temple from Biddlesden to Sir Thos Tyringham at Tyringham 11 Jan 1625/6; STT 2273 Sir Thos Temple from Biddlesden to Sir Richard Neuman at Lambeth 14 Jan 1625/6; STT 581 Sir Thos Denton to Sir Thos Temple at Biddlesden 19 Jan 1625/6; STT 17 Anne Andrewes to George Abbot Archbishop of Canterbury 1626. Eventually the two apparently reconciled; see STT 41 Sir William Andrewes from Lothbury to Sir Peter Temple 13 Nov 1634. See above for other examples of women appealing to their fathers and brothers against their husbands.

39 Mary Beth Norton (1996), *Founding mothers and fathers*, p. 90.

40 HEH, STT 745 Letter from John Farmer to Sir Peter Temple, Kt and Bt at Stowe 28 Dec 1637 from Bradley.

41 R. A. Anselment (2001) pp. 14–24.

42 HEH, STB Box 2, Books 1 and 2.

43 HEH, STB.

44 R. A. Anselment (2001) pp. 22–5.

45 L. Walsh (1979) p. 133.

46 See A. Laurence (1994 reissue 2002) p. 54 for this view.

47 The truth of this rumour seems suspect. In the family register Henry, 2nd Duke, was at pains to state of Duchess Anne who died on 9 Aug 1759: 'Shee left behind her in writing [p. 33b] every thing relating to Lady Augusta's education and conduct in life and every paper relative to Houshold affairs was left in the most exact order for she [left] of her surviving Lord

with directions indexes where to go to each papur, which must have been a work of some months and plainly shewed that she was not insensible of her approaching Dissolution'. See HL ST Personal Box 10 (6).

48 See S. P. Meneffe (1981).
49 C. Chapman (1996) p. 89.
50 C. H. Dayton (1995) pp. 61–2.
51 R. Thompson (1974) pp. 177–9.
52 W. H. Browne, *Archives of Maryland*, 10, p. 464.
53 D. Meyers (2003) p. 91. This example is discussed in more detail in 'Patriarchy', Chapter 7.
54 Browne, *Archives*, 10, p. 503.
55 Browne, *Archives*, 10, pp. 501–4, 555; 41: 20, 50–51, 85; 53: 4, 33–4.
56 C. Peters (2004) pp. 12–14.

CHAPTER 9

Mistress of the household: what wives did all day

Marriage is a merry-age, and this world's paradise, where there is mutual love[1]

Introduction

The above quotation suggests that marriage was a time of pleasure and leisure for husbands and wives. This was certainly an idealised view, far removed from the hard-working and frequently hard-going lives of men and women from the aristocracy down. Nonetheless the cooperation specified in the quotation is an accurate reflection of the manner in which couples were expected to live.

Circumstance proscribed the daily lives of wives as it did those of husbands. This is not to argue, however, that married women were helpless and passive victims in a world shaped by men.

The daily activities and responsibilities of wives would naturally vary according to their social and economic status and according to whether they were rural or urban dwellers. An elite woman might be more or less fully occupied managing the household and estates, raising the children and fulfilling obligations within the community; the wife of a clergyman or a farmer might find her days filled with a mixture of household management and shared activities with her husband. When the Marian martyr Alice Davis described her life as a farmer's daughter she summed up the experience of many a husbandman's or yeoman's wife: 'I have driven the plough before my father many a time.'[2] The wife of an urban tradesman might find it necessary to add to her household duties engagement in an economic activity inside or outside the home. Thus the traditional role of both married and unmarried women in retail was established. For some of these women the transition from maiden to wife to widow was almost seamless.³

The activities and duties of wives would also depend upon whether they were living at a time and in an area affected by unrest or even war. Recent work on Scotland, which has turned on its head the once accepted view of Highland society as wild and uncivilised and Lowland society as disordered and irresponsible, by no means undermines the responsible and resourceful role that its women had to play.⁴ A woman living on the Anglo-Scottish frontier at any time during these centuries had to display 'courage, activity and resolution ... ancient characteristics of the sex on the border', picking up the pieces after midnight raids and starting afresh.⁵ Isabel Ker, Lady of Linton, deputised for her husband in 1547 and Lady Isobel Home of Eccles acted in her husband Sir James Home's absence in 1602.⁶ In January 1598 George Home of Wedderburn's thoughts turned 'homevart' as he served his King. He wrote to his wife that she should 'tak a horse or an ox fra Jhone Orknay till he cum heir and mak his comptis ... Quen thou cumis ower amongst other thingis bring my mekle compt buike with ye ... item my velvet gowne and cloke ... I vot not how our dochter is pleased ... God send all vell and preserve the and all ouris ... Thy George Howme.'⁷ Sir Thomas Ker of Ferniehirst was forced into exile in France for his activities in support of Mary Queen of Scots and he left his wife Janet in charge of family and estates. She signed writs on her husband's behalf and even sent coded messages to Mary. In 1583 she was given full power of attorney.⁸ There were feuds between clans and also within kindred, in which women played key roles. When the Earl of Cassillis accompanied James VI and I to London in 1603 his enemies took the opportunity to capture his wife the countess and to hold her to ransom and also to place his brother under the control of Lady Bargany, his enemy within the kindred. The experience killed his brother! Conflict concerning religion also involved women in danger. In post-Restoration Scotland, Covenanters would frequently take refuge in local houses.

Householders, male and female could not be too careful whom they harboured, as men commonly disguised as Covenanters were sent to seek out Covenanting sympathisers. George Brysson quite understood when an 'honest widow-woman', who 'had some of Mr Renny's men hiding in her house', would not give them shelter 'taking us for dissemblers'.⁹ Slightly earlier Brysson's sister had had to maintain the family farm, eventually relying on the charity of neighbours to keep the cows alive, while George hid in the wood and among the corn and 'sometimes ventured to my bed'.[10] Scottish wives were also caught up in the effects of campaigns against the English throughout the seventeenth and eighteenth centuries. Andrea Knox has argued convincingly that women of the Scottish Highlands and Irish rebel women built up networks to resist the effects of English colonial authority. Agnes Campbell and her daughter, Finola O'Donnell, became Irish rebels themselves through marriage and brought hundreds of Scottish mercenary troops as their dowries with them to Ireland.[11] Maggie Craig has well demonstrated how important female support was to the Jacobite cause. Women raised regiments, acted as spies and passed on information, nursed the wounded and assisted prisoners in escape.[12] When William Graham, Laird of Potento, strove to protect his brother-in-law, Lord Balinsho, after the Jacobite rising of 1715, he nonetheless beseeched his sister Jean, Lady Balinsho, to collect certificates on her husband's behalf. She collected a number of such certificates which, alongside her declaration that she wouldn't 'hazer'd Balinsho and my childrens bread for aney king ever munted the Britih throne, tho I oun I lyk't the pretender', persuaded Lord Stanhope to be lenient.[13] Another aspect of women's reactions to war in their midst is evidenced by the Wedderburn correspondence. A later George Home of Wedderburn addressed his 'lady' in October 1715:

My dearest, we came heir yester night and ar to joyn the English the morrow who ar very strong both in horse and arms . . . I desire ye may take curage and be not dejected, for we doubt not of business proveing to our mind . . . I shall miss no suire occasion to writ to yow. We ar all very weill and wishes to hear the like to yow and the bairns . . . For God's sake be not dejected.[14]

This same Lady Margaret, when her husband forfeited his estates because of his complicity in the Jacobite rebellion, had to petition the King, 'having nine children and having no thing whereupon to subsist my selfe and my children . . . a proper object of your Majestie's pity and compassion', for her marriage settlement out of the said estates.[15] When the king wrote a passport for Home's stepdaughter Flora Macdonald in 1746 (the very same that she used for safe passage for Bonnie Prince Charlie), the king thought it perfectly reasonable to justify it thus: 'I have sent your daughter from this country lest she should be in any way frightened with the troops lying there.'[16]

Indigenous Irish women lived permanently in similar situations. A fair idea of conditions in Elizabethan Ireland can be obtained. Edmund Tremayne in 1571 offered a tabloid diagnosis: 'religion has no place, men have no fear or love of God. They regard no faith, no oath. They murder, ravish, spoil, burn, commit whoredom, break wedlock, change wives, without grudge of conscience.'[17] He blamed lack of true (that is, Protestant) religion, of law and of justice and the propensity of English settlers to foment unrest by siding with one 'native Irish' party or another. The Lord Justice Fitzwilliam and his councillors were more liable to blame lack of money and provisions. Soldiers were heavily indebted to the 'country people'. When soldiers were short of money and victuals they sold weapons and munitions to the enemy and laid waste the countryside.[18] Assessments on the local populace to provision the troops hit all families hard and poorer families most. When Irishmen tried to raise rebellions against English rule, they too seized provisions from the locals. In May 1571 Thomas Stukeley was trying to stage a rebellion in Enniscorthy and among those who were forced to help him with a 'gift' of her entire herd of thirty 'kine' [cattle] and her horses was widow Katherine Kavanagh of Ballyngatte.[19] There was also unchecked and vicious corruption among officials, which accentuated the problems of living in a countryside laid waste by rebels and troops. In Killenbride, for example, the sub-sheriff was said in 1570 to have illegally and 'wickedly' seized for his own use her cow and heiffer and a payment of 13s. 4d. from widow Jowan Ny Worroghe and then a few months later to have similarly targeted her son-in-law.[20] Jowan's and Katherine's cases were specified because they were widows and heads of household but the plight of the wives of the myriad male victims of the rebel and of the sheriff and sub-sheriffs is hidden from history, although no less real for that. Life for all married women, at whatever social level, was hard. Occasionally we see the ways in which Irish women too played a more proactive role in events. For instance, in spring 1571 the wife of Terence (Turlough Luineach) O'Neill crossed to Scotland to recruit soldiers to assist him. She was reported to have been spectacularly successful in this enterprise, gathering a force of 3,000–4,000.[21] She also sent boatloads of provisions to him along with intelligence from Scotland.[22] The following September, Lord Justice Fitzwilliam reported to the English Privy Council that O'Donnell's wife (Agnes Campbell) had also gone over to Scotland to hire Scots soldiers.[23] Perhaps we should be noting here not only the crucial role that these elite Irish married women were playing in the affairs of Ireland but also the fact that the English commentators were totally accepting of this situation, seeing nothing unusual in it whatsoever.[24]

In the early American colonies, life was 'nasty, brutish and short' for many. A woman in New York confided in her diary: 'This day is forty years since I left my father's house and come here, and I have seen little else but hard labour and much sorrow . . . I am dirty and tired almost to death', and Virginians sang, 'The axe and hoe have wrought my overthrow . . . If you do here come, you all will be weary, weary, weary.'[25] In the Chesapeake region of Virginia and Maryland, despite a largely temperate climate, the mortality rate was high. Malaria seems to have weakened the settlers and made them susceptible to every illness.[26] Polluted water brought illness and disease to the settlers of Jamestown.[27] The situation in New England was probably much better. Here childhood and youth were the most dangerous times with perhaps as high as a 23 per cent death rate between infancy and maturity. If an individual survived childhood he or she was likely to live out their natural span of seventy years.[28] Despite these variations in mortality patterns, many settlers throughout the colonies lived in conditions that were unstable when compared to the old country. Whole areas were seized from the indigenous peoples of the Americas as the frontier was pushed back, and, for the pioneers, living implied settlement and conquering an often hostile environment. This could mean that married women were thrust into the thick of conflict. Hannah Duston (1686–1736) was the wife of a Haverhill, Massachusetts, bricklayer and farmer and the mother of twelve children when in 1697 her settlement was raided by native Americans. Hannah was taken captive, her new baby's brains dashed out on a tree, and she along with others was taken on a long trek on foot towards Canada. Two weeks later Hannah and two youths attacked the sleeping Indians with hatchets: reputedly she scalped nine of their captors and took the scalps with her to prove before the General Court in Boston what she had done. She was awarded a bounty of £25 and each of her two male companions was awarded £12 10s., thus acknowledging the primacy of her role.[29] Wars and revolutions here too generally had the effect of emphasising women's key role in colonial public life. Kathleen Brown and Debra Meyers have argued that white women were marginalised in southern politics from the 1660s.[30] Cynthia Kierner, however, has shown that at the revolution they came to the fore in boycotts, fundraising, petitioning and electioneering.[31] All this provides an echo of the situation in Scotland, England and Ireland at times of unrest and war.

Women in most parts of England and Wales lived in rather more settled circumstances for most of these centuries although they too faced turmoil for a long period during the 1640s and 1650s and also at other times. The English borders were always unsettled and women there were affected throughout these three centuries. From time to time during the

Wars of the Roses there was conflict, although there were also periods of calm.[32] In any case the troublesome times of the Wars of the Roses were followed by the relative peace that the Tudor dynasty won and James I maintained. Some were then plunged into the thick of the fray of the English civil wars. In England and Ireland there were, at one social extreme, the female soldiers. Some married women accompanied their soldier husbands to Ireland: Alice Stonier of Leek, Staffordshire, took along her five children when her husband was pressed to serve in the army; when he was killed at Drogheda Alice and her family became a burden on the Dublin coffers.[33] Alice was returned to her native parish as were many Scottish widows and children. At the other extreme were elite women who took an active role in furthering the cause of one side or another and/or defended their homes against attack. Lady Brilliana Harley, in her husband's absence, fearlessly defended her family and her religion against royalist threats.[34] A string of royalist wives, notably Lady Blanche Arundell of Wardour Castle, Wiltshire, Lady Mary Bankes of Corfe Castle, Dorset, and the Countess of Derby at Lathom House, Derbyshire, defended their besieged castles against parliamentary troops.[35] Such experiences were echoed in Ireland, where, during this same period, there are several examples of doughty women defending their estates – Lady Offaly at Geashill Castle in County Offaly; Lady Forbes at Castle Forbes, County Offaly; Lady Fitzgerald at Trecroghan Castle, Westmeath. Mary O'Dowd suggests that Lady Elizabeth Dowdall positively 'relished the opportunity to command a group of men to defend her castle at Kilfenny in County Limerick', even when her husband was clearly at home, and wrote her own exultant account of her organising powers and military achievements.[36]

It was not only during time of war that women had to face violent disruption to their lives. In the fifteenth and sixteenth centuries disputes over the ownership of estates sometimes led to armed sieges. For example, on 12 April 1596 Sir Percival Willoughby

writ his father a long account of his troubles, how when he was from home and had left his wife big with child Sir Francis [her father] had sent a troop to take possession of Middleton, that his servants resisting they went off to ye town after having broke down a wall and two doors.[37]

Historians are most aware of the plight of elite women who defended their estates during the civil wars in the four kingdoms but it was not only the elite who suffered. Billeting of troops upon local inhabitants meant that many a household was disrupted by more than usually dirty, dishevelled, demanding and sometimes desperately hungry men. Mrs Jemima Bourne of Ashover, Derbyshire, was one of the many clerical wives who had to pack up their belongings at short notice and flee from their parsonages in the civil wars. In Ireland, when soldiers were rewarded for their service with Irish lands, it was often the wives of the owners of the forfeited estates who remained on the land to salvage what they could of stock and crops prior to transplantation to the west of Ireland, while their husbands were in forced exile. Women were then frequently responsible for organising the transplantation of their large households.[38] War, civil war and protest certainly brought with them exceptional responsibilities.

The available evidence suggests, however, that the responsibilities that women shouldered during periods of turmoil were exceptional only in their intensity.[39] Lady Elizabeth Dowdall, for example, organised the defence of Kilkenny Castle during her husband's presence almost as if this was a simple extension of her normal role as household manager.[40] Caitlin, wife of Cormac O'Hara, was praised because she 'as made the land prosperous by her management'.[41] Vivienne Larminie has noted how Anne Newdigate in Elizabeth's reign used correspondence to further the fortunes of her family.[42]

Neither must it be assumed that women's lives were disrupted only during war. At a time when it was common enough for men of the landed classes to spend at least a period in the debtors' prison, their wives had to hold the fort at home and often to raise money for their husbands' eventual release from gaol. Rowland Mynors of Herefordshire described to his father-in-law how in the 1610s, when Mynors was a young married man, he was thrown into gaol for debt and his wife Theodosia was left alone for a year to manage his depleted estate.[43]

Women lower down on the social scale were also expected to manage their households and keep the family finances in order. What managing a household implied clearly depended considerably upon the family's economic status and its environment but the differences were those of scale and degree rather than essence. The wife of a London artisan would have different lifestyle and responsibilities compared to, say, a rural husbandman's wife but would still be an essential partner. Contemporary manuals and account books permit us to list some of the individual tasks performed by wives; managing the household and its servants (if any); feeding the household; clothing the household; to some extent furnishing the household; caring for the children and young people; keeping the dairy and the vegetable garden; marketing surplus produce from these.[44] In an urban setting this list would be modified somewhat, partly because the individual households were less self-sufficient and partly because wives would play a role either in the trading activities of their husbands or in by-employments of their own. In the late 1620s, for example, Elizabeth Welsh was married to a London tradesman but ran a lodging house in the parish of St Clement Danes.[45] We do not hear as much about women below the gentry but clearly not all were up to the task. John Bois, one of the translators of the King James Bible, left all practical domestic matters to his young and inexperienced wife, 'Miss Holt', herself a daughter of a clergyman. It was not long before the family was swamped by debt. The ideal wife was someone who was extremely capable and responsible, someone whose contribution to the thriving household was vital.

It might be assumed that aristocratic wives were more removed from daily responsibilities and more pampered than women of the middling and lower sorts. For instance, they had housekeepers and servants to perform many menial tasks. Far from it. Female diaries, memoirs and autobiographies indicate that elite women rose extremely early in order to accommodate all their spiritual and household duties. Account books and estate records support this view of busy women throughout the period. In the early and mid-sixteenth century, women such as Lady Anne Lestrange and Margaret (Kitson Long) Bourchier, Countess of Bath, were occupied constantly in household and estate business.[46] Indeed, Barbara Harris asserts that all the surviving archives of Yorkist and early Tudor aristocratic households show women thus occupied and prominent.[47] The situation had not changed by the seventeenth century. Mary Rich, Countess of Warwick, carefully supervised all the domestic affairs of her Essex manor, including the dairy and henhouse, and checked the annual accounts of the estate. Elizabeth Walker (1623–1690), also in Essex, followed a similar pattern but, being lower on the social scale, did some of the manual work herself.[48] Hester (Sandys) Temple provides an excellent example of the elite wife who managed the household, raised the children and played an active role in the economic activities of the Temple family of Stowe, Buckinghamshire. There were certainly servants but they added yet another responsibility to the many she had already. She may have been spared many manual tasks by her status and she may have enjoyed a relatively comfortable lifestyle with some good clothing and jewels and access to a coach and horses but her life was extremely busy.[49] Throughout her life she had her fingers on the family's pulse. When her several children were young her concern was to educate and raise them and organise their marriages. As she and her husband grew older and her children grew up, Hester's responsibilities changed but they did not diminish.

Hester Temple was one of the two cornerstones of the Stowe connection in the first half of the seventeenth century (the other being her husband Sir Thomas). She entertained close and distant family members and members of the Stowe connection.[50] Often she had to make the practical travel arrangements so that they could visit. She cared for her various grandchildren on a long-term basis.[51] People who sought Sir Thomas's patronage often approached her in the first instance. For example, Robert Higgins, parson of Finmere, wrote to her in 1627: 'I beseech you that you would vouchsafe to speak to the Right worshipful Sir Thomas Temple your husband to be good to the poor orphans my brother's children', by allowing his daughter Anne to remain in the mill her father had worked and his daughter Susan to inherit his copyhold of a tenement 'and close and quarterne land, ten sheep and one cow's common for her life upon that rent that my brother paid which was fifteen pence a year . . .'.[52] When this did not produce the desired result for Susan, Higgins approached Hester again in October with £10 in 'good gold' in full payment of the rent and beseeched her to intervene again on Susan's behalf.[53] There are many other examples – for instance, Lord Chancellor Ellesmere's step-daughter was asked by her child's wet-nurse to intercede with Ellesmere on behalf of her son Timothy Gatte BD 'that your Lordship will be pleased to bestow uppon him a prebend, mastership of an hospitall or any dignity in your Lordship's gifte'.[54] It was probably not only the women of the landed classes who exercised such influence. There are indications that contemporaries throughout our period assumed that the wives of professional men commanded their patronage.[55]

Hester was approached for loans by several family members and made such loans without reference to her husband. She was undoubtedly a key player in keeping these other (nuclear) families afloat financially. The correspondence reveals just how 'cash poor' propertied families often were and how they depended upon other families (and the leading women within them) in the connection for survival. Particularly acute was the plight of Elizabeth, who had married Henry Gibbs. For example, Thomas and Hester Temple allowed their daughter 'Gibs apparel and necessaries for her being now presently to go away to my son Clarke's to board the sum of £50', apparently because the groom's father, Ralph Gibbs, had reneged upon the agreement. She begged Sir Thomas not to make the 'bargain' worse because 'he [Ralph] hath not paid my son his allowance and answereth him that when you be agreed he shall have it. My daughter hath nothing but what we give her, not money to pay her maid's wages nor to buy her soap or starch and in brief never had 2 penny from him nor his son.'[56] She had also had to find £50 for her son Peter's allowance and £20 2s. for her son-in-law Thomas Penistone's expenditure on his two children.[57] Hester was later to lend money to her daughter Anne Andrewes. Her son-in-law, John Lenthall, wrote asking 'Good madam Concerning my self, I was bold to write unto you, to entreat your favours to assist me with some money which my occasions required, which shall be truly allowed you again . . .',[58] and he later explained that unless she underwrote £50 worth of his debts 'if you fail me I am undone'.[59] She brokered a substantial loan to her husband Sir Thomas from her son-in-law John Rous: 'Good madam . . . I remember the speeches that were between us in my chamber at Wolverton and upon those conditions then spoken of I will (God willing) in Easter term furnish Sir Thomas with 2,500li but with more I doubt I shall not be able but for that at our next meeting we shall farther talk And you shall ever find me ready (wherein I have power) to satisfy all your reasonable demands.'[60] The family showed her enormous respect in her own right. 'So with the remembrance of my service to Sir Thomas and your Ladyship I take my leave and remain Your Ladyship's faithful son-in-law to command.'[61] Business letters from both John Lenthall and John Rous were a common occurrence.[62] For instance, in 1629 Rous communicated with her concerning a mortgage.[63] When she was in London on business for the Temples, other members of the connection made use of her services.[64] Her children and their spouses felt able to discuss with her their concerns and felt confident that she would address them appropriately and from knowledge. Her son Peter, later 2nd Baronet, assumed that she would know all about entails on the estate, 'whereby either my father his estate or your jointure, may be questioned . . .'[65] The Temple manuscripts show her moving around the countryside independently and engaging in business and society with tenants and others. For example, in a slightly earlier letter Parson Higgins of Finmere, Oxon, wrote to her as, 'Virtuous lady and my singular good mistress', recalling a discussion that he had had with her and Sir John Lenthall about a particular statute.[66] Being a wife also meant making detailed arrangements for the household's food and other supplies.[67] Historians have debated the self-sufficiency of early modern households on both sides of the Atlantic. It seems probable that elite households in mainland Britain were more self-sufficient than their counterparts in America – especially the southern Plantation households which concentrated on staple crops and had to obtain household stuffs and other foods from elsewhere, including Britain.[68] However, the difference between English and American households was one of degree only and housewives such as Lady Hester found that adequate provisioning took up a good deal of time and effort.

Hester spent considerable time in London taking personal care of court cases in Chancery and other business. She was far from lacking in independence but she took necessary precautions for her health and welfare. Her son Thomas explained in April 1630, 'I have taken you two lodgings 14s a week for 3 weeks in Chancery Lane at the White Horse a chandler very near Lincoln's Inn and to go through the fields . . . I hope I have looked you a place as yet free from infection . . .'[69] Back in Buckinghamshire she assumed the reins of the estate, making leases and collecting rents and issuing instructions to estate personnel:

Mistress Horley, My Lady did wish me to write to you to certify you of the bargain that I made for her with Goodwife Wilmore for Marton lease, which is this: she must have for it, threescore and ten pounds in hand and five pounds to be abated of her Michaelmas rent. And the other ten pounds she is to pay to me for your use.[70]

It is true that Hester Temple seems to have been most active in business and estate matters when, from the mid-1620s onwards, her husband was laid low by heart problems and was unable to travel or undertake strenuous activity. When he was able to function she consulted him for advice and 'instruction' as when she wrote to him in June 1633:

Good sweet heart, I thank God I am well. To Barnind I expected to have received a letter of instructions of your mind but Brus brought me none. Thus with my love to you and mine I leave and ever rest your ever loving wife Hester Temple.[71]

Such could be used to support the view of those historians who believe that wives only shared in such concerns when they became widows with minor children or during their husband's absence. Taken with other evidence, however, it is clear that Hester was regarded as Thomas's natural partner in such activity.

Good madam This present Good Friday I received your letter and black box with two writings in it, the one from Cooke to Millett and the other from Millett to Sir Thomas Temple, both which upon Monday next God willing I will send to Mr Dowdeswell and so soon as the mortgage is drawn I will send it to Sir Thomas and your Ladyship to peruse and correct.

[and in another letter in which Sir Thomas is barely mentioned] If it be to your liking I pray you send it back by this bearer, if otherwise correct it and return it so soon as you may . . .[72]

Moreover, Sir Thomas her husband clearly regarded her in the same light – as his partner in the household and estate and, furthermore, as a partner who could take executive decisions without his intervention so that he could 'rest in this and all others to [her] care with God's help'.[73] A number of documents exist in the Temple collection listing in detail business to be attended to by his wife. He told her on several occasions to make her own decisions: for instance, he wrote 'You may speak hereof what you think good.'[74]

There are, moreover, indications that Hester had particular charge of parts of the estate, probably of those lands around Burton Dassett, Warwickshire, which formed part of her jointure. During the marriage, Sir Thomas acknowledged her control of these lands. In 1632 he wrote to the steward: 'I hear nothing further from my wife concerning Mr Spenser's farm in Northend, and therefore I think she resteth upon her agreement. And if the farm be held but for a year upon the same terms passed, I think my wife will upon reasonable consideration be satisfied therewith, having but some reasonable time for disposition thereof.'[75] When absent, she wrote frequently to Harry Rose, steward, and to William Hart, clergyman and schoolmaster, giving very detailed instructions concerning agricultural matters, the house and its servants, and the tuition of grandchildren and others in Hart's care.[76]

The early seventeenth-century Verneys of nearby Claydon lived in a similar fashion, with a society that revolved around country life with forays into the metropolis on business. In such a society, women spent more of their time in the country than did their menfolk and perforce had to take decisions on a day-by-day basis. During the rest of the century a gradual gravitation towards London occurred. Whereas few were as determined to be fashionable as Lady Anne Newdigate, who leased a house in Hackney in order to launch her daughters into polite society, already, by 1622, the influx of women into the capital city was sufficiently notable that a proclamation described it as 'an innovation and an abuse lately crept in'. Women seem to have been attracted by the shopping and social activity and by the facilities. For example, elite women began to choose to give birth to their children in the capital under the care of male doctors and midwives. In the 1670s and 1680s the Verneys, Temples and Dentons socialised with one another both in Buckinghamshire and in London. By the late seventeenth century, county elite families in this part of Buckinghamshire often lived a rather different kind of life from that of a hundred years or even fifty years earlier – sometimes spending as much as nine months of the year in London and only retiring to the country seat for the hot and dangerous summer months.[77] A study of the Verney's social networks shows that the Buckinghamshire neighbourhood network was transported to London, with the Verneys, Temples, and Dentons living cheek by jowl in Covent Garden during the season.[78] John Verney and his first wife Elizabeth also belonged to other social networks, based on John's merchant connections and on the neighbourhood, Hatton Garden (in the parish of St Andrew Holborn), in which they lived.

The papers and correspondence of James Brydges, 1st Duke of Chandos and his second wife, Cassandra Willoughby, show a woman of even higher social standing building up a number of interconnecting social and familial networks and expending a considerable amount of time and energy in so doing. She and her husband spent time travelling between homes in London, Middlesex, Tunbridge Wells and Bath, cultivating their connections. These networks included the close families and stepfamilies of both Cassandra and her husband (which were in any case closely allied by blood as well as marriage), dukes and duchesses, earls and countesses, courtiers, bishops and lawyers and city financiers, as well as humbler tenants and applicants for assistance. Cassandra, like Hester Temple but on a more exalted scale, acted in many ways as the gatekeeper to her husband's considerable social, economic and financial patronage. Her charm, tact and diplomacy smoothed the Duke's relations with disappointed applicants for his help at all social levels. Her understanding of young people and their needs helped to preserve family bonds that would otherwise have been neglected. Cassandra was acutely aware of the value of the patronage she now commanded and also of the need to cultivate connections.[79] In spring 1722 she rebuked her brother for neglecting a distant female cousin who commanded votes in a parliamentary election and who, because of his lack of attention to her, would not bring the votes to his assistance.[80] Her husband deliberately employed her skills and acknowledged her value.[81] When times were hard, as after the bursting of the South Sea and Mississippi Bubbles in the period 1719–1720, it was Cassandra who wrote letters to a number of well-placed female friends, seeking loans and mortgages to assist her husband.[82]

Cassandra, like her cousin and husband James, was the grandchild of a prominent merchant, Sir Henry Barnard, and she probably served her apprenticeship as woman of affairs under her financially literate mother Lady Emma (Barnard Willoughby) Child, wife and then widow of Sir Josiah Child of the East India Company.[83] During both her spinsterhood and her marriage, Cassandra took care of the financial interests of her Willoughby nephews.[84] Her mother shared this active concern for their advancement.

Looking back in time to the later fifteenth century we can see that married women at that time also lived within and nurtured a series of 'connections' or 'networks'. The Pastons provide well-known examples but even less well-documented families yield suggestive information. Margery Cely married George in 1484 only to find herself left alone in her house for long periods with only the servants for company. She felt lonely and fearful, not daring to go into some parts of the house (which boasted cellars and shops) at night. However, she lived for part of each year in a house in Mark Lane, London, just three doors down from Richard and Anne Cely, George's brother and sister-in-law, with whom relations were close, where the family had long laid down its roots. The remainder of her time was spent in Essex. By 1489, when George died, she had four boys and one 'in the mother belly' so her days were soon fully occupied. One of the couple's servants, Jane Upton, was also a near kinswoman of Margery so she didn't lack for adult female companionship for long. The husbands of both Margery and Anne Cely were indebted both to their wives and their parents-in-law. Margery lent money to George and also invested money for her children's benefit. It is not known whether she had an independent income or whether she was simply saving quite substantial sums from the money George sent her. There are also indications that Margery had dealings with a wider network – with Elizabeth Punt, a connection by her first marriage.[85] When George died in 1489 Margery lost no time in marrying Sir John Halwell, or Halliwell, of Devon, who was a royal servant of Henry VII.

Information regarding ordering of the domestic lives of elite couples is much more plentiful if we look forward. John and Elizabeth Verney enjoyed a good London social life in the early 1680s, sharing visits to art auctions at the Banqueting House and the Lord Mayor's Show, trips to view curiosities such as an East Indian monster or a three-year-old who spoke exotic languages fluently, and 'taking the waters' and the society at Tunbridge Wells.[86] But Elizabeth's role and that of other Verney and Buckinghamshire women was not confined to providing their male relatives with frivolous feminine company. During the day the women of the families 'visited' one another, establishing and cementing relationships. In the evenings they socialised at dinner parties and entertainments.

The Verneys had an established tradition of supporting their penniless female relatives in exchange for other no less important services. For instance, John's father, Sir Ralph (1613–1696), supported his sister Aunt Gardiner with a small annuity and eked out her existence with presents of venison and other largesse. She repaid him and his son by acting as a funnel for gossip and political secrets communicated by her titled friends, relayed in 518 letters between 1696 and 1717. This suggests that not all men were as impatient of women's opinions on politics as was Sir Henry Carey (Carew). In addition, Aunt Gardiner gave her services as a matchmaker on many occasions. Ralph supported his other sister, Aunt Adams, with a £50 annuity and similar gifts. In return she offered gifts of food and imported luxuries such as a coffee mill and lemon syrup. His patronage enabled *her* to become a patron – she used part of the venison her brother gave her to make a gift to her nephew Dr Blackmore, fellow of the College of Physicians, thus asserting her superiority and position as someone worth cultivating in society.

A study of gentlewomen in the somewhat later 'polite society' of Georgian England reinforces this picture of family-based connections and patronage but also shows how the connection reached out beyond them into a gossip network.[87] Of especial interest is Amanda Vickery's analysis of Elizabeth Shackleton's servant information network between 1770 and 1781. This shows how important this gentlewoman's patronage was to women from other classes in the locality. She recommended servants; she answered inquiries about servant availability and suitability; she sought information about servants. This brought her into contact with tradespeople, shopkeepers, gentlefolk and professionals as well as the servant classes.[88] Research into the activities of Cassandra, Duchess of Chandos, in the early years of the eighteenth century shows that she committed a good deal of her time and energy to seeking out opportunities to extend direct or indirect patronage to family and to members of the network. Thus Amanda Vickery's conclusions can be extended back in time.

Clearly, however, the extent to which women were able to carve out an active life for themselves varied. We have the sense that Hester Temple was able to travel a good deal and to maintain family and other relationships. Cassandra Brydges travelled a good deal when she was single and during her marriage. Dorothy Adams, in the early 1600s, was not so fortunate. She longed to travel to see her sister for

there is no woman in the world that she more esteems, but her husband does not care she should go journeys from him and he is more than ever pleased with the country he is in, so she has no hopes of seeing her, but must sit moping at home by her fire side, turning apples and may go to church to pray for her friends.[89]

The emphasis thus far has been on a married woman's role within her immediate household and nuclear family. For many if not all elite married women, this role in many respects was extended to the wider community.

The mistress of the household was a hostess, sometimes on a grand scale. There are indications that managing the provisions and the cooking for dinners was not an easy matter. At Stowe, household and estate retainers would turn up with unexpected guests, and tenants and their wives seem to have been able to claim dinner as of right.

The mistress was also expected to minister to the ordinary medical needs of the whole 'community' dependent on the estate. Timothy Rogers' *Character of a Good Woman* described one who 'distributes among the indigent poor money, books and clothes and physic, as their several circumstances may require [thus relieving] her poor neighbours in sudden distress, when a doctor is not, or when they have no money to buy what is necessary for them.'[90] Sometimes, as in the case of Anne, Countess of Arundel, or the granddaughters of Mary Ferrar of Little Gidding or Lady Grace Mildmay of Northamptonshire, this resulted in the provision of a dispensary.[91] At Cannons in 1725 there was a dispensary with a painting of a corpse on the wall.[92] According to Anne Clifford, her mother was 'a lover of the study of medicine' who prepared 'excellent medicines that did good to many' in the late sixteenth and early seventeenth centuries. Bridget Marbury, wife of a Lincolnshire cleric, gave birth to thirteen children of her own and was (in her free time!) an accomplished community midwife.[93] Somewhat later, John Evelyn, when reflecting on the activities of his mother and sisters when he was a boy, said that preparing medicines occupied them very considerably:

[T]heir recreation was in the distillery, the knowledge of plants and their virtues for the comfort of the poor neighbours and the use of the family.[94]

Hannah Woolley assumed that women needed to know about medicine in much the same way as they needed to know about preserving meats and fruits, cooking and beautifying.[95] Elizabeth Blackwell displayed her expertise in her *A Curious Herball containing 500 cuts useful in the practice of physik* in 1756. There are indications that unmarried women and childless women were expected to share this expertise even when it came to midwifery.[96] As with any other aspect of her duties, the mistress of the household might be assisted by other family members – usually her daughters – but could also employ assistants. The Countess of Warwick, for example, employed Elizabeth Walker who 'was skilled both as a physician and surgeon . . . and she was very inquisitive of other doctors and had many English books . . . which she read'.[97] From the later seventeenth century there were medical books written by women to draw upon, such as Jane

Sharp's *The Midwives Book*.⁹⁸ The Frontispiece of *The Excellent Woman Described* (1692) shows a lady closeted with her library of books, among which works of 'physick' and 'surgery' are prominent.⁹⁹ Professional midwives and physicians would be consulted when necessary.¹⁰⁰ Some women went so far as to seek an episcopal licence to practise surgery and/or midwifery.¹⁰¹ In 1689 Mrs Elizabeth Frances was supported in her application for a licence by two surgeons, two physicians and a male midwife with statements testifying to her theoretical and practical knowledge of midwifery and of women's ailments.¹⁰² Joanna Martin, however, has argued that during the eighteenth century the role of the elite wife as pharmacist had been taken over by the figures of the housekeeper and the local apothecary.¹⁰³ Nevertheless some of the letters of Duchess Cassandra suggest that this transition was by no means complete.¹⁰⁴

Married women and financial matters

In the twentieth century historians became aware of the importance of moneylending in early modern England and of the role of women within it.¹⁰⁵ Barbara Todd showed how wealthy widows in Berkshire invested in property (through mortgages) and in local industry in the late sixteenth and early seventeenth centuries.¹⁰⁶ Recently there has been a flurry of renewed interest in the contribution made by single women to the English economy.¹⁰⁷ Judith Spicksley has argued that during the seventeenth century single women could well have overtaken single men as a source of credit in England as a whole and could have raised their own proportion of the nation's wealth, their possibilities of independence, and their marriage portions as a consequence.¹⁰⁸ Anne Laurence and others (including the author of this work) are adding considerably to our knowledge of women as investors and financial decision-makers in the eighteenth century.

This interest in the activities of the unmarried should not, however, be allowed to eclipse the considerable importance of married women to the economy throughout the period. There is, for example, a good deal of evidence that married women engaged in direct moneylending (formally and informally) and investing in mortgages and the nascent stock market. Two very different women offer excellent examples of stock-market speculation in the period down to 1721. Cassandra, Duchess of Chandos, invested money herself in the South Sea and Africa Companies and in Royal Assurance, and Henrietta Howard, Countess of Suffolk, invested in the Mississippi Project and the South Sea Company. The letters of both women indicate that they understood what they were about and considered themselves to be capable of both giving and taking financial advice. But whereas Cassandra wisely seems to have taken out at least some of her money from the Stock companies and bought instead into assurance, Henrietta was misled by her adviser, Lord Ilay, and lost her considerable investment in South Sea Company stock when the Bubble burst.[109] These two aristocratic examples hide a network of lending and investing that apparently spread throughout polite society. Cassandra, for instance, made it her business to invest money as shrewdly as possible on behalf of those of her nephews who had no inheritance (with money her mother, Lady Emma Child, gave her for this purpose) and female kin who had no marriage portions to speak of. She and her husband the first Duke pursued a deliberate policy of training up their nieces and female cousins, building up marriage portions for them and negotiating attractive marriage settlements. Cassandra kept careful records of precisely what she had done with the money, what the rates of interest were, and expected the recipients of the dividends to accumulate their money in order to increase their investments.[110] She was anxious to ensure that the investments accumulated for the young women remained separate from their husbands' estates.[111]

While some women made their investments personally, others did so through a male intermediary. For example, Henrietta Howard used Lord Ilay as her stockbroker. Mrs Elizabeth (Welwood) Molesworth, wife of Captain Walter Molesworth, wrote congratulating Henrietta Howard on her early successes with South Sea stock and bemoaning her own inability to take advantage of the opportunity for rich pickings. Then she explained her activities. A gift from Lady Sunderland had provided her father with £500 to invest for his daughter's benefit, and he had succeeded in doubling it. She continued:

As greedy as I seem, I should have been satisfied if I could by any means have raised the sum of five hundred or a thousand pounds more, but the vast price that money bears, and our being not able to make any security according to law, has made me reject a scheme I had of borrowing such a sum of some monied friend . . .[112]

Lady Betty Germain rebuked her brother George Berkeley for presuming that she would demand security from him for a much-needed loan of £4,000:

Why, thou fool, puppy, blockhead, George Berkeley, dost thou think I will be troubled with securities? Or can it enter into your no-head that if you were put to distress for four thousand pounds, that I should not think myself happy to be able to serve you?[113]

She dismissed the caution that others urged upon her, confident in her knowledge of her finances:

I have desired the Speaker to let you have what you want. He tells me he fears another such call from the Bank; but even though you should take the four, still I shall have enough without: – they are much higher discount than 13, which most of my last were sold at.

It would be a mistake to assume, however, that a married woman's importance to the economy lay principally in her primarily financial transactions, even at the pinnacles of the social hierarchy. As indicated in a previous chapter, married women spent a good proportion of their time considering how to advance their families in a material sense. Some used unusual means to do so. For instance, family tradition had it that Lady Bridget Willoughby in the late sixteenth century so favoured her younger son Edward that she contrived to purchase one of the family estates in another's name and then settle it upon Edward.[114] Furthering the family interests meant, however, not only a preoccupation with providing handsome portions and arranging suitable marriages for children but also with doing the same for more distant relatives of both master and mistress. When Duchess Cassandra wrote the following response to a letter from one of her own cousins regarding a marriage settlement it was with reference to another cousin.

In Feb 1716 my cousin Bell Coke writ a proposal from her nephew Wilmot who offered to settle £300 per annum in present upon his son and £300 per annum more after his own and his wife's death, for which settlement he thought his son deserved £5,000 or more, of which he should take but £2,000 for himself to provide for his younger children and the rest were the fortune ever so much his son and the lady should keep for themselves besides the £600 per annum which he should settle upon him if this proposal would be approved of for any of our relations it would be a great pleasure to her.

My Answer

I am obliged to you for the thoughts you have of serving any of our relations, but I do not know any relation or friend which has £5,000 fortune, that would be pleased with such a proposal as yours mentions. Sir Hungerford Hoskyns has near four times that estate, and had the other Sister married as my Lord had designed it would not have been to a much less estate than his.

I doubt the gentleman you write about values ladies at a less rate than they do themselves. My cousin Cass Cornwallis is now with me, you know what her fortune is, and truly I should be very sorry to see her marry to a less estate than that which you mention.[115]

Work outside the home

Many married women outside the elite and professional classes engaged in paid by-employment outside the home and from the home. The general view is that women's late medieval role in such work as the brewing industry declined in the sixteenth and seventeenth centuries so that married women retreated into more lowly manufacturing work (often working from home) and in retail.[116] Thus, according to the current orthodoxy, women's role was economically marginalised.[117] Much of the evidence about women's work pertains either to single women or to widows. Married women, however, continued to be important among the lower and middling social orders as dairy and market-garden producers and retailers, and as nurses and midwives, for example. They performed these jobs on top of their responsibilities as wives, mothers and household managers. However, the value of women to the economy cannot be assessed on the basis only of their paid work outside the home. Conduct books certainly did not see wives as unimportant on the economic side of family farms and businesses: for 'two eyes see more than one [and] two hands despatch more business than one'.[118]

Married women in Scotland

The picture of married women as active in domestic and estate affairs seems to be echoed in the case of Scotland. Inevitably we know most about the lives of noble women. One such was Lady Grisell Home, eldest daughter of the earl of Marchmont, who married George Baillie of Jerviswood at Redbraes in 1692, and was the mother of Lady Murray of Stanhope and Lady Binning of Haddington. Grisell was born at Redbraes Castle in December 1665, one of eighteen children. She had had a hard life during the troubles of the later seventeenth century, when her father had been arrested for high treason and had narrowly escaped death at least in part owing to her intervention, which prepared her for the role of wife to George Baillie until his death in 1738. Just after her marriage, Grisell took a course of cookery lessons from a Mrs Addison and another of dancing lessons. While she was young she had devoted two nights each week to dealing with her father's paperwork and it seems probable that she took lessons in book-keeping. After her marriage she not only kept her own and her husband's accounts in good order but also spent weeks setting her father's neglected affairs in order. Clearly she thought this an important part of a woman's duties and she paid for her own daughters' education in book-keeping.[119] Her household books are many and detailed. According to her elder daughter, George relied on his wife absolutely:

In her family, her attention and economy reached to the smallest things: and though this was her practice from her youth, there never appeared in her the least narrowness; and so far was she from avarice . . . that often my father said to her, 'I never saw the like of you, goodwife, the older you grow, you grow the more extravagant; but do as you please, providing I be in no debt'. Nor did he ever ask her another question about the whole management of his private affairs, but 'if his debt was paid'.[120]

Sir John Lauder (1646–1722) was another Scottish lord who, when he was but nineteen years of age, thought his wife's inability to write and do arithmetic was unacceptable: he paid for her to have private lessons to correct the deficiency, so that she could spend the allowance of 10 dollars (50 shillings) on the household.[121]

Grisell had known what poverty was. Now, living an affluent lifestyle, her husband often absent from her in England, she used her wealth to benefit others about her.

She had a cheerful and open cordiality, that made every one easy and happy about her. Her reigning principle appeared here very much; she took all that pains, that she might have more and better things to please other people with.[122]

Elizabeth Ewan has drawn upon burgh court records to examine the lives of more ordinary urban women in the later Middle Ages. She shows how married and single women formed networks through which they acted to provide mutual aid and sociability. This was of great importance during times of crisis, such as plague.[123] Being the mistress of a household without landed property meant much more than remaining in the home to handle domestic affairs or even keeping the household accounts. Married women supplemented the family income in many ways throughout our period. Some of these ways took them outside the home into the community. In eighteenth-century Edinburgh, married women worked in the retail trade; took in lodgers (known as room setting); gave their services as nurses of the sick; as midwives; and as wet nurses and day nurses for the children of the elite and of other working women; and as layers-out of dead bodies and makers of graves clothes.[124] Some of the women had served formal or, more often, informal apprenticeships. John Bell, Edinburgh merchant and linen-draper, kept a ledger from 1707 to 1724 which indicates that he dealt in his wholesale business with no fewer than one hundred female shopkeepers.

Mistress of a household in colonial America

Before the Revolution, homes in the northern colonies were generally timber-built single-room dwellings erected around posts driven straight into the ground. Such homes offered little privacy or opportunity for close emotional family relationships and few home comforts. A central hall would provide the living and working space for the household, which included one or more families and their young servants. Even the mistresses of great Plantations in the North American colonies enjoyed a standard of living that was in most respects considerably worse than that of their English counterparts and had responsibilities that included organising the daily lives of her own children and of young servants. These households might encompass several biological families – that of the Plantation owner, wife and children and those of servants and slaves.

We are permitted occasional glimpses into the married lives of colonial women and the ways in which they were regarded by their husbands. William Byrd II (1674–1744) was educated and spent his young manhood in England but in 1705 returned to his deceased father's Plantation, Westover, in Virginia. He married Lucy Parke, daughter of the colonial governor, and settled there. In 1709 he began to keep a secret coded diary, apparently to exclude his wife from his private thoughts and his sexual peccadilloes. A strange, shy man, he spent his days in solitude and did not share much of his daily 'life' with his wife. There was a place for her but it was allocated and defined by him. At the start of his diary he is angry with his wife for listening into his conversations from the top of the stairs. He refuses to allow her the run of his library. He saw his tempestuous wife as extravagant and wilful. It was her assumption of what he saw as his role that made him so keen to exert his own authority. For example, on one occasion she rebuked a guest for swearing. According to his biographer he used sex to maintain his authority over his wife, recording, for example, on one occasion that he had 'rogered' her and on another that he had given her a flourish on the billiard table. Yet he was also a gentle man, who 'walked with [his] wife in the garden', rued his lapses from the moral code, put up with his wife's many tantrums and tried to curb her unacceptable violence towards the servants. On one occasion she had deliberately burned a young maid with fire irons. In March 1712 Jenny was again her victim:

I had a terrible quarrel with my wife concerning Jenny that I took away from her when she was beating her with the tongs. She lifted up her hands to strike me but forebore to do it. She gave me abundance of bad words and endeavoured to strangle herself, but I believe in jest only. However after acting a mad woman a long time she was passive again.[125]

Clearly Lucy's behaviour towards the servants was intolerable and William's reaction understandable. He did, however, try to bring her round by gentle reconciliation for the most part. Shortly after this terrible scene we find him spending time with Lucy and drinking cider together. He went into society with her on his arm, had 'very merry' times with her and, when she died in London in 1716, he grieved her and wrote to a friend 'how proud I was of her'.

The majority of unnamed colonial women leaving little or no historical record worked on or were dependent on the land as part of a family unit. Women, for whom we do have names, who quietly brought up their children, attended to their home, livestock and kitchen garden, or managed a larger landholding, included Priscilla Alden, Hannah Duston, and Elizabeth Estaugh. In their households they tended kitchen gardens, preserved and collected food, butchered animals, made cider and ale, spun, wove and dyed cloth, made candles, churned butter, made cheese, cared for poultry and dairy animals. They, like their menfolk, bartered with their neighbours for additional supplies. Because their menfolk often worked within the home, these wives learned about business and trade, kept the books and supervised the apprentices. Sometimes they would display considerable initiative, although they might be conscious that this was not socially acceptable. In the early 1700s, for example, Abigail Adams managed all the family property and investments in Massachusetts – buying land, planning additions to houses and farm buildings, hiring and firing labourers, contracting with tenants, supervising farm work: 'Most of these things were accomplished without John's advice and in many cases without his knowledge. She often disagreed with him on the best way to invest their money, and she generally got her way. She also served as John's unofficial, unpaid, but most influential political adviser.' Nevertheless, she constantly sought John's advice and expressed unease about the extent to which she stepped out of women's traditional sphere.[126]

Matriarchy?

Were all aristocratic married women matriarchs? In reality the issue would seem to be a contrast between patriarchal and parental authority within the family rather than one contrasting the dominance of patriarchs and matriarchs. The 'strong women' highlighted in this study did not generally exercise power and influence at the expense of that of their spouses. Rather they exercised roles that complemented those of their husbands. Even so most of the rich evidence relates to the wives of leading aristocrats and it is difficult to assess the roles of other wives. Within a hierarchical society such as England's, where patronage and clientage were so much part of the fabric of life, it is probable that most influence normally belonged to the wife of the propertied male head of household, and that her married daughters and daughters-in-law had somewhat decreasing pools of influence, until such time as they and their husbands created patronage networks of their own. It is perhaps significant that, in the main, Lady Hester Temple communicated about business with the men of the Stowe connection – her husband, her sons, her sons-in-law, the estate agents – and only relatively rarely with her daughters. However, there are indications that they were acting in a similar way to her within their own families, seeking the assistance of their father and mother in securing the future of their marriages and their children. Hester's daughters were certainly involved in keeping their own families afloat financially. Also some of the letters address women on business matters or clearly see them as equal members of a partnership with their husbands. For example, Robert Hickeman informed Mistress Harley of a provision his mistress had made regarding a lease and asked both her and her husband to give their consent.[127]

We know that American societies were somewhat less hierarchical than English in the seventeenth century but insufficient work has been done on the internal workings of early American families to make a sensible assessment regarding the prevalence of a matriarchal as well as a patriarchal structure. Where there is documentation it appears to support the view that husbands and wives acted in partnership. Recent work by Terri Snyder, Debra Meyers, Kathleen Brown and others, however, suggests that assertive wives in seventeenth-century Maryland and Virginia were making husbands anxious and that this anxiety led to attempts to reassert patriarchy both within households and within economy and polity.

Brabbling women, both in print and in practice, illustrate the varieties of female agency in 17th C Virginia and, on a cultural level, reflect the substantial threat women posed to the structures of political and domestic patriarchy. The crises investigated here feature women who challenged both the doctrine of coverture and the practice of mastery: women who entered the political sphere, wives who breached the authority of their husbands, indentured servants who questioned the dominion of their masters, slaves who sought their freedom, and free black women and widows who sought the assistance of the court in governing and protecting their households . . . In a colony intent on shoring up mastery, assertions of political, legal, and domestic authority over women were of critical importance. Yet these declarations did not always have the desired outcome: given the right strategies, women in seventeenth-century Virginia – even unfree women – could prevail.[128]

Childbirth and overlap of generations

Giving birth to, and rearing, children occupied a goodly proportion of the lifetime of women at all social levels.[129] The Duchess of Newcastle wrote that 'all the time of their lives is ensnared with troubles, what in breeding and bearing children, what in taking and turning away servants, directing and ordering their family . . . and if they have children, what troubles and griefs do ensue? Troubled with their forwardnesse and untowardnesse, the care for their well being, the fear for their ill doing, their grief for their sicknesse, and their unsufferable sorrow for their death . . .'[130] Death rates for women were higher during the childbearing years than later although the sources do not allow historians to be certain that childbirth *caused* these deaths.[131] Nevertheless, it is vital to appreciate the commitment of health, time and energy motherhood involved, even when mothers did not breastfeed and even when they had servant help. The precise nature of the work children engendered varied, as Cavendish appreciated, with the stage of their lives and development. Barbara Harris has shown in her study of aristocratic women that the extent of a woman's participation in estate management may have been dictated partly by whether or not she was childbearing. Lady Anne (Vaux) Lestrange, wife of Sir Thomas Lestrange of Hunstanton, Norfolk, played a marginal role in the household during her twenties and early thirties. By 1530, however, her childbearing done, she was 'supervising both the Lestrange household and estates and keeping detailed accounts of her cash transactions'.[132] Teenage girls from lower levels of society frequently gained experience caring for children by caring for siblings or by becoming part of another household as servants.[133] Jane Whittle has shown how female servants were prominent in rural households where there were several young children.[134] For girls from all social classes, practical caring for young children was not only an occupation but also a training for motherhood. Relatively few elite women had as many children as Hester Temple or Elizabeth Clinton but large families were common among the aristocracy of England and Scotland. Apparently this tradition also spread to New England. Anne Hutchinson was the eldest of the thirteen children of her English father, the Revd Francis Marbury and his second wife Bridget, and Anne herself had fifteen children. Rebecca Park, an eighteenth-century resident of Grafton, Vermont (who died at the age of forty) had fourteen children, thirteen of whom predeceased her.[135] Nevertheless, in New England families, commonly between five and seven children of a family would survive to adulthood.[136] The business of childbirth itself was stressful, whether it resulted in live births or not. Childhood and adolescence also took their toll on parents' energies and emotions. Mothers (and fathers) then, as now, did not cease to love and care for their children just because some other person had day-to-day care of them in the household nursery or in the home of a wet-nurse or at a boarding school.

Among the elite the life phase of giving birth was often extremely lengthy and led to important overlaps of generations. This happened often in the Temple dynasty, where the matriarchs had long lives. Susan Spencer Temple was producing children who survived between 1560 and 1589 (probably from her late teens to her mid-forties) and her youngest children, Elizabeth (b.1585) and Peter (b.1589) were born at approximately the same time as her eldest son, Thomas's and his wife Hester's eldest children: Susan (b.1587), Hester (b.1589) and Bridget (b.1591). In many respects the relationship of Thomas and Hester to Elizabeth and Peter was that of parents rather than of siblings. This Peter[137] was deemed a lunatic and Thomas and his brother Alexander were given charge of him and his maintenance, education and marriage. Thomas arranged Elizabeth's and Peter's marriages and the letters of Elizabeth and Katherine, Peter's wife, to Thomas and Hester closely resemble the letters sent by their own children. Hester's years of childbirth spanned at least 1587 to circa 1609/10, by which time three of her own daughters were married and possibly childbearing.[138] Thomas's youngest sister, Elizabeth, aged nine, stood godmother to Thomas and Hester's daughter Martha in 1594.[139] This same Elizabeth as Lady Say and Seale was mother to Bridget Clinton, Countess of Lincoln, who by 1622 had already borne several children and breastfed them.[140]

Conclusion

Throughout the early modern period, aristocratic and non-aristocratic married women often lived their lives in demanding circumstances. They were required to be strong partners in most marriages. There was a biological cycle to married life and this may well have determined the nature of a woman's participation in the partnership. There is good evidence that married women did far more than tend and manage the house and care for the children, albeit these were important and energy-consuming parts of their lives. Wives of tradesmen and artisans took their share of jobs associated with trade and craft. Wives of farmers shared the agricultural work associated with the farm and pursued the retailing of surplus produce. Some married women combined the role of midwife or nurse or gossip[141] or wet-nurse or landlady with those of wife and mother. Wives of labourers took in washing and mending and sewing. Any impression that well-to-do married women lived idle, pampered existences must stand corrected. In the propertied classes, wives managed estates and many had a shrewd eye for business. Their active role in affairs prepared them well for their probable future role as widows. They used their knowledge of family politics often to effect. They acted as gatekeepers to their husbands' patronage. They were active in securing the futures of male and female kin both through investments and through appropriate marriages. The extent to which these women were able to determine their own activities and actions usually depended upon their own inheritances, upbringing, personalities and abilities, as well as those of their menfolk. Many such women negotiated a path through patriarchy that they found bearable. But when disaster threatened, married women were not slow to seize the initiative and seek to save the day. There is little foundation for the belief that colonial women were uniquely resourceful in these respects. The challenges they met were different but colonial women built upon a long tradition of capable wives and mothers already established in England and Scotland.

Notes

1 Rachel Speght, *The Women's Sharpe Revenge*, 1617.

2 John Foxe, *Acts and Monuments*, 1563, 8, p. 495.

3 E. Sanderson (1996) pp. 74–107, shows how young seventeenth- and eighteenth-century Scottish women were prepared during their youth for their later economic activity as wives in charity schools, sewing and pastry schools, and formal and informal apprenticeships. Jane Whittle has shown how servant girls acquired skills for later life. See Jane Whittle (2005b) *passim*.

4 J. Wormald (1981); M. H. B. Sanderson (1982); A. I. Macinnes (1982); Rosalind K. Marshall (1983); J. Wormald (1985); A. I. Macinnes (1986) and A. I. Macinnes (1993).

5 Maureen M. Meikle (1997) p. 173.

6 SRO, GD 267/27/76; *Calendar of the State Papers Relating to Scotland and Mary Queen of Scots*, Edinburgh, 1898–1969, xii, no. 38, cited in Maureen M. Meikle (1997) p. 181.

7 *Historical Manuscripts Commission Report*, 1902, p. 72, Document 145, Manuscripts of Colonel David Milne Home of Wedderburn Castle. In modern English the quotation reads as follows: 'take a horse or an ox from John Orknay till he come here and make his accounts . . . When thou comest over amongst other things bring my middle account book with ye . . . item my velvet gown and cloak . . . I what not how our daughter is pleased . . . God send all well and preserve thee and all ours . . . Thy George Holme.'

8 BL, Cotton MS Caligula C. VII, fo. 338; SRO, GD402/9/66; cited in Maureen M. Meikle, 'Victims, viragos and vamps: women of the sixteenth-century Anglo-Scottish frontier', in John C. Appleby and Paul Dalton (eds), *Government, Religion and Society in Northern England, 1000–1700*, 1997, p. 182.

9 Extracts from Memoirs of George Brysson, merchant of Edinburgh, J. G. Fyfe and R. S. Rait (1928) pp. 325–6.

10 Ibid pp. 322–3.

11 Andrea Knox (2002) pp. 13–31.

12 Maggie Craig (2002) pp. 84–100.

13 *Historical Manuscripts Commission Report* 5, p. 259, 1909, Manuscripts of Sir John James Graham of Fintry, ed. Mrs S. C. Lomas.

14 *Historical Manuscripts Commission Report*, 1902, p. 111, Document 264, Manuscripts of Colonel David Milne Home of Wedderburn Castle.

15 *Historical Manuscripts Commission Report*, 1902, p. 115, Document 271. Manuscripts of Colonel David Milne Home of Wedderburn Castle.

16 Narrative of Flora Macdonald, J. G. Fyfe and R. S. Rait (1928) pp. 442–3.

17 Mary O'Dowd (ed.), *CSP Ireland Tudor Period, 1571–1575*, 2000, Document 65, pp. 45–6, Edmund Tremayne, 'Why Ireland is not reformed', SP 63/32 no. 65.

18 O'Dowd, CSP Ireland, Document 42, Earl of Ormond to Lord Burghley, 23 May 1571; Document 41, Sir John Perrot to Lord Justice Fitzwilliam, 14 May 1571.

19 O'Dowd, CSP Ireland, Document 22, p. 19, c.1571, regarding Thomas Stukeley in Kinniscorthy.

20 O'Dowd, CSP Ireland, Document 108, p. 64, The Book against Robert Harpoole, 21 August 1571, SP 63/33 no. 39.

21 O'Dowd, CSP Ireland, Document 2.4, pp. 6–7, Brian Mac Phelim O'Neill to Lord Deputy Sidney and Council, 19 March 1571, SP 63/32 no. 2 (iv).

22 O'Dowd, CSP Ireland, Document 13.1, pp. 14–15, Nicholas Begenal to Lord Justice Fitzwilliam, 17 April 1571, SP 63/32 no. 13 (I).

23 O'Dowd, CSP Ireland, Document 143, p. 84, Lord Justice Fitzwilliam to Privy Council, 29 September 1571, SP 63/64 no. 15.

24 For an interesting discussion of the ambivalent attitude taken by both English and Irish contemporary male commentators to the political role of native Irish elite women, see Ciaran Brady (1991) pp. 69–90.

25 Donna M. Lucey (2005) p. 43.

26 D. Rutman and A. Rutman (1976) pp. 31–60; L. G. Carr (1992) pp. 271–91, especially pp. 272–6. There were some ways in which inhabitants were better off than in England – for example, food (cultivated and wild) was more plentiful than in England (Carr, 1992 p. 277).

27 Carville Earle (1979) pp. 96–125.

28 John Demos (1978 repr.) pp. 65–6.

29 Cited in Edward T. James *et al.* (eds) (1971) Vol. 1, p. 535.

30 Kathleen M. Brown (1996) p. 291.

31 Cynthia A Kierner (1998) pp. 69–110.

32 Christine Carpenter (1996).

33 Cited in M. O'Dowd (1991) p. 99.

34 J. Eales (2001) pp. 143–58.

35 Cited in Eales (2001) pp. 154–5; see G. Bankes (1853) and E. Halshall (1902).

36 M. O'Dowd (1991) pp. 92–3.
37 HEH, STB Box 2, Book 2, p. 11r.
38 See M. O'Dowd (1991) pp. 104–5.
39 I am grateful to Barbara Donagan for an interesting discussion surrounding this point.
40 M. O'Dowd (1991) p. 93.
41 Bernadette Cunningham (1991), 'Women and Gaelic literature, 1500–1800', 1991.
42 Vivienne Larminie (2001) pp. 94–108.
43 HEH, STB Box 2, Book 3, p. 12r.
44 See, for example, Thomas Tusser, *Five hundred points of husbandry*, 1573; Gervase Markham, *The English Housewife*, 1615; Michael R. Best (ed.), *Gervase Markham, The English Housewife*, 1994.
45 Greater London Record Office, DL/C/622, Consistory Court Act Book, 1626–7, p. 174; for an interesting account of her lodging house see Bernard Capp, 'The Poet and the bawdy court: Michael Drayton and the lodging house world in Early Stuart London', *The Seventeenth Century*, Volume X, no. 1, pp. 27–37.
46 B. Harris (2002) pp. 65–72.
47 Ibid p. 65.
48 S. Mendelson (1985) p. 190.
49 Mavis E. Mate has argued that aristocratic women's clothing prevented them from performing manual tasks and militated against their living an active life. See M. E. Mate (1998) pp. 139–40.
50 HEH, STT 22, 12 July 1630, Anne (Temple) Andrews to her mother, Lady Hester (Sandys) Temple.
51 HEH, Stowe Collection, Temple MSS, STT 19 c.1617–1637 (This must be well past 1617, when Anne married, as she refers to her children. Her father died in 1637.) Anne (Temple) Andrews to her mother, Lady Hester (Sandys) Temple.
52 HEH, HM 46407 Robert Higgins to Hester Temple 8 Mar 1626/7 from Finmere Oxon.
53 HEH, HM 46408 Robert Higgins to Hester Temple (who is at Dassett) 13 Oct 1627 from Finmere Oxon.
54 HEH, El 416 Chandos to Ellesmere.
55 A letter from the Duke of Chandos to his brother Dr Henry Brydges in 1722 indicates that men generally assumed that bishops' wives commanded the patronage of their husbands. HEH, ST 57 Vol. 22, p. 57–8, 16 Aug 1722.

56 HEH, STT 1924 Hester (Sandys) Lady Temple to Sir Thos Temple 1st Bt in 1614.
57 Interestingly, in the same letter she refers to her own 'year's allowance' of £40.
58 HEH, STT 1273, 2 Feb 1627/8 Sir John Lenthall to Lady Hester Temple from Stoke (Warws.).
59 HEH, STT 1276, 22 Nov 1629, Sir John Lenthall to Lady Hester Temple from Stoke (Warws.); see also STT 1283 Sir John Lenthall to Lady Hester Temple at London 1630, in which he asks her to stand surety for a loan and to provide his son with money to undertake business.
60 HEH, STT 1746, 4 Mar 1628/9, Sir John Rous to Lady Hester Temple at Wolverton from Rouslench (Worcs.).
61 HEH, STT 1746, 4 Mar 1628/9, Sir John Rous to Lady Hester Temple at Wolverton from Rouslench (Worcs.).
62 HEH, STT 1747, 30 Mar 1629, Sir John Rous to Lady Hester Temple from Rous Lench (Worcs.).
63 HEH, STT 1748, 4 Apr 1629, Sir John Rous to Lady Hester Temple from Rous Lench (Worcs.).
64 HEH, STT 1277, 20 Jan 1629/30, Sir John Lenthall to Hester Lady Temple (a business note asking her to take care of a payment to his attorney in Chancery).
65 HEH, STT 2057, 28 Apr 1630, Sir Peter Temple, 2nd Bt to Lady Hester Temple.
66 HEH, HM 46407 Robert Higgins to Hester Temple 8 Mar 1626/7 from Finmere Oxon.
67 For example, see HEH, HM 46494 Hester Temple to Edward Ayres from Burton Dassett 22 Aug 1635.
68 C. Shammas (1990), for example p. 95.
69 HEH, STT 2209, 10 Apr 1630, Thomas Temple to his mother Lady Hester from London.
70 HEH, Stowe Collection, Temple Correspondence, STT 1048, 21 June 1630, Robert Hickeman to Mrs Horleye (for whom see Harley). Hester's involvement in estate management during her husband's life and in peace time finds echoes in many gentry and noble households of the sixteenth and seventeenth centuries – for example, the Duchess of Newcastle, Margaret Lucas Cavendish, and her mother, Elizabeth Lucas; Lady Anne Heton Filmer (wife of Sir Robert, the author of *Patriarcha*!); Margaret Long, Countess of Bath (d.1561); Maria Thynne of Longleat; Dorothy (Percy) Sidney, Countess of Leicester; Lady Joan, and Lady Judith Barrington.

71 HEH, HM 46504 Hester Temple to Sir Thos Temple 1st Bt 28 June 1633 plus a note from him.

72 HEH, STT 1749, 14 Apr 1629, Sir John Rous to Lady Hester Temple from Rous Lench (Worcs.).

73 HEH, STT 2308, 16 May 1629, Sir Thos Temple 1st Bt to Lady Hester Temple from Wolverton; see, for comparison, the regard in which the Earl of Bath held his wife Margaret in the mid-sixteenth century: he had her conduct legal and other business for him in London in the 1550s. For this see B. Harris (2002) pp. 70–72.

74 HEH, STT 2308, 16 May 1629, Sir Thos Temple 1st Bt to Lady Hester Temple from Wolverton.

75 HEH STT 2294 Sir Thomas Temple from Wolverton to Harry Rose 30 Apr 1632.

76 See Rowena Archer (1992) pp. 148–81 and also Mavis E. Mate (1998) for interesting discussions of earlier wives and widows in this tradition.

77 Susan E. Whyman (2002 pbk edn) pp. 22, 56–61.

78 Whyman (2002) pp. 67–9. See M. J. M. Ezell (1987) p. 145 for another example of late seventeenth-century family members living cheek by jowl in London.

79 See NLCS, Copy Letter Book of Cassandra, Duchess of Chandos, 1713–1735, no. 1, p. 1, To Stephen Rothwell.

80 See Copy Letter Book of Cassandra, Duchess of Chandos, 1713–1735, no. 123, p. 62a, To my brother Middleton, 16 Mar c.1721/2.

81 See, for example, Copy Letter Book of Cassandra, Duchess of Chandos, 1713–1735, no. 7 p. 6 To the Lady Chandos at Dr [Henry] Brydges' house in Dover Street Jan 1714; no. 107 pp. 55–6 To my cousin Hartstonge 31 Dec [Undated]; no. 191, p. 105 To Right Hon. Lord Carleton, Lord President of the Council 10 Dec [?1724]; no. 354, p. 213 To Sister Chamberlayne 20 Feb 1732/3; and no. 122, p. 62a, To Mrs Brydges of Bosvill Court 15 March 1721/2.

82 See Copy Letter Book of Cassandra, Duchess of Chandos, 1713–1735, no. 81, p. 43 To the Duchess of Bedford 29 Sep 1720 regarding a mortgage on Bolingbroke's estate; no. 82, pp. 43–4 To the Lady Davall 30 Sept [1720] regarding a loan and a mortgage; no. 83, p. 44 To Lady Davall 30 Sept [1720]; no. 84, pp. 44–5 To Lady Davall 14 Oct [1720]; no. 85, p. 45 To the Lady Thorold 1 Oct 1720; no. 86, p. 45 To the Lady Thorold 9 Oct 1720; no. 96, pp. 49–50 To the Duchess of Bedford 20 May [1720].

83 For Emma see Dorothy Johnston, 'Emma Child, née Barnard, formerly Willughby (1644–1725): records of the life of a gentlewoman', in John Beckett (ed.) *Nottinghamshire past: Essays in honour of Adrian Henstock*, 2003.

84 See *Life and Letters of Cassandra, Duchess of Chandos (1670–1735)* R. O'Day, 2007.

85 A. Hanham (1985) pp. 316–17, 404, 412–14.

86 Not all late seventeenth-century wives were kept in the background of their husband's lives as was Elizabeth Pepys but even the Pepyses enjoyed expeditions to the theatre and shops and summer outings. Samuel Pepys taught his wife arithmetic, astronomy and music and found her an apt pupil. He admired her artistic efforts. See Claire Tomalin (2002) pp. 195–214.

87 A. Vickery (1998) pp. 135–47.

88 See Vickery, pp. 385–9 based on Lancaster Record Office, Diaries of Mrs Elizabeth Shackleton in DDB/81/18–20 and 36–7. These points also applied to Cassandra, Duchess of Chandos in the early eighteenth century.

89 HEH, STB Box 2, Book 3, pp. 9–10.

90 Roger Timothy, *The Character of a Good Woman*, 1697, p. 43.

91 H. G. F. Howard (1857), cited in H. Bourdillon (1988) p. 17.

92 HEH ST 83.

93 D. Crawford, *Four Women in a Violent Time*, pp. 11–15, cited in H. Bourdillon (1998) p. 17.

94 BL, John Evelyn, *Diary*, 19 January 1686 (writing of his earlier life).

95 Hannah Wolley, *The Accomplisht ladys delight in preserving, physick, beautifying and cooking*.

96 See NLCS, Copy Letter Book of Cassandra Brydges, *passim*.

97 Anthony Walker, *Holy life of Mrs E. Walker*, 1690.

98 Jane Sharp, *The Midwives Book*, 1671; also Sarah Stone, *Complete Practice of Midwifery*, 1737.

99 Theophilus Dorrington (transl.), *The Excellent Woman Described by Her True Characters and Their Opposites*, 1692.

100 See M. Pelling (1998) for an excellent discussion of women from the lower social orders and medicine in the early modern period.

101 See J. Donnison (1988) for an account of the way in which midwifery gradually ceased to be regarded as women's work from the seventeenth century onwards.

102 O. Moscucci (1990) pp. 8–9.

103 Joanna Martin (2004) p. 167.

104 See, for example, Copy Letter Book, no. 159, p. 82. To the Dutchess of Marlborough 6 Nov 1723.

105 B. A. Holderness (1975/6); B. A. Holderness (1979); B. A. Holderness (1984); R. G. Griffiths (1933); W. C. Jordan (1993).
106 B. Todd (1990) pp. 195–7.
107 See, for example, P. Sharpe (2002).
108 See, for example, J. M. Spicksley (2004).
109 See J. W. Croker (1824) Vol. 1, pp. 42–5 Letter from Archibald Lord Ilay from Paris Sept 1719 to Mrs Howard and p. 45–8 Letter from Archibald Lord Ilay from Paris 16 Jan to Mrs Howard.
110 Croker (1824) Vol. 1, pp. 42–5 Letter from Archibald Lord Ilay from Paris Sept 1719 to Mrs Howard.
111 See Rosemary O'Day, 'Maidens and the Stockmarket: Marriage Portions and Matchmaking, 1700–1735', forthcoming.
112 Croker (1824) Vol. 1, pp. 54–6. Mrs Elizabeth (Welwood) Molesworth, wife of Captain Walter Molesworth, fifth son of the 1st Lord Molesworth, to Mrs Howard from Axminster, 25 June 1720.
113 Croker (1824) Vol. I, pp. 71–3 Lady Betty Germain to George Berkeley, her brother, 17 Oct 1720. This is apparently an edited version of HEH, HM6664 Suffolk Papers letter from Betty Jermain to George Berkeley at the Admiralty Office, receipted 19 Oct (undated but c.1720).
114 HEH, STB Box 2, Book 3, p. 39.
115 Duchess of Chandos's Copy Letter Book.
116 J. M. Bennett (1996).
117 L. Charles and L. Duffin (1985); P. Sharpe (1996); P. Sharpe (1998); P. Sharpe (2002).
118 See William Whateley, *A Bride bush: or, a direction for married persons*, 1623, pp. 83–6.
119 Robert Scott-Moncreiff (1911) pp. xxxiv, 29.
120 Lady Murray of Stanhope (1821) p. 73.
121 Extracts from the journal of Sir John Lauder, Lord Fountainhall, J. G. Fyfe and R. S. Rait (1928) pp. 202–3.
122 Lady Murray of Stanhope (1821) p. 73.
123 Elizabeth Ewan (2002) pp. 117–36.
124 E. Sanderson (1996) pp. 5–64.
125 K. A. Lockridge (1987) p. 49.
126 Lynne Withey (2000) p. xi.
127 HEH, STT 1048, 21 June 1630, Robert Hickeman to Mrs Horleye (for whom see Harley). The lease probably pertained to land 'owned' by Hester.

128 T. Snyder (2003) pp. 16–18.
129 See L. Pollock (1990) pp. 39–67, especially pp. 45–9 and 59.
130 Margaret Cavendish, *Playes*, 1662, p. 160 cited in S. Mendelson (1985) p. 195.
131 See B. J. Logue (1991) pp. 309–43, especially pp. 320–22 which summarise findings for North America.
132 B. Harris (2002) p. 67.
133 Ann Kussmaul estimated that 60 per cent of the early modern 15–24 age group were engaged in service. A. Kussmaul (1981) p. 3.
134 Jane Whittle (2005a) pp. 57–8, 65, 74.
135 D. M. Lucey (2005) p. 38.
136 Richard Middleton (1992) p. 67.
137 Not to be confused with Sir Thomas's eldest son, Sir Peter Temple of Stowe.
138 See parish registers of Stowe and Burton Dassett; Hester's record of her children's births (HEH, STT Personal Box 5, Folder 7 1602 Hester Temple: giving the dates of the births of her first eleven children from 5 Sep 1587 to 11 Sep 1602. Two of these children, John I and Jane Sybila died within weeks of birth); and STT Genealogy Box.
139 In STT Personal Box 5, Folder 7, Hester wrote, 'Martha Temple was borne the 8th of Januarye 1594: betwixt 2:and:3: in the afternoone the godfather was Mr Paule Risley [husband of Thomas's sister Dorothy and therefore the child's uncle]; her godmothers were her aunts mris Susan Denton and mris Elizabeth Temple: maydes', both of whom lived locally.
140 Elizabeth Clinton, *The Countess of Lincolnes Nurserie*, 1622.
141 Women who were paid to sit with the sick and dying.

CHAPTER 10

Mothers

Good Mother

I can not present you with any thing in thankfulness for your much care of me, but an acknowledgement of them, which I will do to the last day of my breath. I obey your command in keeping my father company: which is a great happiness to me, in respect he is so merry and healthful. I should think I had all thing here if we hade your cheerful company: which I hope will be shortly: I am sorry that our businesses proceed no better: but god will teach me to bear poverty: that I may know how to use riches.

In deed forsooth, I think you conceive me to be, light of foot, that you have sent me such heavy soles: these must needs make me a housewife for I can not well roll a broad: but to be serious with you it is for lack of wit if I be not a good housewife for I rise very early and look about and me thinks all things are well: and I am your true obedient daughter Margratt Longvill.[1]
[In the margin is written 'pray some nedells']

Introduction

In this early seventeenth-century letter Margaret Longville of Wolverton, a young married adult, expressed her gratitude to her mother for her loving care and demonstrated her continuing obedience to her mother's wishes. Her letter also indicates the easy relationship she had with her parents as she joked with her mother. One of the main purposes of marriage was the procreation of children, and women early prepared themselves for this. Motherhood was not, however, easy for women. In this chapter we consider what is known about early modern motherhood and what it implied in terms of work and relationships.

The part motherhood played in women's married lives

Women spent much of their married lives taking care of their babies and children. This was true in all these societies and at all social levels. A noble woman might have had wet-nurses, dry-nurses, nannies and governesses in the nursery and rather less direct care of her offspring than did the mother of the middling or lower sorts but she, nonetheless, had responsibility for the manner of their upbringing, the recruitment and supervision of their carers and the nature of their education. A large proportion of children who could read learned to do so at their mothers' knees.[2] A mother's literacy was appreciated by contemporaries as being extraordinarily important for the literacy of her children. It was also she who was primarily responsible for the religious education and moral upbringing of her children. There are examples of this influence at many social levels and throughout the period. It was sometimes indicative of the continuing importance of oral culture. For instance, in the early sixteenth century Mrs Alice Collins of Burford was notable because she could recite the scriptures and many other good books. She was observed to have taught her daughter and also men within the connection. Other relatives – daughters, grandmothers, aunts – and servants frequently shared the day-to-day care of young children in and out of the parental home but their role was normally subsidiary to that of the mother, unless she were dead.

Motherhood came early and often for most wives. The close association between marriage and procreation had been apparent in the pre-Reformation Church in the fact that St Anne was the patron saint of both married couples and childbirth.[3] The number of children a woman had was partially determined by the length of her marriage. It was common for a woman to give birth within a year of marriage and at very frequent intervals thereafter. Hester Temple, who gave birth to fifteen children (thirteen of whom survived and married) between 1587 and circa 1609, was unusual only in the length of her marriage and her success in child-rearing.[4] Historians have examined the sources carefully to establish whether birth control was practised and especially to see whether breast-feeding was consciously employed as a method of natural birth control.

Childbed and churching

Immediately after childbirth the mother was confined, first to her bed and then to her house. For some, such confinement must have represented considerable practical difficulties – the widowed mother of several young children, for example. It was small wonder that in such circumstances mothers made siblings grow up fast and depended upon their own mothers and neighbours for assistance. Even the landed gentry were often poorly supplied with necessaries. When the period of confinement was over, the woman, wearing a veil and bearing a candle, was attended to church for a ritual celebration of the end of her uncleanness that had been occasioned by childbirth. Unless her baby had been born a 'creature' (stillbirth) or very sick, baptism followed thereafter. This was the occasion for more sociability. Each baptised child was given three godparents: two godfathers and one godmother for a boy and two godmothers and one godfather for a girl. The child was customarily named after one of the godparents.[5] Frequently the godparents were also members of the child's wider family. These godparents were expected to concern themselves with the future spiritual well-being of their godchildren. Often young babies died, however, and those who died shortly after baptism were known as 'chrissoms'.

Women as mothers

Woman's role as mother was regarded as both essential and natural. Recent historians have shown how this role was socio-economically constructed. Biologically, of course, only women could give birth but the emphasis on reproduction in a society was not inevitable and neither was the woman's role in the upbringing of children. Patricia Crawford suggests, for example, that aristocratic women were less likely to be economically productive and therefore more emphasis was laid upon their reproductive labour.[6] It was not simply that such women did not have to go out to work: they had the responsibility for continuing and maintaining the family line, for ensuring that the offspring were not only healthy but manageable, for associalisation and acculturation (for transmitting ideas about acceptable behaviour within the family and community). She forgets, however, that bearing children and rearing them successfully was in fact the greatest economic contribution a woman could make to the household at all social levels.

Because giving sucke is a mother's duty, and hindered by breeding and bearing another child, man ought to doe what hee can to containe for that time: yet dare I not make this an inviolable law for man and wife to deny due benevolence each to other, all the time that wife giveth sucke.[7]

The portrayal alive in medieval art of woman as mother offering her breast to her child continued to be enormously powerful in European culture generally. The image of the Virgin Mary nursing the Christ child was extended to include more contemporary relationships. Moreover, this analogy was not only used in Catholic contexts. For example, when Elizabeth of Bohemia was crowned Queen in 1619 she was heavily pregnant with her third child and in a prayer during the ceremony she was declared a nursing mother of the Church. Northern humanists such as Erasmus supported breastfeeding. In his *Puerpera* Erasmus wrote that this was essential to motherhood. Erasmus had enormous influence upon early sixteenth-century English and Welsh society and this influence continued after his works were banned by the Catholics in 1559. Protestant writers adopted his advice. The dialogue was not only available in Latin but also in more accessible English editions of seven Erasmian dialogues, including the *Puerpera* (New Mother), translated by William Burton, Puritan minister of Norwich.[8] Erasmus emphasised the value of breastfeeding to the physical and emotional growth of the young child but women were at least as attracted by its effect as a form of birth control. If the intervals between births are examined it can be established that many women did breastfeed their offspring. For example, despite the huge size of her family, Hester Temple's children were born, with occasional exceptions after an infant died, approximately at two- to three-year intervals.[9] English women who wrote advice books in the early seventeenth century frequently entered into the debate about whether women should nurse their own children or employ wet-nurses. Perhaps the most famous of these was Elizabeth Clinton's, *The Countesse of Lincolnes Nurserie*, of 1622 which gave much attention to this issue. She had not breastfed her eighteen children. She felt 'pricked in hart for [her] undutifulnesse' and certainly suffered in consequence of her many pregnancies.[10] In the early modern period as in the modern there was considerable debate about the wisdom of breastfeeding by the natural mother. It seems that one either loved or hated the idea. There were those who preached 'Mother's breast is best' and those who thought breastfeeding inimical to the health of the mother, to the relationship between mother and family and to the future well-being of the child. Mothers' milk was thought to be the conduit of health, sickness, temperament and sexuality. Early medical writers stressed that breastfeeding by the mother was advisable and acknowledged the emotional bond that was thus created.[11] The milk itself was seen as having almost magical and certainly tonic properties. Lady Katherine Murray in the mid-1680s reported giving both her husband and her son drinks of forced breast milk and in the 1700s Dr Archibald Pitcairn advised an adult patient to breastfeed from a woman. Some husbands and wives believed that breastfeeding destroyed a woman's figure and prevented normal husband–wife relations because sexual intercourse was thought to stimulate menstruation and adversely affect the mother's milk. The eighteenth-century Virginia planter and medic Landon Carter criticised his daughter-in-law for resuming sexual relations with his son while she was still nursing. 'Poor children! Are you to be sacrificed for a partner's pleasure?' Puritan authors, such as William Gouge in the early seventeenth century, who were eager to promote breastfeeding, recognised the sexual needs of both sexes but tried in vain to reconcile the roles of mother and wife, urging husbands to be patient and abstinent for a while. In Virginia as in England some husbands solved the problem by putting their newborns out to wet-nurses. 'I have been a parent and I thought it [having sexual intercourse with a nursing mother] murder and therefore either hired nurses or put them out'. Rosalind Marshall, however, suggests that there is little *direct* evidence to prove these hostile allegations that wet-nurses were employed because of a woman's vanity or laziness.[12]

By the seventeenth century it was generally accepted that breastfeeding *was* best, albeit not necessarily by the mother. Dorothy McLaren argued that wet-nursing was the norm for rearing children of the rich from 1570–1720, while poorer women nursed their own offspring.[13] The health benefits of breastfeeding in the days after birth were unknown to people in the sixteenth and seventeenth centuries. Colostrum, now known to provide immunity to the young baby, was thought by contemporaries to be poisonous. The midwife Jane Sharp wrote, 'It is not good for a woman presently to suckle her child because those unclean purgations cannot make good milk.'[14] In the first days after birth a child would therefore be fed sweetened wine or would be put to the breast of another mother. Even mothers who eventually breastfed their children, therefore, might, if they could afford it, hire a wet-nurse for a period of about two weeks post-partum. This practice made eventual breastfeeding by the natural mother more difficult – because the sucking stimulus that encouraged milk production (lactation) was lacking. It also delayed the formation of the all-important bond between mother and child and rendered the babies susceptible to disease. In addition, women who did not breastfeed for up to two weeks after the birth suffered not only from problems of lactation but also from breast abcesses and other problems. Books of advice recommended many solutions to these problems, from suckling the midwife or puppies (!) to snuffing anemone juice.[15] It was not until the eighteenth century that the benefits of colostrum were recognised in medical circles. William Cadogan's *Essay upon nursing* of 1748 advised that colostrum was essential to a baby's life and his views were extremely influential.

Some women were reluctant to breastfeed their own children because of their knowledge of the contraceptive effects of nursing and their desire to breed frequently. It was also believed late into the seventeenth century that if a mother resumed sexual activity this would have a deleterious effect on a nursing infant.[16] At a time of high infant mortality such concerns were understandable. Maternal mortality or illness also necessitated wet-nursing in all these societies.

Rosalind Marshall has demonstrated that wet-nursing was practised in late seventeenth-century Scotland, although it was certainly not dominant. She used the Poll Tax Records for five Edinburgh parishes in 1694. Of 1,078 families with children, 6.8 per cent (seventy-three families) employed a wet-nurse either in or out with their own household. This practice was more common in the Tollbooth parish (12 per cent) for apparently social reasons. Tollbooth housed more upper-middle class households who kept servants and those families who employed wet-nurses tended to come from such families. 'Social divisions were also apparent in the occupations of fathers who employed wet nurses: of those whose occupations were known, 43% were merchants, 31% were lawyers and 4% were doctors.' One minister and a soldier occurred on the list as did solitary examples of tradesmen such as a candle maker, a baker, a periwig maker and a skinner, suggesting that the practice was gradually permeating down into society at least to master craftsmen. This study indicates that wet-nursing was rare outside the cities but warns that it was still practised in other parts of Scotland.

It was believed in Britain and her colonies that the characteristics of the nursing mother or wet-nurse substitute were passed on to the suckling infant: 'He sucked in his malice with his nurse's milk.'[17] Those English and colonial mothers who could afford wet-nurses chose them carefully to ensure that boys were nursed by wet-nurses who had themselves borne boys (for fear that the child would otherwise grow up effeminate), who were sanguine in complexion and temperament and who were healthy. Rosalind Marshall portrays aristocratic Scottish ladies as 'neurotically anxious about the outcome' of handing a baby over to a wet-nurse. When eventually the idea was rejected that babies consumed the characteristics of their nurse, it was still seen as crucial to choose an appropriate woman 'of middle stature, fleshy but not fat, of a merry, pleasant, cheerful countenance and ruddy colour' with a sociable nature, 'not given to anger but infinitely to playing and singing, she delights much in children, and therefore is the fittest nurse for one'.[18] The diary of the astrologer John Dee shows how important to him and his wife was the whole process of handing a beloved child to a wet-nurse. Far from neglecting their parental duties they agonised over the welfare of their offspring.

4 Aug 1581 (p. 12) 'Katharin was sent home from Nurse Maspley of Barnes for fear of her man's sickness; and Goodwife Benet gave her suck.'
11 Aug 1581 (p. 12) 'Katharin Dee was shifted to Nurse Garret at Petersham, on Friday, the next day afterr St Lawrence Day, being the 11th day of this month. My wife went on foot with her, and Ellen Cole my maid, George and Benjamin in very great showers of rain.'
25 Feb 1581/2 (p. 14) 'Paid Nurse Garret for Katharin till Friday the 23 day; 6s: then remaining due to Nurse for 4 pownd of candle and 4 pownd of soap.'
26 Feb 1581/2 (p. 14) 'Katharin my daughter became very sick.'
22 June 1581/2 (p. 15) 'Nurse Garret had 6s for a month ending the 18 day of May; she is to have for a months wages ending the 15 day of this June. My wife went this Friday hither with Benjamin.'
16 July 1582 (p. 16) 'Jane my wife went to Nurse Garret's to pay her 12s for her wages till Friday last, which was St Margaret's day: and brought her 12d for candles. She went by water; Mistress Lee went with her, in Robyn Jacke's boat.'
8 Aug 1582 (p. 16) 'Kate sickly.'
20 Aug 1582 (p. 16) 'Katharin still seemed to be diseased.'
25 August 1582 (p. 46) 'Katharin was taken home from Nurse Garret of Petersham, and weaned.'[19]

If breastfeeding was not possible, either because of expense or the unavailability of suitable wet-nurses, dry-nursing was regarded as a last resort. Early and mid-seventeenth-century contemporaries associated higher levels of infant mortality with dry-nursing. The child would be fed mixtures of wine, meat or rice broth, cow's or goat's milk, sugar and water through cloth teats and bottles. By the close of the seventeenth century, however, upper-class women in England attributed rising levels of infant mortality to the negligence of wet-nurses and began to dry-nurse their children. This trend lasted well into the mid-eighteenth century, when it became fashionable for well-to-do women to nurse their own children. These fashions followed medical advice.

Despite these fashions in infant feeding among the upper classes in parts of Britain and the North American colonies, historians argue that most mothers in the rest of society breastfed their own children for between one and two years. Weaning was recommended once a woman resumed her menses (monthly periods) for fear that contaminated milk would infect the child. Weaning might be a gradual or a sudden process and was regarded as a notable 'event' by both husbands and wives.

The method of feeding children provides an interesting example of the impact of socio-economic and demographic conditions upon actual behaviour, notwithstanding current thinking about an issue. Many of the Old World books recommending breastfeeding were widely available in the New World. Such views appear to have been resisted. In the North American colonies there seems to have been a general consensus that maternal breastfeeding was harmful for both mother and child. However, because of an acute shortage of women in the settlements, there was no ready supply of wet-nurses and thus no alternative to the breastfeeding they opposed. Ironically the societies least in need of natural birth control were those that could not easily avoid its consequences.[20]

Expectations of motherhood

It is difficult but important for historians to both ask and answer the question: what expectations did women have of motherhood? To some degree such expectations were shaped by the views of 'authorities' such as the Church, and this subject has been touched on earlier in this chapter. However, it is far from certain how much of this had been taken on board by women themselves. Where should we look to discover their own views? Diaries and correspondence could offer useful information. Elizabeth Freke, for example, clearly expected her child to be a comfort to her and was sadly disillusioned by her conflictual relationship with Ralph. She commented on his duty of care and concern and his neglect of her physical and financial well-being. She also expected gratitude from this son and from his wife. They should also have displayed concern for her feelings, with respect, for instance, to the naming of their children and her access to these grandchildren.[21] The point here, of course, is not that all women had disappointing relationships with their children or even that they shared the hopes of what motherhood would bring but that there are ways of discovering these relationships and expectations.

Supportive mothers

There are abundant examples of the close and supportive relationships that mothers had with their children, and especially their daughters.[22] These relations continued once the children had left home and it is often through written correspondence between mothers and their now independent children that the historian glimpses them. Hester Temple of Stowe had a large family of both sons and daughters and maintained close contact with them. She did not always approve of their actions and from time to time had difficult relationships (that were sometimes strained to the limit) with her sons Peter (the heir) and Thomas, both of whom had little or no financial acumen. Her daughters and their husbands tried her patience much less. In the letter from Margaret Longville as set out at the beginning of this chapter on p. 240, we see that odd mixture of formality and familiarity that characterised so much early modern correspondence between parents and children. Most notable perhaps is the joke that Margaret felt able to share with her mother about her own lack of housewifery skills.

Mothers as patrons and benefactors

A mother's blessing might take a practical form. Sons and daughters relied on their mothers to supply deficiencies in their own lifestyle, then as now. The extent to which a mother could oblige would, naturally, depend upon her circumstances, and her willingness to act as benefactor had to be secured by assiduous grooming. For example, Thomas Temple, curate of Bourton on the Water and a bit of a ne'er-do-well, could write to his mother Lady Hester Temple and be fairly certain that she could and would lend him 'the tumbrell carte' and 'greate and small Harrowes' until she 'have use of them'. Thomas parted with obsequious reinforcement of their bond:

So trusting upon your charitable assistance to mee hearein: I humbly begg your blessinges, presenting with all humblenesse of hart my filiall duty to you, and my good father, desiring god to continue yea to increase his blessinges spirituall and temporall upon you both that in the eveninge of your dayes the sunne may shine upon you both to the comfort of you and yours which is a sign of a glorious resurrection and thus I beseech god to graunte you both, and yours, and so I rest

Your sonne that truly honors you and the Lords priest that prays for you[23]

Daughters similarly continually renewed the bond with their mothers. Margaret Longeville wrote thus to her mother, Hester:

Good mother: I am much joyced you are so weell come down in to the contry: and woold have bene exsiding glad to have seen you if it had stood with your convenient sis bot it your kind and loving lines hath much raysed my hart sencs I reseueed them which I givee you most homble thanks for: and I pray you to bee plesed to ad wone hapines more to mee which is to givee mee your blessing and so I rest

Your obedient daughter[24]

The relative importance of the mother's patronage as compared with the father's is uncertain although it seems probable that children courted the parent who seemed to exert most influence and who appeared a 'soft touch'. Children manipulated their parents and exerted a kind of power over them.

Mothers and children

Mothers had special responsibility for the upbringing of children. This included both girls and boys and all ages. Some of this responsibility would be discharged in partnership with the father. So Sir Thomas Temple directed his son Peter regarding the upbringing of his infant son Richard Temple: 'I hope and desire especially you with my daughter your wife will do your endeavours to make him the child and son of God, without which he cannot be happy and with which he shall be blessed, whatsoever fools say in their hearts the contrary.'[25] Diaries and correspondence provide examples of the ways in which mothers fulfilled this responsibility. Sometimes this would be against a background of a difficult family life because early modern families, like their modern counterparts, were not always harmonious. Lady Margaret Denny, for instance, took her son Francis to task for 'swearing, cursing and storming like Bedlam' some days earlier. She 'spake most fully to him; oh why shouldest thou tear the name of God in pieces, did he wrong thee; if I have; better had it been that thou hadst struck me thy mother a box on the ear' on 29 February 1636. Her chaplain Samuel Rogers thoroughly approved her action saying that she spoke 'most wisely and discreetly this and much more'.[26] That this counsel seems to have had little impact upon 'that cursed imp' Francis Denny's drunken, loud behaviour is beside the point.[27] Samuel Rogers despaired of this 'contentious family' saying he was 'almost weary of angry, and furious spirits'.[28] But there are also more charming instances – as when in 1626 Lady Katherine Paston fussed about her son William's health at university[29] or when Elizabeth, Lady Finch, wrote to her husband Sir Heneage from Bath in 1667, reporting that their 'middle' children were enjoying and benefiting from the baths. John Finch was 'the only mirth wee have in the Bath' and 'he is so taken with his guide that teaches him to swimme that he commends him so much'. She goes on to say 'I am glad to heare the little ones are well. I should be very glad also to heare of Daniel and Heneage.'[30]

Severe mothers

The definition of 'severity' or 'strictness' is inevitably variable: a twenty-first-century audience would probably react with horror and disbelief at some of the parenting practices of our forebears but it is important to contextualise those practices and see them as, for the most part, the expression of love and care. Nonetheless sometimes contemporaries and near contemporaries themselves saw particular behaviours as noteworthy and unacceptable.

Mothers were expected to define the boundaries of their children's behaviour and by modern standards to be strict. They were, however, also expected to love, care for and encourage their children to behave well and to seek their children's best interests. There are indications that mothers were not always a source of comfort for their offspring. Elizabeth Paston in the late 1440s was virtually under house arrest by her mother, Agnes, because she refused to marry where her mother had chosen. In the late 1460s another Paston mother, this time Margaret, banned a rebellious daughter (who had married beneath her station) from her house, and ruled her sons strictly. Margaret retained, nonetheless, her children's affection and respect and this suggests that her severity was intermittent.[31]

Winifred Willoughby, over a century later in the 1580s, by all accounts had a most difficult relationship with her mother, Lady Willoughby. Winifred had developed a deep friendship with her brother-in-law, Edward, also confusingly named Willoughby, who became her confidante. She would 'ease her mind by telling him how much she suffered from her mothers severity to her and those unhappy divisions in ye family' and often said that she was suicidal. Then she fell in love with Edward and secured his and her father's agreement to the match. 'The greatest difficulty still remained, and yt was gaining Lady Willughbys consent; Ned writes yt when it was first proposed to her she flew into violent passions both with Sir Francis and her daughter Winifred and would by no means be prevailed with to hear of such a match and for fear least Winifred should steal away to marry privately, she kept her locked up by such hands as he could not convey a letter to her or get one from her and used her most sadly, in so much yt in one of Ned's letters to Sir P W he writes yt he fears by my Ladys severity poor Winifred will be lamed' (p. 36, 18 March 1589). In the end Winifred escaped her mother's clutches and married Edward privately. Her mother threatened Ned with death and destruction. Lady Willoughby also treated her youngest daughter Frances with similar severity and this daughter, too, eloped.[32]

Severe mothers did exist then as now but their severity, when prolonged, was remarked upon as unnatural both at the time and in retrospect. The Willoughby family at that date was what we in the twenty-first century would call dysfunctional. Winifred's father was too heavily influenced by his sister and his servants; her mother was often irrational and cruel and perhaps rendered paranoid by events. Both Winifred's sister Lady Bridget and her brother-in-law Sir Percy helped her and her impoverished new husband. Her late-seventeenth-century relative excused Winifred's and Frances's filial disobedience on the grounds of their mother's cruelty. Mothers and children had reciprocal duties and obligations and these did not include excessive harshness.

Distant mothers

Some mothers had rather distant relations with their children in terms both of space and emotion. Elizabeth Freke's relationship with her only son Ralph was in part shaped by his commitment to residence in Ireland. Strains were also put on their relationship by the arrears from the Irish estates that he owed Elizabeth after his father's death under the terms of his father's will. Elizabeth complained of his 'rude answer' to her request for payment and was compelled to take legal action. It is worth noting not only that this made her unhappy – it had 'broke my hartt' – but also that she saw his behaviour and their strained relationship as unnatural.[33] There are many other examples of mothers' relationships with their children being placed under strain by property matters.[34]

Grandmothers

Mothers, of course, frequently also became grandmothers. Their relations with their grandchildren (and indeed with their adult children) varied considerably as they do today. Mothers-to-be frequently returned to their own mothers' homes to give birth. In many cases grandmothers played an important part in bringing up their young grandchildren, of whichever sex.[35] This could be a shared responsibility with the children's mother. So in 1632 Lady Judith Barrington instructed her mother-in-law 'that if my sons follow not their books well, and carry them selves not well in my absence to you, or others, that you will please to use your authority to chide them. I hear they go much abroad to neighbours' houses to fishing; I should be sorry if the eagerness of that sport should make them the less mind their books, which must not be neglected.'[36] But it could also be the grandmother's particular responsibility. During her widowhood in the later seventeenth century Lady Anne Filmer oversaw the upbringing of her grandchildren and continued to run the estate for her sons.[37] Hester Temple appears to have directed the early education of her grandsons by the vicar of Burton Dassett from the late 1620s onwards, paying for their upkeep and tuition and receiving regular reports of their progress and health. '[I] also have been much absent of late from my school . . .' 'The children are in health, and I hope we shall do well here.'[38] At an unknown date she informed her daughter:

John and Henry are very well and present their duty to you. I also pray you to take into your consideration, and remembrance, 30 li that you received your self and 30 li more I paid to Mr Gutter for the boys' diet etc. there, and their diets clothes and schooling since they came to me . . . Your aged and weake
Grandmother[39]

Hester also preserved a copy of one of the letters she wrote as a young married adult in the early seventeenth century to one of her own grandmothers.[40] This slip of paper reveals both an intimate relationship and an instrumental one as Hester asks her 'Most loving and dear Grandmother' I entreat 'you for to buy me a fan and gloves and mask . . . and a gum for the Baby' 'and a curling iron' and ends with a conventional farewell 'and so I commit you to the great love of the Almighty God I rest Your loving Grandchild Hester Temple'.[41] In this case 'Grandmother' played her humble but essential part in the patronage network of the Sandys/ Temple connection.

Elizabeth Freke, nigh on a century later, assumed that a grandmother had rights with respect to her grandchildren. These rights included access (even the right to care for the children), a strong say in decisions taken concerning the children's careers, and to be consulted and listened to with regard to the naming of the children. When her three-year-old grandson

Jack died in a tragic firearms accident Elizabeth was inconsolable. She had wanted Jack with her when his parents entered lodgings in Norfolk Street; she had warned them earlier that the lodgings were dangerous because the servants mishandled the pistols and would do so again. Elizabeth accused her son and his wife of being responsible not only for Jack's death but also for that of her husband, who never recovered from the tragedy and was also denied a consoling visit from his elder grandson, Percy. Following Jack's death his father and mother did not correspond with Elizabeth.[42]

Mothers' advice to their children

Elizabeth Carey (or Carew) wrote prose advice to her children, of whose company she had been deprived by her husband Sir Henry for much of their childhood.[43] Another mother who expended much energy on written advice for her descendants was Lady Grace Mildmay, who, unlike Carey, had no pretensions to being otherwise an authoress or dramatist. More commonly mothers communicated their wishes for their children's behaviour and future more gradually and sometimes more subtly. Lady Tanfield was not subtle. Horrified by her daughter's public avowal of the Catholic faith and refusal to do her husband's bidding, confirmed in letters to her mother, she wrote, 'I perceive by your last letters . . . that I shall never have hope to have any comfort from you . . . My desire was . . . to have you live with your husband, and to live in that religion wherein you were bred.'[44]

So mothers and grandmothers gave direct advice to their children and grandchildren and much of this advice, being informal, ad hoc and oral, has not survived for historians to inspect. These women, however, provided role models, especially for their daughters and future generations of women, and it is intriguing to note how descendants observed their ancestors' lives. Grace Freke, for instance, had in her possession her grandmother's diaries and remembrances and copied out sections of them for her own edification – and this despite the strained relations between Elizabeth and her parents.[45] Cassandra Willoughby went to great pains to reconstruct and understand the actions and characters of her long-dead female relatives, constantly empathising with them and in some cases apologising for them. It was expected that a mother would act as a role model for her daughters.

When a mother could not or would not act as a role model for daughters, another female relative or friend would stand in. Unusually a father might provide advice. Sir Francis Willoughby, acknowledging that his wife provided an inappropriate model, wrote to his daughter Brigitt at Boreplace in March 1581. In this letter he tells her 'tis not beauty nor fortune but good qualities and a virtuous disposition which makes a Gentlewoman esteemed, therefore tis her good behaviour that must gain her own credit, he desires she will learn by others in time (she may guess who he means) to be wise and not repent too late – that now at first entrance she should frame herself a dutiful wife, and that she should take care to be indeed such a woman as she desired to be esteemed and thus she might increase and long enjoy her friends. In order to which two things were needful, serving God and knowing herself; he bids her therefore serve God first in the morning and last at night with earnest affection even from the heart and not for customs sake. Next he bids her learn to know herself, what is and what is not fit to be done, that she may follow the good and refuse the evil, he bids her be careful to keep good company, because [p. 24r] ill company soon infects those that are well inclined.'[46]

There is also occasional evidence that parents discussed the best advice to be given to their children, whether male or female. Sir Percival Willoughby sent to his wife on 10 June 1604 a copy of a recent book on the subject, which he asked her to explain to their son, Francis. It contains:

Many excellent admonitions to teach him how to live and die. This book he desires she will have read and explained to their son and with him to take good counsel in time and if he looks for more than his brothers will have he must endeavour to deserve more.[47]

Conclusion

In all these societies the role of the mother was acknowledged as profoundly important. The mother produced and reared children. She guided and educated these children to conform to contemporary social mores. She had an important part to play in determining their future marriages and hence the future of the 'house'. On occasion, especially when she became a widow of property, a mother could hold that future materially in her hands. Her role as mother was not fulfilled in isolation, however. On the one hand there was no shortage of printed and homiletic advice in the Old and New Worlds on how best to perform mothering duties. On the other hand there was often a continuing dialogue with her husband about what was best.

Notes

1 HEH, Stowe Collection, Box 8, STT 1410 Lady Margaret Longville (Temple) to Lady Hester Temple c.1631–1637.

2 Margaret Spufford, 'First steps in literacy: the reading and writing experiences of the humblest seventeenth-century autobiographers', in *Social History*, 4, 1979, pp. 407–35; Juliet Fleming, *Graffiti and the Writing Arts of Early Modern England*, 2001.

3 Eamon Duffy, *The Voices of Morebath. Reformation and Rebellion in an English Village*, 2001, p. 69.

4 Hester was reputed, at her death in 1656, to have 700 living descendants. Her marriage lasted from about 1585 to 1637. Her daughter Millicent, the last child to be married and to leave home, was still living unmarried in the family home in 1628/9. (See HL STT 1746).

5 Cassandra Brydges was asked to be a godmother so often, and had so many children named after her, that she wrote to one parent asking that the new child not be named Cassandra.

6 Patricia Crawford, 'The construction and experience of maternity in 17th century England', in Valerie Fildes (ed.) *Women as Mothers in Pre-Industrial England*, 1990, p. 14.

7 William Gouge (1626 edition), *Of Domesticall Duties*, p. 131.

8 William Burton, *The New Mother*, 1606 (2 editions), 1624.

9 See HL STT Personal Box 5 for a list of the first eleven of her children; the remaining four were born from 1602 to 1609.

10 Valerie Wayne, 'Advice for women from mothers and patriarchs', in Helen Wilcox (ed.), *Women and Literature in Britain, 1500–1700*, 1996, pp. 56–79; See also, Dorothy McLaren, 'Marital fertility and lactation 1570–1720', in Mary Prior (ed.), *Women in English Society 1500–1800*, London: Methuen, 1985, pp. 22–3.

11 Mary Martin McLaughlin, 'Survivors and surrogates: children and parents from the 9th to the 13th centuries', in Lloyd De Mause, *The History of Childhood*, 1974, p. 115; and Laurence Stone, *The Family, Sex and Marriage in England, 1500–1800*, 1977, p. 6.

12 Rosalind K. Marshall, 'Wet-nursing in Scotland, 1500–1800', *Review of Scottish Culture*, 1, 1984, p. 546.

13 Dorothy McLaren, 'Marital fertility and lactation 1570–1720', in M. Prior (1985), pp. 22–53, and esp. pp. 26–7, 43.

14 Jane Sharp, *The Midwives Book: On the whole art of midwifery discovered directing childbearing women how to behave themselves*, London, 1671; republished as *The Compleat Midwives' Companion*, 1725.

15 Claire Fox, 'Pregnancy, childbirth and early infancy in Anglo-American culture, 1675–1830', Unpublished PhD Thesis, University of Pennsylvania, 1966, especially pp. 194–8, 221; Valerie Fildes, *Breasts, Bottles and Babies: A History of Infant Feeding*, Edinburgh, 1986, pp. 272–3.

16 W. Harris, *An exact enquiry into . . . the acute diseases of infants*, 1693, p. 17.

17 *A dialogue between a gentleman and a lady, relating chiefly to the nursing and bringing up of children*, 1698, p. 39.

18 Rosalind K. Marshall, 'Wet-nursing in Scotland, 1500–1800', *Review of Scottish Culture*, 1, 1984, p. 546, citing Nicholas Culpeper, *Directory for Midwives*, Edinburgh, 1668.

19 James Orchard Halliwell (ed.) *The Private Diary of John Dee*, 1845, pp. 12–16.

20 Paula A. Treckel, 'Breastfeeding and maternal sexuality in Colonial America', *The Journal of Interdisciplinary History*, XX, 1989, pp. 25–52, especially p. 26.

21 Raymond A. Anselment (ed.), *The Remembrances of Elizabeth Freke, 1671–1714*, Camden Fifth Series, 18, 2001, pp. 24–8.

22 See, for example, A. Beer (2004) on Bess Throckmorton's relationship with her mother Anne; A. Laurence (1994 reissue 2002) p. 86 cites the examples of Lady Anne Clifford (1616) and Alice Thornton (1659).

23 HEH, Stowe Collection, Box 7, STT 2211 Thomas Temple to Lady Hester Temple from Bourton on the Water, Gloucs. 7 July 1630.

24 HEH, STT, Box 3, STT 1409 Margaret Longville (Temple) to her mother Lady Hester.

25 HEH, STT, Box 9, Sir Thomas Temple from Wolverton to Sir Peter Temple 14 July 1634.

26 T. Webster and K. Shipps (2004) pp. 45–6.

27 Webster and Shipps (2004) p. 49.

28 Webster and Shipps (2004) p. 45.

29 R. Hughey (1941) p. 97.

30 See *Historical Manuscripts Commission Report*, 1913, Vol. I, Item 467.

31 Norman Davis (ed.), *The Paston Letters*, Oxford World's Classics, 1999 edition, for example, nos 12, 87, 99, 103, 113, 137.

32 HEH STB Box 2, pp. 34ff. of the wife of Sir Francis Willoughby in the 1570s and 1580s.

33 Raymond A. Anselment (ed.), *The Remembrances of Elizabeth Freke, 1671–1714*, Camden Fifth Series, 18, 2001, pp. 254, 132, 24–5.

34 See, for example, the relations between Jane and William Stonor noted in Christine Carpenter (ed.), *The Stonor Letters and Papers, 1290–1483*, Cambridge, 1996, pp. 53–4.

35 See Chapter 13 on women's formal and informal education.

36 BL Egerton MSS 2644, fo. 31r. In 1628 Sir Thomas had written to his mother asking her to take care of his son Oliver that he might 'be quickly refreshed by God's blessing when he is near your affectionate and tender eye', 2644, fos 297–8.

37 M. Ezell (1987), p. 142 citing Kent County Archives, Filmer MSS U120, F7.

38 For example, HEH, STT, Box 6, 1007 William Harte to Lady Hester Temple 1627. The letter indicates that the school was recently set up.

39 HEH, HM 46497, Hester Temple to 'daughter' >1657 signed 'your aged and weake grandmother'.

40 It is possible that the 'grandmother' was not her own but that of her children, of course, but this would not alter the significance of the communication.

41 HM 46493 Hester Temple to her grandmother 1606. The baby was probably Miles Temple, born c.1605/6.

42 Raymond A. Anselment (ed.), *The Remembrances of Elizabeth Freke, 1671–1714*, Camden Fifth Series, 18, 2001, pp. 27–9; 82, 83, 247, 248.

43 B. Lewalski (1992), p. 185.

44 Lewalski (1992), p. 187.

45 Raymond A. Anselment (ed.), *The Remembrances of Elizabeth Freke, 1671–1714*, Camden Fifth Series, 18, 2001, p. 32.

46 HEH STB Box 2, Book 2 pp. 23r and 24r.

47 HEH STB Box 2, Book 3 p. 7v.

CHAPTER 11

Wives and property

know all men by these present that I, Lady Elizabeth Viscountess Say and Seale, have received of my loving brother Sir Thomas Temple knight and Baronet all such writings as he saith were in his hands concerning my jointure which writings the said Sir Thomas Temple hath delivered to me at my own request and in obedience to an order made heretofore in the High Court of Chancery witness my hand and seal[1]

Introduction

Throughout this book we have uncovered evidence that the role that a woman was allowed to play in her family and in the wider community was very heavily dictated by personal circumstance. During these three centuries legal instruments were increasingly used to protect wives and widows against the vagaries of such circumstance and personal preference. It is difficult, if not impossible, to distinguish completely between the rules of property ownership as applied to wives and to widows. In this chapter we treat, in the main, the rules as they applied to women while their husbands were still alive and the implications of those rules for women's lives. In Chapter 12 we examine the rules as they applied to widows and the ways in which widows seem to have conducted their lives. This was a period in a woman's life when she was most likely to go to law to protect her jointure.

The rules of intestacy: inheritance in England, Wales, Scotland, and Ireland

Until relatively recently historians have been largely concerned with the rules of intestacy regarding the division of freehold property.[2] In most of England (and in Wales after 1536) these rules of intestacy provided that, in the event that the freehold property holder left no will, freehold property would pass to the eldest son and failing a male heir to the daughters equally. This system is known as primogeniture. In some areas, different systems, such as gavelkind (partible multigeniture inheritance) or even borough-English (where the youngest son inherited), prevailed. Now it is accepted that much property was held by copyhold or leasehold (where different rules of intestacy applied) and, moreover, that parents at all points on the social scale attempted to provide for all their children as far as possible, using various legal mechanisms such as the will and the use, and several types of trust. Holding property of various kinds (what we would call spreading one's investment portfolio) was a good strategy that contemporaries seem to have appreciated. For example, in Whitehaven, Cumberland, Joseph Berry, an apothecary, specifically bequeathed his freehold properties to his two younger daughters (because freehold property was devisable by will) but Eleanor his eldest daughter automatically inherited his three customary tenements, which he was not allowed to will away.[3] Widows and orphans in land held by copy of the manor rolls frequently depended upon personal negotiation or mediation with the lord of the manor to ensure continuity of tenure. Such customs varied from manor to manor. One example will suffice. Christine Churches established that in Whitehaven, Cumberland, a new town built after 1660, most land was held by customary tenure. If there were no male heir, the eldest girl inherited and not all the girls equally as under common law. Although testators sometimes tried to vary the custom, ultimately it was the customary court that decided who was the heir.[4] Another example from Whitehaven, where half of all customary tenures were either held jointly or by women solely, shows that it was common for a male customary tenant to negotiate a marriage settlement whereby he surrendered his sole tenure and took out a new 'joint' admittance for himself and his wife. On the other hand, when a woman with customary tenure married, she remained sole owner unless she deliberately surrendered.[5] This meant that often a husband did not need to provide for his wife because she already had a life interest in property. This practice also hints at the canny approach of parents (and young women themselves) in negotiating secure settlements for their daughters. Many English women (from the middling sort and above) entered marriage with property of their own, or inherited such property during their marriage. Moreover, the goods and chattels that women inherited or received as part of their marriage settlements made them important to the economic survival of a marriage and a family even when they had no landed property.

Although land formed an important part of the estate an heiress could bring to a marriage, there were many other forms of property which made a valuable contribution to her new family. Advowsons to ecclesiastical livings were a case in point for they increased the family's influence. For example, in 1611, Thomas Egerton had in his gift (through his wife, formerly Countess of Derby) the right of presentation to the living of Bangor. On her death, by Act of Parliament, this right would pass to her daughters.[6] Then there were commercial interests. When the clergyman son of Robert Whitby married the widow of Mr Gamull, late recorder of Chester, he acquired through her the profits of a mill on the river Dee.[7]

In Scotland women generally kept their own name after marriage whereas in England wives took their husband's surname. A Scottish heiress would be known as the lady of the estate, equivalent to the laird, while in England the heiress would not have quite this status.[8] In both England and Scotland single heiresses and widows were the only women able to hold property in their own right, unless they ingeniously employed legal instruments to the contrary.[9]

The situation in Ireland and in Wales seems confusing to the modern mind and, indeed, there is some evidence that contemporaries were also confused by the clash of jurisdictions, rules and customs. Broadly speaking, in the English Pale of Ireland, English inheritance customs prevailed although there were areas which had been little anglicised where Gaelic customs were followed.[10] Although in areas of English law daughters might inherit land in the absence of sons, in practice, entails were used to circumvent this necessity. In Gaelic Ireland and Wales clans were, as noted in the introduction, agnatic groupings where the links with male ancestors were crucial. Land inherited by female descendants was held for limited, often short, periods only and then redistributed between male heirs. If the co-heirs agreed this partition could be made permanent. Lawyers compared this to the inheritance customs of Kent and called it 'a custom in nature of gavelkind'.[11] By native Irish law and custom, a woman might not inherit the hereditary property of her clan. If she did inherit, this was only for her lifetime; on her death the property passed to the agnatic heirs and not to her children. (The Elizabethan Irish Court of Chancery, influenced by English law, acted contrary to this custom by insisting on the right of a woman to inherit in the absence of sons.) Yet Kenneth Nicholls has indicated that women were granted lands and other property in 'mortgage for the amount required for her dowry' or for that of daughters. Also in purely Gaelic parts of Ireland a married woman had the right to acquire, hold and administer property independently of her husband. Kenneth Nicholls has shown how this right applied until the late sixteenth and even seventeenth centuries when gradually this entitlement was eroded by English common law. Awly MacCoghlan, in order to raise funds to save himself from the gallows, sold half his share in some land in Clonoony, County Offaly, to Mairgreead ni Coirechain, wife of his elder brother. Johan fitz John joined with her husband to purchase lands in Garrynoe, County Limerick, but by her will devised her share to the son of her first marriage, suggesting some real independence.[12] Nicholls also suggests that so much of the stock and farming equipment was settled as part of a dowry that most farms would have been economically non-viable without this property. For example, when Margaret Tobin married Thomas fitz Richard she brought with her eighty cows, twenty-four stud mares, five riding horses, backgammon tables, a harp and household goods.[13] Frequently land was mortgaged to ensure that this dowry would be repaid to the woman if the marriage were to be annulled. In 1546 Ulick O Bruadair gave twenty-one cows, a bull and three horses with his daughter to her new husband Sean mac Donnchadha, for which Sean gave sureties and a mortgage on land as security for repayment. This protected the wife's future interest but also gave her land to administer.[14]

In Scotland heiresses might inherit both estate and title, as was the case of Isabel Murray of Bowhill, Selkirkshire, in the 1520s.[15] In Wales, however, prior to the Act of Union of 1536, women and widows could not inherit property in the same way as in Scotland and England and their chances of independence or influence were seemingly reduced as a result, although further research might reveal that Welsh like Irish women had rights that have been previously unsuspected. Union with England brought the mixed blessing of coverture. After 1536, in theory Welsh women had the right to be treated under English law as regards inheritance and property ownership during marriage, although historians believe that in practice this had less effect upon their position than might have been expected. Under the common law of England a married woman's legal identity was covered by that of her husband. She was feme covert and was not allowed to enter a contract or sue or be sued in common law apart from her husband.[16] Her position was somewhat different under the other main legal systems prevailing in England – ecclesiastical and equity.[17]

Coverture

Under English common law the property that a wife brought to a marriage – such as her dowry or portion or the wardships that she owned – was (unless some legal instrument was employed to protect her rights) legally handed over to the husband's control and use. The chattels (moveables) she lost completely, the leases might revert to her on her husband's death if he had not disposed of them already, the freehold and copyhold land could not be disposed of by the husband without the wife's consent but he received the profits and controlled the use thereof.[18] In Scotland married women could make property transactions only with the consent of the husband.[19] In practice, though, a husband's control over his wife's property was only as good as his control over his wife and this control might also have been limited by the existence of a marriage settlement. What often happened was that men treated the wife's property as part of their estate and sought the wife's consent and signature for transactions. This consent had to be given freely, whether in England and Wales or Scotland. Ann Cranstoun, wife of Andrew Ker of Cessford, surrendered property in Selkirk 'not moved by force or fallen in error . . . of her own free will'.[20] In Yorkshire Adam Eyre had considerable difficulty in persuading his wife to agree to a sale of her property.[21] At Whitehaven the Steward insisted on interviewing privately female customary tenants who wished to surrender their tenancy on marriage, to ensure that they were not acting as the result of coercion.[22] There is also evidence that some women were very active in protecting, managing and controlling their property and that their husbands saw this as a natural (if not always welcome) activity.

It is important not to imply that husbands and wives were at daggers drawn over the control of property – property was a family affair and most husbands and wives sought to protect the eventual interests of their widowed spouses and their children.[23] Francis Willoughby felt that he had let down his wife Emma by accepting a disadvantageous jointure settlement.[24] He tried to compensate for this by allocating her the remaining jointure payment of £2,000. Sir Josiah Child, Emma's second husband, has had a bad press because of his step-children's opposition to his election to the trust set up by their father Francis. Yet it seems that he took great care to invest Emma's £6,000 jointure to her considerable benefit (turning £6,000 into £10,000) and spoke also of his successful management of her

Willoughby jointure estate and monies.[25] Thomas and Hester Temple acted cooperatively in respect of her property. In such harmonious circumstances, wives accepted the latitude their husbands allowed them in the spirit that it was given. For example, in a letter to the parson of Finmere about a lease of her cottage there to Higgins's orphaned niece, Hester wrote:

I have received your letter and 10 li, and my husband's answer to that, is that in respect of his love to you and that you will make him your acquittance for wood mill and warren he is content to make her assurance of the cottage for her life which conditions that if he pay her any time within 7 years £10 again that shall be void and after the first 7 years if he pay £5 at any time it shall be void also; and truly upon my word I have been offered for 21 years £20 in ready money. I pray you make no [of]fer of your money nor of honest performance hereof thus remembering my love to you I rest your very loving friend Hestor Temple Thomas Temple alloweth hereof.[26]

Although women's historians have often seen feme covert as a vehicle of women's oppression, on occasion women might see it as a future protection. For instance, in a letter to the now-widowed Lady Hester Temple in 1642, Sir Thomas Tyrell suspects that she will try to avoid paying him a debt of £900 on the grounds that she had done everything '*femme covert* yet madam remember you are to give shortly an account in another world of your actions where that plea will not serve . . .' 'therefore Madam I pray you recollect yourself and discharge this debt as in justice you ought to do . . .'[27]

Separate estates and other forms of settlement operative during marriage

In many cases in England and Wales some of the property – freehold, copyhold, leasehold – was held by husband and wife as joint tenants. In the case of such a jointure, the widow was entitled to the income from the property. Legal jointures were enforceable in either the common law or the manorial courts and had largely replaced the system of dower by the early sixteenth century.[28] It became common practice for some of the money brought by the bride to the marriage to purchase land to produce an annual income (annuity). Initially this income was used to support the married couple and their family but the land was designated as jointure and provided an annuity for the widow once the husband died. The annuity was usually protected by a trust deed in the marriage settlement. The jointure system was useful in that it protected the wife/widow even where leasehold property was concerned.[29] Such a jointure would often include a separate house (called a dower house) where the young couple could reside.

To add to the complexity of the situation, marriage settlements in England and Wales (created by contract, bond or by will) often protected the right of the bride to different types of property – pin money; a separate estate held in trust for her use and her disposing during marriage;[30] and her personal paraphernalia of clothing, jewels, plate and household linen. As will be seen, such arrangements might give particular women considerable freedom.[31] The chief authority on women's property ownership in England and Wales states that: 'Conveyancing manuals ... demonstrate that the primary purpose of a marriage settlement was to preserve the wife's property rights.'[32] The establishment of separate estates proved unpopular with husbands but were recommended by women as a way of providing both independence and security. Mary More, in her manuscript essay 'The woman's right', advised her daughter in the 1670s that 'the laws of our country give a man after marriage a greater power of their estate than the wife, unless the wife take care before hand to prevent it (which I advise her to doe).'[33] In some cases a separate estate was created by means of a will rather than a separate marriage settlement. For example, Alice Thornton's mother, Alice Wandesford, had bequeathed her a separate estate held in trust and had, moreover, named all her personal property.[34] This protected Alice against the debts which her husband had incurred, when his will was probated. Often, however, the bride's family's motivation did not include liberal consideration of their daughter's 'freedoms': the marriage settlement would incorporate the creation of a separate estate as a means of ensuring that the bride's property from her birth family passed to her children (whoever their father) and that her parents and kin were relieved of the need to provide for her in marriage (if her husband could not stay out of debt or neglected his obligation to provide for her) or her widowhood.[35]

We would be wrong to assume that it was only late in the period that English women sought to protect their property during coverture. In the first half of the sixteenth century Margaret (Kitson Long) Bourchier, Countess of Bath, had her husband sign a pre-nuptial contract 'that included an inventory of all her possessions and gave the right to dispose of them as freely as if she were single'. Under coverture, however, the Countess could not herself enforce such an agreement. Instead, two of her daughters became trustees, with authority to do that for her should the need arise.[36] This use of trustees to protect a woman's rights was a constant motif.

English women's knowledge of the law

English gentlewomen were reasonably informed about the law, especially but not only that relating to property. Parents of daughters saw it as their duty to educate them in this area on the assumption that they would require such knowledge in the future. For example, Anne Docwra, a Cambridgeshire gentlewoman, was only fifteen years old when her father 'appointed her to the great Statute book that lay upon the parlour window and bid her read that; saying it was as proper for a woman as for a man, to understand the laws, because women must live under them and obey them as well as men.'[37] Mary More produced 'The woman's right' in order to educate her teenage daughter Elizabeth so that she would be protected from the worst aspects of the law.[38] Mrs Alice Thornton had clearly been given a clear explanation by her mother of the measures she had taken through a will and through trusts to protect her daughter's rights in a separate estate. As contemporaries stressed the special bond between mothers and daughters, and because girls were left longer in their mothers' care than were boys, it seems reasonable to suppose that a daughter's education in property law as in so much else was left to her mother. Jane Eyre, wife to a farmer, was fully aware of her rights regarding control over her own property when she fought against her husband Adam's attempts to convey it elsewhere.[39] There are several examples of women, married and unmarried, involving themselves prominently in legal wrangles. The involvement of Welsh mothers in fighting for their daughters' wardships tellingly suggests their knowledge of the law. Much later another Welsh woman, Elizabeth Baker, in the 1770s worked with 'a newly appointed solicitor . . . in putting together a damning case against' Robert Lloyd of Swan Hill, Oswestry, who was seeking repayment of a mortgage granted to her close friend Hugh Vaughan, who had given her a home on his estate of Hengwrt. In her diary she carefully recorded all the involved legal proceedings and her part in them.[40]

By the seventeenth century there was a perceived need for texts treating the complicated area of marriage law and the earliest treatise, *The Lawes Resolutions of Women's Rights: or the Lawes Provision for Woemen*, was published in 1632 but it circulated in manuscript for many years before this.⁴¹ This lawyers' manual was also aimed at women readers and it served its purpose throughout the century, because of its use of ordinary English as opposed to law French. When the *The Ladies' Dictionary* was published in 1694 it clearly expected its female readers to have an interest in and, and even some existing knowledge of, property law – entries for coverture, alimony, dowry, dower, feme covert and jointure occurred alongside entries about personal appearance, behaviour and etiquette.⁴²

In 1700 *Baron and Feme: A treatise of the common law concerning husbands and wives* was published, followed by an extended version in 1732 entitled *A treatise of feme coverts: Or, the Lady's Law, Containing all the Laws and Statutes Relating to Women*. The sole work to be produced by a woman (anonymously) and published on this subject during our period appeared in 1735 under the title, *The Hardships of the English Laws. In Relation to wives. With an explanation of the original curse of subjection passed upon the woman. In an humble address to the legislature*. This work was, as the title suggests, a spirited argument for change in this law. It provides evidence that at least some women were aware not only of the law as it affected them but also of its defects.

Historians have often assumed that the family bookshelves were lined with reference books used only by the men of a household but this was not necessarily the case. The small collection of books purchased by the Temples of Stowe in the 1650s was probably used by Lady Hester (whose

1 Sucklyng Poems Extraordinary⁴³	4-0
1 newes booke	-2
1 Almanake	1-6
1 Cooks Reportes⁴⁴	8-0
1 Leonards Reports⁴⁵	7-0
1 Stopes Fables by Ogleby⁴⁶	10-0
1 newes booke	-2
1 Ld Fynes speech	-6⁴⁷
1 Baxter against popery⁴⁸	3-6
1 Laymans Lawyer	2-0
1 Craggs works	4-0
3 newes books	0-6
1 petition	-4
1 Howells discourse⁴⁹	1-0
1 Frobells Arts	18-0
1 Accomplisht Courtier	1-6⁵⁰
1 Cowells Interpreter ⁵¹	6-0
1 Exact Lawgiver	1-6
	3-9-8

Note: HEH, HMT Temple Family Addenda Collection Box HM46553 (Listed as c.1600 but works listed indicate that a date in the 1650s is more probable.)

husband had died in 1637) and included law books as well as news books, poetry and books on religion.

Whereas the contents of the muniment rooms of great houses bear witness to the custom whereby the 'patriarch' archived and maintained the legal papers pertaining to the whole estate and the various marriage settlements and wills that touched upon it, there is also scattered evidence that some women took responsibility for guarding their own legal papers, even going to court to win custody of them.[52] In October 1632 Elizabeth Fiennes, Lady Say and Seale, took charge of papers 'being six sealed writings in parchment and four in paper' concerning her jointure, and her marriage licence from her brother Thomas Temple:

know all men by these present that I, Lady Elizabeth Viscountess Say and Seale, have received of my loving brother Sir Thomas Temple knight and Baronet all such writings as he saith were in his hands concerning my jointure which writings the said Sir Thomas Temple hath delivered to me at my own request and in obedience to an order made heretofore in the High Court of Chancery witness my hand and seal.[53]

Emma Child, mother of Cassandra Willoughby, kept legal and financial papers in her own possession as did Cassandra herself.[54] Hester Temple seems to have kept copies of her own Dassett, Warwickshire leases or at least to have had ready access to them if letters to her from her son-in-law John Rous are to be believed. In one letter he asked her to send him a counterpart of one of the leases to use as template for one of his own. Rous also writes that he will shortly send her and Sir Thomas a mortgage for them 'to peruse and correct'.[55]

Even where they entrusted the original documents to the 'patriarch' it seems that women maintained a lively interest in their own property rights as documented in wills, leases and settlements. Indeed, they were forced to keep track of what was owing to them if they wished to receive legacies and/or annuities from executors and administrators who were often reluctant to pay. So Mary Farmer wrote to her brother Thomas Temple for two more cows 'that shall be young and fit for my profit and purpose so soon as you can possibly because I loose the benefit of my pasture. You shall pay your self what you think good of that money which I am to receive of you and I desire also to know where I shall receive the rest.'[56] Married women would shrewdly pursue the advancement of their children, displaying an acute knowledge of appropriate property settlements. This is evidenced, for example, by the negotiations conducted single-handed and with startling confidence by Christian Temple, second wife of Sir Peter

Temple, for a marriage between her eldest daughter Frances and the Earl of Londonderry:

I have been this day atreating with my Lord of Londonderry and can draw him no lower then two thousand pound which is very small if we were able to secure it. I find his estate in the west is far greater then was reported to us: which he is contented to make all in jointure and five hundred pound a year more in Ireland.[57]

Women at all social levels apart from the very poorest used the law in their own defence and especially had recourse to the ecclesiastical and equity courts. The help and advice they received from their birth families in securing and organising appropriate settlements and in obtaining satisfaction should not, however, be disregarded.[58]

Indeed, women, like their menfolk, sometimes sought expert legal advice. Such occasions were afforded by will-making. For instance, Christian (Leveson) Temple referred in her will to an established trust whereby Thomas Earl of Sussex, Viscount Saville, would pay £200 a year for herself and her younger children's maintenance and her desire that this device should now be used to raise portions for her younger children.[59] Hester Temple's final will of the 1650s demonstrates her suspicion that some of her kin might not be above tampering with its provisions by stating: 'my last will and testament written in four sheets of paper I put my hand and seal (that is to say) my hand under the writing of every sheet and my seal once at the top . . .'[60]

We have already noted that many upper-class English women were involved in estate management, in peacetime and while their husbands were yet alive. Very probably these women had an active role in managing the estates that formed their own jointures. The evidence that survives suggests that they had considerable control over the product of such estates. Even where they did not, such involvement was good preparation for their widowhood.

Examples of similar activity in the Americas are hard come by but there are suggestions that women there had similar responsibilities and also gained considerable knowledge of the law. In America as in England and Wales, it seems, fathers and husbands expected daughters and wives to participate actively in estate management. On occasion this meant that American women assumed tremendous responsibilities, outside the ken of their British contemporaries. In parts of colonial America women left in charge of huge estates were sometimes remote from family support as the example of Eliza Lucas in Chapter 7 showed.[61]

Property in the North American colonies

A comparison between the situation in England and in America is not simple. For instance, we know that prior to the American Revolution different inheritance rules pertained in the various colonies but there is some debate about the nature of these rules. In Virginia, for example, the Rutmans urged that male partible inheritance of realty was the rule at least in Lancaster County, Virginia, while Keim insisted that this colony was keen on primogeniture.[62] Morris, however, had compared the intestate inheritance laws throughout the colonies and modern authorities such as Alston and Schapiro accept his findings.[63]

Occasionally there seems to be confusion based on whether the author is defining rules of intestacy (that is, how the property would be divided if the deceased property owner had left no will) or the practice of testators, who may or may not have observed intestacy rules in their wills.

The situation regarding the use of wills, on the one hand, and marriage settlements, on the other, to secure the future of daughters and widows is also contested. Where colonial parents survived until their children were of marriageable age, it seems that they commonly sought to some

TABLE 11.1 *Colonial inheritance practices*

Colony	Intestate inheritance law	Comment
New England colonies		
Maine	multigeniture	
New Hampshire	multigeniture	
Vermont	multigeniture	
Massachusetts	multigeniture	
Plymouth	multigeniture	
Rhode Island	primogeniture	until 1798 (with interruption 1718–1728)
Connecticut	multigeniture	
Middle colonies		
New York	primogeniture	until 1786
New Jersey	multigeniture	
Pennsylvania	multigeniture	
Delaware	multigeniture	
Southern colonies		
Maryland	primogeniture	until 1786
Virginia	primogeniture	until 1785
North Carolina	primogeniture	until 1784
South Carolina	primogeniture	until 1791
Georgia	primogeniture	until 1777

extent to influence their children's marriage decisions and to negotiate the terms of the marriage settlement. For a variety of reasons this seems to have been less true of seventeenth-century Maryland and Virginia than of New England. Parents frequently survived longer in New England than in the two southern colonies. As girls tended to marry younger than men, it was more often the bride's parents than the grooms who were party to the negotiations around marriage. Often the child's portion was granted to the child on marriage. Wills seem to have been used mainly to make more minor bequests to already married children.[64]

English common law was operative in the American colonies under British control until independence. It might seem fair to assume that American colonists grew so used to this state of affairs that they would continue the status quo ante following the Revolution. Far from it: the evidence points to pre-independence Americans manipulating, and post-independence Americans turning their backs on, fundamental parts of the English law. It seems probable too that, if the colonists changed that law shortly after independence, there must have been a legacy of discontent with that law. In most of the northern and middle colonies a form of inheritance was newly introduced that directly benefited women and ensured that more women brought property to a marriage than previously.

Historians have assumed that the legal rules regarding property ownership and inheritance prevalent in Britain would naturally have migrated to the North American colonies that were under British control. They have speculated why there were marked departures from the existing British laws of intestacy by the second half of the eighteenth century, which required active legislation.[65] The southern colonies maintained primogeniture in its intestacy inheritance laws as did Rhode Island and New York. The New England and middle colonies, on the other hand, adopted partible inheritance rules shortly after independence.[66] It was common in these colonies to follow the Mosaic law, whereby, saving the rights of a surviving husband or wife, a double portion went to the eldest son and half portions or less to daughters.

Wills were commonly used in the early days of the colonies, indicating the desire of the property owner to control the distribution of that property and probably to do so in the perceived interests of all his/her dependants. Many such wills did follow intestacy rules. However, in some cases, they were used in intriguing ways to modify the effects of such rules. For instance, in Virginia where planters were happy with the principle of primogeniture, they were less than satisfied with the fact that under intestacy rules the eldest son would inherit the plantations but not the slaves or personal property. These planters used the will to ensure that the eldest son had the wherewithal to work the plantation.[67]

Later in the period, wills became unpopular as a means of transferring property, because the process was both expensive and complicated. By the end of our period property transfers by will were quite rare.[68] As a result, making sure that the rules of intestacy were acceptable to the ruling elite became a matter of paramount importance. The intestacy laws had to promote the religious, economic and political security of the elite but, if this required the introduction of partible inheritance, the central government of the colony needed to be sufficiently strong to bring in and enforce new legislation.

Alston and Schapiro argue that 'primogeniture promoted large agricultural units' whereas multigeniture 'provided motivation for family labour'. Climatic conditions in the south favoured the growth of labour-intensive crops such as rice, cotton and tobacco, where tasks were simple and slave labour easily monitored. The north could not compete for slaves, and family general farms grew up 'accompanied with multigeniture to motivate family members to remain on the farm and work with little supervision'.[69] This said, even in the south where some historians argue that primogeniture prevailed, plantation owners would seek to keep individual plantations intact but might give the home plantation to the eldest son and distribute other plantations to the remaining children.[70] Also there were geographical exceptions: for instance, in newly British New York the elite turned their back on the multigeniture of Holland in favour of primogeniture because its wealthy estate holders employed non-family labour and in Rhode Island the central government simply was not sufficiently strong to legislate for the desirable multigeniture.[71]

The colonies were short of people and, while primogeniture can be argued to discourage population growth, multigeniture can be supposed to have the opposite effect, encouraging 'little out migration, a high proportion married, early marriages, and large families'.[72] This could have motivated settlers in the northern and middle colonies in their espousal of partible inheritance. While such effects might have been seen in the Old World, where there was easy availability of land in the North American colonies, this meant that under both primogeniture and multigeniture systems alike, younger children could easily marry and set up farms and households of their own so that the impact of inheritance laws on population growth was minimal.[73] However, as Philip Greven has shown in his study of seventeenth-century Andover, Massachusetts, once land became scarce within a colony practising multigeniture, out-migration increased and birth rates fell.[74]

In the northern and middle American colonies it seems that multigeniture was introduced and was felt by the Puritan settlers to be broadly compatible with their religious beliefs. In the southern colonies there is still debate as to whether primogeniture prevailed.

Moreover, until the 1990s, there was a common belief that women of the Old Country were disadvantaged before the law when compared to women of the New World.[75] Authors emphasised that women were regarded as feme covert in England and Wales whereas in the early colonies they were allowed to make and sue contracts made before and after marriage and even to hold personal estate during marriage. Recent work on the situation in England and Wales as discussed above casts real doubt upon the validity of such a comparison. As we have seen, English women also were the beneficiaries of prenuptial contracts and marriage settlements and sometimes retained and administered a personal estate during marriage. Women on both sides of the Atlantic retained use and ownership of their personal apparel, which they were able to dispose of as they wished. Frequently ordinary women accumulated a number of small bequests, usually of clothing, household 'stuff' or farm animals, which made a welcome contribution to their personalty. Members of elite families also received important contributions to their own household economies in this way. For instance, Anne Wharton, daughter-in-law of Anne, Dowager Countess of Derby, was granted by the latter's will of 1,550 expensive wall hangings given to the Countess of Derby by her brother, the Earl of Huntington, and a sable fur. Grandparents frequently favoured younger grandchildren in their wills, presumably assuming that parents would look after the interest of the legal heir. So the same Dowager Countess of Derby gave her married granddaughter, Jane Ratcliff, her second-best set of hangings 'and one trussing bed of black velvet and cloth of gold with the feather bed and all that thereunto doth belong, and one board cloth with the towel and a dozen napkins of all damask work and also my gown of black velvet and my kirtle of tawny satin and my other fir of sables.'[76] Godparents were also the source of many bequests. If women belonged to well-off families they might also receive 'portions' from their grandparents. Thomas Temple's married daughters were willed sums of money by their grandfather, John Temple, in 1604 – payments which took a few years to be paid by his executor. In 1609 Thomas recorded that he had:

paid to my son Clarke for his wife's person at ii payments being given her by my father being paid 1609 – £3 . . . ; paid my mother by my Father's [will] £400; paid my brother [in law] Risley by will of my father 1604 £xxli xi; paid my son [in law] Rous his wife's my son at iii payments in 1606 and 1607 £1100; paid my son Lenthall in march [] his wif £1100 . . . paid in March to my son [in law] Clarke in marriage with my daughter Susan; paid for son [in law] Rous in marriage with my daughter Hester; paid Mr J. Lenthall in marriage with my daughter Bridget . . .[77]

Equally women in Old and New England did not usually make wills, unless they were given permission to do so by their husbands or unless they were widows. In England and Wales the intestacy laws related to freehold property offered married women basic protection but left their younger sons and all their daughters without a claim; the laws related to copyhold and leasehold property offered more hope. In these societies the devices of the will and of jointure and the marriage settlement were commonly used to circumvent the harsh effects of intestacy. The courts could, and did, step in to modify the impact of what they perceived as unjust wills upon widows and children. This pattern seems to have been repeated in Plymouth Colony. 'If any man do make an irrational and unrighteous will, whereby he deprives his wife of her reasonable allowance for her subsistence', the court could 'relieve her out of the estate', especially where she had brought property to the marriage and/or had contributed to its establishment during the marriage.[78] The will was not, according to some authorities, commonly employed in the eighteenth-century colonies to modify the effects of the inheritance laws upon individuals within a family. Instead pre- and post-nuptial agreements were used to protect female descendants further.

In some parts of the colonies women were in a strong bargaining position when it came to provision both for their married life and their potential widowhood, and the common law courts allowed them to use this bargaining power to good effect. Where a prenuptial agreement existed to protect the wife's property, a woman was permitted to administer and use her own property during marriage. Such contracts were not uncommon and included first and second marrieds. John Phillips and widowed Faith Dory of Plymouth Plantation drew up the following contract in 1667:

The said Faith Dory is to enjoy all her house and land, goods and cattles [?chattels], that she is now possessed of, to her own proper use, to dispose of them at her own free will from time to time, and at any time as she shall see cause . . . The children of both the said parties shall remain at the free and proper and only disposal of their own natural parents, as they shall see good to dispose of them.[79]

The southern colonial courts lent support to yet another device which undermined the common law principle of feme covert. They permitted post-nuptial agreements which tacitly acknowledged the separate legal identity of wives. In 1686 Dorothy and Nathaniel Clarke of Plymouth were allowed a judicial separation. The court divided the estate between them by a contract to which Dorothy was a party.[80] Such agreements marked either the separation or reconciliation of spouses: commonly they ordered that partners should not meddle in one another's affairs. In one such case, that of Richardson v. Mountjoy in Virginia, the courts acknowledged that the woman involved thereby became feme sole and could henceforward make contracts. Possibly these concessions to the legal independence of colonial women were necessary if widows and separated women were to rejoin the supply of marriageable women.[81] In seventeenth-century Maryland, as in England, women used the equity courts for protection of their property rights.[82] So in the colonies women adapted and used legal instruments that had been available to them in England.

Conclusion

Women in the early modern British Isles and on the Atlantic seaboard were clearly disadvantaged by the laws of inheritance – especially where the owner of property left no will. In the American colonies the community frequently stepped in to take the place of birth family to protect widows and children who had been left unprovided for. Moreover in England, Wales and the colonies the principle of coverture operated for all women except singletons and widows. A variety of legal instruments (for instance, the trust in equity) were, however, devised to ensure that young women were provided for during and after marriage and were protected from exploitative husbands. A woman's greatest protection in this respect came from her caring and knowledgeable parents and guardians, who experimented with many different devices to secure their daughters' and their daughters' younger children's futures (and their own freedom from further financial encumbrances). In England, education, formal and informal, ensured that young women entered marriage able to conduct themselves confidently. In practice, many women from the propertied classes seem to have had a good working knowledge of the law and their rights under it. Moreover, in all sorts of circumstances (whether they benefited from a separate estate or not), some demonstrated considerable skill in estate management. If they had not had practical experience while still at home, young wives rapidly acquired it after marriage. Husbands at different social levels relied upon their wives in this respect. Naturally, not all women (or men) were equally capable farmers and managers, but comments made by contemporaries suggest that such abilities were generally regarded in a favourable light. Early moderns revered practical, down-to-earth men and women, not frivolous fops and feeble, flighty females. This was even more true of wild and remote colonial settlements, where wives and widows were often the mainstay of a household and family. Modifications appear to have been made to the rights of colonial women under the law to ensure that they rapidly re-entered the marriage market.

Notes

1 HEH, STT Personal Box 8, Folder 22, 12 Oct 1632 Receipt of papers from Sir Thomas Temple, her brother, re jointure of Elizabeth Fiennes (Temple) Viscountess Saye and Seale; and STT Personal Box 8. Folder 23, 13 Oct 1632 William Sprigge's receipt to Sir Thomas Temple of the above writings re Elizabeth Fiennes' jointure.
2 Intestacy was the situation that prevailed when the deceased had left no valid will and testament.
3 Christine Churches (1998) pp. 165–80, p. 169.
4 Ibid pp. 165–80, pp. 167–9.
5 Ibid pp. 165–80, p. 170–71.
6 See HEH, El 227, Letter from Roger Puleston of Emmanuel College to Sir Thomas Egerton, 27 October 1611. The right was being contested by Mr Gittins, parson of Malpas, by the bishop of Chester, and by Puleston himself.
7 HEH, El 398, Letter from Robert Whitbie to Sir Thomas Egerton, 20 January 1616/17.
8 M. M. Meikle (1997) p. 173.
9 Ibid p. 174.
10 S. G. Ellis (1985) p. 47.
11 Ibid pp. 40–41.

12 K. Nicholls (1991) pp. 17–31, especially pp. 17–20 and 26–31.

13 Ibid pp. 17–31, pp. 21–4.

14 Cited by Nicholls (1991) p. 22 alongside other examples of the same.

15 Isabel Murray of Selkirkshire, *Selkirk Protocol Books*, pp. 65–6, cited in M. M. Meikle (1997) p. 177.

16 A. L. Erickson (1995 pbk edn) p. 24. See Chapter 12 for further discussion of coverture.

17 For more information on women and property see Chapter 12: Widows and widowhood.

18 Erickson (1995 pbk edn) p. 24.

19 M. M. Meikle (1997) p. 175.

20 Ibid p. 175.

21 See Chapter 7 for further discussion of Adam Eyre and his wife's property.

22 C. Churches (1998) pp. 165–80, pp. 170–71.

23 See, for example, the partnership between Francis and Emma Willoughby which sought such protection for her estate during widowhood. See HEH, STB Box 2, Folder 1, 1–3 and Chapter 4: Finding a partner among the landed aristocracy.

24 See above.

25 Dorothy Johnston, 'Emma Child' (2003) p. 75 citing Sir Josiah's last will.

26 HEH, HM 46499 Hester Temple to Robert Higgins >1637 entitled 'Coppi of my leter to parson Higinges of Fenmer [Finmere] of my cottege [letter itself not in Hester's hand] [must be prior to 1637 when Sir Thomas Temple died]'.

27 HEH, HM 46529 Sir Thos Tyrrill to Hester Temple from Castle Thorpe 21 Mar 1641/2.

28 Rowena Archer (1984) p. 19.

29 A. L. Erickson (1995 pbk edn) p. 26.

30 Private contracts to achieve such separate estates predate the sixteenth century. Erickson (1995 pbk edn) pp. 106–7.

31 Erickson (1995 pbk edn) p. 26.

32 Ibid p. 104.

33 Margaret J. M. Ezell (1987) p. 192.

34 *The autobiography of Mrs Alice Thornton of East Newton, County York*, 1873, pp. 121, 249.

35 A. L. Erickson (1995 pbk edn) p. 107.

36 B. J. Harris (2002) p. 71.

37 L. Phillipson (1987) p. 21.

38 See N. H. Keeble (1994) *The Cultural Identity of Seventeenth-Century Woman: a reader*, 1994.

39 *The autobiography of Mrs Alice Thornton of East Newton, County York*, 1873, pp. 246–9. H. J. Morehouse (1877) p. 84.

40 S. Clarke (2000) pp. 237–8, citing NLW, Diary of Elizabeth Baker, 1778–1786. See also Chapter 10 for the much earlier example of Lady Hester Temple's involvement with Temple family legal affairs.

41 W. Prest (1991) p. 169. Prest argues that the basic text was in existence in the 1580s.

42 Anon., *The Ladies' Dictionary*, 1694.

43 A major edition was published in 1646.

44 First part published in 1600–1615. Later parts published in 1656 and 1658.

45 William Leonard. His Reports were not published until 1658–1675. See L. W. Abbott (1973) pp. 310–11. The list might coincide with the publication of both Coke's and Leonard's Reports in 1658.

46 This is John Ogilby (1600–1676) a Scot who published, amongst other works, an edition of *Aesop's Fables*.

47 The Lords Fiennes, Viscount Say and Seale were brothers-in-law and nephews of Sir Thomas and Lady Hester Temple.

48 Richard Baxter's *Call to the Unconverted* was published in 1658.

49 This could be James Howell's *Londinopolis: An historical discourse or perlustration of the City of London*, 1657.

50 HEH, Temples MSS Addenda, Box I.

51 First published 1607.

52 See the HEH Library's extensive collection of such documents over two centuries.

53 HEH, STT Personal Box 8, Folder 22, 12 Oct 1632 Receipt of papers from Sir Thomas Temple, her brother, re jointure of Elizabeth (Temple) Fiennes Viscountess Saye and Seale; and STT Personal Box 8. Folder 23, 13 Oct 1632 William Sprigge's receipt to Sir Thomas Temple of the above writings re Elizabeth Fiennes' jointure.

54 For Emma (Barnard Willoughby) Child see UNL, Middleton Papers which contain many of Lady Emma Child's accounts, bills and receipts both before and after her second widowhood: e.g. Mi AV 143/1–42, and Mi A 128 which are her London household accounts for 1717–1720, and Mi A 106 'E[mma]

W[illoughby's] Journal. For Cassandra (Willoughby) Brydges and her comments on her mother's financial activities see NLCS, Copy Letter Book of Cassandra Brydges, Duchess of Chandos, 1713–1735, No. 142, p. 67v To Lady Ann Countess of Coventry [Undated]; No. 211, p. 121 To nephew Henry Willoughby 4 Dec 1725; No. 210, p. 121 To nephew Rothwell Willoughby 4 Dec 1725; No. 212, p. 122 To Brother Middleton 4 Dec 1725.

55 HEH, STT 1748 Sir John Rous to Lady Hester Temple from Rous Lench 4 Apr 1629.
56 HEH, STT 756 Mary Farmer (Temple) to Sir Thos Temple 1st Bt on 27 May 1614–37.
57 HEH, STT, Box 13, 1914 Lady Christian Temple from London to Sir Peter Temple at Stowe 4 Sep 1650.
58 For a fascinating if unusual example see Murphy (2003) pp. 220–30 regarding the settlement for Mary (Howard) Fitzroy, Duchess of Richmond and Somerset, before and after the death of Prince Henry Fitzroy, and the role in it which she and her parents played.
59 HEH, STT Personal Box 10, Folder 15 1648–1655 Draft will of Christian Leveson Temple.
60 HEH, STT Personal Box 11, Folder 13, 26 Sept 1654 Copy Will with probate of Hester Temple.
61 D. M. Lucey (2005) pp. 47–9.
62 R. C. Keim (1968) pp. 545–86.
63 R. B. Morris (1927) pp. 24–51, cited in L. J. Alston and M. O. Schapiro (1984) p. 278.
64 L. S. Walsh (1979) pp. 133–5.
65 L. J. Alston and M. O. Schapiro (1984) pp. 277–87.
66 R. B. Morris (1927) pp. 24–51.
67 R. C. Keim (1968) pp. 545–86.
68 Alston and Schapiro (1984) pp. 277–87.
69 Ibid p. 280.
70 Keim (1968).
71 H. L. Osgood (1904) Vol. 2, pp. 31–3; R. B. Morris (1927) p. 78.
72 M. O. Schapiro (1982) pp. 577–600.
73 Alston and Schapiro (1984) p. 283.
74 P. Greven (1970), *passim*; see P. J. Tracey (1980) which reinforces Greven's argument for the eighteenth century.

75 See, for example, R. B. Morris (1930), Chapter 3, which is cited in John Demos (1970 edn) p. 84.
76 *Historical Manuscripts Commission Report*, Vol. I, 1928, p. 315, Document 1296b, *Manuscripts of the late Reginald Rawdon Hastings esq. of the Manor House, Ashby de la Zouche*, Testament of Anne, Dowager Countess of Derby, 6 September 1550.
77 For example, HEH, STT 1864 Rowse Stratford from Banbury to Sir Thomas Temple at Dassett 10 Feb 1608/9. The accounts written on the dorse seem to bear no relationship to the letter but are probably accounts made by Thomas Temple as executor of his own father's will in the period between 1604 and 1609.
78 W. Brigham, *The Compact with the Charter and Laws of the Colony of New Plymouth* (1836), p. 281, cited in Demos (1970) p. 85.
79 Demos (1970) p. 86.
80 Demos (1970) p. 86.
81 R. Thompson (1974) pp. 166, 180.
82 G. Gampel (1984) pp. 20–35.

CHAPTER 12

Widows and widowhood

[M]y desire is, to leave a testimony to the world of my exceeding desire of leaving peace, especially of God to my posterity, who I desire earnestly, that they would embrace one another in faithful and true love, and to give due respect and reverence to their aged mother my loving wife Albeit I have divided my estate amongst them in my life time, yet for a pledge of my love to every of my children . . . I give every of them a ring of gold of twenty shillings[1]

Introduction

This clause reminds us that it would be dangerous for historians to rely too exclusively upon testamentary evidence in their discussion of family strategies and, particularly, provision for widows and younger children. His will was just a part of Sir Thomas Temple's strategy for pacifying his family and strengthening his widow's position after his decease. Little of substance was passed on by his will, with the exception that he left amounts of money to the eldest son of each of his married daughters and tokens to each of his surviving children. The title and family estate would pass by primogeniture to his eldest son. He had already 'divided [his] estate amongst [his children] in [his] lifetime', and his wife was provided for with jointure lands and leases. His will provided a last vocal and public reinforcement of his desire for Temple family harmony and respect for their mother.[2]

His will not only indicates the limitations of will evidence in any study of family survival strategies but also suggests that widowhood was an important phase, albeit a vulnerable one, in the lives of married women.

Some historians argue that the incidence of widowhood had profound implications for contemporary society. Joel T. Rosenthal discovered that 68 per cent of peers summoned between 1399 and 1500 left widows.[3] Many of these widows were long-lived and it has been argued that the drain they placed on great estates led to the collapse and, indeed, extinction of many peerages.[4] Barbara Harris has contested this view, indicating that most aristocratic widows managed their property profitably during long widowhoods; that when they died they distributed their property within the family; and that 'collectively their activity ensured the survival and continued prosperity of their class'.[5]

Widows are one of the few categories of women who emerge readily from the shadows at all social levels and they do this because of their legal identity and also because, perhaps for a brief period, they appear relatively powerful as acknowledged heads of household in the absence of an adult male. But widows never formed a cohesive, distinct group in society (any more than married or single women did). Rather, widowhood was a prospective life stage for all married women and one for which preparations were made from their childhoods. While the dirigist approach to widowhood (which sees widows as 'powerful') is valid, it is equally important to note that widows were also vulnerable and that the behaviour of widows, provision for them and attitudes towards them, reveal a good deal about contemporary kin bonds. Moreover, the part which the widow-led household played in the family cycle is worthy of consideration. Discovering the role a woman played when she was a widow head of household can tell us a good deal about her marriage and her role as both wife and mother. Moreover, if widowed women were relatively powerful why did they choose to remarry? Were they seekers of protection rather than power? Did they find ways to protect the benefits that widowhood had conferred upon them, while reaping the different benefits of remarriage? What was the fate of a widowed mother who chose not to (or was fated not to) remarry? Historians have focused very much upon this question of the remarrying widow, but there are other matters of interest.

The sources available for the study of widowhood

Studies of widowhood in England have relied very heavily upon court records (especially of the ecclesiastical and equity courts) and registers of marriages. Use has also been made of population listings such as the Norwich census of the 1570s. A rich source of a very different kind has been found in wills and inventories and in family papers, correspondence and personal diaries and autobiographies reaching back into the fifteenth century. For the colonies, too, court records and, after 1740, family and personal papers have proved extremely important. The scarcity of work on widows in Scotland and Ireland seems in part to reflect the inadequacy of the documentation, particularly before the eighteenth century. The paucity of records in Ireland is likely to remain a serious obstacle in the way of work on indigenous Irish women although there is, of course, documentation relating to the Anglo-Irish elite, many of whom lived for some part of their lives in England. Court records and family papers can, however, be used to reveal attitudes to, and, to some extent, the status of widows of all classes in Scotland.

The incidence of widowhood

There is some debate about the incidence and causes of widowhood. Inevitably, it was very common in times of high mortality. On average, one-fifth of households in any English community were those headed by widows, although there was considerable deviation from this mean.[6] In some communities, also, widows lived either in almshouses or as lodgers in other households.[7] There would also be some widows who lived in allocated rooms within their adult children's households.

In seventeenth-century England as a whole, women enjoyed a slightly higher life expectancy than males. The high mortality rate among men was not entirely due to what might be termed normal, natural causes. Men were more vulnerable to plague and other forms of disease than were women. In the plague epidemic of 1603 in London the ratio of male to female deaths was 6 : 1.[8] The incidence of widowhood in the population as a whole was increased by the tendency for wives to be somewhat younger than their spouses.

These, however, are very general statements and when we probe more deeply reveal mortality rates and patterns that were highly class-specific. Marriages among the peerage, for example, were more commonly dissolved by the death of a wife than of a husband. High mortality rates amongst aristocratic women appear to have been associated with childbirth and, particularly, with intervention in childbirth. The rate of such deaths appears to have increased after 1750 once male medics began to assist female midwives, often using forceps for the birth.[9] When elite women were widowed they often rapidly remarried although there are also many well-known examples of elite widows who clung to their status as dowagers.[10] Widowhood, and especially prolonged widowhood which persisted into old age, was, in contrast, extremely common among the poor and in towns. The wording of a licence granted to Elizabeth Livingstone, widow, by the lord of her manor reminds us that in the English, Welsh and Scottish manors, there were still feudal restrictions on widows' remarriage:

We gif and grantis oure full licence, benevolence and fredome to oure lovit widow, Elizabeth Levingstoun, the spouse of . . . Alexander Levingstoun, oure tenante of oure landie and toun of Inchmachane to complete the band of matrimonye with ony lauchfull persoun scho plesis and thinkis expedient without ony hurte or damage to be impute be us to hir tharfor.[11]

Such customs were still persisting throughout rural Britain into the late seventeenth century and beyond, as surviving manorial court books show.[12] On the other hand, it was probably the case that any widow who had inherited property, whether freehold, copyhold or by custom, stood a good chance of remarriage.[13] It was different for the unpropertied and especially the elderly among them. In Norwich in 1570 a listing of the poor detailed twelve times as many widows as widowers over the age of sixty-one. Some 88 per cent of the males over the age of sixty-one were married whereas only 25 per cent of the women over that age were married. Over two-thirds of these elderly married men had wives who were ten or more years their junior.[14] Poor married women lived longer than married males from the same class but poor and elderly widows were not an attractive marriage prospect.

There were also other sex-selective forms of mortality. The low sex ratio in England (that is the ratio of males to females), which was especially characteristic of urban areas, is normally attributed to male vulnerability to disease and a penchant for emigration among males, rather than to fatalities of war, but the last should not be discounted.[15] Involvement in foreign wars took its toll amongst the aristocracy and lower orders in all these societies. English and Welsh troops were variously involved in campaigns in Scotland, Ireland, France, the Netherlands and central Europe at times during the sixteenth, seventeenth and eighteenth centuries. Men and their families knew the risks. When William Trew, husband of Margaret Bagot, prepared to go to France with the Earl of Essex in 1591, he wrote to his father-in-law Richard Bagot, in expectation of death 'this voyage'. Mortality rates among combatants in the three English civil wars in the mid-seventeenth century were high, estimated at 20 per cent overall, comparable with mortality rates during the First

World War. The most recent study gives a figure for English and Welsh troops of 84,830 dead.[16] In peacetime too, men were prone to settle their disputes through combat. Interpersonal violence was common at all levels of society and, because almost everyone carried a potential weapon – a knife – such violence frequently resulted in injury or death. Although duelling did not reach England and Wales until the late sixteenth century and was not anything like as common as it was in France in the first half of the seventeenth century, it did become a serious problem after the Restoration.[17]

Some historians argue that widowhood affected males as much as it did females but that widowers are much less visible in the sources available to historians. This it is said was because widowers remarried much more frequently and much more quickly after the death of a spouse than did widows. The popular proverb 'to thrive thou must wive' indicates why remarriage was so important to a widower. A wife took care of her husband, children and household and she was a vital part of an economic and social partnership. There were also outside economic and social pressures on males to remarry: in the Church of England, for example, bachelor or widowed parish priests were looked at askance – the presence of a wife not only guaranteed an extra pair of hands for parish work but also protection for the wives, boys and maidens of the locality. The law prohibited a widow from remarriage for a full year after the death of a husband (in order to prevent disputes about the paternity of posthumous offspring), but a widower was allowed to marry much sooner following the death of his partner. The imposition of taxes upon widowers from the 1690s onwards might also have motivated men to remarry in greater numbers.[18] Even after the year of waiting was up, many women remained widows. Some of the reasons for this life choice, if such it were, are discussed later in this chapter.

Widowhood as a life stage

Widowhood was, nonetheless, part of the anticipated life experience of a young woman whatever her station in society. Some widowed women undoubtedly did remarry but the attempt to find a second or further marriage partner was less certain of success in some places and at some times than in others.

The North American colonies, for instance, were characterised by great diversity. A high sex ratio (of males to females) has been seen as a feature of the colonial experience in North America, Canada and Ireland, producing often exceptionally male-heavy societies. Demographically it might seem that, as a result, widowhood in the colonies that were male-heavy would be rarely a lasting condition because wives were in such short supply and the normal caveats against men marrying widows were not issued. Hidden widowhood would be as prevalent in the New World as hidden widowerhood was in the Old. In which event, one might expect examples of lasting widowhood to be restricted to the towns which had a more even sex ratio. In general, though, we would expect the American experience to contrast quite sharply with that in England, Scotland and Northern Europe, where lengthy widowhoods were relatively common and where there were attempts to prevent men marrying widows.

On closer inspection, however, the contrast between the colonies and elsewhere was often not so stark. The sex ratio differed somewhat from colony to colony as a reflection of the phase of the colonial experience. For instance, women were far scarcer in late seventeenth-century Virginia than in Massachusetts, and more scarce yet on the New England frontier. The data provided by John Demos and Philip Greven indicates that in New England disruption of marriage by early death was rare and consequent lengthy widowhoods equally rare. The average marriage ended when the wife was sixty-three or the husband seventy and the average eldest child in his or her early forties. This picture contrasts markedly with that painted by the Rutmans for Middlesex County, Virginia. Here median first marriages ended when the wife reached her late thirties or the husband his late forties. Female mortality rates here were higher than male but this did little to change the overall picture of disrupted marriages. Remarriages in this society were exceedingly common. Debra Meyers has indicated that widows rapidly remarried in Maryland just a few months after the death of their spouses. She argues that Marylanders valued the part of women in founding necessary new families in a way not common in the Old World. For instance, Ignatius Causine gave his daughter Jane 150 acres of land if she married a propertyless man so that 'she joined the marriage in a position of authority and also made the marriage economically viable'; similarly, Arminian Anglican Henry Hyde gave his 'loving wife Frances' total control of his estate 'for the childrens use during her life with as much freedom as it were I my self in my lifetime'.[19] Maryland wives were customarily given at least one-third of the estate and often much more 'to be absolutely att the disposall and discretion of my said wife ... to doe with the same what shall seem good unto her'.[20] Moreover there are indications that married women contributed vociferously and cannily to this strategy, which permitted them through multiple marriages to accumulate wealth and property and pass it down to the children. Katherine Wright quizzed the lawyer who had drawn up her husband's will as to whether it protected her right 'to hold the land' and when he replied that the provisions were not watertight, she instructed the lawyer to ask her husband Arthur if he 'would make another will' to ensure her complete control of the estate. Arthur agreed to his wife's request.[21]

Some historians have, however, questioned the applicability of Greven's and Demos's conclusions to the whole of New England. Linda Auers Bissell's study of mobility in Windsor, Connecticut, throws doubt upon their notion that most marriages were lengthy and uninterrupted by showing that 32 per cent of sons inherited land by their sixteenth birthday and after the death of a father, which compares well with the Virginian incidence of orphanhood of minors. This debate will only be resolved through more detailed reconstitution of families.

Did widows have much in common other than the state of widowhood? Widows were not a discreet interest-group as were lawyers, grocers or master builders. Widows, whatever their social class or place of habitation, did share a certain vulnerability. The nature and extent of this vulnerability varied enormously, however, from social group to social group, from country to country, from individual to individual.

Widows and their vulnerability or protection before the law

The laws and customs regarding inheritance in part defined that vulnerability. Much of English and Welsh inheritance continued to rest to a limited extent on parliamentary statutes but mainly on common law precedents and on custom. There were no statutes governing dower, primogeniture, or the order in which collateral kin should be treated when there were no surviving direct heirs of the body, although over the period there were statutes governing intestacy, freedom of testation and distribution of personalty. In England (and Wales after 1536) a widow was entitled under common law and ecclesiastical law to a dower of at least one-third or reasonable parts of the property that her husband had held during the marriage for her lifetime.[22] She was unable to alienate this property and it passed to their children on her death.[23] (Under common law a wife had no right to devise land.) Manorial law gave widows similar rights with respect to copyhold land (usually a more generous 50 per cent) for either her lifetime or unless she remarried. This was known as 'free bench' or 'widow's bench'. The husband could sell property that had been designated as dower but he was required to have his wife sign a deed of release from the dower on it. Marriage settlements and wills were often used to override these rules and to specify particular real property as a jointure or even to create a separate estate for the wife.[24]

Until relatively recently historians would have argued that there was a sharp social divide in the provision made for widows. Widows of the upper class in England and Wales were best provided for. Despite an overriding concern for the transmission of property by primogeniture or some other system such as gavelkind (partible inheritance by sons) or borough-English (inheritance by the youngest son),[25] law, custom and family feeling made sure that widows (as well as younger children) were well cared for and their financial contribution to the partnership (as a dowry or portion) acknowledged and protected. This was something that was dealt with prior to marriage. A wife's birth family frequently acted to ensure this. Walter Bagot refused to continuing payments of his daughter Anne's dowry until her husband made satisfactory jointure arrangements for her widowhood.[26] Women of the middling and lower sorts, it was once argued, were not well provided for and were entirely defenceless because the common law offered them no protection and no rights.[27] The relative absence of marriage settlements of the detailed type for women of the middling sort seemed to support this view.[28]

No historian has contradicted the view that elite married and widowed women were well provided for by their birth families and the families they married into. On marriage a woman's inherited property was controlled (used) by her husband (although he could not alienate this property without her explicit, written consent). On widowhood the woman had restored to her, as of right, this and any lands and properties which were hers by inheritance. Contemporary genealogies illustrate the way in which many aristocratic male lines died out, leaving the freehold estates to pass to female heiresses and co-heiresses. Women also inherited leasehold land, land held by customary tenure, wardships, advowsons and grants of pro hac vice presentations to church livings,[29] shares and moveable property, not only from parents but also from more distant relatives and from godparents. All this was restored to a woman's control on her husband's death. Statute law also gave a widow a right to a dower of a third of her husband's freehold estate for life if her husband died intestate or by his will deprived her of this proportion. In practice, among the middling and the elite, this right was normally waived in favour of an equitable jointure arranged in the formal marriage settlement by the parents of the bride and groom. Concern here was not only for the future security of the wife but also for the passing on of an unencumbered estate to the eldest son of the union. George Stratford, in the later sixteenth century, agreed that his widow should inherit a lease due to George on the death of his brother from the manor of Coldaston, Gloucestershire, and that George 'shall joyne wth hym in purchas the said Alyce of all suche lands wch the said George shall hereafter purchas untill the landes so purchased shall amounte to the sume of one hundred marks to have to the said Alyce for tyme of hyr lyff onely.'[30]

The elite could often make better provision and such a jointure might well include a separate house (called a dower house). So Richard Bagot provided his younger son Anthony with an annuity of £40 and his bride Katherine Lowe with a newly built house which would later become her dower house.[31] The jointure itself was often increased during the course of a happy marriage. Because it involved a contract, this type of jointure was defensible not in the common but in the equity courts.[32] The ratio between the dowry (the sum of money paid by the bride's parents to the groom) and the jointure seems to have risen during the seventeenth century from 5 : 1 in the first half of the century to 10 : 1 in the second half. Lawrence Stone calculated that a bride who in 1550 would have a jointure settled upon her of between £200 and £250 for every £1,000 of her dowry would have only £100 settled on her in 1700. R. B. Outhwaite also suggested a very marked rise in the ratio. This inflation in dowry was perhaps as much owing to the rising cost of land (for the portion or dowry would usually have been used to purchase land to provide an annuity) as to the extremely low sex ratio in the late seventeenth century, which placed wives in a poor bargaining position. As Lloyd Bonfield has pointed out, the true value of the jointure settlement depended on the number of years by which a widow survived her husband.[33]

After 1650 the development of the so-called 'strict settlement' enabled a landowner – while preserving the patrimony for his eldest son, or the closest male descendant of that son, or his daughters as co-heiresses – still to provide security for his bride and make adequate provision for all his legitimate progeny. By laying down precisely what property was inalienable it protected the core estate from profligate and careless heirs who might live extravagantly and sell their inheritance in order to pay off their debts. Such settlements, enforced by the equity rather than the common law courts, treated heirs as tenants rather than owners. Where there were younger sons and daughters, specific provision was made for them either when they came of age or married. However, strict settlements often effectively disinherited heiresses by substituting collateral male kin as heirs to the estate. They also tended to accord widows less favourable treatment than the thirds which she would have inherited for her lifetime under customary law. Marriage contracts (settlements) gradually came to redress this defect of the strict settlement because they often allowed women to control their own property and have some financial independence.

Our understanding of provision for married women and widows of the 'middling sort' has, however, been considerably modified of late. This is, in part, because we now have an improved understanding of the complexity of the early modern legal 'system' and its implications. We know, for example, that relatively little land passed by primogeniture from father to eldest son; that written law and customary law reserved provision for widows; that various legal instruments and wills were used to provide for widows and minor children of both sexes.

The custom of *legitim* governed the inheritance of property in England down to the sixteenth century. Under this custom the childless widow inherited one-half of her husband's moveable goods (including leasehold property) after his debts had been paid, and the widow with children inherited one-third. As this so-called personalty accounted for the entire or largest part of the estate of most husbands and fathers, *legitim* was a very important guarantee of the welfare of widows and children. It is seen in many contemporary wills. For example, in 1504 John Brown of Knotting, Bedfordshire, asked that all his goods be divided into three equal parts, of which one was to be retained to fulfil his testament, one was to go to his widow and one to his sons and daughters. The part for the children would normally be administered by the executors, most often the widow, until the child or children came of age. Where this custom was applied, however, it was unnecessary for a testator to refer to it in his will.[34] Under the custom of *legitim* the will itself may often have been a disposition of the so-called soul's or testator's part alone and be rendered highly unreliable as evidence of a man's estate, of his provision for his widow and children, or indeed of the composition of his family.

By Elizabeth's reign the custom of *legitim* had ceased to be enforced in the Province of Canterbury as a whole although there is evidence that it continued to be observed in the City of London as late as the early 1700s and in Wales in the 1690s. It certainly continued to be enforced by the ecclesiastical courts in the Province of York until at least the 1690s. Even where *legitim* was not formally referred to, however, it may well have continued to be used as a rule of thumb by both will-makers and the ecclesiastical courts who had to make decisions in cases of intestacy and also when inheritance was disputed.

Historians are now aware of the ways in which wills were used in both the late medieval and the early modern period to provide for and protect widows. Judith Ford's study of will-making in Bedfordshire before 1540 showed how testators used the will and devices such as the *use* to do this. At this time, most freehold land was set to descend by primogeniture and much copyhold land descended according to locally accepted custom such as gavelkind (partible or shared inheritance) or borough-English (where the land was inherited by the youngest son). It could not be devised by will. This makes wills an extremely unsafe indicator of property provision for either spouse or family. In general, only bequests of leasehold property (held for term of years) find mention therein. In practice this rule regarding freehold was circumvented by a medieval legal instrument called the *use*. This enabled property owners to provide for all their offspring even where primogeniture was the rule. It transferred the legal title to the property to named trustees (feoffees to *uses*) who held it and administered it for a third party or parties, who were frequently named in the last will or in a separate statement.

I will and bequeath to Alys my wiff all my purchased lands and tenements and all such as be named . . . in my new dede of feoffment with meadows isis pasturys closys rents . . . and all my other land and tenements being in forefeet in eyton . . . of her liff and after her decease to remain all holey . . . unto John Cutlatt my sonne.[35]

In 1536, by the Statutes of Uses and of Enrolments, this right to devise land by *use* was abolished in order to prevent loss of revenue to the crown by evasion of feudal dues. This move was met by outcry and the resulting Statute of Wills of 1540 in fact permitted testation of real property under the common law. All freehold land and two-thirds of land held by knight-service could be willed away, reserving only a third to the heir and any dower settled on the widow. Other property could be freely bequeathed according to the will of its owner.[36] The abolition of feudal tenures, confirmed after the Restoration, swept away restrictions on the remaining third of knight-service land.

Most land was held either by leasehold, the passage of which was specified in the lease,[37] or copyhold, where custom still prevailed. The ever declining amount of land held by copy of the manor rolls made such considerations of diminishing but real importance. (As noted earlier, widows of copyholders had to apply to the lord of the manor to remain in their property and to remarry.) Leases-for-life remained an extremely important instrument whereby families provided for widows and younger children.

There were still a great many customs governing the rights of widows, widowers and children in the partition of other kinds of property. For instance, a widow had a common law dower right (generally a third) in personalty (a term used to describe movable goods and chattels) that was generally upheld. However, Henry Swinburne's *A Brief treatise of testamentes and last willes* (1590 edition) suggests that this right was under attack. Such restraints on the will-maker's freedom to will his moveable goods were said to be illegal unless a locality specifically adopted such mandatory division. Testamentary freedom was advocated, in any event, because it kept wives and children in line.[38] Over the course of the seventeenth century many parts of the southern province of Canterbury accepted freedom of testation of personalty but the old dower custom persisted in the province of York, in Wales and in London.[39] Parliamentary statutes during the 1690s insisted on the complete freedom of the testator to bequeath realty. (Wives, however, had no right to make a will bequeathing personalty without explicit consent from the husband.) Dower rights in personalty were widely ignored in London from the Restoration onwards but remained defensible at law until a specific act outlawing the practice was put on the statute book in 1725.[40] In 1670 a statute provided for the distribution of personalty in the event of intestacy: widows inherited a third forever and children shared the remainder equally. If there were no surviving children, the widow divided the children's portion (two-thirds of personalty) with her husband's kin. (These proportions differed somewhat in London, Wales and parts of the Northern Province.) In the absence of survivors the personalty went to the monarch.[41]

Whereas ecclesiastical historians and historians of equity law have long been aware of the continuing importance in the lives of ordinary men and women of jurisdictions other than the common law, only very recently have other historians understood this fact and followed up on its implications. In the medieval and early modern period several different laws ran and, while the married woman was undoubtedly in a state of coverture before the common law and therefore without identity, rights and property, married women did have legal identities in the church courts. In the equity courts (such as chancery and requests) they could sue and be sued in some circumstances and defend their own interests. Perhaps more important is the fact that study of wills, grants of administration and court records has revealed that women of quite modest means did make marriage settlements to protect their own property and that of children born of previous marriages and themselves in widowhood and did actively defend these settlements. Sometimes these were formal treaties of marriage, such as those made by the London middle classes in the late seventeenth and eighteenth centuries.[42] Lawyers offered women, both single and widowed, advice on protecting their property, their separate estate, suggesting a range of different legal instruments that could be used.[43]

Women were active in litigation in the equity court of Chancery in defence of their separate estates. Such action was expensive and the women involved were generally well-to-do. Half of the female litigants, however, were the wives of professional men, merchants and tradesmen, yeomen and husbandmen and, when compared with the settlements made upon elite wives, the size of marriage portions (ranging from £40 to £3,000) and jointures (ranging from £12 to £200) was low. For those who could not afford to use Chancery, the simplest and most common way of effecting a marriage settlement was to enter a common bond either to pay a specified sum on a given date or to pay portions to a wife's children by previous marriages, or to leave the wife a certain amount on her widowhood, or to create a separate estate for the wife during coverture.

The terms 'jointure' and 'dower' or 'dowry' were only used by people of the yeomanry or above. For example, Susan Gaunt, widow of a prosperous citizen of Lincoln, was left by her husband's will of 1624 'that which I formerly set out to be for and in lew of her joynter and thirds of all my lands in Yorkshire . . . according to a former writing'. Similar examples survive for all social levels down to the humble yeoman of the Suffolk Weald who in 1631 left his wife 'in full recompence of her dower (according as by a certeyne bond I am bound) £3 yearly . . . paid half-yearly for her life'.[44] In some cases wills were used to confirm other arrangements made for wives and children: 6 per cent of clerical wills registered in Lichfield diocese between 1550 and 1700 made specific mention of a portion or jointure or both, excluding the very large number of bequests to surviving wives which may or may not have been pre-arranged. Most of the marriage settlements referred to in the probate documents examined by Amy Erickson were not described as dower or jointure and did not involve cash annuities or lands for life. Rather they referred to 'portions' and provided for the payment of cash lump sums, over which the widow had complete and immediate control.

A full 10 per cent of the married men's probate accounts inspected by Amy Erickson mentioned bonds protecting the property of the wife or her children from prior marriage(s).[45] Several women had made premarital settlements ensuring that a given sum was paid them upon widowhood. This was a wise precaution as one-quarter of husbands died in debt and the bond enabled the widow as executrix or administrator to pay herself out of the estate before doing anything else. This was preferable to relying upon the ecclesiastical law for payment of a third or 'reasonable parts' of the husband's estate because in that case the settlement was only made after all debts were paid. There is some evidence that even very young women played a role before marriage in determining the terms of their marriage settlements.[46] Some more experienced women made marriage settlements to protect the portions of their children from previous marriage(s). Again this was wise because, if the widow remarried, all her unprotected property would effectively devolve to the new husband.[47] Circa 1590 George Stratford married Alice Shakerley, a widow with a son and daughter. Marriage articles were drawn up which provided for a marriage portion of 200 marks for the daughter, Anne, either if George and Alice remained married for six years or Alice brought with her 200 marks' worth of goods to the marriage, after the payment of her late husband's debts and legacies. These articles also provided for maintenance of her son, Richard, until he reached the age of twenty-one, at a staged annual rate of £5 or £10.[48] Articles such as these were carefully filed in the family legal archive and in those of the witnesses to be referred to if a dispute arose.[49] On occasion the probate court acted to protect the property of such children when the remarrying widow had neglected so to do. In some cases remarrying widows actually used their bargaining power with their new spouses to increase the settlements made by their natural fathers on these children. For instance, Elizabeth Doughty's daughter received a bequest from her father John as well as the promise of property worth £4 a year after her mother's death. Elizabeth, however, required a bond from her second husband to pay the same daughter £20 when she achieved the age of twenty-one or married.[50] New husbands were sometimes bound to provide in more general terms for the education and upbringing of their stepchildren. During the husband's lifetime, should he break the terms of any of these bonds, the sureties of the bonds (but not the wife) could sue him in the courts and obtain redress for the wife; on his death, the bonds reverted to his widow as moveable property and she could herself sue for their satisfaction. Bonds, then, offered the wife/widow some power as well as security.

Bonds for the creation of separate estates during coverture survive more rarely although they did occur. More commonly separate estates would be created very simply by will. For example, the father of Margaret Sumner appears to have bequeathed £350 to her on express condition that it was kept separate from her husband's estate. When Margaret died in 1662 she was able to bequeath the £350 as she willed.[51] Thomas Hall, a widower from Yorkshire, in 1642 willed his second daughter Alice Furbanke his dwelling house for her life and then upon her death to his two grandchildren, equally divided between the boy and girl. He specified that George, Alice's husband, was 'debarred and excluded' from claiming or enjoying the house.[52]

Marriage settlements thus provide a good deal of evidence that elite and middling couples and their families discussed provision for both the children of their own union and also those of previous unions prior to testation. Wills also encapsulated the results of similar discussions. Prior to her own death in 1629, Lady Anne Throckmorton observed that her husband, then deceased, had wanted the stock of Luffield Priory to go to their unmarried daughter Katherine and she willed that this should indeed be so.[53] Distribution of portions prior to the demise of the father was, however, an even more secure way of ensuring the future of the offspring of the union and, while not usual, was commonly practised.

Women and especially widows were the most common executors (correctly executrices) of early modern English wills: from the fourteenth to the early eighteenth centuries between 63 per cent and 89 per cent of married men who made wills appointed their wives as executrices.[54] Women would act not only for their deceased husbands but also for fathers and fathers-in-law.[55] During the eighteenth century, however, widows were less likely to be appointed as executrices than previously, suggesting perhaps that this century, far from marking an advance in the independence and power of widows, marked a decline in both.[56]

In England ordinary men were more likely to appoint their wives to this role of executrix than were rich men. When a rich man did appoint his wife as executrix she more often acted jointly with a male executor. Only in New England, in Massachusetts, was this not the case.[57] Historians have suggested that this was because in England the role of the wife as a business partner who was acquainted with financial matters and considered capable of managing them was more accepted in ordinary households than in the marriages of the rich elite. Recent studies of the lives of many elite wives seem *not* to support this reasoning. Scholars have, nonetheless, used the prevalence or non-prevalence of women executors as indicators of the economic importance of women in the household. Alice Clark, on the basis of wills from Worcestershire, Hertfordshire and Middlesex, saw a sharp decline in the appointment of women as executors from the later seventeenth century and deduced a declining role for women in the family economy. Richard Vann saw the very opposite happening in Banbury, and argued that woman's economic importance was increasing. Amy Louise

Erickson has urged caution on the basis of observed wide regional variations and much less obvious chronological ones.

Widows acting as executrices had control over their husband's estates. In many cases, however, will-makers also appointed overseers or supervisors who cooperated and assisted the executrix in administering the will. Their appointment does not indicate that the testator wanted to restrict his widow's control but it could suggest that he felt that she would need the support of practically minded 'friends' during her mourning. The processes of probate made demands on a grieving widow and mother.

It is as well to remember that male and female children also had a vested interest in the protection of their widowed mother's property and rights to pass this on to their heirs unhindered. This issue of their eventual inheritance ensured the lively support of financially-aware children when mothers were laying claim to their rights in open court. In his diary John Dee (aged about fifty) reported:

15 June 1579: My mother surrendered Mortlake houses and land, and had state given in open court until the end of her life: and to me was also the reversion delivered by written contract, and to my wife Jane by me, and after to my heirs and assignees for ever, to understand Mr Bullok: and Mr Taylor, surveyor: at Wimbledon under the tree by the church.[58]

Much later, in the 1720s, Cassandra Willoughby and her brother Lord Middleton were acutely aware of the implications of their mother possibly dying intestate, and exchanged anxious letters about the situation.[59]

In some parts of North America it was considered abnormal for a household to contain more than one married couple. Wills in New England bequeathed houses to individual sons and sometimes left instructions to widows and children to assist in housing their other children and siblings. William Carpenter left his property to his elder son but willed that his widow and this elder son should 'help [Abiah] to build an house, because Samuel hath an house built already.'[60] Marriage settlements provided for the purchase or building of a house for the couple. So Joseph Buckland's father promised to build Joseph 'a convenient house for his comfortable living with three score acres of land adjoining to it'.[61] When her husband died it was expected that a woman would be cared for by one or more of her children and live with one or other of them. William Carpenter gave his house to Samuel but stipulated in his will that his widow would have 'the room I now lodge in and the chamber over it and to have liberties to come to the fire to do her occasions' (that is, cooking and washing and warming rights).⁶² On occasion the whole estate was left to the widow, for her to distribute on her own death 'accordingly as she shall see cause and they deserve in their . . . care of her in her widow's estate'.⁶³

In seventeenth-century Maryland widows and widowers often sought to protect their own interests when providing marriage settlements for their children and some even opted for a form of early retirement. For example, Christopher Kirkly, a joiner, made over his entire estate to his daughter Susannah when she married in 1705. In return Christopher was to have 'meat, drink, washing and apparel' of equivalent quality to that enjoyed by her husband and heirs, and a separate chamber, bed, and gun plus the use of his joiner's tools and any money that he made from his joinery business. More usual was the willing of the estate to the son, with insistence that the widow was well and explicitly provided for (an echo of English practice). Edward Bowles gave his son Edward junior the whole estate on condition that his son kept his mother in the family home 'with sufficient meat, drink and apparel with one room to herself and a good bed and chest'.⁶⁴

In some of the North American colonies it appears that the courts were very active in protecting the rights of wives and widows. For example, in Plymouth Colony the laws provided that the courts might overturn a will that did not provide adequately for the widow, especially if she had brought property into the marriage or had increased the prosperity of the family by her hard work. In 1663, Widow Naomi Silvester had her portion increased because she had been 'a frugal and laborious woman in the procuring of the said estate'.⁶⁵ The courts persuaded children to care for their widowed mothers even when no provision had been made for them by the deceased.⁶⁶

Vulnerable widows

We know that from the Middle Ages onwards both wives and widows knew and used the law to protect their interests. Elizabeth Berkeley, Countess of Warwick, and Lady Isabel Berkeley, for example, were at the centre of a lawsuit between 1417 and 1439 concerning the Berkeley inheritance, with Elizabeth appearing before the King's Council at Westminster to argue her case.⁶⁷ More typical was involvement as widows seeking to secure dower or bequests. For example, between 1473 and 1476 Anne Neville, dowager Duchess of Buckingham, brought suits against twenty-three people for debts.⁶⁸ Margaret, dowager Marchioness of Dorset, in 1540 defended her interests at law in a Leicestershire property suit.⁶⁹ Anne,

Lady Berkeley, in 1535 petitioned Thomas Cromwell to assist her in obtaining a writ for her jointure.[70] Such examples indicate how difficult it frequently was for a widow to lay her hands on the property that would support her during her widowhood.[71]

While the law and well-placed patrons did offer widows potential protection, many widows, especially those of means, were conscious of their vulnerability as the relatives of their deceased husbands attended them like hyenas at a lion's kill. Widows expected their own kin to chase away these marauding hyenas. In the early sixteenth century Anne Clifford Clifton, the recently widowed wife of Robert Clifton of Nottingham, upbraided her brother, Henry Clifford, later 1st Earl of Cumberland, for being neglectful of her plight:

Right worshipful brother, I heartily recommend me unto you, beseeching you to be good brother to me, and having great marvel of your unkindness, that you would not be here your self at this time, nor none for now for here has been all my husband's uncles and brothers and I had nobody to speak in all my cause but myself . . . every gentlewoman might have trusted to help of her brother . . . I pray you that you and my sister will speak together and take your best counsel and advice what you can do for me.[72]

Much later, in the middle of the seventeenth century, Katharine Austen found herself equally without help from her own kin and moaned: 'I am in the hands of potent men. Men skilful to destroy and subtle men, who lay trains to ruin the widow and fatherless. [I am] a woman without alliance of the family to help me. Yet O god help me and make me over come those bands that do environ me.'

The widows of men who lived in tied accommodation suffered from a different kind of vulnerability. Such widows ranged from the wives of farm labourers to the wives of clergy. Unless a clergyman had managed to purchase property of his own (often out of a very meagre income), his widow would be cast out of the parsonage shortly after his death. Such women did not always calmly accept this fate, however. The widow of the vicar of Rosthorne, Cheshire (whose husband had apparently made further provision for her accommodation), insisted that she deserved some compensation for the fact that her husband had improved the vicarage at his own expense and had, as a consequence, left her with debts to settle. In 1649 Adam Martindale became vicar. However, he and his family could not occupy either the vicarage or the glebeland (the fields attached to the benefice) because 'my predecessor's widow was in possession'. Martindale and his growing family were compelled to board at John Bentley's house. Martindale attempted to oust her once 'she could conveniently go to her own estate near Nantwich' but the feisty widow collected together several ministers to argue that Martindale should pay her money out of the arrears of the vicarage. In the event Martindale allowed her a proportion of the stipend of the living for the year before he came, let her live in the house until May Day in 1650, and paid her for 'all the wainscot in the house, flags of the floor, glass in the windows, with all the inner doors, and even the great double door full of nails leading to the hall, or else she would take all these away, and I must either lose them or sue for them . . .'[73]

Widows, although they often maintained separate households, reverted to their birth families on the death of their husbands. The deceased spouse's family may have shown genuine concern but it was for the offspring of the match and not for the widow. So widows from all walks of life sought the help of their birth families and 'friends' and 'patrons'. The widows Lady Ursula (Fiennes) Marrowe and plain Mrs Elnor Taverner, for example, were both equally dependent upon Sir Thomas Temple for help in recovering their property.[74]

In comparison with much of Europe, England and Wales had a tightly circumscribed system for the descent of property – the eldest son under rules of intestacy inherited a large proportion of an estate, the remainder of which passed to the widow during her lifetime and to other children, generally to the exclusion of collateral kin. Will-makers (perhaps a quarter of adult males) certainly used their growing testamentary freedom to provide better for all of their dependants but they still chose to concentrate particularly on portions for younger offspring. Acknowledging that the American colonies' laws regarding testation and intestacy had their roots in this unilinear system of descent, historians still argue about the extent to which they accepted the English preoccupation with obligations towards the dynasty. The continually shifting laws of testation in some of the colonies and the complete absence of testamentary law in others makes 'it very difficult to write very authoritatively about general patterns of colonial inheritance much before the second decade of the eighteenth century'.[75]

We can safely say, however, that in the American colonies there was immense diversity in the levels and types of protection offered vulnerable widows.[76] A leading authority, Marylynn Salmon, argues that Virginians, Marylanders and South Carolinians more closely followed English patterns than did New Englanders because these southerners did not have the ideological commitment to change that was apparent among the 'pilgrims' of the North East.[77] Indeed immigrants to the southern colonies and New York often *wanted* to mimic the institutions and laws of the mother country whereas those of Massachusetts and Connecticut wanted to instigate reform and readily modified English laws and customs where they saw fit.[78] Southerners tended to see themselves as English overseas, whereas for the Puritans this was definitely New and not Old England.[79] This ideological difference helps to provide a general explanation for variations in the provision for and protection of widows on a regional basis. Salmon adds, however, that the laws were changed in response to the circumstances of colonisation and this explains the considerable diversity from colony to colony, notwithstanding the regional distinctions attributable to ideology.

Therefore, even in colonies with similar backgrounds, different rules sometimes evolved. In Virginia . . . slaves became defined as realty[80] for the purpose of apportioning widows' dower, while Maryland retained the [English] common law rule defining all movable estate as personalty. Virginia widows therefore inherited a share of their husband's slaves only for life, whereas widows in Maryland gained absolute rights to some slave property. Because dower in Maryland included a share of personalty as well as the standard widow's thirds in realty, women there had a considerable advantage.[81]

Such differences seem sometimes to have been dictated by the timing of settlement. For instance, when Maryland was developing its laws in the early seventeenth century, it naturally followed current English rules of allowing full dower in moveable goods, whereas South Carolina took over the new English rule brought in during the 1690s in most of England that men had the right to will all of their personalty without restriction.[82]

Demography also seems to have explained variations in the amount and type of protection offered vulnerable widows. Legal historians have noted that the dissenter colonies of New England liberalised the inheritance laws with regard to younger children (by rejecting primogeniture) and that the Chesapeake colonies of Virginia and Maryland 'resisted shrinking widows' dower rights' in accord with new standards in England. Only Virginia and Maryland continued to support a widow's right to personalty and generous support for widows in wills. It is suggested that this reflected the fact that marriageable women were in short supply in the Chesapeake and that remarriage was extremely common.[83] The dower laws which allowed women to retain realty even when they remarried benefited both widows and the men who married them.[84]

Powerful widows

Both the powerfulness and the powerlessness of widows from the late Middle Ages onwards are becoming increasingly evident to historians. For instance, Rowena Archer has drawn attention to the estate administration of numbers of fourteenth- and fifteenth-century aristocratic widows such as Elizabeth de Burgh (d.1360), Lady Margaret Beaufort (1443–1509) and Katherine Neville, Duchess of Norfolk (fl.1412–1422).[85] When Eleanor Townshend assumed control of her deceased husband's estates in 1491, the accounts were kept in English so that she could oversee them until her death in 1499, when they reverted to the usual Latin.[86] Barbara Harris notes, however, that medieval aristocratic women's lack of Latin made them especially vulnerable to fraud.[87] Moreover, we now know that in some cases widows lower down the social ladder were heads of household and were accorded the same benefits and obligations as males in the same position. In Morebath in Devon widowed heads of household were involved in the election of church wardens and on occasion actually served as High Wardens. In 1528, 1542, 1543, 1548, 1557, 1561, 1563 and 1572 there were female High Wardens in that parish and in 1561 and 1572 the junior High Warden was also a woman.[88] High Wardens were responsible for the central parish funds and for keeping accounts, and the post was no sinecure.

There can be no substitute, when seeking to understand the situation of, and provision for, a widow, for careful case studies. When Thomas Ferebe, a well-off Cirencester mercer, died in 1611, he left his son George nothing but a 'black mourning suit' and bequeathed most of his estate, once proper provision had been made for his widow, Elizabeth, to his youngest son Anthony, who was carrying on the family business. Elizabeth went to live with her son Thomas and his wife Bridget, where she remained for the next twenty-three years. Thomas the elder had taken into account, when he made his will, the fact that George was well-established in a church benefice and that Elizabeth had appropriate living arrangements. There was also no need for Thomas to mention in his will realty that had passed to his eldest son or to his widow as of right. A widow's provision often consisted of the use and administration of the whole estate during the heir's minority (as was the case with William Stout of Lancaster's mother); of part of the estate during her life and/or widowhood; of the use for life or viduity of apartments in the family house or of a separate dower house. The more the different types of documentation that surround a case, the more the historian can understand the nature of particular widowhoods.

There are also many examples of widows throughout the period who managed urban businesses left to them by their husbands. Examples from London and the larger cities abound but there are also examples from newer towns. In Whitehaven in the late seventeenth century, several widows were left shares in ships and not only continued the investments but became successful in managing them. In 1680, Madam Gale was left a large house there, a number of shops in a prime position in the market place, a malt-making business and a stone quarry. She directed all these businesses and expanded them considerably.[89] Some of these Whitehaven widows exhibited considerable financial acumen and sought to adjust the distribution of portions to their children. For example, Isabel Boyd bought the freehold of land she had inherited from her father by customary tenure and used her will in 1742 to divide it equally among her daughters (something the custom would not have permitted). Susan Millam decided that her son Joseph had been well provided for and so willed to her daughters money, personal estate, shares in ships and in the sugar house.[90]

Widows had once been wives or even other men's widows, and before that unmarried daughters, and now in their widowhood were frequently the mothers of young children and mature adults. They carried with them into widowhood a whole baggage of relationships, including relations with in-laws and with their own children. How far were they still regarded by their kin, their late husband's kin and their children as authority figures? How far were they now simply treated as dependants? Case studies of particular widows can shed further light on these issues. The first such case study is all the more telling because it is based upon a son's perceptions and his acute observations of the role his widowed mother played in the lives and livelihoods of her sons and daughter.

William Stout of Lancaster (1665–1752) was at pains to recount in his autobiography how his mother and father, who married in Charles I's time, were partners in the management of their yeoman's estate. They had acted to improve the estate specifically for the support of their children. When her husband died, Elizabeth without hesitation continued to run the farm for the benefit of her eldest son, Josias, who was still a minor. In this she was far from unusual. Among Stout's aunts were several widows who ran farms in order to support their young families. On the surface, Elizabeth Stout asppears as a strong, even formidable, mature woman – a veritable matriarch – and her son William, who clearly held her in great love and esteem, paints her as such. If we probe a little further, however, this impression is somewhat dented. Elizabeth acted on her own initiative in keeping the farm but she did not regard herself as sufficiently skilled in husbandry (farming) to organise the farm in more than a general supervisory capacity. This had not been her role when she was a wife and she had not been trained up to do it. Accordingly, she followed the advice of the overseers appointed under her husband's will and employed William Jenkinson as her farm manager. Her prime task was that of ensuring that her young sons were educated to perform his functions in later life. Josias and Leonard worked on the farm until they were twenty-four and twenty, respectively. Her husband and she had purchased land specifically to create a separate estate for Leonard and during the first phase of her widowhood Elizabeth organised work on this land to provide a working farm for the youth. Elizabeth followed the wishes of her late husband in binding William apprentice to Henry Coward. She also trained her disabled daughter in housewifery. Her actual day-to-day work differed little from that she had done as a wife, except that now her children were teenagers and made different demands on her. She was now, however, the figure of authority in the household, the one who made the decisions.

This phase of her widowhood represented Mistress Elizabeth Stout at her most powerful within the family. In theory it ended when her son Josias came of age (probably at the age of twenty-five). Elizabeth technically exchanged her position as head of household with that of housekeeper for her son. Hers was now a servicing role. In practice this was modified by Josias's memory of her authority and his affection for her. Eventually, however, Elizabeth became too old and infirm to do the job properly. Josias initially leased the farm out and went to stay with his brother, Leonard. This experiment collapsed and mother and son returned to their farm to run it with the aid of servants. When Elizabeth could go on no longer she advised middle-aged Josias either to hire a servant or to marry a wife. He was accustomed to obeying his mother and he went ahead and married a wife.

This was when Elizabeth's status truly changed. The third phase of Elizabeth's lengthy widowhood began when Josias brought his new wife into the farmhouse. Strong-willed Sybill was determined to be mistress in her own house and Elizabeth, as William observed, found it difficult to adjust. Even as Josias's housekeeper she had been used to being the one who gave commands. The arrangement lasted only a year. Desperate for peace, Josias asked his bachelor brother William to look after their mother. Elizabeth spent the seven remaining years of her life living with her unmarried son and daughter in Lancaster. She died at the age of eighty-four.

It would be precipitate to claim that Elizabeth Stout was a typical widow. For many widows the period of headship of the household might be absent (if her children had reached majority) or truncated. For others there would be no period of acting as housekeeper for a bachelor son. A widow did not necessarily have children and, even where she did, actual mothering might be a thing of the distant past. A young widow might be excessively dependent upon her birth family and look to her own father or uncle as the authority figure. Nonetheless, Elizabeth's life does demonstrate that a widow's life was characterised by phases. Her period of relative power and authority was not only ended if she chose to remarry; it also depended upon the ages, circumstances and attitudes of her children; upon the relationship she had built up with them and maintained; upon the marital status of the heir and his siblings.

For much of Elizabeth's widowhood, Josias was the titular head of the household yet she seems to have been in many respects the real figure of power and authority. On the other hand, at times (even during the early phase) her actions were hedged by her deceased husband's express wishes, by the strategy which she and he had evolved as partners, by his legal prearrangements, by the advice of the overseers and by the temporary nature of her position as head of household.

The example of Anne or Abigail Baldwin (d.c.1713) is also instructive. Anne had married Richard Baldwin from Buckinghamshire. He was a freeman of the London Stationers' Company from 1675 and was an important Whig publisher by the 1690s. Anne was active in his business during their marriage and, when Richard died in 1698, Anne continued to run it from a shop in Warwick Lane. Between 1698 and 1713 she published 240 works 'mainly concerned with contemporary political, religious and foreign policy issues'.[91] She seems to have shared her husband's radical republicanism – for instance, in 1698 she published a new edition of Henry Neville's *Plato Redivivus*. Amongst other authors, Daniel Defoe published with her. In 1709–10 she controlled *The Ladies' Tatler* which was edited by Mary Manley. Her life, so different from Elizabeth Stout's in many ways (urban, metropolitan, politically active) resembled it in the way that she too was her husband's 'business' partner and, in widowhood, carried on his concerns.

Lady Hester Temple of Stowe had always been a strong and active partner in her long marriage to Sir Thomas and when he died she did not suddenly become a shrinking violet. She had been well-provided for by the terms of her marriage settlement and leases that had been purchased during her marriage, and she lived chiefly at Burton Dassett in Warwickshire (part of her jointure lands) when the estate at Stowe, Buckinghamshire, passed to Peter, her eldest son. Her circumstances were, however, reduced and she found it difficult to respond to all the demands that her married children continued to make upon her. In his will of 1632 her husband Thomas had been concerned to remind those quarrelsome children of their duty towards their mother: 'who I desire earnestly, that they would embrace one another in faithful and true love, and to give dew respecte and reverence to their aged mother my loving wife . . . as they will answer me their earthly [father] and the great God of heaven' 'and be comfortable dutiful and respective to their mother and to suffer her in quietness to enjoy that little I shall leave unto her'.[92]

Although widows were often independent and powerful, some husbands did seek from the grave to curb this independence. They did this not only by making bequests conditional on remaining widowed. So, late in the seventeenth century, Edward, Earl of Conway, willed in trust for her lifetime the whole of his estate in Ireland to his widow on condition that the house at Ragley should be finished 'according to that model and design which I began and carried it on in.'[93]

In her study of marriages in seventeenth-century Maryland, Lorena Walsh argues that nearly three-quarters of male testators gave their wives more than the law required and that this indicates a high regard for, and trust in, their wives, given that they knew that their wives were likely to remarry. Indeed husbands frequently bequeathed their wives either the whole estate or a major part of the estate for their natural lives rather than until they died or remarried.[94]

There are many examples of 'powerful' widows in eighteenth-century America. One of the best known was Sarah Kemble Knight who owned a shop and rented accommodation on Moon Street, Boston, by 1707. She perhaps also acted as a scrivener and amanuensis for the neighbourhood, although the legend that she was Benjamin Franklin's schoolteacher is unsubstantiated. In 1713 her daughter Elizabeth married John Livingstone and in 1714 Sarah sold some of her Boston property and followed them to live in Connecticut. She did not, however, enter into any kind of retirement. Instead she accumulated more and more property, this time in Norwich, near New London, Connecticut, most of which passed to her widowed daughter on Sarah's death in 1727. Her married daughter and son-in-law seem to have lived in her house in Norwich until John died abroad in 1720. She also kept a shop and was sufficiently prosperous to donate a silver chalice to the Norwich church in 1717. She apparently sold liquor and in 1718 was fined 20 shillings for selling alcohol to the local Indians. In the 1720s she bought more land in New London and had a family pew in its congregational church. She also ran an inn in one of her farms there. When she died in 1727 her estate was valued at £1,800. Of course, we have no way of knowing how typical Sarah was. Certainly, even when she had been married, she was already a remarkably independent woman. In the autumn of 1704, at the age of thirty-eight, she had undertaken a lengthy and potentially dangerous business journey on horseback from Boston to New Haven and New York City (where she spent a fortnight). In her diary she recorded keenly and wittily observed details of the arduous trip, 'Bugbears to a fearful female traveller' such as 'Bridges which were . . . very tottering and of vast Length' over swollen rivers, her food, lodging and the company she kept at inns and farmhouses where she stayed, before her return home to an enthusiastic welcome from friends and relatives in March 1705. For a long time she was the focus of attention as she entertained with 'the story of my transactions and travails'.[95]

Another interesting example, this time from New York City, is provided by Maria DePeyester Shrick Spratt Provoost (d.1700) and her daughter, Mary Spratt Provoost Alexander (1693–1760). It shows how these women were both powerful in marriage and in widowhood. Also it makes clear how Old World customs (in their case Dutch) were influential upon their behaviour both as wives and widows. Mary was the daughter of John Spratt, a Scottish Covenanter from Glasgow and Maria DePeyester, from a Dutch family of goldsmiths which had made its fortune in the New World. Maria had previously been married to Paulus Shrick; when Spratt died in 1697 she remarried to David Provoost, a merchant. As was the custom in the Dutch community, Maria carried on the business concerns of her first two husbands until her own death in 1700. At this point Mary Spratt was reared by her DePeyester grandmother and her uncles until 1711 when she married Samuel Provoost, a younger brother of her stepfather. She invested her money in Provoost's business ventures and mixed raising three children with business activities. She was widowed sometime between July 1719 and February 1720 but soon married again. Her husband was James Alexander, descendant of the Earls of Stirling and a major figure in New York politics and business. She took care to protect the interests of her three Provoost children in a prenuptial agreement. During the next thirty-nine years she bore seven more children, five of whom reached maturity, but again combined motherhood with business and being a political wife. Many of her business ventures were independent: she became a major importer of goods, which she sold in her own store. During the French and Indian wars she and her son took advantage of the business opportunities offered and contracted to supply General Shirley's army with horses, food, cannons and so forth.[96]

Preparation of women for widowhood

Separating out the education of women for widowhood is, of course, an artificial exercise: the education a young woman received was designed to fit her for all the roles she would potentially play throughout her life: marriage, motherhood, widowhood and so forth. At least some authors and educators, however, appealed directly to the widow market. Martin Billingsley, for instance, urged in *The Pen's Excellencie* that the ability to write 'at lest in some reasonable manner' will give a widow control over her estate and protection from the deceits practised by agents:

The practise of this art [of writing] is so necessary for women, and consequently so excellent, that no woman surviving her husband, and who had an estate left her, ought to be without the use thereof... for thereby shee comes to a certainty of her estate, without trusting to the reports of such as are usually imployed to looke into the same: whereas otherwise for want of it, she is subject to the manifold deceits now used in the world, and by that meanes plunges herself into a multitude of inconveniences.[97]

Billingsley's counsel would appeal not only to parents and wives but also to husbands whose greatest fear was that, on their death, their children would be cheated out of their inheritance – a competent widow was the greatest security that such a husband could have.

Remarrying widows

How say you if I would help you to a widow, who is come of worshipful parentage and hath twenty pounds a year dowry or jointure, who hath no children and is of years nigh five or six years younger than yourself?[98]

Widowhood has been singled out by historians, myself included, as a life stage in which women were to be seen at their most powerful. It is not, however, really possible to distinguish widowhood sharply from wifehood and motherhood. A remarried widow was also wife to a husband and probably mother to children of two or more husbands. To treat widows as if they formed a homogeneous mass is almost as bad as treating all women as if their lives were identical. Some widows, of course, did live alone or with minor children for many years. Others were very briefly alone, swiftly remarrying. Some of the sources pertaining to widowhood actually inform us about the emotional and economic position of married women as much as they do those of widows.

Widowhood did not come as a surprise to early modern women in any of these societies. It was not, however, for a great many a continuing state. Notwithstanding recent conclusions regarding the increasing reluctance or inability of many English widows to remarry as our period progressed,[99] remarriage of widows did occur frequently and often occurred very soon after widowhood.

Widows, like wives and singletons, held highly diverse lives, as one might expect, because they belonged to diverse age and socio-economic groups. There should be no blanket assertion that widowhood offered opportunities for independence, self-sufficiency and social freedom. Thus only 56 per cent of the widows of London aldermen in the second half of the sixteenth century remarried, and a third of the widows were economically active during their widowhood; whereas the widows of poor craftsmen, labourers and porters appeared as supplicants for charitable relief or as spinners, weavers and servants. Widows became dependent upon unrelated friends and neighbours. If a woman elected to remarry the supposed advantages of widowhood might rapidly disappear, yet there is some evidence to suggest that it was 'need' which eventually pushed many widows into remarriage although they had resisted such action for as long as possible. Barbara Todd's study of Abingdon widows suggests that in sixteenth-century England, male testators quite frequently regarded the remarriage of their widows with equanimity, seeing it as a way of ensuring the future of their loved ones. After 1570, however, there appears to have been a change of attitude, particularly in the case of men of some social or economic standing. By the seventeenth century this trend spread to testators from all social groups: 'these testators made certain that their wives should take none of their wealth into a new marriage by inserting a penalty withholding or reducing the wife's share of the estate if she remarried'.[100]

Widows were themselves only too aware of the implications of remarriage. Katharine Austen, a twenty-nine-year-old London widow with three children, discovered that her husband's will prevented her marrying for seven years after his demise if she wished to avoid harsh financial penalties. When this time was over she considered remarriage but decided against it and remained a widow until her death in 1683. She was attached to her husband's memory and to his family to which she had been 'grafted'. She feared to lose her reputation by remarrying. She felt that if she remarried she would not be free to rebuild her children's fortunes and protect their inheritances.[101] Historians have shown that remarriage was growing less common in the second half of the seventeenth century, just as there was an oversupply of women in the marriage market. They have also shown that marriage was becoming less fashionable and that this may have had economic, as well as demographic, causes. For example, in the 1690s a tax was laid on London marriage licences.[102] Despite such disincentives many women did elect to remarry and attempted to protect themselves and their children from the consequences.

In the Chesapeake region remarried widows probably had difficult lives, juggling as they did the relationships between their new spouses and several sets of children by different fathers. Marriage perhaps brought physical and economic security but it also brought with it its own set of problems. Mary, wife of George Keeble, was born in Virginia in about 1637 and she had seven children by Keeble before being widowed at age twenty-nine. Shortly thereafter she married Robert Beverley and brought to the marriage at least four of Keeble's offspring. She was to have five more children by Beverley before she died, aged forty-one, in 1678. Beverley almost immediately remarried a widow, Katherine Hone, with a young child. By 1680 their household held children from four different unions, including one of their own! Katherine and Robert had three more children before he died in 1687. She then remarried to Christopher Robinson, a widower with four surviving children, and they had four children together, adding eight offspring to the wider family.[103]

Widows taking care of their own offspring

Widows such as Maria Spratt Provoost Alexander tried to protect the offspring of their previous marriages when they entered into new unions. Sometimes wives who feared death were also impelled to take forestalling action to protect the inheritances of their children, not simply by will but by arranging their marriages and settlements. Concerned relatives might offer shrewd advice. 'There is a letter to Sir Francis Willughby's Lady writ in the year 1594 from her son-in-law Spenser – he writes to advise her to hasten the disposing of her daughters, and urges how much reason she has to desire to see them married soon, her illness making her apprehend her life is in danger, and should she [p. 40] die, he tells her tis very likely Sir Francis would marry again, and how much that would be to her daughters disadvantage, she may judge, besides he tells her on this account, she is wholly blamed, and some say if she and Sir Francis had not come together again they would have been as well or better disposed of than the rest of their sisters – he writes she knows of the offers which he had made of such men, both for estates and worth that if he had had sisters he should have been glad they might have had them – which offers she had thought contemptible – insomuch that he says he would never more have meddled in this affair, had not now her dangerous illness prompted him to it.'[104]

In Maryland as in England prudent widows sought to safeguard the estates of their children while they still had legal identity as 'femes soles'. Such a widow might deed shares of their deceased father's estate to his children before she remarried. Or her marriage contract might specify the precise payments that the new spouse had to pay his stepchildren out of their father's estate. Sometimes a widow would fail to take these precautions and her children were left fighting for their livelihood in the courts. Other times a widow might appoint a new husband trustee of funds designed by her late husband for the benefit of his children, thus confounding the purpose of the trust.[105]

While it is true that widows felt an obligation towards their own children, they had to be careful to protect their own livelihoods. Lady Hester Temple was constantly pressured by her eldest son to sign over her jointure lands first to him and then to his children. She gamely resisted such moves.

Conclusion

Widows were in a stronger legal position than wives but their true strength varied according to their age, their property, their prior relationship with their children, and their independence of spirit. As fewer English widows appear to have remarried by the later seventeenth century, the indications could be that women were beginning to appreciate their relative strength vis-à-vis married women but in fact demography could explain why second marriages were on the decrease. The relative scarcity of women in many of the sixteenth- and seventeenth-century colonies probably rendered the propertied widow more powerful and desirable.

The behaviour of widows, especially in relation to the management and protection of their property, can provide a valuable indicator of the involvement of women in such matters throughout their married lives. Indeed, where historians have ample information about the lives of so-called powerful widows, rural and urban, elite and non-elite, British or colonial, the evidence suggests that these women who as widows ran estates and/or enterprises had during marriage been partners with their husbands in similar activities. Inevitably such information survives for only a tiny proportion of the populations and this fact should be taken into consideration when assessing the strength of the evidence.

Notes

1. Will of Sir Thomas Temple, February 1632/3.
2. HEH, STT Personal Box 9 1632–1639 Folder 1 Will and probate copy of Sir Thomas Temple. Will made 4 Feb 1632/3 'calling to minde the mortalitie of man and desirous to settle peace to my posteritie'. In the American colonies also there are strong indications that fathers did not pass on their lands by will but rather provided for their sons and daughters during the father's lifetime.
3. J. T. Rosenthal (1991) p. 182.
4. See Rosenthal (1991) pp. 197–8; K. B. Mcfarlane (1973) pp. 64–6, 204–7; L. Stone (1977) pp. 172–3; R. Archer (1984) pp. 15–35, and especially pp. 23, 25 and 31.
5. B. Harris (2002) p. 127.
6. P. Laslett (1972) pp. 77–8.
7. J. Boulton (1987) p. 129.
8. F. P. Wilson (1963) pp. 3–4; M. F. and Mary F. and T. H. Hollingsworth (1971) pp. 131–46.
9. L. Stone and J. F. Stone (1984) p. 95.
10. For example Anne Clifford. Susan (Spencer) Temple and Hester (Sandys) Temple provide examples of women widowed in later life who continued long lives as widows.
11. *Historical Manuscripts Commission Report 5*, 1909, p. 86, *Manuscripts of Sir John James Graham of Fintry; Manuscripts of Sir Archibald Edmonstone of Duntreath, Strathblane, Bt.*, Licence by Alexander Stewart, Archbishop of St Andrews to Elizabeth Livingstone, 2 Aug 1510. Stewart added a postscript in his own hand that 'al hurting and damge at efter ma follow to us rasarvit'.
12. BL Stowe MSS 847 and 848.
13. See C. Churches (1998) pp. 165–80.
14. Cited in R. A. Houlbrooke (1984) p. 213.
15. D. V. Glass (1965); Roger Thompson (1974) p. 35.
16. Charles Carlton (1992) pp. 204–5.
17. L. Stone (1977) pp. 93–4.
18. *Instructions to be held and observed by the second surveyors appointed ascertaining the duties upon Houses . . . and upon Batchelours and Widowers, pursuant to the Act of Parliament in that behalf*, London, 1697, cited in Cavallo and Warner (1999) p. 11.

19 D. Meyers (2003) p. 56, citing Maryland Wills: Ignatius Causine, 1695, 7: 94; Maryland Wills, Henry Hyde, 1675, 2: 362.

20 D. Meyers (2003) p. 56 citing Maryland Wills, 1702, 11: 210.

21 Meyers (2003) pp. 56–7 citing Maryland Wills, Arthur Wright, 1677, 5: 180.

22 Not to be confused with dowry which was property given to a woman (or her husband) on marriage, usually by her family. A widower received lifetime use of his late wife's property (realty). This customary right was called curtesy. At his death, her property went to her children or, failing them, her next of kin.

23 A. L. Erickson (1995 pbk edn) p. 25.

24 Jointure was used to describe either a joint interest in a piece of specified property, which would be enjoyed by the surviving partner (legal jointure), or an agreed annuity to be paid to the wife for her lifetime should she survive her husband (equitable jointure).

25 Under primogeniture, where there was no son to inherit, daughters inherited in equal shares. In Kent, gavelkind, true partible inheritance (division of the estate amongst the sons in equal shares or, failing sons, daughters) prevailed.

26 FSL, Bagot Collection, la 613 Walter Bagot to Jane Lane.

27 See, for e.g., L. M. Glanz (1973).

28 R. Thompson (1974) p. 164.

29 These were valuable forms of patronage in sixteenth- and seventeenth-century England and Wales, of which there was no direct equivalent in the American colonies or in Scotland after the Reformation. For a discussion of the operation of grants of next (and future) presentations (pro hac vice) see Rosemary O'Day, *The English Clergy: The Emergence and Consolidation of a Profession*, 1979, pp. 105–12.

30 HEH, STT Personal Box 5, Folder 1 >1600 Marriage articles for marriage of George Stratford to Alyce Shakerly, wyddowe.

31 FSL, Bagot Collection.

32 The common law denied a married woman's legal identity and, therefore, any contracts she made were rendered null and void on her marriage. Legal jointures, which were actionable at common law, involved a joint interest in a piece of property by husband and wife (either by lease or puchase) and it is entirely possible that the kind of 'joint purchase' arrangement George Stratford made (and enshrined in the marriage settlement) was a legal jointure defensible in common law.

33 L. Bonfield (1989) pp. 194–8.

34 Neither needed the testator to refer in the will to the freehold lands (or realty) which passed via primogeniture, partible inheritance or Borough-English to his descendants.

35 J. Ford (1992) p. 145.

36 There are indications that a widow might choose her third of her husband's property and that she would be helped to make a sensible choice by her father or the head of her birth household. See, for example, the will of Thomas Ryche, son of a wealthy London mercer, who when he died in 1474 left his widow Elizabeth a third of his residue which she was to choose with the help of her father John Croke. See C. Carpenter (1996) p. 55.

37 For example a lease might be made to three named individuals and the longer-lived of them – thus a wife and child named in a lease who outlived the husband would jointly 'inherit' the lease and, if the child outlived his or her mother, the lease would continue in his or her name only. Sometimes a lease would, instead, be made for a number of years and/or for a specific purpose.

38 Henry Swinburne, *A Brief treatise of testamentes and last willes*, 1590 edition, pp. 105–6.

39 Probate of wills was under ecclesiastical jurisdiction. England and Wales were divided into two provinces: Canterbury (headed by the Archbishop of Canterbury) and York (headed by the Archbishop of York). Each province was divided into bishoprics which were in turn subdivided into archdeaconries and deaneries. At each level of division there were probate courts, from the deanery court which dealt locally with estates of little value to the Prerogative Courts of Canterbury and York, which dealt with probate of valuable estates.

40 See William Blackstone, *Commentaries on the Laws of England*, 1765–1769, Vol. 2, pp. 492–3; Ronald Marchant (1969) p. 91; H. Horwitz (1984) pp. 223–39.

41 *Statutes of the Realm*, 22–23 Car. 2, c. 10; 1 Jas 2, c. 17.

42 Peter Earle (1989) pp. 194–8.

43 A. L. Erickson (1990) pp. 26–7.

44 Cited in Erickson (1995 pbk edn) p. 129.

45 Erickson (1995 pbk edn) p. 130.

46 See HEH STB Box 1, loose letters and notes for letters relating to the controversial marriage settlement of Francis Willoughby and Emma Barnard and for Emma's part in the affair. See also Dorothy Johnston, 'Emma Child, nee Barnard, formerly Willughby (1644–1725): records of the life of a gentlewoman', in John Beckett (ed.), *Nottinghamshire past: Essays in honour of Adrian Henstock*, 2003.

47 Erickson (1995 pbk edn) p. 132.

48 HEH, STT Personal Box 5, Folder 1, Marriage articles for marriage of George Stratford to Alyce Shakerly, wyddowe.

49 It is interesting that the above marriage settlement was in the possession of Sir Thomas Temple, one of the administrators of George Stratford's estate.
50 L. Munby (1981) p. xv.
51 Margaret Jewer wife of John Sumner, Easebourne, WSRO: Epl/29/75/35 as cited in Erickson (1995 pbk edn) p. 136.
52 Thomas Hall (1649) Malton, Rydall, BIHR as cited in Erickson (1995 pbk edn) p. 136.
53 HEH, STT, Personal Box 8, Folder 7, 26 July 1628 Copy of will and probate of Lady Anne (Lucas) Throckmorton. She died in August 1629.
54 A. L. Erickson (1995 pbk edn) pp. 156–7.
55 Erickson (1995 pbk edn) p. 156.
56 S. Cavallo and L. Warner (1999) p. 14.
57 Gloria Main (1989) pp. 77–8.
58 Edward Fenton (1998) p. 5.
59 NLCS, Copy Letter Book, No. 197, p. 111 To Brother Middleton 26 June 1725.
60 Mayflower Descendant, XIV, 231 cited in Demos (1978 reprint edn) p. 63.
61 Mayflower Descendant, XVI, 82 cited in Demos (1978 reprint edn) p. 63.
62 Mayflower Descendant, XVI, 232 cited in Demos (1978 reprint edn) p. 75.
63 Mayflower Descendant, XXXIV, 34 cited in Demos (1978 reprint edn) p. 75.
64 L. Walsh (1979) pp. 134–5.
65 Demos (1978 reprint edn) p. 85.
66 Demos (1978 reprint edn) p. 76.
67 A. Sinclair (1987) pp. 34–50; C. D. Ross (1951); J. Maclean (1883) Vol. II, p. 62, all cited in R. Archer (1992) p. 161.
68 For this and other fifteenth-century examples see Archer (1992) p. 161.
69 See B. J. Harris (2002) p. 146.
70 See Harris (2002) p. 139.
71 See Harris (2002) pp. 134–45.
72 Letter of Anne Clifton to Sir Henry Clifford, 6 March 1518, printed in A. G. Dickens, 'The Clifford Letters' (1957).
73 R. Parkinson (1845) pp. 82, 88.
74 HEH, ST, Temple Correspondence, Box 4, STT 1454 Ursula Marowe (Fiennes) Lady to Sir Thos Temple 1st Bt on 17 Sep 1610, and STT 1901

Elnor Taverner from Paternoster Rowe on 5 Feb 1610/11 to Sir Thos Temple 1st Bt.
75 C. Shammas *et al.* (1987) p. 31.
76 M. Salmon (1986) pp. 1–12.
77 Salmon (1986) p. 10.
78 Salmon (1986) p. 12.
79 See Chapter 16.
80 Commonly used to refer to land and usually freehold land in contrast to personal property or personalty.
81 Salmon (1986) pp. 4–5.
82 Salmon (1986) pp. 5–6.
83 Walsh (1979) *passim*.
84 Shammas *et al.* (1987) pp. 36–7.
85 R. Archer (1992) pp. 171–2 and *passim*; see also B. J. Harris (2002) pp. 127–74.
86 B. J. Harris (2002) p. 38.
87 Harris (2002) p. 38.
88 E. Duffy (2001) pp. 28–9.
89 C. Churches (1998) pp. 177–9.
90 C. Churches (1998) p. 176.
91 Anne Crawford *et al.* (1983) pp. 27–8.
92 HEH, STT Personal Box 9 1632–1639, Folder 1 Probate copy of Sir Thomas Temple's will made 4 Feb 1632/3.
93 *Historical Manuscripts Commission Report*, Vol. I, 1928, p. 321, Document 1306, *Manuscripts of the late Reginald Rawdon Hastings esq. of the Manor House, Ashby de la Zouche*, Testament of Edward Earl of Conway 9 Aug 1683.
94 L. Walsh (1979) pp. 134–5.
95 E. T. James *et al.* (1971) Vol. 2, pp. 340–41.
96 E. T. James *et al.* (1971) Vol. 1, pp. 35–6. See also pp. 384–5 below for examples of eleven widows who supported themselves in the pre-Revolutionary colonial printing trade.
97 Martin Billingsley, *The Pen's Excellencie*, 1618, pp. 35r and v.
98 J. M. Osborn (1962) p. 150.
99 See J. Boulton (1990) for the decline in remarriages in London in the 1690s.

100 B. J. Todd (1985) p. 73.

101 Cited in Todd (1985) p. 77; will of Thomas Austen, PROB 11/285, fo. 338, 15 December 1658; BL Add MS 4454, fos 79v, 110v, 50; will of Katharine Austen, PROB 11/375, fo. 1.

102 See R. B. Outhwaite (1995) pp. 54–73; J. Boulton (1991) pp. 15–29.

103 D. B. and A. H. Rutman (1979) pp. 155–6.

104 HEH, STB 2 Account of unhappy marriage of Sir Francis Willoughby and his first wife.

105 See A. C. Wood (ed.) (1958), *Cassandra Willoughby, A History of the Willoughby Family*.

PART 3

Culture and religion: women's preparation for and participation in contemporary culture

Introduction

This part of the book treats aspects of women's lives that formed a link between the lives of single women, as they prepared for marriage, and those who were already married. Single and married women played a part in the overall culture of these societies but what that part was has yet to be determined. Were women cut off from the predominant male culture or not? Did women carve out a distinctive cultural identity? If so, did this separate them from their menfolk? What effect did marriage have upon a woman's cultural identity and participation? Were there marked regional and national differences? The chapters that follow seek to provide some of the answers to these questions.

In a book that covers such a long period it has not been possible to pursue consistently the policy of comparison. The sources are simply inadequate for this purpose. Where historians have drawn attention to useful indications of female cultural activity in Ireland, Wales, Scotland and the colonies, these ideas have been pursued but the effect is inevitably episodic. For that part of the period when there were very few elite or middling women in the American colonies (before the late seventeenth century), scarcely any points of comparison exist or are meaningful. Enough is available to suggest that elite women in Old World Britain were culturally active and often assertive from 1450 to 1760 and that cultural activity among their American sisters in the eighteenth century was not an innovation.

What is attempted is an overview of women's cultural life which will provoke questions such as those above and suggest some of the ways of answering them. Abundant examples are provided to support this overview.

CHAPTER 13

Women's formal and informal education

nor do I think that she can read well enough to teach Lady Carolina the right way of syllabling her words (but as to that perhaps you will sometimes give yourself the trouble of that which may remove that objection)[1]

Introduction

A definition of education is problematic. The term derives from a Latin word meaning to lead and it is probably most satisfactory to define education as the conscious and deliberate instruction of people in order to prepare them for future life. The years before adulthood were traditionally seen as the period during which such education occurred. Education did not necessarily or even normally take place in schools. Neither was the content of education predominantly academic. In this book there are many references to informal education – for example, the instruction of young women in legal matters by their parents and guardians – and this present chapter concentrates on what is known about the attitude to the education of females and the actual education of girls in a more formal environment.

England and Scotland

English renaissance educational theorists and practitioners certainly saw a place for the education of girls and young women.[2] Richard Mulcaster devoted a chapter to the education of girls. In it he set out four propositions or principles: that girls should be given a basic or primary education; that they needed education for their social role as mothers; that they were rational creatures able to learn; and that the learning of ladies such as the Queen showed that such education was not wasted. He stressed the vocational role of education as much for girls as for boys: all girls should be educated to become wives and mothers; and those who needed a trade or by-employment should be educated for that. If they had a public role then they needed further education to perform it well.³ Sir Thomas More accepted that women were intellectually inferior to men but insisted that education would and should enable them to make the best of what they had. Women had a lasting influence on the world of men and they required education to make that influence benign.⁴ To such ideas (which became commonplace) were added a conviction that all Christians needed an education to support their faith. George Savile's 1688 *Advice to a daughter* is a good example of a text that emphasised this rationale for female education.⁵

In discussing the education of girls and women in England and Wales during this period it is important to realise that home education was not necessarily informal, basic or random. The children of many intellectuals and governors in the sixteenth and early seventeenth centuries received a rigorous classical education from home tutors: Sir Thomas More's three daughters (taught alongside their brother by Dr John Clement followed by William Gunnell and Richard Hyrde); the Princesses Mary and Elizabeth Tudor; Anne, Margaret and Jane Seymour, the daughters of Protector Somerset; Lady Jane Howard; Frances Brandon; Lady Jane Grey; the daughters of the Earl of Arundel; Anne and Mildred, daughters of Sir Anthony Cooke; Lady Anne Clifford; Princess Elizabeth (of Bohemia), daughter of James VI and I, and another Princess Elizabeth, daughter of Charles I. By the seventeenth century, daughters from less illustrious but nevertheless prominent families also on occasion followed a classical curriculum at home. Katherine MacLean, wife of the Earl of Argyll, was said to be 'not unlearned in the Latin tongue, speaketh good French' and had a number of other academic accomplishments. Mary Ferrar (mother of Nicholas) founded a 'Little Academy' for the education of her granddaughters, Mary and Anne Collet. Here the emphasis was upon religious exercises, scripture and moral stories from antiquity although, for example, the girls were taught the story of Katharine of Aragon. Stories were chosen to 'befytt the season and tend to a serious confirmation of our well chosen resolutions'. At Christmas Mary strove

> [t]o make it a merry and a true Christmas both together to your household by delightful and vertuous exercises, that they should have

no cause to envy others greater liberty or better cheere . . . following which the master of their musique play'd on the vyoll.[6]

Anne (Finch) Conway, the posthumous daughter of Sir Heneage Finch, Speaker of the House of Commons, and his second wife, Elizabeth Craddock, was tutored at home in Kensington. Because she exhibited a penchant for academic work, Anne's studies were eventually expanded to include Latin, Greek and Hebrew. Her close relationship with her eldest half-brother, John, led her to correspond regularly with him when he went up to Cambridge University. Through him she was introduced to his tutor, Henry More, who was struck by her brilliance, later stating that he had 'scarce ever met with any person, man or woman, of better natural parts than Lady Conway'. More encouraged her to read and to comment on Descartes and other philosophers, and also recommended other Cambridge tutors to teach her mathematics when her usual method of self-education could not sustain her thirst for knowledge. Henry More dedicated to her his first important prose work, *An Antidote Against Atheism*, in 1652. He noted in the Preface that she was 'one whose genius I know to be so speculative, and wit so penetrant, that in the knowledge of all things as well natural as divine, you have not only outdone all of your own sex, but even of that other also, whose ages have not given them over-much the start of you.'[7] Another example of a learned lady is provided by Mary More, who read both Greek and Latin, and had friendships with Robert Hooke and William Derham in the late seventeenth and early eighteenth centuries. Margaret Ezell speculates that she was educated alongside her brother.[8] Lady Mary Fairfax (1638–1704), however, certainly from an early age had her own tutor.[9] From 1650 her tutor was the poet Andrew Marvell, until he moved on to teach Oliver Cromwell's ward, William Dutton.[10]

Young women from the aristocracy might also have a governess, who would be responsible for supervision of their charges' upbringing and for the acquisition of many skills. The best-known examples are of royalty: Katherine Champernowne, daughter of Sir Philip of Modbury, Devon, for instance, brought Elizabeth I 'up from the cradell to the throne' and actually 'governed' her household for nine years. But the practice extended down the social scale. So in 1554 Sir George Gifford of Middle Claydon, Buckinghamshire, employed a former nun, Joan Deane, to care for his children.[11] In many cases the 'governess' was a servant, albeit an elevated one, rather than a tutor. The ideal might be to appoint a gentlewoman but this was not always realised.[12]

Anne Conway's level of education was not unique but it was unusual. Much more common was the pattern of daughters who picked up a somewhat basic literacy at home, whether from parents, governesses, brothers or brothers' tutors, and built upon this according to their individual aptitude. Thus we can find in the same social milieu women for whom writing and spelling was always a struggle alongside women who composed fluent prose and possibly had some academic pretensions.[13]

David Cressy's and Rab Houston's studies of literacy in early modern England and Scotland permit some instructive comparisons. Cressy demonstrated in his pioneering studies of literacy and illiteracy in London and elsewhere the enormous variations between different communities and different social strata. (Illiteracy was used as the marker because historians cannot identify positively those who could read but only those who definitely could not sign their names.) He posited a 30 per cent active literacy rate overall in seventeenth-century England (that is, an illiteracy rate of 70 per cent). Outside London and Suffolk, no English county had an overall literacy rate higher than 38 per cent of the male population, or lower than 27 per cent. The male literacy rate of seventeenth-century London at 78 per cent (22 per cent illiteracy) was exceptional.[14] Cressy also argued convincingly that literacy did not rise constantly during the period 1530 to 1730.[15] Historians have suggested a 10 to 15 per cent literacy rate in the early sixteenth century. Marked rises in the sixteenth

TABLE 13.1 *Overall levels of male and female illiteracy in England and Scotland, 1550–1760*[16]

	England		Scotland	
	1550–1640	1640–1760	1550–1640	1640–1760
Female illiteracy	90–95%	81%	90–95%	81%
Male illiteracy		42%		32%

TABLE 13.2 *Overall male and female literacy rates in England and Scotland, 1550–1760*

	England		Scotland	
	1550–1640	1640–1760	1550–1640	1640–1760
Female literacy	5–10%	19%	5–10%	19%
Male literacy		58%		68%

century were followed by a levelling off or even a decline in the seventeenth century. Rates of female literacy were everywhere lower than those for males but they probably increased more rapidly.[17]

However, illiteracy rates are postulated on a distinctive definition of literacy. First of all it does not take account of those who could read but not write and historians agree that there were a good many of these. Secondly it excludes all those who could write but only with chalk on a slate or a wall. Juliet Fleming argues that in the paper-hungry society of sixteenth-century England and Wales, paper, pens and ink were priced beyond the reach of most of the population. Instead people practised their writing on walls with chalk and on windows with sharp objects and communicated with family and community in the same way, simply whitewashing over old messages. Thirdly, it relied heavily on the assumption that those who used a mark instead of a signature did so because they could not write their names. This could be an unsafe assumption in an age when little store was set by a signature and a good deal by a witnessed mark or a seal. These arguments should convince us that many more people could participate in reading and writing than the illiteracy rates would suggest.[18] Even more could participate at second or third hand. Reading was frequently a communal or a family activity and both men and women who were technically illiterate would hear books read and sermons preached and even memorise large parts of them. This was especially true of Lollards and early Protestants. For example, Mrs Alice Collins of Burford could recite whole sections of the vernacular Scriptures and did so before a conventicle of men.[19]

Even without such considerations, in English and Scottish aristocratic homes (nobles and gentry) female literacy was relatively high (although not universal), echoing the literacy of their menfolk.[20] When Sir Peter Temple of Stantonbury, Buckinghamshire, in the mid-seventeenth century collected together a large number of medical cures, cooking recipes, and husbandry, hunting and fishing tips, he intended it 'For my dear daughter Elianor Temple'.[21] Not only did he expect her to find the collection highly useful and to be able to read it, he also expected that she would be able to decipher its coded passages.[22] Interestingly, the female servants in such households were also more literate than women of lower status elsewhere. There was also a well-established tradition of female education in both parsonage and manse. So when we examine the culture of upper-class and professional-class women and their servants we can reasonably expect that they were able to participate in literate culture to some degree. (Clearly this is not the same as saying that they did so participate or were encouraged so to do.)

TABLE 13.3 *Illiteracy rates of Northern English and Lowland Scottish women, derived from court depositions.*[23]

	England		Scotland	
	1640–1699	1700–1770	1640–1699	1700–1770
Prof. and gentry	24%	0%	35%	25%
Craft and trade	78%	69%	71%	72%
Farmer/tenant	88%	68%	100%	86%
Labourer	95%	88%	100%	90%
Servant (overall)	85%	75%	92%	88%
Prof. and gentry servants	33%		47%	

Boarding education for girls

In the Middle Ages there had been several well-known and highly-thought-of convent schools. These were a feature of Catholic countries. Examples include Polesworth Convent, Warwickshire (in 1537 said to have educated between thirty and forty gentry daughters), and Oxford (said to have educated the daughters of most of the local gentry). Boarding education for girls seems to have been in abeyance between the dissolution of the religious houses and the later sixteenth century. One of the earliest references to such secular boarding establishments occurs in a letter from Anne Higginson to Lady Ferrar of Tamworth, recommending a boarding academy at Windsor. The curriculum was equivalent to that of a finishing school but it did include writing as well as reading (affirming the importance of letter-writing to a lady of quality) and it did socialise the young women involved.

Her rates are this, sixteen pounds a year a piece, for diet, lodging, washing, and teaching them to work,[24] *reading, writing, and dancing, this cometh unto £32 a year. But for music you must pay for besides . . . she saith she hath now twenty gentlewomen boarders, and half as many more ladies and gentlewomen's daughters come forth of the town and cloisters, for she hath none but such for the meaner sort are not able to reach her rate . . .*

This suggests that there was considerable demand for girls' schools by this time and that it was to some extent being satisfied. By the reign of James VI and I this demand had reached some of the highest in the land. For instance, Robert White, author of *Cupid's Banishment*, c.1617 was probably the master of Ladies Hall private academy in London, at which two of Queen Anne's god-daughters were pupils (Ann Chalenor and Anne

Sandilands), alongside other daughters of the mighty and influential such as Elizabeth Cranfield, daughter of Lionel, and Lea Watson, daughter of Sir Thomas, teller of the Exchequer.[25] By the mid-seventeenth century, at the latest, every English town of any size boasted a girls' academy.

Other sources indicate, though, that the professional and merchant classes were also supporting schools. Contemporaries spoke without surprise of girls from professional families who attended school.[26] Hannah Archer of Snelston, Derbyshire, was sent at the age of twelve to stay with an aunt in London and attend school for her 'better education'.[27] The minister Ralph Josselin's daughters appear to have received their early schooling in the home and at local Earl's Colne school, where their father was headmaster. Anne began to 'learn her book' when she was three years and ten months old; Mary had a 'towardliness to learn' when she was just four and had developed 'an aptness to her book' five months later.[28] Three of the five daughters of Ralph Josselin who survived long enough to leave home around the traditional ages of ten to thirteen years were boarded out (at a cost of about £6 p.a.) in order to attend school at Colchester and Bury St Edmunds.[29] This schooling was of variable length: for example, Jane attended Mrs Piggott's school in Colchester over four years in the mid- to late 1650s. Elizabeth, however, was less than a year at school in Bury St Edmunds before moving with her sister Mary to London. Neither Anne nor Rebecka were sent away to school. Instead they moved away from home to enter service – joining the army of literate female servants in the capital. Clearly what we see in this example is an overlapping of two traditions: formal schooling and service. We shall never know why it was that Josselin gave some of his daughters more schooling than others. Even if girls did go to school, this might be for short periods and to acquire particular skills. Claver Morris, a well-to-do Wells physician sent his eight-year-old daughter Betty to a day school in Wells to learn sewing. Two years later she began to learn singing and violin. In 1708 (when she was thirteen) she went to a dancing school in Salisbury for a year. Somewhere along the way she must have learned conversational French because she had an argument with her father over her refusal to converse. Compared to her, her brother received a grounding at a local dame school followed by a rigorous classical education at Wells Grammar School and Sherborne preparatory to entering Balliol College, Oxford. In total he spent the years 1713 to 1727 in full-time education.[30]

In 1537 an 'Act for the English order, habit and language' was passed which ordered a 'schoole for to learne English' to be kept in each Irish parish. Such schools were used in an attempt to convert the Irish to

Protestantism.[31] Margaret MacCurtain argues that while in Ireland in the sixteenth and very early seventeenth centuries there was a tradition of esteeming female learning both within and without Catholicism, by the seventeenth century this tradition had all but disappeared. Protestants encouraged active literacy sufficient for Bible reading and passing on skills to children, but Catholics neglected all but basic catechising of girls.[32] In large part this was due to the periodic attempts by the English state to extirpate Catholic education under Queen Elizabeth and throughout the seventeenth century. Under Cromwell a 'thorough-going Penal Code, designed to supplant Catholic education, was first devised'. In 1657 Cromwell announced to his Council in Ireland that Catholic children, both rich and poor, should 'at the age of ten years and upwards be taken from their parents and bound apprentices to religious and honest people in England or Ireland'.[33] There was, moreover, a determined persecution of Catholic teachers by the state, in particular from 1693 onwards. The English made a two-pronged attack on Catholic education in an act of 1695 which targeted both Catholics sending children to be educated abroad and also Catholics teaching in Ireland:

[B]e it enacted that no person whatsoever of the papist religion shall publicly teach school or instruct youth in learning ... upon pain of £20 and also being committed to prison with bail or main prize for the space of three months for every such offence.[34]

This act 'found by experience that tolerating and conniving at Papists keeping schools' had resulted in 'natives of this kingdom continuing in ignorance of ... true religion and strangers to the Scripture, of their neglecting to conform themselves to the laws and statutes of this realm, and of their not using the English habit of language.' This was followed by an even more savage act under Queen Anne which condemned Catholic teachers to three months imprisonment plus transportation on a first offence. Should a teacher return to Ireland and be prosecuted a second time, this time for High Treason, then the punishment was hanging, drawing and quartering. Informers were rewarded with £10 apiece.[35] The Grand Jury records of Limerick (1711–1722) and Parliament Returns in 1731 demonstrate how prosecutions of Catholic teachers within Ireland most often resulted in transportation of the accused.[36] Twenty Catholic teachers were prosecuted at Limerick during these years 'for teaching school being a papist'. As a result well-to-do Catholics sought secretly to educate their daughters in convents abroad and any attempts to school other girls within Catholic Ireland itself were covert.[37] In Tralee in 1714 the JPs heard the cases of many Catholics charged with sending their sons to France for education. Perhaps significantly, none had risked prosecution for sending a daughter.[38]

The Convocation of the episcopal state church in Ireland attempted to supplant Catholic schooling with Protestant. In Dublin in 1711 it proposed the compulsory education of Irish Catholic children in free English-language parish schools. Poor Catholics were ordered to send their children, boys and girls, from the ages of seven to twelve for three months in every year; wealthier Catholics were ordered to send their children for six months in each year. All births were to be recorded in the parish register within ten days. Parents of absentees were to pay fines. Children were to be examined on the Church catechism and the English language quarterly.[39] The project, however, fell through and Protestants relied even more upon Protestant charity schools, of which at least 300 were set up between 1710 and 1730. These were most apparent in Dublin where, by 1717, there were fifteen, teaching 513 pupils, a proportion of whom were girls. In 1733 Protestant (and state funded) Charter Schools were also set up, largely in rural areas and with a curriculum clearly designed for members of both sexes. These were originally day schools but, when it became clear that frequent contact with Catholic families rendered the attempt at Protestantisation and Anglicisation futile, boarding education was substituted.[40]

The demand for female literacy and formal schooling in England and Scotland inevitably created a demand for female teachers. We know relatively little about the type of woman who was drawn to teaching, whether by necessity or design. For most female teachers in local schools and in boarding establishments we know little but their names. We do know that there were large numbers of dame schools in England and Wales, where girls learned to read as they sewed with female instruction. A good and unusually full example is that of Meppershall in Bedfordshire where a charity set up by Mrs Sarah and Mrs Elizabeth Emery provided education for both boys and girls. In eighteenth-century Llanwyddelan in Montgomeryshire Alice Hibbot tried to make a pittance by keeping a dame school.[41] The extensive system of parish schools in Scotland may have stretched to the education of girls. The circulating schools (3,325) run by Griffith Jones throughout Wales from the third decade of the eighteenth century were open to girls as well as boys and, in at least twenty-eight cases, teaching was provided by women, often in Welsh.[42] These schools offered three-month courses in the summer months, which coincided with the fallow agricultural season. A good many of the scholars, however, were taught for several hours of an evening after paid work was done. Interestingly, Jones's period as organiser was followed by that of a gentlewoman, Bridget Bevan, until 1779. Eryn White argues that the work of these circulating schools, brought to a halt by legal wrangles at the time of Bevan's death, was carried on by the Sunday schools of the late eighteenth and nineteenth centuries. Some, but not many, established schools in England had long admitted girls as well as boys. By the eighteenth century the Charity School movement provided basic instruction in reading for girls. Throughout the whole period many clergymen ran private schools and possibly arranged for their wives to teach the sisters of boy pupils. In the houses of the gentry and nobility the early education of daughters probably often fell to literate servants and/or to mothers. There is an instructive episode in the Brydges correspondence in the early eighteenth century, pointing both to the expectations such servants were expected to fulfil and the type of preparation many would have had. Cassandra, Duchess of Chandos, opposed the appointment of her own servant Bab Blackley as the personal servant of her step-granddaughter Caroline on the grounds that, although she was a good and honest woman, Bab had inadequate preparation and skills.[43]

First of all, she has no experience of children and, especially, of girls. This experience is necessary to acquire the skills required to guide a young person in terms of morality, religion and appropriate behaviour. It comes from caring for young children and observing their ways.

That she would be careful and diligent I verily believe and that she has good notions of what is just and honest, and I hope a good sense of religion, but I fear her head has never been turned to what is right and proper by way of guiding a young lady (which I think is a peculiar talent and must be acquired by being accustomed to see children and observing their ways which may give one some knowledge of how their tempers may be best worked upon. I don't know that Bab: had the care of any child but her own, or that she ever was in any family where any children were, to have gained herself any experience yt way by seeing or being with young children (<. . .)>.

Secondly, Bab does not have sufficiently advanced literacy to teach Lady Carolina to read, using the syllabic method. This, says Cassandra, may not be an insurmountable objection because Lady Carnarvon may choose to teach Carolina herself.

nor do I think that she can read well enough to teach Lady Carolina the right way of syllabling her words (but as to that perhaps you will sometimes give yourself the trouble of that which may remove that objection).

Probably young women who specialised in teaching gained their own skills via informal or formal apprenticeships within existing schools, where it was customary for the advanced pupils to teach the beginners. For some women teaching in high-class boarding establishments probably offered a reasonably good living but low status.

It should not be overlooked either that some young women received a practical education in the home, especially in professional families, that sometimes resulted in work in the outside world. One of the younger sons of Sir Percival Willoughby of Boreplace, and a distant relative of Cassandra (Willoughby) Brydges, in 1631 married a younger daughter of Sir Francis Trusley of Derbyshire. This gentleman, also confusingly called Percival, was trained in medicine under Van Otten and 'settled in Derby, where he practiced Physic, and lived in great repute, to a very great age'. He also practised in Stafford. He is known to history both for his *Observations in Midwifery*[44] and for the fact that he trained his daughter Eleanor as a midwife, when she was about fifteen years of age, to assist him in his medical practice.[45] 'He had 2 or 3 Sons (but they left no children) and two daughters. The eldest married Mr Hurst, the other married Mr Burton of Derby.' *Observations in Midwifery* and its companion, *'the country midwife's opusculum or vade mecum'*, were packed with case histories from his own and Eleanor's practices and it is tempting to see it as a work he produced for Eleanor's use. Possibly Eleanor's transcript of the work survived until publication.

Formal and informal education in the American colonies

The question of education exercised the founding fathers of Massachusetts and Connecticut. In Massachusetts the first law regulating education was passed in 1647. It stipulated that if parents neglected to teach their children, the selectmen should apprentice the children so that they could 'read and understand the principles of religion and the capital laws of the country'. Connecticut passed a similar law in 1650. As in Old England, the larger towns supported grammar schools, which catered in most cases exclusively for boys. Communities, large and small, were also served by dame schools, run by a female church member, which catered for both sexes.[46] In this way, seventeenth-century New England, made up as it was by small urban communities, developed the basis of an extensive public school system. There were also private boarding establishments in the towns. These multiplied considerably by the eighteenth century. For instance, Mrs Taylor of Philadelphia advertised her girls' boarding school locally and in the southern colonies. The curriculum of such schools focused on needlework and housewifery but also included reading and writing.[47] In addition some young and not-so-young women ran private schools from home. Roxanna Frisbie, a twenty-three-year-old who brought a case for slander in the Connecticut courts in 1780, may have been typical of many single women who combined teaching pupils with other wage labour that could be performed in the home, such as sewing and cooking.[48]

By 1700 literacy in New England was high when compared to England and Scotland. By this date 70 per cent of men and 45 per cent of women could both read and write. Its acquisition was motivated by religion.[49]

In the southern colonies the isolated plantations made such a public school system impracticable. In many ways the educational facilities resembled those found in so many aristocratic English households – private tutors educating the children of the household as well as, perhaps, a few others, black and white. Although there are references to schoolmistresses and female tutors from the 1650s onwards – for instance, Katharine Shrewsbury was employed to teach the son of a Richmond, Virginia, planter in 1693 – Julia Spruill concluded that school dames were rare in the first century of settlement and that both private tutors and school teachers were usually men. Richard Burkland came to an agreement with Richard Kellam for Kellam to give bed and board to, and teach, Burkland's daughter to read, write and cast accounts. Some of the well-to-do sent their daughters to England to complete an education begun in Virginia. For instance, Peter Hopegood's will provided that his daughter be educated in Virginia until 1680, at which time she was to travel to England, live with an uncle, and continue her education. William Byrd sent his two daughters Susan and Ursula to school in Hackney, London, in the 1680s under the supervision of their maternal grandfather. Byrd agreed to send his younger daughter 'Nutty' (aged only four) because 'she could learn nothing good here in a great family of Negroes'. There were also local schools, later known as Old Field Schools, which were accessible on foot by the boys and girls of a whole neighbourhood; and there were scattered private schools with an endowment.[50] The situation in Maryland was apparently worse with religious differences and popular disturbances blocking the establishment of schools. In 1673 Governor Charles Calvert explained to the colony's proprietor that he, Calvert, would encourage a schoolmaster working in his household to try to establish a school in the colony 'but doubt he will not find the people here so desirous of that benefit of educating their children . . . for the remoteness of the habitations of one person from another, will be a great obstacle to a school . . .'[51]

Literacy for both girls and boys does seem to have been a general goal in Virginia. Apprenticeships in seventeenth- and eighteenth-century Virginia provided that both boys and girls be taught at least to read. Rebecca Francis's master and mistress were ordered to provide her with a 'complete year's schooling, to be educated in reading the vulgar tongue', while Anne Chandler's were to ensure that she could 'read a chapter in the Bible, the Lord's Prayer and ten commandments', and Anne Matthews's to see that she could both read and write.[52] North Carolina apprenticeship indentures followed suit but those of Maryland and South Carolina did not require schooling for apprentices. Guardians of orphaned girls and masters of apprentices were brought before the Virginia and North Carolina courts if they neglected formal schooling.

There was, however, widespread female illiteracy in seventeenth-century Virginia, even among the most prominent families. Overall one in three Virginian women was able to sign her name, compared with three in every five men.[53] It is difficult to make a straight comparison with the situation in England and Scotland because of the way in which the statistics are derived and presented, although on the surface such figures do suggest a marked improvement on the position in England and Scotland but still far from universal female literacy in Virginia.

The situation did improve considerably in the eighteenth century as increasing population made established schools more viable. Education was seen as desirable not only for religious but also for commercial reasons. This, however, probably benefited boys much more than girls.[54] Virginia had had some free schools in the later seventeenth century, but

TABLE 13.4 *Male and female literacy in New England and Virginia, England and Scotland, c.1700–1760*[55]

	1700		1760	
	Male	*Female*	*Male*	*Female*
New England	70%	45%		
Virginia	60%	33.3%	67%	33.3%
England			58%	19%
Scotland			68%	19%

the eighteenth century saw the foundation of many more. South Carolina also had free schools. While not all accommodated the education of girls, the South Carolina Society, founded in 1737, did provide for the appointment of a schoolmaster and a schoolmistress who were to educate girls aged eight to twelve, and boys aged eight to fourteen. Similarly a school founded by Mary Smith at Smithfield, Virginia, stipulated a three-year education for boys (in reading, writing and arithmetic) and a two-year education for girls (in reading and writing). Free schools were slow to come to Maryland. Subscription schools also grew up in the eighteenth-century southern colonies. For example, a number of citizens in North Carolina set up the New Bern Academy and built a schoolhouse by private subscription.[56] The same plethora of private day and boarding schools for girls is found in the towns of pre-Revolutionary South Carolina as in those of the mother country. They were to be found in smaller numbers elsewhere in the southern colonies. Often these seem to have been established by school-teachers who had emigrated from England. For example, one of the first private schools advertised in the newspapers of Virginia was set up by ex-Londoner John Walker and his wife in Williamsburg in 1752. He taught the boys reading, writing, arithmetic, geography, history and a classical curriculum and his wife taught girls needlework.[57] Thereafter several women set up schools and taught a variable curriculum, which often emphasised embroidery, music and dancing but also included reading, writing and French. The few private co-educational schools in North Carolina seem to have offered more academic opportunities to girl pupils.[58]

Teaching had long been a job open to women in New England but, as noted, it was not so for southern women. It does seem, however, that women began to see school teaching as a credible career option in the southern colonies in the fifty years before the American Revolution. Potential employers advertised for female tutors in the burgeoning newspapers of the pre-Revolutionary period.[59] Some women advertised themselves in the local press: 'A middle-aged woman, who can be well recommended, and understands music, dancing, and all sorts of needlwork, and can speak four different languages' would 'be glad to engage as a tutoress to children, or if encouraged would keep a school'.[60] A young woman 'of unblemished character, and liberal education' wished to tutor young ladies in a gentleman's household.[61] These advertisements can tell us a good deal about the expectations shared by potential employers.

An English woman between 20 and 40 who has a good education and understands most branches of needlework, tambour, embroidery, etc., writes a good hand and is well acquainted with arithmetic, wants a place as teacher of children. No objection to living in the country.[62]

These were the subjects the schoolmistress would be expected to teach and she had to have the experience and skill to be a suitable model for her pupils to emulate. Her age, character and her English origins were advantageous.

Julia Spruill established that women frequently combined teaching with other occupations. Many teachers were married women. In 1742 Martha Logan sold garden produce and also boarded and taught children in her home, a plantation which she ran ten miles outside Charles Town, South Carolina.[63] Many teachers seem to have made and sold linen, done laundry and mending, made clothes to order, or made and sold hats.[64] Some ran boarding houses and taverns. Probably these patterns echoed those in New England and in the Old World. All were traditional areas of female employment.

The well-to-do still often preferred to send their daughters abroad to complete their education. For example, William Byrd II continued the family tradition by sending Evelyn and Wilhemina to be educated in England. The schools they attended offered a wide curriculum and fashionable extras such as music, dancing and French. Some, like Thomas Jefferson and Charles Carroll, preferred Europe, especially France, to England for their daughters and granddaughters. These young women were both privileged and exceptional. Most colonial women, even if they did attend a school, did so for a period of only a few months to a couple of years and picked up the bare rudiments of learning.[65]

Conclusion

Formal schooling (whether by private tutors or 'private' or 'public' schools) was during this period always less available to girls than to boys. In the sixteenth and seventeenth centuries much education occurred within the home. When girls did attend schools they studied a distinctive curriculum. They also attended for relatively short periods when compared to boys of the same class. The demand for and provision of schools for girls did, however, increase in all these societies over the period in question. Access to schooling depended a good deal upon where the young person lived (because towns generally offered more facilities) or whether their parents were able and willing to pay for them to 'table out'. Literacy among females (in the sense of being able to both read and write) increased everywhere and was seen as a universal goal by ruling elites in the American colonies, for both religious and commercial reasons. Literacy amongst females rose more steeply in urban areas of England than in rural areas. Female literacy was most notable in the low-population but nonetheless urbanised areas of lowland Scotland and the American colonies. Although such literacy was by no means universal, it did provide more and more young women with easier access to the dominant culture. As the next chapters indicate, women also negotiated access to knowledge about the world in a variety of ways.

Notes

1 Cassandra, Duchess of Chandos, 1731.
2 See H. Smith (1996) pp. 9–29; see also R. O'Day (1982).
3 Richard Mulcaster, *Positions*, 1581, pp. 20–21.
4 H. Smith (1996) pp. 25–9.
5 Marquis of Halifax, *The Lady's New Years Gift; or, Advice to a Daughter*, 1688. (Note that George Savile is the Marquis of Halifax.)
6 BL, Add MS 34657 fos 6, 18r and v, 38r.
7 M. H. Nicholson (Sutton edn. 1992) introduction.
8 M. J. M. Ezell (1987) pp. 146–7.
9 Portrait of Lady Mary Fairfax c.1647 by Robert Walker.
10 H. M. Jewell (1998) p. 105.
11 Both examples cited by B. Hill (2001) p. 55.
12 See p. 329 for the employment of Bab Blackley by the Countess of Carnarvon.
13 See A. Beer (2004) pp. 28–9 for Bess Throckmorton's haphazard education and her probable dyslexia.
14 D. Cressy (1980) pp. 72–5.
15 Ibid p. 65.
16 R. A. Houston (1985) p. 57.
17 P. Crawford (1993) p. 47.
18 J. Fleming (2001) pp. 9–10, 29–72.
19 S. R. Cattley (1939) Vol. 4, p. 238.
20 Measuring literacy and illiteracy is always an approximate science because of the small populations available for study. Women from professional and

gentry families, 1700–1770, in Houston's study amounted to a mere ten persons.

21 This Sir Peter Temple (d.1657) was the son of John Temple (d.1632), Sir Thomas Temple of Stowe's second son. Elianor was, therefore, Thomas Temple's great-granddaughter.

22 BL Stowe MS 1077 and 1078, 'Receipts, dated May ult 1656'.

23 R. A. Houston (1985) p. 60.

24 That is, needlework.

25 B. Lewalski (1992) pp. 76–7.

26 See, for example, BL Stowe MS 1077, fo. 76r.

27 Hannah Allen, *Satan his methods and malice baffled*, 1683 cited in Elspeth Graham, 'Women's writing and the self', 1996 p. 217.

28 See Alan Macfarlane, *The Family Life of Ralph Josselin*, 1970, p. 91.

29 A. Macfarlane (1970) p. 49. The daughters who were boarded out were Jane, Mary and Elizabeth.

30 Edmund Hobhouse (1934) pp. 31–3.

31 R. B. Savage (1940) p. 26.

32 M. MacCurtain (1991) pp. 160–78.

33 Oliver Cromwell to the Council in Dublin, 28 Mar 1657, quoted in S. J. Corcoran (1928) p. 29.

34 Act to restrain foreign education, 1695.

35 Statutes of the Realm, Anne 8, c. 3. This act remained on the statute book until 1782.

36 R. B. Savage (1940) p. ix.

37 As in the so-called Hedge Schools. See J. P. Dowling (1935).

38 T. Corcoran (1932) p. 20, cited in Savage (1940) p. 30.

39 Savage (1940) p. 30.

40 Ibid pp. 40–42.

41 Bedfordshire and Luton Archives, Bedford P29/25/1, fos 5v–6, orders of Engagement of Emery Charity School, Meppershall, 1701, with a list of mothers and children. The title 'Mrs' was commonly used for both married and unmarried women. E. M. White (2000) p. 215 citing Melvyn Humphreys (1996) p. 162.

42 E. M. White (2000) pp. 216–18 citing Clement (1978); E. M. White (1997) p. 331.

43 NLCS, Copy Letter Book of Cassandra Duchess of Chandos, no. 321, p. 198 Cassandra Brydges to Lady Carnarvon 16 Nov [1731].
44 This existed in manuscript in 1672 but was not published until 1863.
45 HEH, STB Box 2, Book 3, p. 44r.; A. Wilson (1997) especially pp. 139–40.
46 R. Middleton (1992) p. 256.
47 *Maryland Gazette*, 12 Sept, 1775.
48 C. H. Dayton (1995) p. 314.
49 K. Lockridge (1974).
50 J. C. Spruill (1938) pp. 185–7, 255.
51 'Calvert Papers', Maryland Historical Society Fund Publications, 28, p. 286.
52 L. G. Tyler 'Education in Virginia', *William and Mary Quarterly*, 5, pp. 219–22; cited in Spruill (1938) p. 186.
53 P. A. Bruce, *Institutional History of Virginia*, 1910 pp. 454–7.
54 R. Middleton (1992) p. 257.
55 These figures are based on the best available estimates.
56 *North Carolina Magazine; or Universal Intelligencer*, 6 July 1764, cited in J. C. Spruill (1938) p. 196.
57 J. C. Spruill (1938) pp. 199–200.
58 Ibid pp. 201–3.
59 *Virginia Gazette*, 8 March 1770.
60 *Maryland Gazette*, 24 December 1772.
61 *Maryland Gazette*, 14 June 1764.
62 *South Carolina and American General Gazette*, 28 October 1774.
63 *South Carolina Gazette*, 6 March 1742.
64 J. C. Spruill (1938) pp. 257–8.
65 Cited in Spruill (1938) pp. 205–7.

CHAPTER 14

Women and religion

*She that now takes her rest within this tomb
had Rachel's face and Leah's fruitful womb
Abigail's wisdom Lydea's faithful heart
with Martha's care and Mary's better part*[1]

Introduction

Piety was a virtue of which women, in the eyes of contemporary society, could legitimately boast. Women were perceived as having a special role in the religious life of the household. For most women this role was fulfilled by setting an example of piety and devotion based upon a close reading of the scriptures (tutored by preachers) and the guidance of chaplains and other (male) authorities. So male and female religiosity were seen to stand as two sides of the same coin. The rational and emotional nature of a woman (as contrasted with a man's intellectual and rational characteristics) was believed to suit her to experience true faith. In pre-Reformation times noble and gentle women carried at their girdles miniature books of hours which contained (as their name suggests) prayers to be read on the hour, every waking hour. Many such books of hours contained illuminations which focused the mind of the worshipper. Some brought home the message particularly to women and reinforced it with a memento mori.[2] Many women were drawn to the contemplative life of an enclosed religious community, although there were few convents in Wales, and even by the 1530s, when fewer men and women were attracted to the monastic life, there were 1,600 women in such communities.[3] Within the parishes women played an important if subsidiary role as benefactors. For instance, at Rickmansworth in 1496 Margaret a Dene left an altar cloth, vestments and two tunicles of purple velvet.[4] Their activities in cleaning and beautifying the churches appear to have continued throughout the period 1450–1760.[5] In church, women were also beneficiaries of the system. They both gave and received charity. They could participate in the church's services, including those of the mass, marriage, confirmation and churching. They could borrow the girdle of a saint to protect them during childbirth. They could pray to the figure of a virgin bedecked in damask.[6] They were, however, seated separately from the men of the parish. Fifteenth-century women of all social classes were taught using words and pictures and a special effort was made to appeal to their religiosity through cults of the Virgin and female saints, especially in Scotland and Wales. After the Reformation, there was less use of pictures but just as much acknowledgement of the piety of women. Women in post-civil war times were as assiduous in holding household prayers as they had been in the sixteenth and early seventeenth centuries. The resurgence of the cult of the Virgin Mary among Catholics on both sides of the Atlantic points to the widely accepted importance of providing female models of piety. Women were not encouraged to engage in theological debate although the line between this and a desire to understand properly the meaning of the scriptures and of sermons and religious works, and to promote this meaning and sometimes distinctive interpretation in the household or even beyond, was often crossed. This was certainly an area where men sought to define their womenfolk's subordination but where women themselves resisted such limiting definition.[7]

Women's religious role was never restricted to the privacy of the domestic: women attended church and they went on pilgrimages. An analysis of miracles performed at English shrines in the twelfth and thirteenth centuries demonstrated that 39 per cent of those attending were women and that 86 per cent derived from the lowest social classes.[8] Geoffrey Chaucer's *Canterbury Pilgrims* reflected the place that women of varying statuses played in this public arena. Some women served as wardens of church guilds, as at Morebath in Devon where there was a maidens' guild until the Reformation.[9] Elsewhere there were female church wardens, at least until the 1690s.[10] In some places the wives of the churchwardens performed a public and presumably official role in collecting dues from parishioners.[11]

It has sometimes been argued that religion provided some women with a route to an even more public life and that it did so especially during the Reformation and the conflicts of the seventeenth century. Indeed some historians believe that women, forbidden a secular public role, were attracted to religion for this very purpose.[12] Patricia Crawford has argued that it was the battle for power and authority within religion that allowed women to make gains in the seventeenth century and led them to resist the view that only men could participate in the secular political sphere. Mrs Jane Ratcliffe has been portrayed as a woman who gained local renown and 'emancipation' through her exercise of the faith and the contribution she made through it.[13] Contemporary funeral sermons underline the typicality of this case study. It was perhaps but a short step to emancipation in a more secular sense. Certainly it is possible to show women playing a prominent role in protests and petitions, underlining what we know about women's interest in religious issues and their determination to make themselves heard. In 1566 sixty women of St Giles Cripplegate approached Bishop Grindal to protest his suspension of Mr Bartlett, their lecturer, and they refused to leave until they were asked to do so by a reader. Soon after, Grindal required a warrant to support him against women in another parish.[14] Later, two or three hundred London women went to meet the ministers who had been turned out of their livings for refusing to wear the surplice: they gave them provisions and urged them to stand by their faith.[15] Sects and groupings during the mid-seventeenth century were notable for the activity of women. Bernard Capp, for instance, found that women 'easily outnumbered men' among the Fifth Monarchists.[16] In the Civil War and Commonwealth years some women justified their exceptional public activity on grounds of possessing the gift of prophecy.[17] In Scotland, Lady Anne Cunningham, daughter of the Earl of Glencairn and Marchioness of Hamilton, had been reared in a family noted for its early commitment to Protestantism. This 'notable virago' became renowned for her active leadership in the National Covenant resistance movement against Charles I's introduction of episcopacy. This led her into direct conflict with her son, the 3rd Marquis of Hamilton, who sided with King Charles. When Hamilton tried to land an army in Scotland, she vowed to discharge a pistol into her son if he dared come ashore. She raised a cavalry troop for the Covenanters and led them personally. At the time, contemporaries noted 'how the Ladies and gentlewomen, by her example do all practise their arms, in which new kind of housewifery they are very expert'.[18] Women lower down the Scottish social ladder also intervened in the Protestant cause on occasion throughout the seventeenth century. For instance, fifteen ministers' widows petitioned the Edinburgh council in the 1670s for 'gospel ministry' to be 'provided for the starving congregations of Scotland'. The council did not acknowledge their right to do so, however, but treated their petition as a seditious libel and cast three of their number into prison as an example.[19]

Women often do seem to have been drawn to dissent. Early examples refer to the supposed prominence of women in the Lollard movement. Margaret Aston discovered that women not only belonged to the movement but also that, in the early days, they served as preachers. Arguments were advanced for their admission to the priesthood and rumours circulated that women were administering the sacrament.[20] Evidence from the Lollard trials provides fascinating insights into the relationship between husbands and wives within this sect, with husbands often accepting the role of their wives as instructors and examples. However, this prominence within dissent may have been more apparent than real. This is a sharp reminder that the historian must not take documentation at its face value. First, all-women Lollard groups were rare.[21] Second, female forwardness in religion was newsworthy and probably seized upon with alacrity by male commentators. Third, the evidence that women were especially prominent in 'heretical' sects and in religious protests is now suspect for a number of reasons. There is evidence that in some cases male rioters throughout our period deliberately disguised themselves as women. This may have been because the full force of the law was not normally brought down on the heads of women, as long as they could prove that they had not been incited to act by men.[22] At Exeter in 1536, the women who had vigorously protested the removal of the rood loft from St Nicholas Priory were interrogated to make sure that they had not been 'commanded, procured, advised or abetted by their husbands or by any other men'.[23] As a result it was difficult for the authorities to act against the large number of female recusants in the Elizabethan and early Stuart period. Responsibility for their recusancy was laid at the feet of their husbands and fathers. It had to be because married women had no property ownership. Churchwardens contented themselves with presenting female recusants to the church courts, whereas Justices of the Peace – who, under the 1581 Act to retain the Queen's Majesties subjects in due obedience, indicted female recusants – were ordered not to fine them because they had no property of their own. Only widows might be fined.[24] This could account for the fears expressed by a number of wealthy aristocratic non-juring and possibly crypto-Catholic or High Anglican widows in the eighteenth century who feared the sequestration of their estates.[25] When women were involved in religious protest it was often in association with their menfolk and led by them. For example, the female protest against the prayer book in Edinburgh in 1637 was orchestrated by influential men.[26] Fourth, female resistance was normally condemned and was shown to contradict the proper order, and commentators were eager to make examples of offenders. On occasion it led women into direct conflict with their husbands. An early Reformation example was that of Anne Askew who left her Catholic husband because of her Protestant convictions.[27] The Catholic community in late Elizabethan and Stuart England is even said to have gone through a matriarchal period, during which wives clung to Catholicism despite their husbands' conversion. An anonymous writer in 1658 accused the Jesuit priests who manipulated these wives and daughters of undermining patriarchy. There was certainly a persistent and pervasive anxiety in all these societies about the power of women in religion and it is this anxiety that historians should note.

Nevertheless wives (whether Catholic or Protestant) were increasingly entrusted with the nurture of their husbands' spiritual life and the religious upbringing of sons and particularly daughters. 'Let us all for our application learn of a woman of the weaker sex: especially women imitate her.'[28]

Aristocratic and royal women also acted as patrons of chaplains, preachers and writers and had a complex relationship with them, being on the one hand their 'sponsors' and in some sense their 'authorities', and on the other their 'clients' and 'beneficiaries'.

Although it is possible to build up from printed contemporary works some idea of the ways in which women fitted into religious life (or were intended to do so by male writers), a more detailed picture of women's actual experience in religion and belief has to be painstakingly built up from individual biography and autobiography, from the published and manuscript writings of women and their patrons, from wills, correspondence and family papers, from ecclesiastical and secular court records, from parish accounts, from narratives of the civil wars and from often fragmentary and casual references in manuscript collections. The sources that illuminate these aspects of the lives of women survive rarely and most plentifully for the aristocracy (the gentry and above). While no one example may be regarded as 'typical', such may be seen fairly as representative of a much greater number of occurrences. Historians are also increasingly making use of visual and artefact sources as well as published texts to indicate the models of feminine virtue and religiosity that early modern women were expected to emulate.

There has been a trend for historians, working in a secular age, to argue or assume that women self-consciously used their religion as an arena for personal fulfilment and agency precisely because other avenues were closed to them.²⁹ This approach seems ahistorical: it casts doubt upon the sincerity and depth of women's religious belief in an attempt to show that women were painfully conscious of their subjugation and determined to circumvent it. It is impossible to prove whether women were either as individuals or as a gender thus cynically motivated. Moreover, women had more opportunities for 'agency' than has been assumed. Common sense suggests that it is far preferable to accept that particularly pious women simply took advantage of the role they were allowed within the spiritual realm – a role acknowledged by their menfolk.

Religion and the royals

Good examples of religious women occur amongst the highest in the land of England from the start of our period to the end, although they are less evident at court from the Restoration onwards. Medievalists have drawn attention to the notable piety of late medieval queens.³⁰ Henry VII's mother, Lady Margaret Beaufort, was notable in having played a crucial role in sponsoring the cult of the Holy Name of Jesus, which emphasised the human tenderness and approachability of Christ and which spread through the parishes of early Tudor England. Her grandson Henry VIII's first two queens and his last, and his two daughters, all had reputations for their own learning and their encouragement of the humanist and religious learning of others.³¹ It is important to consider the potential of their role and the limits placed upon it.

Katharine of Aragon had received a humanist education in a country where women had a history of acting as regents. She was an enthusiastic supporter of the New Learning in England, most notably commissioning the humanist scholar Juan Luis Vives to write several handbooks, including *De Institutione Feminae Christianae* (The Instruction of a Christian Woman). In 1523 Vives came to England to educate her daughter, Mary, the heir to the throne of England. As Maria Dowling points out, although Vives shielded women from harmful reading such as romances and emphasised scriptural reading, this work was revolutionary in many respects. It allowed women a huge range of reading material; it maintained that mothers (not nurses or tutors) should educate both sons and daughters; and it saw education as a life-long process.³² It is to Katharine that we owe this landmark in the history of education.

Henry VIII's second Queen, Anne Boleyn, demonstrated great interest in the scriptures and works of devotion. In the popular imagination Anne is more typically seen as a 'teaser' who bewitched a king, yet there was a very different side to her persona. As early as 1530 Loys de Brun praised her:

Chiefly I have seen you this last Lent, when I was in this magnificent, excellent and triumphant court, reading the salutary epistles of St Paul, in which are contained the whole manner and rule of a good life.[33]

She commissioned, as Marquess of Pembroke, a manuscript volume in French and English of the epistles and gospels for the ecclesiastical year. Her chaplain William Latymer said that she was 'very expert in the French tongue, exercising herself continually in reading the French Bible and other French books of like effect, and conceived great pleasure in the same'. She directed the reading of her chaplains and ordered Latymer and others to go abroad to buy books for her. As Queen, Anne was an important patron of humanist scholars, with a reputation for favouring the vernacular scriptures. She certainly paid especial attention to the training of her ladies-in-waiting in the scriptures. The English scriptures (probably Tyndale's New Testament of 1534) were available in her apartments at all times and were read privately; there were discussions at her table, especially in the King's presence, of the vernacular bible. Her ladies, at her wish, hung books of devotion from their girdles: one contained a prayer thanking God for inspiring Henry to bring the scriptures to the people. Anne probably had a humanist education planned for her infant daughter, Princess Elizabeth, and she was charged to the care of Matthew Parker, her humanist chaplain.[34] Of course, as is the way with 'official' biographies, Latymer's account probably exaggerated the Queen's devotion to religion but there is no reason to doubt that this devotion was genuine.[35]

Katharine Parr's contribution to the learning and religion of England's court was very different. Katharine did not herself receive a humanist education and her religion was not based on the New Learning. Maria Dowling describes Katharine's 'anti intellectualist streak', which found expression in her *Lamentations of a Sinner* in condemning those who rooted their faith in academic learning and in declaring 'I have certainly no curious learning . . . but a simple love and earnest zeal to the truth, inspired of God.'[36] Yet, once she married the King, Katharine became conscious of the need to educate herself and to be seen as a patron of religious learning: she began to learn Latin and to practise italic handwriting and she commissioned a translation of Erasmus's *Paraphrases*. She wrote two works of her own, the Lutheran *Lamentations* and the *Prayers or Meditations*, based on Erasmus and Thomas à Kempis. She was noted as one who promoted the translation of the Bible into English. Her household chaplains were noted reformers such as John Parkhurst and Anthony Cope and her ladies too were often learned and pious. All in all, her example helped confirm the role of women in religion and to make learning of a specific kind fashionable among royal, noble and gentle women. Her contribution should not be exaggerated, however. Katharine apparently viewed her marriage to the King as a religious vocation but had relatively little influence on Henry. Katharine engaged the King in theological debate, risking her own life in the process.[37]

These queens, in their different ways and through politics as well as religion, influenced the Reformation in England. Their examples were noted and followed by women of the nobility and gentry, and accepted by many of their menfolk as a pattern for their own wives' behaviour. This pattern was strongly reinforced during the period. For instance, conduct books of the seventeenth century made a great thing of the equality of both sexes before God, of the natural spirituality of women and of their role as spiritual educators and nurturers. Thomas Powell counselled that a mother who was 'a good Huswife, and Religiously disposed' should be charged with bringing up her daughter in a similar way.

Lest we forget, queens who were Catholic also wielded influence. The examples of Queen Mary I, Queen Henrietta Maria and even Catherine of Braganza helped fortify their Catholic subjects, perpetuating Catholicism as a religion within many households and communities, including, in the case of Charles I's queen, within the royal family. This influence was hated and feared by Protestants, who thus acknowledged the important religious role of the mother.

Lollardy and the Reformation

Much lower down in society we find further evidence of female religious life. The precise relationship between Lollardy and the Protestant Reformation in England is contested by historians. Nonetheless it seems clear that in the sixteenth century Lollards (who believed in a vernacular Bible and Christian practices based on the word of Scripture) were absorbed into Protestantism and so it is appropriate to combine a brief consideration of women and belief in both movements. Women played a prominent role in popular Lollardy in the period 1480 to 1531, although the precise nature of their participation seems to have varied from place to place. In Coventry, for example, a third of people charged with, or suspected of, Lollardy were women. These women came from both high and middling social groups. In some cases they shared their beliefs (regarded as heretical by the Church) and the activities associated with them with their husbands but in other cases women operated in all-female 'cells'. There is evidence that they passed on their beliefs to their children and others in their social and occupational networks. Thomas Villers, a spicer, confessed to having been taught heretical opinions by his mother. William Borodall alleged that his parents had drawn him into Lollardy when he was a teenager although he had resisted and screamed at them that they were heretics. Shannon McSheffrey and Norman Tanner suggest that Coventry was unusual in having all-women groups and explain it in terms of the urban setting (which facilitated women and especially single women meeting together) and the high-born and charismatic nature of some prominent women Lollards. In rural areas single women probably found meeting separately much more problematical: they might have to travel a distance away from their home villages and they might incur damage to their reputations. Certainly there were women Lollards elsewhere but they more usually occur in groups with their husbands. This might indicate that female Lollard influence was by the late fifteenth century more generally exercised through the family. In Coventry, Thomasina and Richard Bradeley held gatherings in their home, and other Lollards often referred to the couple in the same breath. Even in Coventry there is the strong probability that women Lollards were protected during their husbands' lives and became subject to court proceedings once this protection was removed. Joan Smyth, the only Lollard to be executed in 1520, had just been widowed. Mistress Alice Rowley, like Smyth, wife of a former mayor of Coventry, was charged in 1506 after her husband's death. Neither Richard Smyth nor William Rowley was sympathetic to Lollardy but their status protected their wives. The complex ways in which women were recruited to Lollardy and maintained within it are exemplified by the case of Joan Warde, alias (also known as) Wasshingburn(e), who testified that she was recruited by Alice Rowley, left Coventry in fear of Rowley's husband, was taken to Northampton by one Robert Bastell, lodged in the home of a leather-dresser there for nigh on six months, travelled to London and stayed in the home of a bedder, whose wife was a Lollard. Within six months Joan married a Lollard shoemaker named Wasshingburn(e), lived in London with him for about three years, travelled to Maidstone, Kent, with him, and was tried alongside him for heresy in 1495. She was branded on the cheek with an H for heresy[38] and it seems entirely possible that he, as a relapsed heretic, was executed by burning. In any case she travelled back to Coventry alone and began once more to associate with Alice Rowley. She continued with Lollard activities and was especially prominent among the women for fifteen years before the authorities caught up with her. She was burned to death as a relapsed heretic in 1520.[39]

Religion and the household

Christianity was a patriarchal religion and nowhere was this more evident than in the household and the family: 'Ye wives, be ye in subjection to obey your own husbands.'[40] The head of the household, normally an adult male, was held responsible by church and state for the religious observance and conformity of his wife, children and servants. He it was who took the family to church and who held family prayers. He it was who was made to pay fines if recusancy was proved. In 1657 Parliament passed legislation to the effect that a man whose wife was a Catholic recusant was to suffer sequestration of two-thirds of his estate. Husbands resented this: 'if my wife turns Papist I shall suffer sequestration'.[41] Husbands and fathers saw it as their duty to order their wives' and daughters' religion. Anne Line, one of the Elizabethan Catholic martyrs, was disinherited by her father for her Catholicism.[42] Lady Tasborough was evicted by her father from his house when she joined the Augustinian canons at Louvain.[43] Possibly these men were using religion as a means of asserting patriarchy. This said, the women of the household also played a key role in household religion, and in some cases seemed to undermine patriarchy, albeit sometimes subtly. Some historians have argued that this household role was more important within Protestantism than within Catholicism but this conclusion seems unfounded.[44] John Scarisbrick, John Bossy and others have emphasised the traditional role of women in the religion of Catholic households.[45]

Contemporary males, particularly but not only in the seventeenth century, paid tribute to the spiritual examples presented by their wives and mothers. Although more examples derive from among the aristocracy (broadly defined as gentry and above) than from among the middling and lower sorts, this is probably a function of the poorer survival of records from the latter than of a real difference in the influence of wives and mothers in spiritual matters. Thomas Hernsted in 1522 declared that his wife had taught him the Lord's Prayer, the Hail Mary and the Creed in English.[46] John Bois, son of secret Marian Protestants William Bois and Mirabel Pooly Bois, wrote in the flyleaf of his mother's Book of Common Prayer:

This was my mother's book. Her name was first Mirable Poolye . . . She had read the Bible over twelve times, and the Book of Martyrs twice; besides other books, not a few.

By the time John was five he could read the Bible through and write in Hebrew. Unsurprisingly he followed a life of scholarship, eventually becoming one of the translators of the King James Bible, and, although he married, he maintained a closer relationship with his Bible-loving mother than with his unintellectual wife.[47] The dissenting minister Isaac Archer acknowledged the virtuous example offered by his stepmother in the seventeenth century. Jemimah Bourne learned her religion in the household of wealthy London merchant Sir Samuel Tryon and his wife Lady Elizabeth Tryon, guided by her future husband, their chaplain Immanuel Bourne. She passed it on to her several children by him. In the 1650s and 1660s Sir Francis Willoughby was devoted to his studies but broke his concentration to attend his mother's prayers at eleven each day.[48] Individuals who declared that they were not influenced by their mothers in religion generally explained this as an unusual situation caused by their mother's absence through death. For instance, Ralph Josselin was born in 1616 but had lost his mother by 1618.

The devotion of women to their religion could lead to considerable hardship. As Patricia Crawford argues, this brought their faith out of the household into the public arena.[49] In the reign of Henry VIII a few Protestant women were actually burned for heresy.[50] Under Mary I about fifty-five Protestant mainly poor women were martyred – twenty-eight of them married women.[51] Women were gaoled under Elizabeth and a few, Anne Line and Margaret Ward among them, were executed. But even when dissent did not bring martyrdom it could bring penury. John Erskine of Carnock heard from his mother in 1684 that the sheriff of Fife had fined her 4,000 marks for not attending church and in the summer 1685 that, when she refused to pay the fine, messengers had been sent to search for her and exact payment. He counselled her to 'walk steadfastly in his way' 'not regarding worldly losses'.[52] Women from the upper social echelons were, however, sometimes protected by their social position. In the 1590s the Dowager Lady Montague not only said her rosary openly but also provided for mass to be said in her home, Battle Abbey, for about 120 people and was scarcely troubled by the authorities.[53]

When we catch rare glimpses of the religious education of women that prepared them for 'spiritual' nourishment of their children we are struck both by its thoroughness and its currency. For example, Grace Sherrington of Lacock, Wiltshire, was presented in her teenage years (by her mother) with four religious 'texts' for detailed study. To us these books, the Bible, Foxe's *Book of Martyrs*, Musculus's *Common Places* and St Thomas à Kempis's *Imitation of Christ,* may seem like conservative classics. Our view may change, however, when we realise that the Bible was the protestant Genevan Bible, available in English for the first time in 1560; that the edition of Foxe was the enormous 1,800-page first edition of 1563; and that the translation of Musculus was undertaken by John Man in 1563. Her religious reading, then, was for the most part hot off the press, and exciting at a time when lay readership of the Bible had only lately been accepted, and acquainted this young girl with the reformed doctrine and the Protestant martyrology during her formative years.[54] Lady Grace Mildmay, as she became in 1567, was never reckoned a Puritan in religion but she was certainly a Calvinist and a proponent of Sabbath day observance and, interestingly, in nine hundred pages of religious meditations and in an autobiography, never mentioned the Book of Common Prayer once.[55] The habits of daily household prayers and scriptural study continued into her life as mistress of her own household at Apethorpe, Northamptonshire, and into her widowhood. We know so much about Lady Grace (Sherrington) Mildmay's religious beliefs precisely because she conceived of this manuscript as an opportunity to educate her daughter and her grandchildren and transmitted it to paper. Whether they ever had the time, the heart, or the stomach required to read and inwardly digest this lengthy work is not known. Margaret Dakins, who eventually became Lady Margaret Hoby, is also frequently cited as an example of an Elizabethan woman who was trained (this time in a household other than that of her parents) to become a good Christian wife and mother, which meant living a life of industrious piety and following a 'rigorous pattern of instruction and observance'.[56] Her diary and those of other female spiritual diarists, such as Elizabeth Bury (1644–1720), Elizabeth Viscountess Mordaunt (1633–1679), Sarah Savage (1664–1745) and Mary Rich, Countess of Warwick (1624–1678), parallel the kind of spiritual account-keeping practised by male diarists such as Ralph Josselin in the seventeenth century.[57] Possibly they followed the advice given to spiritual diarists in books such as John Featley's *A Fountain of tears* (1646). He listed thirty-eight introspective questions that a woman should seek to answer each night before she went to sleep, for example, 3. How devoutly prayed I? 4. What Scripture read I? and so on.

Examples of female religious study and observance appear to be well distributed throughout the sixteenth and seventeenth centuries. Katherine Brettargh read eight chapters of the Bible every day of her life, according to her funeral sermon in 1601.[58] Somewhat later than Lady Hoby and Katherine Brettargh we find Lady Elizabeth Coke, daughter-in-law of John Coke, Secretary of State to Charles I, studying the scriptures and other writings (provided for this purpose by Sir John) alongside her husband with the household chaplain at Melbourne, Derbyshire, in the 1630s.[59] Lady Mary Langham, who died in 1662, read the entire Bible through once a year.[60] The ladies or maids in waiting and servants in such households would share in this religious education. Jemima Bourne engaged in scriptural study alongside Mistress Tryon in the latter's London home and found her own husband in the chaplain, Immanuel. Women in merchant families, such as the Tryons of the early and the Barnards of the later seventeenth century were equally absorbed with religious study and observance. The Middleton papers contain two volumes of theological commentary bearing the signature of Emma Barnard from the days before her first marriage in 1667/8.[61] Later she kept a copy of a sermon made by the family chaplain George Antrobus. Dorothy Johnston observes that there is also 'a notebook dated 1675 containing a collection of prayers, apparently associated with a personal servant of Emma's'.[62] A number of devotional books were directed primarily to a female readership, such as Thomas Bentley's three volume *Monument of Matrones*.[63] These examples underscore the position taken by contemporary males regarding appropriate religious behaviour by women, which was that women must learn and live their faith with proper guidance from male authorities.[64]

While agreeing that women were active in religious observance we should not, however, be misled into thinking that all were as assiduous as, for example, Lady Margaret Hoby, Lady Grace Mildmay, Lady Mary Langham or Lady Emma Child. Nor should we conclude that when a lady is described by contemporaries as 'godly' she was necessarily content to toe the religious line drawn by her closest male religious advisers. When he was a chaplain in the household of, first, Lady Margaret Denny and, second, Lady Mary Vere, in the 1630s the Puritan Samuel Rogers contrasted their respective attitudes to household prayer and meditation. Both of them cared sufficiently for their faith to employ a personal chaplain. Lady Denny and her daughter, Madam Elizabeth Earle, however, rebuked Rogers for making his prayers too long and on one occasion she impatiently made to leave prayers before they were finished. She sometimes interrupted him at prayer and on one occasion burst into his chamber unannounced while he was praying. She otherwise offended him by swearing. Lady Mary's piety was much more to his liking.[65] Another preacher, Samuel Clarke, said that she 'brought her religion and devotion home with her, and did not leave them in her Pew behind her ... as too many do'.[66] Twice daily, religious exercises, each ending with a psalm, were regularly held. The Sunday sermon was repeated to the household and Lady Vere examined them concerning its contents and meaning. On occasion, when Samuel Rogers' spirits were at a specially low ebb, it was Lady Mary who consoled him with her faith.[67] Once again, however, the Vere family objected to Samuel Rogers' tendency to expand too much when he repeated the sermons of visiting preachers on Sabbath afternoons.[68] Perhaps the rebuke was felt all the more keenly because it was delivered by Lady Vere's godly 'secretary' Priscilla Watson. On another occasion Catherine St John, Lady Vere's younger daughter, complained that Rogers' prayers were too lengthy.

The practice of household religion appears to have been strikingly similar in English and Scottish families. Parents were catechised and in their turn they catechised. Parents quizzed their families and servants on the contents of the Sunday and weekday sermons. Whole families prayed together and sang psalms together. The only caveat might be that in Scotland more thorough provision was made both for sermons and catechising and for binding the household more rigorously into this programme than in parts of England and Wales. The threat of excommunication was taken seriously in Reformation Scotland and entire communities thronged to annual communion, bearing tokens which signified that they had 'passed examination' by the minister and elders. Research such as that by Jeremy Boulton indicates that such practices may have been equally common south of the border but further work on English records is required to prove whether this was countrywide.[69]

Thus far we have assumed that all women had an active interest in and knowledge of religion. This was not so, as cases brought against women in the church courts show. Like some men, some women were ignorant of the basic tenets of the faith. Some were charged of pursuing superstitious practices but these were in fact frequently practices that had persisted under Catholicism, such as placing candles around a corpse. Others were accused of refusing to participate in the church's rites. Katherine Chidley, for example, in the 1620s refused to be churched because it was a superstitious, non-scriptural, ceremony.[70]

Husbands probably acknowledged that their wives had a particular role to play in the religious ordering of a household but expected that role to be played out in conformity with their own beliefs and that of the Church to which they belonged. A woman's strongly held religious beliefs could also be a seriously divisive factor in a marriage. Elizabeth Carey's marriage to the Lord Deputy of Ireland Sir Henry Carey foundered largely because of her at first secret and then overt Catholicism, practised against his will. He sent her back from Ireland in 1625 but when she tried to use her influence with Queen Henrietta Maria on his behalf he objected strongly: 'For her abilities in agency of affairs, as I was never taken with opinion of them, so I was never desirous to employ them if she had them, for I conceive women to be no fit solicitors of state affairs . . . for my part I should take much more comfort to hear that she were quietly retired to her Mother's in the country.'[71] When her Catholicism became public he disowned her, took her eleven children away from her, and had to be coerced by the Privy Council to maintain her.

Indeed, if husbands did try to use religion as a way of enforcing patriarchy they were frequently disappointed. In her studies of recusancy Marie Rowlands drew upon the records of the Northern High Commission in 1575. She was able to show that some husbands of recusant women did try to force their wives to attend church but failed. For instance, Christopher Kinchingman dragged his wife to church and George Hall beat his wife in an attempt to make her attend. Even the Lord Mayor of York had to admit that he could not secure his wife's obedience in this matter and was lectured on the disgrace of a man 'set to govern a city who could not govern his household'.[72]

The case of Susanna Hopton (1627–1709) demonstrates the considerable religious influence that some women, not necessarily of noble birth, could have within the family and community, when acting in agreement with their husbands.[73] Susanna was born in Staffordshire and during the civil war was a Royalist and a Catholic convert. However, she married ex-parliamentarian Richard Hopton just before the Restoration and was reconverted to the Church of England. Her husband became a chief justice in Wales. Susanna's house became the centre of a religious society, or 'family', which probably included the mystic and poet Thomas Traherne, then rector at neighbouring Credenhill, who wrote his *Centuries* for her. She organised posthumous publication of his *Thanksgivings* in 1669.[74] She was well read in theological controversy and also in devotional works. Intriguingly she did not generally publish under her own name: some of her work was published anonymously by her friend Dr George Hickes. (This may well have been in deference to the contemporary view that women were excluded from an authoritative theological role.) Together they also produced a manual, *Daily Devotions* (1673), and an adapted Catholic work *Devotions in the Ancient Way of Offices Reformed by a Person of Quality* (2nd edn, 1701), which became very popular and went into many editions. After her death her friend the Revd Nathaniel Spinckes published her *Meditations on the Life of Christ* and also a long letter in which she explained to Father Turberville, her earlier mentor, her reconversion to Anglicanism.

Women who belonged to prominent families frequently exercised a degree of ecclesiastical patronage within either household or community. Sometimes this patronage would not be direct (in the sense of having the legal right to nominate a parish priest) but would consist of the personal influence a woman might be perceived to exercise.[75] In 1622 Lady Dorothy Bacon, seeking to establish the credentials of a suitor for her patronage and that of her sister, said: 'it is a matter that all good men and women ought to be careful of in the choice of a minister in to our houses and parish . . .' She sought good references from a Plumstead preacher on his behalf to ensure that he was a suitable person for her nephew Sir Roger Townshend to prefer to the living of Ranham, Norfolk. Her influence lay in equipping the candidate with good references and with her and her sister's backing, and in ensuring that he presented himself to Sir Roger speedily.[76]

While preachers and husbands concurred that wives had an important role to play in the religion of the household and often promoted the goal of spiritual friendship within a companionate marriage, the simultaneous insistence upon patriarchal relations could be an impediment. 'Passionate friendships [in which the sublimated sexual element was acknowledged] between men and women who were unconnected by marriage or kinship, centred in shared religious practice' developed in the sixteenth and seventeenth centuries as a superior alternative in both Catholic and Protestant countries.[77] Margaret Blagge, later Mrs Sidney Godolphin, for example, lived a devout life while she was one of Queen Catherine of Braganza's maids of honour.[78] Eventually she resigned her position in the Queen's household in order to test her religious vocation, to see whether she should marry or lead a celibate religious life. For two years she met regularly with John Evelyn for prayer and good works and he finally persuaded her that she should marry and thus pursue her vocation. The Evelyn archive and Margaret's correspondence with Sidney Godolphin allow us to see how Margaret revisited the age-old debate about whether celibacy was more pleasing to God than marriage and of how best she could fulfil her religious vocation. Blagge's friendship with Evelyn 'was not a furtive, isolated or eccentric affair. It was conducted in terms quite familiar to their contemporaries and in full view of their families and court circle, who were for the most part supportive and sympathetic.' Margaret claimed that she received enormous benefits from it. It is hard to see her as manipulated by Evelyn, who was her intellectual superior. Indeed, she seems to have introduced in him an internal spiritual conflict which caused a major breakdown.

Women in the parish

The formal religious life of women took place in the parish church. Here they were baptised, catechised, married, churched, confessed. Here they joined others for morning and evening service, and communion. Here they heard sermons and sometimes did public penance, wearing a white shift and carrying a wand, for their offences against the church's laws. Young maidens came to worship before the Virgin Mary, who mirrored their innocence. Eamon Duffy, John Scarisbrick and others have demonstrated the lively religious faith and piety of English people prior to the Reformation. In the later Middle Ages and early Tudor times, cults of the Virgin Mary, of her mother St Anne and of various other female saints appealed particularly to women at various stages of their lives. Eamon Duffy points to the highly personalised nature of this female devotion: Widow Rumbelow, for example, gave her entire estate to the cult of our Lady – kerchiefs, girdles, beads and gowns as well as other property. St Anne, originally a barren woman, who eventually gave birth not only to Mary but also two other daughters, appealed especially to married people anxious to bear children. There were also local female saints, such as Sidwell the virgin in Devon, to whose service the priest of Morebath encouraged dying female parishioners in the 1520s and 1530s to make bequests of altar cloths, candlesticks, banners, wedding rings and rosaries.[79]

Our sense of the relative importance of female religious role models in the various parts of the British Isles, however, has been enhanced recently by Christine Peters. She convincingly argues that in fifteenth-century England the cult of the Blessed Virgin was effectively eclipsed by that of Christ and the Holy Name of Jesus. In Scotland cults of Mary and the saints, including a multiplicity of female saints, continued to prevail and in Wales that of the Blessed Virgin Mary was predominant.[80]

Women were active in the religious life of the parish of Morebath. Not only did widows serve the parish in the highest lay offices – those of senior and junior High Warden – but they also frequently made significant benefactions to the church, some of which remained in the church's possession and some of which were sold before and after the Reformation ordered the removal of images to raise church funds. For instance, Old Dame Rumbelow, who had served as High Warden a year after being widowed in 1556, on her own death left the church at Morebath, Devon, a new image of the Virgin Mary and on another occasion Katherine Robbins's expensive amber rosary beads were left to the church and bought by Mistress Tutlake, wife of her executor.[81] The young maidens acted together to support the Maidens' store, to keep the candles to the Virgin lit, and joined the young men of the parish to raise money from all the unmarried inhabitants to purchase a new chalice (the cup used to celebrate communion) when thieves struck at Morebath church in November 1534. In these pre-Reformation parishes women (especially widows) could, as we have seen, play an important official role. This seems to have been the case in Scottish parishes also. Margo Todd has found that women were required to sign parochial confessions, to swear the covenant and even to join in the vetting of ministers and elders.[82]

Recent historians of English religion in the fifteenth and early sixteenth centuries have suggested that the Protestant Reformation was not welcomed with open arms by the populace. They claim that earlier histories, such as that of A. G. Dickens, which stressed the barrenness of the late medieval church, profound anticlericalism and the growing popular enthusiasm for Protestantism as coincidental with the official Reformation imposed by Henry VIII, have mistakenly overemphasised the views and pious activities of a very few. The truth, as so often, lies somewhere between these extremes. In Scotland too historians have traditionally painted a picture in which the Protestant Kirk, the national church, reigned supreme. A new generation of scholars have urged that in sixteenth-century Scotland the official religion was a minority religion, with the majority remaining faithful to the old religion. The sources are not so rich as those of England but what exists certainly suggests that late fifteenth- and early sixteenth-century religion there shared much with that of Morebath. Moreover, Scotland appears to have lost many of the potential early leaders of Protestantism to a permanent foreign exile.[83] F. D. Bardgett has established that there was a caucus of thirty or so lairds in Angus who were Protestant (and perhaps even formed a secret church) but that this represented a mere 10 per cent of the lairds of Angus. In this clan society the laird would carry with him all his followers.[84] According to historians working in the 1980s and 1990s, Protestantism gained ground quite slowly and at varying regional rates: in Aberdeen it took thirty years to convert the burgh rulers, in St Andrews just ten; in rural Angus, conversion was much swifter than in rural Mearns. James Kirk's study of the ministry suggests that in Scotland, as in England, the key to the success of Protestantism in terms of conformity on the ground really lay in filling benefices with educated and persuasive protestant preachers.[85] This, however, did not automatically mean that the conformists were converts, even after 1560. Scholars disagree regarding the pace of such change. Some historians, notably Michael Lynch, have suggested that Protestantism did not really take root in most of Scotland until the 1620s and 1630s. Margo Todd urges that Protestantism took root much earlier. She argues, on the basis of a careful analysis of parish records, that the institution of the Kirk session from the 1570s and 1580s was 'the single greatest factor in establishing a culture of Protestantism'. It implemented a logocentric programme of sermons, propounding the word of God, and catechising among a predominantly illiterate population but 'eased the transition from Catholicism by linking this to old ritual, by introducing a reformed ritual of communion, Baptism, and Penance, and by approaching popular cultural survivals – such as Yule Day festivities (1 January), nuptial celebrations and baptism feasts – with general sensitivity and only occasional attempts at suppression'. Its impact was felt very early in Scottish towns, which accommodated most of the population. Perhaps its success was to be attributed to the way in which the congregation felt ownership of the Kirk session, bringing before it their problems and not seeing it as an external authority imposing unwelcome discipline.[86]

In other respects, when one reads the accounts of the proceedings of the church courts in England and Wales, one is struck by the similarities rather than the differences with the approach adopted by Scotland's Kirk session and the presbyteries. In England and Wales we know little about the life of the parish after the Reformation because the ecclesiastical records are, in the main, the product of a system of 'visitation' and 'inquiry' imposed from above. Visitation *comperta* of presentations are the closest we come to records made by representatives of the parish, the churchwardens, of those requiring discipline within the parish. A constant Protestant complaint was that discipline was not exercised at parish level. Until proven otherwise, we should probably assume that the lively parish life of pre-Reformation times continued to exist. We do know that church ales and other fund-raising and community-consolidating activities persisted and were generally tolerated until the reign of Charles I and, in all probability, were resumed after the Restoration.

In no part of the British Isles then should one assume radical Protestantism following the Reformation, even in the towns, but remain open to the suggestion of a very mixed religious economy during the sixteenth century and into the seventeenth in which the Protestantisation of society involved tactful negotiation with the popular culture of the past.

House churches in Catholicism

The case of Dorothy Constable Lawson illustrates the dominant role that many women had in the Catholic community and bears out the Catholic maxim that what was important for the survival of their faith was securing the allegiance of mothers. This was all the more true when the besieged nature of Catholicism in Scotland and the North of England pushed it underground into the family and household. Dorothy was the daughter of Margaret Dormer and Sir Henry Constable of Burton Constable, Yorkshire, members of leading Catholic families and she was brought up as a Catholic. In 1597, Dorothy married Roger Lawson, heir of a prominent Protestant Newcastle mercantile and landed family. His family certainly had some Catholic connections, but it was Dorothy who converted the household to her faith. Within a week she had introduced a Catholic priest into the house, and she rapidly converted most of her husband's family. Roger remained a Protestant until just before his death in 1613, when he was persuaded to convert by Dorothy.[87]

Some time after 1605 when Dorothy was living at Heaton near Newcastle and while Roger, a barrister, was absent on business in London, she surrounded herself with Catholic servants and became a very active Catholic proselytiser at home and in the community. There were, for example, daily Catholic religious exercises in her home. All fifteen of her children were brought up as Catholics and two of them became nuns. She fulfilled the normal charitable and medical duties of well-to-do women but took this several steps further to convert the local population. When comforting local women in childbirth she catechised them and ensured that their children were baptised as Catholics. Heaton had not had a single Catholic family in 1605, but had a hundred converted families by 1632. Her national and even international importance was increased when in the early 1620s she built a centre for Jesuit missionaries at St Anthony's near Newcastle.[88] This is doubtless an extreme but nonetheless instructive example of the important role women played in Catholic survival and, indeed, revival in parts of the north and midlands. Marie Rowlands has drawn attention to the role played by Catholic housewives in harbouring Catholic priests.[89] The role of women in Catholic survival in Scotland was no less crucial.[90]

In a good many respects the religious influence of Catholic women in Ireland was similar. After the Reformation the official Church in Ireland was Protestant. The Catholic Church, stripped of its network of parish churches, was forced underground and women found an important role in the Catholic house churches that grew up. Especially in the Pale, wealthy aristocratic women provided safe havens and support for priests. Take, for example, Margaret Bermingham from a Meath gentry family who was married to Bartholomew Ball, a Dublin merchant. She turned their Dublin home into a recusant centre, where children were educated and where priests took refuge. She was arrested twice for her complicity and eventually seems to have died in gaol in 1584. Slightly later, Joan Roche of New Ross and Anastasia Walsh were noted as having kept their houses open for priests and the poor. Higher up the social scale the Dowager Countess of Kildare provided a house for the Jesuits in Dublin. At every social level the home became the main venue for worship and one heavily influenced by women, although most of the examples pertain to the well-to-do.[91] P. J. Corish has indicated that the popularity of the Marian cult is significant in this context, especially as the Irish translation of Mary 'bean an ti' meant 'woman of the house'. It was in the eighteenth century that the 'house mass' of the 'stations of confession' evolved. 'Twice a year, in Lent and Advent, the priest visited designated Houses . . . the neighbours gathered and he heard their confessions and said mass.'[92]

As John Bossy indicated, Catholic women sometimes defied patriarchy through their religion. About a quarter of seminary *responsa* of English Catholic boys in Rome revealed that one parent had been Catholic and the other Protestant and in the great majority of such cases it was the mother who was Catholic.[93] Edward Willoughby of Kinsbury, Warwickshire, in 1615 married Elizabeth Atkinson of Nottingham, a Catholic who contrived to conceal her religion from her husband while he lived. On his death, despite the fact that all her children had been brought up Protestant and were now grown, 'their mother had then influence enough over them to make them all change their religion and turn Roman Catholics, which religion has been professed by all the descendants from that lady to the present time, being AD 1720.'[94]

A few Catholic women deliberately sought to carve out a specific religious role for married women. A good example is that of Mary Ward, a Yorkshire gentlewoman who had been brought up with well-to-do Catholic relatives at Osgodby in the late sixteenth and early seventeenth centuries. Mary had several attractive marriage proposals but in 1605 (aged about twenty) she elected to go to the Netherlands in search of a religious vocation. When she found none of the existing convents to her liking, by 1610 she had founded her own, the Institute of the Blessed Virgin Mary, for which she developed a mission directed particularly at women. The Institute rapidly recruited many young women over the next decade or so. In Europe it focused on the education of girls; in England it sought to support married women in the business of 'domestic reformation'.[95]

Convents

Religious houses, including convents or nunneries, were dissolved at the Reformation in all parts of the British Isles, including Scotland and Ireland. Nevertheless, for Catholics, the religious life became in the seventeenth century once again of great importance for its womenfolk both in exile and to some extent at home.[96] The aristocracy provided dowries for their daughters to enter convents. For example, in seventeenth-century Ireland Sir Christopher Cusack, 4th Viscount Gormanstoun, willed to each of his daughters who decided on a religious life £15 a year, no small sum at that time. His successor did likewise.[97] Such generosity was motivated in part by a desire to see unmarriageable daughters provided for and educated but also by a genuine desire to see Catholicism perpetuated. Certainly nuns were not only the taught but the teachers, who in their turn ensured the Catholic education of future generations.

In the 1590s Father Fitzsimmons encouraged some young women to join a convent in Europe and then he founded the Sodality of Our Lady in Dublin, which lasted into the seventeenth century and had in its midst ladies of 'the first rank'. There were also other groups of religious women in Dublin and Drogheda. In 1629 a group of Irish nuns returned to Newport from their convent in Europe and established a community of Poor Clares in Dublin, with Cecily Dillon as abbess. Almost immediately they recruited twelve new members and eventually many members of the Dillon family joined them. It was not long though before the community was quashed and the Poor Clares dispersed to Loughrea, Galway, Athlone, Waterford and Wexford, where they struggled to re-establish themselves, under a rule translated into Irish, and survive. In the 1640s there was a Poor Clare convent known as Bethlehem in the archdiocese of the Archbishop of Tuam. He noted its popularity with the 'best of the country' and, with dismay, the 'absolute' authority of its abbess. Sixty pious ladies are reputed to have invited the Poor Clares to Drogheda. The Civil Wars brought this period of relative stability to an end. Bethlehem was closed in 1642 and Irish nuns began to leave for the continent or to go into hiding. In 1653 Cromwell ordered nuns either to marry or leave the kingdom and many chose to return to the houses in France and Spain where they had taken their vows.

So women had an important role in the Irish Catholic community but it was still a role circumscribed by patriarchal attitudes. Innovation and authority was suppressed. Women's religious role lay in the home, supporting males and male initiatives, facilitating the work of priests and the spreading of male teachings.[98]

The religious life of colonial American women

When the puritan colonies of New England were founded, church membership for both males and females was restricted to a small number of people who readily submitted to the church's discipline. Members had to adhere to strict moral and religious codes. For example, the separatists who formed the Pilgrim Fathers certainly dissented from the authority of the Church of England, but they obeyed the church elders who had made the Mayflower contract and were united in the desire to build a godly community. The Massachusetts Puritans were not separatists but they sought a reform of the Church of England which would abolish bishops and the prayer-book liturgy and replace them with congregational authority and worship founded on the Bible. They were Calvinists but they modified Calvin's teaching slightly – they believed that they would be saved as long as they lived a godly life and kept the faith. A system of public examination was introduced to discover precisely who within the community was of the Elect of God. Only the Elect could participate in the government of the colony. This government imposed godly rule, making church attendance compulsory for all and punishing immoral and amoral behaviour.

In the mid-1630s there were challenges to the authority of these New England Churches on two fronts: a radical separatist congregation in Plymouth and Salem led by Roger Williams; and the preaching of a married woman, Anne Hutchinson, who joined John Cotton's church when she and her family arrived from England in 1634. Anne Hutchinson dared to criticise the ministers of the church who, she said, preached a religion of deeds rather than one of grace, thus running the risk of suggesting that men and women might earn salvation by their good works. Her opinions and her activities were no more welcome to some of the Massachusetts Puritans than they would have been in England although she had some powerful supporters. Eventually, however, Governor Winthrop examined her in 1637 on her teaching and alleged that she had 'maintained a meeting and assembly in your house that hath been condemned by the general assembly as a thing not tolerable nor comely in the sight of God nor fitting for your sex'. This women's meeting had contained sixty or so members who met regularly in Anne's house in Boston. Either she would submit to the Governor's censure (admit her fault and repent) or she would be banished from the colony. Anne claimed that she had spoken out after God had spoken to her directly and that she had to obey her conscience. Her words were seen as a challenge to the authority of the ministry and the Bible. She was condemned and banished.[99]

This episode is extremely interesting because it not only demonstrates that the position of women in the Puritan churches of Massachusetts was very similar to that of women in the Church of England but also hints at active female resistance on a large scale. Women were certainly admitted to full membership of the church but they were barred from the ministry and from preaching. In civil matters they could not stand for election as magistrate or deputy, become a freeman or vote. Their knowledge of religion would come from listening to ministers and their husbands and modelling themselves upon them. Women were meant to be passive. Only witches were aggressive and 'male'. The views of women were unimportant. 'We do not mean to discourse with your sex', declared Winthrop. But it was not only Anne but also a sizeable number of Boston matrons who gathered together to worship, to discuss and to criticise what the ministry and elders preached in what was probably a natural (if, to the authorities, unwelcome) extension of the puritan practice of studying the Sunday sermon.

Not everywhere or with everyone was such patriarchal discipline exerted. The indications are that Anglicans and Catholics accepted a more active religious role for women. Elizabeth Harris brought Quakerism to Maryland in 1655 and Quaker women there as elsewhere were expected to act as ministers during services and to participate in the work of conversion. In 1682 William Richardson wrote to George Fox lauding the missionary work of five prominent female Quakers. Anne Ayres Chew used her own money to establish a meeting house and travelled with other Quakers at her expense to persuade others to start societies. Ann Galloway was especially prominent in the Society of Friends within the colony. Quaker women were encouraged to model themselves on Old and New Testament female role models such as Rachel and Lydia, much as Catholics were.

In Maryland both Anglican and Catholic women were accepted as important to the colony's spiritual life. Marylander Henrietta Maria Neale's credentials as a card-carrying Catholic were unassailable. Her mother, Ann Gill, had served as Queen Henrietta Maria's Maid of Honour. When Ann married Captain James Neale and gave birth to a daughter, the Queen agreed to become the child's godmother. Henrietta Maria Neale married first Richard Bennet and bore him a son; after Richard's death she married Philemon Lloyd and they had several sons and daughters. Henrietta Maria built a Roman Catholic chapel on her own property (inherited from Bennet) and, when she died in 1697, left bequests to her favourite priests. Philemon, however, instructed his wife in his own will: 'I will that my children be brought up in the Protestant religion and carried to such church or churches where it is professed and to no other during their minority and until such years of discretion as may render them best capable to judge what is most consonant to the good will of Almighty God unto which I pray God of his mercy direct them.' This suggests a relationship between Philemon and Henrietta Maria where her private exercise of her religion was countenanced and even her catechising of the children therein but where the husband was Protestant and envisaged his children of both sexes being able to choose for themselves when they achieved majority on the basis of knowledge of both denominations. Susannah Gerrard, an Anglican, married a Catholic and convinced him that it was a good idea to build a chapel on their property to serve both Anglicans and Catholics.

Like so many of the elite English women we have encountered, Henrietta Maria was a notable patron, her counsel was sought by local priests, and she was generally respected as the family matriarch. As such, she was typical of many propertied Catholic and Anglican wives and widows in seventeenth-century Maryland. 'Wealthier women used their resources of both land and money to build and maintain chapels, while they also supplied and cared for communion plate.'[100] Lord Baltimore seems to have been so worried about land being donated to the churches in this way that he persuaded the Maryland Assembly to legislate limiting the amount of land that could be donated without special permission. Eventually Catholic women founded the first American convent at Port Tobacco in 1790, which drew members from the local elite and its income from their dowries.

In addition Maryland women performed a very important role as educators, especially at a time when priests (both Anglican and Catholic) were in scarce supply. This role was largely played out in the home, as in England. A Catholic named John Parsons willed his wife Mary 'to maintain and educate my said children bringing them up in the fear of God and the holy catholic religion', and an Anglican, Thomas Stockett, declared, 'I surely trust [my wife] will not neglect any endeavour that shall be tending to [the children's] good both in religious education and for the advancement of their temporal fortunes . . .' Husbands also accepted religious teaching from their wives. Walter Smith was a devout and committed Anglican but he had married Rachel Hall, a member of a well-established Maryland Quaker family, and he attended Quaker functions (including a wedding in 1687), and the language of his will in 1711 indicates that he had imbibed some Quaker teaching during their marriage.

The resurgence of the cult of the Virgin Mary that was apparent in seventeenth-century England in sermons and tracts found echoes in Maryland among both Catholics and Anglicans. Father Peter Attwood preached sermons in which he saw the Virgin as a model for earthly mothers and as intercessor with her son, Jesus. 'This son can refuse nothing to his mother.' Attwood cast women themselves as intercessors and urged his congregation to respect the authority of their own mothers. Calvinists on both sides of the Atlantic vigorously criticised the cult as blasphemous.

There is some evidence that suggests the power of Maryland women within the churches themselves and, by inference, within the community. For example, Mary Taney, wife of the sheriff of Calvert County, wrote to King Charles II and the Archbishop of Canterbury requesting £500 to build a church and support an Anglican priest. Intriguingly, both King and Archbishop appear to have accepted Mary as spokesperson of the community without demur and to have sent her the money, the Bibles and texts she requested. In 1715 it was Mary Boone Merriman and Rebecca Colegate who led the congregation of St Paul's Church, Baltimore, to complain about the behaviour of their Anglican priest.

Apart from glimpses such as this, the religious lives of early American women remain very much a closed book. We know that, especially in the early years, women became church members in New England in more or less equal numbers to men. We know that women played a more prominent role in the Quaker meetings. We know that within New England and Middle Colony homes and the Planter homes of the southern colonies, women participated in family prayers and shared a responsibility for the religious upbringing of their children, servants and slaves that was very similar to that shouldered by English and Scottish wives and mothers. But we await more detailed studies of the contribution made by women to the religious lives of their communities.

Mothers and immortality

Laurel Thatcher Ulrich has shown how, in the New World, the role of woman in the spiritual life of her family began with the act of procreation.

For a woman, fruitfulness conferred status upon the extended family. 'May you glorify the Lord in helping to build up the house of Jacob your father', Margaret Thatcher urged her daughter in October 1686. She hoped to see her grandchildren become 'polished stones' in God's house and 'heartily embraced' them. In gentle families women seem often but not always to have assumed responsibility for recording genealogical information.[101] In old age, women looked back at their family, regarding themselves as mothers of both the living and the dead, expecting to meet the dear departed in heaven and adopting, therefore, religious resignation. At the same time they displayed an obsession with the next generations. Anne Bradstreet's poem to her children, written in 1656, is used to show how for this mother immortality lay not only in heaven but also in her own song and in her children's memories:

When each of you shall in your nest
Among your young ones take your rest,
In chirping language oft them tell,
You had a Dam that loved you well.
That did what could be done for young,
And nurst you up till you were strong,
And fore she once would let you fly,
She shew'd you joy and misery;
Taught what was good, and what was ill,
What would save life, and what would kill.
Thus gone, amongst you I may live,
And dead, yet speak, and counsel give.[102]

In Britain the role of women as main conservers of the genealogical record is less well documented. For example, we know that in the case of the Bagot family in Staffordshire, the record of births, baptisms and deaths was in the hand of the patriarch. However, the womenfolk were still revered for their fertility, still obsessed with the lives of their adult children and grandchildren, and still convinced that their own immortality lay with them. Evidence from both the Temple and the Brydges families considered elsewhere in this book, moreover, supports a view that women of the period 1590 to 1730 were frequently intimately concerned with preserving information about their pedigree and even extending considerably the sense of family identity. Alice Thorneton in the seventeenth century also recorded the births (and the deaths) of her nine children and wrote a family memoir. These examples certainly demonstrate a concern for family past and present, dead and alive, amongst English aristocratic women but they do not quite match the poignant preoccupation with immortality displayed in Bradstreet's verse.[103]

Witches and witchcraft

Whether witchcraft should be included in a discussion of female religion is debatable. Many of the so-called 'beliefs' of witchcraft, especially those concerning diabolism or devil worship, are now thought to have been attributed to witches by their accusers. However, the phenomenon of witchcraft, the role of women within it, and the attitude of both men and women towards it certainly warrant mention in this book. Throughout our period and in the five 'nations', rational and often well-educated men and women shared stories about witchcraft and clearly believed in the existence of powerful witches. Robert Woodrow (1679–1734) graduate university librarian of Glasgow recorded conversations with his wife about witchcraft and devilish possession among her friends and solemnly reported that the Countess of Dumfries 'did frequently fly from the one end of the room to the other, and from the one side of the garden to the other . . . The matter of fact is certain.'[104]

Conclusion

Women's involvement in religion was accepted as desirable by contemporary society. Their active role was largely seen as played out within the household and limited by the patriarch, be he husband in the case of the married woman or father in the case of the unwed. This was as true of the American colonies as it was of England, Wales, Scotland and Ireland. It was, however, acknowledged as a vital role and it probably helps explain the survival of Protestantism and Catholicism in particular communities. Some socially prominent women, notably Anne Boleyn, Katharine Parr and Elizabeth I, did, of course, lend their imprimatur to particular beliefs. Women lower down in society played a quasi-public role within the religious life of the community and some held lay offices in the church. In general, however, a very public role was denied women within England after the Reformation. There were opportunities for women to live the religious life in English convents in Europe and in convents in Ireland.

As indicated, women did not always obey their husbands and fathers in the matter of religion. Although husbands and fathers imposed penalties, women with strong religious convictions were in general not deterred by them from following their own religious persuasion. Catholic or Protestant, where their faith was firm they would follow it and their spiritual guides (male preachers), whether it led to marital conflict or not. Anne Vaughan, for example, who married a mercer, Henry Locke, was extremely close to the preacher John Knox. In 1556 Knox set out to persuade Anne to join him in exile in Geneva. Despite her husband's opposition, Anne gathered up her two children and joined the reformer in Geneva. She then spent much of her time translating Calvin's sermons for the use of the congregation there. Later she acted as a channel for Knox's communications from Edinburgh and St Andrews with the Genevan church. From mid-1559 she was back home with her husband in Cheapside. When Henry died in 1571 she married the Protestant preacher Edward Dering.[105] The male reformers themselves were uncertain how to handle the issue of female conscience. Thomas Becon, while he stressed the obligation of the wife to love and respect her husband, nevertheless taught that if the husband ordered the wife to follow Catholicism, she should leave him and, if necessary, suffer death.[106] John Bale praised Anne Askew for deserting her husband for conscience sake.[107] Later Elizabethan writers, such as William Gouge, however, thought it much preferable that the problem be avoided: men and women of different beliefs should not marry in the first place.[108] Within Catholicism the authority of the priest was sometimes set in sharp contrast to that of the husband or father.

From the point of view of this book, women's religious role is important for several reasons. First, it explains one of the activities in which married women were engaged during their daily lives – looking after their own soul's health and the salvation of their spouses, children and servants. This offered an opportunity for agency which might not otherwise have occurred and it was one which most husbands and fathers acknowledged. Second, it helps to explain the contribution married and unmarried women made on a cultural level. Not only did they write or translate religious texts, but they also engaged in reading, study and discussion and also exercised patronage. Although grounded in the household, this did draw them into engagement with the wider world of learning, politics and local patronage. Third, it certainly provided the chief impetus towards female literacy, which once gained could be, and was, the basis of much wider cultural and intellectual activity. The suggestion that attitudes to women's role in religion differed according to denomination – with Puritans asserting strict patriarchal control in matters spiritual and Anglicans, Quakers and Arminians allowing women a much more active and even public role in religion – warrants further investigation.

Notes

1. Inscription on Henrietta Maria Neale's tomb, Maryland, 1697.
2. That is, reminder of death.
3. A. G. Dickens (1989) p. 74.
4. M. Aston (1989) p. 536.
5. See P. Crawford (1993) p. 56.
6. See P. Crawford (1993) pp. 23–5, for an interesting discussion.
7. S. D. Amussen (1995) pp. 48–68.
8. R. C. Finucane (1977) pp. 142–3; See P. Crawford (1993) p. 23.
9. J. E. Binney (1904); see also E. Duffy (2001) for a discussion of the subject.
10. Bishop Hobhouse (1890) p. 6; see also J. C. Fox (1913) p. 7ff. which shows that there were, at Kilmington, Devon, female churchwardens on at least six occasions during Elizabeth I's reign and that there were women churchwardens several times at St Brideaux, Devon, until 1699.
11. C. Welch (1912) pp. 22–4.
12. P. Crawford (1993) p. 97.
13. P. Lake, 'Feminine piety and personal potency: the emancipation of Mrs Jane Ratcliffe', *Seventeenth Century*, 2, 1987, pp. 143–65, *passim*. I thank Professor Patrick Collinson for drawing my attention to this article.
14. CSPD, 1547–1580, pp. 271 and 273: also cited in P. Collinson (1983) p. 274 and P. Crawford (1993) p. 54.
15. P. Collinson (1967) p. 82.
16. B. Capp (1972) p. 82.
17. See K. V. Thomas (1958) pp. 42–62; P. Mack (1992); C. Trevett (1991); Anne Laurence (1990).
18. Cited in A. Crawford *et al.* (1983) pp. 117–18.
19. Extracts from James Kirkton's 'Secret and true history of the Church of Scotland', in J. G. Fyfe and R. S. Rait (1928) pp. 253–4.
20. M. Aston (1984) pp. 49–70.
21. See below.
22. For a discussion of this point see C. Peters (2004) pp. 134–5.
23. R. A. Houlbrooke, 'Women's social life and common action in England from the fifteenth century to the eve of the Civil War', *Continuity and Change*, 1, 1986, pp. 171–89.

24 For this see C. Peters (2004) pp. 138–40.

25 See O'Day (2007), *Cassandra Brydges*, Introduction.

26 Diary of Henry Guthrie in Fyfe (1928) pp. 136–8.

27 See also the case of Anne Vaughan Locke discussed below.

28 Lancelot Langhorne, *Funeral Sermon of Mrs Mary Swaine*, 1611; quoted in J. L. Mcintosh, 'English funeral sermons, 1560–1640: the relationship between gender and death, dying and the afterlife', Unpublished University of Oxford MLitt thesis, 1990, p. 10.

29 See P. Crawford (1993), *Women and Religion*; and P. Lake, 'Feminine piety', 1987, for examples.

30 Ann Crawford (1983).

31 See, for example, Steven W. May (ed.), *Queen Elizabeth I: Selected Works*, New York, 2004, which contains examples of Elizabeth's prayers, translations, essays, poems and speeches.

32 See M. Dowling (1986) pp. 223–5.

33 BL, Royal MS 20 B XVII, Loys de Brun, French treatise on letter-writing, 1530.

34 Later Parker was Elizabeth's first Archbishop of Canterbury.

35 See E. Ives (1986) pp. 302–31; Maria Dowling (1984) pp. 30–46; Maria Dowling (1986) pp. 231–4.

36 Dowling (1986) pp. 235–6.

37 Ibid pp. 66–8.

38 The medieval/early modern painful and humiliating equivalent of electronic tagging, whereby individuals were readily recognised as people on whom the authorities should keep an eye.

39 S. McSheffrey and N. Tanner (2004) Introduction.

40 From 'An Homily on the state of matrimony', 1562, from *Certain sermons or homilies appointed to be read in churches in the time of Queen Elizabeth*, 1908, p. 539.

41 J. T. Rutt (1828) Vol. I, p. 6: cited in P. Crawford (1993) p. 59.

42 Crawford (1993) p. 63.

43 Adam Hamilton (1904) Vol. I, pp. 253–6; also cited in Crawford (1993) p. 59.

44 For a contrary view see Crawford (1993) p. 37.

45 J. J. Scarisbrick (1978), *The Reformation and the English People*, Oxford, 1984, pp. 150–9; John Bossy (1975) pp. 152–8.

46 John Strype, *Ecclesiastical memorials*, Oxford, 1822, p. 61.
47 A. Nicolson (2003) pp. 202–15, citing Anthony Walker, Biography of John Bois, BL MS.
48 A. C. Wood (1958) p. 110.
49 P. Crawford (1993) pp. 62–3.
50 For this view, which seems to be contradicted by the evidence she presents, see P. Crawford (1993) pp. 30–34.
51 Retha M. Warnicke (1983), *Women of the English Renaissance and Reformation*, p. 74.
52 Extracts from the Journal of John Erskine, in J. G. Fyfe and R. S. Rait (1928) pp. 422–3.
53 Richard Smith, *The life of . . . Lady Magdalen Viscountess Montague*, 1627, pp. 27–31.
54 Lady Grace Mildmay's Journal, Central Library, Northampton.
55 I gratefully acknowledge that I owe this assessment to Retha Warnicke.
56 Joanna Moody (1998) p. xviii.
57 S. Mendelson (1985) pp. 185–9.
58 William Harrison, *Deaths advantage little regarded*, 1602, p. 79.
59 Coke MSS (now held by the British Library), Bundle 43, 1639–40.
60 Edward Reynolds, *The Churches triumph over death*, 1662, p. 33.
61 UNL, Mi A 143/27/12, 13. I owe this reference to Dorothy Johnston.
62 See D. Johnston (2003), 'Emma Child', p. 60.
63 S. W. Hull (1982); Thomas Bentley, *Monument of Matrones*, 3 volumes, 1582.
64 See Christine Peters (2004), *Women in early modern Britain*, p. 152.
65 T. Webster and K. Shipps (2004) pp. xxxii, xxxix–xli.
66 Quoted from Samuel Clarke, *The Lives of Sundry Eminent Persons in this Later Age*, 1683, 2nd pag., p. 145 in Webster and Shipps (2004) p. xl.
67 Webster and Shipps (2004) p. xli.
68 Ibid p. xlii.
69 J. Boulton (1987).
70 See P. Crawford (1993) pp. 53–6.
71 State Papers of Ireland, 63, 242/282, quoted in B. Lewalski (1992) p. 185.
72 Marie B. Rowlands, 'Recusant women 1560–1640', in Mary Prior (1985) p. 151.

73 Anne Crawford *et al.* (1983) pp. 207–8.

74 G. I. Wade, *Thomas Traherne* (1946).

75 For exercise of patronage pro hac vice see R. O'Day (1979) pp. 105–12. This system allowed patronage on one occasion to many people who were not ordinarily patrons of church livings.

76 The Letters of Lady Dorothy Bacon, Norfolk Record Society, LVI, 1991, p. 96, Letter 13, which is BL Add. 41654, fos. 50–51.

77 See also P. Collinson (1994) pp. 119–50. Knox's relationship with Anne Locke, Elizabeth Bowes and Rose Hickman, and Dering's with Lady Mary Mildmay, Lady Golding, Mrs Mary Honeywood and Mrs Catherine Killigrew seem to fit into this category.

78 See G. Wright (2003) pp. 221–32 for a discussion of Mary Evelyn's religious life.

79 E. Duffy (2001) pp. 141–51.

80 C. Peters (2004) pp. 141–51.

81 Duffy (2001) pp. 28–9, 10, 98.

82 M. Todd (2002) p. 23.

83 J. Durkan, 'Heresy in Scotland: the second phase', *Records of the Scottish Church History Society*, 2001.

84 F. D. Bardgett (1989).

85 J. Kirk (1989); for England see R. O'Day, 'Ecclesiastical patronage: who controlled the church?', in F. Heal and R. O'Day (eds), 1977, pp. 136–55.

86 M. Todd (2002) pp. 14, 26 and *passim*.

87 J. Bossy (1975) pp. 156–7; W. Palmes, *The Life of Mrs Dorothy Lawson* (ed. G. B. Richardson) Newcastle upon Tyne, 1851; Marie B. Rowlands (1985).

88 J. D. Hanlon (1966).

89 M. B. Rowlands (1985) pp. 156–60.

90 See A. F. B. Roberts, 'The role of women in Scottish catholic survival', *Scottish Historical Review*, 70, 1991, pp. 129–50; and Christine Peters (2004), *Women in Early Modern Britain*, pp. 139–40.

91 P. J. Corish (1991) pp. 212–20.

92 Ibid p. 213.

93 J. Bossy (1975) p. 157.

94 A. C. Wood (1958) p. 53.

95 J. Bossy (1975) p. 160.

96 Bossy (1975).
97 P. Kilroy (1991) p. 195.
98 M. MacCurtain (1991) pp. 160–78; Phil Kilroy (1991) pp. 179–96.
99 L. Koehler (1974) pp. 55–78.
100 Debra Meyers (2003).
101 See, for example, M. Halsey Thomas (1973) Vol. I, p. 292.
102 John Howard Ellis (ed.) 1962, *The Works of Anne Bradstreet*, pp. 400–403.
103 B. Lewalski (1992) p. 185.
104 Extracts from *Analecta*, in Fyfe and Rait (1928) pp. 380–81.
105 P. Collinson (1983) pp. 274–87.
106 Thomas Becon, *Catechism*, pp. 340–41.
107 Henry Christmas (1849) pp. 199 and 238.
108 William Gouge, *Domesticall Duties*, 1634, pp. 193–6; P. Crawford (1993) p. 52, notes that these pages were an addition to the 1622 text.

CHAPTER 15

Contemporary culture: print and non-print, public and private

I am not obnoxious to each carping tongue,
who sayes my hand a needle better fits
A poet's pen all scorne, I should thus wrong . . .[1]

Introduction

In the introduction to this book we noted how important it is to locate the contribution of individual women and women in general within the cultural life of their societies, and some of the reasons why this process has been impeded. In order to do this well we need to know about early modern culture in general. Above all, printed publications have not proved a very promising way of determining the female role within the culture because, throughout our period, the public arena of print was not thought quite proper for either male or female cultural contribution and, proportionately, women published far fewer volumes than men. Both men and women wrote in manuscript. It emerges that, in addition to hand-writing in books, plays and letters, they wrote on walls and windows and communicated through tapestry and embroidery, and, of course, conversation. It was regarded as socially much more acceptable to exchange ideas and writings within a confined arena; as a result much of this cultural production (male and female) disappeared from view after the moment passed and as a consequence had little documented lasting impact on the future. Contemporary accounts also show us men and women engaging in conversation and other oral cultural forms. For example, when John Lauder stayed for a time in the mid-1660s with a

French couple, he described his animated fireside conversations with his host and his wife and the occasions when Madame regaled him with fairy tales and legends peopled by kings, queens and werewolves. 'We have laughed no little at some.'[2] Yet historians traditionally have equated cultural importance with publication.

The following assumptions underlie much of the late twentieth-century writing on the role of women in the culture of early modern Britain. First, there is quite a narrow definition of culture as literary and artistic production and participation. This culture is interpreted as product rather than process. Women are quoted as complaining of their exclusion. For example, an Irish dialogue circulated in the late seventeenth century has a character named Fionuala lament women's relegation to the domestic sphere where they attend 'to our distaffs and spindles, even though many of us are no good about the house'.[3] Women were not active in public culture: when women wrote, painted, composed or performed this was largely in a private, often domestic, context. They were permitted to listen, even to read and write, but not to speak or publish abroad. Women were denied the opportunity to publish because of their sex. This is assumed to be the reverse of male patterns: men wrote, painted, composed and performed for a public audience, and were applauded for so doing.

Print and non-print culture

So what is wrong with this? Certainly, when compared with men, women published and painted very little for the public eye and they were banned from the stage for a large part of the period. And is not that the crucial issue – how much women contributed to the accepted, public canon of the arts and literature? Some historians (especially literary historians) don't think so. They have pointed to the fact that most literature – whether penned by male or female writers – of the sixteenth and seventeenth centuries was in fact circulated in manuscript and that only a tiny proportion went into print.[4] Women played their part as authors and poets. Men, too, frequently worked at least partially within a domestic context. The historians have also shown how women (and some men) played a different role in the production of literature, a crucial role that 'supported', 'facilitated' and 'encouraged' the production of, for example, a collection of poetry or helped spread the works of foreign authors or actually influenced the content of a poem or play or established the canon. Similarly they have shown how women provided an audience for works of literature and art and, because of their active networking, helped to stimulate wider interest and circulation.

This work by literary historians is extremely valuable because it has caused historians to stop in their tracks and ask what part women played in the contemporary culture rather than asking how many books or poems they wrote or how many drawings and paintings they made. Answering such questions, however, poses enormous problems because the processes involved were 'private' and by their very nature ephemeral. Historians have employed considerable ingenuity to reveal women's (and indeed men's) roles. To date, more emphasis has been laid upon women and literary culture but exciting work is being done in the areas of female involvement in art, design, decor, architecture and building, for example, by Rosemary Baird and Anne Laurence.[5] While emphasising the problems of the documentation, Anne Laurence argues that women 'used buildings and building projects to make statements to a wider world about their wealth, ancestry, social aspirations, taste, religious preferences and their ability to deal with directing builders, managing money and the other practical details that go with building projects'. Anne Laurence cites, among others, the interesting examples of Mary Sidney, Countess of Pembroke, 1561–1621 (Houghton Conquest, Ampthill, Bedfordshire); Lady Anne Clifford, 1590–1676 (castles in the north, memorials and churches such as that at Outhgill, Westmorland); Elizabeth Mitton Wilbraham, 1632–1705 (Weston Park, Shropshire/Staffordshire and Woodhey, Cheshire); Mary Somerset, the Duchess of Ormond, 1615–1685 (Dunmore Castle, Co. Kilkenny); and Lady Betty Hastings, 1682–1739 (Ledstone, Yorkshire). Rosemary Baird, in a book which details the building projects of many elite women, has described the 'glamorous furniture' collection assembled by Elizabeth Murray, Countess of Dysart, in the 1660s to furnish Ham House. When Elizabeth married the Duke of Lauderdale in 1672 they together embarked on an ambitious building programme. Notably, Elizabeth provided an apartment in the remodelled house designed to accommodate Charles II's Queen, Catherine of Braganza. Elizabeth selected the furnishings and hangings for the royal bedroom, including a bed made in Portugal, with supreme care. The Queen's tiny closet was intricately carved and given a parquet floor; the ceiling bore a painting of *Ganymede and the Eagle* by Verrio and on the walls were views by Thomas Wyck of various seaports. In the eighteenth century, Elizabeth Montagu (best known for her activities as a 'bluestocking') built 'a sensational new town house' and undertook 'impressive alterations to her country seat at Sandleford Priory in Berkshire'.[6]

Women on both sides of the Atlantic sometimes challenged the assumption that they were better suited to needlework than to penwork, and such work has often been seen by historians as a denial of intellect and as the very antithesis of culture, but scholars have shown how women often used their own embroidery skills for self-expression in writing and art.[7] In examining contemporary female diaries and autobiographies historians have often concentrated on the spirituality of women or their literary activities at the expense of their other cultural outlets. In the case of Lady Margaret Hoby, for example, few have noted the times she spent 'dyinge of stuff' and doing 'worke'.[8] On most afternoons she was engaged in a needlework project.[9] In Wales and England there are examples of sewing parties and collaborative effort. Not infrequently women wrote to other women about their needlework. At sewing bees they recited their own poetry, listened to readings and exchanged invaluable gossip. The importance of embroidery and other needlework in the culture of Europe and the British Isles has been generally acknowledged of late. No longer is it always brushed aside as 'the great feminine time filler'[10] or a mere 'ornamental accomplishment'.[11] There may, however, have been significant regional variations in the manifestations of this culture. Ruth Geuter has suggested differences in its nature between Wales and England, owing in large part to the isolation of the principality until the later seventeenth century.[12] The sampler was a distinctively English form and there are no Welsh examples in the sixteenth and early seventeenth centuries.[13] Much of the English tradition, however, passed seamlessly to the New World. New England farmers' daughters embroidered so-called courting pictures, which showed young gallants courting maidens in gardens within sight of a house.[14] Young women would spend time making decorative hangings for the bedrooms of their future marital home. We have already mentioned the five years that Mary Bulman of York, Maine, spent creating her extravagant vision of paradise on her valence, side panels, head cloth and coverlet.[15] Needlework samplers are perhaps the best-known products of such projects, surviving in some numbers for eighteenth-century England and the American colonies.[16] These were 'training pieces' where an unmarried woman learned her future skills as a housewife and mother. A sampler such as that made by sixteen-year-old Cynthia Burr in 1786 allowed the creator nevertheless to demonstrate her literacy, her morality, her observation, her sense of individual identity, and her creativity as well as her skills. Cynthia left some of the earliest depictions of the State House and Brown University in Rhode Island.[17] But some young women went much further than working a conventional, if exquisite, sampler.

They were able and willing to experiment. Prudence Punderson of Connecticut, who died at the age of twenty-six, left a series of three embroidered self-portraits showing herself in infancy (being rocked in her cradle by a black slave), as a young woman (with sketch book before her), and in death (her coffin by her side bearing the initials P. P.).[18] Colonial school girls, aged between ten and twenty, used their art and their embroidery lessons to become aware of their family identity and of their mortality – a collection of New England pupils' work survives depicting graveyards and the family headstones. The very earliest mourning scenes were embroidered, but in late eighteenth- and early nineteenth-century Connecticut this developed into an established form of water-colour art. By the early nineteenth century we can recover the names of some of these artists. Eunice Pinny in 1809 memorialised her friend, the Reverend Ambrose Todd of Simsbury, Connecticut. Elizabeth Hurlburt in around 1808 in a wonderfully painterly composition portrayed her grief-stricken family as they gathered about the family tombstones.[19] Amanda Vickery, in her study of eighteenth-century English gentlewomen, has shown how cultural activity and production of this kind was the norm in their households. In Revolutionary America women used their needlework skills in the patriotic cause: at public spinning bees, on miniature 'tape looms' and at sewing parties they produced home-spun cloth and obviated the need for English imports. Abigail Foote of Colchester, Connecticut, wove a fine bed cover and also wrote in her diary 'I carded two pounds of whole wool and felt nationaly.'[20]

For women – and Mary Queen of Scots and Bess of Hardwick seem the best-known early examples – the cultural outlet was not only in producing works of embroidery but also in selecting which works of art and tapestry to purchase and hang, which furniture to buy, which decorated ware to place on the table, which jewellery to have handcrafted and wear.[21] Not unimportant was the way in which such choices, commonly made by women (although in some marriages menfolk would join in making some selections),[22] affected the survival of particular works and the persistence of particular styles as the direct result of feminine decisions. Patronage was important not only in terms of the careers of given individuals but also in terms of their 'product'. The effects of such patronage are today only obvious in a very few elite examples (the Antwerp tapestries that the Duchess of Ormond hung at Dunmore Castle, Co. Kilkenny and which are now at Kilkenny Castle, for instance) but were to be seen, to a greater or lesser extent ephemerally, in the much humbler houses of the many women of the middling and even the lower sorts who influenced the look and feel of their domestic spaces.[23]

Indeed research into the decoration of early modern houses indicates that there were ample opportunities for women and men to make such an impact even when they were not among the wealthy. Homes, like churches and inns, were adorned with graffiti and wall paintings. The concept of 'writing on the wall' is foreign to us today, when graffiti writing is regarded as antisocial and abhorrent, and inscriptions on walls are only condoned in churches and public buildings (where interestingly they occur as 'memorials'). In Tudor and early Stuart times it was different. Thomas Tusser's *A Hundreth good pointes of husbandry, lately maried unto a hundreth good points of housewifery*, first published in 1570, contained patterns for 'poesies for the hall', 'posies for the parler', 'poses for the gest's chamber' and 'poesies for thine own bed chamber'. In 1584, at the end of the *Welspring of wittie conceited*, were printed 'Certeine worthie sentences, very meete to be written about a Bedchamber or to be set up in any convenient place in a house'. Such 'posies' were short poems or mottoes written on to something.[24] That contemporaries used these collections as source books for their home decor is evidenced by the discovery of selections from Tusser on the walls of two Hertfordshire farm houses, Pirton Grange, Pirton, and Ansell's End Farm, Kimpton. In both cases the selections are beautifully written and relate directly to emblems. The 'creativity' lay in the selections made. When the selection was written somewhere, the 'posy' was created. Contemporaries derived their sentences from other people's walls and also from manuscript collections. Thomas Coryate copied down verses he had seen written in and about houses on his travels.[25] Bacon sent Jane Lumley a copy of the sentences that he had had painted throughout the long gallery at Gorhambury, because he thought they would be useful to her.[26] What is important is not only that women probably had a role, possibly the dominant one, in choosing these poems from a printed or manuscript book but also that all the occupants of the home, male and female, and their guests were exposed regularly to these moralistic writings.[27] This was much more than decoration. It was serious communication of the moral values and religious beliefs of the household.

Contemporaries were encouraged to use the walls and windows of their houses for writing practice and expression. Indeed, Juliet Fleming argues that 'the whitewashed domestic wall' was 'the primary scene of writing in early modern England' and that this fact has 'consequences for current assumptions about the constitution and statistics of literacy and schooling...'[28] Its high point fell between the years 1530 and 1580. Children of both sexes were taught to read using alphabets written on the walls and were given charcoal and rocks to write and draw there. Adults too also wrote on the walls of their houses and were encouraged to do so. Frequently they 'copied' proverbs and sayings from eminent authors such as Erasmus, from emblem books like those of Whitney, and from collections of wise sentences such as those provided by Tusser and Fister.

On occasion, however, the relationship between the graffiti and the 'true' author is less certain. Proverbs and adages were part of the common store. The sentence 'In the morning earlye serve God devoutlie' occurs in a domestic setting in Oxford but a similar sentiment was recorded by the son of Katharine Dowe, dairywoman of Sibton Abbey, Suffolk, as one of his mother's wise sayings: 'Arise early/Serve God devoutly'.[29] Did the 'writers' of either of these sayings believe that they had thought them up independently or did they know that they were adapting or adopting the common wisdom? Probably it was the latter – just as I am aware that the saying 'If at first you don't succeed, try, try, try again', frequently repeated by my mother, was not of her own making. Yet these wise sayings (sentences) became theirs because they selected them as representative of their own views and values. Fleming also draws attention to a window engraving at Little Moreton Hall, Cheshire: 'Men can no more knowe a woman's mind by kaire / Than by her shadow judge what clothes she weare', which echoes lines in Donne's poem, 'Twickenham Gardens'. She observes that the engraving at Little Moreton Hall could be a free rendering of Donne's poem or Donne's poem could itself be using a contemporary saying as its basis. What was the relationship between Anne Clifford and the great number of 'sentences or sayings of remark' brought out of the 'rich storehouse of her memory' with which she festooned 'her wals, her bed, her hangings, and furniture'? The giver of her funeral sermon acknowledged that these were 'things new and old ... which she had read or learned out of authors' but emphasised that she had caused 'her servants to write them in papers, and her maids to pin them up'. Why had she done this? 'That she, or they, in time of their dressing, or as occasion served, might remember, and make their descants upon them.' What was the effect? She also had many books in her bedroom but rather 'it was dressed up with the flowers of a library'.[30]

So committed were the English and other Europeans of the sixteenth and early seventeenth centuries to graffiti writing that they also frequently used the walls and windows to record matters of importance to them, as they might also use the family Bible, a commonplace book, or a diary. This, however, was much more public a communication and one difficult to escape. The long galleries of English and Scots houses seem to have been used for didactic purposes in much the same way as the Athenian painted gallery. All who walked in them were expected to understand the language they 'spoke'.[31] In the early sixteenth century a genealogy of the Percy family and thirty-two proverbs were written on the walls and ceilings of New Lodge, Leckinfield. Similarly, in Scotland, the long gallery at Pinkie Castel, Musselborough, was adorned with coats of arms, emblems and Latin inscriptions. Joseph Hall's comments suggest that this fashion extended down the social ladder. So while Stoke Poges Manor House had a room filled with painted sayings such as 'Fear the Lord, Obey the Prince', a four-room cottage in Chalfont St Peter also had an inscription in black lettering, 'When any thing thou takest in hand to do or enterpryde / fyrst markewell the fynall end there of that maye aryse. Fear God.'[32]

Painters were employed to produce much of the wall writing in long galleries but ordinarily both men and women also expressed themselves creatively on their walls and windows. One of Queen Elizabeth I's poems was etched on the walls of the palace at Woodstock, Oxfordshire. Richard Braithwaite recorded window etchings made by four 'brave resolved women'. The fashion for writing on windows with specially made pointed writing rings and on walls with coloured stones, candle smoke and charcoal meant that Spenser noted that the English court was covered with 'posies'.[33] So natural an activity was this that when she was delivered from house arrest at Woodstock, Princess Elizabeth was said by John Foxe to have etched in the window with her ring 'Much suspected by me / Nothing proved can be. Quoth Elizabeth, Prisoner.'[34] Lady Jane Grey, with no ring at her disposal, used a pin to moralise about her plight on a window in the Tower of London.[35] Individuals of both sexes would sometimes communicate 'by graffiti': the best-known example of this type of window-writing dialogue is that supplied by Sir Walter Raleigh's 'Fain would I climb yet fear I to fall', which was answered by Queen Elizabeth's 'If thy heart fail thee, climb not at all.'[36]

These practices have significance not only for our understanding of adult literacy in the period but also for the ways in which values and knowledge were communicated and recalled in contemporary culture. The wall and the window might act as the main site of written communication or, being relatively ephemeral because from time to time the wall would be whitewashed over, as a staging post to the permanent commonplace book kept by so many. Conversely it might begin life in a printed work, migrate to someone's commonplace book, and thence to another's wall or window. When placed about the house, the sentiments could be remembered by the device of recalling where they were written.[37] In his *Positions . . . for the training up of children*, schoolmaster Richard Mulcaster advised, in imitation of a classical idea, 'If the nine muses and Apollo their president were painted upon a wall . . . they would serve for places of memorie'.[38] John Willis's *Art of memory* expanded upon such ideas in 1621.

The function of 'writing on the wall' as being much more than aesthetic in purpose is reinforced by what scholars have uncovered regarding emblematic devices as a prominent form of communication in Elizabethan and early Stuart times. Contemporaries were accustomed to thinking in terms of allegory: John Bunyan's *Pilgrim's Progress* is an excellent but late example of this mode of thought. Rosemary Freeman's work on emblem books shows how allegorical devices and short poems interacted to convey 'truths' to contemporaries. The mere sight of an emblem would conjure up in the mind of the beholder the wise sentiment with which it had been linked, so that in effect the emblem became the sentiment. Contemporaries read emblem books, then they repeated emblems in their wall paintings and commonplace books and in the embroidered clothes they wore and the hangings that adorned their homes. Much of the apparent decoration present in Tudor and Stuart homes served in fact a much more serious purpose.

Historians such as Ruth Geuter (with her important work on Wales) have begun to reveal the ways in which women used their ability to create 'works of art' as a way to influence their lives and those of their families to the good. At the highest levels Mary Queen of Scots sought to win Elizabeth I's 'friendship' by gifts of embroidery, for example.

For the historian of women (as opposed to the historian of culture), of equal importance must be the value that women attached to their cultural life. In the Old South of the United States a plantation owner's wife, Sarah Gayle, pictured her young self as 'a wild and happy being, whose dreams of the world were awakened by the reading of novels and poetry'.[39] Was this a new phenomenon? An American phenomenon? An elite phenomenon? Or was it one characteristic of all periods and of all social groups?

The printed word

Let us begin by examining the more traditional view that women were not cultural players because they were prohibited from publishing on account of their sex. Some prominent male authors certainly equated chastity with silence. Thomas Becon, an English preacher, wrote: 'let her kepe silence. For there is nothinge that doth so much commend, avaunce, set for the, adourne, decke, trim, and garnish a maid, as silence.'[40] In Elizabethan times, Thomas Bentley threatened damnation to women who spoke publicly: 'There is nothing that becommeth a maid better than sobernes, silence, shamefastnes, and chastity, both of bodie and mind. For these things being once lost, shee is no more a maid, but a strumpet in the sight of God.'[41] This viewpoint was rooted not only in a belief that women should be meek and humble but also in a conviction that only those with authority should be heard and heeded. Publishing ideas and opinions was tantamount to speaking and to claiming authority for one's views and an audience to heed them. Here women were held in the same regard as males of low social status, who were also denied a voice and an audience. Teaching women and poor men to read but not to write was an effective way of silencing them. Martin Billingsley advised teaching women just to copy rather than to write: women, according to him, had such poor memories that they were incapable of engaging in independent authorship.[42] That men bothered to write condemning the ventures of women into writing and especially into print suggests, however, that not everyone accepted this position and that some women ignored such advice.

It perhaps had the effect of making women defensive and apologetic. In the 1980s Hannay argued that women's publishing activity in most areas was prohibited. That this was true was evidenced by the fact that any woman who did publish was painfully conscious of defying a prescribed role, stressed her modesty and clearly had to overcome as a 'primary obstacle' the 'societal norm which she has internalised'. Even a woman who seemingly openly challenged her husband's assumptions about her proper behaviour, Elizabeth Carey or Carew, meditated in an early published work, *Mariam*, the problem of the appropriate audience for a wife's spoken or written thoughts. The chorus suggests that a wife's words should be heard by 'none but one', who might be her husband (the 'owner' of her mind as well as her body, according to Carey's chorus), God or even herself.[43] There is some evidence that women did internalise these values, or at least that they acknowledged social opposition to female publication and used the modesty topos as a ruse to circumvent it. For example, in the seventeenth century Lucy Hutchinson, although she wrote quite extensively, still saw writing as no business for a woman. In her dedication to her translation of Lucretius she apologised for attempting 'things out of my own sphere' and she was similarly dismissive of the memoirs of her husband as a 'rude draft' drawn by 'an unskilful hand'.[44] It was an attitude that crossed the Atlantic. The American poetess Anne Bradstreet wrote in a preface to a book of poems written in 1650: 'I am not obnoxious to each carping tongue, / who sayes my hand a needle better fits / A Poet's Pen all scorne, I should thus wrong . . .'[45] Quality publication by a woman was considered so exceptional that in the Elizabethan age Sir John Harington, for example, believed that Mary Sidney's version of the Psalms had been produced by her chaplain, despite overwhelming evidence to the contrary, because 'it was more than a woman's skill to express the sense so right as she hath done in her verse'.[46]

What effect did the poor publishing record of women have upon female authorship? Scholars working on the cusp of literature and history have noted that, because of this lack of a presence in the literary canon, women writers have not only gone unnoticed but have also had no traditions upon which to build and no female models to imitate. It meant that women relied almost entirely upon models for production from within their own family and social circle, which might or might not be culturally active. There are a few indications that, for example, when a husband kept a diary or journal, so did his wife. This might be particularly the case if the journal had a spiritual purpose. For instance, two ardent Covenanters from Peebles and Dumfries, William Veitch (1640–1722) and his wife kept diaries.[47] Anne Finch, Countess of Winchilsea, published her poems anonymously in 1713 but knew of no female predecessors except those from Scripture. Such isolation was most apparent if a woman were denied access to a good library of printed books. It perhaps had a detrimental effect on women's creativity and their ability to break away from male literary models.

Women, however, did establish a practice of publishing in some defined areas: works of translation (where the views expressed were those of another, usually male, author) and works of religion, closely reflecting the Word of God. One humanist, John Florio, viewed translation as an inferior activity, suitable for women who had no voice of their own.

To argue that women did not publish at all, therefore, would be absurd. Moreover, women did in fact penetrate areas in which some men would have liked to have seen them banned. They engaged in comedic writing,[48] reflected on the world around them and commented on dangerous political subjects,[49] and even entered into the debate about women's public role.[50] Elizabeth Carey, whose husband Sir Henry wished her to be his quiet, compliant wife, was in 1627/8 the first woman to write a history play and her large dramatic output won the esteem of Michael Drayton and John Marston. Earlier, John Davies had urged her to publish *Mariam* which she had written between 1602 and 1604. She published the work in 1613.[51] Her intellectual prominence in the Great Tew circle of male and female literati, which she helped to bind together in her own person, is renowned. Interestingly, her life and work were memorialised in 1655 by her daughter, Lady Anne Carey, later Dame Clementina, who was a Benedictine nun.

Bold Margaret Fell contradicted the received view that women should be silent. Some women even stormed the bastion of the theatre.[52] And occasionally a woman is to be found actively furthering commercial dissemination of the printed word: for instance, Isabella Whitney earned her living as printer in London in the 1570s and published two volumes of cheap poetry.

Nevertheless, women's published writing largely falls into three areas: works of translation; works of religion; works of child rearing. Published translations included Lady Anne Coke Bacon's, *Fouretene Sermons of Barnadine Ochyne* (1550); and Lady Mary Sidney's translation of Philippe de Mornay, *A Discourse of Life and Death*, (1592). Historians have demonstrated that women, far from simply translating the words of male authorities, mediated the text in such a way as to ensure that their own voices were heard.[53] They expressed their own beliefs and preferences through their choice of works to translate: for example, Margaret Beaufort, Countess of Richmond and Derby, translated from French into English Thomas à Kempis's *Imitation of Christ* in 1504 and Jacobus Gruitroede's Carthusian treatise, *The mirroure of golde for the synfull soule*, in 1506. Jane Lumley's partial manuscript translation of Euripides's *Iphigena in Aulis* in about 1550 consciously drew a parallel with the 'martyrdom' of Lady Jane Grey.[54] Women found public expression in works of religion and meditation, for example, Anne Bradstreet, Mary Sidney, Lady Eleanor Davies, Lady Anne Halkett.[55] Notable works on child-rearing were Dorothy Leigh's *The Mother's Blessing*, 1621; and Elizabeth Clinton's *The Countesse of Lincolne's Nurserie* (1622) Women also found it permissible, on occasion, to express their emotions in print: a good example would be Anne Cecil de Vere's outpouring on the death of her baby son.[56]

These were areas in which women, as wives and mothers and mistresses of households, had some claim upon. They were accorded a special role in the upbringing of babies and children and in the religious life of their households and families.[57] The published translations that they made had for the most part a religious application. It is worth noting also that when a woman did promote a particular cause in print she liked to cite the approval of some male or supernatural authority. Bessie Clerksone's *Conflict in Conscience* was published posthumously in 1631 by her minister, William Livingstone. Lady Clinton's advocacy of breastfeeding was underwritten by Thomas Lodge.[58] Published letters to patrons, real and potential, served both as flattering dedications and as acknowledgements of approval.

As a percentage of work published in the period 1500–1760 female publication was tiny – even tinier if we select the period 1500–1650. Special circumstances could be quoted for almost every example of female publication. If printed publication were the sole criterion by which women's contribution to culture was measured then that contribution would be infinitesimally small.

Women as literary patrons

Women patrons were common throughout the courts of medieval and early modern Britain and Europe, often conjointly with their husbands and sometimes independently. In England, for example, one thinks of Sir George Carey and his wife who were patrons of both Shakespeare and Spenser and their relative, Barbara Gamage, who married Sir Robert Sidney, who was patron in her own right of a number of literary works.[59]

As scholars have observed, it was natural that this role should have fallen to noble and royal womenfolk when their husbands were preoccupied with war.[60] Perhaps the reverse was also true, that as men became less obsessed with war, so they assumed a more prominent role in patronage of the arts. There appears to have been acceptance of women's role as literary patrons in Gaelic society in Ireland. Bardic poems frequently mentioned female patrons. In addition about 10 per cent of obituaries (which were written down to the late sixteenth century) were of female patrons. The daughter of Cuchonnacht Mor Mac Cuchonnacht Macguire was said to be 'religious, hospitable, charitable and a patron'. This role as patron was, however, very dependent upon the status and wealth of the women's husbands or fathers.

Women as printers and publishers

The prominent role that women, often widows, played in the establishment and development of printing presses in the eighteenth-century American colonies seems to suggest lively female interest in this area, although sometimes the evidence is difficult to interpret. Eleven women, mostly widows, supported themselves as printers before the American Revolution. For example, Diana Nuthead, widow of the Maryland printer William Nuthead, moved the press to Annapolis the new seat of Maryland government in the mid-1690s and became printer to that government. However, she signed the papers with her mark, which fact may or may not indicate that she was illiterate and possibly that she provided the business acumen but relied entirely upon others to do the typesetting. In his will of 1750 the Virginia printer William Parks directed his widow and his son-in-law to complete the printing of the Laws of Virginia that he had begun. Elizabeth Timothy when widowed took over the *South Carolina Gazette* in the mid-1730s and ran it as a flourishing concern until her son was of age to assume the reins in the 1740s. Forty-five-year-old mother of six, widow Anne Catherine Green, assumed control of the *Maryland Gazette* in April 1767 and became printer to the colony. She was paid at the same rate as her husband by the Maryland Assembly. She published not only the *Gazette* but also an annual almanac and various political pamphlets and satires.[61] Evidence concerning Clementina Rind's tenure at the *Virginia Gazette* in the 1770s shows her making informed decisions about items submitted for publication, specifically refusing to publish some items because she feared libel suits. Mary Catherine Goddard, who ran the *Maryland Journal* from 1774 to 1784, was described by contemporaries as 'an expert and correct compositor of types'. She also ran a bookstore and acted as postmistress in Baltimore.[62] Cornelia Smith Bradford (d.1755) had been the second wife of a Philadelphia printer, Andrew Bradford. She persuaded her husband to leave her the printing press and also his share of the Durham iron works and a good deal of real estate. Within a week of his death in 1742 the *American Weekly Mercury* was up and running once more. Cornelia was the paper's sole editor and printer for a period between 1744 and 1746. She did miscellaneous printing and bookbinding and stationery sales until shortly before her death.[63] At the very least such women became gatekeepers to these vehicles of cultural expression.

Women and the visual arts

If few women published their written works to a wide public, fewer still were those who painted for a public audience. Joan Palmer Carlisle (1606–1679), daughter of William Palmer, an official in the royal parks, was exceptional: she was probably the first female portrait painter and, to wit, the first female painter to attract the praise of contemporary male artists of the first rank and of royal patrons.[64] Perhaps significantly she married the poet and dramatist Lodowick Carlile, Gentleman of the Bows to Charles I and one of the Keepers of Richmond Park, in 1626, and he sponsored her artistic endeavour. Her *Stag Hunt* shows Lodowick, a keen huntsman, with her and their children, James and Penelope, and their good friend, Justinian Isham. The painting has been regarded as a charming precursor of the eighteenth-century genre of conversation pieces in a landscape.[65] She was not a professional painter (in the sense of being dependent upon painting for her livelihood) but she was acknowledged as an expert in copying the works of Italian masters and reproducing them in miniature, and had many influential patrons. She was also an original portraitist who was heavily influenced by Van Dyck's work. A story goes that Charles I so admired her work that he presented to her and her teacher Van Dyck an ultramarine valued at £500. Certainly Sir William Sanderson paid tribute to her ability in his 1658 survey of contemporary art, *Graphice. The Excellent Art of Painting*, when he observed 'in Oyal Colours we have a vertuous example in that worthy Artist, Mrs Carlisle'. There are other examples. Mary Beale (1633–97) supported her family by portrait painting. Artemesia Gentileschi (1593–1653) and Angelica Kauffman (1741–1807) were foreigners who made a living from painting. Susannah Penelope Rose was an accomplished miniaturist. She was the daughter of the Princesses Mary and Anne's drawing master, Richard Gibson, may have been taught by Cooper, and by the 1690s she was being given commissions, albeit unpaid.[66] Mrs Cawardine (c.1730–c.1800) also took commissions for limning.[67]

If we delve beneath the thin layer of painting for 'public consumption', however, we can see that elite and even some middling-sort women were expected to be able to sketch, draw and paint. (There is little suggestion that painting was regarded as an exclusively male sphere or that men were patronising in their attitude to female art.) These were some of the accomplishments of an educated gentlewoman, especially in the eighteenth century, but also in the seventeenth. Alexander Browne taught several ladies, including Mrs Elizabeth Pepys, to draw. Pepys noted her progress in limning and praised one of her paintings as 'mighty finely done'. Mary Evelyn had made a miniature of Raphael's *Entombment of Christ*, which she was permitted to present to Charles II. In 1701 old John Evelyn showed the visiting Yorkshire antiquary Ralph Thoresby drawings, etchings, miniatures and other paintings in oils made by his wife Mary and by their daughter and youngest child Susanna (b.1669). Susanna may have attended a drawing master on a trip to London in 1685/6 and was almost certainly taught by a professional at some time thereafter. She may have been taught to paint in oils by one of the artists who made portraits of her family, and to paint miniatures by Susannah Rose. She was encouraged by her parents in her art and, on her father's advice, attended a picture auction in Tunbridge Wells in 1689. She specialised in portraits but also executed still lifes, biblical paintings and other works. In common with most amateur artists she copied most from other painters' works and her copies either adorned her home or were given to relatives and friends.[68] In 1694 she copied, on her father's advice, Matthew Dixon's portrait of Evelyn's friend, Margaret Godolphin. Then she progressed to making several copies of a painting of Robert Boyle.[69] Twice-married Mary Waller More (fl.1670s) made no fewer than nine copies of Holbein's portrait of Thomas Cromwell (one of which she donated to the Bodleian Library, Oxford, in 1674 under the misapprehension that it represented Thomas More). A portrait of the historian John Stow at St Andrew's Undershaft, her parish church, has also been attributed to More. It was also noted that 'in the family are her and her husband's portraits by herself'.[70] It appears that a sketch of her son, Richard Waller, that accompanies his manuscript translation of the *Aeneid* could be by Mary.[71] Lady Anne Killigrew painted a self-portrait circa 1686.[72] Lady Burlington painted, for example, a portrait in oils of her daughter.[73] Cassandra Willoughby also copied portraits of family members and seems to have given them away as gifts, much as today we might distribute copies of photographs. Although much has been made of Mary Beale as a 'professional artist', in fact this daughter of a Suffolk rector began in the same way as Cassandra as one who painted not commercially but for family and friends such as the Twisdens, Pierreponts, Cavendishes, Holles, Stillingfleets and Tillotsons. Mary took on commissions only from the middle of the 1660s onwards.[74] (Perhaps many of the anonymous Restoration and Georgian portraits of middling and gentle families were the work of 'amateur' but proficient wives and daughters.) The act of giving away a portrait drew the recipient into the close circle of the Duchess and bound them together.[75] Cassandra also sketched the family home, and was at times very self-critical.[76] An inventory of Cannons, her country home, and a house in St James's Square, her London house, in 1725 indicates that she continued this activity when she was married.[77] Such young women as she were tutored in drawing, painting, music and dancing. It is interesting to speculate on the functions of these 'skills'. Musical prowess enabled a wife to entertain her household and to engage with the interests of others; dancing meant that she might participate in the social round as well as in entertainment, but what of sketching, drawing and painting? These were skills of recording: in an age without cameras, the ability to sketch and record must have been highly valued. For those young women associated with male members of the Royal Society, mere copying was not enough: accurate representations of what and who they observed at first hand were particularly prized.[78] One of Cassandra's paintings was of the Duke's youngest sister as she approached death.[79] Additionally they were skills which enabled women to beautify their homes and make them aesthetically pleasing. Often they used their skills to instruct and to enhance the spiritual life of the home, with visual renderings of Bible and classical stories. On occasion they might employ their skills for more subversive ends.[80]

Indirectly we can see women, young and old, transferring patterns and pictures on to the loom or on to canvas in order to turn them into tapestries and embroidered coverings and hangings. These were activities with a long pedigree that stretched throughout the British Islands at the highest social levels.[81] A fourteenth-century Welsh poem by Iolo Goch pictured Sir Hywell Fwyall of Cricieth's wife and her ladies weaving a standard adorned with fleur-de-lis in bright-coloured silk. Another by a Flintshire poet praised a needlewoman for her beauty and her skill in embroidering birds in fine silk 'as instruction for your young ones'. During the reign of Edward IV Lewys Glyn Cothi asked Anne of Caerleon to make him a bed curtain (a tapestry):

... *a cloth full of designs*
Figures of saplings, of foliages and images
Figures of the birds of the earth in the south, of lions
Below are stags and cross designs
... *The figures of Mary and the twelve apostles seated in thrones are there,*
The figures of saints and Jesus, the figures of female saints.[82]

The tradition was seemingly, however, especially rich in England and France. Mary of Scotland and Bess of Hardwick, with their ladies-in-waiting, spent long hours during Mary's imprisonment creating elaborate panels with designs of their own creation. Amongst other things they accurately copied emblems and animals from 'Icones Animalium' (1562).[83] There was also a propensity for creating visual narratives. Sixteenth- and seventeenth-century English gentlewomen spent long hours embroidering the stories of Biblical heroines such as Judith and Esther, surrounding them with exquisitely rendered images of trees, plants and birds. During the period of the civil war some women created embroidered accounts of events and portraits of political figures, thus expressing their own political allegiances. Sixteenth- and seventeenth-century English women busied themselves creating elaborate samplers of their art, but this tradition seemingly did not spread into Wales. Indeed historians of Wales have suggested that 'decorative domestic needlework apparently played relatively little part in home life in Wales' before the eighteenth century.[84]

There is also mounting evidence of the role women played as patrons of, and customers for, the visual arts. This is especially true, it seems, of portraiture. It was not solely or even mainly the grand set-piece portrait that elite women sponsored. The miniature was as treasured by sixteenth- and seventeenth-century women as the family photograph is today and the exchange of such miniatures was commonplace. So Anne Clifford, Countess of Dorset, had had her own portrait painted purposely to send it to her mother and anticipated her mother awaiting the visit of the peripatetic limnist in 1615 and reciprocating her gift.

I have sent you by Ralph my picture done in little, which some says is very like me, and others says it doth me rather wrong than flatters me. I know you will except the shadow of her house substance is come from yourself. I hope you will requite me with the same kindness and let me have yours when either you come up to London or when so ever any that can draught a picture comes in to those parts where now you are.[85]

A century or so later Cassandra, Duchess of Chandos, was sending family portraits by well-known artists to her friends at home and abroad (and, as we have noted, copying them herself). The popularity of portraiture among women seems to have crossed the Atlantic. In 1734 a widow, Mary Roberts, advertised in the *South Carolina Gazette* as a 'face painter'. In the same magazine in 1772 it was noted that a lady had arrived who was the niece and pupil of the Queen's portrait painter, 'the celebrated Miss Reid', who intended to follow 'the art of painting portraits in crayons in Charles Town'. In April 1773 Mrs Bambridge, wife of a portrait painter, was advertised as 'a very ingenious miniature paintress'.[86]

Evidence of change

There is some evidence that women were playing a more overt role in public culture in the later seventeenth century and in the eighteenth century and that this role was acknowledged by contemporaries. At the turn of the century there was particularly noticeable female activity in the theatre.

In all probability our brief narrative diversion should begin with the 'career' of Margaret Cavendish. Margaret Lucas was the youngest of the eight children of a wealthy Essex family. In 1642 she moved with her widowed mother to Oxford and there she became Maid of Honour to Queen Henrietta Maria. When she followed the Queen to exile in Paris in 1644 she met and married William Cavendish, Duke of Newcastle. In 1653 Margaret began publishing her own work under her own name with *Poems and Fancies* and *Philosophical Fancies*. Later, while she was in exile in Holland, her husband supported and encouraged her to publish her *The World's Olio* and *Nature's Pictures*, prose miscellanies which indicated her adventurous determination to engage in what had formerly been masculine genres (such as the utopian) and particularly in discourses around philosophy and the new science. Indeed Cavendish's works were regarded by many contemporaries as so masculine that they could not have been her own work. If she had written these independent and outrageous works herself (in some of which she contested the ideas of eminent men in the Royal Society and of Descartes and in which she challenged the sexual subjugation of women to the monarchy of men) then 'there are many soberer people in Bedlam; I'll swear her friends are much to blame to let her go abroad'.[87]

Mary Pix was born in 1666, the daughter of an Oxfordshire clergyman, Roger Griffith, and his wife, Lucy Berriman. Fairly typically of young women of her class she seems to have had little formal education but was well versed in poetry, English and French drama and the French language. At the age of eighteen, in 1684, she married a London merchant tailor, George Pix, whose family was associated with Hawkshurst in Kent, where the couple's only daughter was buried in 1690. Between 1696 and 1706 Mary had a career as a successful professional playwright of twelve plays – six comedies and six tragedies. She also produced a romantic novel, poems in *The Nine Muses* (elegies published in 1700 by women poets to mark Dryden's death), and a verse-novelette, *Violenta, or The Rewards of a Virtue*, an adaptation of one of the tales of Boccaccio's *Decameron*. She was an important figure in the theatrical community, being a friend of the writers William Congreve, Catherine Trotter, Delarivier Manley and Susanna Centlivre, and close to the most famous actress of the day, Elizabeth Barry. In terms of quality her works do not compare with those of Susanna Centlivre and Aphra Behn, but her importance 'lies in the quantity of her output, her dedication to her self-appointed role as a professional playwright, and the success that she enjoyed amongst audiences of her day'. Her dramatisation of English history perhaps had a lasting and deleterious influence upon female understanding of the Wars of the Roses, for instance, as in her tragedy *Queen Catharine, or The Ruines of Love* (1698), she reduced the wars to a love quarrel between Edward IV, Owen Tudor and Catherine of France. Her comedies were more convincing, being full of action, intrigue, stage business, and surprises. She was not a feminist and often her female characters seem to reinforce the stereotypical but it has been argued that she did much for women in the English theatre, both because she was a prominent professional playwright and because her plays revolved around female characters caught up in roles of depth and fun.[88] Her works contributed to that acceptance of theatre attendance for elite women that had occurred by the post-Restoration period,[89] when it was ladies who watched the plays.

The work of Susanna Centlivre is somewhat better known because of her apparent status as a protofeminist. Susanna Freeman seems to have been born circa 1670 and brought up in Ireland, although she spent her adult life in London and Holbeach. She may have begun her association with the stage disguised as a boy in a band of strolling players. Her first marriage was to an army officer and her second to a court chef, Joseph Centlivre. Although she was an actress, it is as a dramatist that she is best remembered, for some of her many plays were still popular in the nineteenth century and others had an international audience. Not only was she a crusader for women's rights, and deplored the fact that some women discouraged female writers, but she was also overtly political.

But it is Aphra Behn who is most commonly recognised as the archetypal (and first) professional female dramatist and novelist of Restoration England. From 1670 onwards she produced a large number of stage plays, poems, novels and stories, many of which retained their popularity well after her death.[90] In her novel *Oronoco* (1688) she drew upon her childhood experiences in the 1650s in the household of the Governor of Surinam. Her knowledge of languages presumably made her useful as a government spy during the Anglo-Dutch Wars. She returned to England penniless and made her living entirely from her writing. Her most successful play was *The Rover* (1677) and her collected works, which comprised many plays and novels, lengthy poems and translations from the French, remained extremely popular at the start of the eighteenth century.

Conclusion

Until relatively recently, historians dismissed the cultural and intellectual activity of women on the grounds that little of the published work of the period – books, plays, poetry, large-scale works of art and music – was produced by women. Now historians are revising this view in the light of an appreciation of the relationship between public work that formed the literary canon on the one hand and manuscript works by both men and women that formed the large part of shared literary activity as a whole. The increasing emphasis upon female proficiency in drawing and painting and its use in the consolidation of extended family ties provides an intriguing example of the ways in which 'cultural participation' could straddle the supposed divide between public and private.[91] Moreover, some women certainly did make a contribution to the public arena. At the start of our period there were a few acceptable avenues – works of devotion and translation, for example – while other areas were contested by contemporaries, and women who trespassed into them felt obliged to defend themselves. By the end of the period women were contributing more widely although there were still boundaries that could only be crossed with difficulty and generally by mavericks. In the Americas, colonial women to a great extent shared English culture. It was not until the eighteenth century that there was sufficient population in the colonies to support the kind of cultural environment common to London, Edinburgh and Dublin and to several provincial cities in England. The undoubted prominence of some women in the establishment of American newspapers and printing houses is at least suggestive of female interest in the world of print and of female involvement as gatekeepers of cultural outlets.

Notes

1 Anne Bradstreet, 1615, cited in Margaret W. Ferguson, 1996, Renaissance concepts of the "woman writer"', 1996, p. 153.

2 Extracts from the Journal of Sir John Lauder in J. G. Fyfe and R. S. Rait (1928) pp. 195–7.

3 M. W. Ferguson, 1996 'Renaissance concepts of the "woman writer"', p. 154 describing the work *Parliament na mBhan* (The Parliament of Women).

4 See, for instance, M. J. M. Ezell (1987) pp. 62–100.

5 For the first fruits of her work see A. Laurence (2003) pp. 293–303. Also see R. Baird (2004).

6 R. Baird (2004 pbk edn) pp. 99–106; 188–219.

7 R. Parker (1984).

8 J. Moody (1998) p. 80.

9 Ibid p. 4.

10 S. Mendelson (1985) p. 190.

11 B. Hill (2001) p. 55.

12 See, for example, V. R. Geuter (2000) pp. 167–80.

13 Ibid pp. 160–61.

14 S. B. Swan (1977).

15 See Chapter 6: Attitudes to marriage.

16 G. Krueger (1978) figures 21, 22, 23.

17 Cynthia Burr's Sampler, 1786, Museum of Art, Rhode Island School of Design.

18 Prudence Punderson, 'The First, second, and last scene of mortality', c.1780, Connecticut Historical Society.

19 D. M. Lucey (2005) pp. 76–7.

20 Ibid pp. 58–9.

21 Bess of Hardwick. See Mary S. Lovell, *Bess of Hardwick, First Lady of Chatsworth*, 2005; David N. Durant, *Bess of Hardwick. Portrait of an Elijabethan Dynast*, 1977; and National Trust, *Of Household Stuff. The 1601 Inventories of Bess of Hardwick*, 2001.

22 See, for instance, the joint shopping trips of James and Mary Brydges in the 1680s, to buy drapes.

23 For the Antwerp tapestries example see Anne Laurence (2003) p. 298.

24 They are equivalent to the posy rings and knives which were inscribed with mottoes such as 'Love me and leave me not', William Shakespeare, *The Merchant of Venice*, Act 5, scene 1, 147–50.

25 Thomas Coryate, *Coryats crudités*, 1611.

26 R. P. Sorlien (1976) p. 124.

27 J. Fleming (2001) pp. 29–31.

28 Ibid p. 50.

29 P. M. Johnstone (1932) pp. 75–100; R. Dowe, *A Dairy booke for good huswives*, 1588; both cited in Fleming (2001) p. 46.

30 B. Lewalski (1992) pp. 139–40, citing Edward Rainebow, *A Sermon preached at the interrment of Anne, Countess of Pembroke*, London, 1677, p. 48.

31 See also E. McCutcheon (1977) p. 18.

32 F. Reader, 'Tudor mural paintings in the lesser houses of Bucks', *Archaeological Journal*, 89, 1932, pp. 116–73, p. 120.

33 See J. Fleming (2001) pp. 55–6 for other examples. See H. C. Smith (1908) p. 260 for writing rings.
34 John Foxe, *Actes and monuments*, 1563, p. 1714; cited in J. Fleming (2001) p. 56.
35 Foxe, *Acts and monuments*, p. 922; cited in J. Fleming (2001) p. 56.
36 Thomas Fuller, *History of the worthies of England*, 1662.
37 Michael Bath (1995), 'Alexander Seton's painted gallery', p. 107.
38 Richard Mulcaster, *Positions . . . for the training up of children*, 1581, Aa2v.
39 E. Fox-Genovese (1988) p. 3.
40 S. Hull (1982) p. 142.
41 Thomas Bentley, *A monument of matrones*, quoted in Hull (1982) p. 142.
42 Martin Billingsley, *The Pen's excellencie*.
43 Margaret W. Ferguson, 1996, 'Renaissance concepts of the "woman writer"', p. 157.
44 J. Sutherland (ed.), 1973, Lucy Hutchinson (1618), *Memoir*, pp. 16–17.
45 Cited in Margaret W. Ferguson, 1996, 'Renaissance concepts of the "woman writer"', p. 153.
46 M. P. Hannay (1985) p. 2.
47 Extracts from the Memoirs of William Veitch of Peebles and Dumfries in J. G. Fyfe and R. S. Rait (1928) pp. 297–301.
48 Margaret Cavendish, *Nature's pictures . . .* (1656).
49 Elizabeth Poole, *A Vision: Wherein is manifested the disease and cure of the kingdom* (1648) (in which she advised against the execution of Charles 1 on the basis of her own understanding of divorce law). For this see S. Trill *et al.* (1997) pp. 164ff.
50 Rachel Speght, *A Mouzell for Melotomus* (1617); Ester Sowernam *Ester hath hang'd Haman* (1617); Anon., *The Mid-wives Just Petition* (1643); Margaret Fell, *Women's speaking justified, proved and allowed of by the scriptures* (1666).
51 Elizabeth Carey, *The Tragedie of Mariam, the faire queene of Iewry: written by that learned, vertuous, and truly noble ladie E. C.*, 1613.
52 For example, Aphra Behn and Margaret Cavendish.
53 Betty S. Travitsky (1996) pp. 234–66.
54 British Library MS Reg. 15A.
55 M. Wynne-Davies (1998) pp. 263, 289, 146ff, 266ff.

56 For this and other examples see Wynne-Davies (1998) pp. 273–5; 286; 275; 340–1; 341–46, 267.

57 See Chapter 13.

58 See S. Trill *et al.* (1997) p. 119.

59 Josephine A. Roberts (1983) p. 5.

60 A. M. Lucas (1983) pp. 170–79.

61 J. C. Spruill (1938) pp. 263–6.

62 Ibid p. 267.

63 E. T. James *et al.* (1971) Vol. 1, pp. 219–20.

64 Anne Crawford *et al.* (1983) p. 78.

65 O. Millar (1927).

66 C. Gibson-Wood (2003) pp. 245–6.

67 That is, miniature painting.

68 See Gibson-Wood, pp. 233–54.

69 Ibid pp. 242–4.

70 H. Walpole, *Anecdotes of painting in England*, 1762–1763, Vol. 3, pp. 135–6, cited in J. M. Ezell (1987) pp. 145–6.

71 BL, Add. MS 27347, cited in Ezell (1987) p. 148.

72 For a reproduction see M. Prior (1985) plate 18.

73 Walpole (1762–1763).

74 See Bodleian Library, Rawlinson 80 572, Entries in the journal of Charles Beale in William Lilly's Almanack, 1677 and Charles Beale's Notebook, 1680/1, Library and Heinz Archive of the National Portrait Gallery, London, MS 9535, which relate to the later period. Extracts from earlier notebooks occur in George Vertue *Note Books, Volumes 1–V*, Walpole Society, Volumes 18, 20, 22, 24, 26. For more detail see Tabitha Barber's introduction to David Dewing (ed.), *Mary Beale (1632/3–1699) Portrait of a seventeenth-century painter, her family and studio*, Geffrye Museum Trust, 1999, especially p. 16.

75 There are other examples of women giving portraits to friends. See, for example, HEH, HM6660 Suffolk Papers, Letter from Thomas Killigrew to Henrietta Hobart Howard Countess of Suffolk, c.1715: 'pray let me know madam where the painter lives that drew the picture you gave of your self to Mrs Bellenden'.

76 NLCS, Copy Letter Book of Cassandra, Duchess of Chandos, 1713–1735, No. 161, p. 84. To my nephew [Francis] Willoughby 14 Nov 1723.

77 HEH, ST 83.

78 Mary Beale's husband, Charles, as a member of the Royal Society and their friends included other fellows such as Thomas Flatman and Samuel Woodforde. Cassandra Willoughby was the only daughter of Francis Willoughby, authority on birds and fishes and fellow of the Royal Society. She married her cousin James Brydges who also belonged to, and frequently attended, the Society. For the Society's emphasis on accurate representation see Abraham Cowley's prefatory verses to Thomas Sprat's *History of the Royal Society*.

79 NLCS, Copy Letter Book of Cassandra, Duchess of Chandos, 1713–1735, No. 437, p. 162 To Sister Chamberlayne 8 July 1735.

80 See R. Parker (1984) *passim*.

81 See, for example, L. Ballard (1991); E. Boyle (1966) pp. 52–65; M. Swain (1970); M. Swain (1986).

82 Cited in R. Geuter (2000) pp. 162–3.

83 M. Swain (1973).

84 See R. Geuter (2000) p. 173 and M. Robbins (1974) pp. 2, 663, 666.

85 HMC 11th Report, Manuscripts of Lord Hothfield, ed. William O. Hewlett, Anne, Countess of Dorset to the Countess of Cumberland (Bellbrooke, 10 June 1615).

86 Cited in J. C. Spruill (1938) p. 259.

87 Extract from Dorothy Osborne Temple's letters, cited in Janet Todd (ed.) *Dictionary of British Women Writers*, 1989, p. 497.

88 Janet Todd (1984) pp. 256–7; Janet Todd (1989) pp. 539–40; Anne Crawford *et al.* (1983) pp. 328–9; V. Blain *et al.* (1990) p. 858; J. Shattock (1993) pp. 340–41.

89 See S. P. Cerasano and M. Wynne-Davis (1996) pp. 157–9; Margaret Cavendish could write of female play-going as just another recreation, *Nature's Pictures Drawn by Fancy's Pencil*, 1671, p. 285.

90 See S. H. Mendelson (1987).

91 See my forthcoming article, 'Family galleries: women and art in the seventeenth and eighteenth centuries'.

CHAPTER 16

Women's cultural lives: participation

Sarah Silsbe is my name
I belong to the English nation.
Boston is my dwelling place
And Christ is my salvation[1]

Introduction

The printed work of women was but the very tip of the iceberg of their cultural activity, as indicated in Chapter 15. Women expressed themselves through their embroidery and tapestry-weaving, through their music and their dancing, their drawing, sketching and painting, their conversation, and they did this with family support and encouragement. Because women did not normally commit themselves to print or become professional painters or musicians the survivals of their 'cultural participation' are at best haphazard and at worse few and far between. Here we gather together some of the evidence pointing to the involvement of women in contemporary culture and its varying context.

Family support and expectations

For women writers the importance of economic, locational and family support was paramount. Just look at some of the English, Welsh and Anglo-Irish family groups in which such women were situated – the Sidneys (Mary, Philip and Robert Sidney, Mary Wroth and William Herbert), the Cavendishes (Jane, Elizabeth, William and Margaret); the Cecils (Anne Cecil de Vere and her Coke aunts); Elizabeth I (Henry VIII, Catherine Parr); the Mores (Thomas, Margaret); Anne Kingsmill Finch and Lady Anne

Finch Conway; the Audleys (Maria Thynne and Lady Eleanor Davies), Constance Fowler (Katherine Thimelby Aston, Herbert Aston, Winifred Thimelby); Mary Rich, Countess of Warwick, and Katherine Boyle Jones, Lady Ranelagh (their father Richard Boyle, 1st Earl of Cork and their brothers Robert (the scientist) and Roger (the dramatist) Boyle); the Duchess of Beaufort and her daughters, especially Mary Somerset (later Duchess of Ormond) and Ann Somerset (later Countess of Coventry); James Harris and his wife Elizabeth and daughters Gertrude and Louisa. These families had an active cultural life in which women were expected to participate. Sometimes, as we shall see, Welsh poetesses belonged to families of 'professional' bards.[2] But female members of some English and colonial bourgeois families were also expected to participate – Isabella Whitney, the first woman to publish a book of poetry, and her brother, Geoffrey; Anne Dowriche and her husband; Rachel Speght and her husband and father; Anne Bradstreet; Aemilia Lanyer and the Cliffords.[3] For these women there was little economic security.[4] When families did not provide support, and sometimes when they did, women turned to other women for nurture, whether through friendship, patronage or inspiration – one thinks of the links that can be established between Anne Clifford, Aemilia Lanyer and Mary (Sidney) Herbert; Elizabeth Clinton Lincoln, Anne Bradstreet and Bathsua Makin; Mary Delany, Sarah Chapone, Elizabeth Elstob, Mary Astell and Mary Wortley Montagu; Elizabeth Elstob, Anne Maria van Schurman, Bathsua Makin and Lucy (Davies) Hutchinson; Anne (Marbury) Hutchinson and Mary Dyer; Katherine Philips, (Roger Boyle, Lord Orrery) and Katherine (Boyle) Jones Ranelagh.

One of the best-known examples of women's cultural life in a household setting remains that of the Sidney family through several generations. Indeed Mary Sidney (1561–1621) and her niece Mary Wroth (1587–c.1651) were each actively to initiate the development of such a cultural life and to see this as part of their vocation. Mary Sidney produced her *Antonie* and Mary Wroth her *Love's Victory* 'within the safe surroundings of the Sidney family homes, and they were respected, not as innovative women playwrights, but as inheritors of the Sidney tradition of literary brilliance'. John Aubrey described Mary Sidney's household at Wilton House as 'like a college, there so many learned and ingenious persons. She was the greatest patroness of wit and learning of any lady in her time.'[5] It was here that, in the words of a modern scholar, she reconstructed 'herself as a Sidneian scholar, fully capable of continuing the textual endeavours initiated by her brother [Philip]' and 'rose to challenge with exemplary skill and an extraordinary sense of purpose.'[6]

Literary historians have written of Mary Sidney Herbert's close participation in the conception of her brother Philip's *Arcadia* and of her later continuation of the work. When her niece Mary Wroth wrote in her poetry of the literary partnership of a brother and sister it was to her aunt and uncle that she referred.[7]

Women were also drawn into wider groupings from the household. In her youth Mary Sidney Wroth was part of the circle of James I's wife, Queen Anne, and she took part in court masques and used her influence at court to gain funds to repair her home at Loughton Hall. Wroth knew and was respected by authors, playwrights, musicians and poets such as Ben Jonson, George Chapman, Robert Jones and George Wither. Jonson even dedicated *The Alchemist* to her. She had close connections with the household of Sir Edward Dering, where amateur dramatics were popular. While her affair with her first cousin William Herbert was certainly physical (she reputedly bore him two illegitimate children) it seems that they also shared an active love of learning and good conversation.

The group that surrounded Elizabeth Tanfield Carey at Great Tew, Oxfordshire, has received some attention but it may be unusual because of the depth of its learning rather than because such groups were a rarity. Moreover, there are examples of 'learning circles' throughout the seventeenth and eighteenth centuries. For instance, during the later 1640s and 1650s, Elizabeth Murray seems to have been part of a learning circle to which also belonged Dorothy Long and Ludovic and Joan Carlisle. Dorothy Long said of Elizabeth: 'Our lady has grown a great student. She reads Dr Donne and Sir W. Rawley; works exquisitely in gum work; hath entered herself Head of the 2nd form in our academy ... she knocks me down with my own weapon [that is, her tongue].' Bishop Burnet also praised her qualities as a conversationalist and noted that she was learned not only in divinity and history but also mathematics and philosophy.[8] A further well-known example of a coterie of learned individuals is that of the so-called bluestocking circle that clustered around Elizabeth Montagu in mid- to late-eighteenth century London. Prominent women in this group included Catherine Talbot, Elizabeth Carter, Elizabeth Vesey, Hester Chapone, Anne Donnellan, Fanny Burney, Hannah More and Hester Thrale. It is, however, important to note that the bluestockings included men such as David Garrick, Samuel Johnson, William Pulteney, Earl of Bath, Joshua Reynolds and Edmund Burke, and that these men often drew into the group their own wives and sisters.[9]

While women frequently depended upon the support of male relatives for their cultural participation, it must not be supposed that such support implied a belief in equality of opportunity external to the household. For example, Sir Thomas More recognised and recommended a limited future for his cherished and talented daughter: 'men that read your writings would suspect you to have had help of some other man therein'; he recognised her deep knowledge but was relieved that because of her piety, 'you esteem me and your husband a sufficient and ample theatre for you to content you with'.[10]

Yet the erudition of their wives sometimes provided a secure and acknowledged foundation for a happy and fulfilling marriage partnership. Hyrde did not name Margaret Roper, More's aforementioned daughter, in the preface of her translation of Erasmus into English but did comment on the joy her translation gave to her and her husband by her erudition 'especial comfort, pleasure and pastime, as were not well possible for one unlearned couple, either to take together, or to conceive in their minds, what pleasure is therein'.[11] Margaret Cavendish, whose ideas challenged those of Descartes, was excluded from the Royal Society but found support at home.[12]

How far did women's education serve to acculturate them and fit them to play an active role in that culture? On both sides of the Atlantic and throughout the early modern period, women's academic education was, to the modern eye at least, seemingly haphazard and often informal. To the contemporary eye, however, a woman's education was appropriate for her various roles. By the mid-sixteenth century an English gentlewoman might learn to read and write in English (so that she could correspond with her husband and family as well as read the Bible and make notes on sermons), to do arithmetic (so that she could manage her household and keep accounts), to sew, embroider and cook (so that she could keep her family and household), to recognise and understand the properties of herbs (so that she might make ointments and potions and care for her household's health) and to observe correct deportment, dance and play musical instruments (so that she could be a social player – not just an ornament but someone whose social skills would help build up and cement a family social network).[13]

The balance would vary from household to household. There were unusual households. One thinks, for example, of the family of James Harris in the eighteenth century, where it was normal for the wife and daughters to share the family passion for music and theatre as audience and where in the case of Louisa as singer and in the case of Gertrude as producer and performer in amateur dramatics, active participation was encouraged.[14] In some families reading and writing skills were crucial to a woman's ability to participate in family culture. Abigail Adams, later wife of John Adams, President of the USA, was herself active politically but she complained of her lack of formal education: 'As to points and comma's, I was not taught them in my youth, and I always intend my meaning shall be so obvious as that my readers shall know when they ought to stop.'[15] In common with many daughters of educated men in the British Isles and the Americas, however, she and her sisters Mary (b.1741) and Betsey (b.1750) were taught to read, write and keep accounts (arithmetic) by their mother. Along with their brother William (b.1746) they were given the run of their father's library and learned to appreciate literature, history and theology.[16] In addition they were taught the skills of housewifery, which seemed to extend to estate management.[17] What they were taught fitted women for the cultural life appropriate for their social station. It was assumed that the wife of a gentleman or a professional man should be able to provide her husband with intelligent conversation and companionship as well as to manage the household and educate the children. This was why, in the colonies, it was regarded as so unusual for a slave girl such as Phyllis Wheatley not only to be highly literate but also to be a poetess. Women learned the skills and accomplishments that fitted them for the social and cultural milieu in which they were expected to move – music, languages, needlework, dancing, reading, writing, doing accounts. It also allowed them to display themselves while they were still single to suitable young men, develop their social skills and extend the range of their acquaintance.

When he was a student in Glasgow in the 1740s Alexander Carlyle was fond of dancing and offered his services at Madame Violante's dancing school for young ladies. 'I became a favourite of this dancing mistress, and attended her very faithfully with two or three of my companions, and had my choice of partner on all occasions . . .'[18] This education began early and it was often designed to produce quickwitted and articulate young women. At Christmas in 1663 the Catholic gentleman William Blundell wrote a playlet for his three young daughters, Mall (nine), Franke (seven) and Bridget (four) to perform 'to embolden them in speaking'.[19] The dialogue that they learned encouraged them to use rational argument against their father. It began with William threatening to beat Mall for uncivil behaviour and with Mall arguing that as God forgave her her sins in confession once she had promised to amend, so William should copy God's example. When William agrees, Mall exults in escaping the beating for once and decides to mend her ways. Much lower down the social scale, where grinding poverty circumscribed the lives of both men and women, there was little need or opportunity for the acquisition of knowledge and skills, just as there was little opportunity to use them. For the middling sort, however, there were many opportunities.

Margaret MacCurtain has argued that for women in post-Reformation Ireland there was no widening of educational opportunity or cultural participation but rather a narrowing. Although some notable women such as Margaret Birmingham (1515–c.1584) sheltered priests and had schoolrooms in their houses; although daughters as well as sons appear to have been taught by resident chaplains (such as he who educated the Stanihurst, Barnehurst and Bathe children); and although some noble girls, such as the Westmeaths, attended boarding schools in foreign convents, it is alleged that the dissolution disrupted the long tradition of native convent education of girls and that for the most part seventeenth-century Irish women received catechistical instruction (which included basic literacy) rather than a humanist and liberating education. The few convents that appeared in seventeenth-century Ireland were for contemplative orders rather than teaching orders. An analysis of the convent for Irish Dominican nuns in Lisbon in 1639 nevertheless suggests that its members were expected to read and write, to know Latin, to converse in English, Irish and Portuguese and sing plainsong. The emergence of the bluestocking movement in eighteenth-century Dublin, however, does indicate that some Protestant women had achieved a high standard of education and a love of learning.[20]

Historians have uncovered some evidence of female cultural activity in households at different social levels. For example, Constance Fowler, sister of Herbert Aston of Tixall, Staffordshire, made a miscellany of poetry in the 1630s that was unified by her family, friends and connections. 'Send me some verses, for I want some good ones to put in my booke', she wrote to her brother.[21] In creating her miscellany Constance demonstrated that she appreciated, preserved and passed on poetry of special relevance to her circle. Without her persistence these poems would have been lost and with it all evidence of the cultural life of this county family. She pestered Herbert for his own poems to add to the volume, gently rebuking him for his reciprocal role in the business of passing on poetry, 'pray see how hardly you deal with me, when I have sent you all the verses that I could get perpetually, never omitting the sending of any, that I could get, that were good ones'.[22] The very fact of the limited horizons of such a young woman perhaps made her more insistent than her menfolk on maintaining cultural life. Constance played an important role in collecting and 'recording the poetry of friends and family and of her embattled

Catholic faith'.[23] An example of shared cultural activity, this time from an urban family, is provided by the case of Lady Anne Southwell, who was the daughter of Sir Thomas Harris, a sergeant-at-law, near the top of the legal profession, and his wife Elizabeth Pomeroy. Anne's first husband was Sir Thomas Southwell of Spixworth, Norfolk, and she moved with him to Ireland and made many literary connections there. After Southwell's death, Anne married Captain Henry Sibthorpe in 1626 and established connections in Acton, Middlesex, including Daniel Featley, Roger Cox and Robert Johnson. Anne Southwell's miscellany is interesting because her own poetry formed approximately 40 per cent of its contents, and because her husband was involved in its compilation and intended it for a public audience.[24]

Another example, this time from the urban artisan class, involves the mother of the antiquary Elias Ashmole, Anne Bowyer. She was the daughter of a Coventry draper, Anthony Bowyer, and his wife, Bridget Fitch, the daughter of a gentleman from Ansley, Warwickshire. Anne was the eldest of at least five children. Her miscellany was almost a dictionary of quotations and proverbs, mainly from printed sources.[25] Sometimes, however, the quotations were from manuscript works such as Ralegh's 'The Lie' and Donne's 'A Valediction: forbidding mourning', showing that such poems gained a popular female readership 'well beyond any intended, exclusive, coterie readership'.[26] Interestingly Anne Bowyer also used the book for practical handwriting exercises for her siblings. It took on the character of a veritable 'educational repository for at least three members of a household', bearing out the idea that through commonplace books their compilers helped frame the thoughts of contemporaries and, especially, those close to them.[27] It appears that the situation was little different over the border in Scotland. Although relatively little work has been done on the cultural life of Scotland some evidence has been uncovered that shows the young Margaret Wemyss, daughter of David, 2nd Earl of Wemyss, and his first wife Anna Balfour, collecting and preserving songs for bass viol and voice, poems, and pieces for the lute. Her music teacher perhaps made printed copies of airs by Thomas Campion and Thomas Morley available to her. The pieces are annotated in a way that suggests Margaret was making a musician's decisions and not simply copying the texts.[28]

There are several examples of the activity of Welsh women in the early modern period. Frequently these women focused on poetry in Welsh. Nia Powell has shown that some of the poetesses of the fifteenth to seventeenth centuries belonged to bardic traditions in particular families. For instance, Gwenllian ferch Rhirid was the daughter of two poets, Tudor Penllyn (c.1420–1485) and Gwerful ferch Ieuan Fychan; and Alice, Catrin and Gwen were poet daughters of Gruffudd ab Ieuan ap Llywelyn Fychan (c.1485–1553) who derived from a family of gentleman poets and patrons of poetry.[29] Such women were, then, from unusual backgrounds congenial to female cultural activity. However, by the eighteenth century this pattern was less prevalent. Ann Griffiths (1776–1805) wrote religious verse.[30] Margaret Davies (1700–1778/85) from a yeoman family of Coetgaedu near Trawsfynydd, not only wrote poetry but collected together and copied surviving verse, much of it surviving from the Middle Ages. She showed herself familiar with the work of other female poets and of her eighteenth-century contemporary female poetess, Angharad James (1677–1749).[31] Angharad came from a family of yeoman farmers in Caernarvonshire. She wrote poetry herself, possessed manuscripts and also copied over 116 poems into the *Llyfr Coch Angharad James*.[32] By this time female poets were communicating with others, both male and female, who shared their interests.[33] Powell attributes the poor survival record of Welsh female poetry to the continued strength of the oral tradition in Wales and the reluctance of both men and women to commit their verses to paper.[34]

Examples of the cultural life of women in Ireland are few and far between. Richard Boyle, 1st Earl of Cork, although he aimed to be the patriarch par excellence, succeeded better with his wife Catherine Fenton than with his daughters and sons. He encouraged his children to explore literature and ask questions. For instance, he organised the 'sober education' of his daughters but also presented his daughter Mary with a copy of Sidney's *Arcadia* for study, thus exposing her to the Sidney connection and humanist influences that were strong in Munster. Mary was also very close to her sister-in-law, Elizabeth Killigrew, who married Francis Boyle, and was encouraged by her to read romances. Eventually Mary rebelled against Boyle's insistence that she marry an Ulster settler James Hamilton and eloped to marry Charles Rich, who had been introduced to her by Elizabeth Killigrew Boyle.[35] Perhaps Richard regretted encouraging Mary's inquiring mind! Mary's sister Katherine, Lady Ranelagh, also had a haphazard education which had the effect of fostering her independence and creativity. Richard depended considerably on her until her marriage to a drunken lord. Katherine separated from her husband and found support for her intellectual life in the circle that met regularly at Great Tew, Oxfordshire, and which was heavily influenced by Elizabeth Tanfield Carey.[36] Her example indicates how family support could be supplemented or even replaced by wider networks.

In certain ways women in such family and wider networks might influence, to a greater or lesser extent, the 'canon' of literary works. Barbara Lewalski points to the way in which Edmund Spenser collaborated with Margaret Russell Clifford (mother of Lady Anne) and her sister Anne Dudley to 'reform' his *Fowre Hymnes* (1596) by adding poems in praise of heavenly and celestial love and beauty. Philip Sidney's collaboration with his sister Mary in translating the Psalms (considered below) provides an even more startling example.

Historians have observed from time to time that there were complaints that the English rulers of Ireland did not import their families along with them and that Irish female society suffered as a consequence.[37] No doubt there is some truth in this. However, from time to time we are aware of the important cross-fertilisation of native Irish and Anglo-Irish society on the one hand and English on the other. MacCurtain shows how 'the network of the Kildare Geraldines interacted with the St Johns, the Grays and the Zouches in the English court' to the extent that Elizabeth Zouche, great grandmother of the linguist William Bathe, mastered the Irish tongue, encouraged her son 'Silken Thomas' to learn the harp, and became a patron of the arts.[38]

In the higher echelons of English society women seem to have organised the cultural life of their households throughout the early modern period. For instance, Lady Honor Lisle purchased a text of an interlude called *Rex Diabole* for her household in 1538.[39] It is common knowledge that women performed in masques at the English court during the reigns of the early Stuarts but it is perhaps less well known that they organised such masques. Moreover there is evidence of noble women laying on such entertainments. For example, the Dowager Lady Russell sponsored a pastoral pageant when Queen Elizabeth visited Bisham in August 1592.[40] Rather lower in the social scale but still well connected was the spinster sister of the Bishop of Hereford, Joyce Jeffreys, who employed performers to entertain her own household.[41]

It is intriguing how women would use the, in some respects, limited roles imposed upon them as a springboard for intellectual and creative activity. Women spent so much of their time in the domestic sphere and the birth family that family history and genealogy sometimes became a passion for its own sake and fed the life of the mind. Cassandra Willoughby (later Cassandra Brydges, first duchess of Chandos) spent many hours in her brother Willoughby's study researching her (and his) family history. The circumstances in which she found herself (her father, the naturalist Francis, had died when she was a toddler and, because she hated her mother's second husband, Cassandra kept house for her brothers) meant that she relished this opportunity to establish her own identity. She wrote her book, then, not only in the cause of establishing and recording her genealogy (as any young woman of intelligence and means might) but also out of a special interest. She transcribed large numbers of family letters from the sixteenth and seventeenth centuries and used them to piece together a narrative of the domestic lives of her ancestors and assess their personalities and motivations.

I could not find it does not appear how or when Sir Percivall gained his liberty but by several letters to him in 1609 one may judge he had then money at command and was in such circumstances as allowed him to live very handsomely. He always seems to have been thoughtful of and carefully to make the best provision he could for all his children. He had six sons and five daughters, whereof the youngest is not mentioned in the pedigree, her name was Elinor but I could find no other account of her than that in one of the Earl of London – Derry's letters to Lady Willoughby he mentions her for a Housewife.

Thus Cassandra self-consciously interpreted the documents at her disposal, edited and re-edited her narrative and researched missing facts. For example, she searched parish registers, talked about her work both with her brother and with family members and retainers, and tried to understand what she read.

In one of Sir P:W:s letters to Lady Will: about this time he desires she will send him up to London her clock with plummets [clock with weights] which he will get mended for her if he can. Qu: [query] what other invention they had for clocks before that of weights because by this letter that seems to have been a new invention then.[42]

She perhaps represents a tradition in noble and gentle families whereby the women researched, recorded and preserved the genealogy (of great use in the search for a suitable spouse either for themselves or their brothers) and also a tradition of providing the family with a shared identity through its history. (It may also be indicative of the way in which women converted activities with a practical purpose into creative opportunities.) Intriguingly a very distant relation of Cassandra, Lady Georgiana Bertie, was responsible for the mid-nineteenth century *History of Two Loyal Houses*.[43] Whatever her representativeness, Cassandra played a unique role within her own family, preserving and interpreting its papers for future generations. Her history of the Willoughbys was bound and treasured by her husband's descendants, and her collaborative work (with her mother-in-law and aunt, Elizabeth Brydges) on her husband's family was added to by them and similarly valued.

Another example of the way in which women exploited their accepted roles to create something of great interest to themselves was their shared interest and expertise in practical medicine. Elsewhere we have noted how mothers and daughters were responsible for the health of the family and for preparing potions and salves to cure ills. An eighteenth-century Welsh woman, Ann Griffiths, might have been typical in keeping her own medical recipe (receipt) book.[44] There is a good deal of evidence that such women were not content to keep these skills to themselves. In letters and in conversation they shared their knowledge and created, in effect, a vast database of medical expertise. Sir Peter Temple noted in his 1656 collection of medical and other receipts, 'I often have these receits from women' although he added that these women obtained the recipes from 'men of judgement' as, for example, 'Lady Forsters receits came most from Sir Theodore Mayherne.'[45] This tells us something of Sir Peter's need to defend his cures as emanating not originally from women but from men but, more interesting from our perspective, it indicates the crucial role women played in further disseminating medical knowledge and opinion. At least some of the recipes emanated from his wife and his mother-in-law.[46] He hints at one important channel for such transmission of knowledge with respect to the 'green oyle'[47] used in his own family: 'if I mistake not, Mrs Hitch the midwife sent it my wife, and tis ye lady Norris receite for wounds and itches and all lamenesse . . .'[48] He also legitimised other cures on the basis of proofs provided by the women involved. For instance, in recommending a particularly gruesome cure for red 'moles' that appeared at birth on many a baby's face – gently stroking the marks with the clammy hand of a recently deceased person – he urged 'in a short time it [the mark] will weare away saith ye author and she proved it in her owne daughter'.[49] Perhaps even more fascinating is the fact that Sir Peter clearly regarded medicines (including animal as well as human medicine, the preparation of food, issues of husbandry and hunting, and Paracelsian experiments) as an area in which both men and women might properly engage.

It is not really surprising that, in an age when life was all too often 'nasty, brutish and short', women in their correspondence were frequently obsessed by their health. More interesting is the way that they discussed the nature and efficacy of particular remedies and drew attention to the excellent reputation that particular women had made for themselves in certain areas. This was as true in the eighteenth century (when 'professional' male medicine was well established) as it was in the sixteenth (when 'professional' medicine was still in its infancy). Cassandra Brydges, for instance, identified the Duchess of Marlborough as an expert on gout:

I hope to hear . . . that your Grace is perfectly free from the gout, and that you will pardon me for the liberty which I now take in behalf of a brother who suffers previously under the same disease. Lord Middleton has been confined to his bed near a fortnight with the gout in his neck, shoulders, and breast, and to keep it out of his stomach he is advised to take Sir Walter Rawley's Cordial Electuary and knowing that medicine is no where to be had in such perfection as from your Grace, I beg you will send me (for him) three or four doses of it . . .[50]

The Duchess obliged and also recommended 'Aquebogue'[51] in the gout', but Cassandra replied, 'My brother has formerly taken it with great success, but I fear by often use that is now grown less beneficial to him, which has made those about him desire he may have this cordial by him in a readiness, in case of extremity.'[52]

There is also evidence that women's cultural activity from time to time moved them beyond the gardens of the country house and into the mainstream. For instance, Katherine Philips's poems exist in a complete manuscript copy and probably circulated simultaneously in manuscript and printed form. Robert Overton (c.1609–c.1672) clearly had access to one or other when he used her poetry, along with that of Donne and others, as models for his verse in memory of his wife Anne Overton.[53] Katherine (Fowler) Philips (1631–1664), daughter of a London merchant and married since the age of seventeen to a Welshman, spent her time in her Cardigan and London homes and organised a Society of Friendship which drew in Abraham Cowley, Henry Vaughan and Jeremy Taylor. Her translation of Corneille's *Pompée* was produced on the stage in Dublin and her poetry was published after her death from smallpox in 1664.

Language and a common culture

Drawing any comparisons or contrasts between the cultural role and experience of women in England, Wales, Scotland and Ireland is fraught with difficulties. Not least among these are the scarcity of appropriate source materials for Wales, Scotland and Ireland and, even more serious perhaps, the lack of attention that has been given to the subject by modern historians.

The extent to which women in the British Isles shared, or were able to share, a common culture has, of course, been debated in a broader context.[54] There is a good deal of evidence that colonists in English parts of the Americas thought of themselves as 'of the English nation' before the Revolution.[55] It probably never struck Sarah Silsbe as strange that she could be both English and an inhabitant of Boston across the Atlantic Ocean. Laurel Thatcher Ulrich has shown how American families constructed their English lineages through stories of their ancestors and thus laid a stake in the culture of Old World and New.[56] For a hundred years most of the printed works circulating in the New World were imported from England. The first Bible printed in English America was the Eliot Bible of 1663 and Robert Hunter's *Androborus* was the first play to be printed in the New World. The New England Primer, first printed in 1686, like its English counterparts contained the alphabet, a syllabarium, alphabet rhymes with pictures, the ten commandments, prayers and psalms.

But language was a major obstacle to sharing a culture in the British Isles as a whole. Contemporaries, however, sometimes expressed their respect for difference. For instance, Elizabeth Baker, an Englishwoman living in Merioneth in the late eighteenth century, who was herself excluded by language from aspects of Welsh culture although not from friendships nevertheless wrote, 'my wish is that they may never lose their language'.[57] The fact that 90 per cent of people in the eighteenth century in Wales still spoke Welsh suggests that Welsh culture *was* very different from English or American. Elizabeth's comment in a letter to a friend underlines her awareness of this: 'This country is often called the British Alps, to me it is almost Greenland.'[58] Neither does it seem that Anglicisation had affected the gentry so profoundly as to achieve a social divide surrounding language. Most of Elizabeth Baker's gentle friends spoke Welsh, as did their social inferiors. (We have already noted the prevalence of poetry in Welsh.) The difference could have surrounded binguality: Elizabeth was prevented from having extended and meaningful conversation with social inferiors because of her lack of fluent Welsh and their lack of fluent English, whereas she did not have the same difficulties with gentry friends.

Interesting work is being accomplished on the vitality and isolation of Welsh literary culture. This burgeoning was especially true after 1695 when for the first time the printing monopoly of London, Oxford and Cambridge was broken. Yet this was just a fledgling publishing industry.[59] Some of the books printed in late seventeenth- and eighteenth-century

Wales were translations from English standards. Eryn White has indicated, however, that while many devotional works were rendered into Welsh, very few domestic and marriage guides were. Women were also deprived of discussion in Welsh of women's social or religious role until a methodist preacher, William Williams, published his *Ductor Nuptiarum neu Gyfarwyddwr Priodas* (Guide to marriage) in 1777.[60] For our period, if one wished to discuss gender roles (and indeed many other topics) one had to do so on the basis of reading English texts.

Nicholas Canny, the foremost authority regarding 'Making Ireland British', has demonstrated the prevalence of bilingualism (and hence, to an extent, cross-fertilisation of cultures) within Ireland during the period 1580 to 1650. He maintains that the majority of the Old English from the Pale (and especially those who moved outside it) knew at least some Irish. Even the Earl of Ormond, James Butler, who had spent most of his formative years in a Protestant environment in England, knew some Gaelic and could understand it perfectly. This state of affairs was probably reinforced by intermarriage between English and Irish. Moreover Canny demonstrates that the indigenous population, even within the most Anglicised areas, spoke Gaelic. This was why Irish Catholic priests were trained to use both languages in their missionary work. Gaelic continued to be the predominant language of communication in Catholic culture throughout the social spectrum of Ireland and, indeed, there is some evidence that Catholic leaders wished to keep 'their subordinates ignorant of English'. But many also spoke or understood English because of the practical advantages conferred by bilingualism.[61]

Those of Irish or Scottish birth who have received scholarly attention are generally such as had been subsumed into English society and, therefore, belonged to the Anglo-Irish elite. A good example is that of Lady Katherine Boyle Jones, Viscountess Ranelagh (1613–1691).[62] She was born in Cork as one of the fourteen children of the 1st Earl of Cork and was educated in languages and philosophy. She married Arthur Jones, later Viscount Ranelagh, in 1630, who turned out to be a drunkard. Katherine appears to have moved to live apart from him in London after the birth of their son in 1641 and to have had an active cultural life thereafter. In her case this meant that she turned her house in Pall Mall into a centre for a notable group of Irish Protestants and scientific figures, and herself became interested in contemporary scientific and philosophical debates. Money gave her freedom and influence. She acted as patron to individuals such as Benjamin Worsley, Samuel Hartlib, John Dury and others. She employed Milton and Henry Oldenburg to tutor her son. She was also a major influence on her younger brother, Robert, eminent scientist and a leading member of the Royal Society. In 1668, when he left Oxford, she built him a laboratory. When she died in 1691, he wrote her eulogy, calling her one of the great women of the age.

Women as audience

Over the period as a whole, there was in all these societies an increasing awareness of women of a certain class as audience. In late seventeenth- and eighteenth-century London, Edinburgh and Dublin women took advantage of the development of the season and were an accepted part of the audience at soirées, plays and concerts where professional, as well as amateur, actors and musicians performed. Other towns – such as Bath, Exeter, York and Norwich – echoed this development in miniature. This kind of communal activity was slower to develop in the New World, although by the 1730s Boston had classical music concerts and by the 1750s New York had a series of subscription concerts performed by amateurs. The theatre was frowned upon as immoral in the early American colonies and it was not until 1713 that the first theatre was established in Williamsburg, Virginia. By 1749 a group of actors had toured New England towns with Shakespeare's plays and in 1752 a London company moved to the colonies for a number of years. The colonial woman, therefore, had fewer opportunities to be part of a large audience than did her old-world equivalents.[63]

There is another less formal sense, however, in which women were regarded as an audience. There were as we have seen depressingly low levels of active literacy (especially in the provinces) among women at all social statuses but probably many more women could read than could write. Moreover, much 'reading' was in fact a shared activity, where a book was read aloud to family, friends or fellow workers as part of what was still very much an oral culture. Where today television, film and radio allow illiterate or semi-literate members of society access to a common culture, in the period 1450–1800 cultural cascading occurred around the hearth, around the table, in the church pews and in the work room. A common belief in the old and new worlds was that reading led to madness in women, whose minds were insufficiently strong to stand the strain. Dol Commons's madness in Jonson's *The Alchemist* (1610) was triggered by reading.[64] In 1645 John Winthrop believed that the poet Anne Hopkins was driven insane by her 'reading and writing . . . if she had attended her household affairs, and such things as belong to women . . .

she had kept her wits', for literacy is 'proper for men, whose minds are stronger'.⁶⁵

Those in authority seem to have regarded reading as a potentially subversive act in both sexes. Only members of certain social groups were regarded as part of the 'political nation', the gate to which was, as it were, guarded by literacy. If women were allowed to read anything they chose they might also be tempted into public debate and declaration. Even members of the elite were frequently uncertain about the advisability of allowing women readers a free rein with religious literature. Sir Ralph Verney of Steeple Claydon, Buckinghamshire, advised in 1652, 'let not your young girl learn Latin, nor shorthand: the difficulty of the first may keep her from vice . . . but the easiness of the other may be a prejudice to her, the pride of taking sermons notes hath made multitudes of women unfortunate'.⁶⁶

More unusually, some feared the power of the active reader to influence the text. Jacqueline Pearson shows how 'John Marston's paranoid satyrist Kinsayder in *The scourge of villainie* (1599) is hostile toward his readers, insulting them and criticising them because he fears their power over him and his poem. They are capable in the act of reading of "quite altering the sense", reading into his poem "that which I never meant": ultimately the power of creation is theirs as much as it is the poet's.'⁶⁷ However, as Juan Luis Vives indicated, reading was a useful way in which women's thoughts could be prevented from 'walking and wandering out from home' so long as they received direction by 'wise and learned men' and were prevented from following their own judgment in choice of reading.⁶⁸ This opinion was repeated conventionally.⁶⁹

Evidence of both female and male reading habits is hard to come by, especially for the sixteenth century. Diaries are an important source and sometimes comment on the reactions of the author to the texts. Such journals are few and far between, however, and it is far from certain that a particular diary author would record and comment upon all of her reading. Occasionally an individual would describe early reading experiences as evidence of a misspent youth – for instance, Lucy Hutchinson regretted her childhood enthusiasm for 'witty songs and amorous sonnets or poems', Mary Rich bemoaned her love of romances and the poet Ann Collins in Divine songs and meditations likewise repented her youthful liking for frivolous reading of 'pleasant histories' that she enjoyed although she knew they 'were not true'. There are scattered references in many sources regarding the female audience for particular works. For example, Shakespeare seems to have been widely read – Gary Taylor has traced references to a 'young Gentle Lady' reading his works in 1635, and to Ann

Merricke doing likewise in 1639; and satirical references to Venus and Adonis being popular reading for bored, frustrated middle-class housewives.[70] Cassandra Brydges recommended Pope's *Essay on Man* to her friend Lady Ann Coventry in 1733, when it was hot off the press.[71] She had also read Chaucer and commented that she found the 'old edition ... very hard to read, the English was so very different from our English now'.[72] New England women of the eighteenth century read newspapers, the Bible, works of popular piety such as Walter Marshall's *Gospel-Mystery of Sanctification* (London, 1692) and novels such as Samuel Richardson's *Pamela* and *Clarissa*, demonstrating the continuing and pervasive influence of English culture in the colonies.[73] By the early eighteenth century there was an established newspaper press in the southern colonies and it is inconceivable that the many women who advertised in these papers did not also read them.[74]

In practice, for both sexes, reading was often restricted to what we today might regard as a 'set book' and 'recommended reading list' both by accident and design. Inevitably the character of each family influenced the reading matter of their daughters. The three daughters of Lady Anne Sharington, who was the daughter of Robert Paget, a merchant tailor and a London alderman, were reared on daily readings from the recently translated Geneva Bible, and on recent reformed literature. Well-to-do ladies such as the Puritan Lady Margaret Hoby often read many devotional works but frequently their reading was guided by the household chaplain, the local minister, or the husband. Household libraries were rarely large, exceptions such as those of elite libraries, housed in separate rooms, at Maynooth Castle and the Geraldine castles in sixteenth-century County Limerick proving the rule.[75] The Earl and Countess of Kildare boasted a collection of thirty-four Latin books, thirty-six French texts, twenty-two English and twenty Irish works.[76] For most households there was what amounted to a small and 'approved collection': the Bible, the Book of Common Prayer, Foxe's Book of Martyrs, writings of continental reformers, a few herbals and reference works, to which might sometimes be added a range of devotional and classical works. Sarah Fyge Egerton, an adolescent in a professional home in the late seventeenth century, complained that her parents tried to limit her reading to the prayer book and 'old receipts of cookery'.[77]

Certain women, however, did have the opportunity and the money to develop libraries of their own. Often these would be relatively small amounting to the contents of a small bookcase. Mrs Elizabeth Freke, daughter of a royalist gentleman, held her books dear and catalogued her varied collection of a hundred or so in her diaries for the years 1671–1714. Her books included bibles, sermons, works of theology and devotion, history and geography, poetry by Cowley and Quarles, herbals and medicine, law, translation of the classics and fiction.[78] More unusual still was Mary Astell's friend Ann, Countess of Coventry, who was rich enough, and independent and 'advanced' enough, to build up a substantial library, which included, in addition to the expected and accepted works, modern novels, 128 plays, women's writings and some sexually explicit works such as Ravenscroft's *The London Cuckolds*.[79]

Some households were relatively permissive in their approach to the cultural life of their womenfolk. Katherine Philips, writing within the gentry class, Royalist circle in the 1650s and early 1660s, easily discussed books with friends of both sexes.[80] It has been argued that Dorothy Osborne's shared reading of French romances with her lover William Temple actually strengthened their relationship and their resistance to their families, who opposed the match. Jacqueline Pearson shows how Dorothy used the language of the romances to discuss her own emotions with Temple and to state that she wants him to reciprocate her fidelity.[81] 'Anne Boleyn is said to have given Henry VIII Protestant texts to read that hardened his own views on the relationship between crown and papacy: in such a case it could be argued that women's reading changed history.'[82] Lady Anne Clifford (1590–1676) recorded her reading: intriguingly her portrait defines her life through the twenty-five books she read at its different stages – including Church fathers, Ovid, Chaucer, Montaigne, Don Quixote, Sidney's *Arcadia*, and poetry by Spenser and Daniel.[83] Such examples also illustrate that active reading played a more varied part in the cultural life of some women than what might be supposed if we restricted our attention to 'passive' or 'received' reading.

Occasionally there are indications that such active reading extended well below the elite. The increasing number of parish, dame and charity schools (despite their very restricted academic curricula) were having an impact on female cultural participation. For instance, in 1744 Alexander Carlyle reported being 'alarmed with the [prolonged] howling and weeping of women in the kitchen' while he awaited dinner at an inn in Glasgow. When he investigated the cause, he 'learnt from the calmest among them that a pedlar had left a copy of Peden's Prophecies that morning, which having read part of, they found that he had predicted woes of every kind to the people of Scotland; and in particular that Clyde would run with blood in the year 1744...' He was able to placate them by showing that there was, in fact, no explicit reference to the year.[84]

Other women were actively discouraged from reading. Sometimes the mother forbade the daughter to read or write and the father is shown as encouraging it: for example, Lucy Hutchinson's mother sought to limit her daughter's reading because it was bad for her health and distracted her from needlework; Elizabeth (Tanfield) Carey's mother refused her a supply of candles to read by and her mother-in-law confiscated her books. Margaret Cavendish decided to generalise from this pattern by giving her female character, Sarsaparilla, in *Youths glory and deaths banquet* of 1662, a supportive father and a discouraging mother.[85]

Were women targeted as readers? There is evidence that they were. Between 1475 and 1640, over 1,800 books printed in England were dedicated to women in general or as individuals. These books fell into four categories: devotion; the women question; fiction; and practical guides on such subjects as medicine, midwifery and cookery. Women were advised not to read fiction, but romances were written specially for their consumption. Pocket Books were also marketed to encourage women to organise their everyday lives.[86] Women were also early seen as a potential audience for more ephemeral literature – the magazine or journal.

Coffee houses and journals

Recently a good deal of interesting historical work has been done on the world of the London coffee and chocolate houses in the post-1660 period when they flourished. Helen Berry has become the authority on the place that women played in this world. She focuses upon the activities of The Athenian Society which met weekly at Smith's Coffee House at the London Stock Market. Arising from this John Dunton produced the *Athenian Gazette or Casuistical Mercury* (1691–97) and took the unprecedented step of offering to publish women's letters and comments, and so seemed to be capitalising on the market potential of women as consumers of popular culture. It was the only periodical to appeal to both a male and female readership. This gazette included a half folio sheet of answers to letters and it was available either in coffee houses by subscription or from named women hawkers on the streets.[87] Berry estimates that the gazette had a circulation of approximately 1,000 copies but that it was read by thousands. The Athenian Society was reputedly inundated with readers' letters and at one point declared a moratorium on further correspondence until it had a chance to 'get rid of these cart-loads of questions which are yet upon the file, and likely to press us to death under their weight'.

All this led Berry to seek to answer three questions: Was coffee-house culture exclusively male? Were the letters sent to the *Gazette* women's letters at all? Did the letters and answers presuppose a female audience? We already know that women ran coffee houses and served in coffee houses from the 1650s onwards, but were they there in any numbers in the clientele? Berry believes that many were present but were not encouraged to speak. Studies of coffee-house society indicate that particular houses aimed at specific clienteles, ranging from members of the Royal Society at Garraways, to poets and literati at Duke's and Wills, to financiers at Marine and Lloyds, to Whigs at the Grecian, to Tories at the Cocoa Tree, James Salter's in Chelsea, and to Moll King's where prostitutes were available.[88] Some of these were aimed at the middling sort, where for 1d. a customer received a dish of coffee and a pipe of tobacco and the opportunity for uncensored public discussion and reading of periodical literature.[89] Others prided themselves on the opportunity they offered for social mixing: 'Gentry, tradesmen, all are welcome hither and may without affront sit down together.'[90] We do know that men and women of the middling and lower sorts drank together in taverns and alehouses throughout England and the colonies. For instance, Elizabeth Wyatt, as married midwife, came before the church courts in 1635 for disrupting domestic harmony by constantly drinking, carousing and taking tobacco with Abraham Brand, a married man, in taverns and victualling houses.[91] These were not just women on the margins of society. Respectable women such as the wife of Adam Eyre regularly joined their husbands and married friends at the local alehouses. Possibly this tradition was transferred to the Coffee and Chocolate houses that sprang up in the late seventeenth century in London and had spread to the provinces by the early eighteenth century.

Contemporary male diaries and male and female correspondence do not support the suggestion that these female visitors included elite women. For example, James Brydges customarily went to a variety of coffee houses either alone or with male friends while his wife made social visits.[92] Famously Samuel Pepys frequented coffee houses and the women he socialised with there were prostitutes or servants.

It is entirely possible that the demand for the *Mercury* came mainly from women who read the paper outside the coffee houses and from the wives and daughters of those men who went to the coffee houses and bought the gazette home for their womenfolk. We do know that other forms of writing were specifically aimed at women. For example, advertisements in the post-Restoration press targeted them.[93] Establishing whether all the correspondents who claimed to be female were women

TABLE 16.1 *The subject matter of questions posed in* The Athenian Mercury, *1691–1697*[94]

Subject matter	Absolute number of items	Approximate percentage
Courtship	236	27%
Marriage	153	17%
Sexual behaviour	114	12%
Adultery	48	5%
Reproduction	59	6%
Men – general condition	48	5%
Women – general condition	41	4%
Occupational	40	4%
Medicine/anatomy	37	4%
Superstition	27	3%
Miscellaneous	117	13%
Total	920	100%

is difficult. We do know that some such letters were authentic. And the *Mercury* provided a forum for the female poet Elizabeth Singer Rowe to publish her first poems.[95] More important is the fact that the letters and the printed answers assumed a female audience and were concerned with issues of importance to women as well as men. Very many concerned 'the rules of attraction and boundaries of modest behaviour during courtship'. Others focused on marital violence, the legal grounds for separation, sexual and reproductive knowledge, and the need for women's education. Significantly some of the discussions were aimed at working women: for instance, advice was given to a female apprentice who sought advice on her choice of career.[96] The letters and answers encouraged both sexes to empathise with one another in a public forum. Berry's analysis of the letters suggests that the periodical was aimed at the under-30s of both sexes among the middling sort.[97]

Confident in their abilities

Some women from the sixteenth century onwards were sufficiently confident to use their writing as a means of self-expression, sometimes adapting accepted literary forms to comment on their own circumstances and to present women in a more sympathetic light than did their menfolk. They might choose seemingly innocuous ancient history as a vehicle for their own views. When writing her *Antonie* Mary Sidney (later Mary Herbert, Countess of Pembroke) chose to write in blank verse, thus rejecting her brother's preference for classical forms such as Alexandrine couplets. Moreover, she emphasised the role of Cleopatra and used the tragedy to warn of the effects of civil wars. *Antonie* was popular and went through no fewer than five editions in fifteen years.[98] Mary Wroth's *Love's Victory* has been read as a 'contemporary allegory that represents three decades of the lives and loves of the Sidney family'.[99] Her Urania II used Petrarch's *Triumphs of Love* as one source but also drew upon contemporary materials.[100]

The Sidney example also shows the willingness and confidence of some women to experiment and take intellectual risks. When the Countess of Pembroke completed her brother's project of translating the Psalms of David she undoubtedly owed much to her brother's example but she did more than follow in his footsteps.[101] 'She has a distinctive vision of her own. Her diction is often less dense, but more fluently poised, than that of her brother. Sidney's metrical suppleness was often striking, hers is still more so, as she repeatedly discovers new stanza forms to complement the varying moods of the psalms she is translating . . . Her emotional range is also remarkable . . . She is a poet of celebration – a quality that is uncommon in Sidney's poetry.'[102] Dinah Birch has pointed to the fact that this translation was a private act of devotion and that the work was circulated in manuscript only (finally being published in 1823). As indicated above, this was perhaps the usual way in which written work (by men and women) was circulated and known. Nevertheless, Dinah Birch is probably correct when she sees this closed cultural circle as encouraging the emancipation of Mary Sidney's gifts.

As such works were private we shall never know how many women participated in lively discussion groups and engaged in writing. We do know that their work was more likely to have been encouraged and preserved when their interests were shared by other members of their family and connection. The Conway Letters show how Anne Finch, poet and philosopher, was incorporated in the intellectual life of her own and her husband's family and friends.[103]

What, then, made a few women 'go public'? In her dedication to *The Reply of the Most Illustrious Cardinall of Perronn* (1630) Elizabeth Carey says 'I will confess, I think it well done, and so had I confessed sufficiently in printing it.' While women sometimes felt justified in publishing by their choice of subject and according to its suitability to their prescribed roles, others were moved to publish because their own sense of self-confidence and worth.

Women as correspondents

There was a long tradition of female correspondence in England. When Sir Thomas More counselled William Gonbell on how to direct his daughter's education he emphasised the place of regular and frequent letter-writing: 'when having nothing to write of, you write as largely as you can of that nothing, than which nothing is more easy for you to do, especially being women, and therefore prattlers by nature'.[104] Men wanted to harness this supposed tendency of women to 'gossip' to the needs of their husbands and households.

Women used secretaries or scribes to write their letters in certain contexts when they were available. This was especially true of the Middle Ages but also later in our period. David Cressy, the foremost authority on literacy in early modern England, estimated that approximately 5 to 20 per cent of women throughout England could at least write their name over the whole period 1550–1700. He conceded that such figures did not take account of social differences, of the urban/rural divide, or of rising literacy over the period.[105] Such minimal literacy was therefore most probably exceeded, especially among urban women of the middling and upper sorts, and especially in London in the years 1660–1730.[106] Active or true literacy implies at least the ability to set thoughts down on paper independently in an organised and readable form in a reasonable amount of time. James Daybell has questioned the extent to which early modern English women could write and also their propensity to write.[107] He examined closely the letters sent by 650 female letter writers in the period 1540 to 1603 and concluded that 23 per cent of these writers used scribes for all of their correspondence. At least some of them could not write at all. Daybell thinks that such a one was Mary Harding who wrote: 'humbly beseeching your honour [Elizabeth, Countess of Rutland] not to be offended with me for that I write no oftener to your honour the cause is that I cannot write myself and I am loath to make anybody acquainted with my letters', although it is conceivable that she meant that something else was preventing her writing.[108] Others could probably write but not with sufficient confidence or fluency that they would often do so. At a time when letters had to be written quickly (because the messenger on horseback was impatiently waiting for her reply) and the lady in question perhaps had hands made awkward by arthritis, a secretary with a quick and easy facility for setting thoughts down on paper probably seemed an ideal solution.[109] Nevertheless a substantial proportion of the women surveyed wrote their own letters, especially in a family as opposed to a business or legal context. Anne Dudley, Countess of Warwick, for example, wrote mainly holograph letters to relatives but used a secretary to pen her business correspondence. Perhaps this was true of Lady Cornwallis who, in 1730, was said to have 'employed lady Fry to writ letters for her'.[110] Cassandra Brydges, Duchess of Chandos, however, penned all her own letters and even made copies of many of them, whether they were family letters or not.

Even medieval women who used scribes to write the main body of a letter quite frequently inserted autograph and personal postscripts to their professionally penned letters. Private and personal communications of this kind have a fluency, informality and immediacy of linguistic expression that is startling. When women were literate or desirous to communicate in writing they played an important role in binding together the wider family, the different generations, the neighbours and the 'friends', through letter-writing. This was true even when the letter-writing itself was done by scribes.[111] Alison Truelove had argued that while the letters of gentry women in the Middle Ages may have been stylised and based on written models those of women of the merchant classes were perhaps more influenced by everyday verbal discourse and that even upper-class women were prone to insert informal postscripts into letters based on classical forms.[112] Interesting though the detailed debates concerning active female literacy are, the important issues for this chapter remain whether, when we read a letter from a woman, it represents that woman's own thoughts, unmediated by another party, and whether a woman's ability to communicate those thoughts was hampered by her lack of facility in handwriting. Important also is whether the language and style of female correspondence represent a woman's own reactions to external influences such as Bible or romance reading, or those of her amanuensis.[113]

Over 10,000 items of female correspondence are extant for the period before the English Civil Wars and innumerable items thereafter. It is difficult to place this activity: frequently the content of such correspondence was humdrum and practical and little connected with the life of the mind, yet it also served to improve communication between individuals, to provide a forum for self-expression, to acquaint distant provincial households with the fashions and the fads of the metropolis and the cultural life of the day, to establish traditions and continuities. In the case of the *Athenian Mercury* it seems that London women from many classes of society by the late seventeenth century also used correspondence to reach out to the wider, male society and to seek outside opinions about issues that exercised their minds. Above all, female correspondence demonstrates that women were actively involved in a continuing family dialogue and thereby played an important part in the culture of that family.[114] Even prosaic subject matter provided the occasion for practice and stylistic experiment. Just one or two examples must be sufficient. The sister of John Evelyn the younger was urged by her brother to hurry up and improve her writing skills so that they could communicate properly while he was at university. [!] In 1685 John Erskine of Carnock, Scotland, acknowledged that his knowledge of his brother's voyage to settle Stuarts Town, Carolina, came from letters written to their 'good-sister'.[115] When New Englander Thomas Dudley wrote to inform his daughter Mercy Woodbridge of her mother's death in 1643 he asked her, 'let me have now thy letters as thy mother had and I will answer them', thus acknowledging the important and indispensable role her mother had played in the continuing 'education' of her daughters and the extent to which the mother–child bond was customarily nurtured by letter-writing.[116] In some circumstances women were also using correspondence to help create and maintain a wider network which extended the reach of the family: the importance of Cassandra Brydges' written and verbal communications was fully acknowledged by her husband the Duke of Chandos who saw her as his channel to relatives and contacts. Where women were taught to write, this literacy was put to good purpose.

Women as players

Until the mid-seventeenth century women were not permitted to perform on the public stage. A patent granted to Thomas Killigrew in 1662, however, made it compulsory for women to play the female roles. This apparently positive step in recognition of women's right to participate nevertheless had its negative side. Elizabeth Howe showed how women were then exploited on the stage 'as sexual objects' – and how this voyeurism helped shape the traditions of comedy and she-tragedy in the later seventeenth and eighteenth centuries.[117] We do not know the extent to which this occurred in the American colonies but when theatre arrived in the New World, women were certainly an accepted part of the companies. One of the first actresses to perform in the southern colonies was Mrs Osborne who played leading parts in Annapolis, Maryland, in the early 1750s and also performed with the Virginia Company of Comedians at Norfolk and Williamsburg in 1767–1768 and with the New American Company in Annapolis in 1769.[118] At least some of these women developed careers and gained considerable following among critics and male and female audiences. The response of Marylanders to the acting of Sarah Hallam as Imogen in Shakespeare's *Cymbeline* does not suggest that she was regarded as a sex object but as a serious actress: 'Such delicacy of manner. Such classical strictness of expression. The music of her tongue . . .'[119] They seem to have established acting as a respectable career for a woman. One, Margaret Cheer, obtained a noble Scottish husband and continued to perform for a year after her marriage.

Women and the world

It is clear also that at least some women in the later seventeenth and eighteenth centuries were displaying an active interest in, and flair for, philosophy and scientific inquiry. This was generally stamped upon but in some cases was supported by their husbands and families. An Englishwoman who questioned Cartesian principles was Anne (Finch) Conway (1631–79) whose *Principles of the Most Ancient and Modern Philosophy*, was published posthumously in 1690. A more fundamental challenge to Cartesian thought was launched by Margaret Cavendish. Bronwen Price, among others, has drawn attention to the ways in which Cavendish's 250 *Poems, and Fancies*, 1656, 'examine uncharted, speculative areas of science, the earth and the universe, and the human body. The volume is divided up into thematic areas, which include the inner workings of the brain, atomist theory, the possible existence of other worlds, and battle.' The very choice of poetry as her medium presented a challenge to the Baconian assumption that prose was the appropriate medium for scientific inquiry. Cavendish problematised knowledge, questioned Descartes's principles and saw body and mind as connected. Her poetry questioned the nature and composition of the brain, asked how it operated, whether it was in fact knowable and whether it was gendered. Notably, in the poem 'The Elyzium' Cavendish examined those operations of the brain that Descartes attributed to the insane (dreams, the unconscious, the fantastic, the prophetic). She supported contemporary atomist theory but extended it to explain disease, psychological change, death, life and creation, thus challenging the role of God. Regarded as eccentric, she was denied membership of the Royal Society. On the one occasion that she attended a meeting she was refused permission to participate. Interestingly her husband was much more supportive.[120]

Conclusion

We shall never be able to measure precisely the extent to which women participated in contemporary culture but it is clear that if we concentrate only on their contributions to 'public' culture (or the institutions which fostered the cultural and intellectual life of males) we shall miss almost entirely the important roles they did play. We have seen that in some families on both sides of the Atlantic the womenfolk were encouraged to engage in the cultural life of the household and the network. It seems probable that individual families had differing attitudes to such participation and what was considered acceptable, and it seems dangerous to identify trends in Old or New Worlds. Nevertheless it does seem that a cultural niche for aristocratic married women was established by the Restoration – it was acceptable for women to have an intellectual and cultural life that served the needs of the family and network in terms of education, companionable activity and matching. By the late seventeenth century these opportunities were expanding, especially in urban areas (with the growth of the season), with the emergence of the bluestockings, and with the accessibility and acceptability of amateur and professional drama and music. The dominance of English seems to have ensured access to a common culture among elites throughout the British Islands and colonies but this did not preclude the continuing health of other cultures from which the English-only speaker was excluded. This seems to have been true of Wales in particular but also to a lesser extent in Gaelic-speaking areas of Ireland and Scotland.

Notes

1. Sarah Silsbe's Adam and Eve Sampler, Boston, Massachusetts, 1748.
2. See p. 404.
3. M. Wynne-Davies (1998) p. xxii.
4. Ibid p. 348.
5. Andrew Clark (ed.) John Aubrey, *Brief Lives* (1898 edn) Vol. 1, p. 311.
6. S. P. Cerasano and M. Wynne-Davis (1996) pp. 13–17.
7. Cerasano and Wynne-Davis (1996) p. 93. According to this reading 'the Vale of Tempe in Urania II is a pastoral interlude in which a brother and sister occur who excel in writing poetry' and this theme 'is expanded in Love's Victory where the brother and sister are Philisses and Simeana.' For this see HEH, HM600 which is the sole surviving manuscript copy.
8. R. Baird (2004 pbk edn) pp. 96–7.
9. S. H. Myers (1990); HEH, MO; R. Baird (2004 pbk edn) pp. 188–9.
10. E. F. R. More (1961) p. 155.
11. B. S. Travitsky (1996).
12. B. Price (1996).

13 See, for example, Grace Mildmay's autobiography, Northampton Record Office, for a description of her education. An edited version occurs in *Linda Pollock (ed.), With Faith and Physic: The Life of a Tudor Gentlewoman, Lady Grace Mildmay, 1552–1620*, 1993.

14 D. Burrows and R. Dunhill (2002) p. xxv.

15 L. Withey (2000) p. xiii.

16 Compare, for example, Cassandra Willoughby's studies in her brother's library at Wollaton.

17 Withey (2000) pp. 3–4.

18 Extracts from the 'Autobiography of Alexander Carlyle', in J. G. Fyfe and R. S. Rait (1928) pp. 407–8.

19 M. Blundell (1933) pp. 304–12.

20 M. MacCurtain (1991) pp. 160–78.

21 Constance Fowler's Booke, HEH, HM 904; Constance Fowler to Herbert Aston, 31 July 1638.

22 Constance Fowler to Herbert Aston, 11 August 1636.

23 V. Burke (1997) pp. 135, 139.

24 Lady Anne Southwell's Miscellany, Folger Shakespeare Library V.b. 198.

25 Anne Bowyer's Miscellany, Bodleian Library, Ashmole MS 51.

26 V. Burke (1997) p. 141.

27 A. Moss (1996).

28 Lady Margaret Wemyss's song book, National Library of Scotland, Dep 314/23 cited in V. Burke (1997) pp. 144–5.

29 N. Powell (2000) pp. 134–40.

30 E. M. White (2000) p. 220.

31 N. Powell (2000) pp. 141–5; White, p. 220.

32 Now lost.

33 Powell (2000) pp. 144–6.

34 Ibid pp. 132, 144.

35 M. MacCurtain (1991) pp. 170–71.

36 M. MacCurtain (1991) p. 173.

37 See Chapter 12 for further discussion of bilingualism and biculturalism in Ireland and Wales.

38 M. MacCurtain (1991) p. 162.

39 S. R. Westfall (1990) p. 110.

40 J. H. Wiffen, *Historical Memoirs of the House of Russell*, 1833; cited in Ann Thompson (1996).
41 Thompson (1996).
42 HEH, STB Box 2, Book 3, Genealogical Notebooks.
43 Lady Georgina Bertie, *Five Generations of a Loyal House, Part I, Containing the Lives of Richard Bertie and his Son Peregrine, Lord Willoughby*, London, Gilbert and Rivington, 1845.
44 See NLW, MS 4756B Ann Griffiths's medical receipe book cited in E. M. White (2000) p. 220.
45 BL, Stowe MS 1077, fo. 10, no. 6. Sir Peter was certainly no slavish admirer of male physicians as his other comments on fo. 10 indicate.
46 BL, Stowe MS 1077, fos 68 and 70.
47 That is, a balm.
48 BL, Stowe MS 1077, fo. 68
49 Ibid, fo. 64r.
50 NLCS, Cassandra's Copy Letter Book, no. 157, p. 82. To the Duchess of Marlborough 6 Nov 1723.
51 Usquebaugh. The meaning in Gaelic is 'water of life'.
52 NLCS, Cassandra's Copy Letter Book, no. 158, p. 83. To Lady Diana Spencer 6 Nov 1723. See also Cassandra's detailed descriptions of illnesses in her letters to Lady Ann Coventry.
53 Folger Shakespeare Library MS V.b.231; Princeton U Library; cited in Elizabeth H. Hageman (1996).
54 See Chapter 1.
55 See Sarah Silsbe's Adam and Eve Sampler, Boston, Massachusetts, 1748 as cited in B. Ring (1993) and L. T. Ulrich (2002) p. 9.
56 Ulrich (2002) pp. 5, 9.
57 Diary of Elizabeth Baker quoted in S. Clarke (2000) p. 236.
58 S. Clarke (2000) p. 247.
59 E. M. White (2000) p. 222.
60 White (2000) pp. 221–6.
61 N. Canny (2001) pp. 415–18, 449–55.
62 M. Ogilvie and J. Harvey (2000) p. 665.
63 I. Lowens (1964); H. F. Rankin (1965) For an excellent summary see R. Middleton (1992) pp. 265–6.
64 Ironically, Jonson's play was dedicated to Mary Wroth.

65 J. K. Hosmer (1908) Vol. II, p. 225.
66 Quoted in V. Lucas (1990) p. 235 n. 10.
67 J. Pearson (1996) p. 86.
68 F. Watson (1912) pp. 60–62.
69 For example, Thomas Salter, *The mirrhor of modestie*, 1574.
70 G. Taylor (1990) pp. 91–2.
71 Rosemary O'Day (2007) Cassandra Brydges, letter no. 355, fo. 213 to lady Ann Coventry 3 March 1732/3.
72 HEH, STB Box 2 Book 3, pp. 10–11.
73 Summarised from B. S. Travitsky (1996) pp. 234–66.
74 J. C. Spruill (1938) pp. 256–8.
75 M. MacCurtain (1990).
76 S. H. O'Grady (1926) Vol. I and A. S. Green (1908) p. 251, both cited in M. MacCurtain (1991) p. 161.
77 Sarah Fyge Egerton, 'The liberty', in R. E. Pritchard (1990) p. 112.
78 Mary Carbery (1913). The works of fiction were 'Cassandra, a romance', and Delarivier Manley's *New Atlantis*.
79 R. Perry (1986) pp. 339–54.
80 J. Pearson (1996).
81 Ibid.
82 Ibid p. 95. See Chapter 14 above on women and belief.
83 G. C. Williamson (1922) p. 60.
84 Extracts from 'Autobiography of Alexander Carlyle', in J. G. Fyfe and R. S. Rait (1928) pp. 422–3.
85 J. Pearson (1996) pp. 85–6.
86 See Jennie Bachelor (2005).
87 See Margaret Hunt (1984) for the activities of Dunton's Mercury Women.
88 See H. Berry (2003) pp. 13–15; S. Pincus (1995); J. Harris (2000) pp. 1–13; H. Berry (2001) pp. 65–81.
89 R. Porter (1994) pp. 93–106, 160–70.
90 Anon., *Rules and orders of the coffee house*, 1674.
91 D. Cressy (2000) pp. 84–91.
92 HEH, ST26, Vol. 1, p. 14, 24 Feb 1696/7 is a typical entry: 'I staid at a coffee house in Gerard Street ~~about~~ betwixt six and seven, whilst my wife went and

made a visit to ye young Lady Manchester, from thence wee went to Mr: Gibbons's, who not being within, wee went to my Cozen Gostwyck's, who being abroad, wee went to Mrs Gors's, who likewise not being within, wee came home.'

93 L. Wetherill (1988).
94 H. Berry (2003) pp. 244–5.
95 Ibid p. 39.
96 H. Berry (1997) pp. 257–76.
97 H. Berry (2003) p. 102.
98 S. P. Cerasano and M. Wynne-Davis (1996) pp. 15–17.
99 J. A. Roberts (1983) pp. 3–39.
100 S. P. Cerasano and M. Wynne-Davis (1996) p. 93.
101 There were 128 solely translated by her compared to 43 translated by her brother with, perhaps, her help.
102 D. Birch (1990), Block 8, p. 47; R. Zim (1987).
103 M. H. Nicholson (1992 edn).
104 Cited by H. Smith (1996) p. 21.
105 Cressy (1980) pp. 112–22, pp. 145–9.
106 Cressy (1980) pp. 145–9.
107 J. Daybell (2001) pp. 59–76.
108 *Historical Manuscripts Commission Report*, 1888, vol. 1, p. 301, *Manuscripts of his Grace the Duke of Rutland, Preserved at Belvoir Castle*, 3 Vols, Mary Harding to Elizabeth, Countess of Rutland, 24 July 1592, cited in Daybell (2001) p. 60.
109 Folger Shakespeare Library, Cavendish/Talbot Correspondence, X.d. 428 fo. 38, Susan Grey, Countess of Kent to her aunt Elizabeth Talbot, dowager Countess of Shrewsbury, 26 Jan 1593: 'pardon me that I write not this with my owne hande for that my finger continue the so evell as that I am not able to howled a penn.'
110 HEH, STB Box 1 (2) no. 28. Lettice Cornwallis to Cassandra Brydges, 30 Aug 1730.
111 V. M. O'Mara (1996) pp. 96–7.
112 A. D. Wall (2001) p. 44.
113 See, for example, those of the Paston women's letters in the fifteenth century that appear to echo the language of the Bible.
114 R. O'Day (2001) pp. 127–42.

115 Extracts from Journal of John Erskine, in J. G. Fyfe and R. S. Rait (1928) p. 339.
116 James Daybell (2001) pp. 59–76.
117 E. Howe (1992) pp. 25–6. See also A. Thompson (1996) pp. 100–16.
118 J. C. Spruill (1938) pp. 261–3 citing G. O. Seilhamer History of the American Theatre, 1888–91, Vol. I, pp. 4, 8–10, 235, 258.
119 *Maryland Gazette*, 6 Sept 1770.
120 B. Price (1996), 'Feminine modes of knowing and scientific inquiry: Margaret Cavendish's poetry as case study', pp. 120–5; S. H. Mendelson (1987); S. I. Mintz (1952) 168–76.

Bibliography

Manuscript sources and collections

Bodleian Library Oxford (especially Anne Bowyer's Miscellany, Ashmole MS 51; Lady Elizabeth Delaval's meditations, prayers and occasional memoirs, Rawlinson MS D.78; Samuel Woodforde's Diary, MS Eng. misc. fo. 381; Charles Beale's unpaginated diary entries in Rawlinson 8o 572, being William Lilly's *Almanack* of 1677).

BL Add. MS 27347 (Richard Waller's translation of the *Aeneid*).

BL Add. MS 27351–27356 (Mary, Countess of Warwick's Diaries, 1666–1678).

BL Add. MS 34169–34172 (Diary of Isabella Twysden).

BL Add. MS 34657 Collet MS.

BL Add. MS 4454 (Katharine Austen's Diary).

BL Add. MS 41654 (The Letters of Lady Dorothy Bacon).

BL Add. MSS 78299, 78300, 78433, 78435, 78539 (Correspondence with and about Susannah Evelyn).

BL Coke MSS (Correspondence of Coke of Melbourne, Derbyshire).

BL Egerton MS 2614 (Diary of Lady Margaret Hoby).

BL Egerton MSS 2643–6 (Barrington Papers).

BL Egerton MS 3054 (Account Book of Joyce Jefferies).

BL Evelyn Archive, Diary, Vols 1–2.

BL Harley MS 6828 ff. 510–23 (Mary Beale, Discourse on Friendship, 1666/7, addressed to Elizabeth Tillotson).

BL Lansdowne MS 460 nos 30, 31, 32, 33 (Sir Francis and Lady Elizabeth Willoughby's marriage); also no. 37.

BL MS Reg. 15A.

BL Royal MS 20 B XVII (Loys de Brun, French treatise on letter-writing, 1530).

BL Stowe MSS 847 and 848 (Manorial Court Books).

BL Stowe MS 1077 and 1078 (Receipts [recipes]).

BL Trumbull MSS.

Central Library, Northampton (Lady Grace Mildmay's Journal).

Folger Shakespeare Library, Washington DC (Bagot Collection, L.a.; Lady Anne Southwell's Miscellany, V.b.198; Cavendish/Talbot Correspondence, X.d.; Katherine Digby's spiritual exercises, V.a. 473).

Huntington Library, San Marino, California (Stowe Collection (Temple, Brydges, Grenville); Egerton Papers; Huntington Manuscripts (especially HM 600 (Urania); HM 904 (Constance Fowler's book); HM 6660 (Suffolk Papers) Montagu Papers.

Lichfield Joint Record Office (Wills and inventories).

National Portrait Gallery, Heinz Archive (Charles Beale's notebook, 1680/1, MS 9535).

North London Collegiate School (Copy Letter Book of Cassandra, 1st Duchess of Chandos, and assorted documents).

Nottingham University Library (Middleton Papers).

Papers of the Marquis of Bath at Longleat (Coventry Papers – also available on microfilm at the Library of Congress).

Shakespeare Birthplace Trust Record Office (Cassandra Willoughby's Travel Journal, DR\18\20\21\1 and Cassandra Willoughby's early correspondence DR\18\20\21\2. Copyright Stoneleigh Abbey Ltd).

Staffordshire County Record Office (Bradford Papers).

Printed primary sources

Hannah Allen, *Satan his methods and malice baffled*, 1683.

Richard Allestree, *The Whole duty of man*, 1684.

George Alsop, *A Character of the province of Mary-land*, in Clayton Colman Hall, *Narratives of Early Maryland, 1633–1684*, 1910.

Anon., *Baron and Feme: A treatise of the common law concerning husbands and wives*, 1700.

Anon., *The Hardships of the English Laws. In Relation to wives. With an explanation of the original curse of subjection passed upon the woman. In an humble address to the legislature*, 1735.

Anon., (N. H.) *The Ladies' Dictionary Being a general entertainment for the fair sex*, 1694.

Anon., (T. E.) *The Lawes Resolutions of Women's Rights: or the Lawes Provision for Woemen*, 1632.

Anon., *The Mid-wives Just Petition*, 1643.

Anon., *Rules and orders of the coffee house*, 1674.

Anon., *A treatise of feme coverts: Or, the Lady's Law, Containing all the Laws and Statutes Relating to Women*, 1732 [An extended version of *Baron and Feme*].

Anon., *A Share of Honour, Virginia Women 1600–1945*.

Athenian Gazette or Casuistical Mercury, 17, 24; 23 June 1695.

Lady Anne [Coke] Bacon, *Fouretene Sermons of Barnadine Ochyne*, 1550.

Marion Balderston, *James Claypoole's Letter Book London and Philadelphia, 1681–1684*, Huntington Library, San Marino, California, 1967.

Margaret Beaufort, Countess of Richmond and Derby, transl. Thomas à Kempis, *Imitation of Christ*, 1504.

Margaret Beaufort, Countess of Richmond and Derby, transl. Jacobus Gruitroede, *The mirroure of golde for the synfull soule*, 1506.

Thomas Becon, *A new catechism set forth dialogue-wise in familiar talk between the father and the son made by Thomas Becon* in John Ayre (ed.) *The catechism of Thomas Becon . . . with other pieces written by him in the reign of king Edward the Sixth*, Parker Society, 1844.

Thomas Becon, *Worckes*, 1560–1564, I, DCXVI.

Aphra Behn, *The Rover*, 1677.

Aphra Behn, *Oronoco*, 1688.

Thomas Bentley, *Monument of Matrones*, 3 Vols, 1582.

Lady Georgina Bertie, *Five Generations of a loyal house, part I, containing the lives of Richard Bertie and his son Peregrine, Lord Willoughby*, 1845.

Michael R. Best (ed.), *Gervase Markham, The English Housewife*, 1994.

Francis Bickley (ed.), *Report on the Manuscripts of the late Reginald Rawdon Hastings . . .* , Vol. 3, revised edn 1934.

Martin Billingsley, *The Pen's Excellencie*, 1618.

J. E. Binney (ed.), *The Accounts of the wardens of the parish of Morebath, Devon, 1520–1573*, 1904.

Ruth Bird (ed.), *The Journal of Giles Moore*, 1971.

William Blackstone, *Commentaries on the laws of England*, 1765–1769.

Elizabeth Blackwell, *A Curious Herball containing 500 cuts useful in the practice of physik*, 1756.

M. Blundell, *Cavalier: Letters of William Blundell to his friends, 1620–1698*, 1933.

Maurice F. Bond (ed.), *The Diaries and papers of Sir Edward Dering . . . 1644 to 1684*, House of Lords Record Office Occasional Publications, no. 1, 1976.

Anne Bradstreet, Works. See John Howard Ellis edition.

Richard Braithwaite, *The English gentleman*, 1630.

Richard Braithwaite, *The English gentlewoman*, 1631.

William Brigham, *The Compact with the Charter and Laws of the Colony of New Plymouth*, 1836.

John Brinsley, *A Looking-glasse for good women*, 1645.

William Hande Browne (ed.), *Archives of Maryland*, 72 Vols, Baltimore, Maryland Historical Society, 1883–1972.

Clive Burgess (ed.), The pre-Reformation records of All Saints Bristol, Part 1, *Bristol Record Society*, Vol. 46, 1995.

Donald Burrows and Rosemary Dunhill (eds), *Music and Theatre in Handel's World. The Family Papers of James Harris, 1732–1780*, 2002.

William Burton, *The New Mother*, 1606 (2 editions), 1624.

S. Bury (ed.), *An Account of the life and death of Mrs Elizabeth Bury*, 1720.

Muriel St Clare Byrne (ed.), *The Lisle Letters*, abridged version, 1983.

The Calvert Papers, 3 Vols, Maryland Historical Society Fund Publications 28, 1889–99.

Mary Carbery (ed.), *Mrs Elizabeth Freke, Her Diary, 1671–1714*, 1913.

Elizabeth Carey, *The Tragedie of Mariam, the faire queene of Iewry. Written by that learned, vertuous, and truly noble ladie E. C.*, 1613.

Elizabeth Carey, *The History of the Life, Reign and Death of Edward II*, c. 1627/8.

Elizabeth Carey, *The Reply of the Most Illustrious Cardinall of Perronn*, 1630.

Christine Carpenter (ed.), *The Stonor Letters and Papers, 1290–1483*, 1996, 2 Vols.

S. R. Cattley (ed.), John Foxe, *Acts and Monuments*, 1939.

Margaret Cavendish, *Philosophical and Physical Opinions*, 1655.

Margaret Cavendish, *Natures pictures drawn by fancies pencil to the life*, 1656, 2nd 1671 edition.

Gillian T. Cell (ed.), *Newfoundland Discovered: English Attempts at Colonisation, 1610–1630*, Hakluyt Society, 2nd series, 160, 1982.

S. P. Cerasano and Marion Wynne-Davis (eds), *Renaissance Drama by Women: Texts and Documents*, 1996.

Certain sermons or homilies appointed to be read in churches in the time of Queen Elizabeth, 1908. ('An Homily on the state of matrimony', 1562).

W. Chapell and J. Ebsworth (eds), *Roxburghe Ballads*, 9 Vols, London and Hertford, 1866–99. (Vol. VI, *Love's Downfall*.)

Henry Christmas (ed.), *Select works of John Bale*, Parker Society, 1849.

Andrew Clark (ed.), John Aubrey, *Brief Lives*, 2 Vols, 1898.

Samuel Clarke, *The Lives of Sundry Eminent Persons in this Later Age*, 1683.

A. Clifford (ed.), *Tixall Letters: or the correspondence of the Aston family and their friends during the seventeenth century*, 1815.

Elizabeth Clinton, *The Countess of Lincolnes Nurserie*, 1622.

Jackson I. Cope and Howard W. Jones (eds), Thomas Sprat, *History of the Royal Society*, 1667, 1958 (facsimile).

Thomas Coryate, *Coryats crudités*, 1611.

D. Cram, J. L. Foreng and D. Johnston (eds), *Francis Willoughby's Book of Games*, 2003.

Robert Croft, 'Eulogy', 1638, as cited in C. Belsey, 'The serpent in the garden: Shakespeare, marriage and material culture', *The Seventeenth Century*, Vol. xi, no. 1, 1996.

John Wilson Croker (ed.), *Letters to and from Henrietta, Countess of Suffolk and her second husband The Hon George Berkeley from 1712–1767*, 2 Vols, 1824.

T. Crofton Croker (ed.), *Autobiography of Mary Countess of Warwick*, Percy Society, 1848.

Nicholas Culpeper, *Directory for Midwives*, 1668.

Norman Davis (ed.), *The Paston letters and papers of the Fifteenth Century*, Vol. 1, 1999 edition.

E. S. De Beer, *The Diary of John Evelyn*, 6 Vols, 1955.

Depositions and other ecclesiastical proceedings from the courts of Durham, Surtees Society, 1845.

A dialogue between a gentleman and a lady, relating chiefly to the nursing and bringing up of children, 1698.

A. G. Dickens (ed.), 'The Clifford Letters', *Surtees Society*, 172, 1957.

G. Donaldson (ed.), *Scottish Historical Documents*, 1970.

Theophilus Dorrington (transl.), *The Excellent Woman Described by Her True Characters and Their Opposites*, 1692.

R. Dowe, *A Dairy booke for good huswives*, 1588.

Richard S. Dunn (ed.), *The Laws and Liberties of Massachusetts, 1648*, Huntington Library, 1998.

Alice Morse Earle, *Customs and fashions in old New England*, 1894.

John Howard Ellis (ed.), *The Works of Anne Bradstreet*, 1962.

John Evans, 'An Account of the presents received and expenses incurred at the wedding of Richard Polstead, of Albury, Esquire, and Elizabeth, eldest daughter of William More of Losely, Esquire' in *Archaeologia*, 36, 1855, pp. 36–44.

Margaret Fell, *Women's speaking justified, proved and allowed of by the scriptures*, 1666/7.

Dudley Fenner, *The Order of Household: Described methodically out of the Word of God, with the contrary abuses found in the world*, 1592.

Edward Fenton (ed.), *The Diaries of John Dee*, 1998.

J. Charles Fox (ed.), *Churchwardens' accounts*, 1913.

John Foxe, *Acts and Monuments*, (*Book of Martyrs*), 1563.

Alice T. Friedman, 'Portrait of a marriage: The Willoughyby Letters of 1585–1586', in *Signs: Journal of Women in Culture and Society*, 11, 1986, pp. 542–55.

Thomas Fuller, *History of the worthies of England*, 1662.

Frederick J. Furnivall, *Child marriages, divorce and ratifications etc. in the diocese of Chester, A.D. 1561–6*, Early English Text Society, 1897.

J. G. Fyfe and R. S. Rait (eds), *Scottish Diaries and Memoirs, 1550–1746*, Stirling, 1928 (Extracts from Autobiography of Alexander Carlyle; Extracts from Memoirs of William Veitch; Extracts from Memoirs of George Brysson, merchant of Edinburgh; Extracts from Journal of John Erskine; Extracts from Diary of Henry Guthrie in Fyfe; Narrative of Flora Macdonald; Extracts from the journal of Sir John Lauder, Lord Fountainhall; Extracts from James Kirkton's Secret and true history of the Church of Scotland; John Clerke, *Memoirs of my life*; Extracts from *Analecta*).

C. Giblin (ed.), *Irish Franciscan Mission to Scotland, 1619–1646*, 1964.

William Gouge, *Of Domesticall Duties*, 1622.

William Gouge, *Of Domesticall Duties*, 1634.

Elspeth Graham, Hilary Hinds, Elaine Hoby and Helen Wilcox (eds), *Her Own Life: Autobiographical Writings by Seventeenth-Century Englishwomen*, 1989.

D. G. Greene (ed.), *The Meditations of Lady Elizabeth Delaval*, Surtees Society, 190, 1975.

Jack P. Greene (ed.), *The Diary of Colonel Landon Carter of Sabine Hall, 1752–1778*, 1965.

Richard Greenham, *Treatise of a contract before marriage*, 1599.

R. Griffin, Lord Bray Brooke (ed.), *The Private correspondence of Lady Jane Cornwallis, 1613–44 from the originals in the possession of the family*, 1842.

M. Griffith, *Bethel: or a forme for families in which all sorts of both sexes, are so squared, and framed by the word of God, as they may best serve in their severall places, for useful pieces in God's building*, 1633.

R. G. Griffiths, 'Joyce Jeffreys of Ham Castle', *Transactions of the Worcestershire Archaeological Society*, NS, 10, 1933.

Susan Gushee O'Malley (ed.), *'Custome is an idiot' Jacobean pamphlet literature on women*, pbk, 2004.

Roger Hacket, *Two fruitful sermons, needfull for these times*, 1607, 1–2.

James Orchard Halliwell (ed.), *Autobiography and Correspondence of Sir Simonds D'Ewes*, 1845, I.

Marquis of Halifax, *The Lady's New Years Gift; or, Advice to a Daughter*, 1688.

Clayton Colman Hall, *Narratives of Early Maryland, 1633–1684*, New York, 1910 (includes George Alsop, *A Character of the province of Mary-land*).

James Orchard Halliwell, *The Private Diary of John Dee*, Camden Society, 1845, *Statutes of the Realm*.

James Orchard Halliwell (ed.), *Autobiography and Correspondence of Sir Simonds D'Ewes*, 1945.

Robert Halsband (ed.), *The Complete Letters of Lady Mary Wortley Montagu*, 1967, Vol. 1.

Adam Hamilton (ed.), *The Chronicle of the English Augustinian Canonesses Regular of the Lateran at St Monica's in Louvain*, 2 Vols, 1904.

Patrick Hannay, *The Happy Husband*, 1622.

W. Harris, *An exact enquiry into . . . the acute diseases of infants*, 1693.

William Harrison, *Deaths advantage little regarded*, 1602.

Ruth Haydn, *Mrs Delany, Her life and her flowers*, 1980.

Robert Herrick, 'An Epithalamie to Sir Thomas Southwell and his Ladie', in F. W. Moorman (ed.), *The Poetical Works of Robert Herrick*, 1921.

George Hickes (and Susanna Hopton), *Daily Devotions*, 1673.

George Hickes (and Susanna Hopton), *Devotions in the Ancient Way of Offices Reformed by a Person of Quality*, 2nd edn, 1701.

Samuel Hieron, *The Bridegroome*, 1613.

Historical Manuscripts Commission Report 11, 1887, appendix, part 7 'Manuscripts of Lord Hothfield', ed. William O. Hewlett.

Historical Manuscripts Commission Report, 1888, Vol. 1, *Manuscripts of his Grace the Duke of Rutland, Preserved at Belvoir Castle*, 3 Vols.

Historical Manuscripts Commission Report, 1902, *Manuscripts of Colonel David Milne Home of Wedderburn Castle*.

Historical Manuscripts Commission Report 5 into Manuscripts in Various Collections 5, 1909, *Manuscripts of Sir John James Graham of Fintry; Manuscripts of Sir Archibald Edmonstone of Duntreath, Strathblane, Bt.* ed. Rev. Henry Paton.

Historical Manuscripts Commission Report, 1913, Vol. 1 and 1922, Vol. 2, *Manuscripts of Allan George Finch Esq. of Burley-on-the-Hill, Rutland*. ed. S. C. Lomas.

Historical Manuscripts Commission Report, Vol. I, 1928, *Manuscripts of the late Reginald Rawdon Hastings esq. of the Manor House, Ashby de la Zouche* eds John Harley and Francis Bickley.

Bishop Hobhouse (ed.), *Churchwardens' accounts of Croscombe . . . 1349–1560*, Somerset Record Society, 4, 1890.

Edmund Hobhouse, MD (ed.), *The Diary of a West Country physician A.D. 1684–1726*, 1934.

J. A. Home (ed.), *Letters and Journals of Lady Mary Coke*, 1889, I.

James Kelly Hosmer (ed.), *Winthrop's Journal, 1630–1649*, 1908.

R. Hughey (ed.), *Correspondence of Lady Katherine Paston, 1603–1627*, Norfolk Record Society, 14, 1941.

Sarah Hutton and Marjorie Hope Nicholson (eds), *The Conway Letters. The Correspondence of Anne, Viscountess Conway, Henry More and their Friends*, 1992.

C. Jackson (ed.), *The Autobiography of Mrs Alice Thornton*, Surtees Society, 62, 1875.

Sydney V. James (ed.), *Three Visitors to Early Plymouth*, 1963.

N. H. Keeble, *The Cultural Identity of Seventeenth-Century Woman: A Reader*, 1994.

Lancelot Langhorne, *Funeral Sermon of Mrs Mary Swaine*, 1611.

Dorothy Leigh, *The Mother's Blessing*, 1621.

John Leland, *Collectanea*, V, 1770.

Santina M. Levey and Peter K. Thornton (for The National Trust) (eds), *Of Household Stuff: The 1601 Inventories of Bess of Hardwick*, 2001.

Kenneth A. Lockridge, *The Diary and Life of William Byrd II of Virginia, 1674–1744*, 1987.

G. A. Loundes, 'History of the Barrington family', *in Transactions of the Essex Archaeological Society*, I, New Series, 1878.

Alan Macfarlane (ed.), *The Diary of Ralph Josselin, 1616–1683*, 1976.

Henry Machyn, *The Diary of a Resident of London*, 1847, pp. 243–4, 288.

J. Maclean (ed.), *Smyth's Lives of the Berkeleys*, 3 Vols, 1883.

Gervase Markham, *The English Housewife*, 1615.

J. Marshall (ed.), *The Autobiography of William Stout of Lancaster*, 1967.

Martin Martin, *Description of the western isles of Scotland*, 1695.

Maryland Gazette.

Steven W. May (ed.), *Queen Elizabeth I: Selected Works*, 2004.

Mayflower Descendant, I–XXV.

Shannon McSheffrey and Norman Tanner (eds), *Lollards of Coventry, 1486–1522*, Royal Historical Society, Camden, 5th Series, 23, 2004.

Henri Misson, *M. Misson's memoirs and observations in his travels over England*, 1719.

Joanna Moody (ed.), *Private Life of an Elizabethan Lady*, 1998.

F. W. Moorman (ed.), *The Poetical Works of Robert Herrick*, 1921.

Elizabeth Frances Rogers More, *St Thomas More: Selected Letters*, 1961.

Henry More, *An Antidote Against Atheism*, 1652.

H. J. Morehouse (ed.), A Dyurnall . . . [Adam Eyre], Surtees Society, *Yorkshire Diaries*, LXV, 1877 (1875).

Richard Mulcaster, *Positions . . . for the training up of children*, 1581.

Lady Murray of Stanhope (ed.), *Memoirs of the Lives and Characters of the Honorable George Baillie and Lady Grisell Baillie of Jerviswood, by their daughter, Lady Murray of Stanhope*, 1821.

Marjorie Hope Nicholson (ed.), *The Conway Letters. The Correspondence of Anne, Viscountess Conway, Henry More and their Friends*, New Haven, 1930; revised edition, Sarah Hutton, 1992.

North Carolina Magazine; or Universal Intelligencer.

John Northbrook, *A treatise wherein dicing, dauncing, vaine playes, or enterluds, with other idle pastimes, etc., commonly used on the Sabbath day, are reproved by the authoritie of the word of God and auntient writers*, 1577.

George O'Brien (ed.), *Advertisements for Ireland*, 1923.

Rosemary O'Day (ed.), *Cassandra Brydges, 1670–1735, First Duchess of Chandos: Life and Letters*, 2007.

Mary O'Dowd (ed.), *Calendar of State Papers Ireland Tudor Period, 1571–1575*, Public Record Office and Irish Manuscripts Commission, 2000.

S. H. O'Grady, *Catalogue of Irish Manuscripts in the British Museum*, 1926.

Sir John Oglander, 'Rules for a happy life', 1612 in C. Aspinall-Oglander, *Nunwell Symphony*, 1945.

S. G. O'Malley (ed.), 'Custome is an idiot', 2004.

James M. Osborn (ed.), *The Autobiography of Thomas Whythorne* [1528–1596], 1962.

G. Parfitt and R. Houlbrooke (eds), *The Courtship Narrative of Leonard Wheatcroft, Derbyshire Yeoman*, 1986.

Richard Parkinson (ed.), *The Life of Adam Martindale*, Chetham Society 1845.

Henry Peacham, *The Art of Living in London*, 1642.

Ruth Perry, *The Celebrated Mary Astell: An Early English Feminist*, Chicago and London, 1986. (For correspondence of Mary Astell and Book List of Anne Lady Coventry).

Mary (Griffith) Pix, *Violenta, or The Rewards of a Virtue*, 1696.

Mary (Griffith) Pix, *Queen Catharine, or The Ruines of Love*, 1698.

Plymouth Colony Records, IV.

Plymouth Colony Records, V.

Plymouth Colony Records, VI.

Linda Pollock (ed.), *With Faith and Physic: The Life of a Tudor Gentlewoman, Lady Grace Mildmay, 1552–1620*, 1993.

Elizabeth Poole, *A Vision: Wherein is manifested the disease and cure of the kingdom*, 1648.

R. E. Pritchard (ed.), *Poetry by English Women: Elizabethan to Victorian*, 1990. (Sarah Fyge Egerton, 'The Liberty'.)

Edward Rainebow, *A Sermon preached at the interrment of Anne, Countess of Pembroke*, 1677.

J. Ray, *A Collection of English proverbs*, 1678.

Edward Reynolds, *The Churches triumph over death*, 1662.

G. B. Richardson (ed.), W. Palmes, *The Life of Mrs Dorothy Lawson*, 1851.

Josephine A. Roberts (ed.), *The Poems of Lady Mary Wroth*, 1983.

Amy Edith Robinson, *The Life of Richard Kidder, D.D., Bishop of Bath and Wells: Written by Himself*, Somerset Record Society, 1924.

Timothy Rogers, *The Character of a Good Woman*, 1697.

J. T. Rutt (ed.), *Diary of Thomas Burton Esquire, Member in the Parliaments of Oliver and Richard Cromwell*, 4 Vols, 1828.

Thomas Salter, *The mirrhor of modestie*, 1574.

Robert Scott-Moncreiff (ed.), *The Household book of Lady Grisell Baillie, 1692–1733*, 1911.

Jane Sharp, *The Midwives Book: On the whole art of midwifery discovered directing childbearing women how to behave themselves*, London, 1671; republished as *The Compleat Midwives' Companion*, 1725.

Lady Mary Sidney, transl. Philippe de Mornay, *A Discourse of Life and Death*, 1592.

A. Hassall Smith, *The Letters and Will of Lady Dorothy Bacon*, Norfolk Record Society, lvi, 1991.

Richard Smith, *The life of . . . Lady Magdalen Viscountess Montague*, 1627, pp. 27–31.

R. P. Sorlien (ed.), *The Diary of John Manningham of the Middle Temple, 1602–1603*, 1976.

South Carolina Gazette.

South Carolina and American General Gazette.

Ester Sowernam, *Ester hath hang'd Haman*, 1617.

Rachel Speght, *The Women's Sharpe Revenge*, 1617.

Rachel Speght, *A Mouzell for Melotomus*, 1617.

Nathaniel Spinckes (and Susannah Hopton), *A Collection of Meditations and Devotions on the Life of Christ*, 1717.

Thomas Sprat, *The History of the Royal Society*, 1667.

Sarah Stone, *Complete Practice of Midwifery*, 1737.

John Strype, *Ecclesiastical memorials*, 1822.

J. Stuart (ed.), *Selections from the Records of the Kirk Session, Presbytery and Synod of Aberdeen*, 1846.

J. Sutherland (ed.), Lucy Hutchinson (1618) *Memoirs of the life of Colonel Hutchinson, with the fragment of an autobiography of Mrs Hutchinson*, 1973.

Joseph Swetnam, *Arraignment of Lewd, Idle, Froward and Inconstant Women*, 1615.

Henry Swinburne, *A Brief treatise of testamentes and last willes*, 1590 edition.

Ann Taves (ed.), *Religion and Domestic Violence in Early New England, The Memoirs of Abigail Bailey*, 1989.

Nancy Taylor (ed.), *Cousins in Love: The letters of Lydia DuGard, 1665–1672 With a New Edition of The Marriages of Cousin Germans by Samuel DuGard*, Renaissance English Text Society, 2003.

T. F. Thisleton-Dyer, *Church-Lore Gleanings*, 1892.

M. Halsey Thomas (ed.), *The Diary of Samuel Sewall*, 1973.

The Autobiography of Mrs Alice Thornton of East Newton, County York, 1873.

M. P. Tilley, *A Dictionary of the Proverbs in England in the Sixteenth and Seventeenth Centuries*, 1950.

Thomas Tusser, *A Hundreth good points of husbandry, lately married unto a hundreth good points of housewifery*, 1570; *Five hundred points of husbandry*, 1573.

William Vaughan, *The Golden grove, moralized in three bookes*, 1609.

Virginia Gazette.

Virginia Magazine of History and Biography, VII January 1900.

Anthony Walker, *Holy life of Mrs E. Walker*, 1690.

Horace Walpole, *Anecdotes of painting in England*, 3 Vols, 1762–1763.

Foster Watson (ed.), *Vives and the Renascence Education of Women*, 1912.

Isaac Watts, 'Meditation in a Grove', in *Horae Lyricae*, 1706.

Tom Webster and Kenneth Shipps (eds), *The Diary of Samuel Rogers, 1634–1638*, Church of England Record Society, 2004.

C. Welch (ed. and transl.) The churchwardens' accounts of the parish of Allhallows, London Wall, in the city of London, 33 Henry VI to 27 Henry VIII (AD 1455–AD 1536), 1912.

William Whateley, *A Bride bush: or, a direction for married persons*, 1623.

J. H. Wiffen, *Historical memoirs of the house of Russell*, 1833.

G. C. Williamson, *Lady Anne Clifford*, 1922.

John Willis, *Art of memory*, 1621.

A. C. Wood (ed.), *The Continuation of the History of the Willoughby Family by Cassandra Duchess of Chandos*, Eton, 1958.

Hannah Woolley, *The Accomplisht ladys delight in preserving, physick, beautifying and cooking*.

Secondary works

Books

L. W. Abbott, *Law Reporting in England, 1485–1585*, 1973.

Virginia DeJohn Anderson, *The Great Migration and the Formation of Society and Culture in the Seventeenth Century*, 1991.

Maria Agren and Amy Louise Erickson, *The Marital Economy of Scandinavia and Britain, 1400–1900*, 2005.

Raymond A. Anselment (ed.), *The Remembrances of Elizabeth Freke, 1671–1714*, Camden Fifth Series, 18, 2001.

John C. Appleby and Paul Dalton (eds), *Government, Religion and Society in Northern England, 1000–1700*, 1997.

Margaret Aston, *Lollards and Reformers. Images and Literacy in Late Medieval Religion*, 1984.

James Axtell, *The European and the Indian: Essays in the Ethno-History of Colonial North America*, 1981.

Bernard Bailyn, *The Peopling of British North America: An Introduction*, 1986.

Bernard Bailyn and Barbara DeWolfe, *Voyagers to the West: A Passage in the Peopling of America on the Eve of the Revolution*, 1986.

Rosemary Baird, *Mistress of the House: Great Ladies and Grand Houses*, 2004.

John H. Baker, *Introduction to English Legal History*, 2nd edition, 1979.

Linda Ballard, *Ulster Needlework: A Continuing Tradition*, 1991.

G. Bankes, *The Story of Corfe Castle*, 1853.

F. D. Bardgett, *Scotland Reformed: The Reformation in Angus and the Mearns*, 1989.

Toby Barnard, *A New Anatomy of Ireland: Making The Grand Figure*, 2003.

Caroline M. Barron and Christopher Harper-Bill (eds), *The Church in Pre-Reformation Society*, 1985.

Caroline M. Barron and Anne F. Sutton, *Medieval London Widows, 1300–1500*, 1994.

Anna Beer, *Bess: The Life of Lady Ralegh, Wife to Sir Walter*, 2004.

J. M. Bennett, *Ale, Beer and Brewsters in England: Women's Work in a Changing World, 1300–1600*, 1996.

Helen Berry, *Gender, Society and Print Culture in Late Stuart England. The Cultural World of The Athenian Mercury*, 2003.

Lita-Rose Betcherman, *Court Lady & Country Wife: Royal Privilege and Civil War, Two Noble Sisters in Seventeenth-Century England*, 2005.

Virginia Blain, Patricia Clements and Isobel Grundy (eds), *The Feminist Companion to Literature in English Women Writers from the Middle Ages to the Present*, 1990.

Ian Blanchard (ed.), *New Directions in Economic and Social History*, 1995.

A. Bliss, *Spoken English in Ireland, 1600–1740*, 1979.

Ruth H. Bloch, *Gender and Morality in Anglo-American Culture, 1650–1800*, 2003.

H. Blodgett, *Centuries of Female Days: Englishwomen's Private Diaries*, 1989.

Lloyd Bonfield, *Marriage Settlements 1601–1740: The Adoption of the Strict Settlement*, 1989.

Frances Borzello, *Seeing Ourselves: Women's Self Portraits*, 1998.

John Bossy, *The English Catholic community 1570–1850*, 1975.

Jeremy Boulton, *Neighbourhood and Society*, 1987.

Hilary Bourdillon, *Women as Healers*, 1988.

J. Bradley (ed.), *Settlement and Society in Ireland: Viking and Medieval Times*, 1990.

Ciaran Brady and Raymond Gillespie (eds), *The Making of Irish Colonial Society, 1534–1641: Natives and Newcomers*, 1986.

Xanthe Brooke, *Face to Face: Three Centuries of Artists' Self Portraiture*, 1994.

Terry Brotherstone, Deborah Simonton and Oonagh Walsh (eds), *Gendering Scottish History: An International Approach* [The Mackie Occasional Colloquia Series, 1], 1999.

Kathleen Brown, *Good Wives, Nasty Wenches & Anxious Patriarchs Gender Race and Power in Colonial Virginia*, 1996.

Philip Alexander Bruce, *The Institutional History of Virginia in the Seventeenth Century*, 2 Vols, 1910.

Nicholas Canny, *The Upstart Earl: A Study of the Social and Mental World of Richard Boyle, First Earl of Cork, 1566–1643*, 1982.

Nicholas Canny, *Making Ireland British, 1580–1650*, 2001.

Bernard Capp, *The Fifth Monarchy Men*, 1972.

Bernard Capp, *English Almanacs, 1500–1800*, Ithaca, 1979.

Bernard Capp, *When Gossips Meet*, Oxford, 2003 (references to 2004 pbk edition).

Charles Carlton, *Going to the Wars: The Experience of the British Civil Wars*, 1992.

Charles Carlton et al., *State, Sovereigns and Society in Early Modern England*, 1998.

Lois Green Carr, Philip D. Morgan and Jean B. Russo (eds), *Colonial Chesapeake Society*, 1988.

Berenice A. Carroll (ed.), *Liberating Women's History*, 1976.

C. H. Carter, *From the Renaissance to the Counter-Reformation* (1966).

Sandra Cavallo and Lyndan Warner (eds), *Widowhood in Medieval and Early Modern Europe*, 1999.

Colin Chapman, *Marriage Laws, Rites, Records, and Customs*, 1996.

L. Charles and L. Duffin (eds), *Women and Work in Pre-Industrial England*, 1985.

Maria Cioni, *Women and the Law in Elizabethan England with Particular Reference to the Court of Chancery*, 1985.

Peter Clark, *The English Alehouse: A Social History, 1200–1830*, 1983.

Paul Clemens, *The Atlantic Economy and Colonial Maryland's Eastern Shore: From Tobacco to Grain*, 1980.

Patrick Collinson, *The Elizabethan Puritan Movement*, 1967.

Patrick Collinson, *Godly People*, 1983.

Patrick Collinson, *Elizabethan Essays*, 1994.

Stephanie Coontz, *The Social Origins of Private Life*, 1988.

S. J. Corcoran, *Educational Systems in Ireland*, 1928.

Timothy Corcoran, *Some Lists of Catholic Lay Teachers and their Illegal Schools in the Later Penal Times*, 1932.

Nancy Cott, *Bonds of Womanhood: Woman's Sphere in New England, 1780–1825*, 1977.

Elizabeth Craik (ed.), *Marriage and Property. Women and Marital Customs in History*, 1984.

Anne Crawford *et al.*, (eds), *The Europa Biographical Dictionary of British Women*, 1983.

Patricia Crawford, *Women and Religion in England*, 1993.

David Cressy, *Literacy and the Social Order*, 1980.

David Cressy, *Birth, Marriage and Death: Ritual, Religion and the Life Cycle in Tudor and Stuart England*, 1997.

David Cressy, *Travesties and Transgressions in Tudor and Stuart England*, 2000.

Eveline Cruickshanks and Jeremy Black (eds), *The Jacobite Challenge*, 1988.

Bruce C. Daniels, *The Connecticut Town: Growth and Development, 1635–1790*, Middletown, 1979.

James Daybell (ed.), *Early Modern Women's Letter-Writing, 1450–1800*, 2001.

Cornelia Hughes Dayton, *Women Before the Bar: Gender, Law and Society in Connecticut, 1639–1789*, 1995.

Lloyd De Mause, *The History of Childhood*, 1974.

Carl Degler, *At Odds: Women and the Family in America from the Revolution to the Present*, 1980.

John Demos, *A Little Commonwealth. Family life in Plymouth Colony*, 1970, 1978 repr.

David Dewing (ed.), *Mary Beale (1632/3–1699) Portrait of a Seventeenth-Century Painter, Her Family and Studio*, 1999 (see also Tabitha Barber below).

A. G. Dickens, *The English Reformation*, 1989.

Helen Dingwall, *Physicians, Surgeons and Apothecaries: Medical Training and Practice in Seventeenth-Century Edinburgh*, 1995.

Jean Donnison, *Midwives and Medical Men: A History of the Struggle for the Control of Childbirth*, 1977 and paperbound edition, 1988.

John P. Dowling, *The Hedge Schools of Ireland*, 1935.

Maria Dowling, *Humanism in the Age of Henry VIII*, 1986.

Eamon Duffy, *The Voices of Morebath. Reformation and Rebellion in an English Village*, 2001.

David N. Durant, *Bess of Hardwick: Portrait of an Elizabethan Dynast*, 1977 (Revised pbk edition 1999; reprinted 2000, 2001, 2002).

Peter Earle, *The Making of the English Middle Class: Business, Society and Family Life in London, 1660–1730*, 1989.

Steven G. Ellis, *Tudor Ireland: Crown, Community and the Conflict of Cultures, 1470–1603*, 1985.

Amy Louise Erickson, *Women and Property in Early Modern England*, 1993, 1995 pbk edn.

Margaret J. M. Ezell, *The Patriarch's Wife Literary Evidence and the History of the Family*, 1987.

Valerie Fildes, *Breasts, Bottles and Babies: A History of Infant Feeding*, 1986.

Valerie Fildes (ed.), *Women as Mothers in Pre-industrial England*, 1990.

Margot Finn, *The Character of Credit: Personal Debt in English Culture, 1740–1914*, 2003.

Ronald C. Finucane, *Miracles and Pilgrims. Popular Beliefs in Medieval England*, 1977.

Juliet Fleming, *Graffiti and the Writing Arts of Early Modern England*, 2001.

Anthony Fletcher, *Gender, Sex and Subordination in England, 1500–1800*, 1995.

Jay Fliegelman, *Prodigals and Pilgrims: The American Revolution Against Patriarchal Authority, 1750–1800*, 1982.

Elizabeth Fox-Genovese, *Within the Plantation Household: Black and White Women of the Old South*, 1988.

Antonia Fraser, *The Weaker Vessel Women's Lot in Seventeenth-Century England*, 1984.

H. French and J. Barry (eds), *Identity and Agency in English Society, 1500–1800*, 2004.

Alice T. Friedman, *House and Household in Elizabethan England: Wollaton Hall and the Willoughby Family*, 1989.

Lawrence M. Friedman, *A History of American Law*, 1973.

Yvonne Galloway Brown and Rona Ferguson (eds), *Twisted Sisters: Women, Crime and Deviance in Scotland Since 1400*, 2002.

Dorothy Gardiner, *English Girlhood at School*, 1929.

L. Gent, *Albion's Classicism: The Visual Arts in Britain, 1550–1660*, 1995.

C. Giblin (ed.), *Irish Franciscan Mission in Scotland, 1619–1646*, 1964.

John R. Gillis, *For Better, For Worse: British Marriages 1600 to the Present*, 1985.

D. V. Glass and D. E. C. Eversley (eds), *Population in History*, 1965.

P. Goldberg (ed.), *Women is a Worthy Wight: Women in English Society c.1200–1500*, 1992.

Michael Gordon (ed.), *The American Family in Social-Historical Perspective*, 1978.

Michael Graham, *The Uses of Reform. 'Godly Discipline' and Popular Behaviour in Scotland and Beyond, 1560–1610*, 1996 [Studies in Medieval and Reformation Thought, LVIII].

A. Stopford Green, *The Making of Ireland and its Undoing*, 1908.

Evarts B. Greene, *American Population Before the Federal Census of 1790*, 1932.

Germaine Greer, *The Obstacle Race*, 1981.

Philip J. Greven, *Four Generations: Population, Land and Family in Colonial Andover, Massachuseetts*, 1970.

Philip J. Greven, *The Protestant Temperament: Patterns of Child-Rearing, Religious Experience and the Self in Early America*, 1977.

Paul Griffiths, Adam Fox and Steve Hindle (eds), *The Experience of Authority in Early Modern England*, 1996.

Sarah Gristwood, *Arbella: England's Lost Queen*, 2003; paperback edition 2004.

E. Halshall, *A Journal of the Siege of Lathom House*, 1902.

Alison Hanham, *The Celys and their World*, 1985.

Margaret Patterson Hannay (ed.), *Silent But for the Word: Tudor Women as Patrons, Translators, and Writers of Religious Works*, 1985.

Barbara J. Harris, *English Aristocratic Women, 1450–1550*, 2002.

B. J. Harris and J. K. McNamara (eds), *Women and the Structure of Society*, 1984.

Frances Harris, *Transformations of Love: The Friendship of John Evelyn and Margaret Godolphin*, 2003.

F. Harris and Michael Hunter (eds), *John Evelyn and His Milieu*, 2003.

Anne M. Haselkorn and Betty S. Travitsky (eds), *The Renaissance Englishwoman in Print: Counterbalancing the Canon*, 1990.

George L. Haskins, *Law and Authority in Early Massachusetts*, 1960.

F. Heal and R. O'Day (eds), *Church and Society in England: Henry VIII to James I*, 1977.

Felicity Heal and Clive Holmes, *The Gentry in England and Wales 1500–1700*, 1994.

A. C. Hepburn (ed.), *Minorities in History*, 1978.

David G. Hey, *An English Rural Community. Myddle under the Tudors and Stuarts*, 1974.

John Higham, *Send These To Me. Immigrants in Urban America*, 1984.

Bridget Hill, *Women Alone: Spinsters in England, 1660–1850*, 2001.

W. G. Hiscock, *John Evelyn and Mrs Godolphin*, 1951.

W. G. Hiscock, *John Evelyn and his Family Circle*, 1955.

R. Hoffman and P. J. Albert (eds), *Women in the Age of the American Revolution*, 1989.

James Horn, *Adapting to a New World*, 1994.

W. G. Hoskins, *The Midland Peasant*, 1957.

Ralph Houlbrooke, *The English Family*, 1984.

R. A. Houston, *Scottish Literacy and the Scottish Identity: Illiteracy and Society in Scotland and Northern England, 1600–1800*, 1985.

H. G. F. Howard, *The Life of Anne Countess of Arundel*, 1857.

Elizabeth Howe, *The First English Actresses, Women and Drama, 1660–1700*, 1992.

Susan Hull, *Chaste, Silent and Obedient, English Books for Women 1475–1640*, 1982.

Robert Hume, *Early Child Immigrants to Virginia*, 1986.

Melvyn Humphreys, *The Crisis of Community: Montgomeryshire 1680–1815*, 1996.

Margaret Hunt *et al.* (eds), *Women and the Enlightenment, in Women and History*, 9, 1984.

L. Hunter and S. Hutton (eds), *Women, Science and Medicine, 1500–1700, Mothers and Sisters of the Royal Society*, 1997.

Joel Hurstfield, *The Queen's Wards, Wardship and Marriage Under Elizabeth I*, 1973 edition.

Martin Ingram, *Church Courts, Sex and Marriage in England, 1570–1640*, 1987.

Eric Ives, *Anne Boleyn*, 1986.

Edward T. James, Janet Wilson James and Paul S. Boyer (eds), *Notable American Women. A Biographical Dictionary*, 1971.

Geraint H. Jenkins (ed.), *Welsh Language Before the Industrial Revolution*, 1997.

Francis Jennings, *The Invasion of America: Indians, Colonialism, and the Cant of Conquest*, 1975.

Helen M. Jewell, *Education in Early Modern England*, 1998.

J. Gwynfor Jones, *The Wynn Family of Gwydir: Origins, Growth and Development, c.1460–1674*, 1995.

David W. Jordan, *Foundations of Representative Government in Maryland, 1632–1715*, 1987.

William Chester Jordan, *Women and Credit in Pre-Industrial and Developing Societies*, 1993.

Jenny Kermode and Garthine Walker (eds), *Women, Crime and the Courts in Early Modern England*, 1994.

Cynthia A. Kierner, *Beyond the Household: Women's Place in the Early South*, 1998.

J. Kirk, *Patterns of Reform: Continuity and Change in the Reformation Kirk*, 1989.

David Thomas Konig, *Law and Society in Puritan Massachusetts, Essex County, 1629–1692*, 1979.

Glee Krueger, *New England Samplers to 1840, Old Stourbridge*, 1978.

Allan Kulikoff, *Tobacco and Slaves: The Development of Southern Cultures in the Chesapeake, 1680–1800*, 1986.

A. Kussmaul, *Servants in Husbandry in Early Modern England*, 1981.

A. Kussmaul, *A General View of the Rural Economy of England, 1538–1840*, 1990.

Vivienne Larminie, *Wealth, Kinship and Culture: The Seventeenth-Century Newdigates of Arbury and Their World*, 1995.

Peter Laslett, *The World We Have Lost*, New York, 1965.

Peter Laslett, *Family Life and Illicit Love in Earlier Generations: Essays in Historical Sociology*, 1977.

Peter Laslett, *The World We Have Lost – Further Explored*, 1983.

P. Laslett and R. Wall (eds), *Household and Family in Past Time*, 1972.

Anne Laurence, *Women in England, 1500–1760*, 1994 (pbk edition 1996, 2002 reissue).

Brian Levack, *The Formation of the British State: England, Scotland and the Union, 1603–1707*, 1987.

Santina M. Levey, *An Elizabethan Inheritance: The Hardwick Hall Textiles*, 1998.

Barbara Lewalski, *Writing Women in Jacobean England*, 1992.

Kenneth E. Lockridge, *A New England Town, The First Hundred Years: Dedham, Massachusetts, 1636–1736*, 1970.

Kenneth Lockridge, *Colonial New England: An Enquiry into the Social Context of Literacy in the Early Modern West*, 1974.

Mary S. Lovell, *Bess of Hardwick: First lady of Chatsworth*, 2005.

Irving Lowens, *Music and Musicians in Early America*, 1964.

A. M. Lucas, *Women in the Middle Ages: Religion. Marriage and Letters*, 1983.

Donna M. Lucey, *I Dwell in Possibility: Women Build a Nation, 1600–1920*, 2005.

Margaret MacCurtain and Mary O'Dowd (eds), *Women in Early Modern Ireland*, 1991.

Michael MacDonald, *Mystic Bedlam*, 1981.

Alan Macfarlane, *The Family Life of Ralph Josselin: A Seventeenth-Century Clergyman*, 1970.

Alan Macfarlane, *Marriage and Love in England: Modes of Reproduction 1300–1840*, 1986.

Phyllis Mack, *Visionary Women: Ecstatic Prophecy in Seventeenth Century England*, 1992.

I. Maclean, *The Renaissance Notion of Woman: A Study in the Fortunes of Scholasticism and Medical Science in European Intellectual Life*, 1980.

Peter Malekin, *Liberty and Love, English Literature and Society 1640–88*, 1981.

Ronald Marchant, *The Church Under the Law: Justice, Administration and Discipline in the Diocese of York 1560–1640*, 1969.

Rosalind K. Marshall, *Virgins and Viragoes: A History of Women in Scotland from 1080–1980*, 1983.

Joanna Martin, *Wives and Daughters: Women and Children in the Georgian Country House*, 2004.

Mavis E. Mate, *Daughters, Wives and Widows after the Black Death. Women in Sussex, 1350–1535*, 1998.

Michael McCarthy-Morrogh, *The Munster Plantation, 1580–1641*, 1986.

Elizabeth McCutcheon, *Sir Nicholas Bacon's Great House Sententiae*, 1977.

K. B. Mcfarlane, *The Nobility of Later Medieval England*, 1973.

Marjorie Keniston McIntosh, *Working Women in English Society, 1300–1620*, 2005.

Sara Heller Mendelson, *The Mental World of Stuart Women: Three Studies*, 1987.

Sara Mendelson and Patricia Crawford, *Women in Early Modern England*, 1998.

S. P. Meneffe, *Wives for Sale*, 1981.

Debra Meyers, *Common Whores, Vertuous Women and Loveing Wives Free Will Christian Women in Colonial Maryland*, 2003.

Richard Middleton, *Colonial America, A History, 1607–1760*, 1992.

Oliver Millar, *The Age of Charles I: Paintings in England, 1620–1649*, 1927.

Edmund Morgan, *The Puritan Family: Religion and Domestic Relations in Seventeenth-Century New England*, 1966.

Richard B. Morris, *Studies in the History of American Law*, 1930.

O. Moscucci, *The Science of Women: Gynaecology and Gender in England 1800–1929*, 1990.

A. Moss, *Printed Commonplace Books and the Structuring of Renaissance Thought*, 1996.

Craig Muldrew, *The Economy of Obligation: The Culture of Credit and Social Relations in Early Modern England*, 1998.

Lionel Munby (ed.), *Life and Death in King's Langley: Wills and Inventories*, 1981.

Beverley A. Murphy, *Bastard Prince: Henry VIII's Lost Son*, 2001 (pbk edition in 2003).

Sylvia Harcstarck Myers, *The Bluestocking Circle: Women, Friendship and the Life of the Mind in Eighteenth-Century England*, 1990.

Gary B. Nash, *The Urban Crucible: Social Change, Political Consciousness, and the Origins of the American Revolution*, 1979.

Adam Nicolson, *God's Secretaries. The Making of the King James Bible*, 2003.

Mary Beth Norton, *Founding Mothers and Fathers: Gendered Power and the Forming of American Society*, 1996.

Felicity Nussbaum, *The Brink of All We Hate: English Satire on Women, 1660–1750*, 1984.

Rosemary O'Day, *The English Clergy: The Emergence and Consolidation of a Profession*, 1979.

Rosemary O'Day, *Education for Society*, 1982.

Rosemary O'Day, *The Family and Family Relationships in England, France and the United States*, 1995.

Marilyn Ogilvie and Joy Harvey (eds), *The Biographical Dictionary of Women in Science. Pioneering Lives from Ancient Times to the Mid-20th Century*, 2000.

Diana O'Hara, *Courtship and Constraint: Rethinking the Making of Marriage in Tudor England*, 2000.

Herbert L. Osgood, *The American Colonies in the Seventeenth Century*, Vol. 2, 1904.

R. B. Outhwaite (ed.), *Marriage and Society, Studies in the Social History of Marriage*, 1981.

R. B. Outhwaite, *Clandestine Marriage in England, 1500–1850*, 1995.

Rozsika Parker, *The Subversive Stitch: Embroidery in Women's Lives, 1300–1900*, 1984.

Iain Pears, *The Discovery of Painting*, 1988.

Margaret Pelling, *The Common Lot: Sickness, Medical Occupations and the Urban Poor in Early Modern England*, 1998.

Maria Perry, *Sisters to the king*, 2002.

Ruth Perry, *The Celebrated Mary Astell: An Early English Feminist*, 1986.

Christine Peters, *Patterns of Piety*, 2002.

Christine Peters, *Women in Early Modern Britain, 1450–1640*, 2004.

Kevin Phillips, *The Cousins' Wars. Religion, Politics and the Triumph of Anglo-America*, 1999.

Kim M. Phillips, *Medieval Maidens, Young Women and Gender in England, 1270–1540*, 2003.

Nicola Phillips, *Women in Business, 1700–1850*, 2006.

A. J. Pollard (ed.), *Property and Politics: Essays in Later Medieval English History*, 1984.

Roy Porter, *London: A Social History*, 1994.

Mary Prior (ed.), *Women in English Society, 1500–1800*, 1985.

G. R. Quaife, *Wanton Wenches and Wayward Wives*, 1979.

Hugh F. Rankin, *The Theatre in Colonial America*, 1965.

Marjorie Reeves, *Female Education and Nonconformist Culture, 1700–1900*, 1997.

Kate Retford, *The Art of Domestic Life: Family Portraiture in Eighteenth-Century England*, 2006.

Betty Ring, *Girlhood Embroidery: American Samplers and Pictorial Needlework, 1650–1850*, 2 Vols, 1993.

M. Roberts and S. Clarke (eds), *Women and Gender in Early Modern Wales*, 2000.

Philip Robinson, *The Plantation of Ulster: British Settlement in an Irish Landscape, 1600–1670*, 1984.

James M. Rosenheim, *The Emergence of a Ruling Order: English Landed Society, 1650–1750*, 1998.

J. T. Rosenthal, *Patriarchy and Families of Privilege in Fifteenth-Century England*, 1991.

Neal Salisbury, *Manitou and Providence: Indians, Europeans, and the Making of New England, 1500–1643*, 1982.

Marylynn Salmon, *Women and the Law of Property in Early America*, 1986.

Elizabeth Sanderson, *Women and Work in Eighteenth-Century Edinburgh*, 1996.

M. H. B. Sanderson (1982), *Scottish Rural Society in the Sixteenth Century*, 1982.

Roland Burke Savage, *A Valiant Dublin Woman. The Story of George's Hill (1766–1940)*, 1940.

J. J. Scarisbrick, *The Reformation and the English people*, 1978.

Mechal Scobel, *The World They Made Together: Black and White Values in Eighteenth-Century Virginia*, 1988.

James C. Scott, *Domination and the Arts of Resistance. Hidden Transcripts*, 1990.

George O. Seilhamer, *History of the American Theatre*, 3 Vols, 1888–91.

Carole Shammas, *The Pre-Industrial Consumer in England and America*, 1990.

Carole Shammas, Marylynn Salmon and Michel Dahlin, *Inheritance in America from Colonial times to the Present*, 1987.

Pamela Sharpe, *Adapting to Capitalism: Working Women in the English Economy, 1700–1850*, 1996.

Pamela Sharpe, *Women's Work: The English Experience, 1650–1914*, 1998.

Pamela Sharpe, *A Woman's Worth: A Case Study of Capital Accumulation in Early Modern England*, 19, 2002.

Joanne Shattock (ed.), *The Oxford Guide to British Women Writers*, 1993.

Amanda Shepherd, *Gender and Authority in Sixteenth-Century England*, 1994.

Brenton Simons and Peter Benes (eds), *The Art of family: Genealogical Artifacts in New England*, 2002.

Miriam Slater, *Family Life in the Seventeenth Century, The Verneys of Claydon House*, 1984.

Abbot Emerson Smith, *Colonists in Bondage: White Servitude and Convict Labor in America, 1607–1776*, 1947.

Daniel Blake Smith, *Inside the Great House: Planter Family in Eighteenth-Century Chesapeake Society*, 1980.

H. C. Smith, *Jewellery*, 1908.

R. M. Smith (ed.), *Land, Kinship and Lifecycle*, 1984.

Terri L. Snyder, *Brabbling Women: Disorderly Speech and the Law in Early Virginia*, 2003.

Anne Somerset, *Ladies in Waiting from the Tudors to the Present Day*, 1984.

Julia C. Spruill, *Women's Life and Work in the Southern Colonies*, 1938.

Susan Staves, *Married Women's Separate Property in England, 1660–1833*, 1990.

Lawrence Stone, *Family and Fortune*, 1973.

Lawrence Stone, *The Family, Sex and Marriage in England, 1500–1800*, 1977. (Full and abbreviated editions).

Lawrence Stone and Jeanne Fawtier Stone, *An Open Elite? England 1540–1880*, 1984.

Lawrence Stone, *Uncertain Unions & Broken Lives*, 1995.

Tim Stretton, *Women Waging Law in Elizabethan England*, 1998.

Margaret Swain, *Historical Needlework: A Study of Influences in Scotland and Northern England*, 1970.

Margaret Swain, *The Needlework of Mary Queen of Scots*, 1973.

Margaret Swain, *Scottish Embroidery: Medieval to Modern*, 1986.

Susan Burrows Swan, *Plain and Fancy: American Women and Their Needlework, 1700–1850*, 1977.

Naomi Tadmore, *Family and Friends in Eighteenth-Century England: Household, Kinship, and Patronage*, 2001.

Thad W. Tate and David L. Ammerman (eds), *The Chesapeake in the Seventeenth Century: Essays in Anglo-American Society*, 1979.

R. H. Tawney, *Religion and the Rise of Capitalism*, 1912.

Gary Taylor, *Reinventing Shakespeare: A Cultural History from the Restoration to the Present*, 1990.

Ben Thomas, *The Old Order Based on the Diary of Elizabeth Baker 1778–1786*, 1945.

Ann Thompson 'Women and the stage', in Helen Wilcox (ed.), *Women and Literature in Britain, 1500–1700*, 1996.

Roger Thompson, *Women in Stuart England and America*, 1974.

Roger Thompson, *Sex in Middlesex: Popular Mores in a Massachusetts County, 1649–1699*, 1986.

Janet Todd (ed.), *A Dictionary of British and American Women Writers, 1660–1800*, 1984.

Janet Todd (ed.), *Dictionary of British Women Writers*, 1989.

Margo Todd, *The Culture of Protestantism in Early Modern Scotland*, 2002.

Claire Tomalin, *Samuel Pepys: The Unequalled Self*, 2002.

Patricia J. Tracey, *Jonathan Edwards, Pastor: Religion and Society in Eighteenth Century Northampton* [Massachusetts], 1980.

C. Trevett, *Women and Quakerism in the Seventeenth Century*, 1991.

Suzanne Trill, Kate Chedgzoy and Melanie Osborne (eds), *Lay By Your Needles, Ladies, Taske The Pen. Writing Women in England, 1500–1700*, 1997.

Virginia Tuft and Barbara Meyerhoff, *Changing Images of the Family*, 1979.

Laurel Thatcher Ulrich, *Good Wives: Image and Reality in the Lives of Women in Northern New England, 1650–1750*, 1991 (first published 1980).

Martha Vicinus (ed.), *Suffer and Be Still: Women in the Victorian Age*, 1972.

Martha Vicinus (ed.), *A Widening Sphere: Changing Roles of Victorian Women*, 1980 edition.

Amanda Vickery, *The Gentleman's Daughter: Women's Lives in Georgian England*, 1998.

G. I. Wade, *Thomas Traherne*, 1946.

K. Walker, *Women Writers of the English Renaissance*, 1996.

Retha M. Warnicke, *Women of the English Renaissance and Reformation*, 1983.

Retha M. Warnicke, *The Rise and fall of Anne Boleyn*, 1989.

Suzanne R. Westfall, *Patrons and Performers: Early Tudor Household Revels*, 1990.

Lorna Wetherill, *Consumer Behaviour and Material Culture in Britain*, 1988.

Susan E. Whyman, *Sociability and Power in Late-Stuart England. The Cultural World of the Verneys, 1660–1720*, 1999 (2002 paperback edition).

Helen Wilcox (ed.), *Women and Literature in Britain, 1500–1700*, 1996.

J. L. Williams and G. L. Hughes (eds), *The History of Education in Wales*, 1978.

F. P. Wilson, *The Plague in Shakespeare's London*, 1963.

Lynne Withey, *Dearest Friend: A Life of Abigail Adams*, 2000.

L. Woodbridge, *Women and the English Renaissance: Literature and the Nature of Womankind, 1540–1620*, 1984.

J. Wormald, *Court, Kirk and Community: Scotland, 1470–1625*, 1981.

J. Wormald, *Lords and Men in Scotland: Bonds of Manrent, 1442–1603*, 1985.

Stephanie J. Wright, *A Biographical and Critical Study of the Life and Work of Elizabeth Carey, 1st Viscountess Falkland (1585–1637)*, 1991.

Keith Wrightson and David Levine, *Poverty and Piety in an English Village: Terling, 1525–1700*, 1979.

E. A. Wrigley and R. S. Schofield, *The Population History of England, 1541–1871: A Reconstruction*, 1981.

E. A. Wrigley *et al.*, *English Population History from Family Reconstitution, 1580–1837*, 1997.

Marion Wynne-Davies (ed.), *Women Poets of the Renaissance*, 1998.

Melvin Yazawa, *From Colonies to Commonwealth: Ideology and the Beginnings of the American Republic*, 1985.

R. Zim, *English Metrical Psalms: Poetry as Praise and Prayer*, 1987.

Articles and essays

Lee J. Alston and Morton Owen Schapiro, 'Inheritance laws across colonies: causes and consequences', *Journal of Economic History*, 44, 1984, pp. 277–87.

Susan Dwyer Amussen, 'The gendering of popular culture in early-modern England', in Tom Harris, ed., *Popular Culture in England, c.1500–1800*, 1995, pp. 48–68.

A. E. Anton, 'Handfasting in Scotland', in *Scottish Historical Review*, 37, 1958.

Rowena Archer, 'Rich old ladies: the problem of late medieval dowagers', in A. J. Pollard (ed.), *Property and Politics: Essays in Later Medieval English History*, 1984.

Rowena Archer, 'How ladies who live on their manors ought to manage their households and estates: women as landholders and administrators in the later Middle Ages', in P. Goldberg (ed.), *Women Is A Worthy Wight: Women in English Society c.1200–1500*, 1992, pp. 149–81.

Margaret Aston, 'Lollard women priests?', in Margaret Aston *Lollards and Reformers. Images and Literacy in Late Medieval Religion*, 1984, pp. 49–70.

Margaret Aston, 'Iconoclasm at Rickmansworth 1522: troubles of churchwardens', in *Journal of Ecclesiastical History*, 40, 1989.

James Axtell, 'The ethno-history of early America: A review essay', *William and Mary Quarterly*, 35, 1978, pp. 110–44.

James Axtell, 'Invading America: Puritans and Jesuits', *Journal of Interdisciplinary History*, 14, 1984.

J. Bachelor, 'Pocket Books', *Eighteenth Century Studies*, 2005.

Tabitha Barber, 'Mary Beale', in David Dewing (ed.), *Mary Beale (1632/3–1699) Portrait of a Seventeenth-Century Painter, Her Family and Studio*, 1999.

Michael Bath, 'Alexander Seton's painted gallery', in L. Gent, *Albion's Classicism: The Visual Arts in Britain, 1550–1660*, 1995.

Catherine Belsey, 'The serpent in the garden: Shakespeare, marriage and material culture', *The Seventeenth Century*, Vol. XI, no. 1, 1996.

Judith M. Bennet, 'Feminism and history', *Gender and History*, I, 1989, pp. 259–63.

Helen Berry, 'Nice and Curious Questions' Coffee Houses and the representation of women in John Dunton's *Athenian Mercury*', in *The Seventeenth Century*, Vol. XII, 1997, pp. 257–76.

Helen Berry, 'Rethinking politeness in eighteenth-century England'. Moll King's Coffee House and the significance of 'Flash Talk', in *TRHS*, 6th series, 11, 2001, pp. 65–81.

Dinah Birch, 'Three views of the Psalms', in *Culture and Belief in Europe, 1450–1600*, Open University, 1990, Block 8.

Jeremy Boulton, 'London widowhood revisited: the decline of female remarriage in the seventeenth and early eighteenth centuries', *Continuity and Change*, 5, 1990.

Jeremy Boulton, 'Itching after private marryings? Marriage customs in seventeenth century London', in *London Journal*, 16, 1991, pp. 15–29.

Elizabeth Boyle, 'Irish embroidery and lace making, 1600–1800', *Ulster Folklife*, 12, 1966, pp. 52–65.

Ciaran Brady, 'Political women and reform in Tudor Ireland', in Margaret MacCurtain and Mary O'Dowd, *Women in Early Modern Ireland*, 1991.

Keith M. Brown, 'The Scottish aristocracy, anglicisation and the court, 1603–1638', *Historical Journal*, 36, 1993, pp. 543–76.

Keith M. Brown, 'A house divided: family and feud in Carrick under John Kennedy, fifth earl of Cassillis', *Scottish Historical Review*, 75, 1996, pp. 168–96 (p. 170).

Victoria Burke, 'Women and early seventeenth century manuscript culture . . .', in *The Seventeenth Century*, Vol. XII, no. 2 August 1997.

Nicholas Canny, 'Dominant minorities: English settlers in Ireland and Virginia, 1550–1650', in A. C. Hepburn (ed.), *Minorities in History*, 1978, pp. 17–44.

Nicholas Canny, 'Irish, Scottish and Welsh responses to centralisation, c.1530–c.1640', in A. Grant and K. J. Stringer (eds), *Uniting the Kingdom? The Making of British History*, 1995.

Bernard Capp, 'The poet and the bawdy court: Michael Drayton and the lodging house world in early Stuart London', *The Seventeenth Century*, Vol. X, 1995 no. 1, pp. 27–37.

Bernard Capp, 'Separate domains? Women and authority in early modern England', in Paul Griffiths, Adam Fox and Steve Hindle (eds), *The Experience of Authority in Early Modern England*, 1996.

A. Carlos and L. Neal, 'Women investors in early capital markets, 1720–1725', *Financial History Review*, 11, 2004, pp. 197–224.

Lois Green Carr, 'Inheritance in the Colonial Chesapeake', in Ronald Hoffman and Peter J. Albert (eds), *Women in the Age of the American Revolution*, 1989, pp. 155–208.

Lois Green Carr, 'Emigration and the standard of living: the seventeenth-century Chesapeake', in *Journal of Economic History*, 52, 1992, pp. 271–91.

Lois Green Carr and Lorena S. Walsh, 'The planter's wife: the experience of white women in seventeenth-century Maryland', in Michael Gordon (ed.), *The American Family in Social-Historical Perspective*, 1978.

Lois Green Carr and Lorena S. Walsh in 'The planter's wife: the experience of white women in seventeenth-century Maryland', *William and Mary Quarterly*, 34, 1997, pp. 542–71.

I. Carter, 'Marriage patterns and social sectors in Scotland before the eighteenth century', *Scottish Studies*, XVII, 1973, pp. 51–2.

Christine Churches, 'Women and property in early modern England: a case study', in *Social History*, 23, 1998, pp. 165–80.

Simone Clarke, 'Visions of community: Elizabeth Baker and late eighteenth-century Merioneth', in M. Roberts and S. Clarke (eds), *Women and Gender in Early Modern Wales*, 2000, pp. 234–58.

Mary Clement, 'The Welsh circulating schools', in J. L. Williams and G. L. Hughes, *The History of Education in Wales*, 1978.

Patrick Collinson, 'Not sexual in the ordinary sense: Men, women and religious transactions', in *Elizabethan Essays*, 1994, pp. 119–50.

P. J. Corish, 'Women and religious practice', in Margaret MacCurtain and Mary O'Dowd (eds), *Women in Early Modern Ireland*, 1991, pp. 212–20.

Nancy Cott, 'Passionless: an interpretation of Victorian sexual ideology, 1790–1850', in *Signs*, IV, 1978–9, pp. 219–36.

Nancy F. Cott, 'Eighteenth-century family and social life revealed in Massachusetts' Divorce Records', *Journal of Social History*, 10, 1976, pp. 32–3.

Maggie Craig, 'The fair sex turns ugly: female involvement in the Jacobite rising of 1745', in Yvonne Galloway Brown and Rona Ferguson (eds), *Twisted Sisters: Women, Crime and Deviance in Scotland Since 1400*, 2002, pp. 84–100.

Ralph J. Crandall, 'Family types, social structure and mobility in early America: Charlestown, Massachusetts, a case study', in V. Tufte and B. Myerhoff (eds), *Changing Images of the Family*, 1979.

Ann Crawford, 'The piety of late medieval English queens', in Caroline Barron and Christopher Harper-Bill (eds), *The Church in Pre-Reformation Society*, 1985.

Patricia Crawford, 'Women's published writings, 1600–1700', in Mary Prior (ed.), *Women in English Society, 1500–1800*, 1985, pp. 211–82.

Patricia Crawford, 'The construction and experience of maternity in 17th century England', in Valerie Fildes (ed.), *Women as Mothers in Pre-industrial England*, 1990.

David Cressy, 'The seasonality of marriage in Old and New England', *Journal of Interdisciplinary History*, 16, 1985, pp. 1–21.

David Cressy, 'Kinship and kin interaction in early modern England', *Past and Present*, 113, 1986, pp. 38–69.

John E. Crowley, 'The importance of kinship: testamentary evidence from South Carolina', *Journal of Interdisciplinary History*, 16, 1986.

Bernadette Cunningham, 'Native culture and political change in Ireland, 1580–1640', in Ciaran Brady and Raymond Gillespie (eds), *The Making of Irish Colonial Society, 1534–1641: Natives and Newcomers*, 1986, pp. 152–64.

Bernadette Cunningham, 'Women and Gaelic literature, 1500–1800', in Margaret MacCurtain and Mary O'Dowd (eds), *Women in Early Modern Ireland*, 1991.

Kathleen M. Davies, 'Continuity and change in literary advice on marriage', in R. B. Outhwaite (ed.), *Marriage and Society*, 1981, pp. 55–80.

R. R. Davies, 'The status of women and the practice of marriage in late medieval Wales', in D. Jenkins and M. E. Owen (eds), *The Welsh Law of Women*, 1980.

J. Dawson, 'Anglo-Scottish Protestant culture and the integration of sixteenth-century Britain', in S. G. Ellis and S. Barber (eds), *Conquest and Union: Forging a Multi-National British State*, 1995.

James Daybell, 'Female literacy and the social conventions of women's letter-writing in England, 1540–1603', in J. Daybell (ed.), *Early Modern Women's Letter-Writing, 1450–1800*, 2001.

Douglas Deal, 'A constricted world: free blacks on Virginia's Eastern Shore, 1680–1750', in Lois Green Carr, Philip D. Morgan and Jean B. Russo (eds), *Colonial Chesapeake Society*, 1988.

John Demos, 'Families in Colonial Bristol, Rhode Island: an exercise in historical demography', *William and Mary Quarterly*, 3rd series, XXV, 1968, pp. 40–57.

Maria Dowling, 'Anne Boleyn and reform', in *Journal of Ecclesiastical History*, 35, 1984, pp. 30–46.

Fiona Downie, 'La voie quelle menace tenir': Annabella Stewart, Scotland, and the European marriage market, 1444–1456', *Scottish Historical Review*, 78, 1999, pp. 170–91.

J. Dorkan, 'Heresy in Scotland: the second phase', *Records of the Scottish Church History Society*, 2001.

Jacqueline Eales, 'Patriarchy, puritanism and politics: the letters of Lady Brilliana Harley (1598–1643)', in James Daybell (ed.), *Early Modern Women's Letter Writing*, 1450–1700, 2001.

Carville Earle, 'Environment, disease and mortality in early Virginia', in Thad W. Tate and David L. Ammerman (eds), *The Chesapeake in the Seventeenth Century: Essays in Anglo-American Society'*, 1979, pp. 96–125.

Mary Edmond, 'Bury St Edmunds: a seventeenth-century art centre', *Walpole Society*, Vol. 53, 1987.

Vivien Brodsky Elliott, 'Single women in the London marriage market, age status and mobility, 1598–1619', in R. B. Outhwaite (ed.), *Marriage and Society*, 1981.

S. G. Ellis, 'Economic problems of the Church: why the Reformation failed in Ireland', *Journal of Ecclesiastical History*, 40, 1990.

Amy Louise Erickson, 'Common law versus common practice: the use of marriage settlements in early modern England', *Economic History Review*, 2nd ser., xliii, 1990.

Elizabeth Ewan, 'Crime or culture? Women and daily life in late medieval Scotland', in Yvonne Galloway Brown and Rona Ferguson (eds), *Twisted Sisters: Women, Crime and Devianace in Scotland since 1400*, 2002, pp. 117–36.

Margaret W. Ferguson, 'Renaissance concepts of the "woman writer"', in Helen Wilcox (ed.), *Women and Literature in Britain, 1500–1700*, 1996, pp. 143–68.

Aaron Fogleman, 'Migrations to the thirteen British North American colonies, 1700–1775: New estimates', *Journal of Interdisciplinary History*, 22, 4, 1992, pp. 691–709.

A. D. M. Forte, 'Some aspects of the law of marriage in Scotland: 1500–1700', in Elizabeth Craik (ed.), *Marriage and Property. Women and Marital Customs in History*, 1984.

Alice Friedman, 'Constructing an identity in prose, plaster and paint: Lady Anne Clifford as writer and patron of the arts', in L. Gent, *Albion's Classicism: The Visual Arts in Britain, 1550–1660*, 1995, pp. 358–76.

James Matthew Gallman, 'Relative ages of colonial marriages', *Journal of Interdisciplinary History*, 14, 1984, pp. 609–18.

G. Gampel, 'The planter's wife revisited: equity law and the chancery court in seventeenth-century Maryland', in B. J. Hanns and J. K. McNamara (eds), *Women and the Structure of Society*, 1984, pp. 20–35.

Henry A. Gemery, 'European immigration to North America, 1700–1820: numbers and quasi-numbers', *Perspectives in American History*, I, 1984, pp. 318–20.

Ruth Geuter, 'The silver hand: needlework in early modern Wales', in Michael Roberts and Simone Clarke (eds), *Women and Gender in Early Modern Wales*, 2000, pp. 159–85.

V. R. Geuter, 'Invisible earnings: women's rewards from needlework and spinning in the seventeenth century', in Ian Blanchard (ed.), *New Directions in Economic and Social History*, 1995, pp. 77–84.

Gary G. Gibbs, 'Child-marriages in the diocese of Chester, 1561–1565', *Journal of Local and Regional Studies*, 1988, 8, pp. 32–42.

Carol Gibson-Wood, 'Susanna and her elders: John Evelyn's artistic daughter', in F. Harris and Michael Hunter (eds), *John Evelyn and His Milieu*, 2003, pp. 233–54.

D. V. Glass, 'Two papers on Gregory King', in D. V. Glass and D. E. C. Eversley (eds), *Population in History*, 1965.

Laura Gowing, 'Language, power and the law: women's slander litigation in early modern London', in Jenny Kermode and Garthine Walker (eds), *Women, Crime and the Courts in Early Modern England*, 1994, pp. 26–47.

Elspeth Graham, 'Women's writing and the self', pp. 217–9, in Helen Wilcox (ed.), *Women and Literature in Britain, 1500–1700*, 1996.

Janelle Greenberg, 'The legal status of the English woman in early eighteenth-century common law and equity', *Studies in Eighteenth-Century Law and Culture*, 4, 1975.

Philip J. Greven, 'Family structure in seventeenth-century Andover, Massachusetts', *William and Mary Quarterly*, 3rd Series, XXIII, 1966, 234–56.

Elizabeth H. Hageman, 'Women's poetry in early modern Britain', pp. 190–208, in Helen Wilcox (ed.), *Women and Literature in Britain, 1500–1700*, 1996.

J. D. Hanlon, 'These be but women', in C. H. Carter (ed.), *From the Renaissance to the Counter-Reformation*, 1966.

Barbara Harris, 'Aristocratic women and the state in early Tudor England', in Charles Carlton *et al.*, *State, Sovereigns and Society in Early Modern England*, 1998, p. 11.

Jonathan Harris, 'The Grecian coffee house and political debate in London, 1688–1714', in *London Journal*, 25, 2000, pp. 1–13.

Lloyd E. Hawes, 'Adam and Eve in the decorative arts', *Antiques*, 84, September 1963.

B. A. Holderness, 'Credit in a rural community, 1660–1800', *Midland History*, 3, 1975–6.

B. A. Holderness, 'Elizabeth Parkin and her investments, 1733–66: aspects of the Sheffield money market in the eighteenth century', *Transactions of the Hunter Archaeological Society*, 10, 1979.

B. A. Holderness, 'Widows in pre-industrial society: an essay upon their economic functions', in R. M. Smith (ed.), *Land, Kinship and Lifecycle*, 1984.

T. H. Hollingsworth, 'A demographic study of the British ducal families', in *Population Studies*, 11, 1957, pp. 4–26.

T. H. Hollingsworth, 'The demography of the British peerage', *Supplement to Population Studies*, 18, 1964.

Mary F. and T. H. Hollingsworth, 'Plague mortality rates by age and sex in the parish of St Botolph's without Bishopsgate, London', *Population Studies*, XXV, 1971, pp. 131–46.

Henry Horwitz, 'Testamentary practice, family strategies, and the last phases of the custom of London, 1660–1725', *Law and History Review*, 2, 1984, pp. 223–39.

R. A. Houlbrooke, 'Women's social life and common action in England from the fifteenth century to the eve of the Civil War', *Continuity and Change*, 1, 1986, pp. 171–89.

R. W. Hoyle, 'The land-family bond in England', *Past and Present*, 146, 1995.

Geoffrey L. Hudson, 'Negotiating for blood money: war widows and the courts in seventeenth-century England', in Jenny Kermode and Garthine Walker (eds), *Women, Crime and the Courts in Early Modern England*, 1994, pp. 146–69.

Margaret Hunt, 'Hawkers, bawlers and mercuries: women and the London press in the early enlightenment', in Margaret Hunt *et al.*

(eds), *Women and the Englightenment, in Women and History*, 9, 1984.

James T. Johnson, 'The covenant idea and the puritan view of marriage', *The Journal of the History of Ideas*, 32, 1971, pp. 107–18.

Dorothy Johnston, 'Emma Child, née Barnard, formerly Willughby (1644–1725): records of the life of a gentlewoman', in John Beckett (ed.), *Nottinghamshire Past: Essays in Honour of Adrian Henstock*, 2003, pp. 59–76.

Philip Mainwaring Johnstone, 'Mural paintings in houses', *Journal of the British Archaeological Association*, 38, 1932, pp. 75–100.

Ray C. Keim, 'Primogeniture and entail in colonial Virginia', *The William and Mary Quarterly*, 25, 1968, pp. 545–86.

William Kelly, 'Four needlework panels attributed to Mary Jamesone, in the West Church of St Nicholas, Aberdeen', *Miscellany of the Third Spalding Club*, 2, 1941, pp. 160–82.

Liam Kennedy, 'Farm succession in modern Ireland: elements of a theory of inheritance', *Economic History Review*, 2nd series, 44, 1991.

P. Kilroy, 'Women and the Reformation', in Margaret MacCurtain and Mary O'Dowd (eds), *Women in Early Modern Ireland*, Edinburgh, 1991.

Andrea Knox, '"Barbarous and pestiferous women": female criminality, violence and aggression in sixteenth- and seventeenth-century Scotland and Ireland', in Yvonne Galloway Brown and Rona Ferguson (eds), *Twisted Sisters: Women, Crime and Deviance in Scotland Since 1400*, 2002, pp. 13–31.

Lyle Koehler, 'The case of the American Jezebels: Anne Hutchinson and female agitation during the years of Antinomian turmoil, 1636–1640', in *William and Mary Quarterly*, 31, 1974, pp. 55–78.

A. Kussmaul, 'Time and space, hoofs and grain: the seasonality of marriage in England', *Journal of Interdisciplinary History*, 15, 1985, pp. 755–79.

Peter Lake, 'Feminine piety and personal potency: the emancipation of Mrs Jane Ratcliffe', *The Seventeenth Century*, Vol. II, 1987, pp. 143–65.

Vivienne Larminie, 'Fighting for family in a patronage society: the epistolary armoury of Anne Newdigate (1574–1618)', in James

Daybell (ed.), *Early Modern Women's Letter Writing*, 1450–1700, 2001, pp. 94–108.

P. Laslett, 'Mean household size in England since the sixteenth century', in P. Laslett and R. Wall (eds), *Household and Family in Past Time*, 1972.

Anne Laurence, 'A priesthood of she-believers', in W. J. Sheils and D. Wood (eds), *Women in the Church*, Studies in Church History, 27, 1990.

Anne Laurence, 'Women using building in seventeenth-century England: a question of sources?' in *TRHS*, 6th ser., Vol. 13, 2003, pp. 293–303.

Anne Laurence, 'Women investors, "That nasty South Sea Affair" and the rage to speculate in early eighteenth-century England', *Accounting, Business & Financial History*, Vol. 16, 2006, pp. 245–64.

Anne Laurence, 'The emergence of a private clientele for banks in the early eighteenth century: Hoare's Bank and some women customers', *Economic History Review*, 2007.

Leah Leneman, 'Legitimacy and bastardy in Scotland, 1694–1830', *Scottish Historical Review*, 80, 2001, pp. 45–62.

Barbara J. Logue, 'In pursuit of prosperity: disease and death in a Massachusetts commercial port, 1660–1850', in *Journal of Social History*, 25, 1991, pp. 309–43.

Valerie Lucas, 'Puritan preaching and the politics of the family', in Anne M. Haselkorn and Betty S. Travitsky (eds), *The Renaissance Englishwoman in Print: Counterbalancing the Canon*, 1990.

D. Ludlow, 'Shaking patriarchy's foundations: sectarian women in England, 1641–1700', in R. Greaves (ed.), *Triumph Over Silence: Women in Protestant History*, 1985.

Michael Lynch, 'Response: old games and new', *Scottish History Review*, 73, 1994, pp. 47–63.

Margaret MacCurtain, 'A lost landscape: Geraldine castles and towerhouses of the Shannon estuary', in J. Bradley (ed.), *Settlement and Society in Ireland: Viking and Medieval Times*, 1990.

Margaret MacCurtain, 'Women, education and learning in early modern Ireland', in Margaret MacCurtain and Mary O'Dowd (eds), *Women in Early Modern Ireland*, 1991.

A. I. Macinnes, 'Scottish Gaeldom, 1638–1651: the vernacular response to the covenanting dynamic', in J. Dwyer *et al.* (eds), *New Perspectives on the Politics and Culture of Early Modern Scotland*, 1982.

A. I. Macinnes, 'Repression and conciliation: the Highland dimension, 1660–1688', *Scottish Historical Review*, 65, 1986.

A. I. Macinnes, 'Crown, clans and fine: the civilising of Scottish Gaeldom, 1587–1638', *Northern Scotland*, 13, 1993.

Allan I. Macinnes, 'Early modern Scotland: the current state of play', *Scottish History Review*, 73, 1994, pp. 30–46.

Gloria Main, 'Probate records as a source for early American history', *William and Mary Quarterly*, 3rd ser., 32, 1975, pp. 89–99.

Gloria Main, 'Widows in rural Massachusetts on the eve of the Revolution', in R. Hoffman and P. J. Albert (eds), *Women in the Age of the American Revolution*, 1989, pp. 67–90.

Rosalind K. Marshall, 'Wet-nursing in Scotland, 1500–1800', *Review of Scottish Culture*, 1, 1984.

Christopher McAll, 'The normal paradigms of a woman's life in the Irish and Welsh texts', in Dafydd Jenkins and Morfydd E. Owen (eds), *The Welsh Law of Women*, 1980.

K. B. Mcfarlane, 'The Beauchamps and the Staffords', in K. B. Mcfarlane, *The Nobility of Later Medieval England*, 1973, pp. 187–213.

Dorothy McLaren, 'Marital fertility and lactation 1570–1720', in Mary Prior (ed.), *Women in English Society 1500–1800*, 1985, pp. 22–53.

Mary Martin McLaughlin, 'Survivors and surrogates: children and parents from the 9th to the 13th centuries', in Lloyd De Mause, *The History of Childhood*, 1974.

Maureen M. Meikle, 'Victims, viragos and vamps: women of the sixteenth-century Anglo-Scottish frontier', in John C. Appleby and Paul Dalton (eds), *Government, Religion and Society in Northern England, 1000–1700*, 1997.

Sara Mendelson, 'Debate: The weightiest business: marriage in an upper-gentry family in seventeenth-century England', *Past and Present*, 85, 1979, pp. 126–35.

Sara Mendelson, 'Stuart women's diaries and occasional memoirs', in Mary Prior (ed.), *Women in English Society, 1500–1800*, 1985, pp. 181–210.

Samuel I. Mintz, 'The duchess of Newcastle's visit to the Royal Society', *Journal of English and Germanic Philology*, 51, 1952, pp. 168–76.

Paul Monod, 'The politics of matrimony: Jacobitism and marriage in eighteenth century England', in Eveline Cruickshanks and Jeremy Black (eds), *The Jacobite Challenge*, 1988, pp. 24–41.

Robert B. Morris, 'Primogeniture and entailed estates in America', *Columbia Law Review*, 27, 1927, pp. 24–51.

Michael McCarthy-Morrogh, 'The English presence in early seventeenth-century Munster', in Ciaran Brady and Raymond Gillespie (eds), *The Making of Irish Colonial Society, 1534–1641: Natives and Newcomers*, 1986, pp. 172–89.

David E. Narrett, 'Men's wills and women's property rights in Colonial NY', in R. Hoffman and P. J. Albert (eds), *Women in the Age of the American Revolution*, 1989, pp. 91–133.

Kenneth Nicholls, 'Irishwomen and property in the sixteenth century', in Margaret MacCurtain and Mary O'Dowd (eds), *Women in Early Modern Ireland*, 1991, pp. 17–31.

Mary Beth Norton, 'The evolution of white women's experience in early America', *AHR*, LXXXIX, 1984, pp. 593–619.

Mary Beth Norton, 'Hetty Shepard, Dorothy Dudley, and other fictional colonial women I have come to know altogether too well', *Journal of Women's History* 10, no. 3 (autumn 1998), pp. 141–54.

Rosemary O'Day, 'Ecclesiastical patronage: who controlled the church?', in F. Heal & R. O'Day (eds), *Church and Society in England: Henry VIII to James I*, 1977, pp. 136–55.

Rosemary O'Day, 'Tudor and Stuart Women: their family lives through their letters', in James Daybell (ed.), *Early Modern Women's Letter Writing, 1450–1700*, 2001, pp. 127–42.

Mary O'Dowd, 'Women and war in Ireland in the 1640s', in Margaret MacCurtain and Mary O'Dowd (eds), *Women in Early Modern Ireland*, 1991.

Mary O'Dowd, 'Women and the colonial experience in Ireland, c.1550–1650', pp. 156–171 in *Gendering Scottish history: An*

International Approach, eds. Terry Brotherstone, Deborah Simonton and Oonagh Walsh [The Mackie Occasional Colloquia Series, 1], 1999.

J. Oldham, 'On pleading the belly: a history of the jury of matrons', *Criminal Justice History*, 6, 1985, pp. 1–64.

V. M. O'Mara, 'Female scribal ability and scribal activity in late medieval England: the evidence', *Leeds Studies in English*, 27, 1996.

Jacqueline Pearson, 'Women reading, reading women', in Helen Wilcox (ed.), *Women and Literature in Britain, 1500–1700*, 1996, pp. 80–99.

Margaret Pelling, 'Finding widowers: men without women in English towns before 1700', in Sandra Cavallo and Lyndan Warner (eds), *Widowhood in Medieval and Early Modern Europe*, 1999.

Laurel Phillipson, 'Quakerism in Cambridge before the Act of Toleration (1653–1689)', *Proceedings of the Cambridge Antiquarian Society*, 76, 1987.

Stephen Pincus, ' "Coffee politicians does create" Coffee houses and Restoration political culture', in *Journal of Modern History*, 67, 1995.

Linda A. Pollock, 'Embarking on a rough passage: the experience of pregnancy in early-modern society', in Valerie Fildes (ed.), *Women as Mothers in Pre-industrial England*, 1990, pp. 39–67.

Nia Powell, 'Women and strict-metre poetry in Wales', in M. Roberts and S. Clarke (eds), *Women and Gender in Early Modern Wales*, 2000, pp. 129–58.

Wilfred Prest, 'Law and women's rights in early modern England', in *The Seventeenth Century*, Vol. VI, no. 2, autumn 1991.

Bronwen Price, 'Feminine modes of knowing and scientific inquiry: Margaret Cavendish's poetry as case study', in Helen Wilcox (ed.), *Women and Literature in Britain, 1500–1700*, 1996, pp. 117–39.

F. Reader, 'Tudor mural paintings in the lesser houses of Bucks', *Archaeological Journal*, 89, 1932, pp. 116–73.

A. F. B. Roberts, 'The role of women in Scottish Catholic survival', *Scottish Historical Review*, 70, 1991, pp. 129–50.

M. Roberts, ' "Words they are women and deeds they are men": images of work and gender in early modern England', in L. Charles and

L. Duffin (eds), *Women and Work in Pre-Industrial England*, 1985, pp. 122–80.

Michael Roberts, 'Gender, work and socialisation in Wales', in M. Roberts and S. Clarke (eds), *Women and Gender in Early Modern Wales*, 2000.

M. Roberts and S. Clarke (eds), *Women and Gender in Early Modern Wales*, 2000.

Anne Pollard Rose, 'Crewel embroidered bed hangings in Old and New England', in *Bulletin, Museum of Fine Arts, Boston*, 71, 1973, pp. 101–68.

C. D. Ross, 'The household accounts of Elizabeth Berkeley, Countess of Warwick', *Transactions of the Bristol and Gloucestershire Archaeological Society*, 70, 1951.

Marie B. Rowlands, 'Recusant women 1560–1640', in Mary Prior (ed.), *Women in English Society 1500–1800*, 1985, pp. 149–80.

Daniel Rutman and Anita Rutman, 'Of agues and fevers', in *William and Mary Quarterly*, 3rd Series, XXXIII (1976), pp. 31–60.

Darrett B. Rutman and Anita H. Rutman, '"Now wives and sons in law": parental death in a seventeenth-century Virginia county', in Thad W. Tate and David L. Ammerman (eds), *The Chesapeake in the Seventeenth Century: Essays in Anglo-American Society*', 1979.

Morton Owen Schapiro, 'Land availability and fertility in the United States, 1760–1870', *Economic Journal*, 42, 1982, pp. 577–600.

Roger Schofield, 'Monday's child is fair of face': favoured days for baptism, marriage and burial in pre-industrial England', in *Continuity and Change*, 20 (1), 2005, pp. 93–109.

Carole Shammas, 'Early American women and control over capital', in R. Hoffman and P. J. Albert (eds), *Women in the Age of the American Revolution*, 1989, pp. 134–54.

Pamela Sharpe, 'Marital separation in the eighteenth and early nineteenth centuries', *Local Population Studies*, 45, 1990.

E. Shorter, J. Knodel and E. van de Walle, 'The decline of non-marital fertility in Europe, 1850–1960', *Population Studies*, 25, 1971.

Katharine Simms, 'Women in Gaelic society during the age of transition', in Margaret MacCurtain and Mary O'Dowd (eds), *Women in Early Modern Ireland*, 1991, pp. 32–42.

Alexandra Sinclair, 'The Great Berkeley Lawsuit Revisited 1417–1439', *Southern History*, 1987, pp. 34–50.

Daniel Scott Smith, 'Parental control and marriage patterns: an analysis of historical trends in Higham, Massachusetts', *Journal of Marriage and the Family*, 35, 1973.

Hilda Smith, 'Feminism and the methodology of women's history', in Berenice A. Carroll (ed.), *Liberating Women's History*, 1976.

Hilda Smith, 'Humanist education and the renaissance concept of woman', in Helen Wilcox (ed.), *Women and Literature in Britain, 1500–1700*, 1996, pp. 9–29.

James Smith and Jim Oippen, 'Estimating numbers of kin in historical England using microsimulation', in David Rehere and Roger Schofield (eds), *Old and New Methods in Historical Demography*, 1993.

T. C. Smout, 'Scottish marriage, regular and irregular, 1500–1940', in R. B. Outhwaite (ed.), *Marriage and society: Studies in the Social History of Marriage*, 1981.

J. M. Spicksley, 'A dynamic model of social relations: celibacy, credit and the identity of the "spinster" in seventeenth-century England', in H. French and J. Barry (eds), *Identity and Agency in English Society, 1500–1800*, 2004.

Margaret Spufford, 'First steps in literacy: the reading and writing experiences of the humblest seventeenth-century autobiographers', in *Social History*, 4, 1979, pp. 407–35.

Govind Sreenivasen, 'The land–family bond at Earl's Colne (Essex), 1550–1650', *Past and Present*, 131, 1991, pp. 3–37.

S. Staves, 'Investments, votes and "bribes": women as shareholders in the chartered national companies', in H. L. Smith (ed.), *Women Writers and the Early Modern British Political Tradition*, 1998, pp. 259–78.

Tim Stretton, 'Women, custom and equity in the Court of Requests', in Jenny Kermode and Garthine Walker (eds), *Women, Crime and the Courts in Early Modern England*, 1994, pp. 170–89.

K. W. Swett, 'Widowhood, custom and property in early modern North Wales', *Welsh History Review*, 18, 1996, p. 226.

K. V. Thomas, 'Women and the Civil War sects', *Past and Present*, 13, 1958, pp. 42–62.

Keith Thomas, 'The double standard', in *Journal of History of Ideas*, 20, 1959.

Barbara J. Todd, 'The remarrying widow: a stereotype reconsidered', in Mary Prior (ed.), *Women in English Society, 1500–1800*, 1985, pp. 54–92.

Barbara J. Todd, 'Freebench and free enterprise: widows and their property in two Berkshire villages', in John Chartres and David Hey (eds), *English Rural Society, 1500–1800: Essays in Honour of Joan Thirsk*, 1990, pp. 175–200.

Betty S. Travitsky, 'The possibility of prose', in Helen Wilcox (ed.), *Women and Literature in Britain, 1500–1700*, 1996.

Paula A. Treckel, 'Breastfeeding and maternal sexuality in Colonial America', *Journal of Interdisciplinary History*, XX, 1989, pp. 35–52.

Bruce G. Trigger, 'Sixteenth-century Ontario: history, ethno history, and archaeology', *Ontario History*, 71, 1979, pp. 205–23.

Bruce G. Trigger, 'Response of native peoples to European contact', in George M. Story (ed.), *Early European Settlement and Exploitation in Atlantic Canada: Selected Papers*, 1982.

Alison Truelove, 'Commanding communications: the fifteenth-century letters of the Stonor women', in James Daybell (ed.), *Early Modern Women's Letter-Writing, 1450–1800*, 2001.

Lyon G. Tyler, 'Education in Virginia', *William and Mary Quarterly*, 5, 1976, pp. 219–22.

Laurel Thatcher Ulrich, 'Creating lineages', in Brenton Simons and Peter Benes (eds), *The Art of family: Genealogical Artifacts in New England*, 2002, pp. 5–11.

Garthine Walker, 'Strange kind of stealing: abduction in early modern Wales', in Michael Roberts and Simone Clarke (eds), *Women and Gender in Early Modern Wales*, 2000, pp. 50–74.

Alison D. Wall, 'For love, money, or politics? A Clandestine marriage and the Elizabethan Court of Arches', *Historical Journal*, 1995, pp. 511–33.

Alison D. Wall, 'Commanding communications: the fifteenth-century letters of the Stonor women', in James Daybell (ed.), *Early Modern Women's Letter-Writing, 1450–1800*, 2001.

Lorena S. Walsh, '"Till death us do part": marriage and family in seventeenth-century Maryland', in Thad W. Tate and David L. Ammerman (eds), *The Chesapeake in the Seventeenth Century: Essays in Anglo-American Society*, 1979.

Valerie Wayne, 'Advice for women from mothers and patriarchs', in Helen Wilcox (ed.), *Women and Literature in Britain, 1500–1700*, 1996, pp. 56–79.

Robert V. Wells, 'Marriage seasonals in early America: comparisons and comments', *Journal of Interdisciplinary History*, 18, 2, 1987, pp. 299–307.

Lorna Wetherill, 'A possession of one's own: women and consumer behaviour in England 1660–1740', *Journal of British Studies*, 25, 1986.

E. M. White, 'Popular schooling and the Welsh language 1650–1800', in Geraint H. Jenkins (ed.), *Welsh Language Before the Industrial Revolution*, 1997.

Eryn M. White, 'Women, religion and education in eighteenth-century Wales', in M. Roberts and S. Clarke (eds), *Women and Gender in Early Modern Wales*, 2000, pp. 210–33.

Jane Whittle, 'Housewives and servants in rural England 1440–1650: evidence of women's work from probate documents', in *Transactions of the Royal Historical Society*, Sixth Series, 15, 2005a.

Jane Whittle, 'Servants in rural England, 1450–1650: hired work as a means of accumulating wealth and skills before marriage', in Maria Agren and Amy Louise Erickson, *The Marital Economy of Scandinavia and Britain, 1400–1900*, 2005b.

Susan Whyman, 'Gentle companions: single women and their letters in late Stuart England', in James Daybell (ed.), *Early Modern Women's Letter-Writing, 1450–1700*, 2001.

Adrian Wilson, 'A Memorial of Eleanor Willoughby, a seventeenth-century midwife', in L. Hunter and S. Hutton (eds), *Women, Science and Medicine, 1500–1700, Mothers and Sisters of the Royal Society*, 1997.

Gillian Wright, 'Mary Evelyn and devotional practice', in F. Harris and Michael Hunter (eds), *John Evelyn and his Milieu*, 2003, pp. 221–32.

Susan Wright, ' "Churmaids, huswyfes and hucksters": the employment of women in Tudor and Stuart Salisbury', in L. Charles and L. Duffin (eds), *Women and Work in Pre-Industrial England*, 1985.

E. A. Wrigley, 'Clandestine marriage in Tetbury in the late seventeenth century', *Local Population Studies*, 10, 1973.

Unpublished PhD and MA theses

Vincent P. Carey, 'Gaelic reaction to plantation: the case of the O'More and O'Connor lordships of Laois and Offaly, 1570–1603'. Unpublished MA thesis, St Patrick's College, Maynooth, 1985.

Judith Ford, 'Wills and willmaking'. Unpublished PhD thesis, Open University, 1992.

Claire Fox, 'Pregnancy, childbirth and early infancy in Anglo-American culture, 1675–1830'. Unpublished PhD thesis, University of Pennsylvania, 1966.

L. M. Glanz, 'The legal position of English women under the early Stuart kings and the interregnum, 1603–1660'. Unpublished PhD thesis, Loyola University, 1973.

Sally Gosling, 'Sex and gender roles in gentle and noble families, c.1575–1660 . . .'. Unpublished PhD thesis, Open University, 1999.

Janet Wilson James, 'Changing ideas about women in the United States, 1776–1825', Unpublished PhD dissertation, Harvard University (Radcliffe College), 1954.

J. L. Mcintosh, 'English funeral sermons, 1560–1640: the relationship between gender and death, dying and the afterlife'. Unpublished University of Oxford MLitt thesis, 1990.

Margaret Robbins, 'The agricultural, domestic, social and cultural interests of the gentry in South-East Glamorgan, 1540–1640'. Unpublished PhD thesis, University of Wales, 1974.

Glossary

annuity Annual cash payment, often funded by an investment.

bequest Gift of moveable property by will.

bond (obligation) Simple legal instrument by which person A was obliged to provide person B with something, often money or a service, by a certain date, with witnesses provided by both parties. Failure to honour the bond resulted in a forfeit of (usually) double the amount originally payable. It could be recovered in the common law courts. In the context of women, it should be noted that because a married woman was *fem(m)e covert*, a wife could not sign a bond herself or sue for recovery herself (unless she had become a widow); her trustees had to act for her. For typical uses of bonds see *marriage settlement*, *separate estate* and *wills*.

borough English Also known as 'ultimogeniture'. A manorial custom in some places by which the youngest son inherited *copyhold* land.

copyhold Land held of the lord of the manor, either by custom or by will.

coverture The property (*dowry* or *portion*) a woman brought to a marriage, according to the common law, was immediately under the control of her husband. The chattels or moveable goods were lost permanently; the leases might return to the woman on her husband's death if he had not sold them; the freehold or *copyhold* land came under the husband's control, but he could not sell or alienate it without her consent.

curtesy The widower's equivalent of *dower* rights. On his wife's death, the widower gained control of the whole of his deceased wife's property.

devise To dispose of land through a will.

divorce *a mensa et thoro* (from bed and board) An official separation granted on petition (on grounds of adultery, cruelty or desertion) by the ecclesiastical courts. The courts also sought to ensure provision for the injured party. The parties had to live separately, and remarriage was not permitted.

divorce *a vinculo matrimonii* (from the chains of marriage) This, which permitted remarriage, was rare and obtainable only through annulment (which declared that the marriage had never happened) or (after the Reformation) by private Act of Parliament.

dower Common-law term for the widow's right of a third of her husband's property for her lifetime. (The widower's equivalent was his *curtesy*, by which the widower gained control of the whole of his deceased wife's property.) This was largely overtaken by *jointure* by the 1500s.

dowry Also known as *portion*. The property a woman brought to a marriage.

entail Legal instrument by which specified heirs, in succession, were to inherit property in its entirety. The succession of heirs was thereby forbidden to dismantle the estate.

equity Legal principles drawn up largely in the Court of Chancery in an attempt to provide flexible 'reasonable' solutions that would compensate for the rigidity of both Common Law and Statute Law. By the seventeenth century, the Court of Chancery had become as rule-bound as its common law counterparts (Courts of Common Pleas, King's or Queen's Bench, Courts of Assize, etc.).

fem[m]e covert Under common law, a married woman could not enter contracts, sue or be sued independently of her husband. Although legally this was not the case in other courts (for example, the equity courts), in practice courts such as the Court of Chancery sought to uphold the common law doctrine of *coverture*, choosing to allow a wife to bring actions, make contracts, etc. only when the marriage had broken down completely and the parties were separated officially by the ecclesiastical courts.

fem[m]e sole An unmarried woman who was of age. This included both single and widowed women.

freebench Also known as widow's bench or bench. A widow's right under manorial law to between a third or the whole of her husband's *copyhold* land for either her lifetime or her widowhood.

gavelkind Manorial custom, especially prevalent in Kent, whereby land is divided equally among sons.

jointure By the early 1500s, jointure had normally replaced *dower* rights under common law. Originally it was a form of joint tenure of freehold or *copyhold* land by husband and wife, which allowed the survivor to enjoy the income of the other. By our period, however, it was normally replaced by an *annuity* raised from a rent charge on specific lands. The money that a bride brought into a marriage was used to purchase land to produce an annual income. At first this was used to support the couple. On the husband's death, it was used to support his widow. Jointure had several advantages: one was that it allowed the main estate to remain intact for the heir; another was that it could apply, unlike *dower* rights, to leasehold lands or lands held in trust. The terms of a jointure were normally stipulated in a marriage settlement, which established a trust to protect the *annuity* (which would otherwise disappear under the rules of *coverture*).

intestate Dying without having made a will. Used to describe a person who has died thus.

inventory List of goods made by appraisers appointed by the ecclesiastical probate court soon after a person's death and then exhibited in the court by the executor or administrator of the will.

legitim Term used to describe the thirds due to a widow.

marriage settlement A document or group of documents stipulating the arrangements to be made for the support of the married couple and for the wife (and younger children) in the event of the husband's prior death. It arranged typically for a *jointure* and a trust to protect the widow's rights, and sometimes for the creation of a *separate estate*, a *pin money* allowance and the return of the widow's personal belongings (clothing, etc.). The widow might also be given the right to enter into business for herself as *fem[m]e sole* trader. See also *bond*.

middling sort A term used by contemporaries to describe the layers of society below the gentry. These layers included shopkeepers, some craftsmen, yeomen, clergymen and some husbandmen.

paraphernalia A wife or widow's personal belongings, such as clothing, jewellery, bed linens and plate. This had normally been under the jurisdiction of the ecclesiastical courts, but by our period it was also recoverable under equity jurisdiction.

pin money Annual allowance to a wife, with which to clothe herself and her household, as befitted her husband's rank. This right (set up by a *bond*) was unenforceable during a husband's lifetime, but his widow had a year in which to reclaim it and the arrears after his death.

poorer sort Contemporary term referring to labourers, some husbandmen and some craftsmen.

portion The property a bride took into marriage. See *dowry*. The term 'portion' also refers to the property a child inherited from a parent (more correctly 'filial portion').

primogeniture Inheritance by the eldest son.

probate Process of viewing and proving a deceased person's will and formally registering it in an ecclesiastical court. Wills were proved in a number of ecclesiastical courts, ranging from those of the rural deans, deans of peculiars and the archdeacons (for very small estates) through those of the bishops (for estates of medium value) to those of the provinces of Canterbury and York (for the relatively wealthy).

property, chattels, real Leases of land.

property, personal Called 'chattels' under the common law courts and 'moveable goods' under the ecclesiastical courts. This included money, debts, apparel (clothing), household goods, food and the 'other lumber about the house' referred to so frequently in wills and inventories.

property, real Freehold land.

relict Widow of a named man.

separate estate Specific property held in trust for the wife's use during *coverture*. The provision of this property was set up using a *bond*.

separation Contemporary definitions varied. Official separations were granted by the ecclesiastical courts. However, many marriages disintegrated and the partners lived separately but never obtained *divorce a mensa et thoro* (from bed and board).

strict settlement Settlement designed to keep the main estate intact and passing through the eldest male line and to prevent individual heirs from alienating it. A strict settlement also provided for younger sons and daughters through money portions ('filial portions'). See also *entail*.

third Under ecclesiastical law, a widow was entitled to a third of her deceased husband's estate.

trust A trust separated legal from beneficial ownership of property, allowing a trustee (or feoffee) to hold and manage property on behalf of another (a beneficiary or 'cestuy que use'). It came into being in the late 1530s. Because a married woman was *feme covert* and was not allowed to enter contracts or to sue for their recovery under common law, a device called the 'trust' was used to protect her various kinds of property (set up through *bonds*) and to look after her interests. Put simply, a number of trustees (male and unmarried or widowed female relatives and close friends) were entrusted with her (the beneficiary's) affairs, signed bonds and other legal instruments, received monies on her behalf and made expenditures, investments, etc. on her behalf.

will Unmarried women of age and widowed women were allowed to make a will. A married woman might not, unless she had her husband's express and written permission. This permission was granted in the form of a witnessed *bond*.

Subject index

abuse 176–7, 180, 250–52
Act for the English order, habit and language 326
Act of Union 261
acting 421–2
Acts of Parliament 53, 191, 194, 261–2
Adam and Eve 149–50, 387
Africa Company 221
Anglican(s) 36–8, 44, 157, 189–90, 361, 363
Anglicanism 38, 353
annuity 263–5
annulment 52, 194
apprenticeship 4, 75
architecture *see* building 374
Arminian 60, 158, 189, 285, 366
art 243, 385–9, 392, 397
Athenian Mercury 93, 119, 188, 415–17, 420

baptism 7, 29, 356
bastardy *see* illegitimacy
Bible 173, 327, 332, 345, 348–50, 360–61, 379, 388, 413, 420
　Eliot 409
　Genevan 349, 413
　King James 212, 348
　Welsh language 12
bigamy 43, 44, 61, 63, 132
Book of Common Prayer 48, 62, 349, 413
Book of Martyrs 347–8, 413
books of advice 55, 243–4, 253–5
　see also conduct books
breastfeeding 173–5, 241–7
brothers 154–6, 217
building 374

Calvinists 37, 157–8, 190–91, 349, 360–61, 363, 366
Canadians, French 32
capitalism 3, 4, 5
Catholic(s) 11, 29, 37–8, 42, 44–5, 48, 52, 59–60, 70, 72–3, 114, 148, 157–60, 189–90, 243, 253, 325, 327–8, 339, 342, 357–61, 363, 410
Catholicism 11, 179, 327–8, 345, 351–2, 356–60, 365
charity school movement 329
child marriage *see* marriage, child
childbirth 229–31, 242, 357
Church
　Anglican 51
　Catholic 32, 42, 44, 47, 52–3, 62, 194, 200–201, 357
　Northern High Commission 352
　Northern Province (York) 289, 291
　Presbyterian 51, 356
　of Scotland (Presbyterian) 52, 62, 356
　Southern Province (Canterbury) 289
　of Wales 200
clans 5, 50, 67, 260
class, social 10, 19, 20
coffee houses 415–17
cohabitation 45
colonies 2, 12, 13–15, 16, 17, 31, 142 *et passim*
conduct books 54, 55, 56, 143–4, 155, 243–4
consent 43, 47–8, 52, 56–7, 62, 88–95, 127–134
　see also marriage, consent
convents 359–60, 402
correspondence 416–17, 418–21

courts
  Chancery 157, 215, 258, 267
  Ecclesiastical 96–7, 127, 156–63, 260, 351, 356
  equity 274
  Requests 56–7
  of Wards 50
courtship 67–110, 111–38
  interview 78, 84
cousins 72
coverture 153, 262–65, 273, 274, 292–3
culture 372–96, 397–428
  audience 411–15, 415–17
  family and 398–401, 402–5
  groups and 399–400
  print and non-print 372–96
  public and private 372–96

dancing 401
daughters 63, 71, 72, 74, 77–8, 248
desertion 61, 195–6
diaries 16, 17–19, 265, 349, 412, 416
discourses 8, 9
divorce 52, 61, 156–7, 193–5, 197–200, 476, 477
  see also annulment
dower (widow's) 286–9, 291, 292, 299, 477
dowry 288, 292, 477
  see also portion

East India Company 217
education 198, 216, 241, 252, 254, 275, 293, 320–37, 359, 362–3, 400–402, 403, 404
embroidery 366, 375–7, 397
  see also needlework
executors 294–5

family finance 217–19, 221–4, 225
  see also inheritance, property
family history 406–7
family, nuclear 5, 67
furnishing 49

Gaelic 11, 12, 15, 16, 46, 410
genealogy 170, 287, 406–7
General Assembly (Scottish) 29, 53–4

godparents 78
graffiti 366, 377–80
grandmother 252–3
grandparents 78
guardianship 49, 50, 56

health see medicine
household 5, 170–75, 205–39, 351–2
housewifery 401
  see also wives, activities of

illegitimacy 43, 44, 53, 54, 200
Indian 13–14, 209
individualism 3, 4, 5, 67
individuality 6, 7
inheritance 259–79, 280–309
  legitim 289
  thirds 286–89, 291
intestacy 259–63, 269–71
investment 217, 221–4
  Mississippi Bubble 217
  Mississippi Project 221
  South Sea Company 221–4

James Salter's in Chelsea 416
Jesuit 357–8
jointure 262–5, 287–9, 293, 478

kinship 5, 169–70
Kirk, Aberdeen session 29, 53
Kirk, Cannongate session 53–4

Ladies Tatler 304
language 408–11
law 44, 100–101, 156–63, 265–8, 274–5
literacy 241, 366, 402, 412
literature
  dramatic 390–91, 402, 405, 412–13
  general 390–91, 392
  novel and romance 390–91, 404, 412
  poetry 390–91, 402–5, 408, 412, 417–18
Lollards 324, 341, 345–6
Lord Hardwicke's Marriage Act 128
love, romantic 90–95, 175–8

manuscript circulation 372, 392
Mariam 381–2

marriage
  age at 75, 76, 173–5, 178–9, 223
  arranged 76–90
  attitudes to 95, 114, 146–51, 200
  banns 29, 36, 37, 42, 47–9
  bed 33
  betrothal 29, 42, 44
  broking 79–84, 112
  ceremony 30, 31
  child 95–8, 101
  choice 68, 69, 70, 85–7, 112, 116–19, 127–34
  church 42, 48, 49, 61, 62
  clandestine 28, 43–5, 53
    see also marriage, irregular
  companionate 167–9
    see also partnership
  consent 43, 47, 48, 52, 56, 57, 62, 88–90, 100–101, 127–34
  contract 42, 44–46, 49, 123–4, 190, 193, 273–4, 290
    see also marriage, betrothal; marriage, settlement
  customs 30, 32–35
  definition of 42, 43, 50, 51
  delay 75, 76
  endogamy 69, 70, 71, 72
  feast 30, 32–6
  handfast 29, 44–6, 53, 54, 197–200
    see also marriage, betrothal
  importance of 101, 146–8
  irregular 53
  late 98–100
  legal 53
  negotiations 73, 74, 78–90, 119–23
  Protestant 34, 35
  purpose of 41–66, 67, 68
  sacrament 29, 37, 38
  seasons 28, 29, 31, 32
  second 98–100
  secular 36, 37
  settlement 112, 123–6, 263–6, 291–8, 478
    see also marriage, contract
  sexual consummation of 42, 53, 54
  solemnisation of 28–40
  spousals see marriage, betrothal
  trial 45, 46, 88, 147
  unhappy 176–7
  veto 68, 86–8, 100
  Willoughby–Ridgeway 35
matriarchy 228–9
medicine 220–21, 407–8
monogamy 42, 44
mothers and motherhood 55, 56, 240–54, 363–5
Mrs Piggot's school 326
music 400–401, 403

needlework 149, 375, 401
  see also embroidery
network(ing) 72–5, 216–19, 405

parents 56, 57, 351
  see also consent; marriage, consent; patriarchy
Parliament 163–6, 347
partners
  elite 67–110
  middling-sort 111–39
  professional 111–39
partnership 167, 185–204, 231
patriarchy 67, 152–84, 199–200, 352, 358, 404
patronage 231, 384
  church 213, 287, 353, 366
philosophy 422
plantation 59, 214
poetry 373, 402–5, 408, 412
population 58, 59, 60, 61, 62, 63, 272
portion 30, 287, 288, 291, 293, 479
  see also dowry
portraits 150, 389
Presbyterian(s) 35–8
printing and publishing 384–5, 392
Privy Council 208, 296
property 174
  widows and 280–309
  wives and 258–75
public and private divide 7, 8
publishing/publication 52–3, 380–84, 417–18

Quaker(s) 32, 37, 133, 157, 189–90, 360–61, 363, 366

reading 266–8, 349–50, 352, 366, 401, 403, 404, 412, 413–15, 415–17

recusancy 352, 358
reformation 4, 34, 52, 61, 67, 194, 200, 339, 342, 345, 356–7, 359, 365
religion 338–71
  cults 354–5, 363
  furnishing 355

separate estates 263–5, 287, 293–4, 478, 479
  see also marriage, settlement
separation 194–5, 275
separatists 360–61
servitude, indentured 127–8
sex 114–17
siblings 78, 79, 154, 162–5
singletons 113–14
sisters 143, 154
Smith's Coffee House 415
sources, historical 16–19, 141–5
South Sea Bubble 217
South Sea Company 221–2
Statute of Wills 290
Statutes of Iona 46
Statutes of Uses and Enrolments 290
strict settlement 288–89, 479

theatre 390–91
  see also printing/publication; literature, dramatic
trust 274, 480
  see also investment

Virgin Mary 243, 339, 354–5, 363
Virginia Gazette 385
Virginia House of Burgesses 193

wardships 49, 50, 56, 288
wedding *see* marriage
weddings, big 34
widows and widowhood 55, 56, 280–309
wife sales 196–7
will 122–3, 132–4, 268, 269–74, 287, 289–94, 362–3, 385, 477, 481
witchcraft 365
wives 205–39, 258–75
  activities of 171, 179, 186–90
  jurisdiction of 167
work 224–6, 227–8, 300–6

Index of proper names

This is chiefly an index of women referred to in the text, intended to allow women to emerge from the shadows at last. The index also includes references to some prominent men.

Acheson, Molly 54
Acton, Eliza 30
Adams, Abigail 19, 174, 178, 186, 227, 398, 401
Adams, Peg 94
Addison, Mrs 224
Akers, Elizabeth ('Cousin Thornton') 104, 120
Alden, Priscilla 227
Alexander, Mary Spratt Provoost 305, 308
Allan, Hannah 121
Altham, Joan 172
Andrewes, Anne 159–64, 192, 194, 214
Anger, Elizabeth 36
Ann, Countess of Coventry 413–14
Anne, Countess of Arundel 220
Anne of Denmark 82
Anne, Queen 65, 325, 327, 386, 399
Archer, Hannah 326
Archer, Isaac 348
Argyll, Earl of 321
Argyll, 2nd Duke of 88
Arundel, Lady (Margaret) 79, 143, 195
Arundell, Lady Blanche 210
Ashcomb, Sir William 85–6, 98
Ashmole, Elias 403
Askew, Anne 342
Astell, Mary 414
Aston, Constance 92
Atkinson, Elizabeth 358
Aubrey, John 398
Austen, Katharine 297, 307

Bacon 79–80, 88, 106, 172, 353, 383
Bagot 19, 50, 92, 176–7, 283, 287–8, 364
Bailey, Abigail 174
Baillie, Grisell 19, 194
Baker, Elizabeth 265, 409
Baldwin, Anne (Abigail) 303
Balfour, Anna 403
Balinsho, Lady Jean 207
Baltimore, Lord 59, 60, 131, 362
Bambridge, Mrs 389
Bancroft, Sybil 97
Bankes, Lady Mary 210
Bargany, Lady 206
Barlow, Anna 61
Barnard 73, 350
Barnard, Elizabeth 73
Barnard, Emma 73, 350
Barnes, Isabella 90
Barrington 80, 99, 109, 167, 169, 252
Barry, Elizabeth 390
Basset 77, 90, 173
Bathe 402, 405
Beale, Mary 18, 386, 387
Beaufort 301, 343, 383, 398
Becon, Thomas 148, 366, 381
Bedford, Countess of 82
Benn, Aphra 19, 390–91
Berkeley 297
Berry, Eleanor 259
Bertie, Lady Georgiana 407
Bess of Hardwick 6, 19, 376, 388
Bevan, Bridget 329

Beverley(s) 14, 329
Billingsley, Martin 307, 381
Binning, Lady 224
Blackley, Bab 329
Blacknall, Mary 50
Blackwell, Elizabeth 220
Boccaccio 390
Bois 212, 347–8
Boleyn, Anne 90, 343–4, 365, 414
Bourchier, Margaret, Countess of Bath 212, 264
Bourne 211, 348, 350
Bowyer 403
Boyd, Isabel 301
Bradeley 346
Bradford, Cornelia Smith 385
Bradford, Governor 36, 124
Bradstreet, Anne 364–5, 382, 383, 398
Brandon, Frances 321
Brettargh, Katherine 349
Brew, Margery 90
Bruce, Mary 91
Brydges 78, 91, 108, 187, 195, 320, 329, 364, 407
Brydges, Cassandra *see* Cassandra, Duchess of Chandos
Brydges, Sir James 70, 73, 91, 167, 178, 186–7, 217, 416
Bulman, Mary 150, 375
Bunyan, John 380
Burghley, Lord 84, 233
Burlington, Lady 387
Burnet, Bishop 399
Burney, Fanny 399
Burr, Cynthia 375
Bury, Elizabeth 349
Butler, Eleanor 84
Butler, James *see* Ormond, Earl of
Byrd 14, 128, 226–7, 331, 334

Caerleon, Anne of 388
Calvert, Governor (Charles) 331
Calvin, John 3, 366
Campbell, Agnes 207, 208
Canterbury, Archbishop of 161, 182, 363
Carey 60, 173, 179, 219, 253, 351, 384
Carey, Elizabeth 19, 172, 253, 351, 381–2, 399, 405, 415

Carey, Lady Anne 383
Carleton, Lord, Lord President of the Council 23
Carlile, Penelope 386
Carlisle, Joan Palmer 385, 399
Carnarvon, Lady 329
Carolina (Brydges), Lady 320, 329
Carter 14, 244, 399
Cassandra, Duchess of Chandos 6, 19, 70, 72, 78, 91, 178, 217, 219, 221–2, 223, 253, 267, 295, 320, 329, 330, 387–8, 389, 406, 408, 413, 420, 421
Cassillis, Earl of 49–50, 75, 206
Catherine, Queen 391
Catherine (Huntingdon) 104
Catherine of Braganza 345, 353, 374
Catherine of France 391
Causine, Jane 286
Cavendish 186, 387, 390, 398
Cavendish, Margaret (Lucas), Duchess of Newcastle 9, 19, 229, 390, 398, 400, 415, 422
Cawardine, Mrs 386
Cecil, Anne (de Vere) 93, 108–27, 383, 398
Cely 33, 218
Centlivre, Susanna 390–91
Chalenor, Anne 325
Champernowne, Katherine 322
Chandler, Anne 332
Chandos 78, 91, 94, 197
  see also Brydges
Chapone, Hester 399
Chapone, Sarah 398
Chaucer, Geoffrey 339, 413, 414
Cheer, Margaret 421
Chew, Anne Ayers 361
Chidley, Katherine 351
Child, Lady Emma 74, 217, 222, 262, 267, 350
Churchill, Sarah, Duchess of Marlborough 81
Clarke, Dorothy 274
Clerksone, Bessie 384
Clifford 19, 298, 405
Clifford, Anne 220, 297, 321, 374, 378, 389, 398, 414
Clifford, Anne, Countess of Dorset
  see Clifford, Anne

INDEX OF PROPER NAMES 487

Clifton, Anne Clifford 297
Clinton (Fiennes), Bridget, Countess of Lincoln 173, 231
Clinton, Elizabeth 173, 230, 243, 383–4, 398
Clopton, Anne 96
Coke, Bell 223
Coke, Lady Elizabeth 349
Cole, Ellen 246
Cole, Mary 48
Colegate, Rebecca 363
Collet 78, 174, 321
Collins, Alice 241, 324
Collins, Ann 412
Compton, Lady 83
Congreve, William 390
Conway, Anne see Finch, Anne
Cooke, Anne 321
Cooke, Mildred 321
Cornwallis, Cass 224
Cornwallis, Lady Jane 153, 419
Coryate, Thomas 377
Cotton, John 360
Courtney, Katherine 175
Cowley, Abraham 408, 414
Craddock, Elizabeth 232
Craig, Maggie 207
Cranfield, Elizabeth 326
Cranstoun, Ann 263
Cromwell, Oliver 36, 38, 59, 322, 327, 359
Cromwell, Thomas 298, 387
Cudworth, Mary 111, 112, 118
Culzean 51
Cunningham, Lady Anne 340
Cusacke, Margaret 84

Dakins, Margaret see Hoby, Lady Margaret
Daniel (Samuel) 414
Davall, Lady 236
Davenport, Dame Dorothy 149
Davies, Alice 205
Davies, Anne 30
Davies, Lady Eleanor 383, 398
Davies, Margaret 404
Davis, Dolar 126
Daws, Lady 186
de Burgh, Elizabeth 301

de Vere, Anne Cecil see Cecil, Anne (de Vere)
Deane, Joan 322
Dee 96, 246, 295
Defoe, Daniel 303
Delany, Mary 398
Delany, Mrs 95
Delaval, Elizabeth 95
Denby 168
Denny, Lady Margaret 250
Denny, Mistress 99–100
Denton 161, 203, 216–17
DePeyester, Maria 306
Derby, Anne, Dowager Countess of 272
Derby, Countess of 210, 260, 272
Dering, Edward 81, 366, 399
Descartes 322, 390, 400, 422
Desmond, Earl of 51
Deverell, Katherine 144
D'Ewes, Simonds 96–7, 98
Dickinson, Elizabeth see Stout, Elizabeth
Dillon, Cecily 359
Docking, Faith 154
Docwra, Anne 266
Donne, John 378, 399, 403, 408
Donnellan, Anne 399
Dormer, Anne 169, 191–3
Dormer, Margaret 347
Dorset, Marquis of 49
Dory, Faith 273
Doughty, Elizabeth 293
Dowager Lady Montague 348
Dowager Lady Russell 405
Dowdall Lady Elizabeth 210, 211
Dowe, Katharine 378
Downy, Mary 39
Drayton, Michael 382
Dryden 390
Dudley, Anne, Countess of Warwick 405, 419
Dudley, Dorothy 17
DuGard, Lydia 164–5
Dumfries, Countess of 365
Dunster, Mary 125
Dunton, Elizabeth 188
Dunton, John 188
Dury, John 411
Duston, Hannah 209, 227
Dyer, Mary 398

Earle, Madam Elizabeth 350
Egeton, Sarah Fyge 413
Elizabeth of Bohemia 243, 321
Elizabeth, Countess of Rutland 419
Elizabeth, Princess 82, 344, 379
Elizabeth I, Queen 6, 322, 327, 348, 365, 379, 380, 398, 405
Ellesmere, Lord Chancellor 213
Ellis, Alice 96
Elstob, Elizabeth 398
Emery, Elizabeth 328
Emery, Sarah 328
Erasmus 243, 344, 378, 400
Essex, Earl of 51, 82, 93
Estaugh, Elizabeth 227
Evelyn, John 178, 220, 386, 420
Evelyn, Mary 114, 178, 386
Ewan, Elizabeth 225
Eyre 168–9, 186–7, 262, 265, 416
Eyre, Jane 168–9, 265

Fairfax, Lady Mary 322
Farmer, Mary 192, 194, 267
Featley, Daniel 403
Fell, Margaret 38
Fenn 50
Fenton, Catherine 404
Ferebe 301
Ferniehirst 206
Ferrar 8, 114, 174
Ferrar, Mary 78, 220, 321
Fiennes, Celia 114
Filmer, Lady Anne 154, 252
Filmer, Robert 154–5
Finch 73, 86, 91, 250, 322
Finch, Anne 172, 322, 323, 382, 398, 418, 422
Fister 378
Fitch, Bridget 403
Fitton, Anne 172
Fitzgerald 84
Fitzgerald, Lady 210
Fitzroy, Mary, Duchess of Richmond and Somerset 278
Fitzwilliam, Lord Deputy 51
Fitzwilliam, Lord Justice 64, 208
Florio, John 382
Floud, Rachel 149
Foote, Abigail 376

Forbes, Lady 210
Forman, Andrew, Archbishop of St Andrews 53
Forsters, Lady 407
Fowler 92
Fowler, Constance 19, 92, 398, 402–3
Fox, George 37, 361
Fox(e), John 67, 348–9, 379, 413
Frances, Elizabeth 221
Francis, Rebecca 332
Franklin, Benjamin 305
Freeman, Susanna 391
Freke, Elizabeth 17, 19, 71, 194, 195, 247, 251–2, 253–4, 423
Freke, Grace 253
Frisbie, Roxanna 331
Furbanke, Alice 294
Fychan, Gruffudd ab ieuan ap Llywelyn 404
Fyft, Jonet 54

Gale, Madam 301
Galloway, Ann 361
Galloway, Earl of 87
Gamage, Barbara 384
Garrard, Lady 85
Garrard, Martha 85
Garret, Nurse 246
Garrick, David 399
Gatte, Timothy BD 213
Gaunt, Susan 292
Gay, John 127
Gayle, Sarah 380
Gentileschi, Artemisia 386
George, Earl of Huntingdon 177
Geraldine 405
Germain, Lady Betty 222
Gerrard, Susannah 362
Gibbs 98, 213
Gibbs, Elizabeth 213
Gill, Ann 361
Glamis, 8th Lord 49
Glencairn, Earl of 75, 340
Goch, Iolo 388
Goddard, Mary Catherine 385
Godolphin, Margaret (Blagge) 353, 387
Gouge, William 56–7, 62, 84, 244, 366
Grahame, Anna 79
Gray 405

INDEX OF PROPER NAMES

Green 120
Green, Anne Catherine 385
Greenham, Richard 62, 117
Greenwood 150
Greville 71
Grey, Lady Jane 321, 379, 383
Greystanes, Margaret 121
Griffith, M. 153
Griffiths, Ann 404, 407

Haddington 224
Hale, Lord Chief Baron 152
Halkett, Lady Anne 383
Hall, Elizabeth 77
Hall, Joseph 379
Hall, Rachel 363
Hallam, Ann 123
Hallam, Sarah 421
Hanmer 175
Harding, Mary 419
Harlakenden, Margaret 30
Harley, Brilliana Conway 80, 153, 210
Harley, Mistress 228
Harris, Elizabeth 361, 398
Harris, Gertrude 398, 401
Harris, Louisa 398, 401
Harrison, Sarah 167
Hastings, Lady Betty 374
Hawke, Thomasine 122
Hay, Lucy, Countess of Carlisle 108
Head 127
Heaton 357
Heneage, Mistress 99
Hengwrt 265
Henrietta Maria, Queen 90, 179, 345, 352, 361
Herbert 35, 179, 398, 399
Herbert, Mary 96
Herrick, Robert 39
Heywood, Oliver 36
Hibbot, Alice 328
Hicks, Sir Baptist 70
Hieron, Samuel 56–7
Higgins, Anne 213
Higgins, Hester 263
Higgins, Susan 213
Higginson, Anne 325
Hitch, Mrs 407
Hoby, Lady Margaret 349–50, 375, 413

Holbein 387
Holle 387
Holt, Miss 212
Home 206–7, 232
Home, Lady Grisell 224–5
Home, Lady Isobel of Eccles 206
Home, Lady Margaret 207
Hone, Katherine 309
Hooke, Robert 322
Hope, Christian 96
Hopkins, Anne 411
Hopper, Elizabeth 118
Hopton, Susanna 352
Horley, Mistress 215
Howard, Henrietta Hobart Countess of Suffolk 221–2, 395
Howard, Lady Jane 321
Howard, Rachel 85
Huntington, Earl of 272
Hurlburt, Elizabeth 376
Hutchinson 15
Hutchinson, Anne 19, 230, 360, 398
Hutchinson, Lucy 381, 398, 412, 415
Hyde, Frances 285

Ilay, Lord 222

Jacke, Robyn 246
James, Angharad 404
Jefferies, Joyce 30, 114, 405
Jefferson, Thomas 334
Jeffreys, Joyce *see* Jefferies, Joyce
Johan fitz John 261
Johnson, Elizabeth 196
Jones, Lady Katherine Boyle 19, 398
Jonson, Ben 399, 411
Josselin 121, 178, 326
Josselin, Ralph 36, 120–21, 178, 326, 348, 349

Katharine of Aragon 34, 321, 343
Kauffman, Angelica 386
Kavanagh, Katherine 208
Kay, Isabella 122
Keeble, Mary 309
Kemp, Alice 154
Kennedy 49, 51, 75
Ker, Elisabeth 43–4
Ker, Isabel, Lady of Linton 206

Kidder, Richard, Bishop of Bath and
    Wells 93
Kildare, Dowager Countess of 358
Kildare, Earl and Countess of 413
Killigrew, Elizabeth 404
Killigrew, Lady Anne 387
King, Gregory 113
Kinloch, Lady 79
Kinnersley, Lettice 169, 176, 190, 192,
    193
Kinsayder 412
Kirk, Helen 122
Kirkly, Susannah 296
Knight, Sarah Kemble 305–6
Knollys, Lettice, Countess of Leicester
    104
Knox, Andrea 207
Knox, John 366

Ladies Hall 325
Lane, Jane 311
Langham, Lady Mary 350
Lanyer, Aemilia 398
Latimer, Alice 122
Latimer, Hugh 50
Lawson, Dorothy Constable 357
Leicester, Earl of 51, 88
Leigh, Dorothy 383
Leneman, Leah 121
Lenthall 273
Lenthall John 98, 165, 214, 273
Lestrange, Lady Anne 179, 212, 229
Lettice, Dowager Countess of Leicester
    78
Leveson, Christian 74, 75, 91, 158, 166
Levingstoun, Elizabeth *see* Livingstone,
    Elizabeth
Line, Anne 347, 348
Lisle, Lady Honor 9, 77, 405
Lisle, Viscountess 172
Littleton 143
Littleton, Elizabeth 79, 143, 172, 195
Livingstone, Elizabeth 284, 305, 310
Lockett, Elesabeth 48
Logan, Martha 334
London Stock Market 415
Londonderry, Earl of 69, 81, 268
Long, Dorothy 399
Long, Jane 132

Long, Tabitha 132
Longueville (Longfield), Margaret 74,
    240, 249
Lowe, Katherine 288
Loys de Brun 344
Lucas, Eliza 171, 268
Lucas, Elizabeth Leighton 186
Lucas, Margaret *see* Cavendish
Lufkin, Tabitha 191
Lumley, Jane 377, 383
Lyon, Margaret 49–50

mac Donnchadha, Sean 261
Mac Phelim, Sir Brian 51
MacCarthy 84
MacCoghlan, Awly 261
Macdonald 51
Macdonald, Flora 207
MacDonnell, Arqt 51
Mace, Clove 193
Macguire, Cuchonnacht Mor Mac
    Cuchonnacht 384
Machyn, Henry 34
Mackenzie 51
MacLean, Katherine 321
Makin, Bathsua 398
Manley, Delarivier 390
Manley, Mary 304
Mapletoft, Susanna 78
Marbury, Bridget 220, 230
Margaret, dowager Marchioness of
    Dorset 297
Marlborough, Duchess of 237, 408
Marrowe, Lady Ursula 298
Marston, John 383, 412
Martin, Joanna 221
Martindale 77, 167, 297–8
Martindale, Jane 167
Marvell, Andrew 322
Mary (Argyll) 88
Mary, Countess of Warwick (nee Boyle)
    86, 87
Mary, Princess 386
Mary I, Queen 345, 348
Mary Queen of Scots 206, 376, 380, 388
Mary of Scotland *see* Mary Queen of Scots
Masham, Lady Elizabeth 172
Maspley, Nurse 246
Matthews, Anne 332

INDEX OF PROPER NAMES

Mayherne, Theodore 407
Merricke, Ann 413
Merriman, Mary Boone 363
Meux, Joan 80
Mildmay, Lady Grace 220, 253, 348–9, 350
Millam, Susan 302
Millett 215
Milton 150
Mintham, Christian 123
Misson, Henri 35
Molesworth, Elizabeth 222
Moll King's 416
Montagu, Elizabeth 374, 399
Montagu, Mary Wortley (nee Pierrepoint) 87
Montague, Lady Mary Wortley 147
Montaigne 414
Moore, Giles 35
Moore, Lady Alice 71
Mordaunt, Viscountess Elizabeth 349
More 6, 321–2, 398, 400, 418
More, Elizabeth 35, 265
More, Hannah 399
More, Margaret 398
More, Mary 155, 264, 265, 322
More, Mary Waller 387
Morgan, Joan 156
Morris, Betty 326
Morris, Claver 93, 326
Muir, James, heir to Auchindrain 51
Mulcaster, Richard 320, 380
Murray, Alexander 194
Murray, Elizabeth, Countess of Dysart 374, 399
Murray, Isabel 261
Murray, Lady 224
Murray, Lady Katherine 244
Musculus 348
Mynors, Theodosia 211

Napier, Dr Richard 93
Napier, John 122
Neale, Henrietta Maria 338, 361–2
Neville, Anne 49
Neville, Anne, Duchess of Buckingham 296
Neville, Katherine, Duchess of Norfolk 300

Newcastle, Duchess of 229
Newdigate, Anne 211, 216
ni Coirechain, Mairgreead 261
Northumberland, Countess of 82
Northumberland, Earl of 82–3, 93
Northumberland, Lady *see* Northumberland, Countess of
Nottingham, Earl of 86
Nuthead, Diana 385

O Bruadair, Ulick 261
O'Connor 84
O'Donnell 84
O'Donnell, Finola 207
Offaly, Lady 210
Ogden, Dorothie 196
O'Hara, Caitlin 211
O'Hara, Cormac 211
Oliver, Elizabeth 150
O'Neill 84
O'Neill, Terence (Turlough Luineach) 208
O'Neill, Turlough Brasselagh 51
Orgell, Elizabeth 122
Orknay, Jhone 206
Ormond, Duchess of 376, 398
Ormond, Earl of 233, 410
Oronoco 391
Osborne, Dorothy 414
Osgodby 358

Palmer, Elizabeth 178
Paracelsus 47
Park, Rebecca 230
Parke, Lucy 226–7
Parr, Katharine (Catherine) 344–5, 365, 398
Parsons, Ann 197
Parsons, Mary 362
Paston 8, 70, 52, 90, 143, 218, 250
Pembroke, Earl and Countess of 163
Pembroke, Marquess of 344
Penn, William 133
Pepys, Elizabeth 386
Pepys, Samuel 33, 178, 416
Percy 17, 93
Percy, Dorothy 88, 172
Percy, Henry, 9th Earl of Northumberland *see* Northumberland, Earl of

INDEX OF PROPER NAMES

Percy, Lucy 82–3, 88, 93
Philip, Earl of Pembroke 163–4
Philips, Katherine 192, 398, 408, 414
Phillips 132, 274
Pierrepont 387
Pinny, Eunice 376
Pix, Mary 390
Pomeroy, Elizabeth 403
Pope, Alexander 413
Pope, Mr 93
Post, Mary Titus 17
Powell, Thomas 345
Prence, Elizabeth 128, 129
Price, Bronwen 422
Provoost 305
Provoost, Maria DePeyester Shrick Spratt 305
Pulteney, William, Earl of Bath 400
Punderson, Prudence 376
Punt, Elizabeth 218

Quarles 414
Quincy, Elizabeth 186

Raleigh, Sir Walter 379, 403
Randolph, Dorothy 79–80, 81
Ranelagh, Lady 398, 404–5
Ranelagh, Vicountess see Jones, Lady Katherine Boyle
Raphael 386
Ratcliff(e) Jane 272, 340
Ravenscroft 414
Redyng, Alice 121
Reid, Miss 389
Rhirid, ferch Gwenllian 404
Rich 87, 189
Rich, Elizabeth 50
Rich, Essex 86, 91
Rich, Katheryn 98
Rich, Mary, Countess of Warwick 212, 349, 398, 412
Richardson 413
Richardson v. Mountjoy 274
Ridgeway, Cassandra 69, 86, 173
Rind, Clementina 385
Risley 239, 273
Roberts, Mary 389
Robins, Elizabeth 194
Robinson, Mintham 123

Roche, Joan 358
Roper, Margaret 6, 400
Roper, Thomas, Lord Baltinglass 165
Rose, Susannah 386–7
Rous 273
Rous, John 98, 214, 267
Rowe, Elizabeth Singer 417
Rowley, Alice 346
Royal Society 388, 390, 400, 411, 416, 422
Rumbelow, Widow 354
Ruthven, Katherine 149

Sackville, Anne, Lady Beauchamp 105
Salisbury, Earl of 93
Sandilands, Anne 325–6
Sandys, Hester, see Temple, Hester
Sandys, Miles 71, 81–2, 84, 85
Savage, Sarah (Henry) 95
Say and Seal, Lady Elizabeth see Say, Elizabeth
Say and Seale, Viscountess, Lady Elizabeth see Say, Elizabeth
Say, Elizabeth 172, 231, 258, 267
'Sesell', Mistress (Cecil) 88
Sewall 15
Seymour, Anne 321
Seymour, Jane 321
Seymour, Margaret 321
Shackleton, Elizabeth 219
Shakerley, Alice 293
Shakespeare 149, 411, 421
Sharington, Lady Anne 413
Sharpe, Jane 220, 244
Shepard, Hester 17
Sherrington, Grace see Mildmay, Lady Grace
Shrewsbury, Katharine 331
Sidney 9, 82, 172, 233, 384, 397, 405, 414, 418
Sidney, Mary 19, 169, 374, 382, 383, 397, 398, 399, 405, 417, 418
Sidney, Mary, Countess of Pembroke see Sidney, Mary
Sidwell the Virgin 354
Silsbe, Sarah 397, 409
Silvester, Naomi 296
Skipworth, Jane 108
Smibert 150

INDEX OF PROPER NAMES

Smith, Abigail *see* Adams, Abigail
Smith, Agnes 117, 118
Smith, Anne 132
Smith, Dorothy 17
Smith, Lady Judith 99
Smith, Mary 333
Smith, Rose 199
Smyth, Joan 346
Somerset, Mary, Duchess of Ormond 374, 398
Southwell, Lady Anne 403
Speght, Rachel 205, 398
Spencer, Mr 216
Spencer, Susan 75
Spenser, Edmund 405, 414
Spratt, John 306
Spratt, Mary 306
Spring, Goodwife 61
Stanhope 194, 224
Stanhope, Lord 207
Stanihurst 402
Stanton, Mr 86
Steele 127
Stenson, Mary 116
Stevens, Elizabeth 132
Stillingfleet 387
Stirling, Earls of 306
Stocker, Henry 188
Stockett, Thomas 362
Stonier, Alice 210
Stonor 8, 49–50, 143, 172, 189
Stonor, Elizabeth 189
Stonor, Kathryn 189
Stout 185, 300–3
Stout, Elizabeth 19, 114, 185, 301–3
Stout, Elnor 114
Stout, Sybil 302
Stow, John 387
Stratford, George 288, 293
Stuart, Lady Margaret 87
Stumpe, Elizabeth 173
Sunderland, Lady 222
Swinburne, Henry 291

Talbot, Catherine 399
Taney, Mary 363
Tanfield, Lady Elizabeth 172–3, 179, 253
Tasborough, Lady 347

Taverner, Elnor 298
Taylor, Jeremy 408
Taylor, Mrs 331
Temple 8, 50, 71, 73–5, 81–5, 88–93, 98, 120, 158–62, 163, 165–6, 171, 178, 186–7, 194, 213–7, 230, 248–9, 252, 263, 266–8, 272–3, 280, 298, 303, 324, 364, 407, 414
Temple, Anne 98, 165–6
Temple, Bridget 98, 230, 273
Temple, Catherine 83
Temple, Christian 81, 267
Temple, Elianor 324
Temple, Elizabeth 98, 230
Temple, Frances 81, 269
Temple, Hester 9, 19, 50, 68, 75, 81, 86, 88, 98, 169, 170, 171, 178, 186, 212–16, 217, 228, 230, 241, 243, 248, 252–3, 263, 266, 267, 268, 273, 303, 309
Temple, Katherine 77–8, 86, 98, 230
Temple, Margaret 98
Temple, Martha 98, 231
Temple, Mary 84, 85
Temple, Millicent 98
Temple, Susan 75, 84, 98, 230, 273
Thatcher, Margaret 364
Thimelby, Katherine 92, 398
Thimelby, Winifred 398
Thomas à Kempis 344, 348, 383
Thomas, Earl of Sussex, Viscount Saville 268
Thomas, Jennett 56
Thoresby, Mary 386
Thoresby, Susanna 386
Thorn(e)ton, Alice 95, 264, 265, 364
Thorold, Lady 236
Thrale, Hester 399
Throckmorton 79, 85, 91–2, 88
Throckmorton, Anne 75, 85, 88, 89, 165, 294
Throckmorton, Bess 335
Throckmorton, Jane 92
Throckmorton, Katherine 79, 294
Thynne, Maria 398
Timewell, Margaret 34
Timothy, Elizabeth 385
Tobin, Margaret 261
Townshend, Eleanor 300

Trew 92–3, 176, 283
Trew, Margaret 176, 283
Trotter, Catherine 390
Trumbull, Elizabeth 169, 192
Tryon, Lady Elizabeth 348, 350
Tuam, Archbishop of 359
Tudor, Princess Mary 321
Tusser, Thomas 187, 377, 378
Twigden, Amphyllis 149
Tyrell, Lucy 169
Tyrell, Thomas 50, 263
Tyringham, Sir Thomas 159–60, 161
Tyrrell, Sir Edward 105

Upton, Jane 218

Van Dyck 386
Van Otten, Eleanor 330
van Schurman, Anne Maria 398
Vaughan, Anne 366
Vere, Lady 80
Vere, Lady Mary 350–51
Verney 50, 94, 169, 178, 216–19, 412
Verney, Elizabeth 217, 218
Verrio 374
Vesey, Elizabeth 399
Violante, Madam 401
Virgin Mary 243, 339, 354–5, 363
Vives, Juan Luis 343, 412

Walker, Elizabeth 212, 220
Walsh, Anastasia 358
Walton, Isaak 149
Wandesford, Alice 264
Ward, Cornelius 47
Ward, Margaret 348
Ward, Mary 358
Warde, Joan 346
Warwick, Countess of 220
Warwick, Earl of 87
Washington, George 149
Watson, Lea 326
Watson, Priscilla 351
Watts, Isaac 150
Wedderburn 206
Welsh, Elizabeth 212

Wemyss, Lady Janet 100
Wemyss, Margaret 403
Wharton, Anne 272
Whately, William 55
Wheatcroft, Leonard 30, 36
Wheatley, Phyllis 19, 401
Whitaker 127
White, Eryn 329
Whitmore, Mary 123
Whitney 378, 398
Whitney, Isabella 383, 398
Whittle, Jane 230
Whythorne, Thomas 117
Wilbraham, Elizabeth Mitton 374
Williams, Roger 58, 360
Willoughby 67, 69, 72–5, 78–9, 86, 89, 94, 143–4, 163, 172–3, 177, 195, 210, 223, 250–4, 262, 308, 330, 348, 358, 406
Willoughby, Cassandra see Cassandra, Duchess of Chandos
Willoughby, Cassandra the elder 73
Willoughby, Emma see Child, Lady Emma
Willoughby, Lady Cassandra 143
Willoughby-Ridgeway 35
Wilmore, Goodwife 215
Wilson, Margaret 122
Winchester, Margaret 190
Winthrop, Governor see Winthrop, John
Winthrop, John 58, 360–61, 411
Wisheart, Margaret 43
Wolstencraft, Mary 6
Woodbridge, Mercy 421
Woolley, Hannah 220
Wright, Katherine 286
Wroth, Mary 6, 19, 179, 397, 398, 399, 418
Wyatt, Elizabeth 416

Yarrington 103
Younger, Sarah 196

Zouche, Elizabeth 405
Zouche, 'Silken Thomas' 405